PUBLICATIONS

OF THE

NAVY RECORDS SOCIETY

Vol. 141

THE CHANNEL FLEET AND THE
BLOCKADE OF BREST, 1793–1801

'The Batteries at the entrance to Brest Harbour firing upon H.M. Brig Childers 1793'. Engraving by James Fittler of a watercolour by Nicholas Pocock (1740–1821). Published by Thomas Cadell and William Davies, 20 February 1815. Originals in the National Maritime Museum, London.

THE CHANNEL FLEET AND THE BLOCKADE OF BREST, 1793–1801

edited by

ROGER MORRISS, BA, PhD

Based in part on transcripts made by the late

RICHARD C. SAXBY, BA, ALA

PUBLISHED BY ASHGATE
FOR THE NAVY RECORDS SOCIETY
2001

Published by
Ashgate Publishing Limited
Gower House
Croft Road
Aldershot
Hants GU11 3HR
England

Ashgate Publishing Company
131 Main Street
Burlington, VT 05401-5600 USA

British Library Cataloguing-in-Publication Data

Morriss, Roger
   The Channel Fleet and the Blockade of Brest 1793–1801.
   (Publications of the Navy Records Society; v. 141)
   1. Great Britain. Royal Navy – History – Anglo-French War,
   1793–1801   2. Anglo-French War, 1793–1801 – Naval operations,
   British 3. Anglo-French War, 1793–1801 – Blockades
   I. Title
   940.2'7'45

Library of Congress Cataloging-in-Publication Data

The channel fleet and the blockade of Brest 1793–1801 / edited by Roger Morriss.
     p.   cm. – (Publications of the Navy Records Society; vol. 141)
   Includes index.
   1. Brest (France) – History, Naval – Sources.   2. Blockade – France –
  Brest – Sources.   3. English Channel – History, Naval – 19th century –
  Sources.   4. Napoleonic Wars, 1800–1815 – Proposed invasion of
  England, 1793–1805 – Sources.   I. Morriss, Roger.   II. Series.
  DC153.C48   2001
  940.2'745–dc21   00-057604

Printed on acid-free paper

ISBN 0 7546 0268 0

Typeset in Times by Manton Typesetters, Louth, Lincolnshire and printed in Great Britain by MPG Books Ltd, Bodmin, Cornwall.

NAVY RECORDS SOCIETY
LIST OF COUNCILLORS AND OFFICERS
AS OF 5 JULY 2000

CONTENTS

MAPS AND ILLUSTRATIONS

Frontispiece

'The Batteries at the entrance to Brest Harbour firing upon H.M. Brig *Childers* 1793'. Engraving by James Fittler of a watercolour by Nicholas Pocock (1740–1821). Published by Thomas Cadell and William Davies, 20 February 1815. Originals in the National Maritime Museum, London.

Maps

PREFACE

This volume had its origins in a collection of transcripts of extracts from documents made by the late Richard Saxby. His aim was to provide a forerunner in content to the two volumes dealing with the blockade of Brest between 1803 and 1805 edited by John Leyland and published by the Navy Records Society in 1899 and 1902. Unfortunately, partly on account of his deteriorating health, Richard Saxby's work was not ready for publication by the Navy Records Society at the time he died. It nevertheless contained sufficient material of interest to warrant revision to the standard required for publication by the Society and the addition of further documents to enlarge its scope. It is this enlarged work that is here published, edited by Roger Morriss.

Richard Saxby transcribed 681 extracts of documents at the British Library and Public Record Office, covering the period December 1794 to October 1801. His main focus was the papers of George, second Earl Spencer, which were transferred from Althorp to the British Library during the time that he was working on the blockade of Brest. But he also used the papers of Lord Bridport and letterbooks of Lord St Vincent in the British Library, and made a few transcripts from the papers of Henry Dundas, First Lord Melville, and of William Windham in the same repository. The papers at the Public Record Office provided reports from the Commanders-in-Chief to the Admiralty with some of their enclosures. In making his transcripts Richard Saxby wished to reveal the politics of managing the blockade, particularly that between the Admiralty and the Commanders-in-Chief. He gave considerable attention to the Spithead mutiny, conscious that the correspondence between the Admiralty and Commander-in-Chief on that subject had largely been ignored. Otherwise he was motivated by desires to evoke the atmosphere of the period and to provide the reader with enjoyment.

The volume as published includes a further 160 documents enlarging the chronological period it covers, its substance and purpose. The documents now begin in June 1793 when the Channel fleet was placed on a war footing, and instructions were given to the Commander-in-Chief to proceed 'to the westward'. The volume thus now covers the whole of the operational period of the French Revolutionary War. Documents relating to operations have been supplemented with further letters and instructions from the Admiralty to the Commander-in-Chief, and further reports from the latter to the Admiralty Secretary. Equally important are the addition of Admiralty orders to the Victualling Board, letters from the Victualling Board to the Admiralty Secretary and letters from the Sick and Wounded Board to the Admiralty Secretary. These additions come from both the National Maritime Museum, Greenwich, and the Public Record Office. These administrative documents add dimensions to the blockade which were conspicuously missing from Richard Saxby's work, and cover the challenge posed by the problem of keeping the Channel fleet free of scurvy, and the controversial issue of how to treat sick men once they had contracted disease. They reveal how the increase in Admiralty control, and the movement from an open to a close blockade, was based upon provisions for the welfare of seamen as well as on the routine refitting, repair and supply of ships of the Channel fleet.

The additions made to Richard Saxby's work include transcripts from one personal collection that he ignored: that of the Honourable William Cornwallis at the National Maritime Museum. This has provided transcripts of letters and orders Cornwallis derived from his predecessor, Lord St Vincent. Further letterbooks, orderbooks and a journal relating to the management of Cornwallis remain at Greenwich untapped. A note on these further sources will be found with the list of documents employed in this volume.

In transcribing letters for publication, Richard Saxby concentrated on those parts of letters relevant in his opinion to the blockade. Although invariably neglecting to include an indicative ellipsis (...), he omitted formal preambles and repetitious recitations of orders received; sometimes also parts of sentences that seemed to him superflous. Where possible these have been reinserted. Passages in the original that seemed to him illegible have also been deciphered. Happily, in the editor's experience, the above omissions usually do not damage the sense of the sentences transcribed.

Other omissions arising from decisions by Richard Saxby include letters about patronage and appointments, about cases of wrongful impressment, and about subjects covered by documents already published by the Navy Records Society in the *Papers of George, Second Earl Spencer*. Rightly or wrongly, he omitted letters relating to subjects that he considered subordinate to his main interest in the blockade: for example, documents relating to the refitting of particular ships or the indisposition of captains. More worryingly, he omitted documents that 'would have taken up more space than their importance justified or because they never came to any satisfying conclusion'. This volume is thus dependent in its origin on judgements that were subjective. In partial correction the extra documents that have been added have been transcribed in total. Long instructions, relating for example to contingencies should the French fleet escape from Brest, have been included to show the detail to which the Admiralty came to direct the Commander-in-Chief off Brest. Reports relating to the health of seamen and their victualling are also given their full length in order to show how much consideration was given to such concerns.

In compiling this volume, Richard Saxby made a practice of removing enclosures from their covering letters from the Commander-in-Chief to the Admiralty. Generally they thus stand as independent letters and reports to the Commander-in-Chief. Going back to find these enclosures, usually at the Public Record Office, can be a frustrating task, for Richard Saxby left no reference to the date and nature of the covering letter. In partial mitigation of this practice, the transcripts of documents that have been added maintain the unity of covering letter and enclosures. Three documents which posed a problem even for Richard Saxby were the letters taken by the *Black Joke* lugger from the French vessel *Rebecca* in April 1799 [437, 452, 453]. The first was intended to deceive the Admiralty and send the British fleet on a wild goose chase; the second plainly reveals the deception and the third is, perhaps, ambiguous. Although the means by which the first came into British hands is known, it is uncertain when the second came into British hands. All three are now in Bridport's papers in the British Library but not together. Their location within the sequence of documents in this volume therefore may not be accurate.

Otherwise every attempt has been made to ensure the documents printed here are as in the original. For example, just as contemporaries usually did not underline ship names or print them in *italics*, so those names within the letters printed here are not so rendered. However, consistent with the practice of the Society, names in text added by the editor are rendered in italics. Inevitably, many ships are mentioned in these letters and instructions. They are listed in alphabetical order at the back of the volume. Their dates of build or capture, and number of guns, are taken mainly from the first volume of J.J. Colledge, *Ships of the Royal Navy* (London, 1987), with supplementary details from D. Lyon, *The Sailing Navy List 1688–1860* (London, 1993). The careers of naval officers are derived from *The Commissioned Sea Officers of the Royal Navy 1660–1815*, edited by David Syrett and R.L. DiNardo, published by Scolar Press, Aldershot, for the Navy Records Society in 1994.

This volume could not have been prepared without the assistance of the staffs of the Public Record Office and the British Library, especially the manuscripts department. At the National Maritime Museum, thanks are particularly due to Clive Powell and Alan Giddings who have been more kind and helpful than the strict execution of their duties required. Richard Saxby made much use of the Institute of Historical Research of the University of London, the library of the Royal United Services Institution and Ealing Central Library. He wished to pay tribute to the encouragement of Dr Ruddock Mackay and of Bill Avery of Bethel Island, California. His spiritual mentor was A.B. Rodger of Balliol College, Oxford, who first directed him to the blockade of Brest. During the progress of his work, he gained much support from his membership of St Catherine's College, Oxford. The maps have been drawn by Sue Rouillard, cartographer in the Department of Geography, University of Exeter. Publication of this volume was made possible from the financial assistance of the estate of Richard Saxby administered by NatWest Investments, where particular thanks are due to Mr Boxall and his staff. Michael Simpson, the Honorary General Editor of the Navy Records Society, smoothly guided the volume to publication. Above all, however, it is indebted to the sustained, painstaking scholarship of Mr Tony Ryan, whose interest in the subject matter and scrupulous attention to detail has removed many of the imperfections in the revised text. Without his knowledge, enthusiasm and humour, the production of this volume would have been arduous indeed. Instead, its preparation has been a source of great interest and pleasure, and it is hoped that, as Richard Saxby intended, it will provide similar satisfaction to all those who read it.

1   The Western Approaches and English Channel

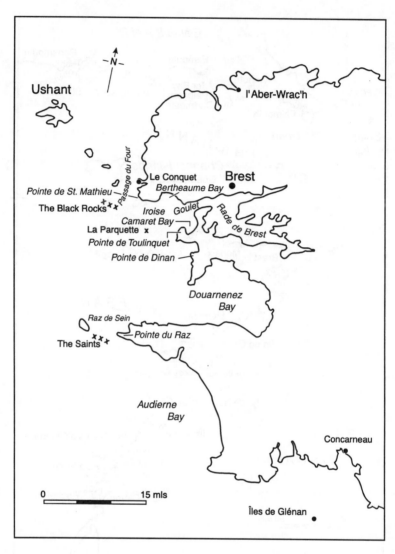

2 *The north-west coast of France*

INTRODUCTION

During the French Revolutionary War the Channel fleet formed the first line of defence of Great Britain against invasion from France; it protected Britain's trade in home waters; and it had responsibility for preventing the French Brest fleet from escaping, either to mount an expedition, to protect French convoys, to succour French colonies, or to reinforce the French fleet in the Mediterranean or in other allied ports. During the war the last of these functions came to predominate, because by it in theory the first two could also be fulfilled. However, like the blockade itself, the strategy within which the Channel fleet operated, the central government bureaucracy which directed it, and the terms upon which its Commanders-in-Chief managed the fleet, only evolved as the French Revolutionary War proceeded. This introduction provides a general outline of these developments with some reference to the careers which lay behind successive commanders of the Channel fleet.

The Strategic Context

A 'western squadron' capable of deterring the emergence of the French Brest fleet, and if necessary of giving battle, has been described as the lynch-pin of British naval strategy in the wars against France between the 17th and 19th centuries.[1] The development of the strategy, with the logistical problems arising from its implementation, has been the subject of numerous studies.[2] The strategy was first mooted during the War

[1]M. Duffy, 'The establishment of the Western Squadron as the linchpin of British naval strategy' in *Parameters of British Naval Power 1650–1850*, ed. M. Duffy (Exeter, 1992), 60–81.

[2]D. A. Baugh, 'Great Britain's "Blue Water" policy, 1689–1815', *International History Review* 10 (1988), 33–58; J. B. Hattendorf, *England in the War of Spanish Succession. A Study of the English View and Conduct of Grand Strategy 1702–1712* (New York & London, 1987); R. Middleton, 'British naval strategy 1755–62. The Western Squadron', *The Mariner's Mirror* 75 (1989), 349–67; A. N. Ryan, 'William III and the Brest fleet in the Nine Years War', in *William III and Louis XIV. Essays 1680–1720 by and for Mark A. Thomson*, ed. R. Hatton and J.S. Bromley (Liverpool, 1968), 49–67; A. N. Ryan, 'The Royal Navy and the blockade of Brest, 1689–1805: Theory and Practice', in *Les Marines de Guerre Européennes XVII–XVIII siècles* ed. M. Acerra, J. Merino and J. Meyer (Paris, 1985), 175–193; D. M. Steer, 'The blockade of Brest and the Royal Navy 1793–1805' (University of Liverpool unpub. MA thesis, 1971).

of William III, when France became Britain's principal enemy. The establishment of Brest as France's principal Atlantic naval base under Louis XIV demanded a strategy which would both defend the English coast and Ireland from invasion, and permit offensive operations against the French Brest fleet should it emerge. During the War of Spanish Succession Admiral Sir Clowdisley Shovell claimed that the most appropriate station for a squadron of line of battle ships should be '20 to 40 leagues S.W. to W.S.W. from Ushant'.[1]

The geographical determinants of this location were best explained by Admiral Edward Vernon in 1745. He pointed out that a fleet 'posted within the Channel between the Lizard and the coast of France' would 'leave all Ireland, the western coasts of this island and even the Bristol Channel and all our East and West Indian trade expected home, open to them [the French] to do what they please'. 'Whereas', he argued, 'a western squadron formed as strong as we can make it . . . and got speedily out into the Soundings, might face their united force, cover both Great Britain and Ireland and be in condition to pursue them wherever they went and be at hand to secure the safe return of our homeward bound trade from the East and West Indies'.[2] It was a location to which Lord Anson in 1755 subscribed. He wrote to Sir Edward Hawke 'the best defence for our colonies, as well as our coasts, is to have a squadron always to the westward as may in all probability either keep the French in port or give them battle with advantage if they come out'. From this belief derived a succession of naval victories, most notably that of Quiberon Bay in November 1759.

This defeat of a French fleet, intended as an escort to an invasion force, demonstrated the efficacy of catching the French soon after they emerged from Brest. However the Quiberon campaign also demonstrated the difficulty with which ships kept station off Ushant. Twice during the autumn of 1759 Sir Edward Hawke had been driven by westerly gales back to the English coast to take shelter first in Plymouth Sound and then in Torbay. The westerly winds which kept the British battle fleet on the English coast also kept the French in Brest. However the easterly wind upon which Hawke sailed from Torbay on 14 November also permitted the French to leave Brest.[3] The fact that Hawke was able to catch the French fleet raised issues that were still being expressed during the French Revolutionary War. Was the British

---

[1] Shovell to Burchett, 20 July 1702, *Calendar of State Papers Domestic*, 1702, 193; quoted in Ryan, 'The Royal Navy and the blockade of Brest, 1689–1805', 181.

[2] *The Vernon Papers*, ed. B. McL. Ranft (Navy Records Society [henceforth NRS], 1958), 459.

[3] Ryan, 'The Royal Navy and the blockade of Brest, 1689–1805', 183.

fleet better preserved in harbour during the gales of winter? Indeed, was the French fleet not satisfactorily opposed throughout the year by a British battle fleet on the English coast?

The answer to these questions depended on whether the wear and tear on ships of the line kept off Brest could be sustained and justified. During the American War of Independence, the combined forces of the Bourbon powers prevented the British navy from blockading Brest, diverted as its strength was to the maintenance of the war in America, to the defence of commerce, and to the reinforcement of remnants of empire. After the war senior naval opinion felt the blockade was better avoided if possible. In 1784 Lord Howe observed that 'stationing a large fleet off the coast of France was a very improper and hazardous measure. The ships, particularly the large ones, were liable to receive great damage, the crews get sickly ... he could affirm from his own knowledge that a station off Brest was a dangerous station, and should never be taken but upon great emergencies'.[1]

However, in 1793, when France was isolated, Britain again possessed superior numbers. While Britain possessed 158 ships of the line, France had 82. Indeed in 1793 the British fleet was exactly equal to the combined battle strength of France and Spain, which then possessed 76 ships of the line.[2] By a sustained programme of investment the British fleet had been repaired and rebuilt and, with stores and equipment ready, was rapidly mobilised.[3] But in 1793 blockade did not seem immediately necessary. The French navy was reduced to virtual impotence by the political conflicts on shore. It had already lost many of its officers by revolutionary purges and emigrations. Its seamen, many of whom were Breton and royalist, were also in short supply. At Toulon the French Mediterranean fleet was surrendered to the British fleet in August. In September the Brest fleet mutinied in Quiberon Bay.[4] The French fleet was not the formidable force it had been. Moreover France was closely beset on land and in no position to undertake serious overseas ventures, least of all an invasion of Britain. About October 1793 Sir Charles Middleton argued that the French 'being much inferior to us in the number of line of battle ships and probably deficient in

---

[1]*The Parliamentary History of England*, ed. W. Cobbett, XX, column 202, quoted in Saxby, 'The blockade of Brest' in the French Revolutionary War', *The Mariner's Mirror* [henceforth *M.M.*], 78 (1992), 25–35.

[2]W. James, *The Naval History of Great Britain from the declaration of war by France in 1793 to the accession of George IV* (6 vols, London, 1859), I, 56–7.

[3]P. L. C. Webb, 'The rebuilding and repair of the fleet, 1783–1793', *Bulletin of the Institute of Historical Research*, L (1977), 194–209.

[4]W. S. Cormack, *Revolution and Political Conflict in the French Navy 1789–1794* (Cambridge, 1995), 143–226.

the great articles of naval stores, their first object will be a general attack upon our trade and supplying themselves by these means of what may be difficult to procure in other ways'.[1] The security of British trade assumed priority in British naval strategy. The instructions given to the Commander-in-Chief of the Channel fleet reflected this priority. Only as an afterthought was he reminded from time to time to cause accurate observations to be made of the force collecting in Brest.

Like priorities determined the operations of the Channel fleet in 1794. It did not leave Spithead until outgoing convoys were ready and once at sea its force was weakened to provide escorts. Having established that the French fleet was still in Brest, it made no attempt to block up that port, focusing its activities instead upon a search for a transatlantic convoy of grain ships bound for France. The French fleet was thus able to leave its base unobserved. Its detection by the British, which led to its defeat at the Glorious First of June, was fortuitous. Only in July 1795, with the necessity to prevent interference with British operations in Quiberon Bay, was a blockade of Brest and Lorient instituted and even then the danger posed by the Brest fleet had constantly to be weighed against the demands of other duties. Indeed the necessity to provide escorts for convoys diminished the reliefs available for the blockade so that ships remaining on the French coast suffered 'a general scurvy'.[2]

Fortunately by the end of 1795 French attempts to strengthen their battle fleet had been thwarted by the loss of 33 ships of the line by capture, wreck or foundering.[3] Consequently, even with French new building, the odds against the British fleet were not as formidable as they might have been. Indeed many of the captures from the French were added to the strength of the British navy.[4] It thus enjoyed a margin of numerical superiority at sea sufficient to compensate for the absence at the dockyards of vessels refitting and undergoing repair. The good condition of the British fleet in 1793 served it well until 1798. However thereafter between a fifth and a quarter of all ships of the line in a

---

[1]*Letters and Papers of Charles, Lord Barham*, ed. J. K. Laughton (3 vols, NRS, 1907–11), II, 365–7.

[2]R. Saxby, 'The blockade of Brest in the French Revolutionary War', 28; *The Health of Seamen*, ed. C. Lloyd (NRS, 1965) 234, 245.

[3]French losses of ships of the line amounted to 15 in 1793, 8 in 1794, and 10 in 1795. W. L. Clowes, *The Royal Navy. A History from the Earliest Times to 1900* (7 vols, London, 1897–1903, reprint 1997), IV, 548–61.

[4]Of 112 ships of the line (64 or more guns) and 99 frigates (20–60 guns) that served in the Channel fleet 1793–1801, 8 of the battleships (7 per cent) and 22 of the frigates (22 per cent) were captured from the French during the French Revolutionary War. See Appendix 1.

condition for sea service were at dockyards.[1] The British victories at
Camperdown, Cape St Vincent and the Nile were thus critical to the
removal of additions to French and allied battle strength.[2] The capture
of French seamen was equally important in weakening the French navy.
It has been estimated that in 1793 France had about 85,000 seamen.[3]
But by 1798 there were over 30,000 French prisoners of war in British
hands; by 1801 over 70,000, nearly all of them seamen.[4] This denial to
the French of an essential resource worked with the blockade for, even
when they accumulated the seamen to man the fleet in Brest, their
crews lacked sea training and confidence, factors which militated against
the safe emergence and escape of ships in any quantity from Brest.

The decision to blockade Brest in 1795 was not taken by the Board
of Admiralty in isolation. Its deployments were calculated with the
sanction of ministers, in particular the Secretary for War, Henry Dundas
(1742–1811). Home Secretary from 1791, he had become Secretary for
War in July 1794, when Pitt's ministry was broadened by the accession
of the Duke of Portland's followers. Until the very end of the war
Dundas was for avoiding involvement in Europe while pursuing British
interests overseas. In July 1793 he opposed reinforcing royalist risings
on the west coast of France because it 'would interfere with the objects
which naturally present themselves either in the West or East Indies'.
Successes in those quarters, he argued, were 'of infinite moment, both
in the view of humbling the power of France, and with the view of
enlarging our national wealth and security'. The West Indies were 'the
first point to make perfectly certain', and even in July 1795, when
British landings were made on the Quiberon peninsula, he remained
adamant that 'complete success in the West Indies' was 'essential to the
interests and I will add to the contentment of this country'. 'By success
in the West Indies alone you can be enabled to dictate the terms of
peace'.

In 1799, as the war dragged on, Dundas continued to justify this
objective. He declared that the very maintenance of 'an extensive and
complicated war' was dependent on 'destroying the colonial resources

---

[1]The proportion of the British sea-going battle fleet out of commission diminished
from 87 per cent in 1793 to 8 per cent in 1797, then increased to 16 per cent in 1798, 20
per cent in 1799, 24 per cent in 1800, and 27 per cent in 1801. R. A. Morriss, *The Royal
Dockyards during the Revolutionary and Napoleonic Wars* (Leicester, 1983), 16.

[2]In 1798 the French lost 14 ships of the line. By the end of 1798 France had lost 49
ships of the line, which amounted to 60 per cent of her battle strength at the beginning
of the war. In total between 1793 and 1801 the French lost 55 ships of the line, the
Spanish 10 and the Dutch 18 ships of the line. Clowes, IV, 552–61.

[3]M. Acerra and J. Meyer, *Marines et Révolution* (Rennes, 1988), part 3.

[4]E. H. Jenkins, *A History of the French Navy* (London, 1973), 241; Clowes, IV, 185.

of our enemies and adding proportionately to our own commercial resources, which are, and must ever be, the sole basis of our maritime strength'.[1] However, as a concomitant of this policy, Dundas remained perfectly aware that, 'unless the great fleet of Brest is kept in its proper subjection by the great fleet of England all subordinate operations must be nugatory'.[2] As in the Seven Years War, the blockade of Brest consequently came to complement the great expeditions to the West Indies that characterised the French Revolutionary War. After 1795 the principle of maintaining the blockade was consistently applied. Even though the resources that could be devoted to it were at times limited by deployments to other stations, there was full recognition that the blockade was indispensable to the maintenance of the British war effort in other theatres.

The Admiralty Administrators

The institution of the blockade in 1795 was preceded by the formation of a team of talented administrators at the Admiralty. The First Lord of the Admiralty when the war began was John Pitt, second Earl of Chatham (1756–1835), the older brother of William Pitt, First Lord of the Treasury and Prime Minister. Chatham was a soldier by profession and had served in Gibraltar between 1779 and 1783 when it was besieged by the Spanish. He had acted as First Lord of the Admiralty since July 1788 without giving offence, but he had a reputation for being distant with colleagues and his talent for business was not equal to the pressures of war. According to William Marsden, second secretary at the Admiralty, when Chatham left the Admiralty in December 1794 many hundreds of unopened letters were found in his house, where they had been carried.[3] Chatham was transferred to the office of Lord Privy Seal and in 1796 became Lord President of the Council.

His successor at the Admiralty, George John, second Earl Spencer (1758–1839), was of very different quality. As Viscount Althorp he had been educated at Harrow and Trinity College, Cambridge. After a tour of the continent, he became MP for Northampton in 1780 and for the

---

[1]Dundas to Richmond, 8 July 1793, British Library Bathurst Papers, Loan 57/107; Dundas to York, 28 July 1795, BL Add. MS 40102; quoted in M. Duffy, *Soldiers, Sugar and Sea Power. The British Expeditions to the West Indies and the War against Revolutionary France* (Oxford, 1987), 25, 161, 371.

[2]Henry Dundas to Lord Grenville, 12 October 1793. *Historical Manuscripts Commission 14th Report. Appendix Part V: the Manuscripts of J. B. Fortescue, Esq., Preserved at Dropmore* (10 vols, London, 1894), II, 444.

[3]*A brief Memoir of the Life and Writings of the late William Marsden, written by himself* (London, 1838), 115.

county of Surrey in 1782. His ministerial career began when he was appointed a junior Lord of the Treasury by the Marquis of Rockingham. He succeeded to the earldom in October 1783. He entered the Cabinet with the Duke of Portland in June 1794 as Lord Privy Seal and was sent to Vienna as ambassador extraordinary. Returning from there he exchanged places with Chatham on 19 December 1794 and remained First Lord of the Admiralty for six years.

Spencer had many natural talents. His first was his administrative ability. He took some time to settle in at the Admiralty and to acquire confidence in his own judgement. But once he had done so, he displayed a clear grasp of the logistics underlying the disposition of Britain's naval forces and a quiet command of policy at the Board. There he was a man of business. Marsden observed that 'no public letter was ever omitted (unless under very peculiar circumstances) to be read at the Board, minuted, answered and despatched, if practicable, on the day of its receipt'. Spencer's private letters were dealt with no less meticulously. At the same time he got on well with those about him, both his professional advisers and the secretaries of the Admiralty. Marsden wrote in June 1800, 'today we all dine with his Lordship: our board is like one family. Business may in former times have been conducted as well in the Admiralty department but certainly never so pleasantly or so smoothly'.[1] His affability stretched to officers corresponding with him from sea. Early in his administration he was ready to indulge Sir Sidney Smith with a private correspondence that was no doubt of interest but really peripheral to the main concerns of the Admiralty at that time.

His second great quality was his diplomacy. He was tactful and courteous, if somewhat short under the most trying provocation. Always he seemed to have carefully considered what was most appropriate from the point of view of the Admiralty and be willing in his private letters to explain that point of view. In a correspondence which must at times have been difficult, he both tolerated and supported Bridport through successive periods of argument and complaint. Likewise he supported both Sir Edward Pellew and Sir John Borlase Warren through their attempts to gain independence from Bridport.

In managing as well as helping these men, it is evident that he had adopted an unstated assumption that was to become characteristic of the naval profession at this time: the principle that personal animosities were not to disrupt the disciplines of service. Spencer and his officers were bound in a common allegiance, an affiliation that put limits on the

---

[1] *A brief Memoir of . . . the late William Marsden*, 97n, 115–16n.

extent to which resentment could be carried. Spencer was not above clearly defining his own position to any captain or admiral, however talented, who formed an opinion unacceptable to the First Lord. Bridport, Lord Keith and St Vincent were all firmly made acquainted with the views Spencer found acceptable. Indeed, by his ruthless readiness to dispense with the services of senior officers like Samuel, Lord Hood and Cornwallis, Spencer demonstrated that, whatever the differences of opinion, he demanded commitment to the Board of Admiralty under the Crown.

Three months after taking office at the Admiralty, Spencer reinforced the secretariat. Philip Stephens (1725–1809), then managing the business of the board single-handed, had begun his career in the Admiralty office as a clerk in 1751. He had become second secretary in 1759, managed alone during the inter-war peace, and became first secretary in 1783. On 3 March 1795 he became an Admiralty commissioner, a position he would hold for another 11 years. His retention as a commissioner represented the embodiment of 40 years' experience. Spencer selected to replace him Evan Nepean (1751–1822). A Cornishman who had served in the navy as a clerk and purser during the American War of Independence, he had become secretary to the port admiral at Plymouth in 1782, whence under Shelburne he became an Under-Secretary of State. In 1794 he went to the War Office and on 3 March 1795 to the Admiralty.

During the eighteenth century the long tenure of secretaries had reinforced the institutional character of the Admiralty. One of the first of a new brand of civil servants, whose ability took them from department to department, Nepean was to become chief secretary for Ireland in January 1804, an Admiralty commissioner from September 1804 to February 1806, and Governor of Bombay in 1812. At the Admiralty from 1795 his office would become the central clearing house for the intelligence that informed British naval logistics in countering French operations. Intelligence was sent to him directly from agents he commissioned,[1] from the offices of the Secretaries of State, and from ships at sea. The unseen hand behind many of the impersonal orders, instructions and letters of information despatched to the fleet, he was not without views of his own on the officers to whom he wrote, his own decided opinion emerging in private correspondence with Spencer.

At the same time as Nepean was appointed first secretary, William Marsden (1754–1836) was made second secretary. Marsden had seen

---

[1] See the Nepean Papers at the National Maritime Museum. NEP/1 and 2 contain letters from agents in Holland; NEP/5 includes a note by Nepean about the cruise of Bruix, May 1799.

service in the East India Company and become secretary to the governor of Sumatra before returning to London and establishing an agency business in 1785. He was to serve as second secretary from 1795 until 1804, when he became first secretary until 1807. Nepean and Marsden would provide the board with administrative support. By the Admiralty patent of 7 March 1795 the board itself was reinforced. The naval officers serving with the fleet, Samuel, Lord Hood and Sir Alan Gardner, were removed from the patent. In their place came the conscientious James Gambier, an evangelical and friend of Charles Middleton, then on the board. Gambier would remain with Spencer until the latter's resignation on 19 February 1801. The same Admiralty patent of 7 March 1795 also brought Lord Hugh Seymour to the board. First Seymour then Gambier later served with the Channel fleet as well as holding seats at the Admiralty. The former in particular, before being posted to command at Jamaica, provided Spencer with perceptive eyes and an articulate voice in the fleet.

In November 1795 the Board of Admiralty lost one of its most able, but also one of its most difficult, members. Sir Charles Middleton (1726–1813) had joined the board in May 1794, under Chatham. He was highly connected. Though fourteen years Middleton's junior, Henry Dundas was first cousin to Middleton's mother. In 1794, owing to the absence with the fleet of those higher than him in the Admiralty patent, he assumed the role of first naval commissioner. Having had 12 years as Comptroller of the Navy, he had a strong grasp of fleet logistics and particular interest in how they applied to the maintenance of a blockade strategy. During the 1780s he had worked closely with Pitt to repair and rebuild the fleet. Moreover, having served in the West Indies, he brought to the board first-hand knowledge of the Caribbean. The reconstitution of the Transport Board in July 1794[1] derived directly from Middleton's experience of four boards competing for the hire of transports during the American War of Independence.[2] However, the former Comptroller was never an easy colleague. Dundas warned Spencer that Middleton was 'a little difficult to act with from an anxiety, I had almost said an irritability of temper'; he required 'to have a great deal of his own way of doing business'.[3] Indeed he could be overbearing, was quite willing to lecture less experienced colleagues, and made no exception of First Lords.[4]

[1]M. E. Condon, 'The establishment of the Transport Board . . . a subdivision of the Admiralty . . . 4 July 1794', *M.M.* 58 (1972), 69–84.

[2]D. Syrett, *Shipping and the American War 1775–1783* (London, 1970), 78, 246.

[3]*Private Papers of George, Second Earl Spencer* ed. J. S. Corbett and H. W. Richmond (4 vols, NRS, 1913 etc.), I, 6.

[4]For his lectures to Lords Sandwich, Howe and Chatham, see *Letters of Lord Barham*, II, 2–10, 178–190, 316–19.

Spencer and Middleton did not get on. Middleton's resignation in 1795 has mainly been associated with the recall of Sir John Laforey from his station in the West Indies against his own opinion of the propriety of the measure.[1] But the explanation for his resignation that Middleton gave Dundas pointed first at the failure of Spencer, by his appointment of Lord Hugh Seymour, to comply with Middleton's objection to officers serving at sea holding seats at the board; second to Spencer's adoption of Seymour's recommendation for the payment of half-pay and other emoluments to surgeons and masters against Middleton's own opinion; and thirdly to the frequency with which Middleton found himself in opposition to Spencer 'and his more confidential friends'. Middleton placed his own interpretation on the conduct of Seymour and Spencer, presuming for example that Seymour's support for the masters and surgeons was 'evidently for the purpose of procuring popularity in the fleet'. In turn Spencer thought Middleton's opposition arose from jealousy: he told him 'with no great delicacy' that he 'opposed the measure because it had not originated with' him. Other differences of opinion followed. Middleton claimed that a confidential 'interior cabinet of admiralty talked over and settled their own plans before it reached the board', and that rarely had he the chance of a discussion with Spencer. Business came to him 'in the shape of letters or notes, without any other explanations, as though I had been the mere secretary of the office'. His pride was hurt. A 'very extraordinary letter ... which could have no meaning but to dispense with' his 'further services' induced his resignation.[2]

He was replaced by Rear-admiral Sir William Young (d. 1821) who, though not possessing Middleton's administrative experience, had Spencer's confidence and a virulent, if caustic, managerial manner. Between 1795 and September 1798, with Seymour away with the fleet, Young acted for much of the time as the sole naval commissioner at the Board. In 1798, with the addition of Rear-admiral Robert Man (d. 1813), the number of naval commissioners was increased from two to three of the seven board members. Their combined naval expertise was perhaps most evident in the voluminous instructions issued to the Commander-in-Chief of the Channel fleet to cover all eventualities should an enemy squadron escape from Brest. However, correspondence directly with the Commander-in-Chief was left either to the secretary of the Admiralty or to Spencer. For without exception the Commanders-in-Chief all

---

[1]*Letters of Lord Barham*, II, 418–24; J. E. Talbot, *The Pen and Ink Sailor. Charles Middleton and the King's Navy, 1778–1813* (London, 1998), 137–143. Duffy, *Soldiers, Sugar and Seapower*, 166–9.
[2]*Letters of Lord Barham*, II, 424–30.

required diplomatic handling. St Vincent made no secret of his contempt for the 'Neptunes at the Board'.

The Growth of Central Control

The strengthening of the secretariat and the naval presence at the Admiralty was accompanied by the progressive increase in the central control of the blockade of Brest. In 1793 and 1794 the movements of the Channel fleet were almost entirely governed by the sailings of large East and West India convoys. The preoccupation of the Channel fleet with trade permitted the Admiralty to allow the Commander-in-Chief relative autonomy in the disposition of his ships. However, the failure to institute a fleet blockade off Brest gave the French independence too.[1] At the end of the 1794 the Brest fleet put to sea when the Channel fleet was at Spithead and captured a great many British merchantmen and one line of battle ship. They were also able to despatch ships of the line to the Mediterranean.

During 1796 the low level of French preparation for sea permitted the Admiralty to rely on squadrons alternately relieving one another. The timing of this relief was to a large extent governed by the needs of ships and the pace at which work proceeded in port. However, the Hoche expedition to Bantry Bay in December 1796, combined with the threat of an impending insurrection in Ireland, persuaded Spencer in March 1797 to demand a more strict and systematic watch on Brest. At the same time the apparent intention of the French to send a fleet to sea required a blockading force of comparative size. Nevertheless the demands of other stations, and the time ships took to refit and replenish, dictated the utmost economy in the number of ships made available to the blockade.

It is tempting to see the Spithead mutiny in April 1797, just as the fleet was about to sail, as a response to the danger clearly presenting itself from Brest. From studies of labour relations in the Royal dockyards, it is clear that strikes occurred at critical times, when the workforce had the Admiralty over a barrel. The Board of Admiralty was not therefore unaccustomed to appeasing its employees.[2] By mid-April 1797 discontent in the Channel fleet had been festering for some months,

---

[1] Middleton to Pitt, 26 Sept. 1794, *Letters of Lord Barham*, II, 408–9.

[2] D. A. Baugh, *British Naval Administration in the Age of Walpole* (Princeton, New Jersey, 1965), 323–32; R. B. M. Ranft, 'Labour relations in the Royal Dockyards in 1739', *M.M.* , 47 (1961), 281–91; J. M. Haas, 'The introduction of Task Work in Royal Naval dockyards, 1775', *Journal of British Studies*, 14 (1969), 44–68; R. A. Morriss, 'Labour relations in the Royal Dockyards, 1801–5', *M.M.*, 62 (1976), 337–46.

and the seamen chose their moment to withdraw their labour. A recent study of mutiny in the home commands of the Royal Navy during the French Revolutionary War acquits the seamen at Spithead of seditious motives.[1] Yet their collective action was beyond the control of the officers on the spot. Despite an initial attempt to have the Commander-in-Chief nip the mutiny in the bud, the Board of Admiralty had to take full charge of negotiations. It had also to obtain the necessary legislation to meet the demands of the mutineers. It was an unavoidable resort to the Crown and legislature that established the terms of employment for seamen for the immediate future.

So rapid was the response of central government to the Spithead mutiny that the seamen delayed the fleet from getting off Ushant by little more than a month. Admiralty anxiety on the score of the delays had only been relieved by its receipt of intelligence of French movements in Brest. Regular reports from informers in Brest reached the Admiralty through Captain Philip D'Auvergne, based in the Channel Islands.[2] They reinforced observations of frigates operating close to the mouth of the Goulet. These ships belonged to two frigate squadrons based at Falmouth of which the Admiralty had retained control. In May 1797 the squadrons were placed directly under the control of the Commander-in-Chief of the Channel fleet, enlarging his force of smaller vessels. But, at the same time, the Admiralty firmly prescribed the use that could be made of these squadrons, maintaining the availability of one for their own use in an emergency. It also denied the Commander-in-Chief disposal of individual frigates to stations inconsistent with Admiralty priorities. Similarly, in November 1797 the Admiralty dictated the disposition of the ships of the line in the Channel fleet. Hitherto the bulk of the fleet had taken shelter for the worst of the winter months. Now the Admiralty directed which ships should remain at sea and which should return into port. Of the latter, two-decked ships were directed to Cawsand Bay, three-deck ships to Spithead.

While enlarging the managerial responsibility of the Commander-in-Chief, the Admiralty thus retained control of the strategic disposition of ships. This trend continued in 1798. An anticipated attempt by the French to mount an invasion of Ireland determined even greater economy and Admiralty control. The strategic advantage of ships returning to Brest from Plymouth, rather than Spithead, was urged on the Commander-in-Chief. Plymouth and Torbay subsequently became the main

---

[1]C. J. Doorne, 'Mutiny and sedition in the home commands of the Royal Navy 1793–1803' (unpub. University of London PhD thesis, 1997). R. Saxby found no evidence of seditious motives in the Spithead Mutiny; see his note in *M.M.*, 76 (1990), 149–50.

[2]G. R. Balleine, *The Trajedy of Philippe d'Auvergne* (London, 1973) 84–94.

base and shelter for ships off Brest.[1] For speed of concentration had become crucial. In 1798, while the squadrons off Brest relieved one another in turn, the Channel fleet had to be further subdivided to supply two new squadrons, one on the coast of Ireland with another ready for sea in reserve. However the French expeditions to Ireland, especially that of Bomparte from Brest in September, demonstrated the limitations of the blockade. Indeed the reinforcement of the Brest fleet from Lorient in the spring of 1799 and the escape of Bruix in April, to return in August 1799 reinforced by a squadron of Spaniards, demonstrated the limitations of Admiralty control and the inadequacy of the loose blockade.

Although the Channel fleet was heavily reinforced, tighter control off Brest could only be achieved through the determination of the Commander-on-Chief on the spot. The appointment of St Vincent to this post was followed by the establishment of the close blockade in the spring of 1800. It was the culmination of the process of increasing Admiralty control of the Channel fleet. Indeed the new Commander-in-Chief's obsession with discipline, both in the fleet and of the blockade, was carried further than even Spencer anticipated. It demonstrated the limits of Admiralty control in the face of a resolute Commander-in-Chief. In September 1800 the Board of Admiralty was challenged, but declined, to give St Vincent an order for his ships of the line to take shelter on the English coast during the winter gales.[2]

The close blockade thus persisted through the winter of 1800. The course of the war on the continent vindicated the policy, for it demanded a demonstration of Britain's determination to oppose French arms by the most extreme measures. The defeat of Austria in November 1800 heralded the collapse of the second coalition against Revolutionary France. The latter seemed once more to be in the ascendant. Indeed fraternisation between France and Russia and the formation of the Armed Neutrality of the North, with the subsequent invasion of Hanover, raised the spectre of new allies to whom the French might wish to send support by sea.[3] The close blockade of Brest was thus an appropriate response to events in Europe as well as the natural product of the personality and circumstances of the Commander-in-Chief of the Channel fleet.

It was made possible by two factors. The first was the establishment of an effective method of feeding and watering the fleet off Brest. By

---

[1] M. Duffy, 'Devon and the naval strategy of the French wars 1689–1815', in *The New Maritime History of Devon*, ed. M. Duffy *et al.* (2 vols, London, 1992–94), 182–191.

[2] *Spencer Papers*, III, 374–6.

[3] I. R. Christie, *Wars and Revolutions. Britain 1760–1815* (London, 1982), 248–9.

1800 convoys of victuallers – small vessels usually 100–150 tons – were escorted to and from Ushant by sloops and cutters. In December 1800 an order required fresh vegetables to reach the inshore squadron off the Black Rocks at least once a month. Though disapproved by senior officers for the spirits they sold, private trading vessels supplemented the cargoes of the victuallers. Otherwise ships reprovisioned by returning into Plymouth Sound or Torbay. Provisions were shipped round from Plymouth into Torbay. There, water was also available at Brixham, although the growth in the amount required by 1800 demanded enlargements to the diameter of piping and length of wharfage available.[1] In 1800 these improvements became the responsibility of the Inspector General of Naval Works, a post established at the Admiralty in 1796.

The second factor facilitating the close blockade was the inauguration in the Channel fleet of the policy of giving seamen lemon juice as a preventive against scurvy. In the Channel, 1800, rather than 1795, was the real turning point in the defeat of scurvy. After the promulgation of the various means by which scurvy could be controlled by James Lind in his Treatise of 1753, the experience of the French Revolutionary War in the Mediterranean had demonstrated the efficacy of lemon juice, paticularly recommended by Lind, as a preventive. The Admiralty's authorisation in 1795 of the issue of lemon juice to seamen has been heralded as a great landmark in the conquest of scurvy. But then it was only issued to fleets on request. Owing to the initial shortage of supplies, ships going on voyages to foreign stations had priority over those on home stations.[2] Furthermore, instructions to surgeons regarding its issue recommended it be given to seamen only as a cure once the symptons of scurvy had begun to appear. Indeed Thomas Trotter, the Physician to the Channel fleet, though an advocate of lemon juice, against the view of the Sick and Wounded Board fiercely opposed its issue as a preventive. Sea officers on blockade continued to despair at the scorbutic state into which their crews deteriorated. Only when St Vincent, fresh from the Mediterranean, assumed command in the Channel was lemon juice demanded for issue on a daily basis as a preventive. Needless to say, though the Commander-in-Chief's criticism of the Physician concerned another matter, Trotter was replaced by Andrew Baird a month later.

[1]M. Steer, 'The blockade of Brest and the victualling of the Western Squadron, 1793–1805', *M.M.*, 76 (1990), 307–15.

[2]K. J. Carpenter, *The History of Scurvy and Vitamin C* (Cambridge, 1986), 54–63, 95; J. J. Keevil, C. Lloyd and J. L. S. Coulter, *Medicine and the Navy 1200–1900* (4 vols, Edinburgh, 1957–63), III, 321–2.

These improvements in the victualling of seamen underpinned the close blockade. Indeed it was in the establishment of the administrative infrastructure that the real achievement of the blockade lay. For the close blockade was not to prove immediately effective. Ganteaume escaped with seven of the line in January 1801. Even so, the extent to which the policy of tight control, both in the fleet and off Ushant, was approved in Government was reflected in the elevation of St Vincent to the Admiralty in February 1801. His successor in the Channel fleet maintained the organisation of the close blockade, established by experience over the previous six years. He was less rigorous about the proximity to Ushant with which the fleet was required to keep station. But he nevertheless complied with the policy, now implemented by St Vincent, of employing the Channel fleet as a weapon wielded directly from London, closely and interminably confronting the French fleet in Brest.

The Managers of the Channel Fleet

The increase of Admiralty control over the disposition of the Channel fleet demanded adaptation on the part of those senior officers who managed the fleet. However, because of the critical role of the fleet in the defence of the United Kingdom, its Commanders-in-Chief were officers of the highest standing. Their seniority made them an age at which there was clearly sometimes difficulty accepting government by a Board of Admiralty consisting of junior officers and statesmen of relative inexperience in naval matters. Moreover, the number of the most senior men with the ability, vigour and motivation to fill the post was limited. Indeed the choice was narrowed in May 1795 when Samuel, Lord Hood (1724–1816) was dismissed as Commander-in-Chief in the Mediterranean for responding negatively to the odds against him there after the French were reinforced from Brest; and further restricted in April 1796 after the Honourable William Cornwallis was court-martialled for failing to carry out the Admiralty's orders to proceed to the West Indies with reinforcements and refusing to sail in a frigate.

The absence of other admirals of comparable seniority and renown accounts for the period for which Richard, Earl Howe (1726–1799) was forced to remain as Commander-in-Chief of the Channel fleet. In 1793 he was the natural choice for the command. His experience was unrivalled, his reputation as a fleet commander second to none. He had joined the navy in time to sail for the Pacific in 1740 with Anson. The ship in which he sailed never passed Cape Horn but with parental interest he had become a lieutenant in 1744 and flag captain to Sir

Charles Knowles before the end of 1748. In 1755 he was with Boscawen when he intercepted the French convoy destined for Canada and, by his offensive action, was alleged to have precipitated the Seven Years War. Howe took the French ship *Alcide* and was credited with firing the first shot in the conflict.

As a rear-admiral in November 1770, Lord Hawke, then First Lord of the Admiralty, appointed him to be Commander-in-Chief in the Mediterranean. During the first two years of the American War of Independence he was Commander-in-Chief on the North American station and joint commissioner with his brother William for the conduct of peace negotiations with the colonists. In 1782 he became Commander-in-Chief of the Channel fleet, and terminated the war by relieving Gibraltar. In January 1783 he was made First Lord of the Admiralty in Shelburne's ministry. Turned out by the Fox–North Coalition, he returned with Pitt at the end of the year and stayed until the Earl of Chatham took over in July 1788. Mobilisation against Spain in 1790 again saw him hoist his flag to exercise the Channel fleet off Ushant where he issued his *Signal Book for the Ships of War*, the final product of his long-nurtured work on a new signalling and tactical system.

Howe possessed the confidence of many naval officers as well as politicians. His *Signal Book* provided the former with a true numerical system of signalling and was to be reissued by others including Hood and Jervis, and to remain the standard book until its contents were amalgamated into the first official Admiralty signal book issued in 1799.[1] However, in 1793 Howe was 67 years of age and his health was to prove a continual problem. Even before his first cruise he asked to resign. He was persuaded to continue after a rest and indeed led the fleet in the autumn of 1793 before retiring to Bath. In 1794 he won the Battle of the Glorious First of June but was left exhausted by the process. Howe went ashore for the last time on 25 February 1795. From this time Howe, though still Commander-in-Chief, lived ashore. Alexander Hood (1727–1814), ennobled as first Viscount Bridport for his part on the Glorious First of June, accepted a role as his deputy, taking the fleet to sea, and receiving instructions from Howe as well as the Board of Admiralty. Howe demonstrated every desire to resign but neither George III nor Spencer, conscious of the credit of his name, would allow him to do so. He was only permitted to resign in April 1797 and even then was brought back from retirement to help settle the Spithead mutiny. By then, he was 71 years of age and was to die two years later.

---

[1] B. Tunstall, *Naval Warfare in the Age of Sail. The Evolution of Fighting Tactics 1650–1815* (ed. N. Tracy, London, 1990), 194.

Alexander Hood, Viscount Bridport, was most affected by the process of reorganisation and amendment to which the Channel fleet was subject after 1795. He was the younger brother by two years of Samuel, Lord Hood,[1] and only nine months younger than Howe. But his career had assumed a very different course to that of his predecessor, though equally indebted to patronage. At the beginning of the Seven Years War he became flag captain to Charles Saunders whose continued interest was evident in 1766 by the former's succession to the latter as Treasurer of Greenwich Hospital, a post Alexander Hood was to hold for 33 years. He also became connected with the Pitt family by his marriage in 1758 to Molly West, 20 years his senior and sister of Temple West. Formerly she had been romantically linked with William Pitt, Earl of Chatham, who remained a family friend.

Alexander Hood was introduced to the blockade of Brest in 1759 when he commanded a frigate under Hawke in the Channel. He established his reputation as a fighting officer in January 1761 when he retook the *Warwick*, a two-decker that had been captured by the French in 1756. During the American War of Independence he again served in the Channel and fought at the Battle of Ushant in 1778. However, his ship was one of the rear division under Palliser and at Augustus Keppel's court-martial Hood was alleged to have changed his log. Although other logs had also allegedly been changed, it was Hood who was known as the man who had tried to affect the verdict by omitting a vital signal. Within weeks, as a friendly act, Sandwich posted him to the North American station. Hood objected to the appointment, however, on the grounds that he was asked to sail as a private captain whereas his status justified the distinction of a commodore's broad pendant, which had been refused. His feelings were further hurt when the Pitts' youngest son, James, was pointedly withdrawn from his protection and entrusted to the charge of Lord Howe. His career was temporarily blighted and might have been extinguished after Keppel succeeded Sandwich at the Admiralty, but Howe came to his assistance. After Kempenfelt was lost in the *Royal George* at Spithead in August 1782, to replace the rear-admiral Howe asked for the appointment of Hood, to which Keppel agreed. Hood thus took part in the last important cruise of the war.

Howe's role in salvaging Hood's career might initially have obtained an amicable response, but by the time of the French Revolutionary War Hood consistently acted towards Howe with antipathy. From 1795, when Hood, now Lord Bridport, deputised for the Commander-in-Chief, the immediate point at issue was Howe's retention of the

[1]D. Hood, *The Admirals Hood* (1942).

prerogatives and remuneration of a command which his health rendered him unfit to exercise. But his ill-feeling may have dated back to an occasion when Howe as First Lord demanded a sum of money due to Greenwich Hospital which was in the hands of Bridport as Treasurer of the Navy. Bridport was adept at revealing his hostility. After the battle of the Glorious First of June he ignored several official letters from the flagship. Between June and September 1795 he failed to keep Howe informed of his proceedings. His rudeness in explaining himself is striking. To alleviate his discontent at deputising for Howe while the latter stayed on shore, in July 1795 he was given a commission as Commander-in-Chief of a squadron to be employed on a particular service. However the commission was cancelled in October with the evident failure of Bridport to respond appropriately towards Howe, and he spent the following 18 months on shore. He was re-employed in April 1797, when Howe was allowed to retire, this time with the full authority and emoluments of Commander-in-Chief.

Bridport was to retire himself in 1800, then aged 73. He brought to the Channel fleet the attitudes of a previous age. He was at his best in managing the seamen of the Channel fleet, for example inducing the Admiralty to come to terms with the seamen during the Spithead mutiny. Afterwards he kept their tributes to him in his private papers. But he reacted against the extension of Admiralty control over the Channel fleet, and especially against its attempts to make innovations in the organisation of the blockade and to control the disposition of all his vessels. Under pressure in 1798 his correspondence with the Admiralty descended into acrimony. He resented having to take responsibility without the resources. In May 1798, on account of a shortage of frigates, he was pessimistic, even negative, about his ability to keep the French fleet under observation and French convoys out of Brest. Yet paradoxically, against Admiralty veto, he regularly proposed disposal of frigates where he thought they would be most useful in taking privateers. Aggravating relations with the Admiralty and his subordinates was his tendency to personalise administrative problems. Over the shortage of frigates his relationship with the commanders of the formerly independent frigate squadrons, Sir John Borlase Warren and Sir Edward Pellew, became at best counterproductive.

The appointment of John Jervis, Earl of St Vincent (1735–1823), to succeed Bridport in 1800 when the combined Franco-Spanish fleet was in Brest achieved through St Vincent's own volition what Bridport, from his reservations, declined to do. Initially St Vincent's energy, drive and determination contrasted markedly with those of Bridport. He almost rejoiced in being permitted to concentrate on the management of the fleet off Ushant while the Admiralty concerned itself with the wider disposition of ships. His difference from Bridport was partly one of personality. Activity and determination had raised St Vincent throughout his career. Sandwich described him as a good officer but turbulent and busy.[1] He was only eight years younger than both Howe and Bridport. He had served under Boscawen in 1755 and accompanied Saunders to Canada in 1759, piloting his squadron up the St Lawrence to Quebec. At Ushant in 1778 he had been stationed immediately astern of Keppel who warmly thanked him for his support. He later observed that the Hoods had ever afterwards been hostile to him.[2] In 1793 he was sent to the West Indies with Sir Charles Grey and played his part in capturing Martinique, St Lucia and Guadeloupe. In the early autumn of 1795 he went to the Mediterranean to relieve Hotham as Commander-in-Chief and on that station ensured by punitive action that the mutinies of 1797 did not spread to his command.

By June 1799 his health compelled him to hand over the Mediterranean command to Lord Keith and return to England. Having recovered, he was ready to succeed Bridport in April 1800. The presence of the combined Franco-Spanish fleet in Brest demanded the utmost vigilance. The close blockade instituted by St Vincent was as much the necessity of the occasion as the product of the Commander-in-Chief's own exacting standards. But the demands of the close blockade on crews off Ushant did, in St Vincent's view, have the additional benefit of deterring the fermentation of discontent among the seamen. However, his obsessive concern with discipline, especially among the officer corps,[3] suggest that his own attitudes were affected by the rigours of the blockade. Indeed by October 1800 St Vincent's health had again broken down and he was obliged to seek permission to exercise his command from Torbay. From there he ensured the standards he had established were maintained. Yet even St Vincent could not force ships and men to persist in the face of the worst winter weather. The escape of Ganteaume early in 1801 demonstrated that, in spite of all the resources and organisational support given to the blockade, even the best-motivated Commander-in-Chief could not close Brest completely.

Yet St Vincent had demonstrated what was possible. When he moved to the Admiralty in February 1801 the Honourable William Cornwallis

---

[1] *The Correspondence of King George III from 1760 to December 1783* (6 vols, London, 1927–28), ed. Sir J. Fortescue, III, 225.

[2] *Spencer Papers*, III, 314.

[3] According to E. P. Brenton 'it was in his situation as Commander-in-Chief of the Channel fleet that Lord St. Vincent lost his popularity among the officers of the navy'. *Life and Correspondence of John, Earl of St. Vincent* (London, 1838).

(1744–1819), who succeeded him, had both an organisation and a standard to work to. Moreover he had a career to resume which St Vincent was ready to promote. The fourth son of the Earl Cornwallis, he had been to the St Lawrence with Boscawen; he was present at the taking of Louisburg in 1758 and at Quiberon in 1759; he fought in most of the West Indian battles between 1779 and 1782; and he commanded in the East Indies from 1789 to 1793 where he took part in the battle of Pondicherry. Returning from India to the Channel fleet, he had demonstrated his seamanship and control of a squadron by his 'masterly retreat' from a superior enemy in June 1795, his manoeuvres contributing indirectly to the subsequent battle of Isle de Groix.[1] He was then sent to the West Indies as Commander-in-Chief but at this point ran foul of Lord Spencer and the Board of Admiralty. Having set sail on 29 February 1796, two weeks into the voyage his flagship, the *Royal Sovereign*, was disabled in a gale. He put back to England and was ordered to proceed in a frigate. He was in poor health and refused. He was consequently court-martialled and acquitted. However, he struck his flag and, though promoted to admiral in February 1799, was not employed again under Lord Spencer.[2]

Cornwallis was not to disappoint St Vincent. The main fleet cruised further off Ushant than St Vincent had been accustomed to require, yet 'always near enough for the purpose' for which it was there. A modest unassuming man, he was not provoked by St Vincent's abrasive manner, nor did he find the faults in his officers and men with which his predecessor had been obsessed. The peace preliminaries of October 1801 permitted him to relinquish his place off Brest, but in May 1803 he resumed that station which he was to hold as the weather and reliefs permitted until 1806.[3]

Cornwallis presided over a fleet off Brest with very different expectations and very different support to that which Lords Howe and Bridport had managed. To those who looked back the contrast was striking. An anonymous commentator observed about 1806 'there was an instance in the early part of the late war of a great portion of the Channel fleet remaining at Spithead five months at one time and now it is to be understood that ships are to return into a King's port but twice a year except when driven in by stress of weather'.[4] The demands of the

[1]Clowes, IV, 256–8.

[2]Ibid., 291n.

[3]James, III, 169. *Dispatches and Letters Relating to the Blockade of Brest, 1803–1805*, ed. J. Leyland (2 vols, NRS, 1899, 1902).

[4]Anonymous to William Windham, Secretary for War and Colonies, c. 1806, BL Add. MS 37890.

continuous blockade on ships, officers and men generated a very different navy from that which had begun the French Revolutionary War in 1793. It was a transition effected partly through an extension of Admiralty control over the Channel fleet. It was a transition that rested on the maintenance of ships and men through efficient dockyard operations and appropriate victualling. The conquest of scurvy was fundamental. So also was the establishment of new standards in the officer corps. It was thus a transition effected by the demonstration of what could be achieved, and this derived from the determination, abilities and leadership of its Commanders-in-Chief, in particular St Vincent and the Honourable William Cornwallis.

1

THE CHANNEL FLEET
12 JUNE 1793–5 JUNE 1795

The National Convention of France declared war on Britain on 1 February 1793. A reciprocal response from the British government ten days later triggered the process of naval mobilisation. At the beginning of the year, Britain had only 26 ships of the line and 135 other vessels in service at sea, but urgent mobilisation rapidly brought many of the ships in Ordinary into commission. The event had been anticipated in the 1780s; owing to the separate preparation and ready availability of the equipment and furniture of individual ships, within a few weeks the ships of the line in commission had doubled and lesser rates increased to over 200. Initially the urgent despatch of squadrons to distant stations took priority over defence in home waters so that it was not until June 1793 that command and direction was given to a nascent Channel fleet.[1] Earl Howe was appointed Admiral and Commander-in-Chief, with Vice-admirals Thomas Graves and Sir Alexander Hood (Baron Bridport from August 1794) second and third in command [1].

As conceived in mid-1793, the functions of the Channel fleet were not exclusively concerned with the blockade of Brest. Initially, the protection of British trade and the destruction of French commerce, along with France's privateers and warships, took precedence. Nor was Brest the primary location of French naval forces to which Howe was directed. The French fleet was anchored in Quiberon Bay and its reinforcement was anticipated from Lorient, Rochefort and Brest. Howe was directed, if possible, to intercept these reinforcements before they reached Quiberon Bay. Nevertheless, as it was from Brest from which the most powerful section of the French northern fleet would issue, Howe was specifically directed to make observations and obtain intelligence about activities in that port.

From the beginning, the Admiralty was the centre to and from which these reports of intelligence were required to flow. Because the operations of the Channel fleet were expected to predominate in the Western Approaches and in the Bay of Biscay, Falmouth was designated the

---

[1]W. James, *The Naval History of Great Britain from the declaration of war by France in 1793 to the accession of George IV* (6 vols, London, 1859), I, 53, 61; R. Morriss, *The Royal Dockyards during the Revolutionary and Napoleonic Wars* (Leicester, 1983), 14–15.

transhipment port for despatches. Howe was directed always to have one of the cutters from the Channel fleet at Falmouth ready to receive information despatched to him by the Admiralty, while the Regulating Captain stationed there was commanded always to be ready to hasten on to London reports sent in by Howe [2].

The first cruise of the Channel fleet, consisting of 15 ships of the line, was terminated early. Sailing from St Helens on 14 July, the fleet was taken aback off Scilly by a squall. *Majestic* fell on board *Bellerophon* which had to be towed into Plymouth, and on the 23rd the fleet put back into Torbay [3]. At this time, convoys, both inward and outward, were the immediate concern of the French as well as of the British fleets. The former, reported to be off Belle Isle, was awaiting one from America and on 25 July Howe, now reinforced to 17 of the line, again put to sea and on 1 August sighted and chased the French fleet before stormy weather intervened and obliged him to put back once more into Torbay. Towards the end of August and between the middle of October and mid-December, Howe cruised twice more off the Scillies, providing protection to an outward bound Newfoundland convoy, an inward West Indian, and troop convoys to the Mediterranean and the West Indies [4]. On 18 October, shots were exchanged with a French squadron before thick weather again intervened. Immediately after losing sight of Howe, the French took 17 Newfoundland ships; however, they failed to intercept the British troop and supply transports destined for the West Indies.[1]

By December Howe had been reinforced to 22 of the line, and when he returned into port only eight of these vessels were directed into Plymouth and the remainder to Spithead [5]. The facilities at Plymouth were still regarded as secondary in importance to those at Portsmouth, partly on account of the number of ships that could moor in relative safety in the lee of the Isle of Wight, and also on account of the greater number of docks in the eastern dockyard. Until 1796 Portsmouth had five dry docks including one double, while Plymouth possessed only three single and one double. To enlarge dock capacity at Portsmouth further, between 1796 and 1801 the basin was enlarged and the number of docks increased to eight singles. The basin and dock gates were made watertight by the use of moveable caissons or floating dams, and a steam engine installed to perform the drainage operations. By 1805 these works would permit Portsmouth to refit twice as many ships as Plymouth: the great margin was then in the number of frigates and sloops; Portsmouth refitted only marginally more ships of the line.[2] But

[1] James, I, 61–8.
[2] Morriss, 19, 44–9.

between 1796 and 1801, when dockings at Portsmouth were diminished while the improvements were taking place, the refitting facilities at Plymouth increased in importance. Their value was enhanced not only by the shortage of docks further east but by the growth in the size of the Channel fleet, the increasing permanence of the blockade of Brest, and the greater ease, so far as distance and winds were concerned, with which the blockade could be served from Plymouth.

Although Brest was kept under observation from sentinel ships during the winter months, the fleet did not go to sea again until 2 May 1794. Then it was to escort convoys down Channel and to intercept if possible a large convoy expected by the French from the United States carrying both food supplies and imports from the West Indies [6]. In anticipation of a cruise that would test the health of his crews, especially their resistance to scurvy, Howe presciently requested the use by the fleet of 'several hundred gallons' of lemon juice in store at Haslar hospital, a request with which the Admiralty complied [7–8]. In the event, the cruise was to last only six weeks. Between 5 and 18 May, having first looked into Brest and found the French fleet still in port, Howe with 26 of the line and seven frigates cruised in the Bay of Biscay across the track which the convoy from America was anticipated to make. On 19 May he returned off Ushant and was informed the French fleet had sailed, in fact only three days earlier.

Howe promptly sailed westward. He feared Rear-admiral Montagu with only six of the line would be taken by the Brest fleet, for Montagu had been directed to cruise between Cape Ortegal and the latitude of Belle Isle [9] after conducting East India ships south as far as Cape Finisterre. Montagu meanwhile on 15 May obtained intelligence that suggested the escort of the American convoy, if joined by a squadron sent out to meet it from Rochefort, would be stronger than himself. Having sent a frigate to gain reinforcement from Howe, and waited as ordered on station until 20 May, Montagu attempted unsuccessfully to find Howe at their rendezvous off Ushant, and then returned to Plymouth. He was immediately ordered to rejoin Howe [10] or, having been reinforced to ten of the line and provided with the latest intelligence, attempt to intercept the convoy himself [12]. However, he found neither Howe nor the convoy from America, which got into Brest safely. Montagu was never employed again.[1]

[1]For the movements of Howe and Montagu, see M. Duffy, 'The man who missed the grain convoy: Sir George Montagu and the escape of Vanstabel's convoy from America in 1794', in *Les Marines Française et Britannique face aux États-Unis (1776–1869)*, (Service Historique de la Marine, Vincennes, 1999), 91–7. See also by M. Duffy in *The Glorious First of June 1794. A Battle and its Aftermath*, proceedings of a conference at the National Maritime Museum in 1994, ed. M. Duffy and R. Morriss (Exeter, 2000).

Howe, on the other hand, on 28 May encountered the Brest fleet under Rear-admiral Louis-Thomas Villaret-Joyeuse and after two days of partial action, engaged it in battle on 1 June [11]. Though evenly matched, each with 26 of the line, the French lost seven ships, one, the *Vengeur*, sinking soon after it was captured. The British fleet was badly damaged too: not until 5 a.m. on 3 June was Howe able to make sail. The fleet was divided between Portsmouth and Plymouth [13, 14] to refit [15] and discharge prisoners, of which nearly 5000 were landed at both places [16].[1] The celebrations surrounding Howe's landing at Portsmouth and his humility in, according to *The Times,* attributing the victory to the British seamen, attest to his personal popularity [14]. Meanwhile, two flag officers of the Channel fleet having been lost through leg amputations, Rear-admiral Cornwallis was placed under Howe's command with a squadron of 12, and continued the business of conducting convoys through the Bay of Biscay into the Soundings [17].

By the patent of 14 May 1794 the Board of Admiralty received a new and significant member, Sir Charles Middleton. He had served at sea, mainly in the West Indies during the Seven Years War, and had been Comptroller at the Navy Board between 1778 and 1790. During the American War he had been the driving force behind the introduction of copper sheathing and contributed to the introduction of carronades. During the following peace he had devoted himself to improving the efficiency of the Navy Office and dockyards and to repairing and re-building the British fleet.[2] His mother had been a Dundas, and his most influential relation was Henry Dundas, now Secretary for War, to whom Middleton addressed his private thoughts on the needs of the navy. Though named third naval commissioner in the Admiralty patent of 14 May, Samuel Lord Hood and Alan Gardner were serving at sea so that temporarily Middleton had disproportionate influence.

On coming to the board, Middleton's thoughts returned to the Seven Years War and his letter to Philip Patton [18] recalls the strategy by which a Western Squadron had blockaded the French Atlantic ports more or less continuously, its ships relieved alternately and supplied on station with fresh provisions. As Middleton suggests, the success of overseas expeditions was attributed to the blockade on the French coast. Now Middleton, with his passion for logistics, sketched out the British naval forces needed on each station, those of the Western Squadron

---

[1]The estimated casualty list for the French fleet, including prisoners of war, exceeded 7000. For an account of the battle of 1 June 1794, see James, I, 138–203.

[2]J. E. Talbot, *The Pen and Ink Sailor. Charles Middleton and the King's Navy, 1778–1813* (London, 1998); P. Webb, 'The rebuilding and repair of the fleet, 1783–1793', *Bulletin of the Institute of Historical Research,* L (1977), 194–209.

coming in his paper before those of any other station [19].[1] He seems to have been the first to have anticipated the scale of the force and the support that would eventually be needed to watch Brest and the other French Biscay ports. To Dundas, he was unabashed about pressing his claims as a naval professional above those of his political superiors, in particular Lord Chatham, First Lord of the Admiralty [21], and asserting the need for a man of his administrative expertise to organise the Admiralty Office [22]. Dundas knew Middleton too well to be dismayed by his desire for autonomy, recommending him to Earl Spencer, who succeeded Chatham as First Lord in December 1794, even though he was 'a little difficult to act with from an anxiety, I had almost said an irritability of temper'. Rather, he simply explained that Middleton needed 'to have a great deal of his own way of doing business in order to do it well'.[2] His confidence was well placed. Middleton was uninhibited in acknowledging the difficulty already being felt in recruiting and pressing sufficient seamen for the fleet and the necessity to cut France's coastal trade in supplies. Above all, he perceived the necessity to increase discipline over captains in the fleet and to impose the will of the Admiralty on its admirals [22, 23].

Middleton's concerns partly reflected the difficulties being experienced with the senior officers of the Channel fleet. In June 1794 Howe requested to be relieved of his command and was permitted to reside at Bath when the fleet was in port. In July Alexander Hood requested the same leave of absence, threatening that his gout, if not given time on shore, might prevent him from returning to sea [20]. In September and November they both managed cruises into the Western Approaches. But in December Howe repeated from Bath his request for permanent relief [24]. News that a large fleet had put to sea from Brest permitted Spencer to persuade Howe to travel to London to provide advice [25, 26, 29]. At the same time Hood, now Lord Bridport, though requesting an extension of leave, was also persuaded to leave Bath for London [27–28]. Conscious of the moral effect, as well as the professional importance of keeping Howe in command, George III wrote to him and and had him visit Windsor for an audience [30, 31]. Though as confounded as everyone else by that 'reserve that at times envelopes his meaning', the King persuaded Howe to continue in service. On being informed of this, Bridport too agreed to return to sea [32–33].

---

[1]The full text of these papers may be found in *Letters and Papers of Charles, Lord Barham 1753–1813*, ed. J. K. Laughton (3 vols, NRS, 1907–11), II, 392–408.

[2]*Private Papers of George, Second Earl Spencer, First Lord of the Admiralty 1794–1801*, ed. J. S. Corbett and H. W. Richmond (4 vols, NRS, 1913–1924), I, 6–7.

The sortie of the Brest fleet about the 24 December 1794 was in fact postponed. The attempt of 35 of the line to pass though the Goulet resulted in the complete loss of a three-decker on the Mingen rock in the middle of the channel. However, the remaining vessels did issue forth on the 31st, only to receive several losses by foundering and much damage from the weather.[1] In response Howe was furnished with a fleet of 31 of the line. However, manning, the distribution of orders, the establishment of rendezvous, the acquisition of information regarding the movements of convoys, and unfavourable winds, all delayed Howe until the end of January 1795 [34, 36]. Bridport's elder brother, Samuel Lord Hood, reported in extreme terms the public consternation in London at the threat posed by the Brest fleet [35]. Howe was able to get down Channel but off Plymouth, where he hoped to take a convoy under his protection, unfavourable winds forced him into Torbay where he remained at least until mid-February [37]. While waiting on the weather, Howe vented his frustration at the choice of Plymouth as a departure point for convoys [37]; at his inability to reconcile the escort of a convoy with looking into Brest; and the apparent failure of the First Lord of the Admiralty to understand the impossibility of doing such surveillance on a westerly wind [38–39]. In winter Torbay was dangerously exposed to easterly gales [40]; nine of his 36 of the line in the bay parted their cables. But on 14 February, adding six more to his fleet, Howe finally departed with his convoys and, having confirmed the Brest fleet was in port, returned to Spithead.[2] There, once more, he left the fleet under the command of Bridport [42].

In the absence of the British fleet, there was little obstacle to sorties by the French fleet which proved dangerous to British shipping. In November 1794 the 74-gun *Alexander* was taken though in company with the *Canada* of equal strength. In January 1795 the French fleet took over 100 vessels, both merchant and naval, on its 34-day cruise.[3] At the same time British frigates remained active and proved quite capable of taking French ships of comparable strength [44]. However French squadrons were sent out specifically to intercept them. Such was almost the fate of the frigate squadron under Sir John Borlase Warren which was operating under Admiralty orders separately from the Channel fleet [38, 45]. Above all, the French could have decisively altered the odds in different theatres by despatching squadrons to, for example, the Mediterranean. One of the purposes of the intended sortie

---

[1] James, I, 258–9.
[2] James, I, 262.
[3] James, I, 203, 261.

of the French fleet in December was to provide escort to six of the line destined for Toulon. They eventually sailed on 2 February.[1] Their safe arrival was the basis of Samuel, Lord Hood's protest at the end of April 1795 at the relative weakness of the British Mediterranean fleet [46].

Hood's protest precipitated serious consideration of a reshuffle of fleet commanders. France's invasion of Holland and the declaration of war against Britain by the Batavian Republic in May 1795 necessitated a commander for a fleet in the North Sea to blockade the Texel and defend convoys to the Baltic. Pending the intended return of Hood, Hotham had been left in command in the Mediterranean. Yet, retaliating at Hood's claim that the best he could do was prevent disgrace, on 1 May the Admiralty ordered Hood to return in *Victory* to Spithead, to return his orders and instructions, and to hand over command of the ships destined for the Mediterranean to Rear-admiral Dickson. In the Channel fleet there was a sense of pleasure that officers were at last being taught the bounds to their authority [47]. Both Jervis and Bridport were considered as potential commanders in the Mediterranean, but the latter, as the younger brother of Samuel, Lord Hood, categorically refused 'to supply his brother's place' [48]. Meanwhile, though remaining in command in the Channel, Howe resided on shore, leaving the sea-going charge of the fleet to Bridport. It was an anomalous situation, creating administrative complications, especially as Howe still expected to have orders to the fleet pass through his hands [49].

At the same time, the medical men in the fleet and at the Sick and Wounded Board were grasping the scurvy nettle. A severe winter and late spring had resulted in a shortage of fresh meat and vegetables, thereby increasing the incidence of scurvy in the Channel fleet even though it was anchored at Spithead [50]. Oranges and lemons were supplied as a curative. Dr Trotter, Physician to the Channel fleet, fearing that all seamen were to a greater or lesser extent liable to scurvy, threatening the operational capacity of squadrons, recommended a two-week crash diet of fresh beef and vegetables when they entered harbour. Conscious that this liability to scurvy arose from a deficiency in the established diet, Trotter proposed the long-term amendment of the diet with the introduction of double-strength beer. He also suggested lemon juice be carried by every ship at sea as a curative [51].

The Admiralty was alarmed at the recurrence of scurvy, raising as it did the necessity to replace its victims with healthy men [52]. The

[1]James, I, 262.

manning problem had already given rise to the Quota Acts of March 1795, placing a levy in men on the counties and seaports of England, Wales and Scotland.[1] Now the Sick and Wounded Board was prompted to state its professional opinion on the best method of maintaining the health of crews. It denied any advantage in strengthening the hop content of beer, and recommended to Admiralty notice a trial of lemon juice as a preventive on a voyage to India and St Helena in 1794 by the *Suffolk* and *Argo*. It consequently recommended lemon juice as a preventive, rather than a cure, defending its cost by reference to that of treating scorbutic seamen. This, after all, included that of recruiting and paying replacements, as well as the management of fraudulent cases. They argued lemon juice should be served daily to crews, and that a special diet, including experimental antiscorbutics, should replace the standard diet for designated portions of crews [53] [2]

The recommendation of the Sick and Wounded Board was to form the foundation of the Admiralty's policy towards scurvy. However, its implementation was to be impeded for five years within the Channel fleet by personality and communication problems within an administrative system that was highly compartmentalised. In June 1795 Trotter revealed his tendency towards managerial autonomy by preventing the Sick and Wounded Board's representative at Portsmouth, Dr Johnston, from receiving the numbers of scorbutic patients in the fleet, to whom at this stage in the war fresh meat and vegetables were limited [54]. Trotter firmly adhered to his belief that lemon juice should be issued only as cure, not as a preventive, for scurvy. Anyway, for some time lemon juice was not to be available in sufficient quantities for it to be issued on a daily basis in every fleet. In consequence, while lemon juice was to be issued by the Sick and Wounded Board to ships going on foreign stations,[3] within the Channel fleet lemon juice was issued only as a cure once symptoms of scurvy had made their appearance. Surgeons were directed to look out for incipient cases. The Sick and Wounded Board did not attempt to alter this arrangement for the Chan-

[1]The first Quota Act of 5 March 1795 placed a levy on each county in England and Wales; the second of 16 March extended it to the seaports of England, Wales and Scotland. The counties and burghs of Scotland were included within the same principle by a third Act. See C. Emsley, *British Society and the French Wars 1793–1815* (London, 1979), 53.

[2]Gilbert Blane, Commissioner for Sick and Wounded Seamen, receives the credit for the Board's recommendation for lemon juice to be issued 'on a far more generous scale than ever before'. See *Medicine and the Navy 1200–1900*, ed. J. J. Keevil, C. Lloyd and J. L. S. Coulter (4 vols, Edinburgh & London, 1957–63), III, 321.

[3]*The Health of Seamen. Selections from the Works of Dr. James Lind, Sir Gilbert Blane and Dr. Thomas Trotter* ed. C. Lloyd (NRS, 1965), 177n.

nel fleet until 1799 [471], and the general issue of lemon juice as a daily antiscorbutic did not remove scurvy as a problem impeding the blockade of Brest until 1800.

1. *Admiralty to Vice-admiral Sir Alexander Hood*

12 June 1793

By the Commissioners for executing the office of Lord High Admiral of Great Britain and Ireland, etc.

You are hereby required and directed to repair forthwith to Portsmouth and, hoisting your flag on board His Majesty's Ship Royal George, put yourself under the command of the Earl Howe, Admiral and Commander in Chief of His Majesty's Fleet employed and to be employed in the Channel Soundings or wherever else His Majesty's service shall require and follow his Lordship's orders for your further proceedings. Given under our hands the 12 June 1793.

2. *Admiralty to Admiral Richard, Earl Howe*

3 July 1793

Commander in Chief of His Majesty's Fleet employed and to be employed in the Channel, Soundings, or whereever His Majesty's Service may require.

Whereas it is judged expedient that, as soon as the fifteen ships named in the margin [*Queen Charlotte, Royal George, Royal Sovereign, Cumberland, Suffolk, Ganges, Montagu, Ramillies, Bellerophon, Edgar, Brunswick, Audacious, Sceptre, Veteran, Majestic*], comprising part of the fleet put under your Lordship's command, and the necessary number of frigates shall be in all respects in readiness for the sea, you should proceed with them to the westward. Your Lordship is hereby required and directed to use your utmost dispatch in getting them ready accordingly, and in proceeding the first opportunity of wind and weather to sea, and you are to employ them either jointly or separately upon such stations as your Lordship shall judge most proper for protecting the trade of His Majesty's subjects coming into or going out of the Channel, and for taking or destroying the enemy's ships of war, privateers or trade going into or out of the Bay of Biscay, or navigating to or from any of the ports of west France.

And whereas intelligence has been received that 8 or 9 ships, from the port of Brest, have already put to sea, with a view, as is supposed, of joining some others (probably to the number of five) from the ports of L'Orient and Rochefort, Your Lordship is to direct your immediate attention to the keeping a strict watch on the said ships in the Bay, and to take care, as far as may be, to prevent their returning to Brest or forming a junction with any other ships or squadrons from thence; using your utmost endeavours, if possible, to attack them separately.

Your Lordship will from time to time cause accurate observation to be made, as well as endeavour to obtain the best intelligence, of the progress of the force collecting in the port of Brest; and you will regulate your conduct accordingly, with due regard to the security of the Kingdoms of Great Britain and Ireland, which, in addition to the other services recommended to your consideration, must always be considered as forming a very material object of your care and attention.

Your Lordship is to transmit to our Secretary before you sail a copy of your intended rendezvous, and of the signals by which the ships and vessels of your squadron are to be known to each other, and you are to send him during your cruise frequent accounts of your proceedings, with such intelligence as you may receive that may be necessary to be communicated to us; directing the Officer who is charged with your dispatches to deliver them to the Regulating Captain at Falmouth, who will be instructed to forward them to this office by express, and also to convey such dispatches as we may have occasion to send to you, as well as to furnish you from time to time with such intelligence as he may learn that may be proper to be communicated to you and, for the better keeping up such an intercourse, you will take care that one or more, of the cutters under your command be always held in readiness at that port.

Your Lordship will continue upon this service until further order, or, hearing nothing from us, will, at the expiration of one month from the time of your sailing, return to Torbay, sending an immediate account of your arrival: but in case any circumstances should arise, which may in your judgement and discretion render your return into port unadviseable, you will (any thing herein contained to the contrary notwithstanding) continue at sea, giving us the earliest notice of your intentions and making such arrangements as may facilitate your being joined, if necessary, by the remaining ships of your fleet, as they may respectively be ready to proceed to sea.

3.   *Admiralty to Howe*

13 August 1793

I received on the 10th instant by Captain Cole[1] of the Eurydice your Lordship's letter of the 7th with its inclosures, giving an account of your proceedings with the fleet under your command to that time; and yesterday I had the honour to receive your letter of the 10th giving a farther account of your proceedings and arrival in Torbay; and having without loss of time laid the same before my Lords Commissioners of the Admiralty, I have it in command from their Lordships to acquaint you that they entirely approve of your proceedings, and of the orders you have given for assembling the ships therein mentioned in Torbay, and getting the fleet in readiness for the sea.

The Alfred is on her way from the Downs to Spithead where orders are transmitted for her to join your Lordship in Torbay.

My Lords had ordered the Marlborough and Russell to Plymouth before your Lordship's arrival, to have their complements completed there; but they have by this post directed Sir Peter Parker[2] to cause the last mentioned ship, if she be not sailed before those orders reach him, to be completed by draughts from the Centurion, and to send her also to join your Lordship in Torbay.

In my letter of the 6th instant (a duplicate of which is herewith inclosed) I had the honour to inform your Lordship that the departure of the Jamaica covoy was delayed until the 24th of June; and I now send you an extract of a letter from Commodore Ford[3] of the 9th of June respecting that convoy accompanied with a private signal that will be made on its meeting any cruisers on its approach to our coasts, for your information.

I likewise send your Lordship a copy of a letter from Sir John Borlase Warren[4] of the Flora respecting the departure of the convoy from Lisbon and Oporto; and also copies of two letters from Mr Consul

---

[1]Francis Cole (d. 1798). Lieutenant 1779; Captain 1790.

[2]Sir Peter Parker (1721–1811). Captain 1747; Rear-admiral 1777; Vice-admiral 1779. He served with distinction in North America and the West Indies. Baronet 1782; Admiral 1787. Commander-in-Chief at Portsmouth 1793 to 1799.

[3]John Ford (d. 1796). Lieutenant 1761; Captain 1773; Rear-admiral 1794; Vice-admiral 1795.

[4]Sir John Borlase Warren (1753–1822). Entered Emmanuel College, Cambridge, in 1769; took his BA 1773, his MA in 1776. He joined the navy in 1771 and for some years pursued a double career, not without complications, since he was at one stage listed as a deserter. He became MP for Marlow in 1774. Captain 1781; Rear-admiral 1799; Vice-admiral 1805; Admiral 1810. Knighted in 1794. He was appointed Commander-in-Chief North America in 1813. In 1795 he was a Commodore.

Hamilton dated the 7th July at Norfolk in Virginia, the one to Lord Grenville, the other to myself respecting the convoy of the enemy from Cape François, for your Lordship's information.

4. *Admiralty to Howe*

12 October 1793

So soon as your Lordship is joined by His Majesty's ships Defence and Bellona, you are hereby required and directed to proceed to sea, and to make such a disposition of the fleet under your command as shall be best suited to fulfil the general object pointed out in our secret instructions of the 3d of July last.

And whereas it is expedient for the purpose of giving protection to the several convoys of troops about to sail in the course of the present month from the ports of England and Ireland to the West Indies and the Mediterranean, as well as to prevent the enemy from attempting to detach to the West Indies, that the fleet under your Lordship's command should keep the sea as long as circumstances may, at this season of the year, permit; your Lordship will continue your cruise as long as the state and condition of the fleet under your command shall render it advisable and then return with it to Spithead for further order, sending such of the ships as you shall judge necessary to Plymouth.

[*Endorsement*]

By Powell the messenger at ¼ p 4 pm.

5. *Admiralty to Howe*

11 December 1793

Notwithstanding any former instructions to the contrary, your Lordship is hereby required and directed on your return with the fleet under your command into the British Channel, to send eight of the line of battle ships including the Cumberland and Ganges, and a proportionable number of frigates, to Plymouth, and to repair with the remainder of your squadron including the Edgar to Spithead, where you are to remain for further orders, sending to our Secretary an account of your arrival and proceedings.

[*Endorsement*]

Original sent to Falmouth. Duplicate to Torbay.

6. *Admiralty to Howe*

17 April 1794

As soon as the several ships of the fleet under your Lordship's command, lately returned from their cruize, are in all respects refitted, you are to put to sea the first opportunity of wind and weather and proceed off of Ushant, giving protection on their passage down Channel to such outward bound convoys as may be at Spithead ready to sail, but more particularly to the East India convoy under the charge of His Majesty's ship Suffolk; and your Lordship is further directed, after having proceeded off Ushant, to detach one of the Rear Admirals of the fleet under your command with such a force as, according to the best intelligence you may be able to procure, you may judge to be necessary for the sake of giving protection to the East India convoy on their passage across the Bay; directing the said Rear Admiral, after having seen them in safety as far as your Lordship shall think expedient, to join you, at such rendezvous, and at such time, as you shall approve.

And whereas intelligence has been received that a very large and valuable fleet of merchant ships may be shortly expected from America under convoy of a French squadron (copies of which intelligence are herewith inclosed) and whereas the attempting to intercept the same is an object of the most urgent importance to the success of the present war, your Lordship is hereby required and directed to give order to the Rear Admiral (to be detached to a certain distance with the East India convoy as aforesaid) after performing that service to cruize, for such time as you may think proper, from Cape Ortegal to the latitude of Belle Isle for the sake of intercepting the same accordingly, or you will make a detachment of any other part of the fleet under your command for the performance of this service, as to your Lordship may appear most adviseable.

Your Lordship is further instructed to make such a general disposition of the fleet under your command and to take such station or stations, and for such time as you shall judge most proper, for the sake of protecting the trade of His Majesty's subjects and of His allies coming into and going out of the Channel, as well as of intercepting, and taking and destroying, the ships of war, privateers and trade of the enemy, bearing always in mind that a due regard to the security of the

Kingdoms of Great Britain and Ireland must ever form one of the most essential and constant objects of your care and attention.

Your Lordship will consider yourself at liberty to send into port, from time to time, such of the ships of your fleet as you may think proper for the sake of refreshment, giving their captains orders to join you again, or otherwise, as you shall judge best for His Majesty's service.

You will also be at liberty to send detachments from you whenever you judge it necessary to cruize on separate stations for the better meeting with the ships of the enemy and to give them such orders as you may think proper for that purpose, and whenever you may return into port you will leave sufficient cruizers for the purpose of watching the motions of the enemy and of protecting the trade of His Majety's subjects.

And whereas Rear Admiral Macbride[1] has been appointed to the command of a separate squadron for the purpose of attending more immediately to the safety of the Islands of Guernsey and Jersey, and of watching the armaments reported to be carrying on in the ports of the opposite coast from Dieppe as far westward as the Isle of Bas; and whereas the said Rear Admiral is instructed to keep up a constant communication with your Lordship, and to co-operate with the fleet under your command for the protection of the coast and the security of the trade of His Majesty's subjects in the Channel, and also to follow such directions as he may receive from your Lordship (not inconsistent with the general object of his instructions), your Lordship is hereby required and directed to communicate with the said Rear Admiral accordingly; to furnish him with copies of your rendezvous and private signals; and to give him such directions for his conduct from time to time as you shall judge most conducive to the good of His Majesty's service, sending copies thereof to our secretary for our information.

Your Lordship will also transmit to our Secretary before you sail a copy of your intended rendezvous and of the signals by which the ships and vessels of the fleet under your command may be known; and you will send him, during your cruize frequent accounts of your proceedings and of any intelligence you may procure that may be necessary to be communicated to us. Your Lordship will continue your cruize so long as you shall judge adviseable according to circumstances and the intelligence you may obtain of the proceedings of the enemy; returning

[1]John Macbride (d. 1800). Lieutenant 1758; Captain 1756; Rear-admiral 1793; Vice-admiral 1794; Admiral 1799.

to Torbay (or Spithead) whenever you may judge it expedient, and holding your fleet in constant readiness to proceed to sea whenever the objects pointed at in these instructions, and the good of His Majesty's service, may render it necessary.

[*Endorsement*]

By a messenger same day at ¾ p 6 pm.

7. *Howe to Admiralty*

The Charlotte, at Spithead, 18 April 1794

Understanding that there are several hundred gallons of lemon juice, and a proportional quantity of sugar, in the stores at Haslar hospital, which had been provided for a particular service now no longer in contemplation, and as the effect of those refreshments is of acknowledged advantage in all scorbutic complaints, I would submit to the consideration of the Lords Commissioners of the Admiralty whether it may not be adviseable to apply the provision made of those articles to the services of the Channel fleet, and request their Lordships' directions may be given to that effect.

8. *Howe to Admiralty*

The Charlotte, at Spithead, 23 April 1794

The permission of the Lords Commissioners of the Admiralty for the lemon juice and sugar deposited at Haslar hospital to be issued for use in the Channel fleet having been obtained too late for the whole quantity to be distributed whilst the fleet, which will put to sea with the first favourable wind, is now likely to remain longer in this port; I am to request their Lordships will be pleased to direct that the remainder of those very beneficial aids for preserving the health of seamen may be put on board a transport and conveyed to Plymouth to be there stored, or otherwise held in readiness for delivery hereafter, when the fleet may be able to take in a farther supply of provisions at Torbay.

Having endeavoured to discover the grounds of the complaint set forth in the petition said to contain the sense of the company of the Theseus, and enclosed with your letter of the 18th instant; but not finding any such appearance of discontent testified by the men, when apprized of the allegation I did not think it necessary to proceed further in that enquiry.

Lemon Juice –
About 900 bottles said to contain from 1½ to 8½ gallons each.

Sugar –
About 60 casks from 10 cwt, 15 cwt and upwards in the gross each.

[*Endorsement*]

25 April. Dr. P.,[1] Portsmouth, to send them to Plymouth accordingly as soon as conveniently may be; own sent and let his Lordship know it.

9. *Admiralty to Howe*

21 May 1794

I[2] received on the 18th instant by express from Falmouth, and lost no time in laying before before my Lords Commissioners of the Admiralty, your Lordship's letter of the 14th giving an account of your proceedings with the Channel fleet up to that time, and informing them of your having directed Rear Admiral Montagu[3] with the detachment under his command to prolong his cruize upon the station assigned him by your Lordship's order of the 18th ultimo, to the 20th instant, and then to repair to your Rendezvous No. 5. In return to which, I have it in command from their Lordships to acquaint you that as no advices have yet been received of the depature of the French convoy from America, it is their direction that your Lordship should order Rear Admiral Montagu to return to the station abovementioned or proceed to such other as to your Lordship may seem more proper, or that your Lordship should send a detachment under the command of a flag officer in his stead, with instructions to cruize thereon until he falls in with the said convoy, or receives credible advices of its having passed to the eastward or that it is not expected to come to Europe.

---

[1]Dr P., presumably at Haslar Hospital, has not been identified.
[2]The Secretary of the Admiralty, at this time Philip Stephens (1725–1809). Admiralty clerk 1751–59; second Secretary of the Admiralty 1759–63; Secretary 1763–83; First Secretary 1783–95; created baronet 1795; Admiralty Commissioner 1795–1806.
[3]Sir George Montagu (d. 1829). Lieutenant 1771; Captain 1774; Rear-admiral April 1794; Vice-admiral 1 June 1795; Admiral 1801.

10. *Admiralty to Rear-admiral Montagu*

2 June 1794

Whereas you have informed us, by your letter of the 29th of last month, of your arrival off the Lizard with the ships put under your orders by Admiral Earl Howe, not having been able to rejoin him on his station, and, by your letter of the 31st following, of your having put into Plymouth Sound; and whereas it is of very great importance that you should return to sea as soon as possible with the said ships, and such of those hereafter mentioned as may be ready to accompany you, you are hereby required and directed to put to sea accordingly and proceed with the utmost expedition to his Lordship's rendezvous No. 5, and to continue thereon until further order, or until you receive any instructions from his Lordship, or such certain intelligence of his situation as may enable you to join him, which you are to endeavour to do.

If, however, you should receive any well grounded information of the approach of the French convoy which may be daily expected from America and the course they are likely to steer, you will, then, make such a disposition of your squadron as you shall judge most likely to intercept the same.

And whereas we intend that you shall be reinforced by His Majesty's ships named in the margin [*Colossus, Minotaur, Swiftsure, America, Druid, Blonde, Perseus, Eurydice, Porcupine*] as soon as possible, you are hereby further required and directed to take them under your command, leaving orders for such of them as shall not be in the way or in readiness to proceed with you, to follow you to the appointed rendezvous; and, in case you should have have left that station, either in pursuance of orders from Earl Howe, of the intelligence you may have received respecting him, or of the approach of the French convoy as aforesaid, you will give directions for the ships (so following and not finding you on the appointed rendezvous) to return to Plymouth Sound for further orders.

[*Endorsement*]

By a messenger at ¼ past 12 at midnight.

11. *Howe to Admiralty*

2 June 1794

Thinking it may not be necessary to make a more particular report of my proceedings with the fleet, for the information of the Lords Commissioners of the Admiralty, I confine my communications chiefly, in this dispatch, to the occurrences when in presence of the enemy yesterday.

Finding on my return off Brest on the 19th past, that the French fleet had, a few days before, put to sea; and receiving, on the same evening, advices from Rear Admiral Montagu, I deemed it requisite to endeavour to form a junction with the Rear Admiral as soon as possible, and proceeded immediately for the station on which he meant to wait for the return of the Venus.

But, having gained very credible intelligence on the 1st of the same month, whereby I had reason to suppose the French fleet was then but a few leagues farther to the westward, the course before steered was altered accordingly.

On the morning of the 28th the enemy was discovered far to windward, and partial actions were engaged with them that evening and the next day.

The weather gage having been obtained, in the progress of the last mentioned day, and the fleet being in a situation for bringing the enemy to close action the first instant, [on 1 June] the ships bore up together for that purpose between seven and eight o'clock in the morning.

The French, their force consisting of twenty-six sail of the line (the Audacious having parted company with the sternmost ship of the enemy line, captured in the night of the 28th) waited for the action and sustained the attack with their customary resolution.

In less than an hour after the close action commenced in the centre, the French Admiral, engaged by the Queen Charlotte, crowded off, and was followed by most of the ships of his van in condition to carry sail after him, leaving with us about ten or twelve of his crippled or totally dismasted ships, exclusive of one sunk in the engagement. The Queen Charlotte had then lost her fore topmast, and the main topmast fell over the side very soon after.

The greater number of the other ships of the British fleet were at this time so much disabled or widely separated, and under such circumstances with respect to those ships of the enemy in a state for action, and with which the firing was still continued, that two or three, even of their dismasted ships, attempting to get away under a spritsail singly, or smaller sail raised on the stump of the foremast, could not be detained.

Seven remained in our possession, one of which, however, sunk before the adequate assistance could be given to her crew; but many were saved.

The Brunswick, having lost her mizen mast in the action, and drifted to leeward of the French retreating ships, was obliged to put away large to the northward from them. Not seeing her chased by the enemy in that predicament, I flatter myself she may arrive in safety at Plymouth. All the other 24 ships of His Majesty's fleet re-assembled late in the day; and I am preparing to return with them, as soon as the captured ships of the enemy are secured, for Spithead.

The material injury to His Majesty's ships, I understand, is confined principally to their masts and yards, which I conclude will be speedily replaced.

I have not been yet able to collect regular accounts of the killed and wounded in the different ships. Captain Montagu[1] is the only officer of his rank who fell in the action. The numbers of both descriptions I hope will prove small, the nature of the service considered; but I have the concern of having to add, on the same subject, that Admiral Graves[2] has received a wound in the arm, and that Rear-Admirals Bowyer[3] and Pasley,[4] and Captain Hutt[5] of the Queen, have each had a leg taken off; they are, however, (I have the satisfaction to hear) in a favourable state under those misfortunes. In the captured ships the numbers of killed and wounded appear to be very considerable.

Though I shall have, on the subject of these different actions with the enemy, distinguished examples hereafter to report, I presume the determined bravery of the several ranks of officers and ships' companies employed under my authority, will have been already sufficiently denoted by the effect of their spirited exertions; and, I trust, I shall be excused for postponing the more detailed narrative of the other transactions of the fleet thereon, for being communicated at a future opportunity; more especially as my first captain Sir Roger Curtis,[6] who is charged

[1]James Montagu (d. 1794). Lieutenant 1771; Captain 1775.

[2]Thomas Graves, Baron (d. 1802). Lieutenant 1743; Captain 1755; Rear-admiral 1779; Vice-admiral 1787; Admiral 1794.

[3]Sir George Bowyer (d. 1799). Lieutenant 1758; Captain 1762; Rear-admiral 1793; Vice-admiral 1794; Admiral 1799.

[4]Sir Thomas Pasley (1734–1808). Lieutenant 1757; Captain 1771; Rear-admiral 1794; Vice-admiral 1795; Admiral 1801. Lost a leg at the Battle of the Glorious First of June 1794 but gained a baronetcy. He became Commander-in-Chief at Plymouth in 1799.

[5]John Hutt (d. 1794). Lieutenant 1773; Captain 1783.

[6]Sir Roger Curtis (d. 1816). Lieutenant 1771; Captain 1777; Rear-admiral 1794; Vice-admiral 1799; Admiral 1804.

with this dispatch, will be able to give the farther information the Lords Commissioners of the Admiralty may at this time require. It is incumbent on me, nevertheless, now to add, that I am greatly indebted to him for his councils as well as conduct in every branch of my official duties; and I have similar assistance, in the late occurrences, to acknowledge of my second captain, Sir Andrew Douglas.[1]

P.S. The names and force of the captured French ships with the fleet is transmitted herewith.

List of French Ships captured on the 1st day of June 1794

La Juste	80 guns
Sans Pareille	80
L'America	74
L'Achille	74
Northumberland	74
L'Impetueux	74
Vengeur	74, sunk almost immediately upon being taken possession of.

N.B. The ship stated to have been captured on the evening of the 28th of last month is said by the prisoners to be the Revolutionaire of 120 guns.

12. Admiralty to Montagu

3 June 1794

Whereas the Earl of Chatham hath communicated to us a letter which he has received from Mr Jones a merchant of Bristol dated yesterday, containing intelligence respecting the French convoy expected from America and the course they were steering on the 12th of last month, we send you herewith a copy of the said letter for your information, and, in case on your arrival on the rendezvous No. 5 (as directed by our instructions of yesterday's date) you should not have received, or receive any orders from Earl Howe, or any further well grounded intelligence respecting the abovementioned convoy, you are, in that event, and on being joined by the Colossus and Minotaur, hereby required and directed immediately to stretch across the Bay with a view of intercepting the said convoy and, in case you should be well in-

---

[1]Sir Andrew Snape Douglas (d. 1797). Lieutenant 1778; Commander 1780; Captain 1797.

formed of its having passed, and there should be no probability of your overtaking it, you are to return immediately to the rendezvous No. 5, and to continue thereon until you receive further order, either from us or Earl Howe, or such certain intelligence of his situation as may enable you to join him which you are to endeavour to do.

And whereas we intend that the squadron under your command shall be further re-inforced by His Majesty's ship Ruby, we send you herewith our order to her captain to put himself under your command, and do hereby further require & direct you to take her under your command accordingly, calling off Falmouth for her on your way to the abovementioned rendezvous, if she shall have left Plymouth when you receive this.

[*Endorsements*]

By a messenger at ¼ past 6 pm.

3 June. Copy sent to Rear Admiral Montagu – see his instructions of this date.
4 June. Return Mr Jones their Lordships' thanks for the communication.

[*Enclosure*]

12a. *James Jones to Earl of Chatham*

Bristol, 2 June 1794

My ship Kelly is just arrived from the Southern Fishery. The Captain informs me that on the 12th of May in Lat. 39.10 Long. 35.36 he saw a large fleet about 150 sail which he is confident were French; they were then standing to the S.E. intending as he supposes to keep to the southward of the Western Islands to be out of the way of our cruisers and after to haul up into the Bay. It blew fresh and they had many heavy sailing ships in tow. They did not chase him. This ship sails very fast. Since seeing this fleet he has had light winds and he thinks they cannot yet be got up to the land.

He saw nothing of Lord Howe's fleet or any of our cruizers. He kept well to the northward to be out of the way of the enemy – this appearing of great consequence I thought it would be agreeable to your Lordship to be informed of it – and I sincerely hope a good account will be given of them.

With the utmost respect.

13.   *Occurrences at Plymouth*

The Times
12 June 1794

This morning arrived here 18 sail of the line, and nine frigates (belonging to Lord Howe's fleet) under the command of Admiral Graves and Rear Admiral Montague . . . The Marlborough is here dismasted – the other ships are much damaged in their hulls and rigging.

14.   *Occurrences at Portsmouth*

The Times
13 June 1794

This morning the conquering fleet, with their prizes, appeared in the offing. Crowds of people soon collected on the ramparts, and when the Queen Charlotte dropped anchor at Spithead the guns on the batteries were fired. About twelve Lord Howe landed at the new sally port, when a second discharge of artillery took place. His Lordship was received with the reiterated shouts of the people: a captain's guard of the Gloucester militia was drawn up on the lower end of the Grand Parade, with the band of the regiment playing, till his Lordship came up to them, *The conquoring* [sic] *hero comes!* The streets, tops of houses, balconies, windows, Grand Parades, and the Ramparts, from the Queen's Battery to the Main Guard, were crowded beyond all example. As his Lordship passed to the Governor's house, when he could be heard, he repeatedly thanked the people for the great respect shewn him, observing that the brave British seamen did the business!

Nine ships of the line of Earl Howe's fleet are ordered into Plymouth and the rest, viz Royal Charlotte, Royal George, Queen, Bellerophon, Russell, Caesar, Leviathan, Bellona, Alfred, with the six prizes, are come into this port. Our ships have suffered greatly in their masts and rigging, and several of them have sustained considerable damage in their hulls . . .

Admiral Pasley just landed at Gosport. We are happy in announcing that the Admiral looks much better than might be expected, and this noble hero waved his hand to the crowd as they cheered him.

15. *Occurrences at Plymouth*

The Times
14 June 1794

All the disabled ships of Lord Howe's fleet that put in here the day before yesterday are gone up the harbour, and their crews are busy employed in unbending the sails, getting out wounded, masts, etc. The greatest exertions are used to get the ships ready for sea again as soon as possible; about 700 prisoners were landed here from them yesterday and this morning, many of whom are much wounded; the greatest part of them are miserable looking creatures, nearly naked, and have not the least appearance of sailors.

16. *Occurrences at Portsmouth*

The Times
15 June 1794

From four o'clock this morning till the evening, the French prisoners taken on the 1st instant have been landing from the fleet, and escorted by the military to Hilsea barracks, where they are to remain till Portchester Castle is fitted for their reception; in the mean time, the troops lying there are encamped on Hilsea Green etc.

The number of prisoners carried to Hilsea barracks this day amounts to about 3,500, who, with the sick, make near 4,000.

17. *Admiralty to Howe*

14 June 1794

Having ordered the Honourable Rear Admiral Cornwallis[1] to repair immediately to Portsmouth and hoisting his flag on board His Majesty's ship Excellent to put himself under your Lordship's command and to follow your orders for his further proceedings, your Lordship is hereby required and directed to take him under your command accordingly, and to order him to proceed in that ship with all possible expedition to Plymouth Sound and to take under his command the nine of H.M. ships whose names are first mentioned in the margin hereof [*Hector*,

---

[1]Sir William Cornwallis (1744–1819). Lieutenant 1761; Captain 1765; Rear-admiral 1793; Vice-admiral 1794; Admiral 1799. Commander-in-Chief of the Channel fleet in 1801 and 1803–6.

Bellona, Arrogant, Theseus, Ganges, Alexander, Audacious, Hebe, Pallas], and also the three others immediately following [*Minotaur, Colossus, America*], whose captains will be directed to follow his orders; and having so done, to make the best of his way with them off Falmouth where he is to take into his charge His Majesty's ships Assistance and Ruby, with the East India Company ships, victuallers and trade under their respective convoys, and proceed with them across the Bay of Biscay using his best endeavours for their protection and security; and then, leaving the said ships and convoys to prosecute their respective voyages agreeable to former orders, he is to return with the ships named in the margin as aforesaid to Plymouth Sound for further order, sending to our Secretary an account of his arrival and proceedings.

[*Endorsement*]

By a messenger next morning at one o'clock.

18.   *Sir Charles Middleton*[1] *to Philip Patton*[2]

27 June 1794

It gives me great pleasure to find my ideas of the naval defence of His Majesty's dominions are similar to yours; and I have been endeavouring to make such an arrangement as the state of the present force will admit. But if the enemy continue to make the exertions which they appear to have been making, from the strength which they have actually shown upon the water about the time of the action of the 1st of June, something more vigorous, and a much more formidable force on our part, will be necessary to oppose them in such a manner as to leave less to the power of chance in the defence of this island. The manning of the navy speedily, and lessening the number of invalid discharges, and desertions, are the great, and I think practicable objects; but these I refer till I have the pleasure of seeing you, and in the meantime confine myself to blocking up the enemy's ports.

---

[1]Sir Charles Middleton, Lord Barham (d. 1813). Lieutenant 1745; Captain 1750; Rear-admiral 1787; Vice-admiral 1793; Admiralty Commissioner 1794–95; Admiral 1795; First Lord of the Admiralty 1805–6. In the Admiralty patent of 12 May 1794 Lord Hood and Sir Alan Gardner were named first and second naval lords but as both were serving afloat the role of Sir Charles Middleton, new to the board by that patent, was enhanced.

[2]Philip Patton (d. 1815). Lieutenant 1763; Captain 1779; Rear-admiral 1795; Vice-admiral 1801; Admiral 1805.

This measure may be made more clearly essential by reverting to what was actually done from the year 1757 to the year 1762; for although several expeditions were undertaken during that period, they were subservient to blocking up and opposing the enemy at home, which were the first considerations, and which were truly the foundation of our successes through the whole war, when the fleet were kept off Brest and in Quiberon Bay. It consists with my own knowledge, that the ships were relieved alternately, and were supplied with fresh provisions, corned beef, potatoes, onions, greens, and beer, during the summer; and Sir Edward Hawke and Admiral Boscawen relieved each other.

In the present state of affairs, such a conduct seems even more necessary, and no less practicable. For such a fleet as my statement No. 1 proposes, two sets of flag officers appear to be requisite, to relieve each other by turns. By this mode of defence, the captains, officers and seamen also relieve each other and are one-fourth part of their time in port, and three-fourths at sea. This is fully as long as it is possible to keep men upon the ocean; because all mankind require a certain relaxation from severe duty, and because it is always in the power of sea officers to obtain that relaxation by permitting disasters to the ships, masts and yards – which neither the most severe discipline nor the most extensive and rigorous authority can prevent. Perhaps it may be prudent to keep the three-decked ships in port from November to March; but even in these winter months, smaller squadrons of two-decked ships may be off Brest in easterly winds, and in Torbay when the winds are strong from the westward.

At present, the whole force of tbe enemy is kept at their ports of Brest and Toulon. They must, therefore, be opposed effectually at home, and in the Mediterranean. According to my ideas, we cannot pretend to keep a force at any of our settlements whilst this is the case, nor can any distant expeditions be undertaken till our naval force is very much augmented. I have, therefore, proposed that the flag-ships upon the stations abroad should only be of 64 guns, and I even doubt if they should be of so great force, especially in the West Indies, where no strength of the enemy can make any impression before ships could be sent after them from the Channel fleet, especially if a certain number of the ships were always kept victualled and stored for foreign service.

You will receive herewith four statements which comprehend the whole naval force now in commission . . . [1]

---

[1]These four statements are printed in *Letters of Lord Barham*, II, 394–401.

19. *Middleton draft memorandum*[1]

June 1794

Western Squadron

From the decided superiority we have lately gained over the enemy's fleet, and supposing things to continue as they now are, I would propose 32 sail of the line and 12 frigates for this service, accompanied by one fire-ship and 6 brigs or cutters, for the purpose of information. Of this force, I would propose 24 sail of the line and 8 frigates to cruise as constantly as possible off Brest, and 8 sail more and 4 frigates to refit at Plymouth, and rendezvous in summer, when complete, at Torbay, and be there kept in readiness to relieve those whose turn it may be to come into port. The three deckers to be confined, as much as circumstances will admit, to long days and summer cruising. With this force, the port of Brest may be generally blocked up, and detachments made after every ship or squadron who may steal out from it or the other ports in the Bay. The squadrons so employed will stand –

3 ships of 100 guns.	6 frigates of 38 and 36,
5 ships of 90 guns.	<u>6</u> of 28 and 32.
<u>24</u> ships of 74 guns.	12
32	

20. *Alexander Hood to Chatham*

Royal George, Spithead, 5 July 1794

I am extremely sorry to acquaint your Lordship that my gouty complaints are of so serious a nature that I am under the necessity of requesting the same leave of absence from my duty as has been given to Earl Howe, it being impossible for me to continue in service unless this indulgence is given me and if I should be so unfortunate as not to feel myself well enough to resume my station before the Channel Fleet shall put again to sea I must in that case request that your Lordship will be pleased to permit me to strike my flag, for I hold it my indispensable duty not to allow my name to be borne on the books of the Royal

[1]This statement is part of a larger document of June 1794 drafted by Middleton also encompassing the forces necessary for the Mediterranean, Coast of Africa, Leeward Islands, Coast of America, Bermudas, Newfoundland, East Indies, Coast of Ireland, Channel and East Coast. See *Letters of Lord Barham*, II, 403–8.

George if I should be unable to serve the King and the Country consistent with public duty.

21.   *Middleton to Henry Dundas*[1]

26 July 1794

Lord Sackville,[2] feeling the disappointments that so frequently occurred in the last war, suggested the propriety of an executive first lord acting under the Marine Minister and that lord a professional man. He was so partial to me as to wish I might then be the person ... Lord Sandwich was as pleasant a man to do business with as ever I met with, and so is Lord Chatham but there are difficulties that neither can remove circumstanced as they are under the pressure of ministerial attendance.

22.   *Middleton to Dundas*

Undated

The fleet being returned into port, this is the time for getting it forward for spring service. My present views are confined to that object and preparing cruising squadrons for the winter. In this way only and by frequent and punctual convoys shall we be able to counteract their depredatory war on our trade. In whatever changes may take place be careful that I am not pinioned nor my plans counteracted by the interference of intrigue or favouritism. Give me power sufficient to command attendance at the Office and that no interruption may be given in the two hours which I have got fixed for letter reading and minuting; let no more ships be commissioned till those now in the ports without men are brought into service. Prepare when Parliament meets to give us aid in bringing forward those ships and who will require 10,000 men.

If those particulars are attended to and I am allowed one sea officer of knowledge and application to assist me I will take the responsibility under Providence upon myself. But without attention to the means I have pointed out I see very little prospect of ending this war with credit.

You remember the last war and what efforts we made against most of Europe.

---

[1]Henry Dundas, 1st Viscount Melville (1742–1811). Secretary of War 1794–1801.
[2]George Sackville Germain, 1st Viscount Sackville, better known as Lord George Germain (1716–1785).

We had then 107 ships of the line in commission and as many thousand seamen employed.

I take no merit to myself but I had the full confidence of Lord Sandwich and I flatter myself I did not abuse it. I directed too in a manner both departments[1] under a man of great abilities and discernment.

The fleet must be at liberty to act or we are undone. The admirals must be directed by the Admiralty and not the Admiralty by their officers.

There are sufficient ones to be found when we are once unfettered. I will add no more but that I am always most faithfully yours . . .

P.S. The visible intention of the enemy is to get, through their number of captures, our best seamen under their power and to deprive us of a use of them. I see evidently the consequence of this in the very few men that are now procured and if not guarded against by a better protection of our trade we must lay our ships up.

What an ill-judged measure has it been to make soldiers of the French seamen[2] when we have at this time at least 20 ships in commission without men and we want of 10,000 to bring them into service.

23. *Middleton to Dundas*

10 December 1794

I need not point out to you the relaxed state of discipline in the fleet. Every day's post manifests it. No inducement for captains to keep the sea. Every reason but duty against it. And every means used by many to evade it.

Under this circumstance prudent but strong measures must be adopted. If not so the trade of the country must be ruined. Your seamen will be all locked up in France. There will be no supply for the fleet and a serious and dangerous invasion must be the consequence.

To counteract all this a system must be immediately laid down and followed up. The fleet must be kept in constant readiness for sea and squadrons of cruisers kept constantly to the westward. The French coast must be guarded and an interruption given to the large supplies of provisions that are carrying coast ways to their armies. The North Sea trade must be better guarded. Your convoys must be regular and strong.

---

[1]The Admiralty and the Navy Office.

[2]French seamen, being mostly from Royalist areas, had, when captured, unsuccessfully asked to transfer to the British Navy.

Your distant possessions must be attended to and men must be procured to man the many ships that are lying useless at the ports. The service must be strong in frigates and small craft. The signal posts on the coasts must be speedily established and many other objects too numerous to name must be attended to.

24.   *Howe to Spencer*[1]

Bath, 17 December 1794

An increased deafness, added to many constitutional infirmities obliged me some time since to repeat my application of last June to be relieved of my command of the Channel Fleet. The answer I received from the Board of Admiralty was confined to the grant of a temporary permission for coming to this place when the fleet was to return to Portsmouth.

My former solicitations remain therefore to be renewed.

[*Endorsed as received on the 18th*]

25.   *Spencer to Howe*

Admiralty, 25 December 1794

The news that arrived here last night from Falmouth of the French fleet being put to sea consisting of 31 or 32 sail of the line and 20 frigates at the same time that it has made it expedient for us to order all our ships that are in any state of forwardness to be expedited as soon as possible has added a strong public reason to the many private ones which I had before for wishing very much to have the honour of seeing your Lordship and to have the great advantage of an early and extensive conversation with you upon what may be fittest to be done upon the occasion.

I have not time at this moment to state, nor indeed could I well do it by letter, the present very critical situation of our very valuable convoys destined to the West Indies and Mediterranean, which have only been prevented by the accident of a contrary wind from proceeding directly into the supposed track of this great fleet of the enemy.

I shall only therefore now apprize your Lordship that orders have been sent to stop their further proceedings on their destination till a sufficient force shall be ready for sea to protect them. In the meanwhile

---

[1]George John, 2nd Earl Spencer (1758–1834). First Lord of the Admiralty 19 December 1794–19 February 1801.

orders have been despatched to the several ports, as I mentioned above, and we hope in no very long time to have a very respectable force fit for sea. Thus circumstanced, I hope your Lordship will excuse my taking the liberty of pressing your return to Town as your advice and, I trust I may add, (notwithstanding the intimation conveyed in your letter which I had the honour of receiving last week) your assistance cannot but be considered as essentially necessary to the public service, not only by myself but by every one of His Majesty's other confidential servants.

26. *Howe to Spencer*

Bath, 26 December 1794

Confined to my room by a feverish complaint which I however hope will allow me to leave Bath next Sunday or as soon after as the heavy fall of snow here will permit.[1]

I will lose no time in my endeavours to be in town for receiving your Lordship's further commands.

My humble opinions I cannot flatter myself would be more worthy of your notice than my feeble powers of personal exertion could be of benefit on the occasion which is the subject of that letter; obliged as I am to repeat my long since declared acknowledgments of incapacity to undertake for a due performance of the professional duties of a situation from which I must still solicit very earnestly to be released.

[*Endorsed as received on the 27th*]

27. *Admiralty to Bridport*[2]

Bath, 26 December 1794

Having laid before my Lords Commissioners of the Admiralty your Lordship's letter of the 24th instant requesting a prolongation of your leave of absence from your duty for the recovery of your health, I am commanded to acquaint your Lordship that the Board are pleased to comply therewith but that as the Channel Fleet is preparing for the sea

---

[1] 26 December was a Friday. It was an exceptionally severe winter, with the coldest January on record.

[2] Alexander Hood was created Viscount Bridport in the Irish peerage on 12 August 1794.

with the utmost expedition their Lordships hope you will hold yourself in readiness to return to Spithead at a short notice.

28.   *Bridport to Admiralty*

Bath, 28 December 1794

I inform you that I have received your letter prolonging my leave of absence from my duty for the benefit of my health but as the Channel fleet is preparing for the sea with the utmost expedition their Lordships hope that I will hold myself in readiness to return to Spithead at a short notice. You will be pleased to acquaint their Lordships that under such circumstances I shall not avail myself of the prolongation of my leave but set out from Bath tomorrow morning for my house in Town, where I shall hold myself in readiness to receive their Lordships' orders. At the same time I must inform them that my health requires the waters of this place where I beg to return whenever the public service shall allow me this indulgence.

29.   *Howe to Spencer*

Bath, 28 December 1794

My feverish complaint not being abated in the degree I had expected yesterday I have been obliged to defer my intended journey to Town for a day or two longer. But as soon as I am able to travel I shall certainly wait upon you there.

[*Endorsed as received on the 29th*]

30.   *George III to Spencer*

Windsor, 15 past 10 a.m., 6 January 1795

As I perceive by the note from Earl Spencer in answer to mine that he concurs in my opinion as to the safest method of addressing myself to Earl Howe, whose health in the present moment is clearly not such as he would safely undertake a winter cruise I shall not fail to form my letter to prevent his retiring at present and I am certain I can put his continuance at the head of the Channel fleet in a light that will secure his taking the part which on many accounts I think highly necessary. As soon as I receive his answer I will communicate it to Earl Spencer that he may speak more positively to Lord Bridport, whose conduct will be highly absurd if he refuses to serve, and I confess, however I may think in general well of his nautical abilities, I do not look on them as superior to those of Vice Admiral Cornwallis.

[Endorsed as received on the 6th][1]

31. *George III to Spencer*

Windsor, 16 past 9 a.m., 8 January 1795

Earl Spencer may be desirous of knowing the result of Earl Howe's conversation yesterday. He is to write an answer to the letters I sent him and I am to have it tomorrow which I believe will contain an acquiescence to continuing to serve. Whether he will be desirous of going out this winter cruise I am not quite certain. Having found more difficulty in persuading him not to lay so much stress on the diminution of his mental and corporal faculties I thought it best not to press this other much to secure the main point, his not retiring entirely. Earl Howe is certainly an excellent man as well as an able officer but not without much reserve that at times envelopes his meaning that it is not at all times easy to bring him to the point as one does not always seize his mode of viewing things.

[Endorsed as received on the 8th at noon]

32. *Spencer to Bridport*

Admiralty, 10 January 1795

I think it my duty to acquaint your Lordship that Lord Howe has agreed to resume the command of the Channel fleet and will most probably hoist his flag at Spithead in a very few days. I hope from what dropped from your Lordship when I had the honour of seeing you here that I am not too sanguine in flattering myself that your Lordship will go out with the Fleet as second in command.

---

[1]The King's idea was to persuade Howe not to give up the command entirely but, even if he did not go out in the winter, to resume active service in the spring. See *Spencer Papers*, I, 26.

33. *Bridport to Spencer*

Harley Street, 11 January 1795

The honour of your Lordship's letter was received last night in my bed, which acquaints me that Lord Howe had agreed to resume the command of the Channel Fleet and would most probably hoist his flag at Spithead in a few days. Your Lordship may depend that I shall hold myself in readiness to hoist mine as second in command whenever the service shall require it but I trust I shall be permitted to remain in Town to the last day as I have much private business to transact which I am anxious to attend to. If your Lordship shall wish to see me I shall be glad to be allowed a short conversation whenever it shall suit your Lordship's convenience.

34. *Howe to Admiralty*

The Charlotte, at Spithead, 22 January 1795

By the messenger Powell I received yesterday the instructions from the Lords Commissioners of the Admiralty whereby I am directed to put to sea with the Channel Fleet as soon as I shall be joined by the ships ordered from Plymouth or such part of them as may complete the fleet to the number of at least thirty-one sail of the line for the services therein specified. As soon therefore as the signals and other necessary regulations for the government of the ships have been distributed the fleet will be ready for sea, the deficiency in the complement of some of them excepted.

I have only at this time to add on the further subject of those instructions that in respect of my appointment to take such station as will facilitate the meeting with other ships sent in quest of the fleet at sea I heretofore submitted to the Board on similar occasions the only manner in which I conceive assurance may be had of being joined by such ships, namely by directions given for them to cruise off of the Lizard during fair weather and when unable to keep that station against strong westerly winds to wait in Torbay in the meantime for returning again off of the Lizard when the weather becomes suitable for the purpose of joining me when I have opportunity to stand over to the British coast or otherwise advising them for proceeding to join me at sea as the circumstances of the case may require. I wrote some days since to Rear Admiral Parker[1] on a supposition that the security of the outward bound trade might be an

---

[1]Sir William Parker (1743–1802). Lieutenant 1766; Captain 1777; Rear-admiral 1794. Vice-admiral 1799. Commander-in-Chief Jamaica in 1795, he returned to England in 1796 and was sent to the Mediterranean, reaching Lisbon in time for the Battle of Cape St Vincent.

object to which my particular attention would be directed and I have been lately furnished with much essential information by him thereon, consequent of orders he had previously received from the Board.

35. *Samuel, Lord Hood[1] to Bridport*

26 January [1795][2]

Many thanks my dear Lord for your affectionate letter of yesterday. I am afraid the Fleet will anchor at St. Helens and if the arrival of more ships is waited for from Plymouth the French fleet will most probably be in port before ours is out. In that case the consequence will be dreadfully alarming. I am just come from the Speaker's, with whom and Lord Camden I had near an hour's very serious conversation.[3] The language abroad is violent in the extreme but I hope and trust the measures Mr. Pitt means to adopt this night will prove salutary and healing. If, however, the enemy returns before Lord Howe gets off Brest the mischief will be great indeed. Impeachment will certainly take place, which heaven avert. I am now about to get an early dinner to be at the House by four.

36. *Howe to Admiralty*

The Charlotte, at Spithead, 27 January 1795

The wind changing and since become very fresh to the westward the movement of the Fleet from Spithead has been prevented since the 25th but I propose to take the first favourable opportunity for getting down Channel, though it should only be to Torbay and nearer the convoys to put to sea with them when the state of the weather may permit.

37. *Howe to Admiralty*

The Charlotte, in Torbay, 1 February 1795

The fleet put to sea from Spithead with a favourable appearance of the weather on the 29th past, the Thalia having been at the same time despatched for advising Rear Admiral Parker thereof.

[1]Samuel Hood, 1st Viscount Hood (1724–1816). Lieutenant 1746; Captain 1756; Rear-admiral 1780; Vice-admiral 1787; Admiral 12 April 1794.

[2]This partly dated letter is misplaced in the Bridport Papers. There is only one year when it could have been written.

[3]The Speaker was Henry Addington, later Prime Minister. Camden was about to take over the Lord-Lieutenancy of Ireland.

When we arrived off of the Start the next morning the wind had shifted from the eastward to the S.E. and more southerly later in the day, which prevented the convoy from getting out of the different harbours of Plymouth and the Sound. It remained between the S.S.E. and S.S.W. the two following days. Fortunately moderate for the most part though with extremely thick weather, placing the fleet in a very critical situation with respect to the land yesterday and this morning. But the wind veering further to the S.W. and west, very fresh in squalls, I was enabled to bring the fleet into this bay today.

If the convoys could have been assembled at Spithead they might have been taken out of the Channel on this late occasion though as the weather has since proved no advance could have been further made in the progress of their outward bound voyages. But as they are now divided a part only could have joined the fleet in case the wind had continued to the eastward at the time of my arrival off of Plymouth as the ships in Hamoaze could not have been moved.

Exclusive therefore of the hazards to the fleet by waiting in the winter season near the coast, the time requisite for being joined by the convoy I would recommend whilst the wind continues to the westward (provided no opportunity for proceeding with them, as I am already directed, speedily occurs) that all those convoys should be appointed to rendezvous with the fleet at Spithead, from thence to put to sea together if the protection of the outward bound transports and trade is still considered as the first object of my attention.

Thinking it not improbable from the appearance of the weather when arrived off of the Start on the 30th that the fleet might be forced to sea without the convoys, I apprized Rear Admiral Parker of the conduct I deemed advisable for the security of the convoys if he should be ready to sail with them in the absence of the fleet. But I now conclude if the wind continues any time to the westward the enemy's fleet will not be found on their late supposed station.

38. *Howe to Spencer*

Torbay, 8 February 1795

Your Lordship's suggestion in your letter of the 6th for looking into Brest is only practicable during an eastern or far northerly wind whilst the enemy may be in force there. The attempt cannot be made from the fleet before our return, after we have seen the convoys out of probable danger. It may possibly be effected sooner by the frigates under Sir John Warren's direction, if not inconsistent with the purpose of his appointment. But of that or the existence of such an establishment I never had any official communication.

[*Endorsed as received on the 11 February*]

39. *Spencer to Howe*

Admiralty, 11 February 1795

The suggestion I took the liberty of making respecting looking into Brest was certainly only meant to be submitted to your Lordship's far better judgment and in case the measure appeared to you practicable or proper. We have since received intelligence from a ship that left Brest as late as the 5th inst. by which it appears that the whole of the enemy's fleet, excepting one or two ships supposed to be lost at sea, made return into that port and L'Orient. If this should be further confirmed, it will naturally occur that so large a force as that under your Lordship's command need not be risked at sea at this unfavourable season of the year. The intelligence is not, however, I think, sufficiently authenticated to act upon it at present. At all events I own I shall be glad to hear that your Lordship and your fleet are safe at Spithead, that being a situation from whence you can avail yourself of a fair wind with the greatest readiness and affording an opportunity of collecting the convoy and taking them out with greater certainty than any other.

40. *Captain Lord Hugh Seymour[1] to Spencer*

Torbay, 11 February 1795

The very blowing weather which we have had since Sunday last will account to you for my not having answered your letter of the 4th . . . Fortunately the gale we have had was to the westward, for if it had been in the opposite quarter as it was on Friday, when we found it impossible to quit the Bay without making a sacrifice of the anchors and cables of all the ships I should have trembled for the fate of our fleet. I am very glad to learn from Lord Howe that you have approved of his moving to the eastwards to collect the convoys as what I have lately seen of this place

---

[1]Lord Hugh Seymour (1759–1801). Captain 8 February 1779; Rear-admiral 1 June 1795; Vice-admiral 14 February 1799. A friend of Spencer and a member of the Board of Admiralty from 7 March 1795 to 10 September 1798. He served at sea while a member of the Board. He died 5 September 1801 in the West Indies.

has confirmed the opinion I have long entertained of its being a very improper one for the rendezvous of large fleets at this season of the year, though it may occasionally serve as a temporary shelter to that employed in the Channel.

[Endorsed as received on 16 February]

41.   *Spencer to Sir Alan Gardner*[1]

Admiralty, 23 February 1795

It is now my duty to acquaint you that a new arrangement of the Board of Admiralty has been fixed upon in which your name is not included. This duty is necessarily become a very unpleasant one for me to execute from the sentiments of respect and esteem which the short acquaintance I have had an opportunity of forming since my appointment here has led me to entertain for you and I hope you will do me the justice to believe that . . .

42.   *Howe to Bridport*

28 February 1795

The present state of my health not allowing me to superintend the concerns of the fleet, I have leave from the Board of Admiralty to go on shore. The charge and government of the fleet will therefore remain with your Lordship during my absence to be carried on pursuant to the directions you may expect to receive from the Lords Commissioners of the Admiralty thereon.

Rear Admiral Sir Roger Curtis will deliver to your Lordship a minute of the several appointments at this time subsisting in the fleet for having the ships completed in all respects for immediate service.

---

[1]Sir Alan Gardner (1742–1809). Joined the navy in 1755, fought at Quiberon Bay and at the Saints. Captain 1766; Rear-admiral 1793; Vice-admiral 4 July 1794. Admiralty commissioner 19 January 1790 to 7 March 1795, but also served at sea after the commencement of hostilities. Created a baronet for his services at the battle of the First of June, 1794. Admiral 1799. Irish peerage 1800, UK peerage 1806. Commanded the Channel fleet in 1807–8.

43. *Warren to Admiralty*

La Pomone, Cawsand Bay, 2 March 1795

I beg you will inform their Lordships that in pursuance of their orders I put to sea on the 12th of February past with the ships named in the margin [*La Pomone, Galatea, Anson, Artois, Duke of York* lugger]. The weather becoming thick with fresh breezes and a heavy sea, on the 14th the Anson carried away her main topmast, which obliged me to heave to and, owing to her damage, I was under the necessity of bearing down the two following days, as she had drifted considerably to leeward, and being unable to repair her defects at sea I ordered Captain Durham[1] to proceed with all possible dispatch to Plymouth.

On the 18th, having fell in with three sail of the enemy's transports, part of a convoy bound from Brest, I hauled the wind and endeavoured to make the land; and on the 21st, the lighthouse on the Isle of Oleron bearing S.E. by E. I discovered a frigate and twenty sail of vessels under convoy close in with the shore, many of them under American, Danish and Swedish colours; I pursued then half way up the Portuis d'Antioche in sight of the Isle of Aix but the tide of flood strong up and the wind right in, I was obliged to tack and captured and destroyed the vessels in the enclosed list. I understand the frigate was the Nériade of 36 guns, 12 pounders, with transports and other vessels for wine and stores to Rochefort and Bordeaux on account of the Convention for their fleet. On the 26th, the Isle of Groix bearing east 6 leagues the squadron I gave chase to six sail of vessels in the N.W.; at 9 a.m. captured the Conventional schooner La Coureuse with the five others. They were bound to Nantes from Brest with clothing for the army.

44. *Lord Henry Powlett[2] to John Colpoys[3]*

Astrea at sea, 14 April 1795

In obedience to your signal from the London yesterday morning I gave chase to the north-east and at 10 o'clock at night came up with and

---

[1]Philip Durham (1763–1845). Captain 1793; Rear-admiral 1810; Vice-admiral 1819. Knighted 1815.

[2]Lord Henry Powlett (d. 1832). Lieutenant 1789; Captain January 1794; Rear-admiral 1812; Vice-admiral 1819.

[3]John Colpoys (1742?–1821). Captain 1773; Rear-admiral 1794; Vice-admiral June 1795; Admiral 1801. He did not serve afloat after the incidents in which he was involved during the mutiny at Spithead in 1797. Knighted 1798; Commander-in-Chief Plymouth 1803–4; Admiralty commissioner 1804; Governor of Greenwich Hospital 1816–21.

engaged La Gloire, French national frigate mounting 26 twelve pounders on the main deck, 10 six pounders and 4 thirty-six pounder carronades on the quarter deck and 2 six pounders on the forecastle, having on board 275 men; after a close action of 58 minutes she struck.

It is very satisfactory to me to be able to say that I had no person killed and only eight men wounded, three of them, I am sorry to add, are in some danger. I am also very sorry to say that the slaughter on board the enemy has been very considerable, the killed and wounded from the best accounts I have been able to collect amounting to forty, among the latter is her captain, Citizen Beens, who received a contusion on the head. He seems an able, humane and intelligent officer.

I have sent Mr. Talbot[1], my First Lieutenant, on board La Gloire, which will I hope meet with your approbation.

45. *Warren to Admiralty*

La Pomone, off Falmouth, 24 April 1795

I beg you will communicate to their Lordships that Le Jean Bart ship corvette, which the squadron captured on the 15th instant, had sailed in company with Le Tyger of 84 guns, Le Zélé of 74 guns, Le Nestor of 74 guns and 3 frigates from Brest only four days for the express purpose of intercepting our squadron. The corvette only parted from her own ships thirty hours, having been sent into Rochefort to order out two frigates and a ship of the line cut down from Basque Road and was upon her return when she was seen by us.

Another squadron, consisting of one ship of the line and four frigates, were also directed to cruise off the Penmarks in consequence of an express which arrived at Brest with information of the convoy from Sebastian having been attacked by us. I understand the ships from that place are in general very valuable, being laden with iron for the foundries of the republic and wood for ship building, Spanish plunder, etc.

46. *Samuel, Lord Hood to the Admiralty*

St Helens, 28 April 1795

I beg to trouble you with the copy of a statement I thought it my duty to deliver to Mr. Pitt and Earl Spencer on the 18th March subsequent to a conversation I had the honour to have with them respecting the force

---

[1]Sir John Talbot (d. 1851). Lieutenant 1790; Captain 1796; Rear-admiral 1819; Vice-admiral 1830; Admiral 1841.

necessary to be employed in the Mediterranean, which I wish to lodge as a record of my sentiments in the Admiralty Office. Since that statement was delivered the French are reported to have launched at Toulon two ships of the line and about six of the line, three frigates and a corvette are known to have arrived at that port from Brest; and the British force is reduced by the loss of the Illustrious, since Admiral Hotham's action with the Toulon squadron in which two of the enemy's line of battle ships were taken and previous to which the Berwick was captured, and as I am ever ready to put my name to any opinions I may have given I owe it to myself to have it upon record, particularly as I am convinced the force under my command, when united in the Mediterranean, will be very unequal to that of the enemy and the various services committed to my charge; but although I have not the shadow of prospect of being able to add lustre to the arms of His Majesty I entreat to have credit for doing my utmost that they are not disgraced.

The force of the enemy at Toulon is at this time eighteen sail of the line and will probably be twenty by the end of May. The British fleet in the Mediterranean consists now but of fifteen sail of the line, inclusive of the Berwick, dismasted, upwards of one thousand, four hundred seamen short of complement. The crews of the ships in a mutinous state and, as force may become necessary to restore discipline and proper subordination, no officer who looks to the honour and credit of His Majesty's Navy and the public service can venture to take upon him the charge and command of the Mediterranean Fleet with one ship less than twenty sail of the line without risk of becoming the instrument of disgrace to the nation by encountering difficulties that appear great and almost insurmountable and which evidently stare him in the face.

Admiral Lord Hood therefore feels it his duty humbly to make this statement and thinks it right to add that the Fortitude, Bedford and Agamemnon (and he believes the other 64 also) require to be sent home upon the arrival of the fresh convoy from England.

47. *Seymour to Spencer*

3 May 1795

I was rather disappointed at not having one line from you yesterday as I had been taught by you to expect that pleasure and then I was anxious to learn the line you had decided upon taking towards Lord Hood. It is now generally understood here[1] that he is not going to the

---

[1]Hambledon or Portsmouth.

Mediterranean but he has had the address to impress people about him that his not doing so is his own act and in consequence of Government not having adopted his advice and the measures which he thought necessary for the defence of the country he was called upon to protect. You will not be surprised at his having assured this too and will be as indifferent about the turn which he gives to the business among his own friends as I am but I think you will agree with me that much inconvenience may arise from his publicly declaring that he quits the command because Government will not place in his hands the power of resisting the enemy, which he imparted to much on his station, and this is, I understand, his language. I begin to form that you will be obliged to reinforce our fleet in that part of the world but the necessity of it should not have been declared to the world in this way. As to his Lordship's quitting the command I believe that it will be attended with no disadvantage whatever to the country and I believe the Navy in general will be pleased at his being taught that there are bounds to the authority of all officers which he had appeared to have lost sight of. I am impatient to learn whom you mean should be his successor and as you know that I now have one object only in the arrangement I shall beg you to give me a hint about it whenever you think it right to name the subject to the Board and before you allow them to absolutely fix the business for you.

[*Endorsed as received on the 4th*]

48. *Seymour to Spencer*

Hambledon, 4 May 1795

I am very sorry to learn that the situation in which Jervis is placed towards the West Indian preparations and merchants makes it impossible for Government to avail itself of his services as I have persuaded myself that he would have done particularly well as the successor to Lord Hood in the Mediterranean command. I had however doubts on the subject and on turning it over in my own mind was led to fix upon the same person to fill that station to whom you have offered it. I believe he would have done very well and I therefore cannot understand the ground on which he has declined it after the language he held lately about his claims to command in chief. His decision will, however, relieve you from one embarrassment in case of anything unpleasant happening on the home station, as Lord Bridport must be considered as forfeiting his claims to that command by the way in which he has received your proposal to supply his brother's place. I hope Hotham's[1] health will enable him to prove that the state of our fleet there is not such as to justify the line of conduct which Lord Hood has adopted of late.

[*Endorsed as received on the 5th*]

49. *Seymour to Spencer*

Portsmouth, 9 May 1795

I hope that whenever you decide in your own mind upon sending out the principal part of Lord Howe's remaining ships that you will write to him on the subject as I conceive from his manner that he will be hurt at their being put under any person's orders without their passing through his hands and the attention is all that he requires on the occasion.

[*Endorsed as received on the 10th*]

50. *Seymour to Spencer*

12 May 1795

You will be sorry to hear that the scurvy makes considerable progress in the ships at Spithead owing to their not having had of late the usual supply of fresh beef and to the want of vegetables occasioned by the severity of the winter. Great pains are now taken to check the complaint and I hope that, with the liberal supply of oranges and lemons which the Sick and Hurt Board are about to supply the fleet with, that its progress will be stopped till the markets are well supply'd with both meat and vegetables.

[*Endorsed as received on the 13th*]

---

[1]Vice Admiral Sir William Hotham (1736–1813) had been left to exercise acting command in the Mediterranean when Hood returned home in the autumn of 1794. 'Lord Hood', in Spencer's words, 'being prevented from particular circumstances' from resuming the command, he held it until, after repeated requests on grounds of ill health, he was relieved in the autumn of 1795 by Jervis. In the meantime he fought two indecisive actions which were more highly rated at home than by Nelson or posterity.

51. *Dr Thomas Trotter[1] to Howe*

Spithead, 15 May 1795

Since the Fleet was supplied with lemons and oranges by order of the Admiralty in consequence of my representations to Sir Peter Parker[2] the cure of scurvy has been easily accomplished on board; in the London and Valiant during the last fortnight upwards of a hundred cases have been cured. But from the particular causes which have excited this disease and the very nature of the distemper itself it is probable every man in the fleet must sooner or later partake of its influence unless means of prevention extend to the whole. The quantity of fruit equal to this purpose appears to me too great to be calculated but I am of opinion it may be effectually done by the following method: from the late rapid progress of vegetation a quantity of vegetables equal to our wants can be procured in this neighbourhood at a moderate expense. Thus, let the pursers serve out to the different messes every day a few bunches of radishes, young onions, lettuces, etc. and let a lb. of fresh beef per man be made into broth three times a week, into which may be put a large proportion of onions, leeks or greens. This plan being persisted in for 14 or 16 days would so correct the juices of the body that the scorbutic taint would be effectually overcome, when the allowance of fresh meat once a week might again be resorted to without the hazard at present to be apprehended; and without some measure of this kind being adopted soon it is to be feared the health of our cruising squadrons may not be equal to that active duty they are at present engaged in.

The occurrence of scurvy in the Channel fleet in this manner being rather unusual, it would seem to put us on our guard lest service may require the ships at sea for a length of time and it suggests some improvements in the diet that are easily accomplished. Thus it would be useful to have sugar or molasses to sweeten the oatmeal gruel in order to encourage the men to use it but this meal might be beneficially superseded by cocoa for breakfast, as done on West India stations. The

---

[1]Dr Thomas Trotter (1760–1832). MD Edinburgh 1788; surgeon's mate Channel fleet 1779; surgeon 1782; served on a slaver where he undertook experiments in curing scurvy with a control group 1782; Physician to Channel fleet 1794–95 when he was injured climbing up the side of the *Irresistible*. Thereafter, until his retirement from the navy in 1802, he served mainly on shore, retaining the title of Physician of the Channel fleet although in 1800, after falling out with St Vincent, the latter had Dr Andrew Baird discharge the functions of that post afloat. Retired to civil practice in the Peace of Amiens.

[2]Commander-in-Chief Portsmouth, 1793–99.

common pickles of red cabbage, walnuts, etc. to be eaten with salt meat would also be valuable and they cost little.

I observe the Sick and Hurt Board has lately furnished the ships going to St. Helens with sugar and lemon juice in very great quantity. I think much of this expense might be saved by supplying beer of double strength with a larger proportion of hops as formerly recommended to your Lordship. This method for our fleet would at this time be attended with peculiar advantages.

In addition to these alterations of diet I beg leave to suggest to your Lordship's consideration an allowance of lemon juice to carry to sea: about 30 or 40 gallons to each ship of the line and 3 or 4 hundred weight of sugar, both for the use of the sick alone, appear to me highly necessary in the present state of the fleet.

52.   *Admiralty to Bridport*

27 May 1795

If you should be at Portsmouth when this reaches you, will you be so good to leave word that a return may be sent up to you to Town of the men on board the different ships afflicted with the scurvy that it may be proper to leave behind for their recovery, that arrangements may be made for replacing them in the ships going to sea from those which are to remain.

53.   *Sick and Wounded Board to Admiralty*[1]

Office for Sick and Wounded Seamen, 27 May 1795

We beg you will please to acquaint the Right Honourable the Lords Commissioners of the Admiralty that in consequence of their Lordships' Order, signified to us in your letter of the 19th instant, to take into consideration what is proposed in an extract of a letter addressed to Earl Howe respecting beer, lemon juice, and sugar, and report to you

---

[1]The responsibility for the defeat of scurvy has been principally attached to Dr Thomas Trotter and Dr Gilbert Blane. See K. J. Carpenter, *The History of Scurvy and Vitamin C* (Cambridge, 1986), 95; *Starving Sailors. The Influence of Nutrition upon Naval and Maritime History*, ed. J. Watt, E. J. Freeman and W. F. Bynum (National Maritime Museum, 1981), 13, 58; *Medicine and the Navy 1200–1900*, III, 321. It is an attribution principally arising from the publicity each gained through their publications, for which see *The Health of Seamen*, 132–4, 214–15. It is thus of note that this letter of 27 May 1795 was signed by the less well known Commissioners for Sick and Wounded Seamen, W. Gibbons and R. Blair. Blane joined the Board in 1795.

for their Lordships' information our opinion thereupon, we sent to the King's brewhouse for a sample of the small beer served to the Royal Navy, and having carefully examined the same; it does not appear to us to be deficient in the quantity of hops; we must also observe that hops, considered in a medical light, possess little or no antiscorbutic virtue, and that the habitual use of any very strong bitter (even supposing the seamen not to object to such innovation) would rather tend to impair, than to improve their health.

Their Lordships have not desired us to take into consideration what is proposed in the said letter, or making the beer double its present strength, it has no doubt occurred to them, that before introducing into the navy so very material a change, the matter ought to be materially weighed in all its probable consequences; and that it might be expedient to make the first trial (if judged necessary) on a small scale.

With respect to the animadversions on the quantity of lemon juice, and sugar, lately supplied by their Lordships' order, to several ships bound on distant voyages, and the expense attending them, we must request their Lordships' permission to be somewhat particular on that subject.

From our own observations, and the experience of ages, we have been led to consider fresh limes and lemons or the juice of those fruits, properly prepared for keeping, as the most powerful antiscorbutic in nature, and know of no instance in which (when administered genuine) it has failed to cure the disease, even in its most advanced stages, either on board ship, or on shore. It is also well ascertained that a certain proportion of lemon juice, taken daily, as an article of seamen's diet, will prevent the possibility of their being tainted with the scurvy, let the other articles of their diet consist of what they will.

Upon this principle, we recommended to their Lordships a trial being made of it in the fleet under Admiral Gardner intended in the year 1794 for distant service, with little probability of procuring refreshments.

The daily allowance for each Man, was to be 3/4 of an ounce of lemon juice, and two ounces of sugar, to be made into an agreeable beverage, with their spirits or wine, and such an addition of water, as the captains might judge expedient.

The expedition under Admiral Gardner not having taken place, we can only judge of the effect of the supply from what happened to the Suffolk, Argo, and Swan Sloop, which proceeded on the voyage.

It appears from Captain Rainier's[1] letter to us, dated Madras Road, 29th of September 1794, that the Suffolk performed a voyage from

---

[1]Peter Rainier (d. 1808). Lieutenant 1768; Captain 1778; Rear-admiral 1795; Vice-admiral 1799; Admiral 1805. See also C.N. Parkinson, *Trade in the Eastern Seas, 1793–1815* (London, 1966).

England to Madras in 19 weeks, without touching anywhere, and arrived in Madras Roads with 15 sick. The scurvy had begun to appear in some instances, notwithstanding the quantity of lemon juice given, but on increasing this quantity its progress was stopped.

The report from the Argo, which went no further than St Helena, is that only one case of scurvy occurred the whole voyage, and that on her return in the Channel, the surgeon observes, that the lemon juice and sugar were duly administered, and he has every reason to conclude that besides their happy effects in preventing the scurvy, they were no less effectual in preventing ebriety,[1] its consequences and many other diseases incidental to a warm climate. No return has yet been made from the Swan sloop.

It is a clear inference, from what happend to the Suffolk, that if the proportion of lemon juice had been somewhat greater, the scurvy would never have made its appearance, notwithstanding the unusual length of her voyage; nor can it be deemed unreasonable to conclude, that if she had not been provided with this antiscorbutic, her voyage must either have been retarded by stopping for refreshment, or she must have arrived in India in a state unfit for immediate service.

We leave it to their Lordships to compare this statement of facts with the allegations of the quantity of lemon juice supplied lately to the Hector and Sheerness being unnecessarily large, and whether or not beer given in lieu of that article would have a better effect in preventing the scurvy will best appear from contrasting the state of Suffolk after being nineteen weeks at sea, with the present state of the Channel Fleet, overrun with the scurvy while laying in port and liberally supplied with beer.

Beer of moderate strength is undoubtedly a very proper article of seamen's diet, and may be considered as a good antiscorbutic, just as new soft bread and fresh meat may be called so, but it is not that powerful remedy and antidote, which even in a small quantity cures the disease in its worst state, and effectually counteracts the tendency which the diet and habits of seamen have in producing it. In regard to the expense attending these supplies, which are desired also to be taken into consideration, it is without doubt an object which deserves serious attention. But we beg to suggest to their Lordships the propriety of taking into account in this discussion the additional service performed by an equal number of seamen, as well as the saving in hospital and recruiting service. In recommending an effectual method of preventing the scurvy, our views are not confined to the prevention of the actual

[1]Drunkenness.

appearance of the disease, but extend to the prevention of that scorbutic taint which, even in seamen apparently in health, converts every slight wound into a foul ulcer. Prime seamen being much exposed to such accidents, much of them are well known to be thus lost to the service, or, which is still worse, they are enabled to make a trade of imposing on Government, by repeatedly receiving the Royal Bounty, and contriving as often (after being long a nuisance in the hospitals) to get themselves discharged as invalids. How can this evil be effectually remedied without going to its source?

In the proposal of sending such a quantity of lemon juice and sugar on board the ships of the Channel Fleet, as will not suffice to prevent the disease, and which it is only proposed to administer to those actually afflicted, we have to observe that such articles sent on board to be dispensed at the discretion of any particular officer are liable to abuse and irregularity in the administration; and we are of opinion that a better mode would be to abolish the use of discretional articles of diet, and in lieu thereof, establish a scheme of diet, distinct from the common salt meat diet, consisting of such articles as have been found by experience most useful and most convenient for carrying to sea. As it would be unnecessary that men who are put on this diet should also receive the common salt meat diet, this improvement might be introduced without any additional charge to government. And when the number of sick will admit of it, the benefit of this diet might be extended by the Captain's discretion, to the men in health, that the active and useful part of the crew might in their turns be indulged with it.

Upon the whole, what we have to offer on the subject of diet is contained in the following propositions.

First. That a sufficient quantity of lime or lemon juice, which has been found to be the most powerful antiscorbutic in nature, and when properly prepared and packed will retain its virtues unimpaired for a great length of time, should be daily administered to the whole ship's company when at sea, or on salt provisions, as the best substitute for fresh fruit and vegetables, and the most powerful corrective of the scorbutic qualities of their common diet.

Secondly, that the discretional administration of essence of malt, sour kraut, molasses etc, should be abolished, and instead thereof a separate diet established, to consist of these articles, or such other as are most approved, which are to be served to the persons put on this diet, with the same regularity as the common diet is served to the rest of the crew. In this diet, trials may be made of such articles as may from time to time be proposed, on a small scale and without incovenience.

We conceive that the establishment of these regulations would afford seamen every advantage with regard to diet, which their situation admits of, and that amongst the good consequences attending them, the disorder called the sea scurvy would be no longer heard of in the Royal Navy.

With respect to the proposal made by the Physician to the Channel Fleet of sending on board a quantity of lemon juice, to be used at discretion, it is what we have already directed to be done in several instances and, till a more regular mode can be adopted, we are of opinion it ought to be continued. But the sugar, which is the most expensive article, is unnecessary where the lemon juice is not proposed to be used as an article of diet, as men who labour under this disorder have naturally a craving for acids. We are further of opinion that if the more effectual plan above mentioned is not adopted, it might be proper to supply the navy surgeons with the acid of lemons instead of the mineral acid, now allowed them, as the latter is an article of little importance.

[*Endorsement*]

29 May. Send copy to Lord Howe for his Lordship's information. Approve of the Sick and Hurt's proposal and send them a copy of the plan respecting the issue of molasses in lieu of oatmeal, directing . . . [*incomplete*].

54.   *Sick and Wounded Board to Admiralty*

Office for Sick and Wounded Seamen, 5 June 1795

We request you will be pleased to lay before the Right Honourable the Lords Commissioners of the Admiralty the enclosed copy of a letter, dated 3d instant, which we wrote to Dr Johnston, resident commissioner for sick and wounded seamen etc at Haslar, respecting the supply of vegetables for the Channel Fleet, together with his answer thereto, and of the papers therein referred to.

[*Endorsement*]

8 June. Refer to the Commissioners of the Victualling in order to consider what steps may be taken in the event of supplying the men in health with vegetables as proposed.

[*Enclosures*]

54a.   *Sick and Wounded Board to Dr J. Johnston*

Office for Sick and Wounded Seamen, 3 June 1795

We have received your two letters of the 31st ultimo and 2nd instant.

We approve of what has been done respecting the supply of salad for the scorbutic patients on board the fleet; we are of opinion that those who are affected with the disorder in a considerable degree ought to be sent to Haslar Hospital and we wish to be informed what number of the seamen are still afflicted with the scurvy it being our intention as soon as scorbutic symptons have disappeared to direct the supplies to be discontinued.

Should the Right Honourable the Lords Commissioners of the Admiralty be of opinion that an extra allowance of vegetables is necessary to the whole fleet, over and above what it has been customary for the pursers to furnish, we apprehend their Lordships will give instructions to the Victualling Board to that effect.

54b.   *Johnston to Sick and Wounded Board*

Royal Hospital at Haslar, 4 June 1795

I have received your letter of the 3rd instant in answer to my letters of the 31st ultimo and the 2nd instant approving of the mode of supplying the scorbutics with salad. I sent you enclosed a copy of a letter I wrote to Doctor Trotter requesting to be furnished with the number of patients that required this supply as regular lists were sent to him on board the Charon every morning signed by the surgeon of such ships in the Channel fleet as had any scorbutics on board.

Instead of any satisfactory answer I received the inclosed letter from him yesterday requiring 5000 weight to be daily supplied but has taken no notice of the scorbutic patients. In order to show my readiness in giving every aid to the recovery of patients in scurvy, I encreased the quantity of vegetables this day to 2006 lbs in which were included 268 lbs of spring cabbages; this last I purpose only supplying tomorrow as Doctor Trotter has stated that the Lords Commissioners of the Admiralty have ordered a pound of fresh beef per man a day; either leeks or greens will of course be supplied by the pursers. I shall therefore confine the supplies in future to the salad and shall write to the Commander of the Channel fleet to be furnished with the proper lists for that purpose, as well as for your information.

Enclosed is a copy of a letter I sent this day to Dr Trotter.

54c. *Trotter to Johnston*

Spithead, 2 June 1795

In answer to your letter of this date, I beg leave to inform you that I have been directed by Admiral Lord Bridport to send an account of what quantity of vegetables I judged necessary for the state of the fleet and it appears to me highly requisite for the immediate prevention of scurvy that not less than 5,000 hundredweight ought to be sent to us daily.

The Lords Commissioners of the Admiralty have ordered a pound of fresh beef per man a day although the price is uncommonly high and the Sick and Wounded Board inform me that they have directed a liberal supply of what vegetables the season could afford by command of their Lordships; I have therefore thought proper to let you know that the fleet now at Spithead may sail in a few days and no time ought to be lost in procuring what quantity of vegetables the neighbourhood can afford.

What you have sent here hitherto has been distributed according to the state of the ships and not to any practical representations from lists sent by the Surgeons.

54d. *Johnston to Trotter*

Royal Hospital at Haslar, 4 June 1795

I yesterday received your letter of the 2nd instant in answer to mine of the preceding day requesting you to give me information of the number of scorbutic patients that required the use of salad that I might be able to ascertain the quantity that may be wanted for each day's supply but as you have not been pleased to give such information I have to repeat the same request.

I have to acquaint you that I am not warranted by any instructions from the Commissioners for Sick and Wounded Seamen to supply vegetables for the ships' companies in health nor by Lord Bridport who desires in his letter of the 28th ultimo that there may be purchased such a quantity of vegetables 'to allow each scorbutic patient such a quantity as Doctor Trotter may think necessary' from which it will appear evident that I am not authorised to supply more than patients of that description require.

This day 2006 lbs were supplied in which are included 268 lbs of spring cabbages but the latter will be discontinued tomorrow, you having stated that 'the Lords Commissioners of the Admiralty had ordered a pound of fresh beef per man a day'; as that will be made into broth, and leeks and greens furnished by the pursers, consequently any further supply of greens will be unnecessary. The salad shall be continued so long as any scorbutic patient remain in the Channel fleet and each person shall have as large an allowance as you may think proper and as the salad consists of mustard, cresses, lettuce and young onions I can have no objection in making such alteration in these articles you may desire.

As Lord Bridport mentioned in his letter that 'you had his direction to consult me on the occasion' I am ready to meet you for that purpose as often as you may think proper.

2

THE BLOCKADE INITIATED
6 JUNE–19 SEPTEMBER 1795

In June 1795 the British government aimed to land an army of 2500 French royalists and emigrés on the Quiberon Peninsula as a means of reinforcing a royalist army of 8000 that was already laying siege to Fort Penthièvre commanding the neck of the peninsula. The operation was conceived as a means of raising a rebellion throughout the Vendée, a threat to both Brest and L'Orient. The operation demanded more than 50 transports and an escort of three ships of the line and the squadron of six frigates under the command of Sir John Borlase Warren. To prevent the Brest fleet interfering with the expedition, the Channel fleet under Lord Howe was ordered to sea early in June [55].

Howe still felt himself too unwell to lead the fleet, and accordingly ordered Bridport to take the fleet to sea [56]. The situation of the royalist army in France demanded support without delay. The transports were ready by the 9th and Bridport was urged to sea, the Admiralty anxiously attempting to remove obstacles which included the payment of crews [57], shortages of seamen [58], and the attendance of captains at a court-martial [59]. The Admiralty was kept informed of proceedings by Rear-admiral Lord Hugh Seymour[1] who had been an Admiralty commissioner since March 1795. His ability to use the Admiralty messenger to carry his letters to the First Lord not only gave the executive board an additional and intelligent view of what was happening in the fleet but some local influence on the deputy Commander-in-Chief. Bridport also had the assistance of Vice-admiral Sir Alan Gardner, until March an Admiralty commissioner of five years' standing, Vice-admiral John Colpoys and Rear-admiral Henry Harvey, for the energy and commitment of all of whom Seymour vouched [60].

Bridport sailed on 12 June. He remained with Warren and the transports until the 19th when, near Belle Isle, he stood out from the coast, leaving Warren on a fair wind for Quiberon. Information had been received from an American vessel that the Brest fleet was out [61], but it was received by Warren with reservations [62], a scepticism echoed at the Admiralty [63]. However, two hours after parting from Bridport,

---

[1]Seymour was flying his flag in the *Sans-Pareil* (80).

when actually in sight of Belle Isle, Warren sighted the French fleet [64]. Why the enemy should have been out in force so unexpectedly was to puzzle all the British officers. Bridport believed the Quiberon expedition must have been discovered [72]. This seemed to be contradicted by the failure of the French to attack Warren and his convoy, and Spencer thought they must have been waiting for a convoy from the United States, as they had a year earlier [68].

From prisoners, Seymour pieced together the real reason [66]. Eleven days earlier the squadron under Vice-admiral Cornwallis had chased a smaller French one escorting a convoy into the shelter of Belle Isle and, on the news reaching Brest, Villaret-Joyeuse with nine of the line had been equipped with all speed and sent to retrieve it. Returning to Brest, now 12 strong, Villaret-Joyeuse on 16 June encountered Cornwallis, who, himself possessing only five of the line, was forced for the next 36 hours to retreat, only deterring the French from an overwhelming assault by a *ruse de guerre* on the morning of the 17th of a frigate signalling to an absent fleet over the horizon. While Cornwallis had then sailed straight for Plymouth, Villaret-Joyeuse had been driven again into the shelter of Belle Isle by a gale.[1]

On sighting the French fleet emerging from the shelter of Belle Isle on 19 June, Warren with his convoy immediately altered course and sent a fast vessel to warn Bridport who promptly requested Warren's three of the line, making his force up to 17 of the line. Only on the 22 June, however, was Bridport able to gain sight of Villaret-Joyeuse who, with his 12, stood towards the land. Bridport gave chase. On the 23rd, Isle de Groix east six or seven miles, an action began which resulted in the capture of three French battle ships [65]. The chase continued so close to the land that shots were exchanged with shore batteries. Later Sir Hugh Palliser drew a comparison favourable to Bridport with the controversial Battle off Ushant in 1778 [71]. Greater sea room may have resulted in more captures before Villaret-Joyeuse took refuge in Lorient [66, 67].[2] Spencer at the Admiralty thought there might be a possibility of attacking them there with fireships [68]. This was denied by Bridport; nevertheless, with the expedition to Quiberon so vulnerable to attack from the sea, it was necessary for the British fleet to keep the French ships penned in L'Orient and Brest [72, 73]. So commenced the close blockade.

Free from interference, on 27 June Warren landed the French royalist army, with 300 British marines and arms and ammunition for 16,000

---

[1]W. James, *The Naval History of Great Britain from the declaration of war by France in 1793 to the accession of George IV* (6 vols, London, 1859), I, 263–70.

[2]James, I, 270–77.

men. Fort Penthièvre commanding the isthmus of the peninsula was taken. However, the royalists failed to take the town of Quiberon at the point of the peninsula and were dependent for their supplies on British ships, which also had the population of the isthmus to consider and could remain only so long as favourable weather continued [73]. Cargoes from captured American vessels had been made available for purchase by the royalist forces in addition to their supply of British stores [69]. Yet, on 17 July the royalists failed to fight their way off the isthmus and were beset by desertion, treachery and counter-attack. On 21 July 1100 of the expeditionary force was re-embarked with 2400 royalist inhabitants [88]. To provide a safe haven for them, the islands of Hoedic and Houat were seized [90]; nevertheless 2000 royalists preferred to be disembarked near L'Orient.[1]

While Warren remained in Quiberon Bay, Bridport cruised off the French coast between Belle Isle and Ushant until 20 September. Sir William Sidney Smith, already better known for his dashing indiscretion [75], though one of Warren's captains, was temperamentally and consciously adverse to the discipline of blockade [76]. His attitude was tolerated at this stage in the war; indeed there was still scope for marauding frigates capable of demonstrating on every possible occasion 'that the frontier of Great Britain is high water mark in France' [80].

Smith's method of manning his ship was to take volunteers from returning East Indiamen [81]. For those who maintained the discipline of the blockade, the preservation of the health of their crews was now dependent on regular relief and supply. For this purpose Cornwallis was ordered to join Bridport [77, 78], permitting him to despatch half of his previous force into Portsmouth and Plymouth. Nevertheless scurvy remained an ever-present fear, prompting regular reminders of the necessity for the supply of fresh provisions [73, 79]. Indeed, on account of the shortage of transports to carry out provisions, Warren's frigates were to return to Plymouth to replenish as necessary [84].

The command of the Channel fleet remained a conundrum. Howe, still in London, in principle remained in overall command, and bothered Bridport to send him the same returns the latter made to the Admiralty [70]. His presence on shore, however, made Bridport suspect he was supplying Spencer with suggestions on how better to direct the fleet [72, 78]. Suspicions and separate loyalties divided the officer corps. Adherence to Bridport may have prompted the discourtesy of Captains Domett and Lord Henry Powlett in sailing from Plymouth with Admiralty despatches for Bridport without paying their respects to

[1] James, I, 278–80.

the Port Admiral, Sir Richard King [74]. Spencer still hoped Howe would resume the active command, but was conscious of Bridport's irritation at a situation where he performed the work without receiving the full credit. Accordingly, he encouraged Bridport to see the advantage of his position by adverting to his opportunity for making prize money [78]. Yet Howe felt more than ever the need to return to Bath [82]. Spencer attempted to pre-empt an official resignation [83], and managed to limit Howe to notifying the King of his continued indisposition and inability to resume a more active role [85].

Howe's sustained invalidity did permit Spencer to suggest for Bridport the title of Commander-in-Chief of a squadron to be employed on a particular service, which carried higher payment and rank [86]. The King approved the suggestion [87] and the commission was sent out to Bridport [89, 91]. It was approved in the fleet, at least by Seymour [99], and had the potential for settling speculation surrounding the higher fleet commands. For the uncertainties of the Channel, combined with Hotham's requested recall from the Mediterranean, perpetuated the possibilities of a rearrangement of admirals [88]. Bridport made no secret of his dislike of acting second to Howe while in effect taking the full burden. He was encouraged by others less involved, who regarded Howe as perverse, desiring to retire yet doggedly retaining the command. To obtain the ultimate command, Bridport was advised to remain in post and at sea [92]. This advice he was to follow. Yet to Spencer, Bridport stated quite categorically that the new commission was overdue, failed to arouse in him either a sense of honour or a feeling of gratitude, and did nothing to alleviate a desire for some further mark of approbation from the King [94]. It was a reply that irritated Spencer [96, 97], and prompted George III to pass judgement on the public spirit of the Hood family in general [98].

On account of complaints about his deteriorating health [91], Bridport was given permission to return into port whenever it became necessary [95]. He might be suspected of such complaints on account of the sanction Howe had received for remaining on shore. But his self-defence, reference to his 68 years of age, preference for remaining with his ship, and anxiety for the health of the seamen serving under him all seemed genuine [101].

Bridport had been afloat since early June. Most seamen had been at sea much longer, and by mid-August 1795 scurvy was again becoming a major concern [99].[1] Bridport required a thorough survey and report

[1] According to Trotter, between March and June 1795 over 3000 cases of scurvy were treated on board ships in the Channel fleet. J.J. Keevil, C. Lloyd and J.L.S. Coulter, *Medicine and the Navy 1200–1900* (4 vols, Edinburgh, 1957–63), III, 324.

from Trotter, Physician of the Fleet, who observed that few precautions had been taken to prevent the incidence of scurvy. He reiterated his recommendation for a universal diet of fresh meat and vegetables, with lemon juice for serious cases. Among other measures, he persisted in his recommendation of strong beer, though this was thought of little use by the Sick and Wounded Board. He also demanded that the necessaries supplied for the sick at Plymouth, Portsmouth and the eastern depots be increased and include known antiscorbutics. The Board of Admiralty was appropriately concerned and directed the supply of antiscorbutics. Perhaps more importantly, it gave maintenance of the blockade priority over other functions of the Channel fleet and directed a squadron under Rear Admiral Harvey to relieve some of Bridport's ships without the convoy it had been waiting for [100].

At the Admiralty there was some surprise that ships which had joined Bridport in July under Cornwallis should also be experiencing outbreaks of scurvy [100, 109]. An explanation came from the *Formidable* whose crew had been turned over from the *Marlborough* which had been at sea off and on since January. Fresh provisions had been issued to that crew only eight times; and even after scurvy had made its appearance, actual delivery of fresh vegetables and lemon juice had been limited to a quantity of lime juice. The urgency to make good these deficiencies lay in the fact that most scorbutic patients were able seamen, of whom the ship was already 40 short of complement [102]. Some looked back even further, to the limited availability of fresh food over the previous severe winter [104].

This threat to the operational capability of ships involved in the blockade was reinforced by falling quantities of water on board ships in the fleet. By the end of August 1795, Bridport was deeply conscious of the dilemma posed by obedience to Admiralty orders to remain off the French coast, and was making preparations for refitting and replenishing [102, 105]. Other admirals in the fleet placed pressure on Spencer [106] and Bridport [107]. The pressure was the greater on account of the apparent neglect of the Admiralty to send Harvey with his relief squadron [109], instead putting its faith in the urgent despatch to the fleet of fresh provisions by the Victualling Board [108], and the purchase of large quantities of lemon juice by the Sick and Wounded Board [110]. Only at the beginning of September was the Admiralty able to report Harvey had sailed [111]. It was to be relief that was psychological as much as physical. The absence of an established system of relief, taking priority over all other demands, added an unwanted anxiety to the tribulations of fleet commanders. Early in September Bridport endorsed the letter of the Victualling Board providing assurance of a supply at sea of fresh provisions: 'Only think what we have suffered by not having received a letter . . . and not knowing the measures of Government' [108].

Bridport was relieved on 10 September. The French royalist expedition, for the protection of which his cruise in June had been intended, had by this time dwindled to nothing [112]. In consequence Warren also left Quiberon with the squadron and transports under his command in the middle of September [113]. By this time the state of the scorbutic patients had become quite desperate [114], a misery contrasting starkly with the sort of warfare being conducted by Sidney Smith [115]. Only a small force under Harvey was left to guard L'Orient and watch Brest. The French ships that had taken refuge in L'Orient had sailed from Brest with only two weeks' provisions and had been obliged to discharge there large numbers of their crews. Towards the end of the year, when on-shore winds forced British ships to remove further out to sea, some of these vessels escaped along the coast into Rochefort and back into Brest.[1]

Bridport occupied himself on his return voyage by writing to his Commander-in-Chief. Only now did he acknowledge Howe's request of 5 July for accounts of his proceedings and returns of the state of his ships. Bridport's deliberate disregard of Howe's request and the apparent insolence of his delayed reply was clearly calculated to offend Howe and deter him from again resuming active command of the Channel fleet over the head of Bridport [116]. To underline Howe's apparent dispensability, Bridport's statement of achievements during the voyage was positively jubilant [117]. However, his withdrawal from the French coast had done nothing to raise him in the estimation of George III who remained fully conscious of the necessity for a strong western squadron to resume station off the French coast to protect British trade [118].

55. *Admiralty to Howe*

6 June 1795

We do hereby require and direct you to put to sea with the ships and vessels named in the margin [*Queen Charlotte, Royal George, Queen, Prince of Wales, Sans Pareil, Prince, Barfleur, Formidable, Orion, Irresistible, Prince George, London, Russell, Colossus, Valiant, Thalia, Crescent, Aquilon, Astrea, Revolutionaire, Babet, Megara, Incendiary,*

---

[1]James, I, 280–81.

Charon] under your command and as soon as you shall obtain information of his [Sir John Borlase Warren] leaving Spithead . . . place yourself in such a situation as may under the circumstances of wind and weather be best calculated for preventing the departure of any of the enemy's ships from the port of Brest and for affording protection to Sir John Warren and the squadron under his orders in the execution of the important service entrusted to his care.

From the information we have received of the state of the transports and troops, it seems probable they will be in a condition to put to sea in the course of two or three days. In the meantime it appears to be desirable that your Lordship should endeavour to inform yourself as distinctly as possible of the state of the enemy's fleet at Brest, and though it may not be necessary previously to the sailing of the squadron and troops that you should remain off that port, it will nevertheless be expedient that whenever the wind shall be favourable for the enemy's sailing from thence you should be on the station before mentioned in order to intercept any force which he may attempt to detach . . .

56. *Howe to Bridport*

7 June 1795

Whereas the yet impaired state of my health does not allow me at this time to resume the more immediate direction of the ships of the fleet under my command intended to be employed for the purposes expressed in the most secret instructions from the Lords Commissioners of the Admiralty dated the 6th instant and other documents conditionally issued for my government on the same occasion which you receive herewith and by which several communications you are to be governed in your future conduct in the same manner as if they had been originally addressed to you.

You are therefore hereby authorized and required to proceed to sea as soon as may be with the ships of the fleet therein specified (whereunto you are at liberty to add the Charon hospital ship if you think fit)[1] for carrying those purposes into execution accordingly, being careful moreover to send notice from time to time of your proceedings in pursuance of this appointment to Mr. Secretary Nepean for the information of the Lords Commissioners of the Admiralty thereon.

[1]Her name is in fact pencilled into the copy of the order in the Bridport Papers.

57.   *Admiralty to Bridport*

9 June 1795

By accounts which have been received from Portsmouth it is stated that your Lordship will not be able to sail for some days on account of the payment of the crews of some of your ships. If that should be the case, is there anything that can be done here to facilitate the payments? It is unlucky that you cannot avail yourself of the favourable wind that at present prevails.

58.   *Spencer to Bridport*

Admiralty, 10 June 1795

The object on which your squadron is destined is so very important in the present critical situation of affairs that I cannot resist, though with the risk, perhaps, of appearing to you over anxious on the subject, writing you these few lines by a messenger to express my hopes that no delay may prevent your taking the advantage of this fair wind. The only delay that from our information in this office I can foresee possible is from the Orion not having men enough and that shall be remedied by an order to lend her some from the Commerce de Marseilles[1] which order will accompany this letter but even if any difficulty remained to prevent her readiness after that I must still advise your putting to sea without her as you will then have thirteen sail of the line, of which 8 are 3 deckers, a force far superior to anything you can have to meet of the enemy.

59.   *Seymour to Spencer*

Portsmouth, 10 June 1795

I am just returned from Lord Bridport, who is doing his utmost to forward the departure of his squadron. He will, however, not be able to move far till Friday at soonest as the payment of the Irresistible and Prince cannot take place till tomorrow and that many of the captains will at the same time be occupied with Captain Cotes's[2] court martial. Lord

---

[1]The *Commerce de Marseilles* (120), captured at Toulon in 1793, though admirable in sailing qualities, was structurally weak and being used as a receiving ship. B. Lavery, *The Ship of the Line* (2 vols, London, 1983), I, 121–2.

[2]James Cotes (d. 1802). Lieutenant 1776; Captain 1782.

Howe having directed two of our frigates, the Crescent and Thalia, to be employ'd between Ushant and Cape Ortegal it is quite necessary that another should be added to our squadron for the purpose of frequently looking into Brest, which it will be our business to watch. I perceive Lord Bridport to be anxious on the subject but he will not apply for *anything at present*. I should therefore recommend the Nymphe being put under his orders, who with the Revolutionaire will perform that service well, being well commanded and of a construction likely to deceive the enemy when near the shore.[1] Captain Murray[2] yesterday told me he should be ready for sea in two or three days, by which time he may certainly join us. The Prince being very short of seamen Lord Bridport has borrowed a few from the Canada for her and he proposes borrowing some from the Impregnable to complete his other ships, which I have encouraged him to do from knowing that you had not disposed of that ship for any immediate service. I am glad to say that our squadron is perfectly ready for sea and the ships' companies are all very healthy. Sir John Warren moves to Cowes today and I do trust that we shall soon be enabled to carry into execution a plan the success of which will depend upon the early departure of the ships from this place, for it appears to me that many people are informed of their destination. As the messenger has received Lord Bridport's letter, which may give you more detailed information about his squadron, I will not risk delaying him.

[*Endorsed as received on the 11th*]

60.   *Seymour to Spencer*

Portsmouth, 10 June 1795

Lord Bridport is really doing what he can to get out and I do trust that the day after tomorrow we shall move from Spithead. I can only describe my eagerness to do so by recollecting and expressing how much depends upon our using the greatest dispatch into carrying your present plan into execution. I am happy to say that everything that I have witnessed or heard since my arrival here assures me that the conduct of the admirals under you gives the greatest satisfaction and diffuses the sort of spirit I ever wish to see pursued in the service I am so much attached to.

[1] Both *Nymphe* (36) and *Revolutionaire* (38) had been captured from the French, the former in 1780 and the latter in 1794.
[2] Sir George Murray (1759–1819). Lieutenant 1778; Captain 1782; Rear-admiral 1804; Vice-admiral 1809. In June 1795 he commanded the *Nymphe* (36).

61.   *George C. Fox to Admiralty*

Falmouth, 16 June 1795

I beg leave to inform thee that the commander of the schooner Eliza of Boston which is just arrived here from Rochelle declares that he sailed from thence ten days since in company with 5 ships of the line, which joined 10 others of the line off Belle Isle on the 8th instant, when they composed altogether about 25 sail, including frigates.

62.   *Warren to Bridport*

La Pomone, at sea, 17 June 1795

I beg leave to acknowledge the receipt of your Lordship's letters of the 16th instant with its enclosures and also of this day's date. I shall pay every attention to the intelligence received, although I am apt to think the American's information is similar to what I have often received from ships of that country and that he has substituted a convoy for men of war.

I have already dispatched Captain Keats[1] in the Galatea to look into Quiberon and also with a chasse marée containing some arms for our friends.

If your Lordship should think proper to cruise off the Penmarks and have any frigates towards Hodierne Bay [Audierne Bay] or the Passage du Raz, which we have always found by orders given to the men of war by the Convention is the route they choose for their convoys and squadrons, it would effectually cover us.

63.   *Admiralty to Bridport*

19 June 1795

Having laid before the Lords Commissioners of the Admiralty two letters which I have this day received from Mr. Fox and Lieutenant Pearson[2], regulating the Impress Service at Falmouth, containing intelligence which they had collected from the master of an American vessel which had arrived from Rochelle, I am commanded to enclose to your Lordship copies thereof for your information, at the same time to

---

[1]Richard Goodwin Keats (1757–1834). Lieutenant 1777; Captain 1789; Rear-admiral 1807; Vice-admiral 1811; Admiral 1825. He commanded in the Baltic in 1807. He was appointed Governor of Greenwich Hospital in 1821.

[2]Richard Harrison Pearson (d. 1838). Lieutenant 1793; Captain 1798; Rear-admiral 1825; Vice-admiral 1835.

acquaint your Lordship that according to the intelligence which had previously been communicated to their Lordships respecting the state and condition of the enemy's fleet they had reason to believe that a force to the extent herein mentioned could not have been assembled at the time and in that situation.

64. *Warren to Bridport*

La Pomone, at sea, 19 June 1795

I had just lost sight of your Lordship's fleet about two hours after we made the Penmarks when I discovered a strange fleet to leeward in the S.W. I immediately despatched two frigates to reconnoitre them. One of the headmost made several signals to our frigates, who were convinced of their being the enemy, consisting of 16 of the line, 7 frigates, 2 brigs and a cutter. They were close hauled, standing to the N.E. and one of the headmost[1] very near the Arethusa. An American ship we afterwards spoke to told us they had an action the day before with some ships which lasted two hours, when the others got off. He says they have been stationed off Belleisle and been out there three days. From the state of the weather and wind it is impossible they could get into Quiberon Bay or Rochefort and are consequently to windward.

65. *A Journal of the proceedings of His Majesty's ship Russell, John W. Payne[2] Esquire Commander, 22–23 June 1795*

At 3 the Aquilon made the signal for a strange fleet bearing S.E. by E. At 4 the Admiral made the signal for the enemy. At 8 the signal for a general chase. At 9 the whole of the enemy in view. At 11 calm and clear, the body of the French fleet E. by S., 6 leagues. Cleared for action.

Tuesday 23rd. Light airs and clear. The enemy right ahead, coming up with them fast. The Admiral made the frigates' signal to annoy the enemy and denote their motions. The frigate ahead made the signal for 13 sail of the line and 11 frigates. The Admiral made the signal to engage the enemy as arriving up. At 12 the Admiral 3 miles astern. At 4

---

[1]Here an indecipherable word is omitted. However it does not appear to alter the sense of the sentence significantly.

[2]John Willett Payne (d. 1803). Lieutenant 1777; Captain 1780; Rear-admiral 1799. His journal is adorned with watercolours of the blockade. Naval logs run from noon to noon. This extract begins in the early hours of Monday, 22 June.

Isle de Groix east 6 or 7 miles. At ½ past the action commenced and the Queen Charlotte, Orion, Irresistible, Colossus, Sans Pareil and Russell keeping up a brisk fire on the Formidable. At ½ past 6 the Alexander dropped close alongside of us when we were engaged on both sides. At 7 the Formidable dropped astern, having lost his mizen mast and on fire abaft. At ½ past 7 keeping up a brisk fire on the Montagne. Observed the battery on shore fire at the Colossus, which she returned. At ¾ past hauled out of the line and repaired our rigging, being cut to pieces. At the close of the action the Royal George, Admiral Lord Bridport, hailed us and desired we would go to leeward of him. At 8 the Royal George delivered his guns to the Tigre and Montagne. The former bore up and struck. At ¼ past the action ceased on both sides. Found the Tigre, Alexander and Formidable prizes. 2 men killed, 6 wounded.

66.   *Seymour to Spencer*

Off Belle Isle, 24 June 1795

On Monday morning when we first discovered the enemy, which we had been taught to believe of 17 sail of the line and 7 frigates, our distance from the shore was so small, being only about twenty leagues, of which they were advanced five, that our hope of closing with them rested entirely upon their numbers tempting them to try their force with ours. A very short time, however, convinced us that they had no thought of doing so, as from first making out our squadron distinctly they did what they could to reach the land. There was very little wind all Monday but the object before us was so tempting that by our squadron having availed itself of every air that blew we had approached to them considerably during the day, at the close of which we distinctly ascertained their force to be only 12 sail of the line with eleven frigates, of which two were razés. Monday night was fortunately calm and clear, which prevented the enemy getting away from us, and a breeze which sprung up at daylight yesterday, and which we got before the enemy, enabled us to get within gunshot of them at about six, when our advanced ships, about six or seven in number, began firing. The chase now grew very interesting, for the distance from the shore was so very small that it was doubtful whether it would be possible to stop any of the enemy before they reached Port Louis (within the Isle de Groix) for which they were pressing with every sail set. Fortunately they were so little satisfied with the sailing of the Alexander that they directed a frigate to tow her, which threw her so much to leeward as to enable our ships to cut her off and, after having fought better than the others did, she fell into our hands. The chase continued with a straggling but constant firing till near eight, by which time the Tyger and Formidable had struck and we were within a mile or two of the shore, which made it necessary for us to stand from it. The prizes having been taken in tow we had not much difficulty in accomplishing our wishes of getting them off, as our ships were hardly out of order, though the enemy's suffered so much. You will, I am persuaded, be happy to know that the Sans Pareil was among the foremost of the eight or nine sail who were enabled to get into action and will not be less so to learn from me that she answers in every respect, excepting in light winds, when I have reason to be dissatisfied with her, as the Queen Charlotte, Orion and Irresistible passed her in the course of the chase on Monday night. Her officers and men have given me much satisfaction by their good conduct in the course of the action and chase. I had the misfortune to have two officers killed, one of which, Lieutenant Stocker,[1] was a great favourite with us all, being an excellent young man and, I think, one of the very best officers I have ever met with at sea. In general I believe the squadron to have suffered very little in killed and wounded and I do not hear that any officer of mark is in either list but Captain Grindall,[2] whose arm is broken. The French are said to have lost a great many men, which I can easily believe from the way their ships are cut up. An officer of the Alexander, who is now with me, assures me that they had 100 killed on board her and that the Tyger must have lost at least that number from the reports which have reached him. Had we been fortunate enough to have fallen in with this squadron two leagues further from the coast I have not a doubt but that the whole of it would have been taken but though we cannot prevent this idea from presenting itself to our minds I think it but fair to say that our success yesterday exceeded very much the expectations of the most sanguine person in our squadron, which you will readily conceive on recollecting how near to the enemy's shore our chase of twenty-seven hours terminated and that one hour's more time would have placed the French beyond our grasp. The enemy's squadron was commanded by Joyeuse de Villaret, the same who fought their fleet on the 1st of June, but on this occasion he removed from the Montaigne into a frigate with the Representant du Peuple, I should think more for the sake of security than with the hope of manoeuvring his ships to greater advantage as *sauve qui peut*[3] appears to have been the only order he gave and no signal was ever better

[1]Charles Maurice Stocker (d. 1795). Lieutenant 1783.
[2]Sir Richard Grindall (d. 1820). Lieutenant 1776; Captain 1783; Rear-admiral 1805; Vice-admiral 1810. Captain of the *Irresistible* (74) in June 1795.
[3]Run for your life.

obeyed. It is singular enough that Cornwallis's squadron should have been the cause of our success by tempting these ships to sea and not what we naturally concluded to be the case, that they had sailed to intercept Sir John Warren. I am not certain about the dates but I understand from our prisoners that Cornwallis's having about a fortnight ago chased into Port Louis the Fougeuse, Tisbe and Nestor, an express was sent to Brest requesting a reinforcement and that in consequence of it Villaret was immediately ordered to sea with nine sail in search of our ships off the Isle de Groix, where they formed a junction with their squadron blocked up and soon after which they got sight of Cornwallis, whom they chased the whole day. During the chase two of the enemy's ships, the Tyger and another, got so near to ours that a running fight took place, in the course of which they admit the firing to have been as distressing to their ships as to ours, two on each side having suffered considerably. This squadron left Brest about nine days ago and was ordered to sea in such a hurry that they have a very small quantity of provisions on board but they were assured that a supply would be ready for them at Rochefort, which they were to have visited very shortly. We are now busy in putting the prizes to rights and in removing their men from them. Sir John Warren is in sight and standing with ourselves towards Belleisle, where I shall hope he would be enabled to make the trial tomorrow on which so much turns. The moment cannot fail to be a favourable one for that object, as the news of our having forced (I was near saying kicked) the Brest squadron into L'Orient will have reached Quiberon before our ships do and Sir John Warren will not act with less confidence from having been a witness to that success. That point ascertained, I suppose that we shall return homeward to land our prisoners and present you with our prizes, which I think will be very acceptable by restoring the Alexander to our fleet and adding to it two of the finest ships I ever saw, one of them a favourite of the French navy on account of her good qualities as well as good construction and the other nearly as good and both two years old only.

[*Endorsed as received on 1 July*]

67.   *Gardner to Bridport*

Queen, at sea, 24 June 1795

I most sincerely congratulate you upon our success of yesterday and have only to lament that the French fleet were able to get so near to Port Louis before the van of our fleet were able to come up with them.

Had they been only four or five mile farther from the Isle of Groix I have not the smallest doubt but that the whole of their line of battle ships would have been captured.

68. *Spencer to Bridport*

Admiralty, 29 June 1795

Your Lordship will easily conceive better than I can attempt to express the satisfaction I received from the perusal of your public and private letters brought by Captain Domett.[1] The anxiety which we all felt very naturally after having heard of Sir J.B. Warren's being in sight of the French fleet subsequent to his parting from your Lordship enhanced in a great degree the pleasure arising from the event, which at the same time as it reflects so much honour on your Lordship and all those concerned in it is of such essential importance to the successful issue of the contest at this very critical moment. So decisive and so brilliant an action under the view of so large a number of the enemy themselves must have given them a very excellent idea of the valour of British officers and I am sanguine enough to hope that the very effect of it on their minds may produce most beneficial consequences to the interests of the country.

We feel so great a confidence in your Lordship's tried abilities that we are not in that [sic] hopes of some further opportunity enabling you to follow up this very successful event and I am sure I ought not to take the liberty of throwing out anything like a hint on the subject to you who not only from your knowledge and experience but from being on the spot are so infinitely better able to form a judgment upon it but as I have heard it represented by several officers who are well acquainted with the local circumstances that it may be possible to annoy a fleet lying at the anchorage within the Island of Groix and that from the difficulty of the entrance into Lorient it may probably have happened that they did not all get in, it might perhaps be well worth consideration whether any attempt, either by fireships or otherwise, could be made on them while in this shattered and dispirited condition.

The whole of this, however, I trust your Lordship will excuse my venturing to touch upon and only consider it in the light of a very

---

[1]William Domett (1754–1828). Lieutenant 1777; Captain 1782; Rear-admiral 1804; Vice-admiral 1809; Admiral 1819. Served under Alexander Hood on board the *Robust* at Ushant in 1778 and was chosen by him to be captain of the *Queen* when he hoisted his flag in 1782. They remained together until Bridport's retirement. In November 1800 St. Vincent moved Domett to the *Belleisle*. He became Cornwallis's first Captain. Served on the Board of Admiralty 1808–13.

confidential and private communication of my ideas which will only be worth any attention if they should happen to be confirmed in any degree by your better judgment.

It seems very difficult (in our present state of information on the subject) to ascertain what the real object of the enemy was on this occasion, for that they must have had some great object in view their not pushing further the great advantage of numbers they possessed over Adml. Cornwallis seems very strongly to indicate and convinced me when I first heard of his encounter with them that they had obtained some intelligence of the expedition with the protection of which your Lordship was charged; but their not having availed themselves of the opportunity which was offered them when they fell in with Sir J. Warren and his convoy seems to contradict this suspicion and it would then almost be natural to conclude that they must have been on the look-out for the long expected American convoy (of the existence of which, however, in any large body there seems reason to doubt) and if that should have been the case I very sincerely hope that your Lordship may have the good fortune to fall in with and intercept them. Their supplies from that quarter are of the utmost importance and the interruption of those supplies of course a most effectual service to this country.

69.   *Warren to Bridport*

La Pomone, Quiberon Bay, 3 July 1795

I have in consequence of an application from the commander in chief, General Comte de Puisaye, that the army would soon be in want of provisions, directed the American ships which had been stopped by our frigates and the Standard in Belleisle Road to come here, in order that the General might purchase as much of their cargoes as he might consider useful. The other part, being goods of no consequence and not coming within the sense of my orders for detaining things going to the enemy's ports, I have directed that the neutral ships might proceed upon their voyage. The army will soon be in great want of stores and powder. I believe with respect to flour and salt provisions the American ships already here will be sufficient to supply them. I am particularly requested by the General also to solicit your Lordship to spare as many of the cannon with their stored ammunition and balls as you possibly could and upon any valuation that might be fixed for them he is ready to give bills upon the Treasury, which he is authorized to do.

70.   *Howe to Bridport*

London, 5 July 1795

Not having been advised by your Lordship respecting the receipt of my instructions of the 6th of last month, forwarded to you by express before you left Spithead, nor of the state of the ships lately under your orders I am to request you will furnish me with such returns of the state of the ships and account of your proceedings in conformity to the tenor of those instructions from time to time when you may be to forward similar advices for the information of the Board of Admiralty.

Desiring to offer my congratulations on the important service you have rendered by your late defeat of the Brest squadron, I have the honour to remain . . .

71.   *Sir Hugh Palliser[1] to Bridport*

Greenwich, 6 July 1795

To think of your old friend during your busy moments on the 25th past so soon after your glorious victory on the 23rd to gratify my anxious wishes to hear you was well was very kind indeed, for which accept my hearty thanks.

Always rejoicing at any occasion to testify that esteem and regard which I entertain for you, as soon as the news of your victory was confirmed I attempted to express my joy by a letter and to congratulate your Lordship on that happy event. I hope that letter will find its way to you. It was directed to Portsmouth.[2] Your victory in the view of all is great and important and in the minds of many must appear wonderful that you should obtain such a victory on that lee shore so much dreaded by a former renowned hero and what adds lustre to the action is your remaining on that coast to block up the enemy's fleet and perform other services to your own country as well as to the distracted country of France, as no doubt it will operate on the minds of those who have the inclination but hitherto want vigour, assistance and resolution to relieve their country from anarchy and confusion.

---

[1]Admiral Sir Hugh Palliser (1723–1796). Keppel's second in command at Ushant in 1778, now Governor of Greenwich Hospital. The disparaging reference is to Keppel's reluctance to pursue the French on the day after Ushant and shows that Palliser, justly or not, still considered himself to have been ill-used.

[2]Not in Bridport's papers.

72.   *Bridport to Spencer*

Royal George, at sea, 7 July 1795

I am . . . strongly of opinion that the expedition under Sir J.B. Warren was known at Paris and the fleet not attacking the convoy when it fell in with it off the Penmarks does not in my opinion contradict the plan but rather makes the object stronger. As the letting of the convoy get into Quiberon Bay the destruction of it with all the ships was certain without hazard or the allowing <u>one</u> to escape. It is possible they may have had in view the arrival of the ships from America but for that object so large a force was not necessary. It has been said, I understand, by the prisoners that the fleet went only to attack Vice Admiral Cornwallis's squadron and to release those ships that were at anchor in Belle Isle Road. But I must go back to my first opinion that the expedition was known and the destruction of all the ships the object.

. . . The ships driven into L'Orient and the road of Port Louis cannot in my opinion be attacked by fireships or ships of force. Whoever has given your Lordship the idea of such a proposal, let the rank of those officers be ever so <u>high,</u> I must suffer with them. I think Lord Howe cannot be one of those officers because I know his Lordship's sentiments for declining to attack the fleet at anchor within the Isle de Groix when he fell in with the enemy's fleet the first cruise of this war. But should his Lordship have changed his opinion since that period and your Lordship should judge it expedient that the Earl should proceed to sea and resume the command of the fleet I shall be ready, as second officer, to support whatever plan his Lordship shall judge for His Majesty's service to undertake or I shall most cheerfully resign my station in the fleet and beg your Lordship's permission to return to England.

. . . The port of Brest should be narrowly watched, as well as all the other ports to the eastward in our Channel, not only for American ships but for such as shall attempt to get out of L'Orient and go through the Passage du Raz to Brest.

[*Endorsed as received on the 14th*]

73.   *Seymour to Spencer*

Off Belle Isle, 8 July 1795

I am very sorry indeed to be obliged so soon to balance the good report which I yesterday made of the progress of our friends in the neighbourhood of Quiberon by the account which I have just received from Captain Durham, but I know it to be so essential that you should be informed of every communication which relates to that subject that I seize the first moment to communicate to you the information I have had and I rejoice the more in having an early opportunity of doing so by the Orion's return to England, from having reason to believe that Sir John Warren will feel averse to sending any account to England which may not accord with the hopes he has taught Government to entertain on the subject of his project which began so prosperously and so much to his wish. On Monday last I understand that the patriots made a most serious attack upon the posts of which the emigrés had possessed themselves on their landing between the River Crac and the Islet de Lazares, of which they soon made themselves masters and with them all the provisions, stores, etc. which our people had not been able to remove from thence in the course of the two days they had been engaged on that service in consequence of our being in possession of the Peninsula of Quiberon, which most fortunately had become ours on the 3rd instant and we at the same time lost some of the quarter deck guns which the Robust and Thunderer had landed for the defence of the Peninsula. The patriots afterwards attacked Quiberon with great spirits but were repulsed with the loss of 370 men. Had our gun boats been on the spot they would by guarding the isthmus have rendered the situation of our friends much less perilous than it proved to be but they unfortunately were engaged upon some service off the Morbihan, where I believe they burnt a corvette or two. This business has, of course, thrown a considerable check upon the spirits of our friends in that neighbourhood, as they now see us reduced and confined to the small peninsula of Quiberon, cut off from all communication with our supposed friends on the continent except by such means as our men of war can provide for them, with the certainty that the 10,000 souls said to be upon Quiberon must depend upon the same support for the supply of provisions they will require. I am certainly not so capable of forming a good opinion of the business as those who have been more immediately concerned in it, whose reports will reach you, but it appears to me that the only thing which remains for us to do at present (and that in its effect is doubtful) is to convey to any spot where Charette and his friends are supposed to be in force all the soldiers, stores and provisions which may be remaining, leaving a garrison capable of defending the Peninsula of Quiberon, while our fleet remains upon this coast to prevent any man of war disturbing them and when the moment or the season arrives which prevents our supplying their wants that they follow the steps and example of their emigré friends by removing to the continent. I am aware that the emigrés will say, remain in the bay and while you supply us with stores and provisions our numbers will increase, but I see no end myself to that speculation and as a limit[1] I should not hesitate in declaring that it is only during the summer months and while we have the command of the sea that we can protect them and with even those advantages I think the game a precarious one if the patriots follow up the work in the way they have begun it. The squadron is still off Belleisle to form with the objects of Government but I fear with little chance of advancing their plan for (between ourselves) the communications between our chief and Sir John Warren will not be more regular than what necessity suggests and I believe that we shall have little to do in this business but in keeping the French squadron in the River of L'Orient, where it now is and not in Port Louis as they were at first described to be. On the subject of our squadron, I cannot help feeling anxious that Cornwallis should join us, not from any idea that our force is not equal and indeed superior to any that is likely soon to be brought against us, but that we may be enabled to avail ourselves of all the advantages which fortune may throw in our way. For this purpose we should have, if possible, twenty sail of the line at sea, five of which might be placed off Brest and the Penmarcks to prevent any supplies going from thence to L'Orient as well as to prevent any of the ships escaping from the latter place, which I have no doubt they will attempt to do singly and by passing within the Glenans will hope to reach Brest. The other 15 sail would effectively guard this coast and, with the assistance of frigates, would make it next to impossible that provisions should be thrown into France within the Bay. Should you see this plan in the same point of view that I do, I have little reason to doubt your being able soon to carry it into execution and I think that Lord Howe's returning to his command, which we all in the squadron most anxiously hope he is enabled to do, would ensure the success I so particularly wish to attend this measure. The necessity of our ships returning to port is the only obstacle to it and that I should hope might be managed by relieving them regularly during the summer when we must have enough of command for the purpose. I presume that Lord Bridport gives himself some credit for not complaining of his want of strength to undergo the fatigues of his present employment from which I apprehend you will not have any difficulty in accommodating him by letting him remain onshore while Lord Howe is afloat. The service will not suffer from their being upon different elements for

[1]Word unclear.

those do not in themselves differ more than the characters of the two officers under whose orders I am likely to act during this campaign.

I am very sorry for the cause of the Orion's return to England, which is a malignant fever carried into her by some of the landsmen who were sent into her before she left Spithead, and by which she has lost several of her crew. This circumstance with many others has tended to confirm the opinion that I once warned to you of our hospital ship not being large enough to receive the number of patients likely to be produced in so large a squadron as she generally accompanies. I wish therefore very much that it suited your arrangements to allot an old 64 to that service as I am sure the service would receive considerable advantage from that measure.

The Charon now returns with our wounded men, which is a step pointed out more by necessity than choice, for at this moment there are so many sick on board her as to render the accommodation of the former very bad, it being necessary to keep them distinct. I hope, however, that small as the Charon is, that you will send her out to us immediately as the scurvy will soon make its appearance and that complaint may be easily checked by the fruit, vegetables, etc. with which she will be provided.

[*Endorsed as received on the 18th*]

74.   *Admiralty to Bridport*

9 July 1795

Admiral Sir Richard King, Commander in Chief of His Majesty's ships and vessels at Plymouth,[1] having by his letter of the 3rd instant represented to me for the information of my Lords Commissioners of the Admiralty that Captain Domett, who had been charged with despatches to your Lordship, had sailed from that port on the 1st of this month in the Thalia; and that neither he or Lord Henry Powlett, captain of that ship, had waited upon or shown the least attention to him, I have it in command from their Lordships to apprize you of this circumstance and at the same time to express their surprise that any officers of their description should have been so deficient in their duty as to sail from a port without communicating such an intention to the Commander in Chief.

---

[1]Sir Richard King (1730–1806). Lieutenant 1746; Captain 1759; Rear-admiral 1787; Vice-admiral 1793; Admiral 1795. He had been at Plymouth since December 1794.

75.   *Spencer to Sir William Sidney Smith*[1]

Admiralty, 11 July 1795

. . . As to frigates building and to be built, those now coming forward were ordered before my time, so I cannot say anything of their properties except that I see two of them are to be like the Leda, one of the fastest sailers we have, two like the Inconstant, of which I have not heard any complaints, and the other two are allowed by those who have seen them and can judge better than I can to be very fine frigates of their class. We have likewise some prodigiously fine French frigates getting ready very fast and are going to lay down more upon the best French drafts; but in all this fashion (for I believe it is more that than anything else) I want to have it explained and I never have yet been able to have it done, at least to my satisfaction, why the French, who are supposed to have arrived at perfection, vary so much from themselves and why no two ships of theirs are like one another, though according to our opinion or rather fancies here, the last we take is always the best possible. For instance, the Sans Pareil was to be everything perfect, and a very fine ship she is, but now she is nothing at all to the Tigre, which is very unlike her, and to show you how much all this is matter of opinion I have it from the authority of some prisoners lately come from Brest their artificers there had actually been employed taking the lines of the Alexander, the ship universally acknowledged to be the worst possible, in order to imitate them, merely because she happened to stand their winter cruise better than most of their own.

. . . Adieu dear Sir Sidney, remember that if not the better part at least very good part of valour is discretion and believe me, yours very faithfully

76.   *Sidney Smith to Spencer*

Diamond, at Spithead, 13 July 1795

I am sorry to find the impression at the Admiralty to be that my late unsuccessful attempt to diminish the force against me was too dashing. Daring I allow it to be, for I hold it right to dare attempt more than the enemy dare imagine possible . . . the nature of the service we are on

---

[1]Sir William Sidney Smith (1764–1840). Lieutenant 1780; Captain 1783; Rear-admiral 1805; Vice-admiral 1810; Admiral 1821. Not yet the prisoner of the Temple or the hero of Acre, in 1795 Smith was active off the coasts of Normandy and Brittany in command of the frigate *Diamond*, plying Spencer with letters on any subject that took his fancy, some of which got replies.

exposes us to the obligation of bearing with the fire of batteries in <u>every</u> attempt we make, we cannot expect to take a single vessel without it and cruising merely for the purpose of blockade is a triste occupation.[1] Our frigate work must resemble hussar service and after the commander has set his force at liberty to charge I hope he is not to be considered as restrained by prudence from having the first cut with his own sabre if he can get it.

77. *Admiralty to Bridport*

14 July 1795

Having ordered the Honourable Vice Admiral Cornwallis, with the ships named on the other side hereof [*Royal Sovereign, Formidable, Triumph, Invincible, Brunswick, Bellerophon, Pallas, Phaeton*] to join your Lordship on your rendezvous and follow your orders for his further proceeding; and it being our intention, on his junction with you, that the squadron to continue with you, independent of frigates, etc., shall consist of the ships named in the margin [*Royal George, Royal Sovereign, Queen, Prince of Wales, Formidable, Prince George, Prince, London, Valiant, Triumph, Invincible, Brunswick, Bellerophon*], your Lordship is hereby required and directed to take the Vice Admiral under your command accordingly and to send into port all the other line of battle ships with La Revolutionnaire frigate, two-thirds of them to Portsmouth and the remainder to Plymouth.

78. *Spencer to Bridport*

Admiralty, 14 July 1795

As it is now a principal object to keep up the command which by the action of the 23rd ultimo you have gained of the seas in that quarter, the plan adopted by Government is to keep by successive reliefs a squadron constantly cruising off the ports of Brest and Lorient and occasionally communicating with the officer commanding in Quiberon Bay. For this purpose I thought it most advisable to specify the ships which you should at present retain with you, equal I should hope and trust to anything which the debilitated naval force of the enemy can oppose to you, in order that by refitting with the utmost despatch those you send

---

[1] In 1798 and 1800 two officers, Sir Charles Hamilton and Lieutenant William Coet, took the same point of view and failed to prevent convoys getting into Brest that they were put on station to stop.

home we may be enabled to escort the several divisions of troops that may be occasionally sent out to the coast of Brittany and relieve other ships of your squadron which may want refreshment or refitting at home. As the Brunswick (one of the ships allotted to remain with your Lordship for the present) appears by the report of her last cruise to be a very bad sailing vessel in the present state of her stowage, orders have been given by which the Mars will be substituted in her stead after she has performed a service she is now ordered out upon.

The notions which I alluded to in my former letter to your Lordship by Captain Domett respecting the possibility of any attempt on the enemy ships at Port Louis were very far from being suggested by Lord Howe, who, in a conversation I afterwards had with him, seemed to be decidedly of the same opinion as your Lordship on that subject. It is very probable that his Lordship may be well enough recovered to go to sea when his ship is again ready (in case she is as I suppose one of those first detached) and in that case, if your Lordship is desirous of returning for a short time and the circumstances of the service will then admit of it, there will be no objection to that arrangement taking place. I think in the meanwhile that you will have had an opportunity of detaining many more of the homeward bound ships laden with provisions, etc. and as there is a great probability of many of them turning out to be French property I hope they may prove valuable captures.

79. *Gardner to Bridport*

Queen, at sea, 20 July 1795, 3 p.m.

As I only came out provided with stock for about six weeks, my last sheep was killed yesterday and although I have no more mutton my stock of hay will not maintain my cow above ten or twelve days longer, otherways I would supply your Lordship with a bag or two. I trust our friends at home will consider our situation and send us a supply of fresh stock by the first ships which may be despatched to your fleet, otherways the scurvy will soon make its appearance amongst us.

80. *Sidney Smith to Spencer*

Diamond, off Cape Barfleur, 21 July 1795

My idea of the application of our naval force is to show that the frontier of Great Britain is high water mark in France. The uppermost seaweed on the beach belongs to us . . .

I am told by everybody that the Tigre is really on the most improved plan, which may be, as she is built since the Sans Pareil. The French have 'varied so much from themselves' I apprehend by allowing their constructors to make various experiments. They have no bad ship in all their variety because they invariably give them dimensions, whatever be the form. We have never varied from ourselves in building cribs till lately that we have boldly increased in size. My lamentation arose from hearing that we were going back to the small ships which, though improved in comparison to those we had when they appeared, are not equal to the last six.

81. *Sidney Smith to Spencer*

Diamond, off Beachy Head, 22 July 1795

I am glad to have it in my power so soon after my lamentations of yesterday to acquaint you that I am no longer in the distressed state I was in for want of seamen. I am not a man to call out to Hercules while there is a possibility of getting out of the mire by putting my own shoulders to the wheel. I accordingly, on the wind coming fresh to the westward, placed myself in the track of the homeward bound trade which I had reason to suppose must have accumulated during the easterly wind. This morning I fell in with several homeward bound Indiamen and have manned myself completely out of them by taking volunteers only.[1]

82. *Howe to Spencer*

Grafton Street, 24 July 1795

Sensible how requisite it must at all times be that your Lordship should have the most early intimation when any change in the command of the Channel fleet is rendered necessary and finding the expedient first recommended for removing the impediment to a further tender of my humble services in that very important office appears now to be without adequate effect but that the remaining endeavours for that purpose will require a stay of some continuance at Bath I therefore trouble your Lordship with this private and prior intimation of the painful necessity I

---

[1]The men he took would know that the Impress Service was likely to take them as soon as they reached port and that they might be better off in the service of an enterprising frigate captain.

am under officially to solicit leave to resign the command of the Channel fleet, which it is unfitting for me to retain when unable to perform the duties of the station.

[Endorsed as received on the 24th]

83.   *Spencer to Howe*

Admiralty, 24 July 1795

I feel equally concerned and surprised at the contents of your letter of this morning; after the conversation I had the honour of passing with your Lordship yesterday I flattered myself that no further obstacle would have offered itself to your returning to a situation in which the whole country as well as the whole navy will, I am convinced be rejoiced to see you. Your health appeared to me to be so perfectly restored since your last indisposition that I cannot without great difficulty persuade myself that you are well founded in the opinion you express of being unequal to perform the duties of your station and I very earnestly entreat you not to send any public letter on the subject to the Board till I have had an opportunity of a few minutes conversation with you, for which purpose I will wait on you at any time tomorrow morning you choose to appoint.

84.   *Admiralty to Warren*

27 July 1795

My Lords Commissioners of the Admiralty, taking it into their consideration the great inconvenience which at this time attends the sending out provisions in transports and hired vessels, command me to signify their direction to you to order the ships and vessels under your command, as they respectively stand in need of supplies, to repair to Plymouth to make good their deficiencies, returning to you the moment they shall have done so. And it is their Lordships' further direction when you send any cutters or other vessels express with despatches that you direct their commanders immediately after they shall have landed the same to make the best of their way back to you as other vessels will be always held in readiness to convey any orders necessary to be sent to you in consequence.

85. *George III to Spencer*

Windsor, 27 July 1795

The enclosed are the letter from Earl Howe and the copy of my answer to him on his notification of intending at least for the present to decline, from the weakness of his limbs, taking again the command of the Channel fleet. Earl Spencer will perceive that in my answer I suppose it only alludes to the present moment; indeed I think it highly proper to be understood to extend no further and I should think this circumstance, as Lord Bridport dislikes commanding under the orders of Earl Howe, gives good ground for Earl Spencer's offering the supreme command of the fleet in the North Sea with an admiral's captain and that Sir John Jervis[1] should command the detachment of the Channel fleet on the coast of France under Earl Howe's orders.

[*Enclosure*]

85a. *George III to Howe*

Windsor, 26 July 1795

I received this morning Earl Howe's letter notifying that the weakness consequent of his late indisposition must oblige him to apply to the Board of Admiralty for leave further to postpone the engagement he is called upon to resume in the charge of the fleet. I cannot but sincerely regret that he is under that necessity but trust he will soon be enabled to resume a command he has so ably and successfully filled.

[*Endorsed as received on the 27th*]

86. *Spencer to George III*

[27 July 1795]

[*Draft*]

Earl Spencer feels it his duty in the present instance to submit to your Majesty whether in consequence of the temporary alteration which

---

[1]John Jervis, Earl of St Vincent (1735–1823). Lieutenant 1755; Captain 1760; Rear-admiral 1787; Vice-admiral 1793; Admiral 1795; Commander-in-Chief Channel fleet 1800–1801, 1806–7; First Lord of the Admiralty 1801–4.

must take place in the arrangement which he had the honour of bringing under your Majesty's consideration on Wednesday last it may not
be the most advisable measure to issue a commission to Lord Bridport
constituting him Commander in Chief of a squadron to be employed on
a particular service, which will give him all the emolument and rank to
which he appears fairly entitled as well by his situation in the service as
by what passed between his Lordship and Earl Chatham before he went
to sea and by the service he has since performed; and will at the same
time avoid conveying to the public any idea that Earl Howe's retirement
is more than temporary.

Earl Spencer cannot help being apprehensive that a proposition to
remove Lord Bridport on this occasion to the North Sea might with
justice be considered by his Lordship as entirely cutting him off[1] from
any chance of ever commanding the Channel fleet in any event, more
especially were his place to be supplied by an officer so much his
junior as Sir John Jervis.

If your Majesty should not disapprove the ideas here thrown out Sir
John Jervis might have the command in the North Sea on the event of
Admiral Duncan's[2] being removed to the Mediterranean.

87.   *George III to Spencer*

Windsor, 12 past 7 a.m., 28 July 1795

I have this instant received Earl Spencer's note in answer to mine on
Earl Howe's declining for a time to resume the command of the Channel fleet; I perfectly coincide with the judicious proposal it contains of
giving a commission to Lord Bridport constituting him Commander in
Chief of a squadron to be employed on a particular service provided he
at the same time shall understand that this will not prevent Earl Howe
from returning to the command of the Channel fleet; and think, on
Admiral Duncan's being sent to command in the Mediterranean, that
Sir John Jervis may succeed him in the North Sea.

---

[1]Word unclear.
[2]Adam Duncan, Viscount Duncan (1731–1804). Lieutenant 1755; Captain 1761; Rear-
admiral 1787; Vice-admiral 1793; Admiral 1795.

88. *Seymour to Spencer*

Off Belle Isle, 28 July 1795

Captain Bertie[1] will of course have informed you of the situation in which he left matters at Quiberon and will no doubt have imparted the sanguine hopes which the emigrés were led to entertain after their having made themselves masters of the Peninsula of Quiberon and which in the height of their success they were flattered into thinking a second Gibraltar. The post is certainly of the first importance as far as England is concerned in the contests upon this coast as it covers the best anchorage upon it and that from its position and form it is capable of being rendered exceedingly strong, being assailable only by a narrow sandy isthmus, easily covered by ships or gunboats. The enemy, having seen it in this point of view, were led to attempt driving us from it and on the 21st attacked the emigrés with such spirit as to carry the place by assault. They then pursued their advantage by putting to the bayonet every man of the army on which our hopes for its defence was founded except about 1000 of the troops who reached our ships in confusion and about 13 or 1400 Chouans who had been induced to join that army. I am ignorant what number the army or garrison was composed of at the time of the attack but a few days prior to that event it was said to amount to 8 or 9000 men. I hear that one of the generals was forward in the embarkation and that those whose spirit induced them to make a more determined trial of their force were either drowned or shot in the water in endeavouring to swim off to the ships while the utmost exertions of the shipping and boats were used to save them, though in vain.

I am very happy to learn from you that Lord Howe is soon to return to his command as I trust that in case of his being to be employed on this coast that he will have the direction of all the naval service which may take place within this station, for the more I see of my profession and consider it upon an enlarged scale the more I am taught to believe that the distinguished preference I have given to three or four officers in it only to have been due to the particular talents they possess when in command. This subject leads me to regret that Hotham, who was on so many accounts well qualified to command in the Mediterranean, should find himself obliged to solicit his recall, and the same idea makes me most anxious to remind you of Sir John Jervis's

---

[1] Sir Albemarle Bertie (d. 1824). Lieutenant 1777; Captain 1782; Rear-admiral 1804; Vice-admiral 1808; Admiral 1814.

powers to fill that station with advantage to the country and honour to himself if the French should really mean to try their force with ours in that part of the world. I am aware of the answer which would be made by many of the Ministry on this occasion but I cannot bring myself to believe for a moment that his connection with Lord Lansdown[1] or Sir John's desire to lower every one to the same level will ever interfere with his duty or indeed occupy his thoughts for an instant when removed from the whisper of his political patron.[2] He is certainly an officer of rare merit and I think that he would do honour to the Minister who avails himself of his talents afloat or I would not recommend him to you so earnestly.

I am much obliged to you, my dear Lord, for your letter, which has just reached me, as it throws some little light upon the probable duration of our cruise, which from its sameness is one of the most tiresome I have experienced for some time. The squadron, however, continues healthy and I trust will remain so till your intentions of relieving it are realized, which on that account I should hope will soon be the case.

[*Endorsed as received on the 6th*]

89. *Admiralty to Bridport*

29 July 1795

My Lords Commissioners of the Admiralty having been pleased to sign a commission appointing you Commander in Chief of a squadron of His Majesty's ships to be employed in a particular service I have the honour to send you the said commission herewith and the fee for it being £5-7-6, I am to request your Lordship will permit your secretary to receive and be accountable to this office for the same.

90. *Admiralty to Bridport*

31 July 1795

Whereas information has been received from Commodore Sir John Warren that in consequence of the unfortunate disaster which has taken

---

[1]Sir William Petty, 1st Marquis of Lansdowne and 2nd Earl of Shelburne (1737–1805).

[2]Lord Lansdowne was a whig and Jervis sat in the Commons as a whig for three constituencies between 1783 and 1793.

place at Quiberon, he has found it expedient to remove with the squadron under his orders and such of the emigrant troops and stores as could be brought away from thence to the islands of Houat and Hédic, where he proposed to remain until he should receive our further instructions for his guidance; and whereas until some determination can be formed in respect to the measures hereafter to be adopted we have judged it advisable that he should continue in that position for the present; your Lordship is hereby required and directed to continue to cruise with the squadron under your command on such station as on a consideration of all the existing circumstances you may judge to be most advisable for affording protection and security to the said squadron and troops, attending at the same time to the other important objects upon which your Lordship has already been instructed either by us or by Admiral Earl Howe, acquainting our Secretary of your intended rendezvous with a view to your receiving from time to time our further instructions for your guidance.

91.   *Spencer to Bridport*

Admiralty, 31 July 1795

Lord Howe having found himself unable to go to sea for the present on account of his not being yet sufficiently recovered from his late illness, His Majesty has been pleased to direct that your Lordship should receive your orders for the present from the Admiralty and I have the satisfaction to add that as a testimony of his approbation of your late services His Majesty has authorized us to give you a commission of Commander in Chief of a squadron to be employed on a particular service. I have at the same time His Majesty's commands to state to your Lordship that this arrangement must be understood not to prevent Lord Howe's return to the command of the Channel Fleet whenever His Majesty's service may require it and his Lordship's health may be sufficiently re-established to undertake that charge.

The late unfortunate event which has taken place on the Peninsula of Quiberon makes it more than ever necessary for your Lordship to keep up communications with and give all the protection and assistance you can to the squadron under the command of Sir John B. Warren and we have sent out a cutter with these despatches to you in order to lose no time in acquainting you with the contents of them and to apprize you that in a very few days you will be joined by another squadron which may enable you to send home those ships of your present squadron most in need of refreshment and refitting.

By intelligence which will be communicated herewith to your Lordship you will learn that there were on the 25th instant in Brest road four sail of the line, five frigates and two sloops, besides a seventy-four taking in her masts in the harbour; those in the road were to all external appearance fit for sea but whether they were manned or not is uncertain.[1]

Your Lordship will best know the state of that division of the fleet which you engaged and beat on the 23rd ultimo and will, from the comparison of these circumstances, form the best judgment of the necessity of keeping an eye to the squadron in Brest. On the return of Vice Admiral Colpoys, who is now cruising for the protection of the homeward bound Jamaica fleet, in case it should then be still necessary to keep your squadron at sea we shall be better enabled to supply the means of providing for both the objects, namely that of continuing to block the beaten fleet in L'Orient and of keeping in check the squadron fitting out at Brest.

In the meantime I have no doubt but that your Lordship will see the necessity, as far as the other objects of the service committed to your charge will allow it, to keep a good look out off those points of the coast which are likely to be made by the Americans and other neutrals who are bringing supplies to France. Many of them by the same information are represented to be in Brest and to be constantly arriving there.

Your Lordship will perceive by what I have been saying that it is very expedient for His Majesty's service that you should continue on your cruise for some time longer. I hope it will not be attended with any inconvenience to your health, which in one of your letters you stated to be such as to require your early return.

If, however, you should, either on that account or on account of the state and condition of the Royal George, judge it absolutely necessary for you to come in to refit, you will be to use your own discretion how far the circumstances of the moment will allow of your return with the ship under your command and in the event of your adopting that measure you will, of course, leave your orders with Vice Admiral Cornwallis for his proceeding during your absence.

---

[1]Intelligence of this nature was gained by observation through telescopes from ships venturing as far up the approaches as they dared and by reports from agents in Brest. A ship's readiness for sea could be gauged by noting her depth in the water and by the state of her rigging.

92.   *Marquis of Buckingham[1] to Bridport*

Camp Portsmouth, 1 August 1795

It was so very difficult in every sense of the word to say anything to you upon the latter part of the very acceptable letter which you sent me by Captain Domett that I rather preferred an absolute silence to the possibility of misleading you upon a point so very interesting to you and upon steps which might perhaps be decisive upon your future situation, and I had less the means of giving an opinion upon those steps which you might think of taking as I did not know except from report what had passed between Lord Spencer and you when you refused the Mediterranean command and again when you solicited a more distinguished situation in the Western Squadron. I collected, however, from the very few words which had passed between us on the road when you was going to London that you meant to urge everything but to take the charge of the squadron under any circumstance not absolutely incompatible with your honour. I have been able to collect from other quarters that you left London much hurt and without having made the impression you wished and the latter part of your letter to me marks the same sentiments. Since that period I have taken much pains to make that impression which I thought might assist you, disclaiming always any commission from you or any knowledge of your sentiments further than they were generally known and understood to be avowed and I very clearly saw that I had succeeded in establishing a wish that some solution should be found for the difficulty, though I could suggest none, and there these conversations (which were not official) always ended. I was repeatedly pressed to endeavour to reconcile your mind to your present situation, which I always refused, adding, however, that as I could do no good I would do no mischief either to your views or to the views of your employers by my advice but that if you asked it and if I were obliged to give it I should recommend to you not to continue to serve under Lord Howe's flag if he was ordered out to join you and not to continue in command unless it was generally understood in the navy that his Lordship was not to go to sea. The reverse of all this was understood, for Lord Howe openly and repeatedly declared his intention of going to sea and I saw with very great regret but with a very decided opinion the great probability that you would return. Latterly I knew that you had conveyed your intentions on that subject to Lord

---

[1]Bridport's political patron. In 1790 the Marquis of Buckingham permitted Bridport to gain election to Parliament in the 'pocket borough' of Buckingham where there were but 13 electors.

Spencer and I have reason to know that persons much in his friendship (but I know not whether it was by his authority) have taken great pains with Lord Howe to induce him not to persevere in his intention of taking the command. This produced no other effect than (what entre nous I expected) a directly avowed intention of going to sea with the first reinforcement. Sir R. Curtis was sent to hoist his red flag in the Charlotte, and to notify to everybody that Lord Howe would be down in ten days, and at that time, viz. the 24th ultimo, I received from my correspondent much regrets at 'the possibility of your throwing away from you that command of the fleet to which (if you did not yourself prevent it) you would without much delay succeed'. I answered it with regrets but with my decided opinion that you would resign unless it was generally understood that Lord Howe did not go to sea. Lord Howe was in London and on the 25th I understood authentically from a very near relation of his Lordship that 'he was still very weak' and that his family was urging him to go to Bath to bring out his gout. My correspondent wrote me word at the same time that his hopes were now sanguine, since which time I have not heard from him. But it is now universally known that Lord Howe is gone to Bath. Sir R. Curtis received on the 29th orders to take under his command the Pompee, Powerful and Canada and the Charlotte was put the same day under the command of Rear Admiral Harvey[1] together with the Prince of Wales, Prince, Colossus and Orion. The Charlotte will not be ready for 7 or 8 days so that Curtis's flag remains on board her but Sir A.S. Douglas[2] reports to Harvey. This has produced universally the sensation which I wished and it is now understood that Lord Howe is not to go to sea and therefore I do not hesitate any longer to urge you to continue in command and on no account to return to Portsmouth till it is necessary. As to Lord Howe's actual resignation I am persuaded that it must soon take place but in the interim the opinion is very strong against his retaining his command by his fireside and you may be assured that this opinion must gain strength and in the same proportion the weight of your claims increases. I have now, my dear Lord, done what I much dislike, viz. to give my advice unasked upon another person's concerns. I can only say in my excuse that it proceeds from my real friendship to you and from the conviction that no one will give you an opinion more dispassionate or more anxious for your fame and success. I will not describe to you the effect of the news from Quiberon. We suppose the

[1]Sir Henry Harvey (1737–1810). Lieutenant 1757; Captain 1777; Rear-admiral 1795; Vice-admiral 1799; Admiral 1804. Commander-in-chief in the Leeward Islands 1796; returned to the Channel in 1800.

[2]Sir Andrew Snape Douglas was at this time captain of the *Queen Charlotte*.

consequences of it will operate most severely in France. I have, however, reason to think that Government will persevere in their operations upon the coast but I fancy that they have learnt the exact degree of confidence to be placed in the French corps. Much is said here and in London of the possibility of an attempt by fire boats to smoke fire craft (with the wind at south west) upon the ships at L'Orient. You are, I am sure, perfectly master of the whole subject and if it is not done it is because it is impossible. I was, however, determined to mention the subject to you as any attempt would be well received even if there was a very small chance of success. The idea is that they would by their confusion be driven on shore as there is no room for them to work in wherever they cast their ships loose.

93. *Abstract of the number of sick*

8 August 1795

		Seamen		Soldiers	
	No.	On board	Hospital ship	On board	Hospital ship
July 28th	493	397	27	64	5
August 4th	787	660	53	72	2
Increase	294	263	26	8	–
Decrease	–	–	–	–	3

94. *Bridport to Spencer*

Royal George, at sea, 9 August 1795

Your Lordship's letter informs me that Lord Howe having found himself unable to go to sea for the present on account of his not being yet sufficiently recovered from his late illness, His Majesty has been pleased to direct that I should receive my orders from the Admiralty and that His Majesty had authorized the Lords Commissioners to give me a commission of Commander in Chief of a squadron to be employed on a particular service. At the same time His Majesty commands to state that the arrangement must be understood not to prevent Lord Howe's return to the command of the Channel fleet whenever His Majesty's service may require it and his Lordship's health may be sufficiently re-established to undertake that charge.

In return to the honour conferred upon me I beg leave to state that my rank and long service were as well known to your Lordship before I sailed from Spithead as they were on the 28th of July and Lord Howe's situation stood exactly the same from the report made to me in a letter I received from Mr. Secretary Nepean. Under these circumstances I thought myself entitled to the commission the Admiralty have been pleased to send out to me before I sailed from Spithead and when I had the honour to converse with your Lordship upon this subject at the Admiralty. When I also consider that soon after the landing the troops on the Peninsula of Quiberon your Lordship was pleased to send out a commission to Sir John Borlase Warren appointing him a commodore with a captain under him for his services I do not think that I am particularly honoured or that my commission comes to me so gratifying to my feelings.

It is not necessary for me to say one word on the subject of Lord Howe's return to the command of the Channel fleet. When that event takes place I shall meet it with humble composure and proper resignation.

The event which has taken place on the Peninsula of Quiberon I shall offer no opinion upon, not being in possession of the circumstances which occasioned so severe a blow to the expedition and so severe a loss in men, stores, provisions, with all other articles, which I am told were carried away immediately in numberless waggons to L'Orient to supply the wants of that place and the beaten fleet.

The objects that I am now to attend to, by your Lordship's letter, are the protection of Sir John B. Warren, the beaten fleet in L'Orient and equipment and operations of the enemy in Brest, together with that of the Americans and all neutral vessels bound into France; and for these purposes it is expedient that I should continue my cruise for some time longer. Your Lordship knows that I have been upwards of eight weeks at sea and more than six since the battle was fought and an important victory gained. I beg leave to observe to your Lordship that it appears to me the same objects will remain at the end of ten weeks as at the end of nine, and so on to twelve. Does your Lordship think that I can keep the sea that length of time without receiving the smallest supply for myself or the squadron or that the crews will not suffer much by the scurvy, which increases every day in the Royal George as well as in every other ship and it must ruin the fleet if not speedily allowed to return into port for refreshments.

If Vice Admiral Colpoys had been directed to cruise off Ushant and from thence to Scilly I am of opinion his squadron would have given full protection to the West India convoys as the cruising at a greater distance and upon the nearer station he would have had an eye to the operations of the Brest fleet, which I foresee I shall not be able to do with the force allotted to me and to attend to such operations as may be undertaken by Sir John B. Warren, with whom I have had no correspondence since the 22nd ultimo but one short letter which was sent to the Admiralty and returned to me on the 7th instant by the Hope. I have only further to add that not only my health but the state of the original squadron require a speedy conclusion to the cruise if further services are expected from me or the ships and I feel it particularly necessary to myself on many accounts and I am also anxious to pay my duty to the King in humble expectation that I shall be honoured with some marks of His Majesty's approbation of my services on the 23rd of June, and in that hope, I have the honour to be . . .

95. *Admiralty to Bridport*

10 August 1795

Though your Lordship's continuance at sea with the squadron under your command cannot but be desirable in many points of view, their Lordships would by no means press such a measure upon your Lordship if your state of health should be such as to require a temporary relief; and I have their commands to acquaint your Lordship that you are under such circumstances at liberty to avail yourself of the first favourable opportunity of returning into port, leaving the command of the squadron in the charge of the officer next in seniority to you, but their Lordships take it for granted that you will not diminish the force upon your coming into port to any further extent than that of the ship in which your Lordship may think fit to take your passage.

96. *Spencer to Bridport*

Admiralty, 15 August 1795

I have already taken so much pains both in the conversation I had with your Lordship before your departure and in my several letters written since you have been at sea to explain the reasons for what has been done respecting your command that it is unnecessary for me to add anything further on that subject.

I have therefore now only to acknowledge the receipt of your Lordship's private letter of the 9th instant which I shall not fail to lay before His Majesty for his information.

97. *Spencer to George III*

15 August 1795

[*Draft*]

Earl Spencer thinks it his duty to lay before your Majesty ... the accompanying private letter addressed to himself on which Earl Spencer does not venture to express any further observation except that of expressing his regret that his Lordship should be disposed to see in so unfavourable light the honour done him by your Majesty to receive those marks of honour which Earl Spencer has ever been desirous of paying him and which his services so justly entitle him to expect in a temper so different from that which they were intended to produce.

98. *George III to Spencer*

Windsor, 22 minutes past 7 a.m., 16 August 1795

I cannot see the private letter to the Earl Spencer from Lord Bridport but in a very different style than one should have supposed the granting him the very favour he seemed to look for must have dictated but it appears too plain that in his family self value is so predominant that all other objects are not sufficiently attended to and as much as I was desirous that Earl Howe's strength may be restored I cannot now but more eagerly wish it as the temper of the next in command is now so clearly seen.

99. *Seymour to Spencer*

Sans Pareil, off Belle Isle, 18 August 1795

I cannot think that a better arrangement could have been made than that which you have fixed upon, as it enables you to have recourse to Lord Howe's talents and service as a sea officer if, contrary to our expectation, the enemy should ever be induced to try their whole naval force with our fleet and Lord Bridport should be as much satisfied with the compliment you have paid him as he is sure to be with the advantages and emoluments which he will derive from his new commission. We are looking most anxiously for the arrival of the ships under Admiral Harvey, which I understand are to relieve us as the scurvy is making great progress in the ships which sailed in June and I much fear will soon prevail as generally in the others. In the Sans Pareil we have upwards of eighty men on that list and the numbers increase daily.

[*Endorsed as received on the 26th*]

100.   *Bridport to Admiralty*

Royal George, at sea, 19 August 1795

I acquaint you for the information of the Lords Commissioners of the Admiralty that the Thunderer and Charon hospital ship joined me early in the morning of the 15th instant when I received a duplicate of Lord Spencer's private letter, together with the intelligence from Sir Edward Pellew;[1] also a list of the Danes and Swedes supposed to be bound to France loaded with iron, plank and other naval articles; but I have seen nothing of the Prestwood cutter.

The moment the Charon came into the squadron, I made the signal for the Physician of the Fleet, and gave him directions to visit every ship in it, and report to me the number of sick, particularly the scorbutic cases, with orders for him to make a distribution of the refreshments he had brought out for their relief, and inclosed I send you his report and observations upon this subject; their Lordships will see by it how necessary it is that almost all the ships of the squadron should go into port the moment Rear Admiral Harvey shall join me, which I have looked for every day from motives of humanity and the public service. In my last letter I thought the squadron brought out by Vice Admiral Cornwallis could have kept the sea ten days or a fortnight longer than the ships that sailed with the Royal George, but their Lordships will see by Doctor Trotter's report that the Royal Sovereign and Invincible have more scorbutic cases than I had reason to expect, and their Lordships will also perceive how much that evil has increased since the last return I sent you, and I own I am seriously alarmed at the rapid progress the disease is making amongst us. I am likewise to state that many ships begin to be short of water. The Royal George has supplied the Nymphe with some butts, also some water, and provisions to the Rattler cutter, and her ground tier is expending fast; when she returns to Spithead, her hold must be broke up; under this circumstance and considering that the bottom of the Royal George has not been seen since March 1793

---

[1]Edward Pellew, 1st Viscount Exmouth (1757–1833). Lieutenant 1778; Captain 1782; Rear-admiral 1804; Vice-admiral 1808; Admiral 1814. From this time Pellew established his reputation as a frigate captain. He was placed in command of one of the frigate squadrons operating out of Falmouth under Admiralty orders.

except upon the heel at Spithead, to repair the damages she received under water on the 1st of June 1794, I am to request that she may be docked, her copper washed down, and her hold new stowed, which I think necessary if their Lordships will permit the measure to take place, for her future services, as we think the ship does not in general sail so well as when she was first fitted out, and perhaps some of her copper may be found defective.

As by their Lordship's order of the 31st of July, I am referred to such as I may have received from Admiral the Earl Howe; I herewith send copies of two orders and one letter which were brought to me by an Admiralty messenger from Porters Lodge; though dated in . . . London, I have thought it right to transmit the whole to you, for their Lordship's inspection, that they may judge how far their contents are necessary for my future guidance, or the guidance of the flag officer who may command any squadron of His Majesty's fleet in my absence.

You will be pleased to acquaint their Lordships that the Semillante arrived at L'Orient on the 7th of June, from New York, with dispatches. She brought no convoy, but took an Ordnance transport . . . and sunk her. She is now at L'Orient but was not with the fleet on the 23d of June.

Enclosed is intelligence gained by different ships of this squadron since my last letter to you of the 9th instant by the Hope lugger; also a list of two American schooners, one snow and a brig laden with fish and provisions, which have been detained since my last dispatch; I have ordered them to Plymouth under convoy of La Nymphe, Irresistible and Rattler cutter. I also transmit for their Lordships consideration a letter from Doctor Trotter to me, which I received this morning. Captain Murray of La Nymphe will be charged with my dispatches.

[*Endorsement*]

Own receipt of his Lordship's two letters of the 24th received by the Aquilon, and let him know that the Board are concerned to find that the scurvy has made such progress in the ships, particularly those which sailed so lately under Admiral Cornwallis, but that measures have been taken for sending out supplies by every opportunity of the necessary antiscorbutics and other refreshments.

Acquaint his Lordship also that Rear Admiral Harvey, having been so long prevented from proceeding to join him, he is now ordered to put to sea without the convoy, which will follow under protection of the Orion and frigates.

Approve of his sending in the Irresistible and La Nymphe for the reasons he has given, and let him know that the latter will be ordered to rejoin him when she has completed her provisions and water. Enclose him order to Admiral Cornwallis for the regulation of that officer's proceedings on his Lordship's return into port. Their Lordships are inclined to think the intelligence he mentions to have seen in regard to the arrival of the Semillante at L'Orient from New York is erroneous, and it clearly appears she was at the last mentioned port so late as 25 May, consequently could hardly have got into L'Orient by 7 June. Approve of his Lordship's arrangements owing to the ill state of Sir E. Gower's[1] health.

[*Enclosures*]

100a.   *State of Health in His Majesty's fleet under the command of Admiral Lord Bridport, 16 August 1795*

Ships	No. in the sick list	Prevailing diseases
Royal George	45	Scurvy
Sans Pareil	36	Do. increasing rapidly
Invincible	52	A contagious fever and scurvy
Valiant	35	Obstinate venereal complaints combined with scurvy
Formidable	22	Very bad ulcers. Scurvy beginning
Irresistible	35	Scurvy increasing fast
London	41	Slight scurvies
Brunswick	30	Scurvy increasing
Royal Sovereign	30	Inveterate cases of scurvy. Upwards of 80 scorbutics doing duty
Queen	43	Scurvy and obstinate venereal complaints
Triumph	29	None
Prince George	53	Scurvy increasing fast. Some very bad cases
Bellerophon	24	Scurvy approaching
	475	

[1] Sir Erasmus Gower (1742–1814). Lieutenant 1762; Captain 1790; Rear-admiral 1799; Vice-admiral 1804; Admiral 1809.

Remarks

It appears from the above state of the fleet that scurvy is making rapid progress in the several ships. Few precautions could have been practiced for the prevention of this disease, which is the common consequence of living for a length of time on salted provisions without recent vegetable matter. Even the mild summer weather seems to have had small share in retarding its approach. It is however to be the more dreaded as the season advances, and cold and rain set in. From the lemon juice supplied at the early part of the cruize, no deaths have happened; from the quantity just distributed we have also a right to expect that no immediate danger may be apprehended; but as the causes which have produced this scurvy have been general in their operation, so the means of relief must be general, and fresh meat with fresh vegetables must be extended to the whole. The sooner therefore that the public service can permit the ships to return to port, the more quickly and the more easily will fresh provisions effectually correct this scorbutic disposition in the habits of seamen.

The sheep and vegetables brought out in the Charon have with other articles been distributed in due proportion according to the situation of the sick in their respective ships, and received with inexpressable satisfaction. To some ships where the most inveterate cases of scurvy appeared, I judged it proper to send a quarter cask of porter; also tea, sugar and rice, where the surgeons' necessaries were expended. The Invincible's fever being of the low kind, she has been supplied with quarter cask of port wine, of a quality superior to that of the ship. I have also, to the different surgeons, recommended a mess of fermented oatmeal (Sowens) for a constant supper to the scorbutics.

The Charon's hospital is now ready to receive patients, and there seems a considerable number of objects in the fleet.

T. Trotter. Physician to the Fleet.

P.S. It also appears from the reports from frigates this forenoon, that the scurvy is gaining ground. I have therefore supplied them with lemon juice and according to their wants.
T.T.

100b.   *Trotter to Bridport*

Charon, 18 August 1795

Lest your Lordship may have thought it necessary to represent the present state of the fleet to the Lords Commissioners of the Admiralty, I beg leave to add to the remarks already given to your Lordship some suggestions which may be of much use on the ships returning to port.

It appears to me that effectual and permanent relief from the prevailing scurvy can be most easily accomplished through the victualling. For this purpose I would recommend that the fresh beef broth should be seasoned with all the vegetables in season, such as cabbages, carrots, turnips and onions; to a quantity as great as the broth will boil. But, besides what may be boiled in the broth, I would employ one of the coppers daily to boil these vegetables, to the amount of one lb. per man, to eat with his meat. This mode of diet will in a short time effectually correct the scorbutic taint, so as to prepare our people for future emergencies; and in cases where the disease has gained farther ground we must trust to lemons or the apple during its acerb state.

Their Lordships will find the present state of the fleet exactly corresponding with sentiments conveyed to them through my letters to Earl Howe, some time before we sailed, when among other precautions I thought beer of a stronger quality, so that double the quantity might be carried to sea, and 2 quarts served instead of the gallon, by which means each ship would have brought eight weeks allowance without danger of spoiling; pickles of cabbage, or any other to be used on the days of salted provisions, and mollasses for mixing with the oatmeal to render its use more general; these articles would have increased the vegetable part of the diet, and retarded as least a disposition to scurvy which a long cruize must otherwise produce.

I find that the form of sick necessaries with which the Channel fleet has been served has never yet been supplied at Plymouth or the ports to the eastward. This form includes many valuable articles not formerly in use, with an increased quantity of others, and excludes what absorbed a great quantity of the expense without being of any benefit. In the arrangement care was taken not to exceed the former sum, and our sick are deriving much comfort without one farthing additional to Government. I judged it necessary to trouble your Lordships on this subject, as ships from all the ports, but Portsmouth, are in the custom of joining us extremely ill provided with these articles.

101.   *Bridport to Admiralty*

Royal George, at sea, 24 August 1795

I feel myself much obliged to their Lordships for their indulgence respecting my health by allowing me to return into port on that account. I desire you will inform their Lordships that it was never my intention to quit the squadron but to continue at sea as long as the Royal George was kept out on service. In their Lordships' order of the 28th of July I was given to understand that a squadron of ships would have joined me long before this time under the command of Rear Admiral Harvey and also by a letter of the 31st from the highest authority I received the same information and that it would enable me to send home such ships as should require refreshments and refittings. I judge from thence that the Royal George must be included in that number as she quitted Spithead the same day with the Queen, Sans Pareil, London, Prince George and Valiant. If these are the ships I am to send into port I really feel it my duty to pay the same attention to the Royal George as she has to my certain knowledge undergone the same important services and I was fully persuaded that I should be directed to return into port with these ships and that they could not have intended that I should remove my flag to any other ship and have kept at sea. In what I am obliged to say I trust I shall give no offence to their Lordships which states that if I am kept out in any other ship it must be without a clean shirt to put upon my back or a morsel of fresh meat to place on my table but I am fully convinced their Lordships cannot propose such a measure.

If it will give their Lordships any satisfaction I have the pleasure to say that my health in general is better than it was a month ago but I beg to appeal to the feelings of every naval officer whether he must not think me in a weaker and a more debilitated state from the length of time I have been at sea, having never set my foot on shore since the 5th of June, the day I returned to Portsmouth from London. But under every circumstance of health and personal feelings I am determined to remain with my faithful officers and to share in the labours of the King's service in the Royal George till she can be allowed to go into port – farther than this I hope their Lordships can neither desire or expect. It is the health of ten thousand men that I am anxious about, not my own, as the King has many distinguished and gallant admirals to fill my station but His Majesty and the public may possibly find it difficult to procure seamen to defend and save the country. I am led to this consideration the more from judging that I may possibly be the oldest man in the ten thousand that I have calculated he has in the squadron and therefore I hope I may be allowed to state my feelings on this subject.

I beg to ask if it would be inconsistent with the discipline of the service if their Lordships were to direct you to state some limited time to my cruise, or to say that I was to remain at sea as long as the provisions and water of the squadron would allow me and whether under these circumstances I am to direct the captains to put their crews to short allowance from the exigencies of the service.

102. *Bridport to Admiralty*

24 August 1795

Enclosed is a copy of a letter I received this morning from the Honourable Captain Berkeley[1] of the Formidable which I transmit for their Lordships' consideration.

[*Enclosure*]

102a. *Berkeley to Bridport*

Formidable, at sea, 22 August 1795

In justice to my ships' company, and that their true situation may be known, I think it my duty to represent to your Lordship that the scurvy has made such a progress amongst them that if they have not a course of vegetable and fresh diet soon, I am afraid the consequences may be very serious; that no blame may be imputed to want of care and attention, it will be proper to revert to the cause, and it will then be found that hardly any other ship's company have had so little opportunity's afforded them of getting the proper diet etc as the Marlborough's crew, of which the greater part of this ship's consist.

The Marlborough sailed from Spithead on the 29th January to Torbay, from whence she returned the 25th February to Spithead. She then was ordered to Plymouth and sailed the 7th March; on the 7th of April she was again sent to Spithead, from whence she sailed with Admiral Waldegrave[2] on the 22d of April, and did not return till the 12th of June. In this period she was served fresh beef as under

---

[1]Sir George Cranfield Berkeley (1753–1818). 2nd surviving son of Earl Berkeley. Lieutenant 1772; Captain 1780; Rear-admiral 1799; Vice-admiral 1805; Admiral 1810. Commander-in-Chief on the coast of Portugal 1808–12.

[2]William Waldegrave, Lord Radstock (1753–1825). Lieutenant 1772; Captain 1776; Rear-admiral 1794; Vice-admiral 1795. Served only briefly in the Channel, being mainly in the Mediterranean.

Feby   14th
March 12
       14
       28
April 2
       14
       17
       30

Men received fresh provisions only eight times; upon her arrival at Plymouth and orders for the men to be turned over to the Formidable, I found the scurvy had begun to make its appearance and immediately applied to have vegetables and acids given to the men. But, notwithstanding the Admiralty ordered them to be supplied, nothing was delivered except twenty gallons of lime juice. I sent twenty-two seamen to the hospital at Plymouth with very inveterate scurvy cases, and since that eight more on board the Charon hospital ship. Our sick list at present consists of fifty seven, most of which are objects which require immediate attention and fresh diet or they will be lost to the service for the whole winter at least, and as the greatest part of the scorbutic patients are able seamen, I need not point out to your Lordship how severely it must be felt in a ship whose numbers are forty short of Able and forty of Ordinary seamen of the proportion allowed by the Admiralty.

Under these circumstances I trust your Lordships will see how necessary it will be to relieve the ship as soon as possible, and hope you will take such measures as may appear best for that purpose and insure the healths of a valuable set of men, as well as the service of so large a ship as the Formidable.

[*Endorsement*]

Royal George, off the Isle of Groix.

103.   *Number of sick in the squadron*

24 August 1795

Ships	Sailors		Soldiers, etc.	
	On board	Hospital ship	On board	Hospital ship
Royal George	28	2	12	–
Royal Sovereign	76	2	4	–

Queen	34	–	3	–
Sans Pareil	60	1	5	–
London	64	7	9	–
Brunswick	32	4	3	1
Bellerophon	23	3	–	–
Valiant	50	1	2	–
Invincible	65	4	7	1
Formidable	48	8	10	–
Prince George	78	5	14	–
Triumph	30	–	–	–
Phaeton	1	2	–	–
Pallas	20	4	–	–
Crescent	8	3	1	–
Thalia	22	4	?	–
Aquilon	9	–	–	–
Porcupine	2	3	–	–
Megara	2	–	–	–
Charon	8	=	=	=
	660	53	72	2
	72	2		
	732	55		

104. *Seymour to Spencer*

Sans Pareil, off Belle Isle, 24 August 1795

I cannot help joining the Admiral in thinking it absolutely necessary that our ships should return into port as soon as possible. Those which sailed with Lord Bridport will soon complete their eleventh week without having received any sort of refreshment, a term infinitely too long for any ships to keep the sea, particularly after such a winter as the last, the severity of which deprived the men belonging to the fleet of their normal supply of fresh meat, vegetables, etc. I know you will be told that in former times our ships were kept upon this coast for a much longer time but it is fair at the same time to remind you that they were frequently at an anchor for many weeks together in Quiberon Bay, where an excellent market was established where they were well supplied with fish and that the men had frequent opportunities of going on shore, there not then being the least risk of their deserting. Our people, everything considered, keep up tolerably well but every day adds some scorbutic patient to the sick list and will, I am persuaded, increase the necessity of their remaining a longer time in port on their return, for it is clear to me that if the ships destined to take our places upon this coast do not arrive soon that you will derive very little advantage from the services of this squadron whenever the bad weather sets in, as the men being even so well as I describe them now to be can only be attributed to the very fine weather which has prevailed during the whole of our cruise.

[Endorsed as received on the 31st]

105.   *Bridport to Admiralty*

Royal George, at sea, 26 August 1795

I am much concerned to state to you, for the information of the Lords Commissioners of the Admiralty, that the squadron of His Majesty's ships under my command must necessarily return into port in the course of a very few days.

The abstract of the weekly accounts, which I sent to you by the Aquilon, will show to their Lordships the number of sick in each ship and in the Charon, hospital ship, which has increased from the 28th of July to the 24th of August from 493 to 787, and I am apprehensive before the end of this month a great many more scorbutic cases will appear; but if the squadron was in the highest health, it cannot stay out longer, as their Lordships will see that some ships have not more than forty one tons of water, which with a number of sick on board is a melancholy and alarming situation; under these circumstances I judged it to be my duty as commander of this squadron to send the London into port and directed Captain Griffith[1] to proceed to Cawsand Bay and to take two detained vessels under his charge; the London quitted me the 25th instant. The next ship I shall send home will be the Prince George to that anchorage, as she has now near one hundred sick and will be soon short of water. It is scarcely possible for the whole squadron to remain on this station, until I can receive your answer to my letter, with their Lordships' directions.

The Royal Sovereign is also very sickly with the scurvy, but she does not want water; it appears to my judgement impossible for me to order Vice Admiral Cornwallis to remain at sea and I do not imagine I can give such orders to any other ships than the Triumph, Brunswick and Bellerophon, and I am afraid their crews will feel the fatal effects of such an arrangement. The Royal George has not more than three weeks

---

[1]Sir Edward Griffith Colpoys (fl. 1794–1812). Captain 1794; Rear-admiral 1812.

water on board, at the usual rate of expence, and has only a small quantity of wine remaining for the sick, but it is my intention to remain out in her to the last days allowance, before she is brought to an anchor, unless I shall receive their Lordships order to return into port. But before the squadron quits this station I will give Sir John Borlase Warren notice of my intentions, if he shall remain in Quiberon Bay when that measure takes place.

I will not attempt to reason upon the importancy of keeping this squadron three months at sea, as I am ignorant of it. It is my duty to obey their Lordships' orders; also I conceive it to be my duty to represent the situation of His Majesty's squadron under my charge and command.

I have ordered all the French prisoners remaining in the squadron on board the Prince George, to be landed at Plymouth, as many of them have the scurvy and they expend our lemon juice as well as our water.

I have sent the Penelope cutter, Lieutenant Burdwood,[1] with this letter, and I have directed him to make the first port he can arrive at in England.

I am to acquaint you for their Lordships' information that this squadron cannot water in Quiberon Bay, if such report has been made to them; neither can it with security water and refit in Torbay, as the holds of the ships must be broke up, which may be dangerous if an easterly wind should blow strong in the month of September, while they are in act of refitting.

N.B. I have directed Lieutenant Burdwood to return and join this squadron without loss of time.

[*Endorsement*]

1 September. Acquaint Lord Bridport that his letters of the 25 and 26 ultimo have this moment been received and that he will have instructions upon the subject contained in the letter in the course of a very few hours after the receipt of this.

106.   *Seymour to Spencer*

Sans Pareil, 29 August 1795

The Prestwood cutter has just joined us from Falmouth but as I understand that she has not brought any London letters and that she does not

---

[1]Daniel Burdwood (d. 1804). Lieutenant 1782.

give us to hope that any ships are on their passage to relieve this squadron I must trouble you once more on the subject of our sick, whose condition will soon become a very grievous one. As I am totally in the dark about the measures which the Admiralty may have adopted about the fleet I now suppose that their arrangements no longer admit of their relieving this squadron and I am therefore led to point out what may afford a temporary relief to the people serving in it. I should, for that purpose, earnestly recommend that directions are given to the Sick and Hurt Board to send out vessels laden with sheep, vegetables and fruit for the use of the sick and above all lemon juice, of which 1500 or 2000 gallons would not be too large a supply in their present state as there are few of the seamen but what are affected by the scurvy, though in a slight degree and that remedy has a wonderful effect if taken early in the complaint.

[*Endorsed as received on the 3rd*]

107.   *Gardner to Bridport*

Queen, at sea, 29 August 1795

As an individual I am very thankful for the frequent opportunities which your Lordship has afforded me of writing to our friends and I only wish that they had the means of replying to half the letters which have been sent home from the fleet. This would be some consolation after having been near three months at sea. It certainly is the longest cruise I ever experienced and, as I conclude from the remains of our water that we cannot continue a much longer time out, there can be no treason in saying I shall be very glad whenever the time may arrive for your Lordship's return into port to enjoy (for a short time at least) the blessings of the land with the fruits of our labours and which, after so unusual a time at sea, I hope we may be allowed to have some small claim. I thank God we continue remarkably healthy on board the Queen but that I fear is not the case with many ships of the fleet, whose boats for some days past have made frequent trips to the hospital ship. I hope to hear that your Lordship continues in as good health as can be expected after having been near a quarter of a year at sea.

108.   *Victualling Board to Warren*

29 August 1795

[*Copy*]

The Right Honourable the Lords Commissioners of the Admiralty having been pleased by Mr. Nepean's letter of the 27th instant to direct us to provide as expeditiously as possible at Portsmouth a sufficient supply of refreshments for the use of the squadron under your command, to be sent out in such ships as Admiral Sir Peter Parker may direct; we beg leave to acquaint you that we have given directions to our Agent to provide with the utmost expedition a considerable supply of vegetables, consisting of potatoes, onions, turnips, cabbages and carrots and to cause then to be properly packed in hampers or baskets and put an board such ships as may be appointed for that purpose, consigning the same to you.

[*Endorsement*]

Only think what we have suffered by not having received letter by the Susan cutter and not knowing the measures of Government. Bridport.

109.   *Admiralty to Bridport*

30 August 1795

... their Lordships are sorry to observe that the scurvy during the late cruise has made such progress in the squadron and particularly that the ships under Vice Admiral Cornwallis, though so lately joined, experience already the effects of the disease.

As the squadron under Rear Admiral Harvey has been so long prevented from joining your Lordship orders have been given for releasing him from the further charge of the convoy, leaving the Orion and frigates for its protection, which will follow the moment the wind will permit.

Measures have been taken for sending out by every opportunity such antiscorbutics and other refreshments as seem most to be required and no opportunity will be lost of supplying the squadron from time to time during its continuance at sea.

110.   *Joseph Stewart[1] to Sick and Wounded Board*

31 August 1795

I beg leave to acquaint you I have seen the persons who supply the Board with lemon juice and that they have engaged to have five hundred gallons of that article ready this week; it shall be forwarded to Portsmouth with all possible expedition.

I understand the Victualling Board have taken measures for forwarding to the squadrons commanded by Admiral Cornwallis and Sir John B. Warren the articles of vegetables I mentioned to you this morning which I presume renders to it unnecessary for any steps to be taken by the Commissioners for Sick and Wounded Seamen to ensure a supply thereof.

[*Endorsement*]

2 September. Sick and Hurt to forward antiscorbutics to Portsmouth; Sir P.P.[2] to send them out.

111.   *Admiralty to Bridport*

1 September 1795

Whereas we have received information that Rear Admiral Harvey with the ships named in the margin [*Queen Charlotte, Prince of Wales, Prince, Orion, Russell*] sailed from St. Helens yesterday for the purpose of joining your Lordship, intending to call off Plymouth for the Marlborough, which ship is ordered to join him from thence; and it being our intention in consequence of your Lordship's representation of the present state of the ships now with you, notwithstanding our order to Vice Admiral Cornwallis of the 30th ultimo, that the squadron to continue at sea should be left under the command of the Rear Admiral and be composed of the ships named on the other side hereof [*Queen Charlotte, Prince of Wales, Prince, Orion, Russell, Brunswick, Bellerophon, Triumph*] your Lordship is hereby required and directed upon his joining you to put the said ships under his command; and having completed such arrangements as you shall judge proper you are to return into port with the remainder of your squadron excepting the Phaeton, Pallas and Porcupine which you are to leave with the Rear

---

[1]Secretary to the Sick and Wounded Board.
[2]Admiral Sir Peter Parker, Commander-in-Chief at Portsmouth.

Admiral, sending into Plymouth one third of the ships which you are ordered to bring with you and repair yourself to Spithead with the rest of the said squadron where you are to remain until you shall receive further orders.

112.   *Warren to Bridport*

La Pomone, Quiberon Bay, 3 September 1795

The situation of the troops, who are dying daily, and the scurvy making rapid progress in the ships' companies, and the General having gone into the country, I have requested to know if he had any further service for the army or what he wished I should do with them, and enclose his answer.

I therefore, if no orders arrive by the 15th, propose returning with the squadron and army to England, a measure which from the necessity of the case I hope your Lordship will approve of.

113.   *Warren to Bridport*

La Pomone, Quiberon Bay, 4 September 1795

I beg leave to acknowledge the receipt of your Lordship's letter of the 3rd instant and in consequence thereof I propose sailing from this place with His Majesty's squadron under my command and the transports on the 14th.

114.   *Cornwallis to Bridport*

Royal Sovereign, at sea, 6 September 1795

The surgeon of His Majesty's Ship Royal Sovereign says the lemon juice he received the other day will last only two days. I have therefore desired Captain Whitby[1] to take the opportunity, now it is calm, to send a boat in hopes of getting some more. The late wet weather has affected the scorbutic men very much; some have had their teeth drop out and I am afraid, if we do not speedily get plenty of refreshments, the ship's company will be rendered useless for many months, if we should be fortunate enough to save the lives of those who are most afflicted.

---

[1]John Whitby (d. 1806). Lieutenant 1780; Captain 1793.

115. *Sidney Smith to Spencer*

Diamond, off Havre, 12 September 1795
Finished at Weymouth, 15th

There is scarce a battery between the Seven Islands and Havre that we have not exchanged shot with to plague them and (except at La Hogue) with perfect impunity, dispersing their ill-formed party with a shell now and then, which astonishes the natives not a little. They will make a mountain of all this and multiply us into many squadrons but the fact is the Diamond's launch alone is the mighty fleet that has annoyed them. My practice is, whenever we anchor on the coast for a calm or a contrary tide, to send her away to seek adventure. . . . The boats' crews are so enamoured of this kind of service that I have a difficulty to select from the volunteers that offer and I find some attempts among the petty officers to slip in and secrete themselves in order to go.

116. *Bridport to Howe*

Royal George, at sea, 15 September 1795

Your Lordship's letter of the 5th of July was brought to me in an Admiralty packet on the 10th instant off Belle Isle when Rear Admiral Harvey joined me.

. . . The point for me at this time to answer is that I have not acknowledged the receipt of your Lordship's instructions of the 6th of June, forwarded to me by express before I left Spithead.

I do not know that I can give your Lordship a more satisfactory answer to that part of your letter than by quoting the words of your Lordship's order – 'Being moreover to send notice from time to time of your proceedings in pursuance of this appointment to Mr. Secretary Nepean for the information of the Lords Commissioners of the Admiralty.'

It is impossible for me to conceive that your Lordship put these words into the order to instruct me in my duty as they manifested to my weak understanding that your Lordship did not expect to be troubled with business in your retirement at Porter's Lodge for the recovery of the yet impaired state of your Lordship's health.

But I find by your Lordship's letter that I am mistaken. I have therefore only to add upon this part of the order that the same Admiralty messenger that brought your Lordship's orders and letter from Porter's Lodge brought me several other documents from Mr. Secretary

Nepean and my acknowledging the receipt of them will be found at the Admiralty in two letters dated the 9th of June, one by the return of the messenger, the other by the regular post. I am moreover to acquaint your Lordship that in consequence of an order I received the 31st of July from the Admiralty which alluded to your Lordship's order I transmitted copies of the two orders and your letter to Mr. Secretary Nepean for the information of the Lords Commissioners of the Admiralty.

I am further to express my acknowledgments for the honour of your Lordship's congratulations on the defeat of the Brest fleet and on the important services rendered to the King and the public upon that occasion.

P.S. I am struggling against an obstinate easterly wind after a cruise of near fourteen weeks which has not given strength to my constitution or ease to my mind.

117. *Bridport to Admiralty*

Royal George, Spithead, 19 September 1795

I acquaint you for the information of the Lords Commissioners of the Admiralty that I arrived here this day . . . after a cruise of ninety-nine days and eighty-eight since the battle was fought off L'Orient by my original squadron when an important victory was gained over the enemy's fleet.

I have the further satisfaction to state that the squadron has given full support to the ships and transports under the command of Sir John Borlase Warren, by blocking up the beaten fleet and thereby given protection to the trade and commerce of His Majesty's subjects.

I have also detained upwards of thirty neutral vessels bound into the ports of France and the detached ships under the command of the Honourable Captain Stopford[1] of His Majesty's Ship the Phaeton, together with the Pallas and Valiant drove a large corvette of twenty-two guns on shore in the Portuis Breton [*Pertuis Breton*], which is entirely destroyed.

[1]Sir Robert Stopford (1768–1847). Lieutenant 1785; Captain 1790; Rear-admiral 1808; Vice-admiral 1812; Admiral 1825. Took part in Cornwallis's action of June 1795.

118.   *George III to Spencer*

Weymouth, 19 September 1795

I cannot help just writing a few lines to Earl Spencer expressive of my approbation of the conduct of Sir Borlase Warren, who by the less proper one of Lord Bridport seems necessitated to return to Plymouth.[1] If the French fleet in Quiberon Bay was nearly ready as Sir Borlase supposes it will be highly necessary to send out part of Lord Bridport's squadron with the greatest expedition to protect the East India ships, which must be hourly expected.

119.   *Report on the returned ships*

September 1795

Ships	No. sick Seamen	No. sick Soldiers	Total No. Sick	Tons of water	No. short
Royal George	47	15	62	16	22
Royal Sovereign	67	13	80	80	9
					Major part of the ship's company afflicted with the scurvy
Queen	74	5	79	10	24
Sans Pareil	66	14	80	20	41
Invincible	277	–	277	7	15
Valiant	92	10	102	20	20
Triumph	103	18	121	22	29
Phaeton	7	–	7	25	10
Pallas	51	–	51	4	16
Megara	2	=	2	5	=
	786	75	861	209	186

[1]The suggestion that Bridport returned to port without orders has been repeated by later authors. It is curious that the clear orders sent to him should not have been noticed any more than Warren's proposal to return without instructions.

3

THE LOGISTICAL PROBLEMS
8 OCTOBER 1795–20 DECEMBER 1796

The Command of the Fleet

The failure of Howe to serve at sea in the summer of 1795, and the employment of Bridport in his place, had demonstrated the need to make a new arrangement for the command of the Channel fleet more satisfactory to all concerned. On shore, the relations of Howe and Bridport were exacerbated by the ability of Howe and his flag captain, according to the established rules of distribution as interpreted at the Admiralty, to share in the prize money made by the fleet [121]. The failure of Bridport to keep Howe informed of his proceedings at sea demonstrated the ineffectiveness, where the will was lacking, of delegation of part of the fleet to Bridport as commander for a particular service [116]. Although the problem cited was the issue of orders while the fleet was in port, in October 1795 the divided command was annulled, Bridport's commission was suspended, and whole of the Channel fleet was again placed under the direct control of Howe [122]. Bridport's sarcastic acknowledgement of the termination of what had been an administrative convenience confirmed the arrangement could no longer be sustained [123]. However, Howe was to command the Channel fleet from on shore for another 18 months.

This was not only due to Howe's reputation and popularity. The number of senior flag officers who could be considered contenders for command of the major fleets was limited. Their number was further reduced in March 1796 by the nomination of Lord Hood to the post of Governor of Greenwich Hospital [134]. George III's acceptance of the nomination [135] indicates the readiness with which both Spencer and the King placed long service and merit above the tendency for an officer on occasion to give offence to social and professional superiors. So too with Bridport. By October 1796, after a year on shore, he was ready to serve again at sea [149] and Spencer was ready to accommodate him with a squadron [150]. However, in the autumn of 1796 a squadron was all that was necessary to match the French force ready for sea in Brest [153], and Bridport was not prepared to suffer demotion from the command of a fleet to that of a squadron. Spencer indulged him by recalling Rear-admiral Pole to act as his first captain [156], whereupon Bridport argued that 'by the general rule of the service' a first captain could only be appointed to a fleet of at least twenty ships. This contest between Bridport's pretensions and the demands of the blockade was abandoned at the end of the year with intelligence of increased activity in Brest [157]. Indeed French operations were to demonstrate the acute danger of permitting the command and method of maintaining the blockade to be dictated by demands other than the threat posed by the enemy.

The Demands on the Fleet

The Admiralty was temporarily able to dispense with a sea-going Commander-in-Chief, albeit the deputy of the admiral on shore, because the activity of the French in Brest at the end of 1795 and for the greater part of 1796 appeared at low ebb. Yet elsewhere there were other demands. With the mobilisation of the Dutch fleet under French control, during 1795 there was the necessity to form and maintain a North Sea fleet.[1] At the end of that year the Admiralty had assumed that the Quiberon venture was over, but the desire in Government in January 1796 to sustain a point of supply to the royalist cause through the anchorage in Quiberon Bay raised the challenge of continuing to support a naval force in the bay [127]. That force had to be powerful enough to match anything the French might send to sea from Brest or L'Orient, to protect its line of supply, and to afford replacements for ships refitting or repairing. Yet these vessels could only be supplied at a cost to the potential demand for ships in the West Indies[2] and for ships in other cruising squadrons [129]. At the time, the war in the West Indies seemed both a way of weakening France by depriving her of colonial trade and a way of obtaining bargaining counters for the negotiation of peace. Yet, though pressed by Dundas as Secretary for War, the West Indian campaign could only be waged with ships surplus to requirements in the North Sea, Channel and Mediterranean.

---

[1]Vice-admiral Adam Duncan was appointed to command the North Sea fleet in March 1795.

[2]The campaign in the West Indies had resulted in the capture of French Tobago in 1793 and Martinique in 1794, and the temporary occupation of Guadeloupe and capture of St Lucia in 1795. A toe-hold was also maintained on St Dominque from 1793. A second expedition was on the point of sailing in mid November 1795 when it was struck by storms; it sailed again early in December 1795 only to be driven back in January 1796. It sailed finally in late February 1796. See M. Duffy, *Soldiers, Sugar and Seapower. The British Expeditions to the West Indies and the War against Revolutionary France* (Oxford, 1987), 199–216.

These outside demands affected the manner in which the Channel fleet operated as much as did the activity of the French in Brest and the weather. During the autumn of 1795 the Western Approaches experienced severe gales [120] and the Channel fleet kept only the squadron under Rear-admiral Harvey off the Brittany coast. After the passing of the worst of the winter weather in 1796, the fleet operated economically in squadrons. During March, the main functions of the squadron under Gardner were to escort the Mediterranean and West India convoys into the North Atlantic, to meet and safeguard the return of the inward Jamaica convoy, and to intercept an outward-bound Dutch convoy sailing north-about round Scotland [132,138]. Vice-admiral John Colpoys resumed the disruption of French coastal trade [139]. Already since March Warren's squadron of frigates, operating out of Falmouth, had been attacking convoys along the French coast [136]. As the weather improved in May, Warren's squadron was able to keep the harbour of Brest under observation [141]. Meanwhile the bulk of the Channel fleet remained at Spithead, where the possible necessity of a sudden departure for the French coast prompted a proposal to organise the available French pilots, paying them appropriately and berthing them in the guardship [140].

The Demands on Squadrons

Intelligence gathered from Brest over the summer of 1796 suggested the French were planning an expedition. Its destination remained a mystery; Portugal, Gibraltar or Ireland all seemed possible. As the French progressively equipped their ships, one squadron of the Channel fleet under Vice-admiral Thompson was stationed off Brest, another under Sir Roger Curtis covered Ireland, with the remainder still at Spithead.[1] In August Gardner took Thompson's place off Brest, the alternation of the squadrons again calling for the timely replenishment of ships [146]. The necessity to maintain a force off Ushant was enhanced by the potential return into Brest of Admiral Richery who had left Toulon in September 1795 and was known to be at Newfoundland a year later [147]. Meanwhile during September 1796 the French were gathering transports and transferring warships when possible from Rochefort and L'Orient into Brest [148].

At the beginning of December 1796 French ships in Brest showed signs of being made ready for sea. A squadron from the Channel fleet

---

[1]W. James, *The Naval History of Great Britain from the declaration of war by France in 1793 to the accession of George IV* (6 vols, London, 1859), I, 341.

under the command of John Colpoys remained off Ushant. Short days and long nights at that time of the year made the task particularly trying [154]. Ships from Colpoys's squadron occasionally looked into the entrance to the harbour; some officers had now become quite familiar with the waters of the Goulet. Meanwhile frigate squadrons under Sir John Warren and Sir Edward Pellew, though acting independently and responsible directly to the Admiralty, maintained a more regular station off the harbour mouth and reported their observations to Colpoys. Suspicion of a major expedition was confirmed by the apparent absence of French ships from the sea off the Brittany coast. Had they been prohibited from sailing both to secure their seamen and to prevent information of the expedition getting out [155]? On 11 December the fleet in Brest water was reinforced by five of the line and three frigates under Admiral Richery, who had already put into Rochefort. Four days later, undeterred by Colpoys's squadron off shore, a French expedition put to sea.[1]

The Preservation of the Health of Seamen

By this time steps had been taken towards the preservation of the health of seamen during and after long cruises. In December 1795 Trotter, Physician of the Channel fleet, took the initiative by ordering a supply of fresh vegetables for the sick of the squadron intended to relieve Harvey. He was reproved by the Admiralty which by then had not looked far enough ahead to consider whether another squadron should take Harvey's place, let alone what ships should constitute that squadron. However Trotter's initiative did provide the Sick and Wounded Board with the opportunity to remind the Admiralty of the propriety, already proposed in September 1795, of the Victualling Board supplying all fresh meat and vegetables for the crews of ships [124]. This clarification of responsibilities was confirmed by the Admiralty early in January 1796 [125].

That month Harvey's return from a long winter cruise on the coast of France confirmed that crews could be kept healthy on a supply of fresh provisions, especially when they were able to take shelter from the worst of winter weather [126]. To ensure the health of Harvey's seamen, Trotter proposed that all ships returning from long voyages should be placed upon a vegetable diet for two weeks after their return into port [128]. It was a proposal that was implemented at the end of March 1796 [137], and routine by September, when Trotter was given

[1]James, II, 4.

authority to use his own discretion in allocating vegetables to ships returning into port [145].

Steps were also taken by the Sick and Wounded Board to improve the care available for seamen who could not be cured on board their ships or in the hospital ship and had to be brought on shore. The naval hospitals at Haslar and Plymouth served the fleet anchorages of Spithead and Plymouth Sound. But the use of Falmouth as a port for the frigate squadrons operating off the French coast, and for the receipt of cartels of prisoners from France, now demanded a hospital there. Local inhabitants opposed the rent of an existing house and in March 1796 a double-walled wooden shed capable of accommodating 50 men was proposed and approved [133].

The Production and Distribution of Lemon Juice

However, the main initiative of the Sick and Wounded Board was to set in motion a production and distribution process by which lemon juice might be supplied to all the seamen in the fleet as a preventative of scurvy. Hitherto it had been supplied only to the sick. The Board outlined its convictions and proposals in February 1796. Two years earlier the efficacy of lemon juice as a preventative had been only a 'probable supposition'. Trials of its powers since then had established them to the satisfaction of the Board as 'an established fact'. To avoid the risk of adulteration and to obtain the juice most economically, the Sick and Wounded Board preferred to have the lemons squeezed at their own establishments in England. They now knew the daily dose required by each man, the total quantity required annually, its cost, the amount of sugar needed to mix with it and the cost of the sugar. After deducting savings that could be made in dispensable items of seamen's diet, the whole cost amounted to less than £28,000 [130]. The Board was accordingly permitted to set in motion a production process.

The Board of Admiralty was kept closely informed and was itself able to inspect and question the manner in which the juice would be made available to seamen [130,131]. By the end of May 1796 the Sick and Wounded Board had made ready the first delivery of juice to the Victualling Board [142]. Production and issue arrangements having been agreed with the former board, the Victualling Board had remained in ignorance of what was expected of it. On being informed, it was immediately able to contribute an improvement in the method of dispensing the juice [143]. The Victualling Board then began the distribution to ships with urgency. In June the first delivery of the juice to a ship specified by the Board of Admiralty had to go overland to Portsmouth. Notwithstanding delivery to the ship within a week, the commander of that ship refused to receive it as the vessel was under way [144]!

Nevertheless by November 1796 the Victualling Board had established the distribution process to ships and had issued pursers with printed instructions for issuing and accounting for the juice and sugar [151]. Meanwhile the Sick and Wounded Board was exploring the cheapest means of securing lemon juice. The first tender it received for supply by a contractor was more than twice the cost of production in its own establishments. It accordingly investigated through its own agents and through Commanders-in-Chief the quantities and costs of lemon and lime juice in the Caribbean, Mediterranean, and at Lisbon [152].

120. *A Journal of the proceedings of His Majesty's Ship Russell,*
J. W. Payne, Esqr. Commander

2–3 October 1795

Friday 2nd. Squally with loud claps of thunder. At 1 we were taken aback in a very heavy squall. At the same time the ship was struck by lightning which split our main and mizen masts all to pieces, split the main topsail, also killed our first lieutenant and two men. Several others much wounded. At 2 made the signal of distress. Dark, cloudy with a fresh breeze from the N.E. A.M. moderate and clear. Bore up for Quiberon Bay but the wind heading us could not get in.

Saturday 3rd. Moderate breezes and fine weather. The carpenters from the different ships came on board and examined our masts. At 7 parted company with the fleet. Committed to the deep the bodies of Lieutenant Charleston[1] and two men. Hard gales with thunder and lightning and hard showers of rain.

121. *Seymour[2] to Bridport*

Admiralty, 8 October 1795

Having given all the attention of which I am capable to your Lordship's statement of the doubts entertained of Sir Roger Curtis being entitled to share in the prizes taken on the 23rd of June, I am led to believe that

---

[1]Dederick Charlesson (d. 1795). Lieutenant 1781.
[2]Although he served in the Channel fleet under Bridport, Seymour also acted as an Admiralty Commissioner between 7 March 1795 and 10 September 1798.

while Lord Howe, his chief, can claim for those captures that the Captain of his Fleet must equally do so and this opinion seems to prevail in the minds of my brother officers whom I have had an opportunity of conversing with on that subject.

122. *Spencer to Bridport*

Admiralty, 20 October 1795[1]

The great inconvenience which is found to arise in the transmission of orders to the several parts of the Channel Fleet at the time they are at Spithead or in Portsmouth Harbour from the divided state of the command as it stands at present has induced the Board of Admiralty to come to a determination that all the ships which are meant in the present state of affairs to be employed in the Channel shall again be put under the orders of Lord Howe, through whom the several orders necessary to be given to them may pass to the senior officer who happens to be at Portsmouth at the time, with the exception of sailing orders which it is intended shall be issued from the Admiralty to the officer commanding whatever squadron is to sail on any service that may be required. I thought it an attention due to your Lordship to trouble you with a few lines stating the intention of the Board in order to apprize you fully of what was meant by it and to point out the reason which has made it necessary for us to come to this determination, the effect of which will be for the present to suspend your commission of Commander-in-Chief of a squadron till circumstances arise from which it may be expedient to His Majesty's service for you to resume such command.

123. *Bridport to Spencer*

Cricket Lodge, 22 October 1795

I am honoured with your Lordship's obliging letter of the 20th instant and I beg leave to return my best thanks for the attention your Lordship is pleased to show me. On the determination the Board of Admiralty intend to come to respecting the issuing of orders and the sailing of His Majesty's ships of the Channel Fleet, if I understand the

---

[1]This letter has been misplaced, which possibly accounts for some of the confusion which has arisen from time to time about Bridport's status in the Channel fleet between the end of his cruise in 1795 and his becoming Commander-in-Chief in April 1797.

intention of the Board I readily concur in the measures in future to be adopted as they appear to me to be exactly what I urged to your Lordship when I was going to sea with fifteen ships of the line besides frigates, etc. and with three admirals under my orders. If my wishes and expectations had then been complied with every difficulty which is now stated to exist in the issuing of orders would have been obviated and no commission to me necessary. In which case I should, as well as the admirals under me, have reaped the full reward of our services instead of Lord Howe, Vice Admiral Waldegrave and Sir Roger Curtis. Your Lordship will, I hope, excuse the stating my feelings upon this subject.

As Lord Howe's health is established, I am glad His Majesty is likely to have his Lordship's services in this time of public warfare which calls for the experience and abilities of meritorious officers of every rank.

With respect to myself, I shall be ready to serve the King as long as my health and faculties will allow me. When they shall require me to return to a private station I will give your Lordship no possible trouble but solicit His Majesty's permission to retire from his service as under such circumstances of bodily infirmities I will never receive the public money or take the reward of other men's labours.

124.   *Sick and Wounded Board to Admiralty*

Office for Sick and Wounded Seamen, 9 December 1795

We request you will be pleased to lay before the Right Honourable the Lords Commissioners of the Admiralty the enclosed extract of a letter dated the 8th instant, which we have received from Doctor Trotter, Physician of the Channel Fleet, representing that he has ordered a proportion of stock and vegetables to be given for the use of the sick to each of the ships belonging to the squadron intended to relieve Rear Admiral Harvey on the coast of France.

In our letter to you dated the 29th of September last, we submitted for their Lordships consideration the propriety of the officers of the Victualling Board at the different ports supplying in future such vegetables as it might be thought necessary to furnish to the crews of His Majesty's ships in addition to what is found by the pursers, and we now beg leave further to submit whether it may not also be adviseable for such live stock as is judged requisite to be supplied to any of His Majesty's ships, except hospital ships, to be in future provided by the officers beforementioned.

We have already paid bills, out of money appropriated to pay for medicines, bedding, provisions and necessaries, for hospitals and hospital ships, to the amount of £295.1.0 for live stock, put on board the Charon at different times, great part of which appears to have been issued from thence to His Majesty's ships for the use of their sick, as far as we collect from the vouchers sent us, the defectiveness of which cannot perhaps be entirely avoided in issuing discretionary supplies of this kind.

[*Enclosure*]

124a.   *Extract of Letter from Dr Trotter to the Commissioners for Sick and Wounded Seamen dated 8th December 1795*

This squadron being intended to relieve Rear Admiral Harvey, and as it is probable the Medusa cannot be ready for sea as an hospital for a length of time, I have thought it necessary to order a proportion of stock and vegetables to be given to each for the use of the sick.

The ships now here are in perfect health, but from the time it is expected for them to remain on the coast of France the scurvy may return and it is my duty to use the proper precautions should this be the case.

[*Endorsement*]

10 December. Their Lordships are much surprised at the measure taken by Dr Trotter as their Lordships are unapprized of any squadron being ordered to proceed to the relief of Admiral Harvey or for any other service and that the Dr ought not to have exercised any direction of the nature alluded to.

That in future the supplies will be ordered through the regular channel.

That in case any squadron should hereafter be ordered, Dr Trotter will receive a communication from the commanding officer of the term for which the supplies are to be provided.

125.   *Sick and Wounded Board to Admiralty*

1 January 1796

We have received your letter of the 26th ultimo signifying the directions of the Right Honourable the Lords Commissioners of the Admiralty for us to order a proper supply of vegetables, refreshments and antiscorbutics (in addition to the quantity usually granted) to be supplied to the men now serving on board the ships named in the margin, who were lent to complete the complement of the ships of the squadron under the command of the Honourable Vice Admiral Cornwallis, during the late cruize.

We beg you to inform their Lordships that on receipt of your beforementioned letter, we gave immediate orders for a supply of oranges and lemons being forwarded to Haslar, and desired Dr Johnston to give directions for the seamen belonging to the said ships, who stood in need of them, being liberally supplied therewith, but as we were informed by your letter of the 10th instant that in future all supplies of stock and vegetables would be ordered through the proper channels, we have not given directions for any vegetables to be provided for those ships, the place used for the receipt and issues of them having been given up, in consequence of our having intimated to Dr Johnston that they were no longer to be furnished by us.

We beg to observe that we have received a letter from Dr Johnston dated 31st ultimo informing us that the fleet under Sir Alan Gardner's command appears to be free of scorbutic complaints at present.

[*Endorsement*]

2 January. Victualling Office to provide the beforementioned. Physician of the Fleet to point out to the agent at Portsmouth the quantity ncessary.

126.   *Harvey to Bridport*

Prince of Wales, Spithead, 3 January 1796

I have the honour to acquaint you that I arrived yesterday at Spithead with the squadron under my command, having embarked on board the different ships of the squadron the troops that were on the Isle Dieu and it was very fortunate during the embarkation that the weather was favourable, for with the usual gales that prevailed on the coast it would have been impracticable. I am sorry I have it not in my power to announce to your Lordship any success. The only matter of that kind has been the recapture of the Albion Jamaica ship by the Orion and a part[1] of a Conventional brig taken by La Pomone when the Latona, Melampus and Thalia and Aguilon were in sight.

The Latona and Melampus had a long chase and drove them into Rochefort at that time the brig was taken by La Pomone.

I have great satisfaction in acquainting you that the squadron has been very healthy during the long cruise, which was I think chiefly owing to the refreshments that were sent out and partly to the shelter we took in Quiberon Bay during the hard gales that prevailed in October and part of November. Indeed, had the squadron been at sea during the whole time they must long since have been crippled and unfit for service.

127. *Seymour to Spencer*

Admiralty, 4 January 1796[2]

I was about writing to congratulate your Lordship on the safe arrival of Harvey's squadron in port and of our being delivered from the cares which the employment of our fleet at Quiberon had made us experience when I had the mortification to learn that those scenes of anxiety and disappointment were to be resumed. Two days ago when Warren came to town he admitted that it was at present impracticable to land any stores upon that coast and we in consequence directed the arms etc. which had been put on board the squadron under Captain Robinson[3] to be landed, but it is now determined that some attempt should be made to effect that point and we are called upon to say when it will be possible for us to furnish a force sufficient to drive the enemy's fleet from Quiberon, supposing then to be in possession of that anchorage. The answer to this question appears to me obvious, that while it is an object of the Government to give protection to the outward bound convoys it is impossible to recall the orders given to Gardner and that it will be nearly so to collect a sufficient number of ships before the probable time of his return to match the squadron which the French may send to sea or to Quiberon from Brest and L'Orient. Should the Government continue to wish our fleet to be employed upon the coast in the Bay during the winter we may prepare the ships for that purpose and on Gardner's return have them in readiness to proceed under Lord

---

[1]Harvey refers to the element of prize money due to *La Pomone*.
[2]Dated 1795.
[3]Mark Robinson (d. 1834). Lieutenant 1776; Captain 1790; Rear-admiral 1807; Vice-admiral 1812; admiral 1825.

Bridport or Cornwallis, and Warren's frigates may by that time be equipped for the service on which they have so long been employed. Sir John wishes Keats (during his absence) to have the charge of the Pomone, Anson, Concorde and Galatea for that service but is desirous of giving them orders, which I conceive cannot be admitted, both because you had decided that on his return he was to cease to have his broad pendant and because, exclusive of the irregularity of the measure, it would be depriving Keats of an opportunity of adding to the credit he has obtained in the minds of all those who have been employed with him, though his not being the senior has prevented the world from knowing how ably he has served.

[*Endorsed as received on the 5th and answered the same day*]

128.   *Henry Harvey to Admiralty*

Prince of Wales, Spithead, 5 January 1796

I enclose you a letter which I have received from Doctor Trotter Physician to the Fleet stating that a supply of vegetables for the use of the seamen serving in His Majesty's Ships lately arrived from sea under my command would be highly beneficial to their health.

I have therefore to request that their Lordships will be pleased to give such directions as they may think proper in order that the seamen may have the supply of vegetables which the Doctor thinks will be of such importance to them.

[*Enclosure*]

128a.   *Trotter to Harvey*

Portsmouth, 4 January 1796

Although the ships of the squadron under your command have brought into port a smaller number of sick than could have been expected, from the weather they have experienced and their long absence from England, it would still appear of the first importance to their health that every ship's company should have an allowance of vegetables in addition to that usually furnished by the purser. For this purpose I would beg leave to propose that on every fresh-beef day, two hundred weight of cabbages and a half a hundred weight of onions should be boiled in the broth of each ship of the line and an equal proportion for smaller ships. This form of diet after a fortnight's use might be changed for the common allowance.

It is worth remark that the savoy cabbage, from the mildness of the winter is in great plenty and perfection in this neighbourhood. The cases of scurvy in the squadron which have been numerous have all been successfully treated with aid of lemons and confirm the general reports already collected on this important subject.

129.   *Seymour to Spencer*

Admiralty, 6 January 1796

I can have no doubt of the practicability of our fleet occupying the anchorage of Quiberon the whole year round but I have many of that being an object of sufficient importance to purchase at the rate at which we shall attain it, for to hold it with security it will be necessary for us to constantly employ at that port as many ships as the enemy is capable of putting to sea, besides those which will be necessary for the protection of the supplies required there, as well as to replace such as may be in need of docking or refitting. On looking to the list of the fleet it appears fully equal to that service but when I turn my thoughts to that of the West Indies, where the change of system in conducting the war will not only require more active ships for the present but may eventually lead us into a situation which will require the support of a very large fleet,[1] I am led to fear that we shall have some difficulty in providing for all these objects and by making Quiberon so principal a point in our arrangements we shall lose all the advantages which we have so long promised to ourselves from active cruising squadrons, the success of which distinguished the early part of your administration.

Could a sufficient force be spared for the purpose of establishing a post at Quiberon, there is no doubt but that it would interrupt the coasting trade in that neighbourhood but during the winter it is not possible, I apprehend, to effectually block up their principal ports and Harvey has proved to us how very difficult it is to throw the supplies into France which the Royalists have been taught to expect from us, for he was several weeks endeavouring to do so.

[*Endorsed as received on the 7th and answered the same day*]

---

[1]Spencer wrote to Dundas at some length on the subject. *Spencer Papers*, III, 223.

130.   *Dr Blair[1] to Admiralty*

Somerset Place, 4 February 1796

Doctor Blair presents his compliments to Mr Nepean, is sorry that the statement respecting the lemon juice is not so full as it would have been had there been more time.

He is convinced from the conversation he had with Mr Cherry[2] that the lemon juice must at first be prepared and packed by the Sick and Hurt Board, very great attention being necessary till the workmen get into the way of it.

[*Enclosures*]

130a.   *Remarks on the intended general supply of lemon juice to the fleet as an article of diet for the prevention of scurvy.*

Preliminary Observations

About two years since it was mentioned as a probable supposition, that a seaman who daily consumes a given proportion of lemon juice will never have the scurvy, let the other parts of his diet consist of what they will.

From trials since made this supposition may now be considered as an established fact.

Mode of Supply

Guarding against adulteration. In procuring this article it is absolutely necessary that it should be genuine, and the most certain method of guarding against adulteration is to have the juice squeezed under the eyes of proper officers, which precaution has been taken hitherto.

The difference of expence between squeezing the lemons abroad and at home amounts nearly to the freight of the lemon skins.

To keep an establishment abroad to see the juice squeezed and packed would probably cost more than the above mentioned freight, and there would be much more danger of adulteration, because the preparation and package would then be removed from under the eye of the board.

Quantity required

Three quarters of an ounce was the quantity supplied to the four ships on which the trial was made. This quantity was found sufficient to

[1]Blair was a Commissioner for Sick and Wounded Seamen.
[2]Chairman of the Victualling Board.

prevent the Scurvy in all the ships except the Suffolk; as this ship made a direct passage from England to Madras, Admiral Rainier found it necessary to increase the allowance in a few cases.

One ounce of lemon juice may therefore be fixed on at present, as the proportion required for each man daily.

Expence of this Lemon Juice

The Paper No.1 is a tender for lemon juice, from which it appears that in the most plentiful season it may be had at four shillings per gallon.

This sum may therefore be taken as the probable price of lemon juice, squeezed in London; and perhaps by contracting for the lemons, it may be had still lower, though at present the freight and insurance are high.

It is proposed that those seamen only shall have a regular allowance of lemon juice who are upon spirits or wine.

Mr Cherry mentions 60,000 seamen as the probable number at present upon spirits or wine; and therefore 60,000 ounces is the required daily allowance of lemon juice, and 171,093 gallons is the required annual allowance.

The price of this quantity of lemon juice at four shillings per gallon is £34,218.

Sugar

To make the above lemon juice into punch negus, or sherbet, will require a daily allowance of two ounces of sugar to each man.

The sugar supplied with the lemon juice already sent was good muscovado or raw sugar.

The annual allowance of sugar for 60,000 men is 43,800,000 ounces, or 24,441 hundred weight. The price paid per hundred weight was sixty four shillings so that the whole expense of the annual allowance of sugar, at the above price, is £78,211; as the duty is not to be taken into account there ought to be a proportionable deduction from the above sum.

Articles which may be discontinued upon the introduction of Lemon Juice.

Essense of Malt

I received from Mr Cherry the printed Paper No. 2, from which it appears that the Victualling Board is at present authorised to supply a quantity of the above article, to the amount of £37,682 and I understand that ships abroad are actually so supplied. The proportion for foreign service amounts to £22,609.

The whole of this supply ought to be discontinued, being very little use in preventing the scurvy, and liable to great abuse.

Notwithstanding what is mentioned of the surgeons being required to account to the Commissioners of the Sick and Hurt for the expenditure of this article, not a word was known of the matter in that office until I brought in the paper this day.

There is no other article which could with propriety be discontinued entirely at present.

About 150 tons of *sour croat* were issued last year; this costs about £1,350; as it is both antiscorbutic and nutritious, it ought not to be discontinued.

A little mustard is supplied for East India voyages, which is very proper.

Articles of diet which may be diminished

It appears improper to diminish any other articles of seamen's diet except oatmeal, and even that is now doubtful, as I understand that molasses are at present served in lieu of half the oatmeal.

The officers of the navy will be the best judges in this matter; the question to be determined is whether or not the molasses and oatmeal now allowed are actually consumed by the seamen.

If any other article of diet is discontinued some other article equally nutritious ought to be substituted for it. Seamen's diet upon the whole is not too plentiful.

The value of a seaman's annual allowance of oatmeal at the price given by the Victualling Board is 17 shillings nearly.

The annual saving from discontinuing half the allowance of oatmeal to 110,000 men is £46,750.

The whole saving on the		
discontinuance of the essence of malt is	£37,682	
and on half the oatmeal	46,750	
		84,432
The whole expence of the sugar is	£ 78,211	
The whole expence of the lemon juice	34,218	
		112,429
Expence not compensated		£27,997
Deduct the duty of the sugar		

Board by which these Stores should be supplied

The Victualling Board may without any difficulty supply the sugar; but as the lemon juice requires to be squeezed and mixed with a proportion of spirit, and then packed in bottles with much care, it seems doubtful whether it would not be better to continue it for some time under the Sick and Hurt Board.

This may be done at the Soup House, or other convenient warehouse, and may then be either delivered to officers appointed by the Victualling Board, and sent to the different ships in their hoys, or it may be conveyed to the Royal hospitals and thence sent on board the different ships. Charging it on the pursers and superintending the expenditure ought to rest with the Victualling Board.

130b.   *Blair to Nepean*

Somerset Place, 6 February 1796

Doctor Blair presents his compliments to Mr Nepean, begs leave to send him a seaman's allowance of lemon juice and sugar mixed up in the three different modes of punch, negus and sherbert; in one or other of which it is intended that it should be served to them. Perhaps Mr Nepean or their Lordships may wish to examine it. The lemon juice is a specimen kept in the office of that which was sent on distant voyages.

The board proposes inserting the advertisements on Monday, in order to give the merchants as much time as possible.

131.   *Sick and Wounded Board to Admiralty*

Office for Sick and Wounded Seamen, 16 February 1796

We have received your letter of the 14th instant, suggesting the propriety of using square bottles for packing the lemon juice. We beg to acquaint you, for the information of the Right Honourable the Lords Commissioners of the Admiralty that we have maturely considered this matter, and give the preference to bottles of a cylindrical form because they are much less liable to breakage than bottles with flat sides of equal thickness: strong half gallon bottles, stowed in cases, with a separated square for each bottle, are what we propose to employ.

132.   *Spencer to Gardner*

Admiralty, 25 February 1796

I write a line by the cutter which takes this packet out to you just to say that we have two objects in view in the instructions we send for your guidance. One is the chance of falling in with the Dutch outward bound fleet, which I suppose from the intelligence we have received is destined either to the Cape or to the West Indies and from going north about will be likely either to make the Western Islands or pass a little way to the westward of them; the other the protection of our homeward bound Jamaica fleet, who were to sail from that island the 15th of January last under convoy of one frigate, the Penelope. Both these objects you will see are of great importance and I think the time you will be on the station assigned seems likely enough in all probability to cover them both. The Dutch fleet sailed on the 23rd from the Texel and, on a moderate calculation, going north about with a fair wind may probably reach the latitude you are hereby directed to cruise on in about 16 or 20 days; I reckon you will remain about that situation till towards the 24th or 25th of March, unless anything should happen to bring you from it and I should imagine that if they have a good passage and do not fall in with a squadron which we have sent to intercept them if possible they will by that time have passed to the southward of that latitude.

133.   *Sick and Wounded Board to Admiralty*

Office for Sick and Wounded Seamen, 11 March 1796

Doctor Cochrane, surgeon and agent for Sick and Wounded Seamen at Falmouth, having represented to us the necessity on account of the increase of patients of some further provision being made for the accommodation of sick and wounded seamen at Falmouth, we directed him to make inquiry amd let us know whether any house could be rented to serve as a temporary hospital and we beg leave to enclose for the information of the Right Honourable Commissioners of the Admiralty a copy of a letter dated the 5th instant which we have received from him and copy of an estimate for erecting a temporary hospital, the expence of which amounts to the sum of £179.9.6, and as there appears a necessity for some steps to be taken without delay to provide for the reception of such patients as may be sent on shore at Falmouth, we request permission to recommend to their Lordships our being authorised to cause a temporary hospital to be erected as proposed by Dr Cochrane, unless their Lordships should think proper to sanction our renting the land mentioned in our letter to you of the 2nd of February last, for the purpose of building an hospital on it.

[Endorsement]

Approve of the proposal.

[*Enclosure*]

133a.   *Trotter to Sick and Wounded Board*

Falmouth, 5 March 1796

... In consequence of your letter of the 26th February I have made every enquiry for a house proper for a temporary hospital for the sick and wounded seamen but in vain. If there is an empty house it is refused for this use or from the inhabitants' clamour against the proprietor who may incline to let one.

Under the circumstances, as it is absolutely necessary that something should be done immediately from the number of sick increasing and which may be the case for some time, I see no other alternative than erecting as soon as possible a wooden double shed, in the roughest style adjoining the present building capable of containing 50 men.

With this view I have employed a carpenter to furnish me with an estimate which amounts to £179-9-6 and he says the whole may be done in four or five weeks.

Considering the lumber to be used here will be equally suited for the intended hospital the difference will be only in the carpenters work, which is trifling compared to the advantages that will result to the service. Indeed I am so harassed to find quarters for those the hospital cannot contain that I trust you will readily agree to do everything for the men's as well as my own convenience, for at present matters are very uncomfortable to both.

Another cartel came in here last night and have landed twenty-one men who are so bad with fluxes and fever that I have been obliged to scatter the men belonging to the squadron and convalescents over the town to make room in the duty hovel we have for the worst cases as no person will receive them.

I shall be glad if you will send the iron cradles and bedding as soon as you come to a determination respecting the plan I propose.

P.S. At present on this station: frigates 11 and a 44 gun ship, with gun boats, luggers etc.

134.   *Spencer to Hood*

Admiralty, 20 March 1796

Desirous at all times of showing every mark of attention in my power to the wishes of Lord Chatham and understanding from your Lordship that had the present vacancy at Greenwich Hospital taken place while he presided at the Admiralty he had intimated his intention of recommending you to the King for that appointment I shall on that ground feel great satisfaction in fulfilling Lord Chatham's intention by laying before His Majesty your Lordship's pretensions to succeed Sir Hugh Palliser.

My satisfaction would have been more complete on this occasion if I could have removed the impression made by the conduct your Lordship thought proper to adopt when you were about to resume your command in the Mediterranean last year. I am however perfectly ready and willing in this instance to pass over an occasion concerning which it is impossible for me ever to alter my opinion and to draw His Majesty's attention only to those antecedent public services which had deservedly entitled your Lordship to so high a credit in your profession.

135.   *George III to Spencer*

Windsor, 20 minutes past 7 a.m., 23 March 1796

The answer of Earl Spencer to the letter of application for the Government of Greenwich Hospital from Lord Hood is so liberal and at the same time so just that though the last military transaction of Lord Hood greatly tarnished his former good conduct I will not object to his receiving this employment. Earl Spencer will therefore give him notice that he may appear at the levée this day on his appointment.

136.   *Warren to Admiralty*

La Pomone, Falmouth, 24 March 1796

I beg leave to inform you that on the 15th instant in consequence of my letter to their Lordships from Falmouth I stood over to the French coast in search of the Artois, who joined me on the 18th and on the 20th at daybreak, having discovered from the masthead several sail of vessels in the S.S.E, the Saints bearing N. by E. 3 or 4 miles, I made the signal to the squadron under my command, consisting of the ships named in the margin [*Artois, Galatea, Anson*] for a general chase and upon our nearer approach perceived them to be a convoy of the enemy steering in for the land. At 10 a.m., being up with part of the merchant ships, I captured four and ordered the Valiant lugger to proceed with them to the nearest port. I continued in pursuit of the men of war who were forming in line ahead to windward and kept working to come up with the enemy, who I soon perceived were endeavouring to preserve their distance from us and to avoid an action by their tacking at the same time with our ships but being at length arrived within half gunshot to leeward, the two squadrons engaged and passed each other upon opposite tacks. Immediately upon our sternmost ship being clear of the enemy's line I made the signal to tack and gain the wind, which by making a very short board on the starboard tack was obtained. Perceiving them rallying round the commodore close in shore and beginning to form again I made the signal for ours in close order to endeavour to break their line by cutting off the rear ships and directed the Galatea to lead course for that purpose. But the enemy bore away and made all sail possible from us and stood into the narrow part of the Raz de Fontenay among the rocks. I was, however, enabled to cut off their rear ship. Night approaching, and being unacquainted with the passage, I did not think it proper to continue the pursuit further at the risk of losing some of our ships in so difficult a pass.

137.   *Admiralty to Victualling Board*

29 March 1796

[*Abstract of order*]

To cause the different squadrons of His Majesty's ships to be supplied for 14 days after their return from every cruise with cabbage and onions.

138.   *Gardner to Spencer*

Portsmouth, 30 March 1796

I had the honour this morning of receiving your Lordship's private letter of the 25th ultimo which I find was forwarded by a cutter that was sent in quest of me after I had sailed from St. Helens with the Mediterranean and West Indian convoys which I had the good fortune to escort safely across the Bay, and as far to the southward as I was directed to see them, and parted from the latter on the first instant; and having received information from Mr. Nepean of the sailing of the Jamaica convoy on the 15th January it was my intention after separating from the outward bound convoy not to have returned immediately home with the squadron but to have stood to the northward and westward of the Western Islands and to have cruised in that track until the 25th instant in the hope of meeting with the Jamaica convoy or the Dutch outward bound fleet supposed to have sailed north about; but the accident which happened on the 8th instant to Sans Pareil and Triumph's lower masts frustrated my intentions and in the crippled state of those ships I thought it prudent to proceed homewards with them under as easy sail as possible and I got into the latitude of the Channel on the 16th twelve degrees to the westward and did not reach St. Helens until nine days after, at which time the Jamaica convoy must have been at sea ten weeks, the usual length of a passage from that island.

139.   *Colpoys to Admiralty*

London, at Spithead, 14 May 1796

You will please to acquaint the Lords Commissioners of the Admiralty with my arrival here accompanied by His Majesty's ships named in the margin [*Caesar, Prince, Fame, Pompee, Bellerophon, Impregnable, Niger*] the Melpomene and Thalia frigates having separated from the squadron at different times in chase in the course of the last week (the whole of which the weather has been very bad) the defects of the line of battle ships increasing from day to day and the weather not giving me any hopes of being able to keep my station I thought it most prudent to return into port.

140.   *Seymour to Spencer*

Portsmouth, 14 May 1796

As some difficulty attends the procuring French pilots when ships are suddenly ordered upon that coast, I have prevailed upon Sir P. Parker to order a return to be made to him of those now employed in the fleet and have desired him to receive them all into the Royal William.[1] An Admiralty order will be required for the purpose of accomplishing my plan, which, if you approve, I shall beg you to send to him. It is that all

---

[1] Guardship at Portsmouth.

those who profess themselves to be pilots should undergo some sort of examination and on being found equal to taking charge of a man of war that they should be enrolled as such and received on board the Royal William, where a berth may be fitted up for their reception and where they may mess together, which would not only tend to their comfort but their improvement by conversing about their profession. When a ship is ordered upon the coast of France a pilot should be sent on board her from this number and on the return of that ship the man should go back to the Royal William. While they are on board the ship at sea they should be paid as pilots and when at Spithead in the guardship should be borne for A.B.

[*Endorsed as received on the 15th and answered an the 18th*]

141.   *Keats to Warren*

Galatea, at sea, 19 May 1796

In execution of your order of the 17th to reconnoitre and ascertain the force of the enemy in Brest Water I arrived with the Galatea and Valiant lugger off the Porquet last night but finding when the weather cleared away as we entered the channel this morning between St. Mathews Point and those rocks three frigates, two ships and a brig corvette at anchor in Bertheaume Road, some of which made preparations to get under sail I could not proceed much nearer the Goulet than St. Mathews Point. We had, however, by varying our situation a pretty distinct view of the ships in Brest Road. Their force as far as my own judgment and that of my officers go (and I believe it is pretty correct) consists of eight ships of the line, five or six frigates or cut down ships and four or five corvettes. One only had her yards and topmasts struck, the others appeared to be complete in their masts and rigging and apparently ready for sea.

Besides the abovementioned men of war I saw about a dozen merchant vessels and transports of various sizes at anchor, seemingly rather higher up.

142.   *Sick and Wounded Board to Admiralty*

Office for Sick and Wounded Seamen, 25 May 1796

We request you will be pleased to acquaint the Right Honourable the Lords Commissioners of the Admiralty that we are ready to begin delivering the packages containing lemon juice to the Victualling Board, agreeably to the arrangement proposed in our letter to you of the 11th March, and approved by their Lordships and we request their Lordships will give directions to that Board to receive the said packages into their store rooms as inconvenience begins to be experienced from want of room at the warehouses where the bottling and packing of the juice is now carrying on.

As their Lordships were pleased to interest themselves about the mode of packing this article, we have sent one of the boxes for their inspection; and we beg of you to observe that 88 of these boxes will contain the proper allowance for 600 men for six months, and will require for their stowage a cubical space of between seven and eight feet.

The quantity of juice intended for the general use of the ships' company amounts, as has been already stated in our letters above referred to, to 14,000 gallons and will suffice for 10,666 men for six months; from which their Lordships will be enabled to judge what number of ships can be supplied with lemon juice in the course of the present season, as well as the quantity of sugar necessary to be provided by the Victualling Board; and we beg leave to suggest the expediency of our being acquainted with the names of the ships so supplied that we may send proper instructions to their surgeons on that head.

The whole process of squeezing and preparing the juice having been conducted on the present occasion with great care and without precipitation, and the bottles being of uncommon strength, we are under no apprehensions of its receiving any damage or suffering any diminution of its virtues though it should be kept for a very great length of time.

[*Endorsement*]

26 May. Send copy to Victualling Board. Direct them to receive the cases into their stores and to furnish the names of the ships and vessels to which the lemon juice is to be served agreeably to the request of the Commissioners for Sick and Wounded.

143.   *Victualling Board to Admiralty*

Victualling Office, 27 May 1796

We have received your letter of the 26th instant inclosing one which you had received from the Commissioners for Sick and Wounded Seamen, acquainting you for the information of the Right Honourable the Lords Commissioners of the Admiralty that they were ready to begin delivering the packages containing lemon juice agreeably to the proposed arrangement, and signifying their Lordships direction to us to cause the said packages to be received into our stores, and to furnish the names of the ships and vessels to which the lemon juice shall be served agreeably to the request of the said Commissioners.

In reply to which we beg leave to acquaint you that we are entirely ignorant of the arrangement that has been made and of almost every circumstance respecting the business except what has transpired in a conversation with the Sick and Hurt Board; and we have therefore to request you will be pleased to move their Lordships to inform us of the particulars of the arrangement and to give us full instructions upon the subject.

With regard to the suggestion made to the Commissioners for Sick and Hurt for their being acquainted by us with the names of ships furnished with lemon juice in order to their sending proper instructions to the surgeons on that head, we beg leave to submit to their Lordships whether it would not be more expedient for the instructions to be forwarded by that Board to us in order to our sending the same with the lemon juice, as otherwise during the interval between the time of putting the juice on board, acquainting them therewith, and their sending the instructions to the surgeons, the ships may sail and much inconvenience arise for the want of proper directions for the use of the juice.

[*Endorsements*]

20 May. Direct them to receive the packages into their stores and distribute it to the ships in such proportions according to their respective rates and services as shall be pointed out by the Sick and Hurt who will be directed to supply them with that information and also with instructions to the surgeons for the use of it.

Orders conformably to the Sick and Hurt.

144.   *Victualling Board to Admiralty*

Victualling Office, 15 June 1796

The Right Honourable the Lords Commissioners of the Admiralty having been pleased to direct us by their orders of the 6th and 7th instant to cause a proper supply of lemon juice to be sent on board His Majesty's ships Mercury and Adventure and the Commissioners for Sick and Hurt Seamen having on the 3rd instant caused ninety cases, each containing eighteen two quart bottles of the said juice – which quantity is all that we have hitherto received from that board and is only sufficient for the supply of about six hundred men for six months – to be delivered into our stores at Deptford, we beg leave to acquaint you that on the receipt of their Lordships' beforementioned orders we gave directions for the juice to be forwarded to Portsmouth by land carriage and on the same day directed our agent to cause a proportion thereof to be supplied to the Mercury and Adventure respectively as soon as it arrived, at the rate of one ounce of juice to each man daily for six months, agreeable to which ratio we were informed by the Sick and Hurt Board that the same was to be issued.

We understand however by a letter which we have this morning received from our agent that immediately upon the arrival of the juice he caused the proper quantities to be shipped, but that the Mercury being under way before the vessel laden therewith could get alongside, Captain Byng[1] refused to take any part of it on board.

[*Endorsement*]   18 June. Acknowledge receipt.

145.   *Victualling Board to Admiralty*

Victualling Office, 6 September 1796

Our agent at Portsmouth having informed us by his letter of the 5th instant that in consequence of one he received on the day preceding from Doctor Trotter, Physician to the Fleet, acquainting him that the Right Honourable the Lords Commissioners of the Admiralty had been pleased to authorise him (the Doctor) to exercise his discretion in the supply of vegetable refreshments to the ships and desiring that the four named in the margin [*Princess Royal, Argonaut, Swiftsure, Arethusa*], which are recently returned from foreign voyages, might be supplied with the usual allowance, he had accordingly given orders for their being furnished with the same proportion as – in consequence of a letter we received from Doctor Trotter dated the 3rd April last – we directed should be issued in the case of ships composing the Channel fleet returning from a cruise, being at the rate of fifty pounds of cabbages and greens and ten pounds of onions per day for every hundred men on board each ship. We have to request you will be pleased to acquaint their Lordships therewith and that you will move them to signify to us whether our agent is to comply with any demands that may be made by Doctor Trotter of the like nature in future.

[1]George Byng, Viscount Torrington (d. 1831). Lieutenant 1790; Captain 1795; Rear-admiral 1814; Vice-admiral 1825.

[*Endorsement*]

7 September. To direct their agent accordingly, reporting from time to time the different applications he may receive for that purpose.

146.   *Gardner to Spencer*

Royal Sovereign, at sea, 16 September 1796

Having obtained yesterday afternoon some intelligence which I think may be depended upon from the master of a small vessel under American colours who left Brest the 13th instant, and having some reason to believe this person has been employed for the purpose, I have taken copies of the papers he put into my hands and forward them in my official letter to Mr. Nepean (by Lord Henry Powlett of the Thalia) together with the originals, which by desire of Thomas Le Feuvre, the master of the above vessel, I have put under cover to Mr. William Huskisson.[1] If the Thalia would not be wanted for other service I have to hope she may be ordered to join me again, so soon as her water and provisions are completed, as I have before stated the want of ships of this class.

Having now been nearly five weeks at sea, in case the enemy at Brest should delay their sailing a month longer, I think it proper thus early to submit to your Lordship's consideration the state of the water at that time throughout the squadron, which will be so much reduced as to put it out of my power to pursue the enemy to any considerable distance to the westward should they escape us in the night, in thick or foggy weather, or by passing to the northward or southward of the British squadron as it may happen to be, the doing of which the odds are greatly in their favour.

It is true I am directed by my last orders when any of the ships under my command are in want of water or provisions to send them by two at a time into Cawsand Bay to complete, but, situated as I am at present, with an enemy ready to put to sea from Brest equal if not superior to the force under my orders, with a probability of their being joined by Monsieur de Richery's squadron,[2] I do not think I should be justified in sending any of my squadron into port under the very great uncertainty of their being able to join me again. This is a matter (according to my

---

[1]Under-Secretary at War.
[2]Richery's squadron left Toulon in September 1795 and was a concern both in European and West Indian waters until it entered Brest in December 1796.

judgment) of some consideration and having communicated my ideas to your Lordship I beg to submit whether some means may not be devised to obviate the difficulty which in another month I apprehend the squadron will be under; and if the men could be supplied by means of the hospital ship with some refreshments, such as potatoes, onions, cabbages and a few sheep for the sick it would very much contribute to the health of the squadron, an object I suppose of the utmost importance at this juncture.

147.   *Spencer to Gardner*

Admiralty, 23 September 1796

I have to acknowledge the receipt of your letter of the 16th instant and am much obliged to you for it, as well as for the information contained in the enclosure. You will have perceived that the person who gave you that information, being employed on a very hazardous and confidential service, it will be right that as little as possible should be known concerning the manner in which the information is procured and, as he will continue his proceedings for that purpose, it will naturally seem to you to be very necessary that the nature of his employment should be kept secret, even if possible in the fleet.[1]

. . . You will, before this reaches you, have heard of Richery's squadron being at Newfoundland. It is just possible (though not in my opinion very probable) that he may return to France and if so I have great hopes that the position you and Sir R. Curtis will have taken in pursuance of our last orders may give one or other of you a very fair chance of intercepting him. The probability, however, is that he has proceeded to the coast of America and the West Indies and I do not therefore feel in any degree apprehensive on a comparison of the strength of your squadron and what the enemy may be able to push out of Brest.

148.   *Admiralty to Gardner*[2]

7 October 1796

Their Lordships having received intelligence of the sailing of two sail of the line from Rochefort on the 20th of last month and of three more from

---

[1]In the following year Le Feuvre decided that he had become such an object of suspicion that it was no longer safe for him to visit French ports. See G. R. Balleine, *The Tragedy of Philippe d'Auvergne* (London, 1973), 86.

[2]Addressed to Gardner at Spithead.

L'Orient on the 30th, said to have been bound to Brest, I have their Lordships' commands to desire you let me know, whether by any observations made by the ships which you had sent to look into Brest or by information you may have obtained by other means, you have had reason to believe that they have arrived in that port. Their Lordships, having also received intelligence that a great number of transports have arrived at Brest from the southward, it is their further direction that you let me know whether you have any reason to believe this intelligence to be true.

149. Bridport to Spencer

Cricket Lodge, 24 October 1796

As the Royal George is returning to Spithead I wish she might not again proceed to sea without my flag, but on this subject I will say no more, trusting that your Lordship will call upon me when His Majesty's service shall require me to repair to my duty.

[*Endorsed as answered on the 26th*]

150. Spencer to Bridport

Admiralty, 26 October 1796

I expect Sir Roger Curtis with part of the fleet now out to return in a few days and we shall then, I believe, have occasion to collect a squadron of ten or twelve sail of the line to relieve the other which remains out, of which, of course, the Royal George will be one and, as your Lordship wishes it, I shall feel great satisfaction in seeing that, or a larger squadron if circumstances should make it necessary, under your orders. When the ships in question, therefore, are come in we shall call upon your Lordship to hoist and again take the command of them preparatory to their going to sea. This is at present my idea but of course I need not observe that any such arrangement must necessarily be subservient to whatever change of circumstances may arise.

151. Victualling Board to Admiralty

Victualling Office, 8 November 1796

The Right Honourable the Lords Commissioners of the Admiralty having been pleased to direct us, by their order of the 7th instant, to cause such of His Majesty's ships and vessels as may from time to time be destined for foreign stations to be supplied with a quantity of lemon juice in proportion to their respective complements and length of voyage, and to let their Lordships know the regulations under which the same is at present issued; we have to request you will inform their Lordships that we shall pay due attention to their directions by the furnishing of lemon juice and sugar to such of His Majesty's ships and vessels as may be ordered upon foreign stations accordingly.

With respect to the regulations under which lemon juice and sugar are supplied, we beg leave to add that as soon as the beer on board the ship – directed to be furnished with the two former articles – shall have been expended they are to be issued to the ship's company in the proportion of two ounces of sugar and one ounce of lemon juice per man a day, and are to be mixed with the allowance of grog or wine, or to be issued as sherbert, according as the captains in their directions shall think proper to direct; which proportion has been established by the Commissioners for Sick and Wounded Seamen, as stated in their letter to this board of the 8th June last.

For their Lordships' further information we herewith transmit one of the printed instructions which we have caused to be prepared for the government of the pursers of His Majesty's ships and vessels in the issuing, and properly accounting for, the lemon juice and sugar which they may in consequence supply.

152.   *Sick and Wounded Board to Admiralty*

21 November 1796

Having lately caused publication to be made giving notice of our intention to receive tenders from persons willing to furnish us with lemon juice for His Majesty's ships, we request you will acquaint the Right Honourable the Lords Commissioners of the Admiralty therewith, and that we only received one tender for this article; the quantity offered is 10,000 gallons at fifteen shillings per gallon, but we do not think proper on account of the high price to accept such tender, without stating to their Lordships the present stock remaining and receiving their directions on this subject.

Having delivered to the Victualling Board 14,085 gallons of lemon juice for the purpose specified in our letter to you of the 11th March last, there is now remaining in store for the use of the sick on board ships 10,682 gallons. It appears 2,403 gallons have been issued for this service since the middle of April last. Calculating that in store to be issued in like proportion, it is sufficient to last two years and a half.

The juice delivered to the Victualling Board, and that remaining in store, cost seven shillings per gallon.

We addressed letters in the month of September last to our agents at the undermentioned places, desiring them to inquire and let us know what quantity of lime or lemon juice could be procured in a given time, and at what price; and in order to obtain the best possible information we have written to the Commanders in Chief in the West Indies and in the Mediterranean requesting them to favour us with such information as they are able to get on this subject.

Barbadoes
Antigua
Jamaica
Martinique
Lisbon.

153.   *Spencer to Bridport*

Admiralty, 5 December 1796

As the time is approaching when it will be absolutely necessary for Admiral Colpoys and a considerable part of the ships composing his squadron to be relieved from their station off Brest I write a line to your Lordship to apprize you that you may expect soon to be called upon to hoist your flag at Spithead in order to proceed to sea with a squadron for that purpose. As the equipment of the enemy in Brest has lately fallen off from their activity and extent (from what cause is not exactly ascertained), I believe that about twelve or fourteen sail of the line will be as many as need be appropriated at present to this object, but for that as well as for any further particulars which it may be necessary to make part of your Lordship's instructions I must refer you to the official letter you will receive from the Board, only meaning at present to give you as early notice as I could of their intention that your flag should again be hoisted.

154.   *Colpoys to Spencer*

London, at sea, 7 December 1796

The account this morning from Brest looks as if the enemy meant to take the sea air, which if they should, I hope it may be by day light, for to be sure, blocking up a port with 14 hours night is trying work to an admiral's nerves.

155.   *Colpoys to Spencer*

London, at sea, 11 December 1796

Just now the Surprise sloop has joined me from Plymouth with their Lordships' orders to Captain McDougal[1] to proceed to Spithead, there to put himself under the command of Admiral Lord Bridport. When your Lordship and the Board come to consider the reports made to me by Sir John Warren and Sir Edward Pellew of the enemy's force at Brest, and which accompany this I trust I shall be thought justified in not parting at this moment with the Edgar. Should my next account from the lookout frigates give me any reason to suppose that the enemies' intentions – if coming out – may be done away – I shall in that case send in either the Marlborough or Edgar or both according to circumstances.

This last 24 hours we have had very light and variable winds and for some time it seemed disposed to blow from the S.W. Just now it is very moderate and we are in sight of Ushant light, the wind at south. The Board by this conveyance will have extracts from Captain Stopford's journal. He and Sir Harry Neale[2] have acquitted themselves very much to my satisfaction on the station which I allotted to them and have made themselves so well acquainted with the entrance of Brest water as to make it an object to employ them at any time when the necessity of the service may require it on that part of the coast.

The Thalia departed from me some time since in chase. I hope her absence has not been increased by any accident in the course of the severe eastern gale we had.

Sir Edward Pellew accompanied his report of the 8th with a private letter wherein he assures me that from the clearness of the weather I may perfectly depend on the account he sent. He was so near in that a frigate in Camaret Bay fired at him, as did the forts from each side. Three of the line of battle ships hoisted their topsails but did not pursue.

[1]John McDougal (d. 1814). Lieutenant 1772; Captain 1783; Rear-admiral 1805; Vice-admiral 1810.
[2]Sir Harry Neale (1756–1840). Lieutenant 1787; Captain 1793; Rear-admiral 1810; Vice-admiral 1814; Admiral 1830. Originally named Burrard, he took the name of Neale when he married Miss Neale in April 1795. That year he took command of the 38-gun frigate *St Fiorenzo* which had been captured the previous year. He was to be Captain of the Channel fleet in 1808.

I apprehend there must be an embargo at Brest, for none of the fleet, lookout ships or frigates, have spoke with anything from thence for more than a month and as we generally spread from twenty to five and twenty leagues in the day and indeed nearly as much at night, particularly now that we are blessed with moonlight, I don't think anything can well have escaped us.

156.   *Spencer to Bridport*

Admiralty, 19 December 1796

Having some time ago indicated through Lord Hugh Seymour that it was your Lordship's desire, in the event of your commanding a squadron of more than fifteen sail of the line, to have Rear Admiral Pole[1] for your first Captain, that officer was in consequence ordered home from the West Indies; and as it is now intended that your Lordship on your arrival on the station off Brest should have a number of line of battle ships exceeding fifteen under your command, the Board will, if I receive your Lordship's concurrence to the proposal, appoint Admiral Pole to that situation, that he may be ready to go to sea with you when you sail.

I am happy to see by the returns which have reached us today that the ships intended to sail under your orders are all in so forward a state as to give us hope that they may sail by the latter end of the week.[2]

157.   *Bridport to Spencer*

Portsmouth, 20 December 1796

I have received the honour of your Lordship's letter on the subject of Rear Admiral Pole to be my first Captain. Before he went to the West Indies and when I had under my command eighteen ships of the line I judged it was possible that I might have twenty, and under that circumstance I thought of a first Captain, and it being conveyed to me that Rear Admiral Pole wished that situation I was happy in the prospect of being able to concur in his wishes. This I communicated to Lord Hugh Seymour as a measure that would be agreeable both to the Rear Admiral and myself. In order that the appointment might take place and be

[1]Sir Charles Morice Pole (1757–1830). Lieutenant 1777; Captain 1779; Rear-admiral 1795; Vice-admiral 1801; Admiral 1805.
[2]The 19th was a Monday.

justified by the general rule of the service I have to express my wish that twenty ships of the line may be immediately put under my command and that Rear Admiral Pole may receive his commission as first Captain to that fleet. Though I might proceed to sea with a less number, if I may be allowed to judge on the activity of the enemy from the intelligence I have received from the Admiralty for my information, I do not think that twenty ships of the line too many to secure success, supposing the Brest fleet should put to sea and a battle should take place. But this subject must have been so fully weighed that I shall leave it to your Lordship's consideration and the sentiments of the Admiralty and Government.

Whenever your Lordship shall think it expedient to appoint Rear Admiral Pole as my first Captain it will give me particular satisfaction.

I shall sleep on board this night that I might give all possible despatch to the ships at present under my orders.

[Endorsed as received on the 21st]

4

TOWARDS A SYSTEM
20 DECEMBER 1796–13 APRIL 1797

The French expedition that put to sea on 16 December 1796 consisted of 17 ships of the line, 13 frigates, six corvettes and seven transports: in all, 44 ships under Vice-admiral Morard-de-Galles. Between them they carried an estimated 18,000 troops, both infantry and cavalry. The fleet anchored for the night of 16–17 December at the mouth of the Goulet, spread between Camaret and Bertheaume bays, the greater part passing through the passage du Raz during 17 December. As early darkness fell, Morard-de-Galles attempted to divert the remainder of his fleet through the wider passage d'Iroise, but was only partly successful. One 74 was lost on the rocks at the mouth of the passage du Raz with the loss of about 680 lives. The confusion arising from signal guns and firing for distress was enhanced by rockets and guns from the British frigate *Indefatigable* commanded by Edward Pellew who kept ahead of the French as they made their way through the passage du Raz and hauled close round the Saintes. In turn he had sent his two companion frigates to warn Colpoys with his squadron of ships of the line but he had been blown off Ushant, and there was no response. Later correspondence revealed that Colpoys remained in ignorance of the French departure until at least 18 December [163]. In consequence, on the morning of 17 December, Pellew sent a lugger with warning to Falmouth, then sailed for Falmouth himself.[1]

The Admiralty sent the news to Bridport at Portsmouth just after midday on the 20 December [158]. He gave immediate orders to the squadron under his command at Spithead to prepare to sail at the shortest notice [159]. He was ordered to join Colpoys, whom he was to take under his orders, and, in the absence of certain intelligence of the expedition's destination, search for it off Ireland [160] where rebellion was brewing. If he did not find Colpoys, he was still to search off Ireland, ensuring reports of observations of Brest harbour and all other intelligence was sent to the Admiralty [161]. Bridport had hopes of getting out on 24 December [162], but an easterly wind and adverse

---

[1]W. James, *The Naval History of Great Britain from the declaration of war by France in 1793 to the accession of George IV* (6 vols, London, 1859), II, 7–8.

tide combined to prevent him. Indeed the attempt to get from Spithead to St Helens resulted in five ships being involved in collisions, grounding or accidents [164], and he did not make St Helens until 29 December.

By then Vice-admiral Kingsmill, Commander-in-Chief on the coast of Ireland, had written from Cork to the Admiralty to report the arrival of the French fleet in Bantry Bay on 24 December. On the 31st the news was relayed to Bridport [168], who was directed to take all the officers and pilots acquainted with the coast of Ireland into his ships [169]. Colpoys, meanwhile, had searched vainly for the Brest fleet and had chased instead a squadron from Toulon that put into L'Orient. He arrived back at Spithead on 31 December, still in time to reinforce Bridport [170, 171] but not in sufficient numbers either to permit the release of intended escorts for convoys [173], or for admirals in the fleet to feel comfortable about the size of their force. Bridport was able to accumulate only 14 of the line under his immediate command before leaving port, which number, with the need for detachments and the risk of ships parting company during chase, was too small to meet the French fleet in full force [175].

Bridport sailed finally on 3 January 1797. As instructed, he made for Ushant to check reports of the whereabouts of the French; sailed northwest for Cape Clear; looked into Bantry Bay on 9th; unsuccessfully chased two French frigates on the 10th; and returned off Ushant by the 13th where he remained for about a week. On the 13th the last contingent of the French fleet returned into Brest without having landed its army and having lost about a quarter of its ships through foundering, grounding or capture.[1]

Buffeted by heavy seas, Bridport returned at the end of the month to Torbay, whence he was ordered back to Spithead to escape the stormy weather and to refit. Only one ship of the line and five frigates were directed to remain out to safeguard the return of convoys, the East India ships in particular [176, 177]. After all the difficulties of getting out, Bridport was disappointed at the cruise [179]. A French expedition, though kept secret, had been suspected. Yet, when it happened, the British blockading forces had still been taken by surprise. Neither Colpoys off Ushant nor Bridport in Spithead had been able to intercept the main French force. Only the winter weather had prevented the French from taking greater advantage of their departure. The danger posed by an enemy expedition roaming at will on the seas around Britain for almost a month was evident. For some time afterwards sightings of enemy transports were reported to the Admiralty [180].

[1]James, II, 8–24.

Concurrently, criticisms and fresh ideas arose for making the Channel fleet more effective.

The commanders of the frigate squadrons, Warren and Pellew, reporting independently to the Admiralty, both recommended the close blockade of Brest by a British force anchored in Douarnenez bay, immediately to the south of the Goulet. Warren had his idea sown by officers who had blockaded Brest during the Seven Years War [166, 172, 174]. The reunification of the blockading squadrons under a single sea-going commander was also encouraged by an incident that occurred while Bridport had been attempting to intercept the French fleet. On 27 January his squadron had chased and then been left by a British frigate squadron which had made the private recognition signals but failed to respond to Bridport's signals to join him [178]. The squadron was Warren's [187] and he simply had not seen Bridport's signals [190]. Warren and Bridport had been acting under separate orders and had different preoccupations. At the time, however, Bridport was inclined to regard Warren's conduct as disobedience. It was no coincidence, therefore, that at the end of February 1797 Bridport was appointed to the head of a fleet which not only reflected his own command requirement but was sufficient, even after detachments, to meet a French fleet of the size that had sailed for Ireland in December, and included his own squadron of frigates [181].

At that time another expedition was reported to be under preparation in Brest. Bridport was directed to keep those preparations under observation with his own frigates [182]. Flag officers and captains were appointed immediately for a further cruise [183]. Still theory outran practice. Though potentially equipped with 25 ships of the line, by the end of April only 14 were ready for sea and no frigates [184]. Nevertheless reassured and encouraged by Spencer [185], Bridport put to sea again on 3 March to establish a presence off Brest. His frigate captains, led by Sir Harry Neale, once more seized command of the waters close in-shore [186]. They established that preparations in Brest were not so far advanced as intelligence had suggested. Bridport accordingly returned to Spithead on 30 March. For the time being, a squadron was deemed all that was necessary to watch Brest and Sir Roger Curtis was despatched with nine of the line on 6 April.[1]

The intelligence about Brest available to the Admiralty was increased at this time by that emanating from Captain Philip d'Auvergne, Prince de Bouillon [185]. A native of Jersey he had entered the British navy in 1770. He had been captured by the French in 1779 when the *Arethusa*

[1] James, II, 25.

was wrecked on the Brittany coast, and there had met and been adopted by the Duke de Bouillon. In 1794, now a captain of ten years' standing, he was given command of a small squadron operating in the Channel Islands where he maintained contact with the Chouan and French royalist forces. Informers in Brest kept him supplied with information about what was happening in Brest dockyard and harbour with a regularity that became fundamental to the blockade of Brest.[1]

The establishment of a squadron of frigates within the Channel fleet under Bridport unsettled both Warren and Pellew who commanded squadrons operating out of Falmouth and Plymouth and reported directly to the Admiralty. Pellew now felt relieved of some responsibility for the watch on Brest and wanted to be permitted 'to run loose for a cruise' in search of merchant prizes [188]. Spencer, as ever, was sympathetic but skilful in denying him that pleasure [189]. He maintained that the role envisaged for Pellew in the Channel fleet permitted considerable independence [193]. Warren too wanted a cruise 'that we may be thrown into Fortune's way'. Having clearly offended Bridport by his failure to see his signals [190], the last thing he wanted was to be placed under Bridport's command. If he was not to have his liberty under Admiralty authority, he wished to be placed under another commander, preferably Lord Hugh Seymour or Sir John Jervis, on another station [191, 192].

Spencer's response to these requests referred to several imperatives for the blockade: necessities to improve the reliability of intelligence, the range of ships available to the commander off Ushant, and the efficiency of communication between the British forces. Information coming out of Brest indicated a need 'to keep a much stricter and more systematic watch on that port by the means of frigates than we have heretofore done' [189]. The enemy was sending out larger bodies of ships and the British force prepared to meet them had to be increased in size to the same degree. Moreover the information that passed between the observing frigates and the Channel fleet had to be direct, rapid and reliable: in other words, to a standard set by the officer commanding off Brest. Spencer was quite clear on these priorities. The whole demanded a reorganisation of the squadrons available to the Admiralty.

However, the Admiralty did not have Bridport's complete concordance. In his opinion a more strict watch on Brest was not consistent with maintaining a more close blockade. During his recent March

---

[1]Philip d'Auvergne, Prince de Bouillon (d. 1816). Lieutenant 1777; Captain 1784; Rear-admiral 1805; Vice-admiral 1810. At the conclusion of the Napoleonic War, he returned to Bouillon to claim the estates of his father but his claim was rejected. G.R. Balleine, *The Trajedy of Philippe d'Auvergne* (London, 1973).

cruise Bridport had experienced strong easterly winds favourable for the departure of the French fleet from Brest harbour. He pointed out that in such winds British ships of the line could no more keep station off Ushant than frigates could keep station off the mouth of the Goulet. Nor had he any more faith in intelligence. Observations made down the Goulet could be deceptive, while information gleaned from French seamen was liable to be propaganda put out by the French authorities [194]. Bridport's sceptism was based on almost two years' experience. But it had been accepted during those years that the blockade had to be abandoned by ships of the line in the worst winter weather, and that they sought refuge at Spithead even though that anchorage was over 200 miles from Brest and was difficult to get out of in an easterly wind favourable to the French. Yet Bridport had commanded a frigate squadron of observation with his ships of the line for only a single voyage.

Moreover, to these limitations must also be added an arrogance that blinded Bridport to acts of friendship [178] and prevented him from easily making service allies, in particular Warren and Pellew. Had Bridport developed a closer rapport with these frigate commanders, his views might have been different. Their recommendations for the use of Douarnenez bay during north and easterly winds implied a capability of maintaining a close blockade even under winter conditions. Operating from Falmouth and Plymouth, further west than the main fleet base, they were not only less susceptible to easterly winds but half the distance from Brest. They had maintained a watch on the French base that had been denied the main fleet.[1] Their capability, moreover, was favoured by the provisions being made by the Victualling and Sick and Hurt Boards for the prevention of scurvy. Their very desire to be released from the regime of watching Brest reflected demands on the frigate squadrons that had hitherto only occasionally been made on the main fleet.

These were themes that no doubt surfaced in discussions between Bridport and Spencer [194].[2] That Bridport looked back to a former regime while the Board of Admiralty looked forward to a 'stricter and more systematic' system was reflected in the latter's anxiety at the end of March 1797 for all officers of the Channel fleet to remain with their ships in order that they might put to sea with the shortest notice [195]. The Board of Admiralty was conscious of the example set to his subor-

---

[1]For Pellew's operations on the coast of France, see C. Northcote Parkinson, *Edward Pellew, Viscount Exmouth, Admiral of the Red* (London, 1934), 99–248.

[2]No light is shed on these anticipated conversations by the contents of the *Private Papers of George, Second Earl Spencer*, ed. J. S. Corbett and H. W. Richmond (4 vols, NRS, 1913 etc.).

dinates by their admiral, but was ready to tolerate Bridport's deviation from the ideal just as it balanced his other limitations against his more positive qualities [196]. For the time being the Board adhered to Bridport, and indeed early in April was able to present him with a commission as Commander-in-Chief [197]. Howe wrote formally to relinquish the post on 8 April. It was a step that was intended to mark a new beginning.

158. *Admiralty to Bridport*

20 December 1796

My Lords Commissioners of the Admiralty having received intelligence from Sir Edward Pellew that the French fleet had put to sea from Brest on the 16th instant, and had escaped the squadron under the orders of Vice Admiral Colpoys, supposed to have been driven to the westward, I am commanded by their Lordships to acquaint you therewith, and to signify their directions to you to use every means in your power to get His Majesty's ships under your command put into a state of readiness to proceed to sea the moment they shall be in a condition for that purpose.

[*Endorsement*]

By a messenger at ½ past one p.m.

159. *Bridport to Admiralty*

Royal George, Spithead, 21 December 1796

I have received your letter of the 20th instant communicating the intelligence that the French fleet had put to sea from Brest on the 16th instant and had escaped the squadron under the orders of Vice Admiral Colpoys, supposed to be driven to the westward. I have in consequence given directions to the captains of the squadron at Spithead under my orders to use every exertion in getting their several ships ready for sailing at the shortest notice and I trust I shall be able to go to sea on Saturday or Sunday should the wind be favourable, as the report from the Atlas informs me she cannot be ready before Friday next.

160. *Admiralty to Bridport*

22 December 1796

Your Lordship is hereby required and directed to put to sea without loss of time with the ships and vessels named in the margin [*Royal Sovereign, Royal George, Prince George, Formidable, Sans Pareil, Namur, Colossus, Prince, Atlas, Caesar, Mars, Triumph, Orion, Robust, Irresistible, Phoenix, Stag, Proserpine, Triton, Thalia, Unité, Megaera, Incendiary*], and proceed with all possible dispatch down Channel, calling off Plymouth for the Raisonable (the captain of which ship is ordered to join you on your appearance) and use your best endeavours to join Vice Admiral Colpoys upon his rendezvous, a copy of which you will receive herewith, and upon falling in with the Vice Admiral to take him and the ships and vessels belonging to his squadron under your command. In case upon your Lordship's arrival on Vice Admiral Colpoys's rendezvous you should not find the Vice Admiral and have good reason to believe he has quitted his station in quest of the enemy, you are to proceed with, and make a shew of, your force off Brest, remaining there such time as your Lordship shall judge best for the abovementioned purpose, and having so done you are, in case you should not have been able to obtain any certain intelligence of the French fleet being in that neighbourhood, to proceed with the squadron under your command off Cape Clear, sending a frigate into such port in Ireland as you shall judge most likely to gain intelligence of the enemy, and to use your best endeavours to take or destroy them should they be upon that coast; but not obtaining any information thereof which may be relied on, your Lordship is to return with the ships and vessels under your command off Brest, and take such station off that port for the protection of the trade of His Majesty's subjects, and the annoyance of the enemy as you shall judge most eligible, sending to us by every opportunity accounts of your proceedings and the state and condition of the squadron under your command.

161. *Admiralty to Bridport*

24 December 1796

In addition to our orders to you of the 22nd instant, your Lordship is hereby directed, if the Raisonable should not be ready to join you when you appear off Plymouth, to proceed without her to the rendezvous of Vice Admiral Colpoys, and so soon as you shall have joined the Vice

Admiral and taken under your command as many of the ships of the line of Vice Admiral Colpoys' squadron as will complete that under your Lordship's command to 17 sail of the line, you are to proceed off Cape Clear as directed in our orders abovementioned, without losing time in endeavouring to show your force off Brest, and if you should not very soon fall in with the Vice Admiral, you are, without suffering any delay of looking for him, to proced off Cape Clear with the ships now under your command, and to act as directed in that case, in our said order. If on your arrival on Vice Admiral Colpoys' rendezvous you should receive information on which you may depend, that the enemy's squadron is on the coast of Ireland, you are immediately to proceed in quest of it, without proceeding to the Vice Admiral's rendezvous. In addition to the frigates now under your Lordship's orders, you are hereby authorized to take under your command any other two frigates you may meet which are not employed on any particular service, and if you should meet with any of His Majesty's ships near Brest, your Lordship is to direct the captain of one of them to look into port and having so done to proceed to the nearest port in England and send to our Secretary such information of the force remaining there as he may have been able to obtain. If you should receive certain information of the enemy's squadron having returned into port, or of its having gone to the southward so as to make it impossible that it should be destined for Ireland, you are to acquaint us thereon and cruise off Brest till you receive further orders.

162.   *Bridport to Admiralty*

Royal George, at Spithead, 24 December 1796

I have received your letter of the 23rd instant expressing their Lordships' directions that I should report for their information the occasion of the delay in the equipment of His Majesty's ship Prince George. Since that ship has been under my orders I have had two conversations with Captain Irwin[1] and pressed him very strongly to use every exertion in getting ready for sea and by his personal attentions at the dockyard in getting off her stores for foreign service she is now completed, as their Lordships will see by the enclosed report. The Prince George's weekly account stated her not to be ready before Sunday night. She was paid on Friday and the Orion yesterday, which made it impossible for me to move with the ships under my orders before Monday, but in

[1]John Irwin (d. 1812). Lieutenant 1779; Captain 1796.

consequence of Captain Irwin's letter, which was received last night, I made the Night Signal to unmoor and I hope the whole squadron will be passed St. Helens before the close of day.

163. *Admiralty to Kingsmill*[1]

24 December 1796

I am commanded by my Lords Commissioners of the Admiralty to send you the inclosed extract of a letter dated the 18th instant, which I have received from Vice Admiral Colpoys, being the only account of his proceedings that has come to hand since my letter to you of the 22nd instant, and by which it appears he still remained without positive information of the departure of the enemy's fleet from Brest

I have it also in command from their Lordships to acquaint you that Admiral Lord Bridport, if the wind and weather should permit, will put to sea from Spithead tomorrow, or on the following day, with 16 ships of the line, and that his Lordship is directed in case of not receiving any satisfactory information respecting the destination of the enemy's squadron on his getting out of the Channel to proceed with the ships under his command off Cape Clear, in search of the said squadron, and to follow it if it should have proceeded to any part of the coast of Ireland.

164. *Seymour to Spencer*

[St. Helens], 27 December 1796

When I closed my letter yesterday I did not expect to have had an opportunity of writing to you for some time, as the Prince George was then unmoored and she was the only ship likely to prevent the squadron going to sea; the tide, however, served so late and the wind was so far to the southward that very few of the ships got even so low as St. Helens. In the course of working down several accidents took place, which I much feared would have reduced the force of the squadron but I now believe that when the wind moderates we shall move together. The Prince, having missed stays when she, with the Sans Pareil, was close over upon the Isle of Wight shore, came on board her and for

[1]Robert Brice Kingsmill (1730–1805). Formerly Robert Brice: took the surname Kingsmill, that of his wife, on the death of her father in 1766. Lieutenant 1756; Captain 1762; Rear-admiral 1793; Vice-admiral 1794; Admiral 1799. He had fought off Ushant in 1778. Commander-in-Chief on the coast of Ireland 1793–1800; this letter was thus addressed to him at Cork.

some minutes the ships were locked in the most unpleasant way, the bowsprit of the former being placed just before our mainmast. Fortunately the weather was moderate enough to admit of my casting off all our main shrouds but one, when by the Prince anchoring we got clear of each other, the Sans Pareil without having received the most trifling damage and the Prince only such as I trust will be put to rights in the course of this day.

. . . The Atlas got onshore on the Stourbridge sand on the Mother Bank and after sticking for three hours got off without having received any injury and the Formidable was equally lucky after having carried away the Ville de Paris's jib boom and having been hooked to her for some minutes.

. . . It now blows very hard and I have my doubts whether we shall be able to move today, the wind at about S.E. by E., a charming gale for the French if they are not bound for Ireland and I think will produce half the advantage of a victory to us if they are exposed to it.

[*Endorsed as received on the 28th*]

165.   *Seymour to Spencer*

Sans Pareil, St. Helens, 29 December 1796

The squadron has at last reached St. Helens but most unfortunately not till the easterly wind was ended and that the new moon had brought the appearance of very bad weather from the S.W. quarter, where it now blows hard.

[*Endorsed as received on the 30th*]

166.   *Warren to Spencer*

Falmouth, 30 December 1796

I hope you will excuse my taking the liberty of stating that the surest, safest and fastest mode of our fleet blocking up the French would be at any time by their being anchored in the Bay of Douarnenez; a place as well sheltered and as large as our Torbay; the same wind would carry out both fleets and by advancing frigates anchored and relieved occasionally off the Black or Toulinquet Rocks, with a cutter or lugger within them, no enemy could escape without being seen or have the start of us 10 hours. This, however, is no new plan but recommended and stated at full by that able officer, the late Lord Knight,[1] who was long upon that station and knew it fully. I have his remarks in which this circumstance is mentioned and if ever your Lordship should think it of use or worthy your attention I shall have great pleasure in showing it to you.

[Endorsed as received on 2 January and answered the same day]

167.   *Seymour to Spencer*

Sans Pareil, 31 December 1796

The arrival of the Phaeton so soon after that of the San Fiorenzo occasioned such a general sensation throughout our squadron that I could not resist opening Admiral Colpoys' letter to the Board, to which I was prompted not by curiosity only but by the hope that it contained some information which it might have been necessary immediately to communicate to Lord Bridport. Unfortunately the contents of his despatch did not quite come up to the expectations we had formed on hearing Stopford speak of the French fleet through his trumpet, which words owing to the wind, to the distance and to his stuttering we were sanguine enough to interpret in a manner much more favourable to our wishes than when he made his report to me in my cabin.

The wind seems now so determinedly set in to the S.W. with the appearance of bad weather that I cannot help wishing that Admiral Colpoys may come into port, as very little advantage can be derived from his remaining upon his rendezvous with a westerly wind which I think is likely to blow during the whole of this moon.

[Endorsed as received on 1 January]

168.   *Admiralty to Bridport*

31 December 1796

I am commanded by my Lords Commissioners of the Admiralty to acquaint your Lordship that dispatches have been received from Vice Admiral Kingsmill, dated Cork the 29th of this month, giving an account of the arrival of the French fleet on the coast of Ireland, which had anchored in Bantry Bay on the 24th and had sailed from thence on

---

[1]Probably Sir Joseph Knight (d. 1775). Lieutenant 1740; Captain 1746; Rear-admiral 1775. Knighted 1773.

the 27th and had not afterwards been seen, nor had any intelligence been received of its particular point of destination. The force which had anchored in the Bay consisted of 17 sail, the particulars of which, and of the fleet as it sailed from Brest, are described in the inclosed papers.

Their Lordships are desirous that you should be apprized of this intelligence with all possible dispatch. I therefore send it by a special messenger, and I have their Lordships' commands to signify their direction to you to put to sea without a moment's delay and proceed in quest of the said fleet according to the best intelligence you may be able to obtain and use your best endeavour to fall in with and intercept it.

169. *Admiralty to Bridport*

31 December 1796

My Lords Commissioners of the Admiralty having directed Admiral Sir Peter Parker to put any of the frigates now at Spithead in readiness for sea under the command of your Lordship, and to cause to embark on board the ships of your squadron as many pilots or other officers acquainted with the coast of Ireland as he might be able to furnish, I have their Lordships' commands to communicate the same to you for your information.

170. *Admiralty to Colpoys*

31 December 1796

I this day received and lost no time in communicating to my Lords Commissioners of the Admiralty your letters of the 23rd and 24th instant, the former a duplicate, giving an account of your transactions with the squadron under your command from the 17th instant and I have it in command from their Lordships to acquaint you that they approve of your proceedings.

171. *Admiralty to Bridport*

1 January 1797

Whereas information has been received of the arrival at Spithead of the squadron under Vice Admiral Colpoys, and judging it expedient that the squadron under your Lordship's command should be reinforced, and having in consequence ordered Sir Peter Parker to cause the stores,

provisions and water of the ships named in the margin [*Impetueux,
Edgar, Minotaur, Swiftsure, Majestic, Defiance*] to be completed without a moment's delay (either from the ships not under orders for sea or
from H.M. stores on shore, which can most shortly be done) intending
that they shall compose a part of the squadron under your command,
your Lordship is hereby required and directed to take the said ships
under your command accordingly and having so done you are to put to
sea with them and such other ships of your squadron as may be ready
and carry into execution the orders you have already received as soon
as the wind and weather will permit, without waiting for the completion of the full proportion of stores and water on board the said ships
provided they shall in other respects be in a fit condition to accompany
you. If from any intelligence your Lordship may receive you shall find
that the French squadron shall have left the coast of Ireland, you are in
such case to proceed off Brest, for the purpose of intercepting any of
the enemy's ships of war or transports belonging to it, or any other of
the enemy's ships or vessels which may attempt to enter that or any
other of their ports in that neighbourhood. And whereas we have directed the captain of H.M. ship Ville de Paris to put himself under your
Lordship's orders you are required and directed to take him and the
said ship under your command accordingly. But if from the state of the
crew, or any other circumstances, she should not be ready to accompany you at the time of your sailing, you are not to wait a moment for
her but to direct her commander to remain at Spithead for further
orders, using all dispatch in getting that ship ready for sea.

172.   *Spencer to Warren*

Admiralty, 2 January 1797

Thank you for your hint about Douarnenez Bay; but I want to know
whether a fleet of any size could anchor there so as to be clear of shells
from the shore. If they could, I think I should agree entirely with your
opinion on the subject, which by the by is Pellew's too, who mentioned
it to me not long ago in one of the letters I had from him from off Brest.

173.   *Bridport to Spencer*

Royal George, 3 January 1797

I received the honour of your Lordship's letter yesterday afternoon but
too late for me to acknowledge the receipt of it by that day's post. And

as I am under weigh I have but a moment to say that I shall proceed down Channel with all possible haste and I shall send a frigate ahead to call off Plymouth to order the Raisonnable and Scourge sloop to join me. Your Lordship will know by Sir Peter Parker's return of the ships at Spithead that only the Impetueux and Majestic are arrived there with Vice Admiral Colpoys. It is therefore impossible for me to detach Rear Admiral Sir William Parker and the squadron ordered to accompany him to Lisbon or to allow him to call off Falmouth for the convoys for that port. But whenever the Ville de Paris or any three more shall come to me to comprise a part of my squadron that object shall be immediately complied with.

[*Endorsed as received on the 4th*]

174.   *Warren to Spencer*

Plymouth Dock, 12 January 1797

In answer to the question respecting the possibility of ships laying in Douarnenez Bay out of the reach of shot or shells I take the liberty of stating that the late Lord Bristol[1] whose directions for that place are, I believe, lodged in the Admiralty; he has given his decided opinion in behalf of such a measure and from every observation I could form in being twice all round it appears to possess great advantages capable of containing any number of men of war. There are differences in particular places but as it is larger than Torbay it is impossible for shells to range far enough to annoy shipping.

175.   *Seymour to Spencer*

Sans Pareil, 16 January 1797

I have only one moment to write, having just left the Admiral in the greatest degree of impatience to get away to the southward and westward in company with Admiral Parker, whom I hope we shall set at liberty tomorrow. The Ville de Paris, Duke and Raisonnable are joining which will make our force 13 sail of the line but I cannot help wishing that we may on our return to our rendezvous be enabled to pick up

---

[1]As Captain the Honourable Augustus Hervey, he had served with Hawke in 1759. For reminiscences of the blockade then see *Augustus Hervey's Journal*, ed. D. Erskine (London, 1954), 300–304.

ships to the number of 15 as at this time of the year it is difficult to keep together all the ships of a <u>chasing</u> squadron and it may become desirable to detach 4 or 5 sail, which we cannot do without our force is increased. If on our return we should find the French returned would it not be a good thing for our squadron to show themselves off Cape Clear? By this we should make that ground secure and then be enabled to return into port if neither the state of our trade nor that of the enemies' ships at Brest made it necessary to keep the sea and really at this time of the year without a good object we are better at Spithead if truly ready for sea.

176. *Admiralty to Bridport*

28 January 1797

Whereas we have judged it expedient that the squadron under your Lordship's command should return into port in order that the defects of the respective ships may be made good, and their stores and provisions completed, leaving at sea only one ship of the line and five frigates to cruize on such station as you shall judge best for the protection of the homeward bound convoys which may be expected shortly to arrive, your Lordship is hereby required and directed to return with the said squadron excepting the ship of the line & frigates abovementioned to Spithead accordingly, and remain there until you shall receive further orders. And whereas we think fit that the ship of the line to be stationed as abovementioned (and which you will observe is not to be either the Sans Pareil, Triumph or Raisonnable) shall, in case of falling in with the East India Company's ships from St Helena, accompany them to Spithead, or in case of not meeting with them to lose no time in repairing to that anchorage, if information shall be received which may be depended upon, of their having passed up Channel; and that on her quitting the station, the frigates shall be left to cruize for the space of 14 days after her departure, but that in no case either of them should continue at sea later than the end of the next month; your lordship is hereby required and directed to leave the ships abovementioned on such station as you shall judge best for those purposes, and to give orders accordingly, directing the senior officer of the said ship to take the first opportunity after your leaving your station of sending such of the frigates as he may judge necessary off of Brest, for the purpose of looking into that port and ascertaining the state of the enemy's force there, and to transmit a particular account thereof by the first opportunity to our secretary for our information.

177.   *Admiralty to Bridport*

28 January 1797

I have received and communicated to my Lords commissioners of the Admiralty your Lordship's letter to me of the 24th instant inclosing a statement of the defects of H.M. ship Majestic, and acquainting me, for their Lordships' information, with your intention of sending her as one of the first ships of your squadron which you should order in to Plymouth; at the same time representing that from the condition of the Duke and Atlas, you were of opinion it might be proper that those ships also should be ordered into port; and I am commanded by their Lordships to refer you to their instructions forwarded to you by this day's post, by which you will observe that an arrangement has been made so as to admit of your sending in the three ships for the purpose of being refitted.

178.   *Seymour to Spencer*

Sans Pareil, in Torbay, 1 February 1797

I meant in my last letter to have mentioned to you that on the 27th we fell in with a squadron of frigates which for some time employed six or seven of our ships in chase under a press of sail and led the whole squadron to entertain hopes that we had at last crossed upon a part of the enemy's fleet which has engaged our thoughts so much of late but that impression was done away in the course of two hours by the headmost of our chasing ships having exchanged with them the private signals and by his pronouncing them to be friends. Every signal that was applicable to ordering them to join us was made in vain by the Admiral, who at last directed the Triumph and three frigates to bring them into the squadron but in endeavouring to effect that purpose they parted company from us without succeeding in their object, the frigates having pressed away from them and escaped in the night.

I am yet ignorant what are the ships which acted in this most reprehensible and un-officerlike manner but I take it for granted that our Chief, who cannot fail to have been much hurt with it, will apply publicly for an enquiry in the conduct of the officer commanding them. I am sure that he should do so and that notice should be taken of so glaring a breach of discipline and a piece of disobedience which should be reprobated on every occasion and more especially under the particu-

lar circumstances of time and place when we fell in with this detachment of our fleet.

I am afraid that Lord Bridport's report of some of the ships under his
orders will not be a very flattering one but as he may not have an
opportunity of writing to the Admiralty this post I will endeavour to
give you a just account of them.

The flagships with the Triumph, Mars and Formidable and
Raisonnable are all in good condition and fit for sea except their rigging, which a few hours will put to rights. The Ville de Paris turns out
so well that I have not a doubt but she will become a very favourite ship
when in good order but at present she is in bad plight – wanting
caulking, having a very mutinous sick ship's company which the officers, who are strangers to each other, have yet found it very difficult to
manage at all. I have made Captain Hood[1] sensible of your kind intentions towards him by appointing him to her but I might work from this
day to the end of my life in endeavouring to make Lord Bridport feel
the compliment you meant to pay to him through your attention to his
nephew without making him acknowledge it.

[Endorsed as received on the 4th]

179. *Bridport to Spencer*

Royal George, Spithead, 3 February 1797

As I have written so fully to Mr. Secretary Nepean on all that has
passed since I left St. Helens I have nothing to add to your Lordship on
public subjects further than to say that I have with an anxious solicitude
served the King and the Kingdom to the best of my judgment, of which
I trust your Lordship, the Admiralty and the Government will do me the
justice to give me credit for.

[Endorsed as received on the 5th and answered on the 6th]

---

[1]Alexander Hood (1758–98). Lieutenant 1777; Commander 1781; Captain 1781 (flag
captain to Samuel Hood). A cousin, not nephew, of Lord Bridport. He entered the Navy
in 1767 and sailed on Cook's second voyage in 1772. One of the officers put ashore
during the Spithead mutiny, he was killed in action off Brest the following spring.

180. *Admiralty to Lieutenant Miles*[1]

21 February 1797

By a letter which has been received this morning from Admiral Sir Peter Parker at Portsmouth, he reports that signals have been made denoting that the enemy's transports were seen yesterday morning off Beachy Head, and my Lords Commissioners of the Admiralty being desirous of obtaining the most precise information on the subject, I have received their commands to direct you to let me know the number and description of ships and vessels which were discovered from your signal post and every particular respecting them which came within your observation.

In case such vessels were off Beachy Head as could have induced you to make the signal reported to have been made from your station, their Lordships can hardly suppose you would have neglected to send an Express with information thereof.

181. *Admiralty to Bridport*

25 February 1797

I am commanded by my Lords Commissioners of the Admiralty to acquaint your Lordship that the ships mentioned on the other side hereof are intended to compose the fleet under your Lordship's command, and to signify their directions to you to hasten their equipment by every possible means, sending from 6 to 8 of the first 17 line of battle ships mentioned in the list under a flag officer as soon as they can be got ready to St. Helens, there to remain until they shall be joined by your Lordship.

As the 8 last mentioned ships of the line are ordered to be fitted for foreign service, it is their Lordships' direction that they should remain at Spithead until your Lordship may be ordered to sail, to enable them to keep their stores and provisions complete.

Their Lordships' orders in form will be transmitted to you as soon as they can conveniently be prepared; in the mean time your Lordship will make such arrangements and give such orders in respect to the said ships as the circumstances may be found to require.

---

[1]Thomas Miles (d. 1817). Lieutenant 1779; superannuated commander 1814. Letter addressed to Miles at Beachy Head.

Royal George	Ganges
Royal Sovereign	Ramillies
London	Hector
Queen Charlotte	Russell
Formidable	Ville de Paris
Glory	Defiance
Duke	Alexander
Pompee	Sans Pareil
Mars	Triumph
Impetueux	Theseus
Caesar	Bellerophon
Minotaur	Swiftsure (on her arrival)
Marlborough	

Nymphe
Concorde
St. Fiorenzo
Stag
Unité
Triton
Melpomene
Phoenix
Incendiary } fireships
Megaera

182.   *Admiralty to Bridport*

26 February 1797

Whereas we have received intelligence that the enemy are preparing an expedition at Brest and are using every exertion in the equipment of their ships; and whereas we think it necessary that you should put to sea with such of the ships under your orders as are now ready, without waiting for those which are not so, your Lordship is hereby required and directed to put to sea the moment wind and weather will permit with the 15 ships of the line [*Royal George, Royal Sovereign, Queen Charlotte, London, Duke, Glory, Pompee, Minotaur, Impetueux, Defiance, Ramillies, Marlborough, Ganges, Russell, Mars*] and frigates [*Nymphe, St Fiorenzo, Concorde, Triton, Unité, Thames; Megaera* and *Incendiary*, fireships; two cutters] named in the margin accordingly, and proceed with them as expeditiously as possible off Brest, in order to prevent any squadron or ships of the enemy from sailing from that port and to use your best endeavours to take or destroy them, should they attempt to put to sea. You are to take the first possible opportunity of sending such frigates as you shall judge proper to look into Brest, and to transmit to our secretary, for our information, an account of the state of the enemy's fleet there, as soon as you shall have been able to obtain it. If your Lordship should obtain certain information of the enemy's fleet being at sea, and of its actual situation, you are immediately to proceed in quest of it; but if you only gain intelligence that it has sailed without being able to learn its course, you are in such case to make the best of your way to Cape Clear, and then repair off the Lizard for further orders, transmitting to us as expeditiously as possible an account of your arrival and proceedings. If you should discover that the enemy's squadron has not left Brest, your Lordship is to cruize off that port with the force under your command, in the best situation you may be able for preventing their putting to sea as long as the wind shall continue to the eastward, but on its shifting to the westward and appearing to be fixed in that quarter, you are to proceed off the Lizard and wait for further orders, sending a frigate into Falmouth or Plymouth with intelligence thereof to our secretary for our information. But if the wind should blow so strong as to render it difficult for you to keep your station there, you are, in such case, to repair to St. Helens. If however whilst you are proceeding to the station off the Lizard, or on your way to St. Helens, the wind should change from the westward to the northward or eastward, so as to enable the enemy to put to sea before you receive orders from us, your Lordship is to return as expeditiously as possible off of Brest, and act in like manner; and if during your cruize off Brest, you should be drawn to the westward by strong easterly winds, you are to use every possible exertion to return to the eastward again, in order prevent the enemy from availing themselves of that opportunity to escape. Your Lordship is to keep frigates constantly cruizing (if possible) within sight of the enemy's ships at Brest, in order that you may receive the earliest information of any movements the enemy may make; and you are to give the strictest orders to the captains of such frigates that one at least of them should keep sight of the enemy until he shall be able to ascertain, as well as circumstances will permit, to what coast they appear to be destined, and then to lose no time in acquainting you therewith. If from any accidental circumstances either of the before mentioned ships of the line should not be in a condition to put to sea, your Lordship is to take with you the Robust, or any other ship not under orders for foreign service that may be ready so as to make up the number (with those that may be in a proper state to accompany you) to 15 sail of the line. If however your Lordship cannot make up your force to 15 sail of the line without detaining the squadron you are to put to sea immediately.

183. *Admiralty to Bridport*

26 February 1797

. . . having ordered the Flag Officers named on the other side hereof[1] to put themselves under your Lordship and follow your orders for their further proceedings, your Lordship is hereby required and directed to take them under your command accordingly and to order them to hoist their flags on board such ships as you shall judge proper.

184. *Bridport to Spencer*

Royal George, Spithead, 28 February 1797

Vice Admiral Colpoys went to St. Helens last night and some ships followed him early this morning but I am afraid I shall not have ready fourteen before tomorrow and scarcely any of the frigates are ready for sea . . . I have no doubt but the Brest fleet will soon be at sea, if not already sailed. I am no judge of its force but the intelligences sent on from the Admiralty make the number 25 of the line. I hope this is not true as I had much rather attack than defend against a superior fleet both for myself and the country.

185. *Spencer to Bridport*

1 March 1797

I am very glad to hear that you are likely to be so soon at sea, though I think it less probable than it was that the French fleet should have sailed from Brest and if they do sail I am persuaded their number will not exceed 14 or 15 of the line. The idea of their amounting to 25 I presume your Lordship to have collected from a letter that came from the Prince of Bouillon which states that they wished to make up that number but from all the accounts both from him and from other quarters it does not appear that they have either men or stores enough to go to sea.

. . . I agree with your Lordship entirely on it is much better to attack than defend and I feel under not the smallest anxiety of the event of any attack you may be enabled to make.

---

[1]Copies sent to Vice-admiral Sir John Colpoys and Rear-admiral Sir Roger Curtis. Similar orders were sent to 12 captains.

186. *Bridport to Spencer*

Royal George, at sea, 10 March 1797

We have done something in a small way, much to the honour of Sir Harry Neale and Captain Cook[1] who attacked and took Le Resistance and Le Constance close in with Brest after they had taken a full view of the enemy's force in that port. I am under the necessity of sending the San Fiorenzo and Nymphe into port with their prizes and prisoners. I shall want them much as indeed I have no [others[2]] for the various services attached to this squadron.

[Endorsed as received on the 17th and answered an the 18th]

187. *Spencer to Warren*

10 March 1797

I wish you may be able to give us a satisfactory account of the encounter you had with Lord Bridport's fleet on the 27th January. We shall be obliged to call upon you to explain it as Lord Bridport has made a formal complaint upon the subject and a good deal has been said about it by several of the officers in the fleet.

188. *Pellew to Spencer*

Indefatigable, off the Land's End, 10 March 1797

I shall entreat from you the indulgence of a cruise to the southward for a month or six weeks and I ask it in the following considerations. Your Lordship hath presided over the naval department about two years. During this period I refer myself to your Lordship's judgment if I have not taken my full share of the fag of the service. In the present moment I see many of my juniors placed in situations to make prize money. I have never for the whole war been permitted to run loose for a cruise. I may add to it the promises of the former Admiralty of being placed in a situation where I might reasonably expect some emolument. It hath never happened to me to capture a merchant ship for the war, unless

---

[1]John Cooke. There were two. The first (d. 1805); Lieutenant 1779; Captain 1794. The second (d. 1834); Lieutenant 1781; Captain 1795; Superannuated Rear-admiral 1814.
[2]Word indecipherable.

indeed a few empty chasses marées may be called so and all I have made I have fought hard for. I have watched the port of Brest and performed a hazardous service at Quiberon. The French fleet owe not their escape to me. Give me then my Lordship the first time in my life a chance of getting a prize.

I think there is no reason to doubt the information of Mr. Inglis. His story of the galley slaves[1] proves this, and he assures me a hundred times there was not one ship in the port of Brest which was not crippled, and all of them unrigged. They were working upon none but six, which they reported to be intended for India. If I can fetch Ushant I shall now look into Brest and be at Falmouth or Plymouth in a few days. I left the latter without paying my people, which will take me only a few hours.

This seems to be the moment of my expectations. I throw myself on your Lordship to realize then, and am with grateful respect . . .

189.   *Spencer to Pellew*

Admiralty, 14 March 1797

I am sorry that I cannot say anything more satisfactory than I feel my duty calls upon me to do. The naval service and more particularly that description of it in which you are employed with so much credit to yourself is and always must be a lottery as to profit. Your station from the opportunities it frequently affords of meeting with objects of pursuit and capture has ever since I have been at this Board been looked upon by all the officers in the navy as the most desirable in my appointment and accordingly scarce a day passes that I have not some application or other from officers to be placed upon it; to all these applications I make it an invariable rule to return the same answer, namely that the particular destination of ships can only be determined by considerations arising out of the exigencies of the public service and not by ones of a more private nature and I really do not know (if I should with propriety change your station or destination on any grounds other than public ones) where I could employ you with a better chance for your gaining emolument as well as distinction and credit. As to cruising more at large nothing can be more precarious, as you well know; the

---

[1]Peter Inglis was a West Indian privateer captain, rescued in January by Pellew from his captivity in the *Droits de L'Homme*, who said that there had been nearly 2000 galley slaves on board the French frigates which landed men near Fishguard in February 1797. The slaves rejoiced under the name of the Black Legion. See *Fleet Battle and Blockade. The French Revolutionary War 1793–1797*, ed. R. Gardiner (London, 1996), 160.

war with Spain has now been long enough made public[1] to put them on their guard and that therefore is pretty near over. Besides, it would be unjustifiable to allow any ships from the Channel for the purpose of cruising only to go into the limits of Sir John Jervis's[2] orders.

Your conjectures about Brest were well enough formed on the premises on which you formed them but we have very late and very authentic information which materially differs from what you have collected and which will probably make it necessary to keep a much stricter and more systematic watch on that port by the means of frigates than we have heretofore done. This will probably cut out some more employment for the Falmouth squadrons of the description they have lately been called upon to fulfil but I would not by any means have you suppose from thence that you will not be in the way as much advantage and success as I am sure you highly deserve to meet with.

190.   *Warren to Admiralty*

La Pomone, 14 March 1797

I beg leave to acknowledge the receipt of your letter of the 11th instant requesting that I would give my reasons for not answering the signals made by some ships of the fleet under the command of Lord Bridport on the 27th of January last.

I request that you will state to their Lordships that on that day, being far to windward, I made the signal established in the Channel to a ship to leeward, which was answered.

I then tacked, conceiving that our services were not required by the Commander-in-Chief and therefore proceeded with all despatch to fulfil the orders I had received from their Lordships: and the day being dark and hazy I did not observe any other signals addressed to us.

I am extremely sorry if any inadvertence or error be imputable to me and it grieves me that the Commander-in-Chief can suppose that I should not both from duty and inclination pay every attention to his commands.

I assure their Lordships that in future I shall make it my best object when any of the fleet may be in sight to go down and receive the Commander-in-Chief's orders and to which I shall ever show the strictest attention.

---

[1]Spain had declared war in October 1796.
[2]Jervis had taken over the Mediterranean command from Hotham in November 1795. He became Earl of St Vincent for his victory on 14 February 1797.

191. *Pellew to Spencer*

Falmouth, 18 March 1797

I had received before my excursion to Wales your Lordship's directions upon the intended system of watching Brest and I trust in the execution of them your Lordship will make me responsible only to the Board over which you preside without putting the squadron under the orders of the admiral who may be stationed in the vicinity. When I received my minutes on my last tour of duty off Brest my reasons for this desire are greatly strengthened.

[*Endorsed as received on the 22nd and answered on the 28th*]

192. *Warren to Spencer*

Stapleford Hall, 24 March 1797

I trust you will pardon the liberty I take in stating to your Lordship that having been employed since the commencement of the war, and the three last years of it constantly at sea that it has borne hard upon my health and particularly so since I have been deprived of the assistance of a captain. In the present period of the war there seems no probability that my little squadron should have the opportunity of being distinguished should it be ordered off Brest; more especially as the frigates attached to Lord Bridport's fleet are now as well acquainted as ourselves with that part of the coast of France and most probably may perform that service with much more <u>satisfaction</u> to the Commander-in-Chief than we could hope to do.

I therefore trust and rely upon your Lordship's kindness on allowing me to own that it would essentially serve us if we were favoured with a cruise off the island of Madeira that we may be thrown into fortune's way. We could afterwards remain off Cape Ortegal or between that place and Ireland so as to cut the line of Rochefort and Bordeaux with great advantage to the service.

If that cannot be I should be glad to serve with Lord Hugh Seymour in any station or be with Lord Jervis upon the coast of Spain.

I am, my Lord, advancing high upon the list[1] and it would be hard indeed now that I have unfortunately incurred the displeasure of Lord

---

[1] Of captains, a list that operated in seniority order.

Bridport that I should serve under him in a post that is liable to much misconstruction.

[Endorsed to be answered personally when he comes to Town]

193. *Spencer to Pellew*

28 March 1797

While the enemy sent only small squadrons to sea it was sufficient for us to keep detached squadrons cruising and they were better employed by being independent of each other but as there now appears an intention again of forming their Brest fleet into a large body our Channel fleet must also be enlarged and being so cannot be kept up in succession as the smaller divisions of it have been. Quick and authentic information of what is doing at Brest becomes absolutely necessary in such a state of things and the only way that suggested itself for that purpose was the plan detailed in your orders. From this statement I think you will readily perceive that you are not intended to be constantly under the orders of the Channel fleet admiral; on the contrary from the sort of cruising which that fleet will be to carry on during the summer it will very probably be but seldom that you will meet unless you seek him for the purpose of giving intelligence.

194. *Bridport to Spencer*

Royal George, Spithead, 30 March 1797

The squadron under my command arrived here this day as I have stated in my letter to Mr. Nepean, by which your Lordship will see I was driven far to the westward of my station by the strong easterly wind; during which time the Brest ships might have put to sea if they had received orders and were in all respects prepared for sailing. It was my intention to have sent two ships to look into Brest on the 25th but it blew so strong that day I did not think it prudent to give orders for their proceeding. Your Lordship will perceive how impossible it is to keep frigates cruising in sight of the enemy's ships at Brest or even to preserve a station within a correct distance.

There is no reliance on the appearance of ships at anchor. I mean such as are not apparently ready for sea. Neither is there any dependence to be placed on the reports of prisoners. They speak the language they are told. The captain of the Volant privateer states that Admiral

Richery was expected daily at Brest and was to sail with a small squadron on some secret service. Indeed there appears, by the reports of Sir Harry Neale and Captain Cook, that number ready for sailing.

When I have the honour of seeing your Lordship I will submit my sentiments upon the subject of cruising off Brest. And as Lady Bridport has lost a near relation during my cruise which will occasion some material business for me to transact I must request the Board's leave of absence from my duty for that purpose, which I shall apply for as soon as I have made my arrangements at Spithead.

In case of my absence I must request that the squadron under my orders may be regulated and commanded by Sir Alan Gardner and when he shall be absent by Vice Admiral Colpoys or such other flag officer as may be put under my command. I have many reasons to offer for the adoption of this plan which I hope will meet with your approbation.

[Endorsed as received on the 31st and answered the same day]

195.   *Spencer to Bridport*

31 March 1797

Your Lordship will perceive by the answer the Board has returned on the subject of Captain Thornbrough's[1] application for leave of absence that we deem it very important to keep all the officers of the fleet under your command as much together as possible in order that you may be in constant readiness to put to sea on any occasion which may arise for it and at the shortest notice. Under these circumstances I own I should have wished your Lordship to have remained with them as I know of how much efficacy the presence of the Commander-in-Chief becomes in order to keep everything as it should be, especially in a case like the present where at any moment an urgent call may happen for the sailing of the fleet. I hope therefore that unless the business to which you allude is of a very pressing nature indeed your Lordship will not apply for leave of absence and in case it is absolutely necessary for you to do so your absence may be very short. The command will in that case of course devolve on Sir Alan Gardner as you desire.

---

[1]Sir Edward Thornbrough (1754–1834). Lieutenant 1773; Captain 1782, Rear-admiral 1801; Vice-admiral 1805; Admiral 1813. Knighted 1815.

196. *Seymour to Spencer*

Sans Pareil, 2 April 1797

I have endeavoured to impress Lord Bridport's mind with the necessity of his remaining at Portsmouth in his command and by his example inclining the officers under his orders to hold their ships in constant readiness for sea, which object he assures me he has at heart as much as we have. His private business, however, requiring his presence in town on account of the death of some near relation of Lady Bridport's, he proposes availing himself of your permission to go there for a week. I hope that during that time you will have an opportunity of arranging every matter relating to his fleet, of which I suppose he will become Commander-in-Chief <u>in form</u>,[1] as there are certainly many reasons which recommend that measure, though we are not ignorant of the <u>contre</u> which may be urged to balance them.

197. *Bridport to Spencer*

Royal George, Spithead, 13 April 1797

I have received the commission which the Board of Admiralty has been pleased to sign for me and I hope my health will enable me to execute the duties of my station to the end of the war, though I must own I sometimes feel checks to that explanation.

[Endorsed as received on the 13th]

---

[1]This anticipates Howe's formal resignation as Commander-in-Chief in a letter dated 8 April 1797.

5

THE SPITHEAD MUTINY[1]
13 APRIL–15 MAY 1797

There were several reasons why the first of the great fleet mutinies of 1797 occurred in the Channel fleet. The largest single concentration of the British navy, it received the widest influx of ideological influences amid the seamen induced into its service. Its regular anchorage at Spithead facilitated communication between ships and the shore, and the winter months provided a time for organisation. Administrative reasons included the dual command of the fleet until April 1797, the poor relations that had existed between Lords Howe and Bridport, and the reluctance of the latter to shoulder responsibility for difficulties that he felt had been precipitated by Howe and the Board. In consequence Bridport and the Board both looked to the other to settle the mutiny. This had arisen among seamen from rising expectations regarding their victualling and the care of their sick, so much the recent concern of the Victualling and Sick and Wounded Boards, as well as from anxiety about their rates of pay. These had remained static since 1653 and were being increasingly devalued by the rising rate of inflation of the 1790s. Inseparable from these concerns was the pride many men felt in their indispensable role as defenders of their country from invasion. Many also remained loyal to Howe as their admiral, an association that permitted the *Queen Charlotte*, Howe's former flagship, to have a disproportionate influence in the initial proceedings.

These administrative factors, in particular the conflict between senior management, have hitherto gone largely unrecognised as a source of the mutiny. This is because the correspondence between the Board of Admiralty and the Commander-in-Chief at Spithead has, until recently, remained largely unknown.[2] Owing to the dual command of the Channel fleet, Bridport had remained in ignorance of the petitions that had

---

[1]For complementary papers relating to the Spithead and Nore mutinies published earlier by the Navy Records Society, see *Private Papers of George, Second Earl Spencer*, ed. J. S. Corbett and H. W. Richmond (4 vols, NRS, 1913 etc.) II, 101–74.

[2]The historiography and background of the mutiny are briefly examined in R. C. Saxby, 'Lord Bridport and the Spithead Mutiny', *The Mariner's Mirror*, 79 (1993), 170–78. Some background to the grievances of the seamen are explained in C. Lloyd, *The British Seaman 1200–1860. A Social Survey* (London, 1970), 225–6.

been sent to Howe by the seamen in March 1797. Disclosure of their despatch to Howe came to him as a disturbing surprise [198]. Howe later stated unclearly that he had written to 'the officer at Portsmouth to whom I was naturally to expect such applications would, in my absence, be addressed'. This may have been Sir Roger Curtis, his former first captain, but it was Lord Seymour, as an Admiralty commissioner serving in the fleet, who told him there was no sign of general discontent and who forwarded the petitions to London.[1] There, as Spencer admitted, the Board of Admiralty decided to take no notice of them, hoping by this means to permit the discontent to dissipate [199]. But with evidence of rising discontent and a likely strike, the Board simply hoped the ships' officers would nip it in the bud [200].

Discontent in Ireland, combined with intelligence of preparations in Brest, on 15 April gave urgency to the necessity for a squadron to get to sea [201]. But the delicacy of the labour situation was equally impressed upon Bridport [202] and, unlike the Board, he was inclined to give the petitions an immediate answer. In his opinion, had the Board done likewise the 'ill-humour' with which he was faced would have been pre-empted [203]. Contrary to Board orders, he ignored directions to proceed to sea and, reluctant to sacrifice a willingness on the part of the seamen to sail provided their petitions were answered, committed the Board to providing an immediate answer [204]. This answer was non-committal; indeed the Board returned the responsibility to Bridport to answer the men and still charged him with getting a squadron to sea [205].

Bridport felt obliged to send his first captain to London to explain to the Board a situation in which his best officers were rendered totally powerless, and would be exacerbated by a continuing failure of the Board to respond to the petitions [206]. His alarm was heightened by information of the complicity and binding by oaths of the marines and of the length of time that had been allowed to pass since the seamen had presented their first petitions [207]. Under the impact of further petitions and letters from other officers, the Board was at last induced to take stock of the situation [208]. Meanwhile Bridport attempted to prevent a further deterioration of relations. He placed responsibility squarely with the Board by stating to the seamen precisely what was happening. Already, although only two days after he had been rendered powerless by the threat of mutiny, Bridport had been convinced that the demands of the petitions had to be met [209].

In London debate about how to manage the situation had spread beyond the Board of Admiralty. Spencer was advised to use persuasion

[1]James, II, 26.

as well as force [210]. By then, with other members of the Board, Spencer had decided to convene at Portsmouth [211]. There on 18 April they took receipt of a new petition, drawn up by the fleet delegates sitting in the flag-officers' cabin of the *Queen Charlotte* the previous day. This petition claimed increased rates of pay, a supply of victuals at the rate of 16 ounces to the pound and of a better quality, more vegetables and no flour while in port, better care and provision for the sick, an allowance of shore leave on returning into port, and payment of the wounded until cured or discharged.[1] The minutes of the meetings of the Board of Admiralty between 18 and 21 April trace the means by which the Board was persuaded of the necessity to make concessions, the process of negotiation through the delegates, the decisions to stand firm against further demands and to divide the seamen by a measure of intimidation, and the subsequent role of the fleet captains in persuading the Board that concessions were needed with respect to the victualling as well as the wages of the seamen and marines. The terms upon which the negotations were conducted with the delegates are detailed elsewhere.[2] Evident here is the source of two influences on the seamen: their desire for a guarantee of immunity from punishment and the views of the crew of the *Queen Charlotte* [212].

With delegates meeting on the *Royal George*, Bridport felt obliged to strike his flag on 21 April [214]. Bridport's honest representations to the seamen had nevertheless maintained an element of trust between him and the delegates, and he was to rehoist his flag in the *Royal George* on the 23rd. By contrast, Gardner's forceful attempt to press the delegates while disunited into committing themselves to terms had aroused distrust and a determination to achieve all the demands of the petitions as well as a royal pardon [215]. On returning to London on 22nd, Spencer had attended a Cabinet where the Admiralty's concessions were approved. These were in turn granted by the King. He was now concerned to restore loyalty to the Crown [216]. Happily, only the day after the Board had returned to London, Bridport was able to report the seamen of the fleet were satisfied by the concessions [217]. Congratulations seemed to be in order, especially as six ships had been able to move to St Helens preparatory to sailing [218, 219], for the large number of ships ready for sea in Brest harbour made the departure of a British squadron now a matter of urgency [213].

However, congratulations were premature. At the point when the mutiny seemed to have been settled, new petitions emerged from sev-

---

[1]This petition is printed in full in J. Dugan, *The Great Mutiny* (London, 1966), 102–4.
[2]James, II, 27–8.

eral ships at Spithead including Bridport's own, the *Royal George*, reiterating demands for meat instead of flour, more vegetables, an increase in the amount of out-pension issued by Greenwich Hospital, and the punishment or reprimand of unpopular officers. The Admiralty was not inclined to grant lightly any of these new demands [220], although the Victualling Board was soon to have more fresh beef available [221, 222]. Rather, Spencer believed regular duty at sea would remove discontent.

This appeared all the more important as ships at Plymouth had decided to join the mutiny in solidarity with those at Spithead [223]. The latter moreover wanted to secure the concessions they had won. Thus, for example, they wished to ensure they gained their full 16 ounces to the pound by receiving new weights and measures [224]. Spencer was worried that discontent was stimulated by disaffected persons going on board His Majesty's ships. He was most concerned about United Irishmen being put on board ships on the Irish coast [225]. Regarding the Channel fleet, sensibly he realised that peace would only be fully restored by convincing the seamen that everything possible had been done so far as constitutional procedures permitted to achieve what had been promised. His anxiety to reassure the men of the stages which the grant of their different demands had reached bespoke a genuine desire for an honourable settlement [226]. Bridport was equally willing and prompt to inform the men of the progress of their demands [227]. In consequence by 6 May peace seemed to be restored to the ships at Spithead and at Plymouth [228].

Again, however, the Board of Admiralty and the admirals commanding the fleet were disappointed. This time the ships at St Helens were reported to be out of the control of their officers, the mutineers spreading their resistance to the ships at Spithead by rowing back against orders [229]. They refused to sail without confirmation that the House of Commons had granted the funds to provide their increased rates of pay and provisions [230]. On the *London*, six seamen were shot when Colpoys attempted to resist the mutiny. In vindication he produced Admiralty instructions of 1 May to suppress further disorder and bring its leaders to punishment. The repressive orders gave new life to the mutiny.[1] Officers were turned out of their ships which again came under the control of delegate meetings [231]. However, at the Admiralty the despatch of official notice of the unanimous vote of the House of Commons of 8 May, and the receipt of information of the movement of some ships from Spithead to St Helens, gave grounds for optimism [232, 233].

---

[1]Dugan, 142–3.

This hope was to be fulfilled. Bridport was to reveal qualities of management which at this time more than offset the difficulties of his character.[1] He was meticulous in keeping faith with the seamen, in particular over the date from which their increase in pay and provisions would take effect [234]; and he insisted on the replacement of officers and restoration of authority before he attempted to take the fleet to sea [235, 251]. Through the generosity of both Admiralty and seamen, in each respect he gained his point [237, 239, 247]. Spencer was fully alive to the danger of misunderstanding in rapidly changing circumstances, and to the delicacy of winning back the allegiance of the seamen. The use of Lord Howe for this purpose was potentially a grave imposition on Bridport, one which Pitt as Prime Minister attempted to mitigate [238]. Bridport accepted the gesture with sense and good grace. By the standard of his successor as Commander-in-Chief, his belief that it was wiser 'to soothe than combat disturbed and agitated minds' was positively gentle, but was undoubtedly appropriate at this time [240].

Howe arrived on 14 May. His task, as he saw it, was to quiet 'the most suspicious but most generous minds I think I ever met with in the same class of men'.[2] He elicited the fears of not being pardoned and of being forced to receive back the officers ejected from their ships [241]. Howe was able to wave a copy of the Act of Parliament of 9 May and quote the Admiralty proclamation of indemnity from prosecution. The question what to do with the officers who had been turned out remained debatable [244]. But, through Howe's good offices, by the middle of May most ships were restored to order.

Bridport remained reluctant to take these ships to sea, from an awareness that they would be followed by those still disaffected [243]. He was thus given the option of keeping these disaffected ships or returning them to Spithead [245]. The Admiralty was anxious for Bridport to get to sea and had continued to urge him to sail [244]. This was partly to act as a signal to the squadrons at Plymouth and in Torbay under Sir John Orde and Sir Roger Curtis that the mutiny was over [246]. To promote that end, on 14 May the Admiralty ordered a general amnesty on all acts of disobedience, mutiny, neglect of duty, forbidding any seaman or marines from being 'disquieted by any reproof or reproach' in respect of such deeds.[3] Combined with the influence of Howe, the order had the desired effect: 15 May was

[1]See also G. E. Manwaring and B. Dobrée, *The Floating Republic. An Account of the Mutinies at Spithead and the Nore in 1797* (London, 1935), 99–100.
[2]Manwaring and Dobrée, 142.
[3]Manwaring and Dobrée, 118.

something of a fete day. Even the squadron of Sir Roger Curtis that arrived on 15th was persuaded not to mutiny.[1] Congratulations were once more in order [247].

Little did the Admiralty know that delegates from the North Sea fleet attended Spithead shortly before the mutiny was terminated. For the time being, however, the Channel fleet was restored to order. Though by no means all, many of the officers were received back into their ships. Bridport had been much upset by events, but had the satisfaction of receiving from the seamen a statement of thanks for his considera-tion and indulgence [249]. He had also felt harassed and reproached by the Admiralty's repeated orders to sail [248, 250]. Yet his consistent objective had been to ensure the fleet would be in a condition to engage the enemy when it did sail [251]. It was a professional priority which ensured the discontent in the fleet was not ignored, as the Board of Admiralty attempted, but was addressed squarely. It was a policy which made a principal contribution to the settlement of the Spithead mutiny. Though overshadowed in popular opinion by the influence of Howe, Bridport's professional view had a major influence on the return of the Channel fleet to operational effectiveness. His approach ensured the Spithead mutiny was kept distinct, and had a very different outcome, from the subsequent mutiny at the Nore.

198.   *Bridport to Spencer*

Royal George, Spithead, 13 April 1797

I am sorry to inform your Lordship that a circumstance reached me yesterday which gave me much concern. It has been stated to me that representations have been made by the crews of the Channel fleet to Lord Howe and the Admiralty for an increase of pay. If this should be the case it would be very desirable for me to know what steps have been taken in consequence thereof. I am particularly anxious to receive such instructions as your Lordship and the Board may think expedient with as little delay as possible as I yesterday heard that some disagree-able combinations were forming among the ships at Spithead on this subject.

Captain Glynn[2] will deliver this with the utmost expedition to your Lordship. He is not acquainted with the contents.

---

[1]James, II, 30–31.
[2]Sir Henry Richard Glynn (d. 1856). Lieutenant 1790; Captain 1797; Rear-admiral 1821; Vice-admiral 1837; Admiral 1846.

P.S. It is reported that this subject proceeded from the Queen Charlotte.

199. *Spencer to Bridport*

14 April 1797[1]

Captain Glynn delivered to me last night your Lordship's two letters of yesterday and I am much concerned at the contents of that which relates to the letters written to Lord Howe on the subject of the seamens' pay. The fact, as far as I am acquainted with it, is as follows. Some time ago Lord Howe transmitted by Lord Hugh Seymour several letters (in number eleven) purporting to come from the crews of the ships mentioned in the enclosed list, bearing date as is therein expressed. The letters are all in nearly the same words and have much the appearance of being composed by the same person though they are written in different hands. Lord Howe, of course, took no other notice of them but by putting them into Lord Hugh Seymour's hands for the private information of the Board and as it appeared impossible to do anything officially on the subject without running the risk of unpleasant consequences by a public agitation of so delicate a topic it was judged most advisable by the Board to take no notice of the circumstance, hoping that it might go no further.

Your Lordship not having mentioned any particulars of the reports which have reached you on the subject renders it impossible for me to do more at present than, having acquainted you with what I have already mentioned, to transmit to you the letters in question for your inspection and to desire that your Lordship will be so good as to let me know a little more, particularly what information you may have received and whether any individuals are pointed out as leading in the business.

On a matter of this kind I am sure it will be needless for me to recommend to your Lordship the great necessity of circumspection in whatever measures it may be proper to adopt on a business which is liable to so much difficulty and which, if not very carefully watched, is too likely to produce the most disagreeable consequences.

[Enclosure]

---

[1]This letter, like some others, is taken from a draft in the Board's minutes. There seems no reason to doubt that it was sent.

199a.   *List of ships which had written to Lord Howe with the dates of*
their letters

Feb. 28th 1797	Queen Charlotte
	Royal George
	Formidable
	Ramillies
	Minotaur
Mar. 4th	Audacious
Mar. 6th	Juste
Mar. 7th	Theseus
	Sans Pareil
	Triumph
Mar. 10th	Bellerophon

200.   *Admiralty to Bridport*

15 April 1797

Having received and communicated to my Lords Commissioners of the
Admiralty a letter from Admiral Sir Peter Parker of yesterday's date
acquainting me for their Lordships' information of a private intimation
having been made to you that the crews of some, if not all, ships at
Spithead who had petitioned for an increase of wages were dissatisfied
and intended to refuse doing their duty until their request should be
complied with and that a correspondence is represented to be secretly
carrying on between the different ships' companies in consequence of
which he had communicated with your Lordship and would give private directions to all the captains to sleep on board their respective
ships, I am commanded by their Lordships to acquaint you that they
have approved of his doing as he has proposed and to signify their
directions to you to order the several captains and commanders and
every subordinate officer belonging to the fleet under your Lordship's
command to remain constantly on board their respective ships so far as
their necessary duties will admit and upon discovering any disposition
to mutiny amongst the crews of their said ships to take immediately the
most vigorous and efficient measures for checking its progress and
securing the ringleaders, preventing as much as may be any communication between the seamen belonging to the different ships and also
between them and people from the shore who may possibly have in
some degree been instrumental in exciting the present discontent.

201. Admiralty to Bridport

15 April 1797

Your Lordship is hereby required and directed to hold yourself in constant readiness to put to sea at the shortest notice and to give immediate orders to Vice Admiral Sir Alan Gardner to drop down to St. Helens with eight sail of the line.

202. Bridport to Spencer

Royal George, Spithead, 15 April 1797

I have this instant received the honour of your Lordship's letter on the subject of mine delivered to your Lordship by Captain Glynn, together with eleven letters from different ships therein expressed.

I very clearly see that great delicacy is necessary in their contents and it was on that account I could not state more than I did in my letter to your Lordship, not knowing whether any steps had been taken to meet the subject at the time they were written.

The particulars that have reached me since are that communications have been kept up between all or most of the ships at Spithead and a plan formed to take effect whenever the fleet shall again be ordered to sea and the signal is made to weigh, and the ships are to take the lead from the Royal George and to give three cheers, which is the signal for refusing to weigh the anchor.

This information was brought forth by a boatswain's mate of the Mars, whose name is Brown, and who refused to enter into the plan of mutiny though he was, I believe, a promoter of the letters written to Lord Howe for an increase of pay. The coxswain of the barge belonging to the Mars has been employed in carrying letters to some of the ships and I believe there are two men on other ships who are supposed to be the leaders in the plan.

As Sir Peter Parker told me yesterday that he had received some information of a mutiny which he should transmit to Mr. Nepean, the Board of Admiralty are now in possession of more particulars than have reached me. I shall certainly be watchful and pay attention to this disagreeable subject and shall wait to receive instructions upon it for my guidance in conjunction with the Commander in Chief at this port, who may receive an answer to his letter by tomorrow's post.

P.S. I have this instant received orders by telegraph to prepare to sail tomorrow and the signal will be made for the purpose immediately.

203.   *Bridport to Admiralty*

Royal George, Spithead, 15 April 1797

Herewith I return you eleven anonymous letters transmitted to me by this morning's post from the Admiralty. You will also receive a petition delivered to me by Vice Admiral Colpoys from His Majesty's ship the London and one from the crew of His Majesty's ship Royal George, bearing my flag, to which I have pledged myself that an answer will be given, as I consider the latter to be the sense of the fleet from the best information I have received. I have very much to lament that some answer had not been given to the various letters transmitted to Earl Howe and the Admiralty, which would in my humble opinion have prevented the disappointment and ill humour which at present prevails in the ships under my orders. I therefore conclude their Lordships will not direct the squadron to proceed to sea before some answer is given to these petitions as I am afraid it could not be put in execution without the appearance of serious consequences which the complexion of the fleet manifestly indicates. I have not time to enter further into the particulars of this painful subject, being anxious to save this night's post, to which I hope to receive an answer by express if their Lordships shall deem it necessary.

You will also herewith receive a petition which has this moment been transmitted to me from the Queen Charlotte, whose people have taken the lead in this business.

[Endorsed as received on the 16th by express]

204.   *Bridport to Admiralty*

Royal George, Spithead, 16 April 1797, half past 12 a.m.

I have received their Lordships' order and your letter of yesterday's date by an Admiralty messenger directing me to hold the squadron under my command in constant readiness to put to sea at the shortest notice and to give immediate orders to Vice Admiral Sir Alan Gardner to drop down to St. Helens with eight sail of the line. And in answer to your letter I beg to refer their Lordships to mine of yesterday's date and its enclosures by which the present disposition of the crews of the several ships under my orders are fully stated and I trust vigorous measures will not be necessary as the men on board the Royal George, Queen Charlotte and seven other ships on the remonstrance of Vice

Admiral Colpoys and Rear Admiral Pole, my first Captain, and their several commanders have no objection to go to sea provided an answer is given to their petitions.

I state this in my bed and the several flag officers and captains of the fleet have received my private directions to sleep on board their respective ships.

Enclosed I transmit for their Lordships' information the copy of a memorandum I caused to be delivered yesterday afternoon to the respective captains of the squadron under my command.

[*Enclosure*]

204a. *Pole to respective captains*

Royal George, Spithead, 15 April 1797

Lord Bridport desires me to inform you that if your ship's company will immediately send to him the letter they intended addressing to him on Monday next stating their grievances or wants, his Lordship will transmit it to the Admiralty and he has no doubt he shall have an immediate answer but his Lordship, in undertaking to do this must in return rely on their perfect obedience to all orders which may be issued in the intermediate time. Signed C. M. Pole.

205. *Admiralty to Bridport*

16 April 1797

I received this morning by express and immediately communicated to my Lords Commissioners of the Admiralty your Lordship's letter of yesterday's date returning eleven anonymous letters which had been sent to you from hence and transmitting a petition which had been delivered to you by Vice Admiral Colpoys from His Majesty's ship the London together with one from the crew of the Royal George, bearing your flag, to which you have pledged yourself that an answer should be given, considering that letter according to the best information you had received to be the sense of the fleet. The petition from the Queen Charlotte to which your Lordship refers accompanied your said letter.

I have their Lordships' commands to acquaint you in return thereto that if, as you state in your letter, your Lordship should on a consideration of all the existing circumstances think it absolutely necessary that an answer should be given to any of the petitioners such answer should be confined to the acquainting them that their application has been communicated to their Lordships and that the subject will have that serious consideration which its importance requires.

Whatever your Lordship may determine with respect to the communication which you propose should be made, their Lordships are of opinion that no change ought to take place in the orders which have been given to your Lordship for sending a part of your squadron to St. Helens.

206. *Bridport to Admiralty*

Royal George, Spithead, 16 April 1797

In the present situation of His Majesty's fleet at Spithead I have judged it expedient to send Rear Admiral Pole, my first Captain, to town to state to the Lords Commissioners of the Admiralty all that has come to my knowledge and to lay before their Lordships the petitions that have been transmitted to me since my letter to you of yesterday's date. He is also charged with a letter from Vice Admiral Sir Alan Gardner to me describing the disorderly behaviour of the crew of the Royal Sovereign.

With respect to the using vigorous and effectual measures for getting the better of the crews of the ships at Spithead their Lordships will see that is impossible to be done or securing the ringleaders. I therefore see no means of checking the progress of this business but by complying in some measure with the prayers of the petitions. For further particulars I refer their Lordships to Rear Admiral Pole.

[*Enclosures*]

206a. *Gardner to Bridport*

Royal Sovereign, Spithead, 16 April 1797.

Your Lordship having signified your intentions of ordering me to proceed with a part of the fleet to St. Helens, I gave the necessary orders this morning to prepare the ships for sea and to hoist the launch in, which orders the ship's company have absolutely refused to obey and to a man have declared that it is their determined resolution and the resolution of the seamen and marines of the whole of your Lordship's fleet not to proceed to sea until such time as their grievances are redressed and the prayer of their petitions attended to. When the ship's company were all upon deck and standing around me I made use of every argument in my power to convince them of the impropriety of their conduct and stated to them in the strongest manner I was able the disgrace and mischiefs they were about to bring upon themselves and their country and the encouragement which this very extraordinary and unexpected conduct would give to the enemy and I am sorry to say my admonition and friendly advice was rejected in a manner which has hurt my feelings exceedingly. After a long conversation with the whole of the ship's company I selected all the good and leading men in the ship and pointed out the necessity of their good offices being employed in bringing the less informed men to a sense of their duty and that I looked upon them to do so. Their reply was that they were fully determined not to go to sea till such time as their petitions were attended to and complied with, that the seamen and marines of the fleet had been neglected and that they conceived themselves equally entitled to the notice of their country with the Army and Militia. I told them that I understood their petitions had not been sent in due form and that it was impossible that the Admiralty could give any answer whatever to anonymous letters or remonstrances and that all they could possibly expect in answer to the several petitions which I understood your Lordship had sent officially to the Admiralty would probably be that their Lordships would take them into their consideration, in reply to which they said such answer would not be satisfactory to the fleet. I think it my duty to state these matters to your Lordship and with great concern to add that the whole of this ship's company is in a state of mutiny and that their temper and disposition is materially changed for the worse since yesterday.

206b.   *Gardner to Pole*

16 April 1797

Since closing my letter to Lord Bridport it has been mentioned to Captain Bedford[1] by one of the ship's company that he has overheard below that it is at present determined by the men of the fleet to wait until Tuesday for an answer to their petitions and in case it does not arrive by that day's post that a signal with a Union [flag] and two guns is to be made on board the Queen Charlotte, when the whole of the officers are to be secured and sent on shore.[2]

---

[1]William Bedford (d. 1827). Lieutenant 1781; Captain 1794; Rear-admiral 1812; Vice-admiral 1821.

[2]It seems that this information was given to Captain Bedford of the *Royal Sovereign* by Captain Colby of the Marines on board that ship, who had heard it from one of his men.

It is proper, I think, to apprize you for Bridport's information with every circumstance that comes to my knowledge relative to the present unfortunate and very deplorable situation of the fleet.

207. *Bridport to Admiralty*

Royal George, Spithead, 17 April 1797

I received this morning at 6 o'clock by an Admiralty messenger your letter of yesterday's date acknowledging the receipt of mine of the 15th instant with the several papers transmitted with it.

It is with the greatest concern I acquaint you for their Lordships' information that the marines of this ship and I suppose in all others of the fleet have taken a decided part in favour of the seamen and been forced to take an oath to that purpose.

As I thought it expedient to send my first Captain, Rear Admiral Pole, to town with all the papers and information which had then come to my knowledge I defer entering into further particulars until he returns to Spithead.

You will herewith receive an anonymous letter sent to me from the ship's company of the St. Fiorenzo expressing their wishes with the rest of the fleet for an increase of pay.

The Queen Charlotte's people continue to take the lead in this business and in which ship all the meetings of the fleet are held as well, I believe, as persons from the shore.

I have been informed that the plan was to have taken effect before the fleet sailed from Spithead in December last and it is reported to me that petitions were presented six months ago for an increase of pay, of which I was totally ignorant 'till I wrote my first letter on this subject.

208. *Admiralty to Bridport*

17 April 1797, one a.m.

I received about an hour ago by Rear Admiral Pole and immediately communicated to my Lords Commissioners of the Admiralty your Lordship's letter of yesterday's date with the letters which had been received by you from Vice Admiral Sir Alan Gardner, Captain Payne and Captain Hood, together with further petitions which had been received from the crews of some of the ships at Spithead since your last despatch. And I am commanded by their Lordships to acquaint you that under the present circumstances they feel it impossible for them to authorize your Lordship to give any further answer to the petitioners than that their applications will be taken into immediate consideration but that the subject is of a nature that cannot be decided upon without mature deliberation. In the meantime their Lordships trust that every means will be exerted to restore the discipline of the fleet and for carrying their Lordships' order into execution of sending a part of it as speedily as possible to St. Helens.

209. *Bridport to Admiralty*

Royal George, Spithead, 17 April 1797

I have received your letter of this day's date by Rear Admiral Pole and in consequence of their Lordships' authority I have issued a memorandum to the ships under my command, a copy of which you will herewith receive and which has been read to the crews of the respective ships and I am exceedingly concerned to state that at present it appears to have made little or no impression on the ships' companies of the Royal George or Queen Charlotte, and the latter seems to guide the whole fleet and are determined not to go to sea until their grievances are redressed unless they knew the French fleet were on the coast. Their Lordships desire me to use every means in my power to restore the discipline of the fleet. Would to God I had influence sufficient for this important object, which nothing in my opinion will be able to effect but a compliance with their petitions.

By tomorrow I shall be able to learn whether the memorandum I have issued will be attended with happy consequences.

Herewith you will receive the petitions which have been transmitted to me since closing my despatch by the Admiralty messenger and I understand they are the last I shall be troubled with.

[*Enclosure*]

209a. *Bridport to crews of ships of the Channel fleet at Spithead*

Copy   Royal George, Spithead, 17 April 1797

I am to acquaint the crews of His Majesty's ships under my command that I have transmitted their petitions to the Lords Commissioners of the Admiralty and I am authorized to assure them that their petitions will be taken into serious consideration as their importance requires.

And the Commander-in-Chief trusts this answer will be satisfactory and that the different ships' companies will immediately return to their duty as the service of the country requires their proceeding to sea.

210.   *William Windham[1] to Spencer*

Bath, 17 April 1797

We have just had a little council at Burke's, who from his couch of sickness, that couch, I fear, from which he is never to rise, has been talking with all the wisdom and energy of his best times and impressing deep on us who heard him, Wilberforce, Dr. Scott, Dr. Lawrence and myself, the nature of those powers which the world never so much wanted and of which I fear they cannot long have the benefit.

He conceives, what is indeed the obvious opinion, that whatever is done must be by union of persuasion and force, by persuasion urged through the medium of all the most esteemed and accredited naval characters and by force kept in reserve to second the effects of persuasion and composed rather of mixed bodies, sailors, if they are to be had, as well as soldiers, than of any description of troops.

211.   *Admiralty to Bridport*

18 April 1797

I have received and communicated to my Lords Commissioners of the Admiralty your two letters to me of yesterday's date with the papers therein referred to on the subject of the very extraordinary proceedings of the companies of some of His Majesty's ships at Portsmouth and Spithead and in pursuance of their Lordships' commands I have transmitted the same to Mr. Marsden to be laid by him before Earl Spencer and the other members of the Board who are now with his Lordship at Portsmouth.

212.   *Minutes of the Board of Admiralty at Portsmouth*

18th April

About noon the Board of Admiralty arrived at Portsmouth. Lord Bridport and the other flag officers came and reported the state of the fleet: that

---

[1]Secretary for War 1794–1801. He followed Grenville after 1801 and served as Secretary for War in the 'Ministry of All the Talents'. A leading supporter of the French emigrant cause.

the officers were no longer obeyed in any thing beyond the internal duty of the ships, that a committee, consisting of two delegates from each line of battle ship, meeting regularly in the Admiral's Cabin of the Queen Charlotte, regulate everything and have entire command of the fleet. They issue their orders to every ship, which are exactly obeyed. They have ropes reeved to the yards of every ship to hang up any person who shall attempt to resist and it is said they have it in contemplation to put all their officers on shore and that a signal is agreed for that purpose. At 8 o'clock every morning and at sunset every evening they man the yards and cheer. The ships are in the completest order possible and they punish drunkenness and every other offence against discipline with the utmost severity. At first they would not permit any frigate to move but they have since issued their orders that all frigates may proceed according to their orders with any convoy under their protection as it was not their intention to interrupt the commerce of the country.

Lord Bridport and the other admirals stated the disgraceful situation in which they stood, as well as every other officer in their respective ships, and that it was their decided opinion that the only chance of bringing back the fleet to subordination and the seamen to their duty was by complying with the demands made in their petitions.

After long and serious deliberation it was determined that the Board should give an order to Lord Bridport stating what they meant to concede and directing his Lordship to make the same known to the fleet. This was done accordingly by Sir Alan Gardner, Admiral Colpoys and Admiral Pole going on board the Queen Charlotte and communicating a copy of the Board's said order to these delegates, who did not appear to be satisfied with the contents but said they must consult their several ships' companies and that they would return an answer by ten o'clock tomorrow morning.

Wednesday 19th.
After waiting with great anxiety 'til about one o'clock we then received a note from Sir Alan Gardner to inform us that the delegates said they could not give in their answer before 4 o'clock. About ½ past 5, while we were at dinner, the Admirals Gardner, Colpoys and Pole came to let us know that they were not satisfied with the offer made and delivered to us the paper which they had received as their answer, which contained a variety of new matter and some things quite foreign to the subject and the King's service.

At the close of this anxious evening, the whole of which was spent in the most serious consideration of all the circumstances connected with this most alarming business which was every hour assuming a worse appearance and big with the most fatal consequences, the disposition to concede evidently producing new and unreasonable demands, it being clear that a stand must be made somewhere Lord Spencer and the rest of the Board unanimously came to the resolution to declare that, having granted as much as in reason ought to satisfy the fleet, no further concession should be made and that this determination should be made known to Lord Bridport in an order directing him to communicate the same to all the ships under his command, apprizing the seamen at the same time of the consequences that must inevitably attend their persisting any longer in a state of disobedience and mutiny.

It was at the same time resolved to call all the captains on shore the next morning early that the Board should hear from them individually the state of their ships' companies and also exhort and urge them upon the delivery of this order to take immediate advantage of any favourable impression it might make upon the men and, if possible, to get their ships under weigh or to slip their cables and run down to St. Helens, by which they would be removed from the influence of those that might be still refractory and continue at Spithead.

However, upon conference with the captains the next day, viz. Thursday the 20th, their unanimous opinion taken, seriatim, as well as two of the admirals, viz. Colpoys and Pole (Sir Alan Gardner delivering himself doubtful and Lord Bridport saying that it might be tried) that even complying with their petitions for increase of wages to the full extent of their demand, there was not any chance of the men returning to their duty, from the effect of the proposed order abovementioned without the concession of 1/8th of provisions which they have asked, and also a considerable concession to the marines while on board, and the captains in general declaring it to be their firm opinion that, their requests being complied with, the men would immediately and cheerfully return to their duty without regarding the other extravagant demands contained in their petitions, the Board were reluctantly induced to change their opinion of the night before and to grant what is expressed in the margin, the latter part of the order remaining as before.

Friday 21st, 11 o'clock a.m.
Captain Holloway[1] of the Duke is this moment come in and informs us that the offer has been well received by his ship's company, that he was in great hopes that he should have prevailed upon them to have

---

[1] John Holloway (d. 1826). Lieutenant 1771; Captain 1780; Rear-admiral 1799; Vice-admiral 1804; Admiral 1809.

declared themselves satisfied and to have immediately returned to their duty but that one of the men who kept in the background called out that they must do as the Queen Charlotte did, and he soon found that it would be in vain to prevent their waiting for the decision of the delegates on board the latter ship before they returned to their obedience.

Presently after Lord Bridport came in and showed us a letter he had just received from Admiral Pole in the Royal George, saying that the offer was very well received in that ship and appeared to satisfy the people but as to the rest agreeing with Captain Holloway's report. Upon this it occurred to us that it might possibly have a considerable effect upon their delegates if something of the nature of the paper was to be in this state of things immediately stated to them by Admirals Gardner, Colpoys and Pole, who were gone to them on board the Queen Charlotte. That paper was therefore in great haste drawn up and sent off by Captain Holloway to them, as also a memorandum from Lord Spencer to show and convince them that the pardon held out to them by the Admiralty was quite sufficient to secure them from any punishment for their mutinous and disobedient conduct on this occasion.

In the evening of this day the Admirals Gardner and Pole came to us at Sir Charles Saxton's,[1] where we had dined, and Sir Alan Gardner related that their offer had been received with the greatest apparent satisfaction by his ship's company but that they reserved their decision 'til the meeting of the delegates in the Queen Charlotte had been held. The two from Sir Alan's ship (the Royal Sovereign) went thither immediately and promised directly to send their determination to him. However, after waiting a long time he determined with the Admirals Colpoys and Pole to go on board the Queen Charlotte and once more endeavour to make some impression upon them. He found them all assembled but four, viz. those from the Queen Charlotte and those from the Royal George, who were gone ashore. The remainder expressed themselves perfectly contented and satisfied and Sir Alan Gardner prevailed upon them to let him draw up a paper for them to sign, expressive of their submission and gratitude for the benefits conceded to them. Before this paper was finished the other four delegates returned from the shore and immediately went below amongst the people and persuaded them that the admirals were come on board to impose upon and deceive them and that unless they actually had the King's pardon they could have no security on submission, that the

---

[1] Sir Charles Saxton (d. 1808). Lieutenant 1757; Captain 1762. Commissioner Portsmouth dockyard 1791–1806.

mutineers on board the Culloden had been deceived with hopes of forgiveness and afterwards some of them executed.[1] Sir Alan Gardner appears to have exerted himself as much as man could[2] to counteract the false amd mischievous insinuations of these men but all to no effect, and after experiencing much disrespectful treatment, even expressions of 'Off, off, we won't have him', etc. from the people of that ship the admirals came away.

The delegates soon returned to their respective ships but some time afterwards a red flag was hoisted at the foretop of the Royal George (the signal for them to repair on board that ship) upon which Captain Domett immediately struck Lord Bridport's flag.

About this time Admirals Gardner and Pole left the fleet to come and make their report to the Admiralty of all that had passed. Admiral Colpoys continued on his ship, the London.

[*Enclosures*]

212a. *Gardner, Colpoys and Pole to delegates*

Portsmouth, 21 April 1797

That the effect already produced by the liberal offers of the Admiralty on the several ships' companies is evidently such that they will be ultimately accepted by the fleet and therefore that if the men from the several ships now assembled in the Queen Charlotte do not immediately accede thereto (they being all well known) they may rely upon it that they will be brought to condign punishment and suffer the utmost vengeance of the law. But on the contrary should they submit with alacrity they will experience the forgiveness for which the Board of Admiralty have publicly and solemnly pledged their faith to them.

212b. *Spencer to delegates*

[21st April 1797]

Sir Alan Gardner having signified to Lord Spencer and the Board of Admiralty the universal good disposition and satisfaction that had showed itself throughout the fleet on the very generous offer which has this

---

[1]The crew of the *Culloden* (74) mutinied in December 1794. After three admirals had failed to obtain their surrender Captain Thomas Pakenham succeeded. Five of the ringleaders were hanged in January 1795.

[2]He manhandled at least one person.

morning been made to them and understanding that the only obstacle that prevented their immediate return to their duty was the doubt which still remained on their minds of a free pardon up to the present time for their late illegal conduct – in consequence thereof Sir Alan Gardner has just now received the following declaration which he judges it expedient to communicate and trusts it cannot possibly fail of fully satisfying every man's mind in the fleet (viz.): the Board of Admiralty having under their hands promised forgiveness on the ships' companies complying with the conditions offered if immediately returning to their duty will most completely secure them from punishment if they comply with those conditions because under that promise no court could pronounce sentence against them even if they suppose it possible that the Board of Admiralty, having publicly pledged their faith and honour to them, could ever be brought to break it.

213.   *Keats to Warren*

Galatea, at sea, 21 April 1797

Report of the enemy's naval force in Brest water, April 21st 1797.
Ships of the line in Brest water 18, whereof completely rigged 15, nearly complete 1. Fitting with topmasts struck, one of these a three decked ship, 2.
    Frigates or cut down ships 8.
    Corvettes 3.
    Total rigged and fitting 29.
    Not more than two of the line of battle ships had their sails bent. One only of the abovementioned ships has 3 decks.

214.   *Bridport to Spencer*

Portsmouth, 10 o'clock a.m., 22 April 1797

I have reason to believe that the fleet at Spithead is in the same state as when Vice Admiral Sir Alan Gardner left it last night. Rear Admiral Pole will go to Spithead immediately to collect the temper and disposition of the crews of the ships; and if any satisfactory alteration shall have taken place I will write to your Lordship or Mr. Nepean by this night's post.
    It appears the stumbling block at present is the King's pardon. When that is offered I hope we shall have no further interruptions to our authority. My flag is still down and I think it will be better not to hoist

it again till our authority is fully restored and your Lordship is convinced that no time should be lost for its being accomplished.

[*Endorsed as received at 5 p.m.*]

215.   *Delegates of the fleet to Bridport*

[22 April 1797]

We think it our duty as well as highly proper with your Lordship's permission and to prevent misrepresentations to state to your Lordship the cause of our confusion that happened last night and which we do not hesitate to say really originated from the endeavours of Admiral Gardner to sow division and mistrust in the fleet and in fact to separate our interests which being discovered by the whole fleet has called forth such a spirit as his Lordship little is acquainted with. Nothing now but the most rigid performance of all the articles will satisfy, whereas before they were inclined to comply with the Admiralty proposals. This second instance of the failure of an officer almost universally believed to be the seaman's friend has convinced us that we have nothing to depend upon but our own vigorous assertions to obtain redress of grievances intolerable and insupportable and which the noble Admiral himself surely confesses to be just at the very instant he is manoeuvring for our destruction.

We trust however that your Lordship will consider the whole fleet as universally and zealously attached to your Lordship as their father and their friend and in short as a nobleman willing to assist and further our honest endeavours.

We beg leave to conclude by assuring your Lordship that but for the unfortunate cause abovementioned there is every reason to believe that before this time every tittle of the business would have been settled but at present it is the resolution of all not to offer to lift anchor till every article is rendered into an Act of Parliament and the King's free pardon to all concerned.

We beg your Lordship would be pleased to forward the enclosed to the Lords Commissioners of the Admiralty as it is the final answer of the fleet.

216.   *Spencer to Bridport*

Admiralty, 22 April 1797

Immediately on my arrival in town this morning a Cabinet was summoned and in consequence of their recommendation the measures of which your Lordship will be apprized by the official letters sent herewith have received His Majesty's approbation.

A memorandum communicating to the several ships under your command at Spithead His Majesty's having been graciously pleased to order the arrangements for the better management of the seamen and marines serving on board His Majesty's fleet to be carried into effect should first be read to them by their respective captains and then the proclamation signed by the King himself and under his Great Seal offering his full and gracious pardon to all those who shall return to their duty; and a private intimation might be given to the captains who read the proclamation to avail themselves in the spirit of the concluding sentence of the proclamation, 'God save the King', in order if it be yet possible to rouse again in the minds of those deluded people that loyalty which it may be too much to be apprehended the late melancholy events may have damped, though I have the greatest confidence they have not extinguished it.

I would suggest (unless your Lordship should see any strong reason to lead you to a contrary opinion) that your again hoisting your flag on board the Royal George and being yourself on board in this occasion may be of material effect and advantage, but this I must entirely submit to your own judgment on the spot. If anything more should be said on the subject of the removal of officers from particular ships each captain must be instructed to inform their men that after their complete return to their duty in the terms of the King's Royal proclamation if there is any real grievance or complaint that can be fairly and properly stated through their Commander in Chief all due attention will be paid to it but that no officer can possibly be removed in any other manner than what is presented by the established rules and invariable practice of the service.

217.   *Bridport to Spencer*

Royal George, Spithead, 23 April 1797

I have undergone so much fatigue this day that I have hardly strength to write a line to your Lordship but I cannot let the messenger go with my public letter without giving my congratulations to your Lordship that about six o'clock this afternoon the whole painful business was settled at Spithead. The first intelligence I received was from Captain Holloway soon after I landed and after I had addressed the Royal George's crew twice before I left Spithead and the men there seem perfectly satisfied but they were kept in awe by the crew of the Queen Charlotte till the happy moment arrived of their submission. I will write to your Lordship more fully tomorrow.

[P.S.] Lieutenant Becker[1] is this moment come to me with a confirmation of the above joyful tidings.

218.   *Spencer to Bridport*

Admiralty, 24 April 1797

A great multiplicity of business having pressed upon me today owing in a great measure to some arrears of correspondence which had accumulated during my absence at Portsmouth makes it utterly impossible for me to do more at this moment than most sincerely to congratulate your Lordship on the termination of the mutiny at Spithead or to express the great additional satisfaction that I feel at hearing by the telegraph[2] that a part of the fleet was actually in motion this morning. I shall reserve anything further I may have to say till after the letter which your Lordship has given me reason to expect tomorrow.

219.   *Bridport to Spencer*

Royal George, Spithead, 24 April 1797

I have the satisfaction to acquaint your Lordship that the mutiny in the ships at Spithead under my orders is happily put an end to; but we have many personal complaints against officers which I judge arises from the late tumultuous conduct of the seamen and marines. I have transmitted one from the Minotaur and another from the Marlborough by this post to Mr. Nepean and I have directed an enquiry to be made by Vice Admiral Colpoys into that of the crew of the Nymphe. The Queen Charlotte's conduct is a subject of great consequence to the fleet and which in my opinion calls for the most serious attention as she is not to

[1]Alexander Becher (d. 1827). Lieutenant 1791; Captain 1802.
[2]The telegraph between London and Portsmouth was brought into use late in 1796. A full account of the system can be found in Geoffrey Wilson, *The Old Telegraphs* (London, 1976).

be pushed in service. I have often thought that had she been under the buoy of the late Royal George it would have been a blessing to the country. Indeed, I cannot help suggesting to your Lordship to pay her off and the men moved into other ships. I do not know the officer that would wish to command her. I have many things that I wish to impart to your Lordship personally, if the service would permit my being in town for a short time. Vice Admiral Gardner is gone to St. Helens with six ships, as I have told Mr. Nepean; Vice Admiral Colpoys will remain at Spithead till the whole squadron shall move from thence as he may be necessary to carry on certain duties as the second officer now with me.

I am sorry to inform your Lordship that we shall have many enquiries, if not court martials, and I cannot get the Minotaur to proceed to St. Helens from those circumstances. The crew of the Royal George have taken a dislike to Doctor Johnston, her surgeon, and it was with difficulty Captain Domett could prevent his being turned out of the ship. As he is, I believe, a very good surgeon it would relieve his mind much could he be removed to any hospital, as he appears miserable on board.

I have taken the liberty to send enclosed the names of two gentlemen in the Royal George who have passed for the station of lieutenants and I find there is a vacancy for one in the Mars. I recommend Mr. Thomas Bell Sullivan[1] to be appointed to this ship as he has served with Captain Hood.

[P.S.] I am afraid the subject of flour will occasion further discontent.

[*Endorsed as received on the 25th*]

220. *Admiralty to Bridport*

24 April 1797

I received yesterday by express and lost no time in communicating to my Lords Commissioners of the Admiralty your Lordship's letter of the 22nd instant enclosing a petition which your Lordship had received from the Royal George, said to be the final answer of the ships therein named, together with three letters to you from Captains Brine,[2] Thornbrough and Nicholls[3] on the subject of the proposals which had been made known to the crews of their respective ships.

[1]Thomas Bell Sullivan (d. 1857). Lieutenant 1797; Captain 1814.
[2]James Brine (d. 1814). Lieutenant 1766; Captain 1779; Rear-admiral 1799; Vice-admiral 1804; Admiral 1809.
[3]Sir Henry Nicholls (d. 1829). Lieutenant 1780; Captain 1788; Rear-admiral 1807; Vice-admiral 1811; Admiral 1825.

The fortunate turn which has taken place in the state of affairs on board the said ships since the representations above mentioned were made renders any explanations on these points almost unnecessary but in order that your Lordship may be apprized of the opinion their Lordships entertain I have their command to acquaint you that after the very liberal additions made to the wages and to the allowance of provisions to the seamen in His Majesty's ships their Lordships cannot but look upon these further demands to be very unreasonable. The request that the further issue of a proportion of flour in lieu of meat may be discontinued cannot at this time be complied with, it being impossible to procure a quantity of the last mentioned article of provisions sufficient for the consumption of the fleet but whenever the present difficulties in that respect can be removed it has always been their Lordships' intention to cause the full proportion of fresh beef to be supplied. The quantity of vegetables now served to seamen in port is much greater than was ever served in any former war and a proper quantity will always be furnished but instead of unreasonably asking for more they ought to be most thankful for that with which at a great expense to the country they are now supplied.

With respect to an increase of out pensions of the Royal Hospital at Greenwich I am to state to your Lordship that the present revenues of the said Hospital do not admit of a compliance with this request and when the burdens which must necessarily be laid upon the public in consequence of the increase of wages are considered it cannot be expected that any additional sum can be appropriated to this purpose or that the expedient proposal can be resorted to for removing the difficulty. On the subject of the complaints which have been made against the different officers it must be understood that all such complaints ought to be made to the Commander in Chief and there can be no doubt should the circumstances appear to justify it that the officers complained of will be brought to courts martial. Without that mode of enquiry into the merits of the different cases their Lordships' regard for justice will not admit of their inflicting punishment or censure. But as the characters of officers are not to be lightly attacked the seamen should be admonished not to prefer any complaint against them without having good cause for so doing. In consequence, however, of the favourable change that has taken place in the situation of things, their Lordships are inclined to hope that all animosities have ceased and that the complaints which were brought forward in a moment of ill humour may now be suffered to drop, more especially when the seamen reflect upon the zealous part which their officers have taken in prevailing on their Lordships to consent to the indulgences which have been granted to them.

221. *Spencer to Bridport*

Admiralty, 25 April 1797

The uneasiness which prevails in London on account of the fleet remaining at Spithead and still more the very great alarm in Ireland on the expectation found in that country from a variety of circumstances of an almost immediate attack from the enemy make it a matter of absolute necessity for your Lordship to show yourself at sea with as large a squadron as the present state of things will admit of.

Your orders therefore to sail go down by this post and we have directed the London, the Marlborough, the Ramillies and the Minotaur to remain at Spithead for the present in order if possible to get the better of the separate complaints of some of those ships or to bring them into a state of regular enquiry. I have in my own mind very little doubt that when at sea the unpleasant agitation of mind naturally the consequence of what has passed will by regular and constant employment subside and that if any good chance should throw an enemy in your way every man in the fleet will have no other object but the most active and effectual performance of his duty.

. . . I am happy to learn from the Victualling Office that it will very soon be in their power to return to the issue of the usual quantity of fresh beef in port and whenever that is the case we shall on every account be very glad to avail ourselves of the opportunity of doing so.

222. *Bridport to Spencer*

Portsmouth, 26 April 1797

This morning the messenger brought me the honour of your Lordship's letter of yesterday's date and I am happy to hear that fresh beef will soon be issued to the fleet instead of a proportion of flour as I am well informed that measure will give perfect satisfaction. I rejoice also that the notification of the proposed regulations was received with becoming satisfaction and gratitude from all the ships at Plymouth.

I was fully prepared to receive the Board's order for proceeding to sea as soon as wind and weather will permit but at present we have a strong gale at south-west with much sea at Spithead. The moment it is moderate I will move to St. Helens with the remainder of the ships I am authorized to take with me.

The circumstances of the Nymphe will not, I apprehend, allow her to accompany me to sea but I have reason to expect the Jason will as soon as proper surveys can be taken on the Boatswain's and Gunner's stores, after the removal of the two officers turned on shore and the appointment of two others.

[*Endorsed as received on the 27th and answered next day*]

223.   *Spencer to Bridport*

Admiralty, 28 April 1797

As I collect from your letter of the 26th that it is still possible this should reach you before your departure from St. Helens I think it right to acquaint your Lordship that we have this morning received an account from Sir John Orde[1] at Plymouth that notwithstanding the very favourable appearances of everything remaining right at that port the ships in the Sound and Cawsand Bay had been induced by some very strong letters received by them from Portsmouth (during the mutiny I suppose) to come to a determination not to weigh (except for Spithead) till the people at Portsmouth were satisfied. Sir John Orde adds that the weather on the 26th prevented him from going on board but that he was in hopes on the next morning to bring all to rights again by authoritatively acquainting them that all was happily terminated at Spithead. Your Lordship's appearance off Plymouth will be a very strong confirmation of that intelligence and I should hope that the Edgar will join you according to her orders without any difficulty, but as it may be as well for you to be apprized of the circumstances which have taken place I hope this may reach you in time.

224.   *Bridport to Admiralty*

Royal George, St Helens, 1 May 1797

It having been represented to me that the companies of the several ships under my orders might refuse going to sea when the signal should be made for that purpose unless the proper weights and measures were received in their respective ships and as there appeared to me no means of preventing so alarming a circumstance I judged it expedient to have

---

[1]Sir John Orde (1751–1824). Lieutenant 1774; Captain 1778; Rear-admiral 1795; Vice-admiral 1799; Admiral 1805. Became Governor of Dominica in 1783 but returned to serve in the Channel in 1793. Sent home from the Mediterranean in 1798 after a quarrel with St Vincent. Served briefly at sea in 1804–5 but was otherwise unemployed.

the enclosed memorandum delivered to each captain, which I hope will meet with their Lordships' approbation.

In the several petitions of the fleet the terms 'full weight and measure' and 'of a better quality' are made use of and I beg to observe to their Lordships that two thirds of a pound of Cheshire cheese is equal to one pound of Suffolk, though the former in quality is generally very little superior to the latter. I therefore wish to be informed if this distinction is to be continued or whether they are to have full sixteen ounces to the pound in that species of provisions.

225.   *Spencer to Kingsmill*[1]

Admiralty, 4 May 1797

In addition to what I said to you on the subject of having one or two of your frigates constantly sweeping the north-east and northerly coasts of Ireland I think it right to call your attention to a circumstance which will require your notice not only with respect to the ships so employed but very probably to all the others on your station. I mean the persons who may be put on board them under the late acts[2] passed for that purpose on a suspicion of being disaffected.

I am very credibly informed that many persons of this description very willingly go on board the ships of war with intentions of doing mischief by seducing the other men from their duty and prevailing on them to enter into combinations to take oaths, etc., some symptoms of which have appeared in the late alarming mutinies at Portsmouth and Plymouth though we have not yet been able absolutely to trace them to any particular persons of this description.[3] These men therefore (whom it is necessary for the quiet of the country to receive on board the fleet) should be most narrowly watched and you will do well to put the several captains under your command in a confidential manner on their guard about them. As few of them as possible should be allowed to be together on board any one ship and some note should be taken of their

---

[1]Commander-in-Chief on the coast of Ireland 1793–1800.

[2]The two Acts of 18 December 1795 were against speakers inciting people to contempt of the King, constitution or government, and against unauthorised meetings of more than 50 persons. See E. P. Thompson, *The Making of the English Working Class* (Harmondsworth, 1963), 158–9.

[3]For an examination of whether the Spithead mutiny was motivated by political disaffection or demands for improvements in material conditions, and for the number of Irish seamen tried by courts martial for opposition to authority, see C. Doorne, 'Mutiny and Sedition in the Home Commands of the Royal Navy, 1793–1803', unpublished University of London PhD thesis, 1998.

names that they may be known and traced in whatever ships they may be removed to.

226. *Spencer to Bridport*

Admiralty, 4 May 1797

I am very sorry to perceive by your Lordship's secret letter (written in your own hand) received today that so much dissatisfaction still prevails on board the fleet under your command.[1] I think it extremely essential that, if possible, the men should be convinced that every thing which was promised them not only is intended to be performed but actually has been, as far as it possibly could be, carried into execution. The Order giving sanction to the regulations proposed by the King in Council passed the Council yesterday, which was the earliest day it could, as the forms required it to be referred to a Committee of Council before it could be ratified. The estimate of the charge to be incurred is now preparing at the several offices and Mr. Pitt means to lay it before the Committee of Supply tomorrow in the House of Commons, who will vote money upon account of it; which is all that is necessary to give it full force; and as commencement of the augmentation of wages is to be fixed on the 24th of last month and the victuals at whole allowance have actually been ordered to be issued the whole of the arrangement is really at this moment as much in force as the nature of things will allow it to be. Every man who was now to be paid off or turned over is as much entitled to his increased pay from the 24th ultimo as ever he was to his pay on the former footing and they must feel that they are really in possession of the augmentation of victuals: the weights and measures necessarily take a considerable time in making but I am assured by the Victualling Board that a considerable number of weights will be ready to be sent down by Tuesday or Wednesday next.

It might probably not be amiss to apprize all the officers of these facts that they may be enabled to satisfy their ships' companies upon them if they find it necessary and I trust that after what has happened they will all see and feel the necessity of the utmost vigilance in being beforehand with any commotion or disturbance which may be attempted to be incited among their people and in informing themselves accurately of the particular men who are most busy in holding the very

---

[1]The letter concerned a report by James White, Surgeon's Mate of the Mars. See Bridport's letter of 5 May.

dangerous language which is represented to have been held on board of one of the ships.

This wind is very unfortunate for us, as I am persuaded being at sea would be the best prevention against further disturbances. I hope, however, it will not be of long continuance. Our accounts from Brest seem to point at some expedition being in contemplation and we have private intelligence from the Continent of the same tendency. It is said to be intended for some time in the course of this month; whether they will be ready so soon or no is uncertain but if it be true (as it appears likely to be) that the Emperor has concluded a separate peace they will not long be restrained for want of men, at least for that part of the expedition which belongs to the land service, whatever may be the case in respect to seamen.[1]

227. *Bridport to Spencer*

Royal George, St Helens, 5 May 1797

The honour of your Lordship's letter of yesterday's date is this instant received and I have the satisfaction to inform your Lordship that the ships under my command in appearance seem to be satisfied with what Government has done for the seamen and marines respecting an increase of pay and full allowance of provisions, as have been liberally promised them by the Board's order of the 20th of last month.

The reason of my sending the papers, enclosed to Mr. Nepean, in a letter written with my own hand, was occasioned by that delivered to me by the commander of one of the ships, which I thought should not be publicly known. There are likewise some bad and mischievous men in the fleet and if possible they should be selected from those whose minds are perfectly satisfied and strictly obedient but there may be some difficulty in adopting such measures at present.

I have very fully explained to the ships the time necessary to be taken before the whole business can be arranged and I have assured the crews that what has been promised will be faithfully performed and I have great reason to believe that the crew of the Royal George are convinced of the truth of it.

We have had very blowing weather yesterday and all this day, which has prevented my having a communication with the ships of the squadron and has delayed the delivering out the Board's order of the 1st instant but I hope it will be more moderate tomorrow and allow me to

---

[1] Preliminaries of peace were signed at Leoben on 18 April.

carry the fleet to sea as I am anxious to make an appearance off Plymouth.

[Endorsed as received on the 6th and answered the same day]

228.   *Spencer to Bridport*

Admiralty, 6 May 1797

I had the honour of your Lordship's letter of yesterday this morning and I am truly happy to find that at length tranquillity and order seem to be perfectly established in your squadron. We have received a very good account today of the ships in Plymouth Sound and Cawsand Bay and on your Lordship's appearance off that anchorage they will, I have no doubt, most cheerfully join you.

We have had a very severe lesson in this business and I trust all the officers in the fleet will feel the effect of it. A relaxation of discipline will sooner or later produce mischief and the only way to remedy what is past will, I am fully persuaded, be by a very steady and invariable adherence to the strictest rules of the service. It has ever been my desire to make the service as far as I thought consistent with its interests as agreeable as possible to all those engaged in it and I may perhaps have been misled by this principle in some degree to give a little more indulgence than could in strictness be justified. The example which the late events have exhibited to us must necessarily produce more caution on this head and I trust that the effect of it will be what we must all most sincerely wish it to be.

229.   *Bridport to Spencer*

Royal George, St Helens, 7 May 1797

When I did myself the honour of writing to your Lordship on the 5th instant I concluded the squadron under my orders had no grievance to complain of but yesterday some reports were brought to me that gave me much alarm and which I transmitted to Mr. Nepean for the information of their Lordships. Before I had the honour of your Lordship's letter, received this morning, the crews of all the ships here were in a state of mutiny and all that Rear Admiral Pole as well as myself could say, on this ship, or effect by other means, we could not stop their proceeding to adopt the same disorderly measures as took place at Spithead. What will be the consequence, God only knows, but I am told the fleet will not obey my signals, when made, for proceeding to sea.

I find, with some distress and pain, that I cannot command the Channel fleet with credit to myself or advantage to the public. I suggest to your Lordship whether it might be better for the King's service that I should be permitted to strike my flag and go on shore. I write these thoughts privately to your Lordship for candid consideration as indeed my health has been so much impaired by the late and present painful trials as to render me unfit for public employment, having gouty pain in every limb with very restless nights.

We have a light breeze of wind easterly and it was my intention to have carried the squadron this day to sea if these fresh disturbances had not taken place. I have ordered copies of the vote in the Committee of Supply to be issued to all the ships but paper and words seem to have no effect in the present disposition of the people and I am fully persuaded they are governed by documents from the shore.

I am informed the boats are gone to Spithead to bring the Marlborough to St. Helens. Your Lordship knows the conversation that passed in the Monarch[1] and I am told the people have said they will humble the pride of England.

[*Endorsed as received on the 8th and answered the same day*]

230.   *Bridport to Admiralty*

Royal George, St Helens, 7 May 1797

I am unable to express my feelings upon sending the enclosed letters and papers which have been brought to me and I am overwhelmed with the most painful concern in stating to you for their Lordships' information that the whole fleet is returned again into the highest pitch of mutiny and disobedience to every officer of the fleet.

I have endeavoured to prevent this mischief by every argument in my power but without effect and I cannot command the fleet as all authority is taken from me. I intended to have made the signal for the fleet to weigh this morning as the wind was easterly but I am compelled to remain here unless the Vote of Supply in the House of Commons for the increases of the seamen's pay and provisions should arrive and give the crews of the fleet satisfaction. The boats are now rowing round the fleet in the same manner as they did this day fortnight. My mind is so deeply

[1]Ship name unclear.

wounded by all these proceedings and I am so unwell that I can scarcely hold my pen to write these sentiments of despair.

Immediately after the newspapers arrived I caused the motion referred to the committee of supply for the increase of seamen's provisions to be copied and transmitted to the several ships under my orders.

The boats, after going on board the different ships at this anchorage, are gone to Spithead against all authority.

231.   *Bridport to Admiralty*

Royal George, St Helens, 8 May 1797, 5 p.m.

I am sorry to acquaint you for the information of the Lords Commissioners of the Admiralty that the fleet is in a more disorderly state than when I wrote to you yesterday, as their Lordships will see by the enclosed copy of a letter from Vice Admiral Colpoys which I received last night together with one from Captain John Cooke, who is turned out of the Nymphe, and it is with deep concern I inform their Lordships that the captains and officers of the Duke, Terrible and Mars are turned out of their ships together with the 1st, 5th, 6th and 7th Lieutenants and the Lieutenant of Marines of the Pompee and I am afraid these examples will be followed by other ships.

The red flag was hoisted this morning on board the Royal Sovereign, where a boat from every ship repaired. It was afterwards hoisted on board the Mars, where the people calling themselves delegates have been nearly the whole of this day assembled. The red flag has also been hoisted in the Terrible as well as in the Defiance, these signals from the different ships indicate a serious combination and represents a sad situation to me and the officers that shall be allowed to remain in the fleet.

The London, Marlborough and Nymphe are now under weigh for St. Helens and the Monarch anchored here this morning.

232.   *Spencer to Bridport*

Admiralty, 8 May 1797, 10 p.m.

I trust that the official notification which will be made to you of the unanimous vote of the House of Commons today will remove all the difficulties which have so unexpectedly again risen in the fleet under your command and that you will be enabled to put to sea, which on all accounts becomes more desirable every day.

With regard to the particular subject of your Lordship's letter of yesterday I can only at present say that the considerations involved in it are of too much importance for me to take any decisions hastily upon it. However I may always be disposed to attend to any wishes you may express; the present moment is such as to make the maintenance of the discipline of the service an object of the first consideration and indeed paramount to every other and I do not see any means at present so likely to obtain the very desirable end of restoring order and subordination in the fleet as their being at sea where their situation will necessarily find them constant employment and bring them back into their old habits of regularity and obedience to their officers.

We understand by the telegraph today that the ships at Spithead are gone down to St. Helens, among which is the Marlborough, several of whose officers have been put on shore. If you should be enabled to sail before you hear further from us it will be advisable for your Lordship to appoint others to act in their room, which may perhaps (under the present circumstances) be as unobjectionable a way of getting that ship to sea as can be adopted.

233. *Admiralty to Bridport*

9 May 1797

I received this morning and laid before my Lords Commissioners of the Admiralty your Lordship's letter of yesterday's date acquainting me for their Lordships' information that since the preceding day the disorders on board the fleet had increased, that proceedings had taken place indicating a serious combination among the crews of the different ships and enclosing copy of a letter from Vice Admiral Colpoys, together with one from Captain Cooke of the Nymphe, who, with the captains of the Duke, Terrible and Mars and several other officers had been turned out of their respective ships. These unfortunate proceedings have filled their Lordships with the deepest concern but they hope and trust that the communication of the unanimous vote of the House of Commons and of the Order of His Majesty in Council to which it refers and which were last night sent off to your Lordship by a messenger will have produced some favourable consequences and convinced the crews of the ships who have been misled by false representations that the regular steps have been taken for enabling His Majesty to carry his gracious intentions into effect and that the men will lose no time in giving proofs of their loyalty and obedience.

234.   *Bridport to Admiralty*

Royal George, at St Helens, 9 May 1797

I have received your letter of yesterday's date transmitting to me an attested copy of the vote of the House of Commons for granting to His Majesty a sum towards defraying the expense to be incurred by an increase in the wages and provisions to the seamen and marines of the fleet according to His Majesty's Order in Council of the 3rd instant, a copy of which I have also received, and acquainting me if under any circumstances it should appear to me desirable that the Marlborough should accompany me to sea that I should supply the deficiency of officers on board her from any other ships which may be under my orders.

As several of the ships of this squadron are in the same unfortunate situation with respect to officers as the Marlborough it is impossible for me to form a squadron and carry it to sea under the present circumstances and I submit it to their Lordships' consideration as to sending officers without delay to supply the vacancies of those who have been turned on shore if they shall deem it necessary.

I see by the Order in Council the increase of pay and provisions to the seamen and marines of the fleet does not take place before the 24th of April but their Lordships' order to me was dated the 20th and I have always stated to the people of this ship that the increase would commence from that day, which I hope will take place.

It blows strong at E.N.E. with too much sea to have any communication with the ships by signal this day, the topgallant masts and lower yards being struck.

235.   *Bridport to Spencer*

[19 May 1797?]

I have this instant received the honour of your Lordship's private letter of yesterday's date, which I am unable to answer as I ought. But I think your Lordship and the Board of Admiralty must see how impossible it is for me to carry a squadron to sea either in justice to myself or safety to the country under the state of the ships, without captains or officers, Vice Admiral Gardner sent on shore and his flag struck but hoisted again at the whim of the ship's crew and Vice Admiral Colpoys, his captain and four of his lieutenants in close confinement and their lives threatened, which circumstance I find no notice is taken of by Mr. Nepean's letter which I have just received.

If I could restore order and discipline it would give comfort and happiness to the end of my days but that cannot be done in a moment and the being at sea is no security to that object or safety to the King's service. I shall exert my feeble efforts to serve the nation if I can, which is all that I can offer to your Lordship upon the subject.

[Endorsed as received on the 10th]

236. *Admiralty to Curtis*

9 May 1797

By the messenger who is charged with this letter you will receive an order from my Lords Commissioners of the Admiralty for putting to sea with the squadron under your command and proceeding off the Lizard for the purpose of preventing the execution of any plans the enemy may have formed. Their Lordships have, however, directed me to inform you by this secret letter that although they consider it important on that account that the squadron should put to sea it is not less necessary for the purpose of keeping, if possible, the crews of His Majesty's ships under your command, as well as those under the command of Rear Admiral Lord Hugh Seymour out of the way of communication with the crews of the ships at St. Helens now in a state of mutiny. But as your carrying that order into execution must in a great measure depend upon the state of obedience in which the crews of the different ships under your command may be when this letter reaches you their Lordships must leave you to act upon it or not, according to circumstances.

237. *Admiralty to Bridport*

10 May 1797

I received this morning by the messenger and lost no time in communicating to my Lords Commissioners of the Admiralty your two letters of yesterday's date . . . acquainting me that in the unfortunate situation of the squadron with respect to officers it appeared impossible for you to form a squadron and carry it to sea, expressing at the same time your hope that in consequence of the assurances given to the crew of the Royal George the increase of the pay and allowances should take place from the 20th instead of the 24th of last month as directed by His Majesty's Order in Council of the 3rd instant. In answer to these letters

I have the honour of acquainting you that their Lordships will take into their immediate consideration what may be proper to be done in respect to the several officers who have been sent on shore and that in consideration and on the grounds of the assurances held out by your Lordship in respect to the time of the commencement of the additional wages and allowances an addition equivalent to the amount of the pay and allowances for the four days will be made to the seamen and marines belonging to the fleet.

238. *Spencer to Bridport*

Admiralty, 10 May 1797

I have to acknowledge your Lordship's letter without date by the return of the messenger who carried out the copy of the unanimous vote of the House of Commons and can only say that I am perfectly sensible of the great difficulty and very disagreeable nature of your situation at the time it was written. In a business of this kind when every moment may produce a change of circumstances it is impossible for a person at any distance to draft his expressions in such a manner to the circumstance of each moment as not to make them very liable to be on their arrival very much misplaced and the observation contained in my letter of the day before yesterday to which this of your Lordship's is an answer, having been founded on the information I had derived of the state of things on the day before (with the addition by telegraph of the movement of the ships from Spithead) became subject to this inconvenience and consequently inapplicable to the altered situation in which you were when it reached you.

It is partly on such consideration as the above that His Majesty's servants have determined to advise the King to send down Lord Howe with instructions under the Sign Manual to communicate with the fleet and if possible to avail himself of those favourable dispositions which I am happy to find by the letter received today have again begun to manifest themselves, in order to bring them back to their duty and a proper subordination to their officers. These instructions would have been directed to your Lordship as Commander-in-Chief of the Channel fleet if it had not (in the most serious and mature deliberation we could give to the subject) been decided that the circumstance of your being their commanding officer on this occasion suggested many reasons against your being personally charged with the execution of this measure. I understand that Mr. Pitt has written today to your Lordship upon it and I shall therefore at present (being very much pressed in point of time) confine myself to adding that I most sincerely hope and trust that by the time this letter reaches you the favourable appearance yesterday will have been very much increased and confirmed by the very extraordinary mark of attention which the legislature has paid to the wishes of the seamen by passing through all its stages in one day the Act for confirming what had been before granted to them by His Majesty.

239. *Spencer to Howe*

Admiralty, 10 May 1797

We are informed by the messenger who returned a few hours ago from Portsmouth that late last night several boats came on shore from the Royal Sovereign earnestly to request Sir Alan Gardner to return on board and hoist his flag and that a similar request had been made from the Duke to Captain Holloway, who is likewise on shore at Portsmouth by the same cause. I am very glad to hear this as it seems to promise better for the success of your mission to which I need not add I most sincerely and cordially wish the happiest possible termination.

240. *Bridport to William Pitt*

Royal George, St Helens, 11 May 1797

I feel myself much honoured by your most obliging and affectionate letter of yesterday's date.

I hope the appearance of Earl Howe at Portsmouth will fully answer the expectations of the public by restoring regular order in the fleet at Spithead and at this anchorage. His Lordship will find me ready to give every assistance in my power to assist this most important and necessary object which I hope the measure will produce without delay. In many respects we are better than when I wrote to the Admiralty yesterday but still the authority is in the hands of the people.

I have had, my dear sir, a most anxious time and much to encounter with and if I had not kept quiet, calm and composed the consequences would have been more alarming. I have always considered peevish words and hasty orders detrimental and it has been my study not to allow the one or issue the other. I wish that rule had guided the conduct of those in higher situations as I think 'tis wiser to soothe than combat disturbed and agitated minds.

While I have the honour to command His Majesty's fleet I shall steadily pursue this line of conduct and to the last moment of my life it will be my pride as well as my duty to manifest my loyalty to the King and my rooted attachment to our excellent constitution.

241. *Howe to Spencer*

Portsmouth, 11 May 1797

Not being yet sufficiently advanced in the purpose of my recent appointment to be provided with suitable materials for an official despatch to be addressed to the Secretary of State I trust I shall be excused for preferring this less formal mode of communication in making known the progress of my endeavours for the purpose of my instructions.

Having been in conversation with the delegates (as they are termed) of the discontented seamen in the presence of Lord Bridport and such of the crew of the Royal George as were willing to attend on the tenor of my instructions the chief retardment to a satisfactory conclusion regarded two points: the one created by a doubt the seamen entertained whether they were to deem my declaration of the King's pardon competent to their security, in place of which some of them pressed for the possession of a printed copy of the King's expected proclamation. I would therefore submit whether I should not be most speedily furnished with about 20 of such printed copies deemed by some of the more wrongheaded men as the only unquestionable act of the sovereign and to be issued by me on the condition which would only justify me in any similar service of a power with which I am already provided. The other very important object in my apprehension was the consent of the seamen to receive back the officers they had dismissed from their ships. Without entering into the particular and under great doubts on the event of any modification yet occurring to me on the subject I wish to know whether if I prevail for the readmission of the officers on condition that I should profess to use my endeavours to obtain their removal forthwith into other ships it is judged fit for me to settle our differences in that manner? Whether they can be appointed directly to other ships or different officers nominated by the Admiralty to the deficient ships; how far I must possess the assent of the seamen to the reception of those officers as a condition without which I am not to restore the delinquent seamen to the King's peace; or finally if I am to acquiesce in the resistance to the reinstatement of other accused officers. Furnished with the intentions of Government on these points I shall make the best stand I am able for obtaining the most preferable alternative.

Much would under other circumstances be requisite for me to add in excuse for sending such an undigested letter. But I am really so fatigued with the occupations of the day that I cannot attempt to render it more intelligible.

Upon the whole I was received with the utmost consideration. Almost all my propositions were concurred in at times but fresh exceptions started to them and we finally separated with the professions of the seamen to consult their principals and communicate the result when I return to them tomorrow.

About 40 or so Irishmen of the class of Defenders it is thought in the Duke seem to be our most exceptionable opponents.

[Endorsed as received on the 12th by a messenger]

242.   *Victualling Board to Admiralty*

11 May 1797

We have received your letter of the 9th instant inclosing an extract of one which the Right Honourable the Lords Commissioners of the Admiralty had received from Rear Admiral Sir Roger Curtis, dated Torbay the 7th instant representing that fresh beef was not ready to be issued to the squadron under his command, and signifying their Lordships' direction to us to take effectual measures for supplying the said fleet in a regular and proper manner.

In return to which we beg leave to acquaint you for the information of their Lordships that in consequence of your letter of the 2nd instant, which we did not receive until the 3rd, we gave immediate directions to the contractor with this board for furnishing fresh beef to His Majesty's Ships at Torbay, to be prepared with sufficient cattle against the arrival of the before mentioned squadron, to comply with the demands of fresh beef that might be made upon him; who, on the same day, wrote to his agent to be provided with the requisite supplies of cattle, but whose letter could not be received until the 5th.

The contractor having attended the Board this day upon the subject, it appears, from what he has stated to us, that he has taken every step in his power to be prepared with proper and adequate supplies of fresh beef for the said squadron, though we fear it would not be possible for him to commence upon the issue thereof, in the proportion required, before Tuesday last.

243.   *Bridport to Admiralty*

Royal George, St Helens, 13 May 1797

I received your letter of yesterday's date at 3 o'clock this morning acquainting me that if such difficulties should still remain with respect to any particular ships as may prevent their sailing immediately whether it may not be advisable to leave some of the most refractory behind if I should think fit, it being of the utmost importance in the present moment that the fleet should put to sea with the least possible delay. In answer to which I am of opinion if the refractory ships were left behind at St. Helens when the Royal George proceeds to sea that they would follow her and I ground this opinion upon the circumstance of the London, Marlborough and Nymphe being brought from Spithead to this anchorage by their respective crews from the idea that they were to remain there for some particular purpose.

I am as anxious for proceeding to sea as their Lordships can be but under the present existing circumstances of the fleet I see no immediate prospect of my being able to execute the order I am under and I own I feel rather hurt on being so often pressed upon that object, which rather indicates neglect of my duty.

244.   *Chatham to Bridport*

Berkeley Square, 13 May 1797

I received your letter this morning and not without some disappointment as I had rather flattered myself a more rapid progress would have been made in restoring tranquillity in the fleet. It is not necessary now to look back to the past, which is now matter of vain regret but which I shall be glad to talk over with you whenever we meet, nor shall I say anything as to Lord Howe's mission, as he is actually gone, more than to express my earnest wishes that he may be able to settle things speedily, for every hour's delay is pregnant with mischief incredible. I have not much time to write. I will therefore only remark upon what particularly strikes me in your letter. I am, with you, perfectly aware of the delicate situation in which an officer is placed who is to carry the fleet to sea. I hope, though, that in presence of an enemy they would do their duty well but I perceive difficulties in any long and arduous services. With a view, however, to the public I should consider any change in the command of the fleet as most unfortunate. With regard to your conduct in all this unhappy business I am happy in thinking there is but one opinion and I am sure that your continuing in your present situation, however painful to yourself, must ensure you the approbation of every well-wisher to his country.

There is one circumstance on which I differ a little from you and which you will excuse my mentioning, which is the idea you suggest in the case of officers turned out of their ships that a court martial should decide upon their merits. I do not like the principle that an officer should be put on his trial at a time that a general amnesty is granted to the fleet for the most heinous offence of which seamen can be guilty. I doubt much its giving satisfaction, for if the officers are acquitted partiality would be imputed and at the same time the contention would be kept alive. I hope, therefore, some more summary way may be found. I own I hardly see how, unless the men consent unconditionally to take back all the officers the Admiralty shall choose, there can be the remnants of anything like discipline in the fleet. At the same time it may be prudent at this unfortunate conjunction not to send back any man whose imprudence may have given any just ground of complaint against him, but all this turns on the ability with which the thing is managed and with regard to which, after the sad experience we have had I cannot be sanguine. The infinite pains taken by the disaffected to inflame the minds of the men on prize money, etc. makes one more and more anxious for the fleet, if it be possible, to get soon to sea. I must now conclude but not without assuring you of the unceasing anxiety with which I have watched all this business with regard to yourself personally and how deeply I have felt for the many trying situations in which you have stood.

245. *Admiralty to Bridport*

13 May 1797

I have received and communicated to my Lords Commissioners of the Admiralty your Lordship's letter of yesterday's date, inclosing a letter to you from Captain Campbell[1] of the Terrible relative to the proceedings of the crew of that ship towards him and his officers, with other papers upon the same subject and also a petition from the crew of La Nymphe, and desiring to know whether it is their Lordships' intention that upon your proceeding to sea with the rest of the fleet, you should take the London with you; in return thereto I am commanded by their

---

[1]Sir George Campbell (d. 1821). Lieutenant 1778; Captain 1781; Rear-admiral 1801; Vice-admiral 1806; Admiral 1814.

Lordships to acquaint you that they are pleased to authorize you to take the London with you to sea, or to send her to Spithead, whichever you may judge to be most adviseable.

With repect to the appointment of officers to the Terrible and La Nymphe as so [listed[1]] by the crews of those ships, their Lordships demand me to refer you to the directions of my letter of the 11th instant by which you will perceive that it is left to you to act as in your discretion may seem most adviseable.

246. *Admiralty to Bridport*

13 May 1797

I have received and communicated to my Lords Commissioners of the Admiralty your Lordships' letter of the 11th instant acquainting me that Admiral Earl Howe had in that day come on board the Royal George for the purpose of carrying into execution the commission with which his Lordship is charged.

By letters which have been received this morning from Rear Admiral Sir Roger Curtis (copies of which are enclosed) it appears that dissatisfaction had shewn itself amongst the crews of the ships of the squadron in Torbay in consequence of which their Lordships have sent directions to him, if he cannot prevail upon them to remain for the present at that anchorage, to repair to Spithead.

The ships named in the margin[2] which were intended to have joined the Rear Admiral off the Lizard, from Plymouth, have, as you will perceive by the inclosed letter from Rear Admiral Sir John Orde, proceeded to that rendezvous: and if upon your Lordship's sailing from St. Helens you should fall in with either, or both, of those squadrons, their Lordships are pleased to allow you to take them under your orders

Their Lordships trust that from the message communicated by telegraph this afternoon from Earl Howe, order will shortly be restored; and as it will be extremely important that the earliest information of that event should be given to the ships at the different ports, I have it in command to desire that you will take the most speedy means of sending notice thereof to Sir John Orde at Plymouth, and also to Torbay, taking the chance of finding Sir Roger Curtis at that anchorage.

If your Lordship should happen to fall in with the squadron under the orders of Rear Admiral Lord Hugh Seymour, it is their Lordships'

[1]Indecipherable.
[2]Not named in the draft.

direction that you do order his Lordship to make the best of his way with the said squadron to Spithead.

247.   *Spencer to Bridport*

14 May 1797

From the arrangements which have taken place (as I am informed by Lord Howe) to bring to a termination the unhappy disorders in the fleet and the steps which have been taken by Government and the Board of Admiralty in consequence of that information I trust that I may now have the satisfaction of offering my sincere congratulations to your Lordship on their return to their duty under your command.

I hope you will have been enabled from a reference to the Board's letter on that part of the subject to supply the deficiency of officers which may occur by availing yourself of the services of any captains or other officers belonging to ships in a state of refitting or on half pay who may be proper for the purpose and within reach, and that no further impediment will exist to your putting to sea, which considering the great urgency of the present moment it is needless for me to repeat is become essentially necessary for the interests of the country.

248.   *Admiralty to Bridport*

14 May 1797

I have received and communicated to my Lords Commissioners of the Admiralty your letter of yesterday's date and in answer thereto I have their commands to assure you that no expression in either of the letters which I have had the honour of writing to your Lordship lately on the urgency of your leaving St. Helens was intended to imply that any delay on your part had taken place.

249.   *Delegates of the fleet to Bridport*

14 May 1797

We embrace with eagerness the first opportunity of expressing to your Lordship the very high sentiments of gratitude we feel to your Lordship for the very open and generous behaviour you have manifested on this occasion and the attentions your Lordship has paid to the complaints of the men under your command. Your Lordship has evinced thereby a true spirit of affection and friendship for those whom your Lordship has so often conducted with honour on various and hazardous services. We therefore humbly thank your Lordship for your protection afforded us with the most unfeigned sincerity and rest ourselves assured that we shall always find a real friend and a zealous protector in the person of your Lordship whom we believe to be ever ready to give every indulgence to us that can be expected and to use the authority placed in your Lordship with that humanity which always distinguishes true greatness.

250. *Spencer to Bridport*

14 May 1797, ¾ past 5 p.m.

After I wrote to your Lordship this morning by the messenger we received your letter to the Board of yesterday's date and I cannot avoid taking the first opportunity to assure you that the inference you appear to have drawn from the repetition of pressing orders to you to sail as soon as possible is one which it was very far from the intention of the Board or of myself to occasion. We felt it our duty to express whenever it was possible the very urgent desire we entertain that the fleet should get out but we were fully persuaded at the same time that your Lordship, being aware of all the causes of our anxiety on that head, would partake in that wish at least as much as we could do and it was written in order to show that none of the circumstances which were taking place made any variation in our opinion, than that we doubted in the least of your disposition to carry your former orders into effect, that the subject was so much dwelt upon.

251. *Bridport to Spencer*

Royal George, St Helens, 15 May 1797

I have received the honour of your Lordship's two letters of yesterday's date while Lord Howe was on board the Royal George. I made the signal to unmoor but when I shall be able to carry the squadron to sea I cannot at this moment say as twenty-one lieutenants are wanted to fill the vacancies of officers passed on shore and are with no return to their respective ships. There is also one master, three captains of marines and three lieutenants, two surgeons and a greater number of quarter-deck gentlemen. This is conceded to the people by Lord Howe and this is the condition of the ships under my orders and that I am immediately expected to carry to sea to meet the enemy who may be already sailed from Brest. I have written a second letter to Sir Peter Parker on the subject of the officers and I am told he has only five lieutenants to spare and I have only two to appoint that are qualified.

I am too much hurried to write more and I feel too much hurt at the various circumstances that have taken place to make my letter acceptable to your Lordship. While I remain in command I will do my duty to the King and the public.

[*Endorsed as received on the 16th*]

6

THE GROWTH OF CENTRAL CONTROL
15 MAY 1797–19 MAY 1798

The Spithead mutiny delayed Bridport from sailing from Spithead by one month. He got into the Channel with 15 sail of the line on 17 May 1797, and immediately made an appearance off Brest, which had been under the surveillance of Sir John Warren's frigates. The latter's squadron was now to be taken under the command of Bridport [252], as also was Pellew's squadron. With these additions, Bridport was to be responsible for the protection of trade in the Channel and Western Approaches, as well as the containment of the French in Brest [254]. However, he was never to feel comfortable with the forces made available to him for this purpose, especially as the Admiralty kept control of the disposition of ships under his command, a potential source of conflict only avoided by Spencer's firm explanation of Admiralty logistics and Bridport's reluctant deference to higher authority. The Admiralty, when the fleet was in Torbay, was less than 24 hours away [267, 268] and the correspondence between the Admiralty and Commander-in-Chief reveal how Spencer and his Board gradually imposed government priorities on Bridport.

Although the Spithead mutiny was over, by no means was discontent in the Channel fleet totally removed. Mutiny was to break out again in the *Pompee* which had to return into port [256] in spite of her reputation for loyalty [263]. At Plymouth the crews persisted in refusing to receive the officers sent on shore and the Admiralty, though forbidding the use of force, declined further conciliation [253]. In June the *Mars* threatened to become disorderly [261]. Though physically distant, the Channel fleet could not avoid being influenced by the Nore mutiny which reached its height in June. There the patience of the Board ran out: attempts at negotiation were abandoned and a policy of coercion adopted which had the effect of dividing the ships [255].

Nevertheless the Admiralty was careful to avoid provocation. On board the *Pompee* the cause of discontent was the amount of pork issued and in June 1797 the Board of Admiralty was careful to ensure adequate provisions were ready for the Channel fleet when it put into Torbay [257]. Later in September Bridport would make recommendations for improving the issue of tobacco [295]. The Admiralty also realised the opportunities of dividing difficult crews. For example, it took advantage of Bridport's desire to increase the number of flag officers available to manage the fleet [258, 263] by appointing Lord Keith to the *Queen Charlotte*, permitting him to replace about 100 of her crew with his own followers [262]. Keith, who had been raised to the Irish peerage as recently as March 1797, saw his services during the mutiny as sufficient to justify further honour [270]. Spencer was not of the same mind [275]. On the contrary, the crews of the Channel fleet long harboured antipathy towards some officers forward in trying to settle the mutiny: even in March 1798 Colpoys's unpopularity in the fleet remained a factor influencing the choice of ship in which Colpoys hoisted his flag [325, 326].

On account of French readiness for sea in force, Bridport was urged in June 1797 to remain off Ushant. To enable him to do so, the Admiralty ordered that ships returning from refitting and replenishing should carry extra provisions to the fleet off Brest, and recommended to Bridport that, rather than his whole force sailing for England together, ships should return to replenish in pairs [259, 260]. Scurvy had returned by early July. The Sick and Wounded Board was able to provide a supply of lemon juice for the sick, but also wished the Victualling Board to send off supplies of vegetables from Plymouth. To ensure regularity of supply, the Transport Board was ordered to provide 'a vessel or two' to carry the vegetables out to Ushant [265]. In addition the hospital ship *Medusa* was used to shuttle patients from Ushant to Plymouth and carry vegetables back to the fleet [276].

When Bridport returned to Torbay in early July 1797, as directed by the Admiralty, he ordered Sir John Warren off Brest with a frigate squadron strengthed by ships of the line [266]. Warren was immediately successful in seizing the greater part of a convoy bound for Brest with naval stores, and in clearing French vessels from the waters off Brest [269, 271]. These operations helped to impede the supply of the base and the town with war materials and provisions of all kinds. Warren was also able to collect intelligence concerning the apparent readiness for sea of 19 sail of the line, probably to support a major expedition to Ireland [272]. As a result, Bridport was again off Ushant by the end of July.

Here differences between Bridport and the Admiralty soon emerged. He complained of a shortage of frigates. He had command of both the frigate squadrons based at Falmouth; however, they were not his to do with precisely as he wished. While Warren was placed off the Penmarks in anticipation of the arrival of a large convoy, the Admiralty ordered Pellew's squadron to be returned to Falmouth for refitting.

Moreover, Bridport was directed always to leave one squadron at Falmouth available for any pressing service [274]. The frigate shortage was enhanced by the dangers of the Brittany coast: late in July one frigate operating close in-shore was lost [278]. It was also potentially exacerbated by the policy, still sanctioned by Bridport, of permitting favoured captains to go on cruises in search of prizes [273]. Yet, as the Admiralty had demonstrated with respect to both Warren and Pellew [189, 193], this was a policy it could no longer afford and which it declined to endorse.

Bridport tended to express his frigate difficulties in personal terms. The tension between the Admiralty and the Commander-in-Chief was thus matched by an equal one between Bridport and his frigate commanders. As both Pellew and Warren had anticipated, Bridport was not tolerant of their former independence and indeed, on account of their seniority, hinted at the desirability of their promotion out of their frigate commands [263, 264]. Warren saw this as a natural way of getting out from under Bridport and shifted into a 74 in September [297]. However, Pellew was less amenable to movement and, perhaps on this account, Bridport took opportunities to blame or complain of him, though the causes of his complaints were usually beyond Pellew's control. He thus suggested Pellew remained too long at Falmouth, a delay which he implied was due to disobedience rather than the practical difficulties of supply or weather [280]. Falmouth was not an easy port to negotiate. Bridport preferred Cawsand Bay as the frigates could get to sea more easily from Plymouth Sound [279]. The Admiralty consequently changed the frigates' base from Falmouth to Cawsand Bay to please Bridport [294].

On joining Bridport off Brest, Pellew proposed that two ships of the line continued to be employed with his own in-shore frigate squadron, a strength that would help to drive into Brest the French squadron which anchored in Bertheaume Bay [281]. However, complying with Admiralty orders, Bridport ordered Pellew's squadron into port [283] to which he attributed an immediate outing of the Bertheaume squadron [285] and the need to recall Sir John Warren from his station off the Penmarks [284]. Bridport's animosity was not lost on Pellew. When the fleet was blown off Ushant in mid August and met Pellew by arrangement off the Lizard, without apparent explanation Bridport took the frigate squadron with him into Torbay [286]. It was a demonstration of his subordination that prompted Pellew literally to place himself under the protection of Spencer [287]. The First Lord could only counsel patience [288].

Two days later the Board firmly reiterated its orders to Bridport for a frigate squadron to be left in reserve at Falmouth or Cawsand Bay

[289], and for that squadron to be operational, not refitting [294]. At the same time, it also required a frigate squadron to be stationed south of Belle Isle [290]. To facilitate these deployments, at the beginning of September Bridport's frigate force was increased to 15, thereby permitting both the reserve squadron in port and the southerly patrol [292].

Bridport also felt short of ships of the line. Initially the Nore mutiny exacerbated this shortage, for while it was in progress three vessels under Sir Roger Curtis were diverted to reinforce Admiral Duncan in the North Sea [276]. After that the Brest fleet was always larger and grew more quickly than his reinforcement. At the beginning of August 1797 Bridport had 16 ships of the line under his command to combat a potential 22 [279, 282]. A month later there were still 20 French battleships and at least ten frigates ready for sea [291]. In October Camperdown [298] released some pressure by removing one of the enemy forces available to cover a French expedition to Ireland. But in November the Admiralty reinforced the coast of Ireland at the cost of the Channel fleet. By then, after five months at sea, Bridport had returned to Spithead [300], leaving Sir Roger Curtis with a squadron off Brest. And here economy was enforced by strict control. So familiar had the Admiralty become with the local stations necessarily taken by the blockading force, Curtis was instructed precisely in which positions to station his ships and to which places on the coast of Ireland and England they were to resort in the event of a breakout [299].

In December when Curtis was recalled to refit and replenish, just a frigate squadron under Keats was left on station [302]. The disposition of these frigates was aimed variously at protecting British shipping, stopping the French convoys and coasting trade, watching the port of Brest and the more southerly French ports and estuaries. French privateers were very active, and many of the merchant ships taken were British or those of allies [304, 314]. For the Admiralty, the achievement of economy in ships through control of their disposition depended on the discipline of captains in maintaining their stations. It was thus prompt in calling to account Captain Neale who deviated from his station [303], and, on finding that deviation sanctioned by verbal permission, equally severe in recording their displeasure with Bridport for providing that permission. The strictures of the Admiralty were understandable. For, where written instructions were overridden and ignored by both the Commander-in Chief and individual commanders, the Admiralty could not find its ships when needed. Their absence meant British shipping passing through their stations was jeopardised, and other ships had to be called in to fill the void, dissipating all attempts at economy [308]. Yet Bridport was quick to challenge the restrictions. He pointed to differences in the size of stations, and claimed that success on an unofficial cruise in taking enemy warships might easily turn criticism into praise [309]. His deviance was not encouraged. Indeed later in May 1798 the Admiralty realised the necessity of ensuring flag officers gave clear priorities to ships, for tight station-keeping for the observation of Brest was not usually compatible with other duties like the protection of trade routes [340].

At the end of 1797, while the three deck ships returned to Spithead, the two deck ships were required to replenish in Cawsand Bay. The value of a westerly base, less prey to westerly winds, was accentuated in December 1797 by a private letter to Spencer proposing a base for ships blockading Brest in the Isles of Scilly [305]. It was a consideration underlined in January 1798 when Vice Admiral Sir Charles Thompson – now commanding a squadron, much to the displeasure of Lord Keith [301, 316, 317] – was instructed to hasten off Brest owing to preparations to sail. He received his orders at Spithead on 13 January, reached St Helens on the 16th, sailed but met a south-west wind and had to put back into St Helens on the 22nd, sailed again, was joined by a contingent of ships from Plymouth Sound but was again forced back into St Helens on the 25th. He sailed with success soon after, but had effectively taken 12 days to get to sea, and still had to get off Brest, over two hundred miles south-west [310–313, 315].

In March 1798, when Bridport returned to sea, there was even greater necessity for the Admiralty strictly to control the availability of frigates and the disposition of ships of the line [318]. Fear of invasion of Ireland, combined with attacks in the Channel, made a main fleet and tightly controlled squadrons essential to defence [319]. The collection and manning of transports in the French Biscay ports, the movement of troops from Italy to Bourdeaux, and the mass manning of the ships in Brest appeared extremely threatening [322].[1] In the circumstances, Bridport did not protest unduly [323]. Indeed Admiralty control of ships on the home stations was now universal [324]. Moreover, with the Irish anticipating imminent assistance from France, the coast of Ireland had to be reinforced from Bridport's command with a squadron under Curtis [327], and a reserve created for relieving or reinforcing Bridport's main force. With French preparations and approaching better weather, the main fleet was again to be stationed off Ushant, for which purpose Spencer still considered the proposals to support it from the Scilly

[1]For intelligence received relating to French intentions, and for proposals for the defence of Britain and Ireland, February to April 1798, see the *Private Papers of George. Second Earl Spencer*, ed. J. S. Corbett and H. W. Richmond (4 vols, NRS, 1913 etc.), II, 221–36.

Islands or Douarnenez Bay [328]. However, Bridport maintained objections to the use of both places [331].

A sailing date for the French expedition after mid-April suddenly made a close blockade essential. The capture of a French 74, *L'Hercule*, by the *Mars* was encouraging, even though it left dead Captain Alexander Hood [332]. The Irish coast was placed on full alert and Lord Hugh Seymour again joined Bridport from the Admiralty [330]. Cleverly, Seymour acted to impose Admiralty preferences on Bridport, while at the same time ensuring Bridport still retained some sense of control over the ships under his command [333]. His letters to Spencer permitted the latter to reassure Bridport about the strength of the force at his disposal, its disposition, the nature of the vessels he would get, and the intended system of reliefs [334, 335]. So supported, Bridport helped to improve arrangements for the dissemination of intelligence from observations of the enemy fleet and to ensure the Admiralty could understand his own thinking in selecting particular ships for the stations within his command [336]. It was thinking to which Seymour in his letters to Spencer contributed [337], permitting the Admiralty and Commander-in-Chief between them to fine tune the blockade strategy.

However, in spite of the state of high tension attending the blockade, Bridport did not naturally adapt to the discipline demanded of the whole officer corps. For example, he wanted to take leave on shore while the *Royal George* was being paid, which seemed to Seymour an unhelpful precedent [337]. Also, apparently for his own convenience, he wanted his ship to be paid at Spithead, otherwise in Torbay. Spencer had to persuade him of the geographical advantage of Cawsand Bay for returning to Brest in an emergency [341]. He did not take kindly either to an apparent loss of status arising from the reduction of his force. In May 1798, when the situation in the Mediterranean demanded the shift of Curtis's squadron from the coast of Ireland to Cadiz [338], he complained of the reduction in flag officers under his command and the consequent burden of work that fell to him [339]. Spencer defended Admiralty priorities, and promised what he could, for example in the provision of English-built, as opposed to French-built frigates [341]. Yet such favours, performed at the cost of others, were hardly appreciated. Bridport took his privileges for granted. As Evan Nepean, Secretary of the Admiralty, observed when implementing one such favour, Bridport 'ought to be pleased, though is never likely to be so' [293]. Nature had not equipped Bridport to adapt easily to the growing centrality of control over the Channel fleet.

This growing centralisation was facilitated by a reduction of the problem of manning. The shortages of men that occurred were filled from sources within the grasp of captains [277]. Total numbers disguised significant proportions on some ships of under-sized, over-rated men brought into the fleet by indiscriminate recruitment and the Quota Acts. These proportions could be diluted by discharges and exchanges with other ships [307]. More persistent was the recurrent problem of scurvy [265]. Although vegetables were supplied by pursers and when possible by shipment to the fleet, the quantities and regularity of the supply was deficient. The Victualling Board now maintained a large stock of lemon juice [306] but it was still dispensed in the Channel fleet only as a cure when the first symptons of scurvy made their first appearance.[1] Furthermore the residence of Thomas Trotter, Physician of the Fleet, mainly on shore from 1795 owing to an accident, physically removed the medical conscience of the fleet.[2] Indeed Bridport in March 1798 was prepared to dispense with the attendance of a hospital ship, a suggestion Spencer was ready to consider [320, 321].

Increasing central control and the reduction in size of the Channel fleet was facilitated by a growing confidence in the intelligence about the Brest fleet available to the Admiralty. However, it was driven primarily by a very real need to use the ships available to the country with the greatest economy. The financial difficulties of the country in 1797, the threat of invasion early in 1798, and the deteriorating state of Ireland, all encouraged administrators to consider how resources could be extended further. By the calculations of the Comptroller of the Navy, the Channel fleet was more expensive to maintain than fleets sent abroad [329]. Greater rigour in the resort of ships to port discouraged excesses in the consumption of stores. Central control of the blockade of Brest was consistent with a tendency towards greater control throughout government. It was a control that would be regarded as all the more necessary after the French demonstrated their continuing capability to sail from and return to Brest at will.

252. *Admiralty to Bridport*

15 May 1797

Notwithstanding any former orders, your Lordship is hereby required and directed to put to sea without a moment's loss of time with the squadron under your command and proceed off Plymouth, for the ships named in the margin [*Atlas, Saturn, Powerful, Majestic, Edgar, Unité*],

---

[1]See introduction to Chapter 1.
[2]*The Health of Seamen*, ed. C. Lloyd (NRS, 1965), 214.

and upon their joining you to take them under your command; but if the said ships should have left Plymouth before you arrive there, your Lordship is to proceed off the Lizard where you may expect to fall in with them, and upon so doing take them under your command and proceed immediately with the whole of your force off Brest, for the purpose of watching the motions of the enemy at that place, and using your best endeavours to take or destroy any of their ships should they attempt to put to sea . . . If however on your arrival off Brest, you shall have good reason to believe that the enemy's ships have left that port, or if at any time during your cruise they should put to sea and by escaping your observation you should not be able to ascertain their course, you are in such case to make the best of your way with the squadron under your command to the coast of Ireland . . . Your Lordship is to continue upon the abovementioned service until you receive further orders, taking every precaution in your power to prevent the squadron under your command being driven far to the westward so as to admit of the enemy passing between you and Ushant, and by that means getting into the English Channel . . . Your Lordship upon falling in with Sir John Warren (who is now cruising off Brest) is to take him under your command, and to keep them with you (if you shall find it necessary) until they shall be relieved by the squadron under the command of Sir Edward Pellew, who will have directions to proceed and join you on your rendezvous, a copy of which you will take care to transmit as soon as possible to our secretary for our information.

253.   *Admiralty to Orde*[1]

20 May 1797

I have received and communicated to my Lords Commissioners of the Admiralty your letter to me of the 18th instant giving an account of the situation of the crews of H.M. Ships under your command subsequently to the departure of Captain Pakenham, and I have it in command from their Lordships to repeat to you their desire that you should exert every means in your power to persuade the seamen of the different ships to receive again all the officers who have been sent on shore; or if you cannot succeed with respect to the whole, to procure the return of as many as possible. If however this point should be strenuously opposed, and remain the only obstacle to an accommodation and the return of the seamen to their duty, it must be conceded to the seamen at

---

[1]This letter was addressed to Orde at Plymouth.

Plymouth, as has already been done to those at Portsmouth, on the ground of the officers themselves, disgusted at the unjust accusations brought against them by their crews, having requested to be superseded.

If on the return of the men from Portsmouth, or the appearance of Lord Bridport's squadron off Plymouth, the seamen should, contrary to their Lordships' expectation, persist in their disobedience and, refusing to return to their duty, should forfeit the benefit of the pardon offered to them by His Majesty, you are to inform them that all the reasonable requests of the seamen having been granted them, with which the seamen of all other ships were not only satisfied, but for which they had shewn themselves highly grateful, no further concessions would be made; but on the contrary, that if, unmindful of the very liberal addition made to their wages and provisions, insensible to His Majesty's clemency in pardoning the offences they have committed, and forgetful of the duty they owe to their country, they still persist in their present unjustified conduct, they will be made answerable for all the melancholy consequences which such a conduct must necessarily occasion.

Their Lordships desire it to be understood that you are not to use (unless it be to prevent some very dangerous attempts) any mode of coercion, by which the ships may be disabled, but to take, in conjunction with the Commander in Chief of H.M. Land Forces at Plymouth, every posssible precaution to prevent the seamen from doing mischief in the dockyard, the victualling office, or the town, if they should attempt to land.

254.   *Admiralty to Bridport*

27 May 1797

Their Lordships are pleased to approve of your having detached the Phaeton and Melpomene to watch the motions of the enemy at Brest and have directed me to inform you that Sir Edward Pellew will be ordered to join you with his squadron from Falmouth the moment he shall be in a fit condition so to do; with the assistance to be derived from this squadron their Lordships conceive you will be enabled, while keeping your station off Brest, to afford the necessary protection to the trade of His Majesty's subjects.

255. *Admiralty to Bridport*

10 June 1797

I have received the commands of my Lords Commissioners of the Admiralty to acquaint your Lordship that the mutiny which took place on board the Sandwich and the other ships with her at the Nore, of which your Lordship was apprized previously to your sailing, has extended itself to the most considerable part of Admiral Duncan's squadron and the consequence has been that the several ships named in the margin [*Montagu, Repulse, Nassau, Standard, Lion, Monmouth, Belligueux, Ardent, Agamemnon, Leopard, Isis*] have left the Admiral, and excepting the Glatton (the crew of which ship has since returned to its duty and rejoined the Admiral) have proceeded to and united in the mutiny at the Nore.

As soon as this mutiny had taken a serious shape, their Lordships thought it right to proceed to Sheerness, hoping (as indeed they were led to expect before they left town) that their presence would have tended to put a stop to those proceedings; but instead of producing any good effect, new propositions were brought forward, of a nature so extravagant and calculated, so directly to overturn all naval discipline, and the behaviour of the persons calling themselves delegates, who came on shore, appeared so improper in all its stages, that their Lordships thought it right to leave that place, without publishing His Majesty's proclamation offering them pardon, which they have been authorized to do on the conditions which were granted to the fleet under your Lordship, having neither power nor inclination to accede to any new proposition.

Notwithstanding every proper and consistent means have been exerted on the principle above stated, of resisting any further propositions to bring these people to a sense of their duty, they have proceeded to acts of the most atrocious nature, by stopping the trade of the River, and even by firing upon the King's ships, an instance of which will be stated to your Lordship by Sir Harry Neale, who will be the bearer of this; and in consequence of which His Majesty found it expedient to authorize a communication to Parliament, which has produced the Acts accompanying this, together with the declaration of their Lordships' contained in the inclosed Gazette; and measures are now taking by their Lordships, assisted by all the commercial bodies in the metropolis, whose opinions are stated in the inclosed resolutions, to reduce the mutineers to a state of obedience by force.

I have the satisfaction of acquainting your Lordship that by an express received this morning from Sheerness, it appears that the Repulse,

Ardent and Leopard have left the Nore in the course of last evening, the first and last of these ships under a very heavy fire from most of the other ships. But by the returns which have been made it is hoped that no material mischief has been done and only a few persons wounded, among whom it appears there are two lieutenants. Several of the ringleaders of the mutiny are now in confinement, and will be brought to trial immediately there is reason to suppose that some other ships now at the Nore feel the same disposition, but have not found a convenient opportunity to separate themselves.

P.S. Since writing the above, their Lordships have received information by telegraph that all the ships at the Nore have hoisted their proper colours, indicating (as their Lordships' hope) the intention of their crews to return to their duty.

256. *Admiralty to Bridport*

10 June 1797

I have read and communicated to my Lords Commissioners of the Admiralty your letter to me of the 6th instant, inclosing two letters which had been written to your Lordship by Captain Vashon[1] of H.M.S. Pompee, giving an account of a mutinous and treasonable combination which had taken place on board the said ship; and acquainting me that in consequence thereof you had judged it necessary to make preparations for sending her to Spithead, submitting at the same time to their Lordships' consideration whether in consequence of some representations that have been made upon the subject the allowance of pork in the fleet should not be the same as is given in beef.

In return to which I have it in command from their Lordships to express to you their concern that after having granted the requests of the seamen that they should have full allowance of provisions, without any deduction being made for waste or leakage, any dissatisfaction on account of provisions should be observed in the ships under your command. The full allowance of pork for each man is two pounds per week which, by the late regulation, is to be issued without deduction for waste; and if it is so issued, the men having all that is their due, cannot possibly have any reason to complain.

Their Lordships fully approve of your intention of ordering the Pompee to return into port, and direct me to acquaint you that on her

[1]James Vashon (d. 1827). Lieutenant 1774; Captain 1782; Rear-admiral 1804; Vice-admiral 1808; Admiral 1814.

arrival such steps will be taken as the circumstances may appear to require.

Captain Colnett,[1] late of H.M.S. Hussar, who left Brest on the 5th instant, has arrived in Town and confirms the report which had reached your Lordship of the return of the ships which had left that port. The further information respecting the state of the French fleet is contained in his letter to me of this date, a copy of which I have the honour to inclose.

257. *Admiralty to Bridport*[2]

11 June 1797

I have received and communicated to my Lords Commissioners of the Admiralty your letter of the 7th instant acquainting me for their Lordships' information of your intention to stand over to the Lizard as soon as the wind should set in to the westward, and to proceed to Torbay with the squadron under your command.

I have their Lordships' commands to acquaint you that directions have in consequence been given to the Victualling Board to take measures for supplying such provisions as the squadron may stand in need of during its continuance at the anchorage.

Their Lordships further command me to express their extreme concern at the circumstances stated by your Lordship, in that and your former letters, from which you have found yourself under the necessity of returning into port; and to signify their direction to you to return to your station the moment the circumstances and situation of your squadron shall enable you so to do, there being the greatest reason to suppose that the enemy's fleet, or a part of it, will avail itself of the earliest opportunity of putting to sea.

258. *Bridport to Spencer*

Royal George, off Ushant, 18 June 1797

I have taken the liberty to send the enclosed for your Lordship's consideration as well as for my own justification. As I am given to understand that I may expect the Brest fleet at sea in great force, in which case I

---

[1]Captain Colnett does not appear in Syrett and DiNardo. However the 'Warship Histories' at the National Maritime Museum record that James Colnett was captain of *Hussar* in October 1796. The *Hussar* was wrecked near Isle Bas on 27 December 1796.
[2]Addressed to Bridport in Torbay.

may be [forced[1]] to fight a serious battle, the success of which the safety of England may depend. Your Lordship must allow me to say that I feel myself unsupported, having only Sir Alan Gardner with me. I will add no more upon the subject but to say that I will do my best for the King and the Country.

[*Enclosure*]

258a.   *Bridport to Spencer*

Brest Fleet commanded by one Admiral, two Vice Admirals, one Rear Admiral.

Channel Fleet commanded by one Admiral, one Vice Admiral, one Captain hoisting a distinguishing pendant by Lord Bridport's appointment, one Admiral, Captain of the Fleet.

Dutch Fleet commanded by three Flags, one Broad Pendant.

North Sea Fleet commanded by one Admiral, one Vice Admiral, One Rear Admiral.

Earl Howe when he commanded the Channel Fleet had six Flags flying under him.

One Admiral, Captain of the Fleet.

That number was under Earl Howe when Lord Bridport commanded a detachment of the Channel Fleet and shared with him on the 23rd of June for the prizes taken that day off L'Orient.

Earl Howe, Commander in Chief. Admiral Lord Bridport, Vice Admiral Cornwallis, Vice Admiral Sir Alan Gardner, Vice Admiral Waldegrave, Rear Admiral Harvey, Rear Admiral Lord Hugh Seymour, Rear Admiral Sir Roger Curtis.

[*Endorsed as received on the 22nd and answered on the 29th*]

259.   *Admiralty to Bridport*

20 June 1797

I have received and communicated to my Lords Commissioners of the Admiralty your two letters to me of the 15th instant and I have their

[1]Word omitted in original.

Lordships' command to acquaint you that they feel great satisfaction in finding that your Lordship has returned to your station off Brest instead of proceeding to Torbay.

By letters which have been received from Plymouth it appears that the Defiance has arrived in Cawsand Bay and that as soon as she shall have completed her provisions and water will rejoin you on your rendezvous with such additional supplies as she can receive on board for the rest of the squadron, as will the Medusa[1] as soon as possible with such sheep and refreshments as she can take on board for the use of the sick.

As it is of the greatest importance in every point of view that the squadron under your Lordship's command should for the present continue at sea, their Lordships direct me to recommend it to you rather than return to Torbay with the squadron that you should from time to time send two or more ships of the line in want of provisions into Cawsand Bay and on their rejoining you to send in the same number for the purpose of recruiting their provisions and obtaining refreshments, supplies of every description having been provided and are in readiness to be put on board at the shortest notice.

260.   *Victualling Board to Admiralty*

Victualling Office, 21 June 1797

We have received your letter of the 20th instant informing us of His Majesty's Ship Defiance at Plymouth having been ordered to rejoin the squadron under the command of Admiral Lord Bridport, and signifying to us the directions of the Right Honourable the Lords Commissioners of the Admiralty to cause her to be supplied with such of the provisions intended to have been sent to Torbay for the supply of the said squadron in addition to what may be wanted by the crew of that ship as she can conveniently receive on board to be disposed of on his joining the Admiral as his Lordship shall direct.

In reply to which we beg leave to acquaint you, for the information of their Lordships, that it appears by a letter we have this morning received from our agent at Plymouth that His Majesty's said ship Defiance sailed from that port on the evening of the 18th to rejoin the fleet under Lord Bridport's command.

[*Endorsement*]

[1] A 50-gun ship built in 1785 used as a hospital ship.

22 June. Own receipt and direct them to send out supplies by any of the other ships which may be ordered to join him.

261.   *Alexander Hood to Bridport*

Mars, at sea, 26 June 1797

I think it my duty to inform your Lordship that since His Majesty's ship Mars under my command parted from the fleet that part of her crew have shown a disorderly disposition and I am sorry to say all the advice I and my officers have been able to give them and all the punishment my instructions allowed me to inflict have had very little good effect; and it is the opinion of the officers as well as myself that we could not be answerable for the safety of His Majesty's ship in the present disorderly state of her crew if she separated from the fleet; the contemptuous manner and indifference with which the late Acts of Parliament and His Majesty's Proclamation were received further convinced me of their evil disposition as it appeared to me and the officers that they doubted of their authenticity from the silence observed after being repeatedly asked to promise good behaviour in future; and still a further proof of their discontent I have the honour to enclose two letters which were last evening brought me by William Heather, Carpenter's Yeoman, (who was in the late mutiny at St. Helens one of the Mars's chosen men but who now appears to be satisfied). He told me that he found the letters some days since put under the Store Room door when he went into it in the morning. I therefore suppose they have been wrote by some person in the Mars with an intention to create dissatisfaction among the people.

I also have to inform your Lordship that I cannot place any confidence in the party of marines. They consist of four French, four Dutch, and most of the rest very troublesome Irish.

I therefore beg leave to submit to your Lordship's consideration if it would not be proper to order the Mars into port that my Lords Commissioners of the Admiralty may make such changes in her crew as they may think fit. I have reason to suppose if about one hundred and fifty, besides the Marines, were changed the ship would be fit for any service.

262.   *Spencer to Bridport*

Admiralty, 29 June 1797

I am well aware of the inconvenience which has attended your having only one flag officer in the squadron under your command and should have been glad to have been able to obviate that inconvenience sooner. Lord Keith[1] will join you and put himself under your orders as soon as possible and after one or two courts martial now depending in Portsmouth are over Sir John Orde will also join you and will either hoist his flag in the London or Princess Royal. Lord Keith will hoist his on board the Queen Charlotte and on pretence of his followers going along with him from the Monarch an opportunity may be taken of changing about 100 of her crew, which may perhaps be a good thing in many points of view and had better be effected at sea than elsewhere.

263. *Bridport to Spencer*

Royal George, off Plymouth, 30 June 1797

I have been under the necessity of sending the Queen Charlotte into Cawsand Bay to get new boilers, Captain Lock[2] having represented to me that her old ones are worn out. I entreat your Lordship not to allow that ship to return to me without having an Admiral's flag. But should no Admiral choose to take her I must desire that a captain might be appointed to the Queen Charlotte of high rank in the List as I do not think that ship should any longer be commanded by a young acting captain.

It appears to me very strange that Sir John B. Warren and Sir Edward Pellew should continue in frigates so contrary to the usual practice of the service on their standing in the list of captains.

I am also to request that the Pompee may be ordered to return to me when circumstances will allow of her coming to sea as I feel very anxious to have this ship with her faithful officers and loyal crew in this fleet that their conduct may appear a bright example to all the ships under my command. I wish also to have the Incendiary fireship and Medusa hospital ship as soon as they are fit for sea, as the former was one of the repeaters and has carried away a set of colours.

[Endorsed as received on 2nd July and answered the same day]

---

[1]George, Viscount Keith (1746–1823). Born George Keith Elphinstone. Lieutenant 1770; Captain 1775; Rear-admiral 1794; Vice-admiral 1795; Admiral 1801. Commanded the expedition sent to capture the Cape of Good Hope, returning in time to become involved with Hoche's attempt to land in Bantry Bay. Received an Irish peerage as Baron Keith in March 1797. Was sent to deal with the mutinies at the Nore and at Plymouth. Succeeded St Vincent in the Mediterranean. Raised to the United Kingdom peerage 1802. Commander-in-Chief in the North Sea 1803; Channel 1812.

[2]Walter Lock(e) (d. 1835). Lieutenant 1778; Captain 1795; Rear-admiral 1814; Vice-admiral 1825.

264.   *Spencer to Bridport*

Wimbledon Park, 2 July 1797

The service upon which the squadrons under Sir John Warren and Sir Edward Pellew have hitherto been employed was of a description which seemed to require their experience and ability to conduct it, which I should think would easily account to your Lordship for their being continued upon it.

265.   *Sick and Wounded Board to Admiralty*

Office for Sick and Wounded Seamen, 4 July 1797

We request you will be pleased to acquaint the Right Honourable the Lords Commissioners of the Admiralty that Mr Milligan, surgeon of the Medusa hospital ship, has informed us by his letter dated Plymouth the 1st instant, that very bad ulcers and the scurvy are likely to be general in the fleet under the command of Admiral Lord Bridport, that the scurvy had appeared in some ships, with the worst symptoms, before coming to Torbay, and that the people were only supplied with the purser's allowance of vegetables and what cabbages were brought round in the Medusa.

We have ordered a supply of lemon juice for the use of the abovementioned fleet, to be sent from Portsmouth and Plymouth and we beg you to observe to their Lordships that we are of opinion it will be conducive to the health of the ships' crews in general for the Victualling Board to be directed to send supplies of vegetables from Plymouth as often as opportunities may offer.

[*Endorsements*]

5 August. Own letter and approve of their having so done, acquaint them that directions are sent to the Victualling Board to send out the supplies of vegetables.

Order to the Victualling Board to provide supplies of vegetables and apply to the Transport Board for a vessel or two to be employed from Plymouth in carrying out the said supplies.

266.   *Bridport to Admiralty*

Royal George, in Torbay, 5 July 1797

I received this day at noon by a messenger their Lordships' order of the 3rd instant for increasing the squadron under the orders of Sir John Borlase Warren to two, or three, sail of the line and six frigates and to direct him to cruise very diligently off the port of Brest for the purpose therein mentioned. And to order Sir Edward Pellew to return to Falmouth for his squadron being refitted; also directing me, after making these arrangements, to repair with the remainder of the squadron under my command to Torbay.

I acquaint you for their Lordships' information that, agreeably thereto, I have forwarded orders to Sir John Borlase Warren at Falmouth by express and enclosed directions to Sir Edward Pellew to return to Falmouth accordingly.

I have ordered the captains of the ships named in the margin [*Robust, Defiance, Edgar, Jason, Triton, Nymphe*] to put themselves under Sir John B. Warren's command and they will sail to join him at Falmouth or off Ushant as soon as the weather will permit; at present it is very rough and blowing.

It was my intention to have left two line of battle ships and two frigates at sea to cruise off Ushant had not the weather prevented my making this arrangement.

267.   *Bridport to Admiralty*

Royal George, in Torbay, 14 July 1797, 8 p.m.

I have this moment received your packet containing an order and letters dated 'Admiralty Office, 13th July, by a messenger at ½ past 8 p.m.', together with a despatch for the Earl of St. Vincent which were delivered to me by a farmer who found them near Teign Bridge.

268.   *Bridport to Admiralty*

Royal George, in Torbay, 15 July 1797

Yesterday evening at 8 p.m. I acknowledged by express the receipt of your despatch of the 13th instant together with two packets addressed to the Earl of St. Vincent and at 10 p.m. the messenger came on board this ship, having heard of the packet being found and delivered to me. I understand it was from mere accident the packet was dropped and arose from the messenger unbuttoning his coat, the weather being extremely warm; and he had used so much expedition that he would have been on board this ship by 5 o'clock yesterday afternoon but for the misfortune.

269.   *Warren to Bridport*

La Pomone, at sea, 18 July 1797

I beg leave to acquaint your Lordship that in obedience to your commands I continued off Ushant with His Majesty's squadron under my orders, consisting of the ships and vessels named in the margin [*La Pomone, Artois, Anson, Sylph, Dolly* cutter] until the 16th instant, when, hearing the report of many guns to the southward, I stood round the west end of the Saints and at daybreak on the morning of the 17th I discovered a frigate with a ship corvette and brig having 14 sail of vessels under convoy in Hodierne [Audierne] Bay, eight of which were captured.

I am sorry to add that the ship corvette and brig escaped round the Penmarks and the frigate by cutting away her masts and being otherways lightened, ran on shore; a brig laden with ordnance and naval stores came to an anchor near her, where it was impossible for the Anson and Sylph to follow. The brig, however, was sunk and the frigate (La Calliope) much damaged in her hull by the shot of the abovementioned ship (whose officers and men behaved with the greatest zeal and activity) which induces me to hope that the enemy will not be enabled to get her off, as the wind soon after changed to the south-west with a great swell upon the beach.

I was obliged to burn La Freedom, a large ship armée en flute, laden with squared timber as the enemy had run her on shore at high tide and the crew, with the wounded, got away in their boats.

270.   *Keith to Spencer*

Queen Charlotte, at sea, 20 July 1797

I beg pardon for troubling your Lordship at a busy moment and particularly when it relates to myself but the pending negotiation[1] gives a

---

[1]Between 4 July and 18 September 1797 Lord Malmesbury was conducting negotiations, eventually abortive, with French plenipotentiaries at Lille. See J. Ehrman, *The Younger Pitt. The Consuming Struggle* (London, 1996), 59–65.

reasonable prospect of peace, a time when men of my profession can have but little chance to distinguish themselves.

I assure your Lordship I shall ever feel very grateful for having given me an opportunity of being useful and I trust I suffered no occasion to escape that presented itself during my late command abroad.

Of late my employment has neither been pleasant or brilliant but perhaps not less important and I am happy some success has attended my endeavours to execute your commands.[1]

I am extremely sensible of the repeated marks of favour that have heretofore been conferred on me. At the same time when I look round and find other officers who have been successful in chief command and even some in subaltern situations have been rewarded by peerage, an honour extremely desirable if creditably attained; may I therefore request your Lordship's recommendation to the Minister provided you think me deserving and if through your Lordship I am fortunate enough to obtain his consent perhaps now or at the close of a war is a time when little inconvenience would be felt whilst I should be excessively gratified.

I have taken the liberty to consult the Duke of Portland and Mr Dundas on this subject and hope if your Lordship should feel inclined to favour my views they will not object.

[*Endorsed as received on the 29th and answered on the 30th*]

271. *Warren to Bridport*

La Pomone, at sea, 24 July 1797

I take the liberty of informing your Lordship that being to westward of the Saints on the 22nd instant with His Majesty's squadron under my orders, a brig and a sloop were discovered in Hodierne Bay to whom I immediately gave chase, which the enemy observing ran on shore. I made the Artois's and Triton's signals to burn the brig which was completely effected by the boats of those ships under a heavy fire from the batteries and musketry, and the sloop was destroyed by the boats of this ship.

I have the satisfaction of acquainting your Lordship also that I had an opportunity of seeing that La Calliope, Republican frigate of 36 guns and 250 men that was left on shore on the 17th by the Anson and Sylph is totally destroyed, having separated in the midship body and part of

---

[1]Keith was employed to assist in bringing the mutinies at the Nore and at Plymouth to an end.

her sunk. The crew are encamped near her to save such stores as may be driven on shore.

I am particularly indebted to Captain White[1] of the Sylph brig who having anchored with springs on his cable within pistol shot of the said frigate on the above day and for some hours kept up an incessant and well-directed fire which was at every convenient opportunity returned by her.

272.   Captain John Gore[2] to Warren

Triton, at sea, 24 July 1797

The vessels you ordered me to chase by signal this morning proved two Danes from Brest bound to Bordeaux in ballast and sailed yesterday evening. The master of one of them informed the lieutenant of His Majesty's ship under my command who examined her that the fleet in Brest consists of nineteen sail of the line and seven frigates perfectly ready for sea in every respect except being very short of seamen, which deficiency will be supplied with 40,000 soldiers who are expected daily at Brest to embark on an expedition against Ireland; that their intention is not kept secret, for he heard it publicly spoken of and generally disliked. Besides this fleet there is an 84 (the Mount Blanc) in Camaret Bay with seven frigates. One three decked ship and two seventy-fours (one the Berwick) are fitting in the harbour and will be sent out in five or six days. He says the town of Brest is much distressed for provisions and felt the loss of the convoy you intercepted very severely. That a fleet of thirty sail, laden with stores and provisions is expected in the course of a week from Bordeaux and they cannot do without it.

This information is strongly corroborated by a man who did belong to the Amazon[3] and made his escape from prison a week ago, since which he has been in Brest and says he made it his business to examine everything respecting their fleet, being certain he should be taken out of the Dane by one of our frigates. He says the fleet in the road of Brest consists of nineteen sail of the line, six of which are three decked ships, and seven frigates, two of which are large razées, that in the harbour are one first rate and two seventy-fours. In Camaret Bay the Mont Blanc, a razé and five frigates. During his stay at Brest he lived with four Irishmen, who were pilots to some of the ships; one of the Lion, 110 guns, and one of

---

[1]Sir John Chambers White (d. 1845). Lieutenant 1790; Commander 1795; Captain 1799; Rear-admiral 1830; Vice-admiral 1837.

[2]Sir John Gore (d. 1836). Lieutenant 1789; Captain 1794; Rear-admiral 1813; Vice-admiral 1825.

[3]A 36-gun frigate wrecked on the French coast six months earlier.

the Formidable of 84 and had been employed in the same capacity on the former expedition: he learnt from them that the fleet would sail in about ten days, that they had all six months' provisions on board for 1,000 men and were going to Ireland with 40,000 soldiers but were very short of seamen, that the few they had were kept on board by guard boats filled with soldiers and moored round the fleet, which has every sail bent and topgallant yards across. Each ship has an Irish pilot and it is expected they will rendezvous in Bantry Bay. This man also says there is a razé mounting 50 guns (twenty-four and eighteen pounders) lying in the outer road of Brest perfectly ready for sea going to cruise on the Banks of Newfoundland, that she is fitted out by the merchants as a privateer and has been detained there three weeks for want of men: that they have frequently endeavoured to prevail on the prisoners to enter for her and last week forty-five did enter, in consequence of which she has moved outside and will sail in a day or two.

This man's statement appears so correct and invariable that I am induced to pay the more attention to it.

273. *Bridport to Spencer*

Royal George, off Ushant, 27 July 1797

I am persuaded your Lordship and the Admiralty will be much pleased with the success of the squadron under the orders of Sir John B. Warren, the particulars of which I transmitted to Mr. Nepean by the Lurcher cutter yesterday. I have sent directions to Sir Edward Pellew to join me the moment he receives my orders as I am in want of frigates for the various services which I am called upon to attend to, having sent Sir John B. Warren with <u>four</u> and the Sylph Brig to cruise off the Penmarks for the purpose of intercepting another convoy from Bordeaux bound for Brest. I should be very glad to set the Unité at liberty to cruise on some detached service but as she is my repeater I cannot at present allow her to separate from the squadron. But if your Lordship could spare me one of the twenty-four gun ships for a repeater and order the Incendiary to rejoin me I should be able to detach the Unité and as she sails well and being much disposed to show some favour to her captain I submit this subject to your Lordship's consideration.[1]

[*Endorsed as received on the 30th and answered the same day*]

---

[1]Perhaps a typical instance of the way in which a cruise was regarded as a reward for faithful service or as a mark of favour.

274.   *Admiralty to Bridport*

29 July 1797

I am commanded by my Lords Commissioners of the Admiralty to signify their direction to your Lordship, upon being joined by the Melpomene or Virginie to order Sir Edward Pellew to proceed with his squadron to Falmouth, their Lordships judging it necessary that a squadron of frigates should always be at that port in readiness to proceed upon any service that may offer.

275.   *Spencer to Keith*

St Albans, 30 July 1797

In answer to your letter of the 20th which I have just received I can only at present express my disposition to attend to and promote your wishes on any occasion where it may be on full consideration thought consistent with propriety to do so. On the subject to which your letter particularly relates I am not prepared at present to give a decided opinion. You have so lately been distinguished by the mark of His Majesty's favour which you now hold that it just now perhaps appears a little premature to think of the other step you mention, not but that I am well persuaded that your late successful exertions on the occasion of the mutiny have given to His Majesty as well as to all his servants a very favourable impression of your energy and activity on his service and if any opportunity should offer itself of a more brilliant nature I have no doubt of making a good use of it.

Upon the whole it appears to me that such an application would be made with better effect and more prospect of success at some future period than at the present moment and as this is my genuine opinion on the subject I trust you will do justice to the motive which induces me to communicate it to you.

276.   *Spencer to Bridport*

St. Albans, 30 July 1797

I have to acknowledge the receipt of your Lordship's letter of the 25th and am very glad to learn of the success of Sir John Warren's squadron, which I hope will continue on the station to which you have detached him.

Other ships and frigates will be sent out to you as they can be got ready. The Mars has already sailed and as the court martial on the Saturn is terminated I hope it will not be long before that ship is ready, as well as the Leviathan. Orders have been sent out to Admiral Duncan to send in Sir Roger Curtis with the Prince, Formidable and Sans Pareil as soon as the ships now on the point of sailing from the Nore shall have joined him, so that your squadron will shortly be increased and strengthened and I hope by keeping the Medusa backwards and forwards between the fleet and Plymouth the health of the people may be effectually preserved.

277.   *Pellew to Admiralty*

Indefatigable, 30 July 1797

You will be pleased to announce to their Lordships the arrival of a French cartel from Rochefort having on board two hundred men and officers released from captivity. About fifty of this number are soldiers, the rest masters of merchant ships and seamen.

After completing the complement of His Majesty's ship under my command, which required about 30 men, I have sent the remainder in the Dover cutter to Plymouth to Sir Richard King, directing her commander to pursue his former orders after their discharge.

The weather is such as to prevent the possibility of the ships sailing but they only want a favourable moment for doing so.

278.   *Sir Edmund Nagle[1] to Warren*

Sylph, at sea, 31 July 1797

I beg leave to inform you that in obedience to your signal made this morning to reconnoitre in the N.E., His Majesty's ship Artois, under my command, in consequence of the pilot's ignorance of the distance that the rocks lay from the coast, unfortunately struck upon the Balleine Rocks and I am extremely concerned to inform you that notwithstanding every exertion in my power, with that of my officers and crew, the rudder was carried away and the ship soon after by striking very violently was bilged, which rendered it impossible ever to get her off.

As you had made the signal that the enemy who lay in the Portuis [Pertuis] d'Antioche, consisting of one line of battle ship and five

---

[1]Admiral Sir Edmund Nagle (d. 1830). Lieutenant 1777; Captain 1783; knighted 1794; Rear-admiral 1805; Vice-admiral 1810; Admiral 1819.

frigates, had sailed; and finding every effort to remove her ineffectual, I judged it prudent to set her on fire to prevent any part of her stores from falling into their possession.

I have the satisfaction to say that by the speedy arrival of the boats from the different ships of the squadron the whole of the crew were saved.

I have sent the pilot on board La Pomone to be kept in confinement until there may be an opportunity of trying him by a court martial.

279. *Bridport to Spencer*

Royal George, at sea, 6 August 1797

I have been cruising near three weeks with only fifteen ships of the line. Sir Edward Pellew's intelligence of the Brest fleet, which is this day sent to Mr. Nepean, will inform your Lordship that the number is upwards of twenty with a large appearance of frigates. I repeat again to your Lordship that my situation is critical in that respect. Your Lordship states to me the Prince, Formidable and Sans Pareil. I wish they were with me and also the Leviathan. I think they are all necessary for the public service. I find I am directed by Mr. Nepean's letter, received this day, to send Sir Edward Pellew's squadron into Falmouth, their Lordships always wishing to have a squadron there in readiness. Their directions shall be complied with but I would rather they were in Cawsand Bay from my own judgment, as from that anchorage it can always get to sea but from Falmouth can easily not, and the Revolutionnaire got on shore upon coming out of that hole, as Sir Edward Pellew calls it, when the squadron sailed the other day.

[*Endorsed as received on the 10th*]

280. *Bridport to Admiralty*

Royal George, at sea, 8 August 1797

Enclosed is a copy of my order dated the 24th of July to Sir Edward Pellew to join me off Brest; at that time he had been twelve days at Falmouth and he did not sail from thence before the 2nd of August and joined me on the 3rd. Their Lordships had therefore full time to have sent an order to Sir Edward Pellew to have remained in port if that measure was judged necessary.

But I conclude when ships are put under my orders I am authorized to direct their proceedings to the best of my judgment for the services committed to my charge as long as they shall remain a part of my squadron.

281.   *Pellew to Bridport*

Indefatigable, off Brest, 8 August 1797

I do not imagine the advanced squadron in Bertheaume would wait any serious attack but will either run under the batteries of Camaret or up into Brest Road whenever any force superior to their own shall show itself within Point St. Mathieu. I should also conceive your Lordship would not choose to hazard the line of battle ships in serious action between the Parquette Bank and the north shore as an accident to a mast might eventually endanger their getting out again before a reinforcement could arrive from Brest to attack them. While they continue to anchor in a loose way we can certainly cause them considerable disturbance and should they run up, which I have no doubt they will, we may reconnoitre with more accuracy the ships in the road. I shall upon the opening your Lordship has afforded me presume to suggest if the addition of two ships of the line to this force might not become very desirable for other objects, not, however, losing sight of the first – for instance, if the convoy from Bordeaux was to appear in the Bec du Raz the enemy's advanced guard would come out and prevent our effecting any attack upon them but they would continue at rest if they saw two ships of the line with us and, should your Lordship entrust such a charge to me, I should be careful to use it with prudence for the honour of His Majesty's service.

282.   *Bridport to Admiralty*

Royal George, at sea, 9 August 1797

Their Lordships will see by Sir Edward Pellew's last report that the fleet at Brest consists of twenty-two ships of the line, besides a great number of frigates apparently ready for sea; and by the intelligence from Sir John Warren there are in Basque Road one seventy-four and five frigates ready for sailing, which has been confirmed by other intelligence. My force is but sixteen ships of the line. I therefore submit to their Lordships' consideration the strengthening my hands as soon as possible with more line of battle ships and frigates, as I think it would be advantageous to His Majesty's service if I could send ships to cruise as far to the southward as Bordeaux, Bayonne and Bilbao, as there are a number of privateers out of those parts and many vessels have been captured by them, as I am informed.

283.   *Bridport to Admiralty*

Royal George, at sea, 13 August 1797

You will be pleased to acquaint their Lordships that Sir Edward Pellew with his squadron joined me this morning and I have ordered him to proceed immediately to Falmouth with the ships named in the margin [*Indefatigable*, *Phoebe*, *Revolutionnaire*] to complete them with all possible despatch and to be held in constant readiness for sailing.

I have directed Captain Pellew[1] of the Cleopatra to proceed to Plymouth with Mr. J.H. Dore, late surgeon of the Atlas, and some other of the squadron and objects for the hospital and given him liberty to remain at that port for the payment of his ship and then to rejoin Sir Edward Pellew at Falmouth.

As these frigates are taken from me I judge it necessary to concentrate the force under my command and to keep it within reach of my signals.

284.   *Admiralty to Bridport*

16 August 1797

I have received and communicated to my Lords Commissioners of the Admiralty your letter of the 10th instant acknowledging the receipt of their Lordships' orders for sending Sir Edward Pellew and the squadron under his command into port and acquainting me for their information that, being short of frigates, you should be under the necessity of recalling Commodore Sir John Warren's squadron from off the Penmarks to take the station off Brest; and I am commanded by their Lordships to acquaint you that the Melpomene has proceeded to join you and that the Stag will follow in a few days.

285.   *Bridport to Admiralty*

Royal George, at sea, 16 August 1797

I acquainted you by my letter of the 13th instant for the information of their Lordships of my having ordered Sir Edward Pellew's squadron of

[1]Sir Israel Pellew (d. 1832). Lieutenant 1779; Captain 1793; Rear-admiral 1810; Vice-admiral 1819; Admiral 1830.

frigates into port and they left me on Sunday noon. About 3 p.m. of that day signals were made for seeing several ships in the S.E. quarter, when I directed the Cumberland, Marlborough and Pique to reconnoitre them: soon afterwards the signal was made for their being enemy's ships and that some of them were of the line. From the representations made to me by Captain Montagu[1] they must be the Bertheaume squadron venturing out further than usual as I had no ships close in shore after I had recalled Sir Edward Pellew from his station. They consisted altogether of eight sail, including a lugger, and they returned again to their anchorage.

286. *Bridport to Admiralty*

Royal George, off the Lizard, 20 August 1797

As the winds have blown strong from the western quarter since I received their Lordships' order of the 12th instant I judged I should more effectually give protection to the Leeward Islands convoy expected in the Channel in a few days by standing to the northward than remaining with the fleet off of Brest as if any ship had sailed from that port or any other they would be quite out of my reach and would probably have stationed themselves in the mouth of the Channel. Reasoning therefore as I have done I left Ushant on Saturday the 19th at noon and on the 20th at noon I made the Lizard, where I shall remain some days for the above purpose and if I learn that the convoy has passed up Channel and the wind should continue to blow as it now does it is my intention to bear up for Torbay.

The frigates that I have ordered to cruise off Brest are named in the margin [*Melpomene, Anson, Pique, Dolly* cutter] and Sir Charles Hamilton[2] has directions to put himself under the command of Sir John Borlase Warren whenever he shall join the Pomone off of Brest and on his going to Falmouth with the Sylph brig Sir Charles Hamilton will resume his command.

---

[1]Robert Montagu (d. 1830). Lieutenant 1779; Captain 1781; Rear-admiral 1799; Vice-admiral 1805; Admiral 1810.

[2]Sir Charles Hamilton (d. 1849). Lieutenant 1781; Captain 1790; Rear-admiral 1810; Vice-admiral 1814; Admiral 1830.

287. *Pellew to Spencer*

Indefatigable, Torbay, 25 August 1797

Nothing can excuse me for troubling your Lordship so soon after my letter from Falmouth but that I cannot help thinking your Lordship will be surprised to hear the Indefatigable is at Torbay. Upon my joining his Lordship off the Lizard with the Cleopatra we were directed to follow him to this place and without your Lordship's protection I fear very soon to see myself a repeater to the fleet. His Lordship is excessively angry with me for being directed to return to Falmouth by your Lordship's Board and thinks I had made representations on that subject to your Lordship which induced it. If your Lordship was aware of the great pains that are taken to break up your small squadron at Falmouth and the jaundiced eye with which they are viewed I am satisfied you would see how much we stand in need of your protection and I venture to hope the zeal with which we have served may flatter us with attaining so desirable an object.

[Endorsed as received on the 28th]

288. *Spencer to Pellew*

Admiralty, 28 August 1797

I am concerned to find by your letter that the Commander-in-Chief has disposed of the Indefatigable in a way so little suited to your wishes but for the reason mentioned in my last letter I cannot possibly interfere with those details of his Lordship's arrangements and if I could I doubt whether it would do any good.

I must therefore recommend it to you to have patience for a little while till we can supply his Lordship with some more frigates (which among other reasons the King's residence at Weymouth renders at this moment more peculiarly difficult)[1] and restore you to a post more congenial to your inclination.

---

[1]Frigates had to be provided as guardships while the King was on holiday at Weymouth.

289. *Admiralty to Bridport*

30 August 1797

I am commanded by my Lords Commissioners of the Admiralty to signify their direction to your Lordship on your leaving Torbay to cause three or four of the frigates under your orders to be kept constantly at Falmouth or in Cawsand Bay to be in readiness to put to sea upon any emergency which may require the service of ships of that description.

290. *Admiralty to Bridport*[1]

2 September 1797

I am commanded by my Lords Commissioners of the Admiralty to transmit your Lordship herewith a copy of intelligence this day received from the master of a West Indian trader who lately left the port of Nantes; and in consequence thereof to signify their directions to you to detach at least three of the frigates of your squadron to cruise between the latitude of Belleisle and the entrance of the Garonne for the protection of the trade of His Majesty's subjects and the annoyance of the enemy in that quarter for the space of one month, at the expiration of which period, should circumstances appear to render it necessary, it is their Lordships' further direction that you appoint another detachment of equal force to relieve the former upon the same station and service.

291. *Captain Duckworth[2] to Bridport*

Leviathan, Ushant E.N.E. 5 leagues, 3 September 1797

Since I had the honour of writing your Lordship by the Phaeton the winds have been so adverse and the weather so unseasonably tempestuous that it was out of my power to approach the port of Brest till yesterday afternoon when I directed Sir Charles Hamilton in the Melpomene with the Anson to lead in as near the roads as he could with safety, accompanying him in the Leviathan with the Pompee, which service he, with Captain Durham, executed in a most officerlike manner

---

[1]Addressed to Bridport in Torbay.
[2]Sir John Thomas Duckworth (1748–1817). Lieutenant 1771; Captain 1780; Rear-admiral 1799; Vice-admiral 1804; Admiral 1810. Commander-in-Chief Leeward Islands 1800. Governor of Newfoundland 1810–13.

and I should judge when recalled they could not be more than three miles from the enemy's ships, as the Leviathan had Bertheaume Castle a point abaft her beam, with the frigates more than a mile ahead of her and their captains state what I also distinctly saw, that there were three flags flying one at each masthead and the squadron by their pendants in divisions consisting in all of 18 or 20 sail of the line and either 10 or 11 sail of frigates and corvettes and among the whole 14 with their sails bent, but there is a difference of opinion as to the number of three deckers, Sir Charles Hamilton reporting only two and the rest of the captains four. There were no ships either in Bertheaume or Camaret Bays and I con-clude the late blowing weather had caused them to remove into the road.

As the Pique's water grows very short and she has only a sprung mizen topsail yard left I have directed Captain Milne[1] to return to Plymouth to complete and wait your Lordship's orders. He takes in with him a Prus-sian loaded with masts of very large dimensions for Ferrol but going into Brest and another with hemp. Captain Durham has also sent in a ship under Danish colours from Marseilles bound to Hamburg which had been carried into Gibraltar by an English privateer and manned with thirteen Frenchmen, in which state he boarded her.

292. *Admiralty to Bridport*

8 September 1797

I have received and laid before my Lords Commissioners of the Admi-ralty your letter of the 6th instant and I am commanded by their Lordships to acquaint you in answer thereto that His Majesty's ship Melampus has been ordered to proceed to Falmouth and follow such orders as she may receive from your Lordship. By the addition of this ship they perceive that your Lordship will have no less than 15 frigates and two brigs under your orders, of which three or four of the former only are directed to be left at Plymouth (the selection of which they mean should rest with your Lordship) and that with the remainder they con-ceive you will not be likely to be exposed to any difficulty in making the detachments mentioned in their Lordships' order to you.

I have their Lordships' further command to acquaint you that as you give a preference to the anchorage of Cawsand Bay to that of Falmouth for the frigates which are to remain in port, your Lordship will send directions to their commanders accordingly and to appropriate only

---

[1]Sir David Milne (1763–1845). Lieutenant 1794; Captain 1795; Rear-admiral 1814; Vice-admiral 1825; Admiral 1841.

three to that service. The Pallas, now at Plymouth, is nearly ready and will be sent to your Lordship and her commander will be directed to follow your orders.

293. *Nepean[1] to Spencer*

Admiralty, 11 September 1797

You will receive a letter from Lord Hugh Seymour about the arrangement of the succession to the command of the Raven and the opinion of the Board on the case of the man under sentence of death. I have only, therefore, to add on the subject of your Lordship's note that the three commissions mentioned in it have been forwarded by this post to Lord Bridport, who ought to be pleased, though he is never likely to be so.

294. *Admiralty to Bridport[2]*

13 September 1797

I have their Lordships' commands to acquaint you that they are desirous the three frigates which they have directed your Lordship to station in Cawsand Bay should be composed of ships in a state of actual readiness and not of those in a state of refitting and that your Lordship is to make your selection accordingly.

295. *Bridport to Admiralty*

Royal George, Torbay, 14 September 1797

It having been represented to me that the several ships' companies of this squadron are very much in want of tobacco, that there is not a hogshead to be purchased at Plymouth and under the present arrangement it can only be received from the customs house of the port the ship may be at, and that only at London, Rochester, Portsmouth and Plymouth.

On enquiry I find that the pursers are under great difficulties in supplying this article not only by the increase of price but from the

---

[1]Sir Evan Nepean (1751–1822). First Secretary to the Board of Admiralty. Entered the navy as a clerk, becoming secretary to Sir John Jervis. Turned to politics and became under-secretary of state in the Shelburne ministry. Appointed Admiralty Secretary 3 March 1795 and resigned 20 January 1804 on appointment as chief secretary for Ireland. Returned to the Board of Admiralty as a commissioner September 1804 to February 1806. Governor of Bombay 1812–19.

[2]Addressed to Bridport in Torbay.

great shrinkage and length of time they remain unpaid for what may be issued, generally near three years and sometimes longer, by which a purser of a third rate has upon an average seldom less than £400 due to him for this article only and often a larger sum: I therefore beg to call their Lordships' attention to this subject and would recommend that the pursers may receive the amount of tobacco issued at the payment of the ship, when it is stopped from the men, which would then leave an arrear of six months.

I understand large quantities of seized tobacco are sometimes burnt at the different customs houses. I therefore submit to their Lordships' consideration if it might not be supplied to the navy and charged to the pursers at such a rate as may in that case be judged necessary; and as the fleet may frequently rendezvous in this bay it would be very convenient if the ships could be supplied with this article from Dartmouth in the same way as from Plymouth or Portsmouth.

296. *Spencer to Bridport*

Admiralty, 18 September 1797

The season of the year begins now to be rather too advanced for Torbay, therefore when your Lordship shall come again into port I think there will be no sort of objection to the measure you propose respecting the ships being paid.[1]

297. *Spencer to Warren*

Admiralty, 22 September 1797

You shall be appointed to the Canada in a few days and as your ship and the ship you move into are at the same port the regulated number of followers will be allowed to remove with you. Lord Hugh Seymour has written to you on this subject, therefore I will not repeat what he has said but since he wrote an opening has offered by which your boatswain may be promoted into a third rate (an unusual favour from a 5th rate except in very particular cases) and he may then exchange for duty with the present boatswain of the Canada. The case of the purser will be more difficult but when a proper opening offers for it some arrangement shall be made by which you may have him with you.

---

[1] That is, sending them either to Spithead or Cawsand Bay to be paid.

298.   *Windham to Spencer*

14 October 1797

I will offer no congratulations to you on your victory unless you will take measures to have an illumination. I feel at the same time the objection to having an illumination for Admiral Duncan[1] (which some I dare say do not partake of) when there was none for Lord St. Vincent and likewise enter into the sentiment which slackens all exultation in their successes; namely that they make very little difference as to the sum of things. To those who are masters of Europe a fleet more or less is certainly of little consequence. Still the habit should not utterly be lost of rejoicing in national success; nor the principle become perfectly established that we are never to express any sentiment that may be displeasing to our enemies. Our enemies do not altogether return our courtesy but in the midst of our most pacific communications call our King a despot and the nation a nation of shopkeepers who ought to be driven out of the system of Europe but they are privileged people – Graeci, quibus est nihil negatum – it does not become us to say towards them what may be very proper from them to us.[2]

299.   *Admiralty to Bridport*

11 November 1797

Your Lordship is hereby required and directed in addition to our order to you of the 7th instant for repairing with the ships therein mentioned to Spithead to send His Majesty's ships Leviathan and Cumberland forthwith to Berehaven with directions to their respective Captains to put themselves on their arrival under the command of Vice Admiral Kingsmill, Commander in Chief of His Majesty's ships and vessels employed at Cork and on the coast of Ireland, and follow his orders for their further proceedings.

Having so done your Lordship is to order Vice Admiral Lord Keith to repair to Spithead in the Queen Charlotte, accompanied by the Sans Pareil and Saturn, and to remain there until he shall receive further orders, leaving the remainder of the squadron under the command of Rear Admiral Sir Roger Curtis with instructions to him to station three ships of the line and a frigate to the northward of the Passage du Four, a proper number of frigates off the Saints and to cruise himself with such

---

[1]Duncan won the battle of Camperdown on 11 October 1797.
[2]Undoubtedly Windham had read Adam Smith.

ships as shall then remain with him to the westward of Brest for the purpose of preventing the sailing of the enemy's frigates lying there.

Your Lordship is to direct Sir Roger Curtis to give instructions to the senior officer of the frigates which he may station off the Saints to look frequently into Brest and if he should perceive any appearance of the enemy's ships of the line re-equipping for sea to send to him immediate information thereof, a copy of which the Rear Admiral is to transmit as expeditiously as possible to our Secretary for our information.

The Rear Admiral is also to direct the senior officer of the ships stationed off the Saints in case he should receive intelligence that may be depended upon of the sailing of the enemy's frigates from Brest to lose not a moment's time in giving him, as well as the senior officer of the ships stationed to the northward of the Passage du Four, information thereof and if no certain account can be obtained of the destination of the enemy the Rear Admiral is to proceed immediately off Cork for intelligence and the ships stationed off the Passage du Four are to proceed off the Lizard for the like purpose and if either the Rear Admiral or the senior officer of the ships last mentioned should obtain intelligence that may be depended upon that the enemy has proceeded either to the coast of England or Ireland he is to repair in quest of them and any transports which may have accompanied then.

You are in addition to the above instructions to direct Sir Roger Curtis not to risk unnecessarily the disabling of the ships under his command but on the appearance of strong gales of wind from the westward to repair either to Mevagissey Bay or to Torbay as may be most convenient, putting again to sea and returning to his station as soon as the wind shall change so as to enable the enemy's ships to sail from Brest, giving such directions on that head as may be proper to the senior officers of the ships stationed off the Saints and the Passage du Four.

300. *Bridport to Spencer*

Royal George, Spithead, 14 November 1797

After having been at sea near twenty-one weeks and having never slept one night out of the Royal George since the 27th of April last nor had my foot upon the shore for more than ten hours since that time and under circumstances, as your Lordship knows, the most painful and afflicting to an anxious and feeling mind, I therefore hope your Lordship will not think me unreasonable in requesting some time of break from public business and soliciting a leave of absence for the recovery of my health by going for a short time to my house in the country and afterwards to Bath, as I conclude I shall not be wanted in Town upon any public occasion.

[Endorsed as received on the 15th and answered the same day]

301.   *Keith to Bridport*

Harley Street, 25 November 1797

I was much astonished when I came to Spithead to find Sir Charles Thompson[1] in the port. I had enjoyed under your Lordship's command and which (when I was sent for by Lord Spencer) I was told I <u>was</u> to exercise the command of a division in the Channel fleet where I cannot return without some explanation which I expect this day but if it ends in my resignation I beg your Lordship to accept my sincere thanks for your attention so long as I had the honour to serve in the fleet under you.

302.   *Admiralty to Curtis*

29 November 1797

In addition to former orders you are hereby required and directed so soon as the wind shall become westerly with a probability of its staying in that quarter to proceed with the three decked ships under your command to Spithead for further orders, sending all the two decked ships under your command to Cawsand Bay with directions to their commanders to cause the utmost despatch to be used in making good their defects and in completing their stores and provisions for Channel service and having so done to hold themselves in constant readiness to put to sea at the shortest notice.

Upon your quitting your station off Brest you are to leave thereon such of the frigates as may have been put under your orders with directions to the senior captain to employ them in watching very diligently the motions of the enemy at Brest, taking care to send to you as well as to our Secretary frequent accounts of his proceedings and every intelligence he may be able to obtain proper for our knowledge.

---

[1]Sir Charles Thompson (c.1740–1799). Lieutenant 1761; Captain 1772; Rear-admiral 1794; Vice-admiral 1795. Sent home from the West Indies in July 1795 by Sir John Laforey and promised a court-martial, which was abandoned after Laforey's death. He was second in command to Jervis at Cape St Vincent and created a baronet but relieved in September 1797 at St Vincent's request because he objected to the hanging of mutineers on a Sunday. He served in the Channel both in 1796 and 1798.

303. *Admiralty to Bridport*[1]

29 November 1797

I have it . . . in command from their Lordships to acquaint you that Sir H. Neale of the St. Fiorenzo appearing to have disobeyed your orders by leaving his station and proceeding so far to the southward and eastward as to be in sight of the Isle of Rhé and Light House of Cordovan and the Clyde as far as Cape Machicaco, their Lordships have thought proper to call upon him to account for his conduct.

304. *Commander John White to Bridport*

Sylph, in Cawsand Bay, 2 December 1797

I beg leave to acquaint your Lordship that we sailed from this anchorage on the 19th ultimo in order to rejoin the squadron under Captain Keats but owing to thick and blowing weather I was not able to fall in with him before he quitted the rendezvous. I have further to acquaint your Lordship that since the above period we have made the following recaptures (between the latitude of Belleisle and Rochefort) and with the last of them we arrived here this morning.

On the 21st November Active (schooner) from Newfoundland bound to Teignmouth laden with fish and oil. She was captured on the 14th November by La Constance (brig) privateer of Nantes.

On the 22nd November Durude Gruins (Prussian galliot) from Amsterdam to Lisbon laden with wheat. Captured by Le Buonaparte (ship) privateer of Bordeaux on suspicion of the cargo being Portuguese property. This vessel being very leaky and her cargo much damaged I suffered her to proceed (after taking out the Frenchmen) to her original destination.

23 November. The brig Diarma from New Providence bound to London laden with cotton, sugar and coffee. Captured on the 12th November by the Felix (cutter) privateer of 14 guns belonging to Nantes. Beside the Diarma she had taken three English vessels from Newfoundland and two Americans westbound.

30th November. The ship Henniker from London bound to Martinique laden with provisions on account of Government. Was under convoy of the Trent and Amphitrite and captured in latitude 42.27 and longitude 21.50 by the Francois (ship) privateer of Nantes on the 23rd November.

[1] Addressed to Bridport at Bath.

The prisoners taken in the Diarma inform me that Le Felix (the privateer to which they belonged) was upset on the night of the 16th November in a sudden and violent gust of wind and though not a quarter of a mile from her prize, not one of her crew were saved, which consisted of one hundred and fifteen men, exclusive of whom, I am sorry to add, perished twenty-three British and American seamen belonging to the vessels this privateer had captured.

305.   *Nicholas Hall to Spencer*

2 December 1797

At this particular period I take the liberty of suggesting to your Lordship the propriety of the fleet intended to watch the motions of the Brest fleet during winter being moored for that purpose in the roads and harbours in the Scilly Islands.

In looking at the chart you will see the advantage a fleet must have stationed there. At once looking into Brest and the Bay of Biscay, the English, Irish and Bristol Channels and Ireland. Fixed there during the winter, our cruisers will always know where to carry them intelligence of the enemy's motions, which can never be the case to a certainty when the fleet is cruising.

For strong gales of wind, which prevail in some winters from the eastward, must drive them several degrees of longitude to the westward of their station, which cannot be <u>prevented</u>. In the year 1784 or 1785 I came from the West Indies master of a ship and made Scilly the 12 to 15 February, the wind then came to the eastward and from the longitude six I was driven by the same gale to the longitude 17 in a good ship and well manned. If a fleet had then been cruising off Brest they must have shared the same fate. As it was impossible nor did any vessel of war or other get into the Channel from the westward till about the middle of April following. This fact you may look into and judge whether it will not be proper to guard against the possibility of its happening to our fleet.

I hope from the list I have given you, you will cause two of the most experienced pilots to come to you from Scilly to be examined and I think they will tell you a fleet of 25 to 30 sail of the line can be moored there in the greatest safety and put to sea from thence with any wind.

It must strike you the advantage it will be to have a fleet fixed there only 35 leagues from the Brest fleet, always in condition to follow them if they put to sea.

And you might communicate with our fleet by a telegraph to the Land's End and the Longships the same as you now do to Portsmouth.

It may require larger signals guns or smoke to be seen from thence to St. Agnes Light House.

I am sure if you mention this to any naval gent they will tell you it is a dangerous place and not practicable, which arises from the little use most of them have made of it. I give them great credit for their gallant conduct an all occasions, yet I know they prefer laying at Portsmouth or Plymouth. They will therefore create difficulties that don't exist. Ships stationed there should always have a pilot from the islands on board that should go to sea with them, by which means they might put in and out as they pleased without fear. I should propose for the ships exceeding 74 guns to be victualled only for six weeks or as much as will put them in easy and proper trim. That stock might be constantly kept up by supplies from the western ports, of which Penzance will be a very useful one as vessels from it can reach Scilly when they can't do it from Falmouth or Plymouth and in any emergency the lesser ships might supply the larger ones so that the whole fleet might average two months provisions always on board. Express boats might also be stationed there to aid the telegraph in thick weather and carry despatches.

I will now suppose a strong gale to blow from the westward. In it our fleet must be forced into Portsmouth or Plymouth. The French take the advantage of sailing when it comes a little moderate even with the wind at W.S.W. or S.W., they can get to Ireland or any part of the west of England and land an army and our fleet cannot get down Channel to prevent it. But if our fleet was moored in Scilly it could follow them the same as though the two fleets had come from Brest together. I am aware that your Lordship is often troubled with letters by people who may want employment or advantage. I am actuated by a sincere love for my country and no interested views and I take the liberty of referring you for a confirmation of it to Sir Richard Neave, to whom I am well known.

306.   *George Cherry*[1] *to Admiralty*

Victualling office, 20 December 1797

Mr Cherry presents his compliments to Mr. Nepean and begs leave to acquaint him that the lemon juice remaining in the several victualling stores at Deptford, Portsmouth and Plymouth, is sufficient to serve

[1]Chairman of the Victualling Board.

20,000 men for 234 days according to the proportion in which the same is directed to be issued; and which was particularly stated in the Victualling Board's letter of 8 November 1796 – a copy of which is herewith.

307.   *Curtis to Admiralty*

Prince, at Spithead, 31 December 1797

I request you will represent to the Lords Commissioners of the Admiralty I have found upon observation on service as well as by particular inspection that the Prince, bearing my flag, is very inferiorly manned, notwithstanding she has more than the number of petty and able allowed upon the first outfit of His Majesty's ships of her class: but I have thereon to remark to their Lordships that the foundation of the Prince's complement was about four hundred men she received from the Princess Royal, in which ship every man had been rated an able seaman, though many of those of that description turned over to the Prince were not strictly entitled to such qualification: and, moreover, the men of the Prince are in general slight and undersized. I am, therefore, humbly to request their Lordships will be pleased to give directions that about 30, or 25, of the most exceptionable men might be discharged from the Prince and that their Lordships will be pleased to direct her to be supplied with an equal number of seamen in their room.

308.   *Admiralty to Bridport*

2 January 1798

I have received and communicated to my Lords Commissioners of the Admiralty your letter of the 31st ultimo respecting Captain Sir H. Neale of His Majesty's ship St. Fiorenzo and I am commanded by their Lordships to acquaint you that they were displeased at the conduct of Sir H. Neale for having quitted the station on which he had been directed to cruise, as it did not appear by the copy of your Lordship's order that he was authorized so to do; but as it appears by your letter abovementioned that he had permission verbally to proceed to a much greater distance than his order expressed, their Lordships no longer see any reason for being displeased with Sir H. Neale's conduct.

I have their Lordships' further command to observe to you that, although it may perhaps in some particular instances be attended with advantage to His Majesty's service to allow ships to leave their stations on receiving information of the enemy's cruisers, yet as a general principle it cannot but be attended with inconvenience, for if captains are allowed to leave the stations appointed for them it will be impossible to be sure of finding them in case they should be wanted for any other service and it may frequently happen, as in the instance of Sir H. Neale it did, that one part of the sea where our merchant ships are likely to pass will be left unprotected and exposed to the enemy's cruisers, while the ships appointed for their protection are gone to the station to which others have been ordered; and I am to signify their Lordships' directions to you to order the commanders of His Majesty's ships and vessels under your command to confine their cruising generally within the limits specified in your Lordship's orders and not to exceed them in any degree without very certain information to occasion the same and in such case to return to their proper station as soon as possible and on no account to leave the same entirely for the purpose of cruising on any other station.

309. *Bridport to Admiralty*

Bath, 5 January 1798

I have received your letter of the 2nd instant acquainting me that their Lordships no longer see occasion for being displeased with Sir Harry Neale's conduct, which gives me particular satisfaction to hear.

I agree entirely with their Lordships in opinion that as a general principle captains leaving their stations may be attended with inconveniences. For instance, if I give an order for a ship or ships to cruise to the northward of Ushant to guard the Passage du Four it would be attended with manifest inconveniences to allow the captains to leave that station. The same off Brest, the same off the Saints, and I hold the same principle to be served with respect to myself, though their Lordships know that I am justified in seeking the enemy wherever I can find it if a fleet should get out of Brest unobserved. Lord Howe did the same and their Lordships likewise know how many days passed before the two large fleets met on the 28th of May,[1] though diligently endeavouring to fall in with the enemy's. But with regard to frigates cruising from the latitude of Belle Isle to that of the Garonne, it does not appear to me in the same point of view. Neither does it with ships which have three or four degrees of latitude given them and five or six of longitude. Under these circumstances I apprehend it cannot be injurious to His Majesty's service if from intelligence such ships extend those limits, taking care

[1]1794.

not to go and remain on stations where other frigates are cruising, which I think could not be the case with Sir Harry Neale because I know that Captain Keats and his squadron were returning into port, if not returned, when the St. Fiorenzo and Clyde, the only frigates then at sea under my orders went to the southward and eastward. However, I do not approve of those ships making the Isle Rhé, the light house of Cordovan and the Clyde as far as Cape Machicaco. At least they should not have remained an hour in sight of those places. I have repeatedly given directions to the captains of the frigates cruising to the southward and eastward to avoid being near the land. I have reason to believe the Concorde and Nereide must have fallen into the hands of Captain Stopford and his squadron had they been further from the land when they chased these two frigates.

As far as I am able to judge from the contents of your letter there does not appear to be a shade of difference in the principle of the service between their Lordships and me. I have but one principle for the government of my conduct, which is to serve the King with zeal and fidelity and the public with unshaken attachment. Having stated these feelings with respect and candour, I hope it may be allowed to ask, if Sir Harry Neale and Captain Cunningham[1] had fallen in with the Concorde and Nereide in their sailing from Rochefort, had attacked and taken them after a spirited and well fought action, whether these two excellent officers would not have met with approbation from their Lordships instead of calling upon Sir Harry Neale for having disobeyed my orders and whether the verbal latitude I had given him would have merited the animadversions I have received.

310. *Sir Charles Thompson to Admiralty*

Formidable, at Spithead, 13 January 1798

At one a.m. I received by express your letter of the 12th instant directing me to have the ships named in the margin [*Formidable, Prince, Sans Pareil, Caesar, Pompee, Defiance, Saturn, Lion, Stag, Pallas, Mars, Marlborough, Terrible, St. Albans, St. Fiorenzo, Triton*] ready for proceeding off Brest in consequence of information from Captain Keats of the enemy's preparations at that port, together with an order addressed to Lord Bridport directing his Lordship to take the Lion and Pallas under his command. And have this moment received their Lord-

---

[1]Sir Charles Cunningham (d. 1834). Lieutenant 1782; Captain 1793; Commissioner Deptford dockyard 1806–23; Retired Rear-admiral 1829.

ships' order and your letter of yesterday's date which shall be put into execution with all possible despatch. Have also received a copy of Captain Keats' letter of the 10th instant to Lord Bridport.

I have ordered the Stag to proceed to Plymouth with directions to Captain Hood to have the ships named in the margin [*Mars, Marlborough, Terrible, St. Albans, St. Fiorenzo, Triton*] ready to join me on my appearing off there, I have also wrote Sir Richard King to hasten them accordingly. The Caesar, I am afraid, will not be ready to go with me as two lighters with her guns have grounded in coming out, which circumstance and paying her people will prevent her being ready before Monday night at soonest. The Pompee is also to pay. I have sent to request the Commissioners would do it as soon as possible but as their books only came down this morning Captain Vashon fears they will not be ready before tomorrow. In that case I don't intend waiting for either.

311.   *Thompson to Admiralty*

Formidable, at Spithead, 14 January 1798

In answer to your letter of yesterday I am to request you will acquaint their Lordships that I had . . . purposed sailing this morning with such ships as might be ready, provided the wind had been fair. It now blows strong at west; had it been moderate should have gone to St. Helens this forenoon, which I intend doing either this evening or early tomorrow according to the state of the weather, having been at single anchor for that purpose ever since five o'clock this morning. The wind came to the northward yesterday afternoon.

312.   *Thompson to Admiralty*

Formidable, at St. Helens, 16 January 1798

I request you will inform their Lordships that yesterday forenoon His Majesty's ships named in the margin [*Formidable, Prince, Pompee, Lion, Pallas*] anchored here from Spithead. The Caesar I expect down tomorrow.

313.   *Thompson to Admiralty*

Formidable, at St. Helens, 22 January 1798

I am to desire you will please to acquaint the Lords Commissioners of the Admiralty that His Majesty's ships named in the margin [*Formidable, Prince, Caesar, Pompee, Defiance, Saturn, Lion, Sans Pareil, Pallas*] under my command arrived this day at St. Helens, from whence we sailed on Saturday evening with light airs from the northward and every appearance of a northerly wind but it came to the southwest in the night, in which quarter it has continued ever since, with very thick and foggy weather. Seeing no prospect of getting down Channel and great risk of parting company I thought it prudent to take advantage of the weather clearing up to bring the ships to St. Helens to wait for a more favourable opportunity of putting their Lordships' orders into execution.

314.   *White to Bridport*

Sylph, Plymouth Sound, 23 January 1798

I have the honour to acquaint your Lordship with my return to this port accompanied by the schooner Mercury, letter of marque, of ten guns, laden with different kinds of merchandise from Bristol to Martinique, which we retook on the 17th instant in latitude 47° 12′ North and longitude 7° West, having separated the preceding day from the Phaeton and La Nymphe in chase of a cutter which under cover of the night and thick weather effected her escape and, having forty prisoners on board, I thought it most expedient to return with this vessel to Plymouth, which I trust will meet your Lordship's approbation.

It was in the close of day I lost sight of the Phaeton and Nymphe. They were then in chase of a ship and brig, and from the appearance I judge the former to be a privateer; the Mermaid separated the night of the 16th instant from the squadron.

The Prize Master of the Mercury, who belonged to the Zele, ship privateer of Nantes, acquaints me that on the 1st instant sailed from the Loire three frigates viz. La Porte, La Semillante and La Loire, all of eighteen pounders. They were fitted out for a long cruise and their destination, it was reported, was off the Western Islands in quest of some Portuguese ships they expected from the Messailles.

315.   *Thompson to Admiralty*

Formidable, at St. Helens, 25 January 1798

I am to desire you will please to acquaint the Lords Commissioners of the Admiralty that the ships named in the margin [*Formidable, Prince, Caesar, Terrible, Mars, Pompee, Defiance, Saturn, Marlborough, St. Albans, Lion, Sans Pareil, Pallas, St. Fiorenzo, Stag* and *Cygnet* cutter] under my command anchored here this day. On Saturday afternoon we got down in sight of Plymouth and sent the Pallas to make a signal for the ships from thence to join. The Terrible, Mars, St. Albans, St. Fiorenzo and Stag, being in Cawsand Bay, got out that evening and joined in the night, the Marlborough, being in the Sound, did not get out 'till next morning. She joined last night, in the course of which, it blowing very strong from the south-west with every prospect of its continuing and thick weather, I thought it advisable to bear up in the morning for this place where we anchored about noon. In bringing up, the Caesar fouled her cable and the Lion carried away her main yard this morning, which is all the damage I yet know of except splitting a few sails as I have had no communication with the ships since we anchored, it continuing to blow very hard.

316.   *Spencer to Keith*

Admiralty, 15 February 1798

Your Lordship being out of service at this time was entirely your own act and not at all in consequence of any desire of mine and I am afraid that it will be impossible for me to make an arrangement of the flag officers under Lord St. Vincent which would admit of your hoisting your flag under his command at present.

317.   *Spencer to Keith*

Admiralty, 19 February 1798

Whenever your Lordship shall think fit to make an offer of your services generally, without any stipulations or restrictions, if the dispositions and arrangements of the naval force at the time shall be such as to admit of it I shall be very glad to avail myself of your offer, being persuaded that the service allotted to you will be well executed.

318. *Bridport to Spencer*

Portsmouth, 4 March 1798

By yesterday's post I acquainted Mr. Secretary Nepean of my arrival here and had caused my flag to be hoisted. As the Board have ordered the Ramillies and Stag into this harbour to be docked, which leaves me at Spithead with only the St. Fiorenzo for any immediate active service. Your Lordship knows that six frigates have been taken from me and only three put under my orders. If your Lordship and the Board shall judge it expedient to allow more frigates to the Channel fleet there is at Spithead, I understand, the Naiad, commanded by Captain Pierrepoint,[1] also the Ethalion. It is possible intelligence may be communicated from the signal posts or by other means which may require an immediate detachment but from the present orders of the Board I have no authority to send a single ship to sea, signified to me by letter from Mr. Nepean of the 21st ultimo that I am not in future to send 'any of the ships under my command to sea without receiving directions from their Lordships for so doing' and I hold myself bound strictly to obey these directions as long as they shall remain in force. Your Lordship will excuse my stating these particulars lest they should not have come to your Lordship's knowledge or in the hurry of business have escaped your memory. I shall take the earliest occasion to forward the equipment of the ships at Spithead under my orders and promote the full intention of the Admiralty.

319. *Spencer to Bridport*

Admiralty, 5 March 1798

The very great variety of services for which frigates are now wanted makes it impossible to put as many as we should otherwise wish to do under your Lordship's command but as a great proportion of the frigates which are under your orders are cruising off Brest they would be free to join you if any emergency should require your proceeding to sea with the fleet.

The reason for the order to which you allude was the necessity that appeared of our being perfectly apprized of what force we had to make use of at any time when any part of it might be wanted at the same time. I do not imagine that any pressing emergency which might absolutely require a part of your Lordship's force on a sudden and on which it was

---

[1]William Pierrepont (d. 1813). Lieutenant 1789; Captain 1794; Rear-admiral 1812.

necessary to act without previously consulting the Board would not be justly considered as a justification for sending such force to sea, though I must observe that it will be essential as much as possible to keep the ships under your orders together and ready to move as a fleet on any intelligence which may be received here and which may appear to require your going to sea.

Your Lordship will readily conceive what is meant by this idea, which is grounded on the expectation that whenever the enemy shall be prepared to make the threatened attack on this country they will probably make it in several parts at once and it is most likely that the principal attempt may be proceeding from Brest to Ireland at the same time as several smaller bodies may make their appearance in different parts of the Channel. It will therefore be of great importance to have the main force of the country (which in such case must be employed to counteract their principal attack) kept in a body to move as occasion may require, while it is equally necessary to have at the same time several smaller squadrons separately stationed on different points in a state of readiness to watch the enemy's motions and counteract their smaller attempts if they should make any. This is accordingly the sort of plan on which we intend to proceed and under this plan it will be unadvisable that your Lordship should be called upon to detach on any sudden affair in the Channel a part of the force to which we must look whenever a serious attempt is made for defeating the principal operation of the enemy.

320. *Bridport to Spencer*

Portsmouth, 6 March 1798

In these times of serious warfare, which must occasion heavy expenses to the nation it seems proper that every person should communicate his thoughts who is engaged in a professional line. I therefore presume to suggest to your Lordship what has struck me on the subject of the expense of an hospital ship to the Channel fleet. I understand it is not the intention of the Admiralty to keep the fleet out cruising longer than a month or six weeks, probably not so long. Under this plan for the employment of the fleet I do not see the necessity that the Medusa should attend it, in which case the Physician should be put on board one of the three deck ships not bearing a flag, either the Glory or Atlas, placing the one or the other in the centre of the fleet that the Physician may be ready to attend it when required, who will be allowed the captain's apartments for his accommodation. If these sentiments shall meet with your Lordship's approbation and be adopted by the Board the Medusa in the present call for transports may be employed on that service without any additional expense and the fleet will always have the benefit of the skill and abilities of the Physician instead of his being attached to the hospital ship.

321. *Spencer to Bridport*

Admiralty, 9 March 1798

I am very much obliged to your Lordship for your hint respecting the hospital ship and if it should appear certain that such an establishment will not be wanted for the fleet this summer I shall coincide certainly in your opinion that it would be better to put an end to it. In the meanwhile there does not appear any objection to using her for convoys and such like services near home.

322. *Warren to Admiralty*

Canada, anchored near Basque Roads, 14 March 1798

Intelligence respecting the enemy collected by Commodore Sir John Borlase Warren Bt K.B.

There are 15 or 20 transports laying at Bordeaux waiting to go to Brest, and all the men belonging to privateers at that port have been taken for the use of the fleet at Brest.

All privateers as they arrive at other ports also have their people taken from them for the above purpose.

About a week or ten days ago 8 thousand seamen were marched by land to Brest.

Troops arrive daily by the canal from[1] the army of Italy, intended to serve on the expedition against England or Ireland, and are to embark on board the transports at Bordeaux.

Some vessels are also fitting at Rochefort and Rochelle.

Seamen are collected every where very diligently.

Some transports have already sailed with naval and ordnance stores and provisions for the fleet and armament at Brest, some of which I conjecture were captured by the Amelia.

---

[1] 'Toulon to' inserted here in a different hand.

323. *Bridport to Spencer*

Royal George, 21 March 1798

Your Lordship will allow me to suggest what forcibly strikes me in the present state of things. Ireland seems to be the place the enemy mean to attack. It seems therefore highly proper that the naval commander in that station should not in this awful crisis be permitted to send one ship to move from the coast but to keep all cruising off every port to guard and protect it against invasion.

I feel much for your Lordship's situation and also for the safety of this part of His Majesty's dominions threatened by internal and external enemies. Forgive my sending to your Lordship these thoughts which are offered from the present motives of zeal and respect.

I am much surprised that I have received no letter from Captain Sir H. Trollope[1] since he sailed from Plymouth and I am rather anxious to have some report from him on the observations he or his cruisers have made on the force of the enemy in Brest. I do not learn that Captain Sir Charles Hamilton, who is lately arrived at Plymouth, saw the Russell or any of the squadron on the Brest station.[2]

P.S. I understand that Lord St. Vincent has changed many of the signals that were established by Lord Howe. If this should be the case and he should be to unite with the Channel fleet upon a moment of great importance to the country I am afraid great confusion may arise, attended with fatal consequences.

[*Endorsed as answered on the 23rd*]

324. *Spencer to Bridport*

Admiralty, 23 March 1798

The Commander-in-Chief in Ireland has been very particularly directed respecting the employment of his ships very much on the principles to which your Lordship points and, except when his frigates have necessarily been employed in escorting outward bound convoys a certain

---

[1]Sir Henry Trollope (d. 1839). Lieutenant 1777; Captain 1781; knighted 1796; Rear-admiral 1801; Vice-admiral 1805; Admiral 1812. Trollope quarrelled with St Vincent and went ashore. Gout put an end to his active career. In later life he became eccentric and in November 1839 he shot himself.

[2]Sir Henry Trollope had been deputed a month before to cover the frigates off Brest. For what had happened to him, see the Admiralty's letter to Bridport of 17 May [340].

part of their course and thence returning to their stations, I believe they have been generally confined to the limits prescribed.[1]

I am rather surprised that we should not have heard from Sir H. Trollope since he sailed but I take it for granted it will not be long before we do.

325. *Bridport to Spencer*

Portsmouth, 31 March 1798

I cannot let a post go from hence without communicating to your Lordship the conversation that has reached me from various persons on the subject of Vice Admiral Colpoys, who is, I am informed, to hoist his flag in the Bellona. I have seen Captain Wilson,[2] who tells me there is a gloom amongst his men with the appearance of discontent. I state these particulars with delicacy and feelings of anxiety. I submit it to your Lordship's consideration whether it might not be more advantageous to the King's service as well as to the Vice Admiral if he did not hoist his flag till the Northumberland was ready to receive it, as that ship is fitting out for that purpose and every man belonging to her is apprized of it. I beg pardon for the painful liberty I have taken in stating my sentiments to your Lordship.

326. *Spencer to Bridport*

Admiralty, 1 April 1798

It is fortunate that from considerations of a different nature we had determined that Vice Admiral Colpoys should wait till the Northumberland was ready in order to hoist his flag before the information alluded to in your Lordship's letter had reached us from any authority.

Your Lordship will hear by this day's post that Sir J. Warren is returned to Plymouth having captured and destroyed another convoy with wine and brandy from Bordeaux and driven on shore a French frigate which was bilged. I am sorry, however, to observe that in the latter service he struck the ground himself and the Canada must consequently go into dock. It is lucky that Captain Payne had sailed to relieve him on that station as I think it clearly appears to be very beneficial to

---

[1]That is, they were not expected to take prizes within the limits of Bridport's command.

[2]George Wilson (d. 1826). Lieutenant 1776; Captain 1780; Rear-admiral 1799; Vice-admiral 1804; Admiral 1809.

our service to keep a squadron on that part of the enemy's coast. The interruption of their convoys with supplies for Brest must necessarily be attended with considerable inconvenience to their preparations.

327.   *Spencer to Bridport*

Admiralty, 7 April 1798

You will receive by this post an order from the Board not to consider Sir Roger Curtis and the squadron just put under him as any longer under your command and I think it necessary to trouble you with a line to explain what is meant by it. An urgent necessity has arisen from information which has been obtained from France to reinforce for a short time the squadron on the south and west coast of that kingdom [Ireland] and to do so it seemed requisite to put for that time the whole of the ships which we meant to station there under the command of the Vice Admiral commanding on the station. He is, however, directed after a fixed period to send back Sir R. Curtis and his squadron, who are by no means intended to be taken from the Channel fleet in any other manner than what I have above described to your Lordship.

Some of the disaffected in Ireland appear so confident that the enemy means to come over in the course of this month that I should not be surprised if they were to make their attempt against that kingdom sooner than we have reason to expect or indeed than their preparations as reported to us at present would warrant us in expecting. It is therefore highly expedient for your Lordship to keep the ships under your command at Portsmouth and Plymouth in as complete a state of readiness for sea as possible that if the enemy on the wind changing should push out, which is not very improbable, you may be ready at the shortest notice to proceed in search of them.

328.   *Spencer to Bridport*[1]

Admiralty, 9 April 1798

From the intelligence last received from Brest and which has been communicated to your Lordship it does not appear that it will be necessary for you at present to take a greater number of ships with you than are mentioned in the orders sent down by this day's post, in which,

---

[1]Letter much torn and numerous words illegible or obscure. Suggested wording is given in brackets.

however, you will observe that under certain circumstances you are authorized to send for the other two ships at Plymouth.

If the enemy should intend to avail themselves of the present fair wind for the purpose of carrying their threats of invading Ireland into execution it is clear that they can only do so with a much smaller force than they will hereafter be enabled to put to sea or one which will necessarily be considerably inferior to that portion of your Lordship's force with which it is now intended you should proceed. Under these circumstances we judge it more expedient not to add the Bellona and Robust to it because by that means we shall have a reserve of force either to relieve or to strengthen you if it should appear necessary.

As the season advances and the equipments at Brest get forwarder it will become more and more desirable to take the most effectual means possible for watching the operations from that port and ensuring as far as is practicable their not moving without being closely followed by our Channel fleet. On this subject many ideas have occasionally been suggested and among them none which has appeared to provide so much likelihood of success as stationing the squadron destined to watch Brest in the road at Scilly. I take the liberty of enclosing for your Lordship's perusal and consideration a paper which I some time ago received from a very good seaman on this subject and I should be very glad to know your opinion [about] it at your leisure; if this station could be thus [made] use of in the summer months it would be a great [saving] of the wear and tear of our ships from cruising off Brest and by a chain of frigates and other vessels constantly kept up from Brest to Scilly we should be as nearly as possible to a certainty of knowing their motions early enough to defeat them.

I have heard from some officers that the Bay of Douarnenez would be a good station for the purpose of blocking Brest but being on the enemy's coast and so near one of their arsenals I should be a [little] apprehensive of the squadron anchored in that bay being a little liable to sudden attacks from fireships or gun boats and perhaps also to annoyance from mortar batteries on shore.

I am fully aware of my incompetency to enter into the discussion of these subjects with your Lordship but I much wish you to turn them in your mind and give them a very full consideration because I cannot help being persuaded that if the result should [become] favourable to your adopting (when an occasion [shall] offer) either of these ideas a very effectual advantage would be thereby gained for this country in a naval [contest] with France.

329.   *Sir Andrew Hamond[1] to Spencer*

Navy Office, 13 April 1798

I have been maturely considering the question whether a fleet abroad is more or less expensive than the same number of ships on the Channel service and the more I examine the subject the stronger my opinion is that a fleet of twenty sail of the line with a proportion of frigates, once properly equipped and sent abroad, will cost much less in the space of three years than if they had remained at home. It is true the part of the world they are sent to serve in will make some difference by increasing perhaps the difficulty of supplying them with stores and provisions but as it is a well known fact that ships on foreign service make every article of their stores and furniture last considerably longer than when they have frequent opportunity of being supplied from the King's dock-yards I should apprehend the balance of expenses would be in favour of the fleet abroad and the circumstance of the ships' companies not being paid wages abroad makes a considerable saving on the interest of money.

330.   *Admiralty to Bridport*

15 April 1798

I have received and laid before my Lords Commissioners of the Admiralty your Lordship's letter of the 13th instant, inclosing a copy of your intended rendezvous and desiring that Sir Richard Bickerton[2] in the Terrible may be ordered to join you, as also the frigates under your command, at Portsmouth as soon as they shall be ready for sea. In answer to which I have the honour of acquainting your Lordship that their Lordships have ordered the Stag to join you immediately, and as the Terrible is not in a condition at this moment to put to sea, their Lordships have directed the Saturn to proceed and join you without a moment's delay.

By secret intelligence which has been received, it appears that the enemy will sail from Brest for the purpose of an attack on Ireland the first opportunity after the middle of this month, and I have their Lord-

---

[1]Sir Andrew Snape Hamond (1738–1828). Lieutenant 1759; Captain 1770; superannuated Captain 1806. Commissioner Halifax 1780–84; he served as Comptroller of the Navy 1794–1806.

[2]Sir Richard Hussey Bickerton (1759–1832). Lieutenant 1777; Captain 1781; Rear-admiral 1799; Vice-admiral 1805; Admiral 1810. Succeeded to a baronetcy in 1792. Admiralty commissioner 1805–12; Commander-in-Chief, Portsmouth, 1812–15.

ships' commands to signify their direction to you not to lose a moment, after the wind and weather will allow it, in repairing to your station off Brest, and carrying into execution their Lordships' orders to you of the 9th instant.

Rear Admiral Lord Hugh Seymour has been directed to take his passage in the Stag to rejoin your Lordship and hoist his flag on board the Sans Pareil; and instructions have been sent to Vice Admiral Kingsmill at Cork to direct Sir R. Curtis with the ships of the line under his orders to be ready to intercept the enemy in the event of his escaping from Brest unobserved by your Lordship and proceeding to Ireland.

331. *Bridport to Spencer*

Royal George, at sea, 18 April 1798

I have fully considered the subject of the road of St. Mary's, Scilly, and the Bay of Douarnenez. When I was captain of a frigate I have frequently anchored her in Camaret Bay and have often reconnoitred Douarnenez Bay, which I consider as unsafe to anchor the King's fleet in except in the pursuit of an enemy. What supplies can it receive when at anchor in that bay? And are the proposers of this plan sure that the watching the port of Brest is obtained by that anchorage?

With respect to the road of St. Mary's I perceive the very good seaman confidently asserts the security of the anchorage and who doubted it? But then he draws in and tells your Lordship that in putting to sea with the wind westerly there is not room for line of battle ships to cast and they must slip their cables. I ask this very good seaman how and when the ships are to get their anchors and cables again?

With respect to supplies, he tells your Lordship the fleet would be hove as at sea. Even water cannot be had, either good or in quantity. The circumstances were all known but then he has a remedy. Recourse must be had to Penzance, which is a plentiful market, or, in easterly winds, to St. Ives.

Your Lordship, I am sure, is aware of the uncertainty of these supplies of water and also of the expense that will probably arise in bringing water down in casks for vessels to load, the same, I suppose, as in Torbay. It may also be judged necessary to have a brewery at one or other of these ports, except Plymouth shall be able to supply the Scilly Fleet with beer.

Upon the whole of this subject I cannot give my consent to hazarding the King's fleet in Douarnenez Bay or to risk the loss of it in detail on the rocks of Scilly.

I do not assume the character of a very good seaman but I humbly consider myself a practical one and I must own that the above plan appears to me to be calculated for the [benefit[1]] of Cornwall by some enlightened seaman of that county.

The anchorage of St. Mary's road has been known for ages past, having been carefully surveyed and practically considered by several able seamen, upon which established opinions have been formed.

[*Endorsed as received on the 26th and answered on 1 May*]

332.   *Bridport to Admiralty*

Royal George, at sea, 22 April 1798

I have the satisfaction to acquaint you for their Lordships' information that L'Hercule of seventy-four guns was taken by His Majesty's ship Mars last night.

The enclosed copy of a letter from Lieutenant Butterfield[2] will best show to their Lordships the spirit and judgment manifested upon this occasion. No praise of mine can add one ray of brilliancy to the distinguished valour of Captain Alexander Hood, who carried his ship nobly into battle and who died of the wounds he received in support-ing the just cause of his country. It is impossible for me not to sincerely lament his loss as he was an honour to the service and universally beloved. He has fallen gloriously as well as all those who are so handsomely spoken of by Lieutenant Butterfield. I have ap-pointed him to the command of L'Hercule to carry her into port and I have given a temporary appointment to Captain George James Shirley[3] to command the Mars.

333.   *Seymour to Spencer*

Sans Pareil, off Ushant, 25 April 1798

Lord Bridport is, as you imagine, rather uneasy at his fleet being reduced so low in numbers but I think that I have raised his spirits by teaching him to expect the Terrible and Impetueux soon with some of

---

[1]Word indecipherable.
[2]William Butterfield (d. 1842). Lieutenant 1794; Captain 1802; Retired Rear-admiral 1837.
[3]George James Shirley (d. 1845). Lieutenant 1790; Captain 1798; Retired Rear-admiral 1825; Vice-admiral 1840.

his ships which are now at Plymouth. He asked rather vaguely about the return of the Canada, which, being followed by some conversation about the convoys expected at Brest from the southward, leads me to believe that he will employ her there if she should join and I agree with him that we should always have a squadron there if it is possible.

[*Endorsed as received on 1 May and answered on the 14th*]

334. *Spencer to Bridport*

Admiralty, 1 May 1798

The pressure of the present situation of the country in all parts of the world makes it extremely desirable to husband our ships as much as possible and in order to do so frequent reliefs are very desirable, especially if there is no means of finding an anchorage in such a situation as to enable the fleet to watch Brest without constantly wearing itself out by cruising. It does not appear from the information we have at present of the force of the enemy at Brest that a larger number of ships than are at present with your Lordship are immediately requisite. Some, however, of those that you mention will be ordered out to you as they get ready and it will be desirable to send in some of those with you which may most require it, provided no fresh appearance in the port at Brest should require your squadron being increased.

335. *Spencer to Bridport*[1]

Admiralty, 1 May 1798

We shall endeavour to supply your Lordship with frigates as well as we can as they come forward and I am happy to find that you have sent Captain Stopford to the southward as I am persuaded much good will result from watching that part of the enemy's coast.

We must make the best use we can of all the frigates and other ships we have and it may therefore be difficult to make such arrangements as shall always place English frigates in the fleet under your Lordship; I shall, however, be happy to endeavour to accommodate your wishes as much as I have it in my power to do consistent with other necessary points of the service.

[1] A separate letter from document 334.

336.   *Bridport to Admiralty*

Royal George, at sea, 4 May 1798

By the release of the Naiad out of quarantine I sailed from Spithead with that frigate only and when I came upon my station I found the Jason on it under the orders of Captain Rowley[1] of His Majesty's ship Ramillies, Captain Gore of the Triton having judged it expedient to proceed to Plymouth with the observations he had made on the state of the enemy's ships at Brest, upon the construction he had put upon the discretional words of his order from Captain Rowley. But in my opinion it would have been of more importance to the service if he had endeavoured to have given his intelligence to his senior officer, in which case I should have received it and have had the Triton for the execution of such orders as I should have had occasion to give Captain Gore. The Clyde was the only frigate then to the southward, being ordered there by Captain Payne when he was off Plymouth, and afterwards returned to Spithead in consequence of my first order to him. As soon as the Mermaid joined me Captain Newman[2] was ordered to repair to the rendezvous given him by Captain Payne. Since which I have sent the Phaeton on that station and also the Stag. Their Lordships will therefore see that I have anticipated their directions on that subject.

The enclosed copy of a letter from Captain Cunningham will show to their Lordships that he has driven into Port Louis a large convoy, where I understand it still remains, by Captain Yorke's[3] account to me. The Boadicea I sent off the Penmarcks the moment she joined me and Captain Keats has for some days had the Revolutionnaire with him and I shall put the Pique immediately under his orders as I consider that station of importance for intercepting the coasting trade of the enemy as the whole from the southward to Brest must pass the Penmarcks. He has also the Nimrod cutter and Captain Stopford[4] the Cygnet. The Naiad is cruising to the north of Ushant and when I have a cutter to spare I intend sending one to Captain Pierrepoint and another would be advantageous if one could be spared for the various services I have to attend to.

---

[1]Bartholomew Samuel Rowley (d. 1811). Captain 1781; Rear-admiral 1799; Vice-admiral 1805; Admiral 1810.

[2]James Newman Newman (d. 1811). Lieutenant 1789; Captain 1794.

[3]Sir Joseph Sidney Yorke (d. 1831). Lieutenant 1789; Captain 1793; Rear-admiral 1810; Vice-admiral 1814; Admiral 1830.

[4]Stopford commanded the *Phaeton*.

337. *Seymour to Spencer*

Sans Pareil, Torbay, 15 May 1798

Lord B proposes to avail himself of the leave he has received from the Admiralty tomorrow when his ship will proceed to Plymouth for payment. I cannot but be sorry this measure has been adopted as I fear that it may be claimed in future by other ships and depend upon it that it will if repeated, without there is some additional reason to that of the payment of the ship, and now the whole squadron knows that to be the only one, from his going from us. He wishes much to have the power of placing two or three ships of the line off Brest when he quits that station. His idea is that these ships with the frigates would prevent the Bertheaume squadron or any other squadron of that kind from coming out, and if they should escape from thence, immediately on their quitting that ground they would drive from their stations all the frigates we have cruising to the S.W. As we shall frequently have recourse to this place during the summer I do not think the plan a bad one if the squadron is confined to the neighbourhood of Brest and he has two captains that he wishes much to employ on this sort of service.

[*Endorsed as received on the 18th and answered on the 26th*]

338. *Admiralty to Bridport*[1]

15 May 1798

I am commanded by my Lords Commissioners of the Admiralty to acquaint your Lordship that in consequence of the intelligence which had been received of the preparations which have for some time past been making by the enemy in the Mediterranean, their Lordships have judged it expedient to order Rear Admiral Sir Roger Curtis with the ships named in the margin [*Prince, Leviathan, Centaur, Montagu, Powerful, Edgar, Marlborough, Lion, Success, Incendiary* fireship] to leave the station on the coast of Ireland and proceed and join the Earl of St. Vincent off Cadiz and follow his orders. The Polyphemus with the frigates which had been before on the station will remain there under the orders of Vice Admiral Kingsmill.

My lords have thought it necessary that your Lordship should be apprized of this arrangement, for the regulation of your conduct in case

[1]Addressed to Bridport in Torbay.

any circumstances should arise which may have reference to the squadron employed on the coast of Ireland.

339.   *Bridport to Spencer*

Royal George, Torbay, 17 May 1798

With respect to the number of ships necessary for watching the port of Brest that object must be left to those who know the state of the enemy at that port but if no more than ten or eleven ships are to cruise at one time it does not appear to me to require three admirals. Indeed, if this plan is finally fixed what relief can I expect during the whole campaign? But I will stand it as long as I can with zeal and fidelity let the difficulties be what they may.

The Channel frigates should be strong and in perfect condition. What occasioned my desiring English built frigates arose from the consideration of the boisterous seas they had to encounter and knowing that I have six French built frigates already with me and that I find them oftener and longer in port at a time than our own built frigates. I believe on the Irish station there is not one French built frigate. I therefore do not think my request unreasonable in having no more than six. Neither do I wish to have one more than the service requires as I can clearly see the various calls for frigates on the various and extended services your Lordship must attend to.

340.   *Admiralty to Bridport*[1]

17 May 1798

Having laid before my Lords Commissioners of the Admiralty your letter to me of the 15th instant and the paper accompanying it respecting the conduct of Sir Henry Trollope,[2] Captain of His Majesty's ship Russell, in deviating from the orders of Vice Admiral Sir Charles Thompson for watching the motions of the enemy at Brest; I am commanded by their Lordships to acquaint you that they agree with you in opinion that Sir Henry Trollope would have acted more proper by endeavouring to keep his station off Brest, as the wind and weather

---

[1]Addressed to Bridport in Torbay.

[2]Under Admiralty orders of 21 February 1798 Trollope had been posted off Brest by Sir Charles Thompson. He misinterpreted instructions from Curtis to cover an Oporto convoy and went south to look for it. Bridport strongly demanded that he be removed from the Channel fleet but Spencer refused.

would admit of his so doing, than by endeavouring to get into the route of the Oporto convoy; but that it appears to their Lordships that his not doing so proceeded from his misconceiving the information sent to him by Sir Roger Curtis to be an order to look for the Oporto convoy in the route pointed out that he might protect it. Their Lordships also agree in opinion with your Lordship that great caution should be used in putting together two services incompatible with each other and that on that account intelligence of the nature of that sent by Sir Roger Curtis to Sir Henry Trollope either should not be sent to officers employed on services which they ought not to leave to attend to other duties or, if sent for their information, should, to prevent such mistakes in future, be accompanied by directions which may point out to the officer how far he may deviate from the orders he is under in consequence of it.

341. *Spencer to Bridport*

Admiralty, 19 May 1798

With respect to the exact number of ships necessary to cruise off Brest it must so entirely depend on the circumstances of the moment that I do not see how it can be possible to fix upon any precise arrangement beforehand. All I can say in that matter therefore is that in the present state of our force it will be necessary to make such arrangements as shall be calculated for wearing out the ships as little as possible.

There cannot be a wish on my part either to curtail the number of frigates under your Lordship's command by reducing it more than is absolutely necessary from the other numerous calls of the service, nor can I conceive what object I can be supposed to have of appropriating French built frigates rather than English ones to any particular station. On that point, however, I can only repeat that I shall be very happy, as far as the service will admit, to accommodate your Lordship by putting under your command any frigates whose officers you may be particularly desirous of having with you and which may in other respects be suited to the station. Those on the Irish station have as many bad gales to encounter, especially in the winter season, as those in the Channel.

The reason for our wishing the Royal George not to go to Spithead was because in case of a sudden occasion arising for the fleet to return off Brest. Cawsand Bay is more to the westward than Spithead would be and as your Lordship was desirous that the ship should be paid I think it would have been as well if you had determined to take her into Cawsand Bay at first, which you are empowered to do; whereas by ordering the ship for Torbay for the express purpose of being paid a pretence will possibly be given to the men of other ships to expect a like indulgence when it may not be so convenient to the service to allow of it.

7

THE FRENCH EXPEDITIONS TO IRELAND
28 MAY 1798–6 FEBRUARY 1799

In May 1798 French preparations at Toulon for a major expedition prompted the British government to re-enter the Mediterranean. Until the destination of this expedition was established, the preparations at Toulon seemed a possible threat to Ireland. Early in May this prompted the transfer of a squadron of eight ships of the line under Sir Roger Curtis from the coast of Ireland to the command of Lord St Vincent. It would soon be replaced by a new squadron independent of Bridport's fleet [345]. Meanwhile Curtis's arrival off Cadiz permitted St Vincent the opportunity to criticise the state of discipline among the officers of the Channel fleet and the quality of their leadership [342]. His undisguised criticism of Bridport echoed the difficulties Spencer and the Board of Admiralty had experienced in bringing Bridport to appreciate the necessity for the Commander-in-Chief of the Channel fleet to place discipline in the fleet before his own personal desires [337, 341].

Late in May 1798, hastened by reports of open rebellion in Ireland[1] and the demand for unprecedented vigilance off Brest [343], Bridport responded with appropriate haste in returning from Plymouth off Ushant in 21 hours. There he joined Gardner and Seymour with 15 ships of the line [344]. Early in June French ships took station in Bertheaume Bay outside the mouth of Brest harbour. Though urged to prevent their escape, and happy later to declare he had driven them back inside, Bridport was cautious in expressing confidence of his ability to do so [346, 348]. Indeed caution characterised Bridport's attitude to all the tasks expected of him. Hitherto the French capability of assembling naval forces had been hindered by interception of their convoys of naval stores into Brest [347]. However, the blockade of these convoys in ports further south demanded frigates and cutters [351]. Conscious of his shortage in this respect, and of being deprived of ships of the line [352], he denied any ability to protect British convoys expected in the Western Approaches, unless specifically ordered to use ships for that purpose [349].

---

[1] For detail of the Irish rebellion see C. Dickson, *The Wexford Rising in 1798. Its Causes and Its Course* (London, 1997).

By July 1798 the tenor of correspondence between Bridport and the Admiralty had become personal and acrimonious. Bridport for his part felt obliged to cite his own experience in defending his preference for the use of robust English-built frigates on the French coast and the advantages of Torbay as an anchorage in all winds [350]. There is no doubt that the Admiralty acted towards Bridport with fairness. The Board supported his complaint, for example, that St Vincent was authorising ships under his orders to cross into waters where the Channel fleet had the prerogative over prizes [354, 361]. Yet at the Board he had a reputation for putting a 'stronger and unfavourable construction on some things than they were meant to convey', a charge that turned Bridport to consider the strain placed upon him personally from a blockade that demanded he remain at sea, if need be shifting his flag, while ships under his command were refitted and replenished in turn [352]. What provoked Bridport was that this strain, common to all fleet commanders but peripheral to the immediate concerns of the Admiralty, was insufficiently understood. His responsibility for managing and maintaining a fleet on station conflicted with the inevitable wear and tear of ships, and with the agitation of captains to have their ships refitted or replenished. While attempting to do his duty by the Admiralty, Bridport was subject to the pressure of subordinates and especially to that of those connected with him socially to use his influence on their particular behalf [359].

In this respect, he was undoubtedly prey to his inclination 'not to irritate but smooth the execution of public measures' [352]. As the commanding officer on the spot, his judgement mattered in selecting ships for relief. Although many of their problems were similar, a distinction existed between frigates and ships of the line. Frigates were kept on station all year, but they were alternated in turn and their size permitted them to be refitted quite quickly and in relatively high numbers. To be sure, their problems still increased as the season advanced, with some unable to sail from a foul bottom or sprung mast, or to keep station from a shortage of water [351, 355, 358]. But the problems of ships of the line were more long term. For them, the blockade was still seasonal, from late spring to late autumn, and they too suffered by the failure of relieving squadrons to appear [353]. Yet their problems grew as hostilities wore on from year to year. After over four years at sea, ships like the *Royal George*, *Mars* and *Formidable* that were in good condition at the beginning of the war had deteriorated seriously, for ships of the line were usually refitted about every two and half years and recoppered every four to five years. Inevitably their sailing qualities were affected [365]. Yet the refitting of a 74, including docking, took on average four months, a first or second rate probably longer.[1] Furthermore, such work could not be rushed, cut short or compromised. The *Queen Charlotte* sailed crank after being fitted with longer masts than she had had previously [362].

While Bridport sparred with Spencer and the Board, squadrons of ships of the line under Seymour, Thompson and Gardner relieved one another off Ushant as a matter of routine [360]. From the Iroise, Brest was kept under the observation of frigates [353, 356]. A strong frigate squadron was also stationed off Pointe de Penmarche. Early in July 1798 the 38-gun *Jason*, commanded by Captain Charles Stirling, and the 36-gun *Pique* under David Milne, with the later assistance of the *Mermaid*, took the French 42-gun frigate *La Seine* just arrived with troops from Isle de France, though with the loss by grounding of the *Pique* near Pointe de la Trenche. The arrival after the action of another squadron of frigates under Stopford demonstrates the very saturation of the area by British warships [357]. Frigates ranged along the whole of the French Atlantic coast, from off Cape Finisterre [378] to the Channel, their crews entering the most difficult harbours to cut out French naval vessels [366]. Pellew in the *Indefatigable* continued to prove his capability as a frigate commander, and indeed, though still subject to Bridport, had managed to achieve relative independence in the far south of the station [367, 370]. However, the frigates were firmly in the grasp of the main battleship commanders. Gardner brooked no disregard of station keeping [371], and, though this was still not the first consideration of Bridport, he was quick to align himself with the Admiralty on this demand [372, 376].

In late July 1798 naval attention in England momentarily focused on the Mediterranean, whence came reports of Nelson's pursuit of the French Toulon expedition eastward [359]. The direction of French ambitions towards the Middle East diverted attention from the threat facing England from an invasion of Ireland. Outside government, the threat facing India was not yet fully realised. However, steps were being taken to meet this danger. The ships under Bridport were directed to intercept envoys from Tippoo Sahib said to be travelling to France in a Danish vessel [363].

Only in early August was the Admiralty given specific details of the 74-gun ship and six frigates that were being prepared in Brest harbour to provide supplies to the Irish rebels [364]. Several ships of the line were to follow the frigate squadron from Brest harbour. Distant recon-

---

[1] R. Morriss, *The Royal Dockyards during the Revolutionary and Napoleonic Wars* (Leicester, 1983), 18–21.

naissance confirmed large numbers of ships in harbour, but could not distinguish which were ready to sail [368, 369]. In the event it was from Rochefort that three frigates sailed on 6 August to land 1500 soldiers under General Humbert in Killala Bay, north-west Ireland, on 22 August.[1] The troops were to surrender to a superior military force at Ballinamuck on 8 September. News of the landings, with directions to close Brest to the returning frigates, was sent to Bridport on 27 August. For the present, Bridport was directed to concentrate his frigates at Brest and Rochefort [380–82].

Off-shore, the intentions of the French were anticipated by the crews of the blockading ships of the line. The opportunity of mutineers to assist the Irish cause by crippling the British force, or even by taking British ships into enemy ports, again aroused apprehensions in ships with a large proportion of their crew Irish. The captains of the *Neptune* and *Defiance* were particularly worried [373, 374]. The Admiralty responded with the demand for a survey of the number of Irish on board the different ships, and of an estimate of the number who might be 'evil disposed' [375]. It elicited replies that revealed a high proportion of Irish seamen did not necessarily correlate with the danger of mutiny [377]. But it also revealed plots and conspirators, 70 of whom from four ships including the *Defiance* were tried by court martial.[2]

The Admiralty was pleased at the way in which the Brest fleet had been closely watched during August, and in September was planning to ensure the ships of the line off Ushant were saved as much as possible from the autumn and winter gales by permitting Bridport to use his own discretion in ordering them to take refuge in Torbay [384]. However, their self-satisfaction was short-lived. Just as the Admiralty was beginning to relax its guard, on 16 September the 74-gun *Hoche* and eight frigates, of which the Admiralty had intelligence a month earlier, sailed from Brest [385].

These vessels, commanded by Commodore Jean Bompart, carried 3000 soldiers destined for Ireland. Passing through the Bec du Raz, they did not go unnoticed. Leaving the *Ethalion* and *Sylph* in trail, Keats sailed to inform Bridport. The French took a false course south and the trail was joined on 20 September off Belle Isle by the 44-gun

---

[1]W. James, *The Naval History of Great Britain from the declaration of war by France in 1793 to the accession of George IV* (6 vols, London, 1859), II, 138.

[2]The operations of United Irishmen were revealed on the *Defiance*, *Caesar*, *Captain* and *Glory*. Seventy conspirators from these four ships were tried, and 50 per cent of the Irish who were tried were convicted. In March 1800 the *Danae* would be taken into Le Conquet by mutineers. See C. Doorne, *Mutiny and Sedition in the Home Commands of the Royal Navy, 1793–1803* (unpub. University of London PhD thesis, 1997), 121–4, 187, 246.

Anson which was destined to track the French squadron for three weeks. The news was relayed to Plymouth by 23 September where Sir John Borlase Warren was despatched to reinforce the Irish squadron. *Anson* was sighted and taken under the command of Warren on the north-west coast of Ireland on 11 October, but that night lost sight of the French. However, they were rediscovered the next morning [387], and after a general chase in which two French vessels were slowed by gale damage, by daybreak on the 12th Bompart's squadron was almost surrounded by British ships. These comprised three ships of the line and five frigates. In the melee that ensued, Bompart's 74, the *Hoche*, was reduced to a wreck and surrendered, along with three French frigates, to which a fourth was added on the 14th.

While these prizes were being escorted into Lough Swilly, on 15 October two fugitive French frigates from Bompart's squadron were discovered off Blacksod bay on the north-west coast of Ireland by two British frigates and a brig-sloop. The French ships separated, and in thick, squally weather the British frigates lost their prey. On the 16th, however, the French 40-gun *Loire* was rediscovered and disabled by the 32-gun *Mermaid*, to be forced to surrender after a crippling action on the 18th with the 44-gun *Anson* [388]. Another of Bompart's frigates, the 40-gun *Immortalité*, was also intercepted by the 38-gun *Fisgard* and forced to surrender on 20 October before she could get into Brest. All seven prizes from Bompart's force were eventually got into Plymouth Sound safely.[1]

The credit for the destruction of the expedition to Ireland did not fall to Bridport. After his arrival off Ireland, Warren acted under the orders of Kingsmill, Commander-in-Chief on the Irish coast [389]. His failure to give Bridport precedence in reporting to him was repaid by Bridport to Warren's cost [405, 406]. Moreover on 12 October the French put a third expedition to sea to aid the Irish insurgents, this time from Rochefort. Four frigates reached Killala Bay. But, on learning the fate of the two earlier expeditions that year, their commander made again for Rochefort which, notwithstanding a skirmish with a British squadron off Broadhaven, north-west Ireland, they reached on 3 November.[2]

After the exertions of these events, Bridport took leave ashore. Early November anyway saw the beginning of the winter gales and Gardner, with the fleet off Ushant, was forced into Torbay [390] whence supplies of provisions were immediately ordered [391]. Although he returned off Ushant, in December when the wind was settled from the west, he

[1] James, II, 139–60.
[2] James, II, 164–5.

was again permitted to take shelter, to be replaced by a frigate squadron [392]. Bridport would have liked to have reinforced the frigates with one or two ships of the line but the Admiralty judged such reinforcement unnecessary [394] and potentially dangerous. The winter weather had already taken a toll in the loss of the *Colossus* in St Mary's Bay in the Scilly Isles. It permitted Bridport to raise again his adverse opinion of that anchorage, much to the irritation of Spencer. Other capable seamen like Pellew and Gardner did not agree with Bridport as to the security of the anchorages available to the Channel fleet [393, 395, 397]. This included Torbay, which in winter served as a positive disincentive to Gardner to take shelter there [396]. Moreover, the loss of the *Colossus* was a reminder of the necessity for ships to be supplied with enough anchors and cables of the appropriate strength, and drew attention to the demands of the battle ships at sea for refitting [396].

These concerns ran through the winter blockade into 1799. While in the new year Bridport went to Bath [398, 401], Gardner remained off Brest [400] and, although in January he returned into Torbay, the Admiralty still felt a duty, when the wind turned favourable for the French, to send a squadron of battle ships to stand off Ushant [402]. Meanwhile, the number of frigates standing guard in the Iroise was reduced in late December to just Pellew in the *Indefatigable* [396], the result of both shortage and refitting [394]. Those frigates available were guarded jealously by the Admiralty. Bridport's desire to post more on the north coast of Spain was firmly opposed [403]. Prizes on that station were plentiful and, although Bridport may not have needed the money they brought himself [399], he was able to place his friends in their way [400]. Instead the Admiralty directed frigates to patrol the coast of France between Belle Isle and Rochefort, the Penmarcks and L'Orient, to intercept convoys [403]. Pressure of work and delays at Plymouth dockyard prevented others from being refitted quickly [407]. Nevertheless, by the end of January Admiralty parsimony permitted it the luxury of 12 frigates in port available for service [404].

Thanks to supplies of fresh vegetables, the turns taken by ships returning to port to replenish, and the treatment of scorbutic symptons with lemon juice, scurvy had been kept at bay. The number of sick sent into the hospitals at Haslar and Plymouth in the first nine months of 1798 was lower than that for 1797. The figures suggested a *more* healthy fleet [386], corresponding with an overall trend during the French Revolutionary and Napoleonic Wars.[1] It raised a question mark over the role performed by the Physician of the Fleet, Thomas Trotter

[1]*The Health of Seamen*, ed. C. Lloyd (NRS, 1965), 198–9.

who had resided mainly on shore since an accident in 1795. Bridport was inclined to have him act on shore not just to superintend and survey the sick, but as an inspector of medicine chests and of the quality of 'necessaries' supplied by contractors for the use of the sick [379]. Spencer recognised the incompatibility of such duties on shore with the role of the Physician at sea [383]. However, Trotter was to remain in post, though still on shore, until temporarily relieved in 1800.

342. *St Vincent to Spencer*

Ville de Paris, at anchor before Cadiz, 28 May 1798

The squadron your Lordship has sent me under the orders of Rear Admiral Sir Roger Curtis exhibits a lamentable specimen of the state of your fleet at home . . . unless your admirals and captains are compelled to sleep on board their ships and keep all their officers tightly to their duty when at Spithead, Plymouth Sound and Cawsand Bay your navy will be ruined past redemption. There is a dreadful licentiousness in the conversation of the officers which is very soon conveyed to the men and I attribute in a great degree the disgraces which have befallen your fleet at home to this decay of discipline and unless you have an officer at the head who has vigour and disposition to lay the axe to the root of this evil and you give him the most unequivocal support there will very soon be an end to all activity or energy in the natural defence of the country.

343. *Admiralty to Bridport*[1]

31 May 1798

I have received and communicated to my Lords Commissioners of the Admiralty your letter of the 20th instant acquainting me for their Lordships' information of your arrival at Plymouth and of your intention of proceeding in the Royal George with the other ships therein mentioned to your station off Brest; and I am commanded to acquaint you that they approve of your so doing.

I inclose to your Lordship for your information the Gazettes which have lately been published containing accounts of the disturbances which have taken place in Ireland; and as it is probable that the enemy will in consequence endeavour to support the rebels, and to furnish them with supplies to enable them to hold out until they can be more

---

[1] Addressed to Bridport at Plymouth.

effectually supported, it is their Lordships' commands that you should exert your utmost diligence in preventing the sailing of the enemy's fleet from Brest, and their furnishing the rebels from thence with any supplies; and for this purpose that you should keep your frigates as near to the port as possible for the purpose of conveying to you the earliest intelligence of the enemy's movements or probable designs that you may be ready to take such steps as occasion may require, agreeably to the orders you are now under.

344.   *Bridport to Admiralty*

Royal George, at sea, 31 May 1798

In my letter of the 29th instant, I acquainted you for the information of their Lordships that I had caused my flag to be rehoisted when Captain Domett informed me that Commissioner Fanshawe[1] finished the payment of the Royal George at half past 3 o'clock p.m. on the 28th instant. That night I arrived at Plymouth Dock and before I went to bed I sent directions to Captain Domett to make the signal to unmoor and for such ships as were in Cawsand Bay to follow the motions of the Royal George. At half past one p.m. on the 29th she got under weigh accompanied by the Dolly cutter and I now acquaint you for their Lordships' information that I made Ushant at 10 o'clock a.m. the 30th and before the close of day I was joined by Vice Admiral Sir Alan Gardner and Rear Admiral Lord Hugh Seymour with the ships named in the margin [*Royal Sovereign, Sans Pareil, Atlas, Glory, Neptune, Barfleur, Caesar, Ramillies, Terrible, Canada, Pompee, Defiance, Triumph, Impetueux, Saturn, Diana, Triton, Nymphe, Amelia, Megaera, Lurcher* cutter] and herewith you will receive a return of their state and condition by which their Lordships will see the number of men each ship is short of complement notwithstanding those who have been sent to the squadron and distributed by Sir Alan Gardner before he joined me.

. . . Many of the frigates must also be sent into port to refit, which will leave the enemy at liberty to get the coasting convoys, I am afraid, round to Brest. The Clyde is cruising with the Phaeton. I have ordered her into port as soon as the Anson joins on her station. The Mermaid I left in Plymouth Sound under some repairs which I understood from Captain Newman would not be completed before the latter end of the next week.

---

[1]Robert Fanshawe (d. 1823). Lieutenant 1759; Captain 1768; Plymouth dockyard commissioner 1797–1823.

345. *Spencer to Earl Camden*[1]

Admiralty, 4 June 1798

As it is not impossible (though I confess I cannot help thinking it improbable) that the grand armament from Toulon, of the departure of which on the 19th ultimo you will read an account in the French papers, may be intended for an attack on Ireland we are taking as effectual measures as we can to replace for a time the deficiency of protection which has arisen from the measure taken in the beginning of May, of which your Excellency was informed by the Duke of Portland, and in a few days you will have a strong squadron of line of battle ships off Cape Clear again exclusive of what are cruising off Brest with Lord Bridport. I must, however, caution you against forming too sanguine expectations of our being able to keep such a force on that station permanently, for the present state and disposition of our fleet will not allow of it.

346. *Admiralty to Bridport*

5 June 1798

I have received and laid before my Lords Commissioners of the Admiralty your Lordship's letter of the 2nd instant enclosing for their Lordships' information an extract from the journal of Captain Faulknor[2] of His Majesty's ship Diana and I have their Lordships' command to signify their direction to you to take particular care that the ships thereinmentioned stated to have been seen under Point St. Mathieu do not escape and proceed to sea from that anchorage.

347. *Stopford to Gardner*

Phaeton, at sea, 5 June 1798

Our cruise hitherto has not been attended with any success. The enemy's privateers are mostly laid up for want of hands and their frigates are too cautious to venture far from the land. A very considerable

---

[1]John Pratt, second Earl Camden (1759–1840). An Admiralty commissioner 1783–88, he was Lord Lieutenant of Ireland from March 1795 to June 1798, when he became a minister without portfolio. On the outbreak of the rebellion in Ireland, he requested to be replaced by a military man and was succeeded by Earl Cornwallis.

[2]Jonathan Faulknor (d. 1809). Lieutenant 1777; Captain 1782; Rear-admiral 1804.

convoy is nearly ready to depart from the Loire destined for Brest and I am informed that a line of battle ship and two frigates are to come from Brest for the purpose of convoying them as far as Concarneau Bay, from whence they intend to send their cargoes over land as they have done in the instance of the convoy lately chased into Port L'Orient. The blocking up of these convoys seems the most effectual and certain method of preventing their arrival at Brest. The many causes that may prevent a ship from coming in with the land after stretching at all in the offing may enable the enemy by watching their opportunity to creep along shore in perfect safety. From the reluctance with which their seamen go to their ships of war and from the numerous desertions that take place amongst them I do not think there is much chance of a meeting between the two fleets this summer. Having anchored the other day in Quiberon Bay I was favoured with a visit from our former allies the Governors of the islands of Hédic and Houat, who told me that the Chouans were beginning to collect again but at the same time lamented the fate of two of their chiefs who have been lately shot at Vannes. Our late failure will, I hope, be sufficient warning to us not to undertake anything in that quarter without having good grounds to proceed upon.

348.   *Bridport to Admiralty*

Royal George, at sea, 11 June 1798

I have received your letter of the 5th instant acknowledging the receipt of mine of the 2nd enclosing an extract from the journal of Captain Faulknor of His Majesty's ship Diana and directing me to take particular care that the five ships of war seen under Point St. Mathieu be not suffered to proceed to sea from that anchorage. And in answer thereto I acquaint you that the port of Brest is, and has been, as closely watched as possible and I consider the five ships stated by Captain Faulknor to have been seen under Point St. Mathieu was the enemy's advanced squadron in Bertheaume Road.

I certainly shall use all the means in my power to prevent the above squadron or any other ships sailing from Brest but their Lordships must know the difficulty and that I cannot assure them that they shall not proceed to sea from that anchorage.

349. *Bridport to Admiralty*

Royal George, at sea, 11 June 1798

I have received your three letters of the 4th and 5th instant with the papers therein mentioned relating to the convoy intended to sail from St. Christopher on the 15th of last month and that from Oporto on the 7th instant and directing me to afford such protection to the said convoys on their approaching the Channel as they may stand in need of. And in answer thereto I acquaint you that it will not be in my power to afford protection to the above convoys unless their Lordships are pleased to direct me to detach ships from this squadron for that service.

350. *Bridport to Spencer*

Royal George, at sea, 19 June 1798

It is hardly necessary for me to make any reply to your Lordship's observations on the subject of the hard gales of wind the frigates have to encounter in the Irish station more than to say that I have often experienced them when lieutenant of a twenty gun ship. I think I saw her docked twice if not three times at Kinsale. And the Bridgwater quitted that station at the peace of 1748 when the officers of that yard were brought to England under the protection of that ship. I have also cruised off Cape Clear as captain of a frigate in the winter season and have anchored her at the Cove of Cork. Your Lordship knows that I have been on the coast of Ireland as a flag officer and that the ports are all friendly to His Majesty's cruisers. Those in the Bay on the coast of France are all hostile and that if an accident was to happen to a frigate by carrying away her masts or [she] meets with serious distress and cannot clear the land and driven on shore the officers and crew must be made prisoners if they escape being drowned. These are natural reflections under the above circumstances.

Your Lordship tells me what interest you can have on the allotment of French frigates. I must certainly answer none. And I am sure I can have none but what comes from my anxiety for the welfare of the public service. In a pecuniary light if that was my object, it is supposed that French frigates sail faster than English built ones. But they are confessedly weaker, are oftener in port and not able to keep the sea on long cruises as they stow little and, having no orlop deck, they must move their cables whenever they want to get at the water that is stowed under them, which is sometimes difficult at sea. These are my reasons for giving the preference to English built frigates which I have taken the liberty to state to your Lordship.

In a former letter which I had the honour to receive from your Lordship the want of a good port to the westward seemed to weigh much on your Lordship's mind. We have the same ports in this contest as we had in the last or the preceding one. But our navy and trade have been much increased since those periods, which I am happy to grant.

For a great national object I know no place so proper as Torbay, where the whole navy of England may anchor as well as its trading ships, where water is plenty both at Brixham and Torquay. The country surrounding the bay full of riches in the fruits of the earth. Corn, apples, vegetables of the best sort and every other production for ample supplies. I am so great an advocate for making a secure anchorage in this bay with all winds that I should cheerfully subscribe if a plan was adopted for the accomplishment of so useful an undertaking. As to Scilly, it is a vain and useless speculation where nothing is to be had from those barren rocks but dangerous prospects.

351.   *Bridport to Admiralty*

Royal George, at sea, 28 June 1798

Herewith you will receive a copy of a letter from Captain Stirling[1] of His Majesty's ship Jason, also copies of two letters from the Hon. Captain Stopford of His Majesty's ship Phaeton, which are transmitted for their Lordships' information together with the state and condition of the ships named in the margin [*Phaeton, Stag, St Fiorenzo, Anson, Pique*] by which their Lordships will see how difficult it is to keep frigates constantly cruising on the enemy's coast, as all the frigates at this time cruising under the orders of Captain Stopford require to be relieved and the Pique must also soon return into port, now with the Jason off the Penmarcks. The Triton has been out eight weeks and will soon be in want of water, Captain Gore is cruising off the port of Brest with the Ambuscade.

In my letter of the 4th of May last I stated my reasons for desiring their Lordships would spare another cutter or lugger to be under my orders, to which request I have received no answer but I find by letter

---

[1]Charles Stirling (1760–1833). Lieutenant 1778; Captain 1783; Rear-admiral 1804; Vice-admiral 1810. He was appointed Commander-in-Chief Jamaica in 1811 but was subject to a court-martial for corruption two years later and sentenced to remain on the Half Pay list and not to be included in any future promotions.

from Lieutenant Hamilton,[1] commanding the Cygnet cutter, that she is taken from me and ordered upon other service. I apprehend in these arduous moments for the execution of the service under my charge and direction I cannot have too many frigates and cutters to watch the coast from Bordeaux to the northward of the Passage du Four.

The Stag joined me yesterday afternoon and as she is short of water I have ordered Captain Yorke to proceed to Cawsand Bay to complete her stores and provisions and then to rejoin me on my station off Brest.

352. *Bridport to an Admiralty Commissioner*[2]

Royal George, at sea, 2 July 1798

On the subject of taking ships from me and placing others under my orders I must say something in justice to my own feelings. Before I sailed from Spithead in April last the Robust was taken from me to lay guardship at St. Helens and the Russel was put under my orders. Both ships were then at Plymouth, Captain Thornbrough had been a Channel cruiser, I believe, for the last ten years of his life. He commanded the Latona and the Robust under the orders of Lord Howe and myself the whole of this war. Sir Henry Trollope was never employed on service off Brest before he was selected to relieve Sir Charles Thompson and he has shown that his talents were not suited to that station.[3] The next ship of the line that was taken from me was the Ramillies, when the Captain was in Plymouth Sound, *paid*, and ready for sea and under no orders. Captain Rowley had been serving with me for some time and was extremely desirous to continue with the Channel Fleet. The Captain was of equal force, in perfect repair and her commander had never been under my orders. You must allow me, my dear sir, to make my observations on these points and to say that they do affect the general welfare of the service. I am ready to allow the difficulties the Admiralty have to encounter but I see no necessity for creating them when they can be avoided by clear and simple operation. You tell me that I put a stronger and unfavourable construction on some things than they were meant to convey. In answer to that suggestion I take leave to assure you that I require nothing to stimulate me to the strict execution of my orders and the

---

[1] Sir William Hamilton (d. 1822). Lieutenant 1781; Superannuated Commander 1816.

[2] This unaddressed letter was not written to Lord Spencer or the Secretary of the Admiralty but to a member of the Board.

[3] For Trollope's inadequacies, see Chapter 6.

words in Mr. Nepean's letter to me of the 5th of June directing me to take particular care that the five ships of war under the Point St. Matthieu be not suffered to proceed to sea from that anchorage were unnecessary. It gave me particular satisfaction to know that before I received this additional charge I had with my whole squadron driven that squadron from its anchorage into Brest road and I have reason to believe that it has not ventured out from it since. It is therefore far better not to irritate but smooth the execution of public measures. I beg to be understood that I anxiously feel the warmest desire to contribute to the utmost of my power to relieve the Admiralty from every difficulty as far as relates to the service placed under my authority and I request also to assure you that I shall ever entertain the highest opinion of your upright intentions concerning me personally. I cannot, however, perceive from the words of the last Admiralty order to which I see your name that I have the smallest chance of a little relaxation from my labours on the arrival of Sir Charles Thompson but on the contrary if that order is strictly to be put in execution I am to send as many ships to Cawsand Bay as he brings and when they are refitted as many more, and the Royal George is to remain off Ushant for the whole year or if I send her into port I must shift my flag as the word implies that I must keep the sea. However, I cannot suppose that is meant, though I will venture to say the present order implies it.

353.   *Bridport to Admiralty*

Royal George, at sea, 5 July 1798

Since my letter to you of the 28th ultimo I have received one from Captain Gore of the Triton of that date, stating that he had only six days water left and communicating the observations he had made since his former report on the enemy's force at Brest, of which the enclosed is a copy. As it is my intention to send the first frigate which joins me from Plymouth to relieve the Triton I have caused her to be supplied with four tons of water for her present expense. And I have directed the Pique to join me, that she may also be supplied with water from some of the ships which will go to Cawsand Bay on the arrival of Vice Admiral Sir Charles Thompson off Brest, but I have received no intimation when I might expect him, though their Lordships' order for taking him under my command is dated the 22nd of last month. At present it is my intention to send the ships named in the margin [*Royal Sovereign, Neptune, Pompee, Canada, Terrible, Defiance, Megaera*] to Plymouth when the Vice Admiral and his squadron shall join me, as they are in want of sails, topmasts, or in course of pay.

[*Endorsement*]

9 July. Own receipt and approve of what he has done. Send copy . . . to W. Huskisson for Mr Dundas's information.

[*Enclosure*]

353a.   *Gore to Bridport*[1]

Triton, 20 June 1798

The weather having been so very unfavourably hazy, which together with a heavy swell from the westward, spring tide, and light baffling winds, has prevented my reconnoitring the enemy's force in Brest so minutely as I would wish.

On Sunday last, I stood in to the southward of the Parquette, from whence I observed two ships (in addition to my last report) laying close off the arsenal with their topmasts struck. One of them appeared of the line, and the lieutenant at the mast head informed me she was so, though I am inclined to think he could not exactly determine it, owing to the haze. On that evening a frigate got under sail from off the entrance of the arsenal, and anchored in the southern part of Brest water.

I observed on Friday and Saturday last that the ships in Brest loosed the sails on one mast at a time, then furled them, and loosed the others. I have thought this circumstance worthy your Lordship's knowledge as it may in some degree corroborate the information respecting their want of men. I have not seen any kind of vessel go in or come out of Brest during the last week.

354.   *Bridport to Admiralty*

Royal George, at sea, 11 July 1798

I acquaint you for their Lordships' information that His Majesty's ship Caroline came into my squadron on the 9th instant when I anxiously expected to see the Naiad or some other frigate from Plymouth. Cap-

---

[1]This enclosure is headed 'Extract of a letter from Captain Gore . . . '.

tain Locke, who commands the Caroline, put his orders into my hands, a copy of which is herewith enclosed. I must confess I was not aware that Lord St. Vincent's command reached from the Dardanelles to Corunna and under certain circumstances occasioned his cruisers to approach the British Channel but was of opinion that Corunna and the north coast of Spain properly belonged to the Channel fleet.[1] I apprehend their Lordships are informed that the Caroline recaptured a homeward bound East India packet near to St. Sebastian and has sent her into Falmouth. The packet was taken in latitude 46° north, longitude 27° west by a Bordeaux privateer. I understand likewise that His Majesty's ship Aurora, Captain Digby,[2] has taken a good prize on the Corunna station, which I have always thought should have been occupied occasionally by Channel frigates under my orders more especially at this time as the French privateers send their prizes into Spanish ports to avoid my cruisers off the Garonne.

[*Endorsement*]

We do not consider the north coast of Spain as under the orders of Lord St. Vincent.

355. *Bridport to Admiralty*

Royal George, at sea, 11 July 1798

As the St. Fiorenzo has lost her character for sailing from her being extremely foul, having been more than two years since her bottom was cleaned or her copper examined, I take the liberty to express my wish that their Lordships will be pleased to allow her to go into Hamoaze to be docked, as I consider a frigate of no use as a cruiser if she cannot come up with in chase every vessel that is seen and I understand all the frigates to the southward outsail the St. Fiorenzo. She is also in the course of pay and I think the time of docking ought not to require more than ten days if she shall want no repairs.

---

[1]St Vincent had ordered the *Caroline* to cruise off Corunna and the north coast of Spain.
[2]Sir Henry Digby (d. 1842). Lieutenant 1790; Captain 1796; Rear-admiral 1819; Vice-admiral 1830; Admiral 1841.

356. *Bridport to Admiralty*

Royal George, at sea, 11 July 1798

I acquaint you for their Lordships' information that I have directed Captain Keats of the Boadicea to relieve the Triton in watching the motions of the enemy at Brest and to take the Ambuscade under his command.

357. *Bridport to Admiralty*

Royal George at sea, 11 July 1798

The inclosed copies of letters will inform their Lordships of the taking of La Seine and the loss of His Majesty's Ship Pique. On both these events I can add nothing more than to express my satisfaction on this important capture, and real concern for the accidents that have attended it. Captain Milne with all his officers and people are on board La Seine, and as the Jason must be docked I have ordered Captain Stirling to proceed to Spithead taking La Seine with him, and see her safe into Portsmouth Harbour, considering that port also convenient for Captain Milne and his people.

[*Endorsement*]

Own receipt and acquaint him that their Lordships are highly satisfied with the conduct of the captains of the Jason and Pique and the spirit of the officers and men who were engaged in the action, and have only to regret that the prize had not been taken without the loss of one of H.M. ships.

[*Enclosures*]

357a. *Milne[1] to Bridport*

On board La Seine, late French frigate, 3 July 1798

It is with real concern I have to inform your Lordship of the loss of His Majesty's Ship Pique, under my command on the night of the 30th ultimo in action with the French frigate La Seine by running on shore in the passage Breton [Pertius Breton], where at low water she was entirely bilged. For the transactions of that day, I leave your Lordship to Captain Stirling's dispatches, but must take the liberty of mentioning the entire satisfaction I had from the steady and cool behaviour of the officers and men I had the honour to command, particularly Mr Lee,[1] 1st Lieutenant; Mr Devonshire[2] 2d and Mr Watson[3] acting 3d, and Lieutenant McDonald of the Marines, as likewise Mr Edeveen the Gunner, whose conduct in his department deserves my warmest praise; the guns were supplied in the properest manner with ammunition, by his exertions in pointing them very few shots were thrown away, and I am confident had we remained singly engaged our superior fire would have in a very short time made her strike to the bravery of British seamen, although of so much superior force in men and guns.

It is some small satisfaction to me, my Lord, for the loss of His Majesty's ship that the prize was got off by the assistance given from the St Fiorenzo, and her being a very strong and nearly new ship she docs not appear to have received any material damage in her hull except from shot, as she makes very little water.

I have the honour to inclose a list of the killed and wounded of His Majesty's Ship Pique.

I have to request, my Lord, you will be pleased to apply to my Lords Commissioners of the Admiralty for a court martial to be held on myself, officers and crew for the loss of His Majesty's Ship.

357b.   *Return of killed and wounded on board His Majesty's Ship La Pique in the action with the French frigate La Seine on the 30th of June 1798*

Men's names	Qualities	Killed or Wounded
James Collins	Sailmaker	Killed
Mr Robinson	Boatswain	Wounded
Thos Andrews	Boatswain's Mate	Ditto
Benjamin Lockwood	Seaman	Ditto
William Richards	Seaman	Missing
Benjamin Masland ⎫		
Robert Sallas ⎬	Marines	Wounded
Joseph Fursman ⎭		

[1] Either James Lee (d. 1809), Lieutenant 1795; or William Lee (d. 1816), Lieutenant 1796.

[2] Henry Devonshire (fl. 1796–98). Lieutenant 1797.

[3] Possibly William Watson (d. 1846). Lieutenant 4 August 1798; retired Commander 1840. However, at this time there were four other lieutenants named Watson.

357c. *Stirling to Bridport*

Jason, Pertius Breton,[1] 2 July 1798

On Friday last at 7 a.m., His Majesty's squadron under my command gave chase to a French frigate off the Saintes, but neither of us could get up till 11 at night, when the Pique brought her to action, and continued a running fight till the Jason passed between the two. At this instant the land near Le Point de la Trenche [Tranche] was seen close on our larboard bow, and before the ship could answer her helm she took the ground close to the foe, which was immediately perceived had grounded also. Most unfortunately, as the tide rose, we hung only forwards, and therefore swung with our stern close to the enemy's broadside, who although he was dismasted did not fail to take advantage of his happy position, but a well directed fire was kept up from a few guns abaft, and at half past 2 victory declared in favour of royalty.

Our opponent, called La Seine, was commanded by Le Capitaine Bigot, her force 42 guns, eighteen and nine pounders with carronades, and 610 men, including troops. She sailed from L'Isle de France three months ago, bound to L'Orient.

In the early part of the battle, I had the mortification to be wounded and was obliged to leave the deck; but my misfortune is palliated by the reflection that the service did not suffer by my absence, for no man could have filled my place with more credit to himself, and benefit to the state, than my first lieutenant, Mr Charles Inglis,[2] whom I beg to recommend in the strongest manner for his bravery, skill and great exertions . . .

I come now, my Lord, to the painful part of my narrative, which I am necessitated to make more prolix than I otherwise should from the peculiar circumstances attending the engagement, and first I mention the loss of the Pique, whose officers and crew deserved a better fate. Captain Milne had led her to the fight, and continued the pursuit to admiration, and it was his misfortune that the main topmast being carried away obliged him to drop astern; but ardour urging him on to renew the combat, he did not hear me hail him to anchor, and the ship therefore grounded on our off side, near enough to receive the enemy's shot over us, although very awkwardly situated for returning the fire. In the morning every attempt was made to get the ships off, but the Jason

[1]North of La Rochelle.
[2]Probably Charles Inglis (d. 1833). Lieutenant 1794; Commander 1800; Captain 1802. However there was also Charles Inglis (d. 1810), Lieutenant 1792; struck off Admiralty list 1804.

was alone successful. I therefore on finding the Pique was bilged directed the captain to destroy her, and to exert his abilities and activity to save the prize, which he with great difficulty got afloat yesterday evening after throwing her guns overboard.

The carnage on board La Seine was very great. 170 men were killed, and about 100 wounded, many of them mortally. I inclose a list of the sufferers on board the Jason, and it is with great concern that among the killed I place the name of Mr Anthony Richard Rebotier,[1] my second lieutenant, who died fighting gloriously, and by whose fall is lost a most amiable man and excellent officer. Lieutenant Riboleau[2] commanded on the main deck afterwards, and behaved with great spirit, as did Mr Lockwood the Master. My other officers of every description behaved vastly well, and the bravery and excellent conduct of the crew deserves much praise.

In mentioning the loss of the King's ship and the risk which the others ran, I cannot attach any blame to the pilotage, but must take the consequences to myself. I saw from the beginning of the chase that the enemy was pushing for this place; I was aware of the danger of the navigation with the wind on shore, and the probability of his getting near one of the batteries which are scattered along the coast, but I considered him an object and determined to pursue him to destruction, and I trust I shall be justified in the opinion.

The Pique was exceedingly shattered in her rigging, and the Jason has not one mast or yard but what is much damaged, nor a shroud or rope but what is cut, with all the sails torn to pieces; and indeed the lower masts are so bad that should we meet with blowing weather I much fear we shall lose them. If our ship could have remained in her first position, or our companion could have occupied the situation he wished the business must have been sooner finished without so much injury being done aloft.

It is but justice to observe that every effort was made on board the Mermaid during our long chase to approach the enemy, and I feel much indebted to Captain Newman for heaving this ship off, as that was the only possible means to save her. So soon as we were afloat, the squadron under Captain Stopford was seen in the offing, and being called in by signal was of infinite service; and as I understand that there is a superior force in this neighbourhood I have detained them till we can tow the prize clear of the land.

[1]Anthony Richard Robotier (d. 1798). Lieutenant 1794.
[2]There was John Ribouleau, of whom we know only that he was made a lieutenant in 1797, and Peter Ribouleau (d. 1847), Lieutenant 1793; Commander 1796; Captain 1802; Retired Rear-admiral 1837; Vice-admiral 1846.

358. *Bridport to Admiralty*

Royal George, at sea, 19 July 1798

I am sorry to acquaint you for their Lordships' information that the Ambuscade, having sprung her mainmast in so dangerous a manner that the carpenters of this ship, the Boadicea and Ambuscade are of opinion that it cannot be secured for service by fishing. I am therefore under the necessity of ordering her into Hamoaze for the sole purpose of getting a new one, unless the dockyard officer shall take it out without her going into the harbour. Their Lordships will see how much I am in want of frigates to carry on the various services attached to my command.

359. *Sir Harry Neale to Lady Bridport*

Plymouth Dock, 20 July 1798

I will not send the enclosed without telling you that Lady Neale and myself are very well and often think of you. If Lord Bridport is likely to return to Cawsand Bay remember we have a very good spare bed. I mention this that should you come here before his arrival it will be a thousand times better than any at the inns. I think I need not add what pleasure we should derive from your company.

The old St. Fiorenzo is in Hamoaze to be docked and I expect she will be turned out very gay and sprightly. I was obliged to get my good friend Lord Bridport to interpose his influence to effect so great an event, not daring to encounter the Board myself lest I should be made to account for the grass upon her bottom. Lord Onslow[1] is our next door neighbour and entertains us every day during dinner with his band of music. They are but a motley set but now and then hobble over a tune tolerably well together.

If I should sail before Lord Bridport returns to port I will let you know. Lady Neale desires her best love to you.

[*Enclosure*]

359a. *Lady Neale to Lady Bridport*

My dear Lady Bridport, Sir Harry is gone on board and has left this unsealed and I cannot resist telling you that the Port Admiral here has

[1]George Onslow, first earl of Onslow (1731–1814), politician.

just sent round the following written message to the Captains – 'Capt. Grey[1] is just arrived in the Pumperck sloop of war with intelligence from Earl St. Vincent of Admiral Nelson having fallen in with the French fleet returning from Malta – that the ship in which Bonaparte was is taken and a large number of transports'.

How anxiously must all wish that this news may be true and none more truly than you and I who feel so much of our domestic happiness interrupted by this long war. Unless upon good grounds I think Rear Admiral King ought not to have sent round and would not. And since I have written the above I hear it is Captain Grey, Lord St. Vincent's Captain, that has brought home the news and therefore I think we may certainly credit it. Believe me ever, my dear Lady Bridport . . .

360. *Spencer to Seymour*

Admiralty, 21 July 1798

I should have taken some measure for sending out beer to you in consequence of the suggestion in your letter if I had not found the Victualling Board extremely averse to it as they have an idea that in summer it cannot keep good. I believe if we had not had a fair prospect of relieving your ships pretty constantly I should have still tried the experiment but as Thompson was on the point of joining and as Sir Alan will now in a very few days enable you to send in all the ships that have been long out the necessity of the measure becomes less urgent.

361. *Bridport to Admiralty*

Royal George, at sea, 24 July 1798

I have received your letter of the 16th inst. acknowledging the receipt of mine of the 11th, acquainting me that their Lordships do not consider the north coast of Spain within the limits of Lord St. Vincent's command and that I should perceive by the directions given for the employment of Sir Edward Pellew that their Lordships have anticipated my suggestion of sending some ships to cruise on that coast.

---

[1]Sir George Grey (d. 1828). Lieutenant 1781; Captain 1793; Sheerness dockyard Commissioner 1805–6; Portsmouth dockyard Commissioner 1806–28.

362.   *Thompson to Admiralty*

Queen Charlotte, at sea, 26 July 1798

I request you will inform their Lordships that His Majesty's ship Queen Charlotte is so crank that in a common breeze of wind she lays down so as to prevent her lee ports being opened, this I conceive in a great measure owing to her masts being longer than they were when Lord Howe's flag was on board, at which time I understand she answered very well in every respect.

I am therefore to request that the first time she returns to port their Lordships will be pleased to give directions to remove the masts she has at present and that they may be replaced with masts agreeable to the establishment of a first rate, such as she formerly had.

363.   *Admiralty to Pole*

29 July 1798

I am commanded by my Lords Commissioners of the Admiralty to send you herewith a copy of a paper respecting a Danish vessel said to bring from the East Indies a Frenchman and two envoys from Tippoo Sahib and to signify their direction to you to order His Majesty's ships and vessels under your command to detain the said vessel in the event of their falling in with her and to secure the persons mentioned in the said paper.

364.   *Intelligence Report*

Substance of information respecting force at Brest and its neighbourhood transmitted by Captain D'Auvergne, dated 30th July 1798.

The Hoche of 74 guns, the Fraternité, Bellone, Resolue, Ambuscade, Loire and Immortalité of 40 guns are lying in the road with foretopsails loose, destined to throw succours into Ireland. The 4 line of battle ships (Mont Blanc, Révolution, Wattigny, Fougueux) ordered for a second division have had their crews completed from the ships in the harbour. Forty waggons with cases of arms, etc. arrived yesterday with 4 million of livres in specie. The three decked ships are disarming in order to equip the rest. The ships in the road consist of 16 sail of the line, including the Hoche.

365.   *Bridport to Admiralty*

Royal George, in Torbay, 31 July 1798

In my letter of the 29th instant I acquainted you for their Lordships' information with the allotted stations of all the ships under my orders. I feel it now to be my duty to state the condition of some of them. The Formidable sails so ill as not to keep her station in the common order of sailing, as the Rear Admiral commanding the larboard division of the squadron can testify. The Mars sails also very ill; both these ships have not been in dock for near four years. Indeed the Mars is on her launching bottom. The Royal George was beat by all the three deck ships in coming from Ushant to Torbay, so much so as to spare half their sails. On this appearance, I directed Captain Domett to heel and scrub her bottom, and indeed in his report on what was taken from her copper their Lordships will observe the Royal George has not been in dock, but once, since she was commissioned in February 1793, and in that time her copper is in many places holes, and mussels and grass will collect again in a short time. I therefore conclude their Lordships will be of opinion with me that the Royal George should be docked whenever she can be spared, and I apprehend must be new coppered, as the Queen Charlotte has lately been.

I beg also to observe that the keeping three deck ships cruizing nine weeks to occasion them to begin upon the ground tier of water causes great trouble and time in the refilling them, and produces scurvy in their crews and the breaking out of old sores. I wish therefore that it could be avoided upon every public consideration.

[*Endorsement*]

2 May. Own receipt and acquaint him that when the service will admit of it, the ships in want of it will be docked.

366.   *Captain Sir Charles Hamilton to Bridport*

Melpomene, off Abreverack,[1] 4 August 1798

After a cruise of nearly nine weeks off the coast of Brittany without a prospect of success but by the most hazardous means I at length determined to make an attack with the boats on the port of Corigeou, where

---

[1]Probably the estuary of the River Aber-Wrac'h, on the north-western point of the Brittany coast.

a national brig and several vessels under protection were at anchor. On the evening of the 3rd instant I ordered the boats of His Majesty's ship Melpomene and Childers sloop[1] to be manned and armed and at 10 p.m, dispatched them under command of Lieutenant Shortland,[2] who proceeded in the most judicious manner to the attack, which took place about 3 a.m. The badness of the night from heavy rain, vivid lightning and frequent squalls very much favoured the execution of the design. They boarded the brig in different places nearly at the same moment and carried her, though not without more resistance than such a surprise gave reason to expect. The forts which command this inlet being now alarmed and the wind having unfortunately veered round to the N.N.W. and blowing fresh directly into the passage, the merchant vessels no longer became an object of acquisition and the intricacy of the channel made it doubtful whether the corvette even could be got out. The attempt, however, was made and after working to windward under a heavy fire from the batteries for upwards of two hours it was at length with great perseverance effected. The brig appears to be L'Aventurier carrying 12 four-pounders and 79 men, commanded by Citoyen Raffy, Lieutenant de Vaisseau. As no merit can redound to me from this enterprise I do not hesitate to announce it to your Lordship as one of the most gallant of its nature ever performed and on which no encomiums of mine can do sufficient justice to the conduct of Lieutenant Shortland, the officers and the men who performed this daring achievement. Lieutenant Ross of the Marines, Mr. Bromley, purser of the Childers and Messrs. Morgan, Palmer and Erskine particularly distinguished themselves.

Captain O'Bryan,[3] whom I had appointed to cover the boats, gave all the assistance that the circumstances could possibly admit of and not without great risk from the badness of the night and the dangers of the coast. Our loss is one man killed, one missing, Mr. Frost, Midshipman, and three seamen wounded. The enemy have 16 wounded and several mortally.

---

[1]The watercolour by Nicholas Pocock of the *Childers* under fire from the Brest forts in January 1793 illustrated the first naval engagement of the wars 1793–1815. See frontispiece.

[2]Probably Thomas George Shortland (d. 1827). Lieutenant 1790; Commander 1799; Captain 1802. But there was also John Shortland (d. 1810). Lieutenant 1793; Commander 1801; Captain 1805.

[3]John O'Bryen (d. 1804). Lieutenant 1777; Captain 1797.

367.   *Pellew to Gardner*

Indefatigable, at sea, 5 August 1798

I have much pleasure in communicating to you the capture of the French ship privateer L'Heureux, mounting 16 guns and manned with 112 men, a very handsome ship, coppered and perfectly new, and in every respect fit for His Majesty's service.

I fell in with this ship at daylight on the 4th instant on her return from a cruise in company with a merchant ship her prize, called the Canada (John Sewell, Master) from Jamaica to London (last from Charlestown) laden with sugar, rum and coffee.

These vessels separated upon different courses, the latter steering direct for Bayonne, the former after a circular chase of 32 hours led us in sight of Bayonne and the Canada, which ship, after exchanging the prisoners, we drove on shore under that town, where at least her cargo must be destroyed as the sea ran very high and the wind dead on the shore.

I am now returning along shore to the northwards in hopes of meeting the Cambrian and Triton and whenever I send the former into port I shall return my prisoners by her, which I hope will meet your approbation.

368.   *Keats to Gardner*

Boadicea, at sea, 6 August 1798

I have the honour to acknowledge the receipt of your letter of this day by the Clyde. Yesterday and this day favourable circumstances of wind and weather having afforded opportunities of looking into Brest, the ships on both days approached the Goulet as near as could be done for the enemies' batteries.

I beg, therefore, to transmit the enclosed as a more correct statement of the enemy's force than that which under circumstances less favourable I had the honour of sending the 4th instant.

Though many, <u>most</u> of the enemy's ships of the line have their sails bent, still they do not in general appear to be down in the water and according to the judgment I am enabled to form I do not think more than six or eight of them bear the appearance of ships ready to put to sea.

Report of enemy's force in Brest water, reconnoitred by His Majesty's ships Boadicea and Mermaid, 6th August 1798.

Ships of the line   16, 2 of which are of three decks.
Frigates   12
Corvettes   4
      Total   32

369. *Gardner to Admiralty*

7 August 1798

. . . P.S. Enclosed is Captain Thornbrough's report of the force and situation of the enemy's fleet in Brest, as observed by him on Saturday the 4th instant which I did not receive until I had closed my last dispatches.

[*Enclosure*]

369a. *Thornbrough to Gardner*

Robust sent to reconnoitre the fleet in Brest the 4th August 1798

Situation of the fleet in Brest Harbour beginning to count them from the SE ship or uppermost ship near Point Espagnole.
1 Ship of the line
1 Ship of the line
1 Ship of the line
1 Frigate
1 Corvette
1 Corvette
5 Ships of the line all together or more
1 Frigate
2 Ships of the line with Rear Admiral flags
1 Ship of the line
1 Ship of the line Vice Admiral flag
4 Frigates
2 Corvettes or small frigates under weigh
1 small corvette ship
      Total   12 Ships of the line
            6 Frigates
            2 Corvettes
            2 Corvettes under weigh
            <u>1</u> small
      23

All appeared ready for sea topsails furled in body. I am not certain if one or two of the 5 ships of the line had sails bent.

370.   *Pellew to Gardner*

Indefatigable, at sea, 8 August 1798

I have great pleasure in communicating to you the capture of the French National corvette La Vaillante, commanded by the Lieutenant de Vaisseau la Porte, mounting 20 nine pounders, pierced for 22, and manned with 175 men.

This ship sailed from Rochefort the 1st, from Ile de Rhé, the 4th instant with 25 banished priests, 27 convicts and Madame Rovère and family for Cayenne. We fell in with her at day break on the 7th between Bordeaux and the Ile de Rhé and the chase continued 24 hours when she struck after firing a few guns. She is of large dimensions, only 18 months old, coppered and copper fastened, sails fast and will, I trust, be found fit for His Majesty's service.

The prisoners being more numerous than my own people I thought it prudent to return in order to land them, which I hope will meet your approbation.[1]

371.   *Gardner to Admiralty*

Royal Sovereign, at sea, 9 August 1798

Enclosed is the copy of a letter I received in the afternoon of the 7th instant from Sir Charles Hamilton Bt., Captain of His Majesty's ship Melpomene, which he forwarded to me on the 4th instant by the Childers brig. However gallant and determined the conduct of the officers and men who were employed by Sir Charles Hamilton to execute his orders and however meritorious this enterprise may have been, the particulars of which, I conclude, are before their Lordships, yet I cannot approve of the manner in which Sir Charles Hamilton has judged fit to quit his station and to proceed to Cawsand Bay for the purpose (as stated in his letter) of landing the prisoners and wounded, his station being only a few leagues to the eastward of the fleet (upon which he was ordered on the 8th June to remain until he should receive further orders or be called in by signal), having been directed to come occasionally in sight of Lord Bridport's

---

[1]*La Vaillante* was taken into service as the *Danae*. In March 1800 her crew mutinied and carried her into Le Conquet, near Brest.

flag or of the officer commanding for the time being. I conceive he has judged very improperly in proceeding to Cawsand Bay without his having previously obtained my approbation for his quitting his station and if their Lordships should concur with me in thinking so I hope they will signify their opinion of the matter to Sir Charles Hamilton Bart.[1]

372.   *Bridport to Admiralty*

Cricket Lodge, 9 August 1798

I transmit a copy of a letter from Sir Charles Hamilton, Captain of His Majesty's ship Melpomene, on the taking of L'Aventurier corvette brig for their Lordships' information and which appears to do so much credit to the officers and men employed in the execution of this service.

N.B. I have directed Sir Charles Hamilton to refit in Cawsand Bay and to join me off Brest without loss of time.

373.   *Gower to Gardner*

Neptune, at sea, 9 August 1798

I desire leave to enclose you a letter that was left upon one of the guns upon the quarter deck this morning before daybreak. Tynan and other Irishmen I have had suspicions of for some time past and lament that I can't bring sufficient proofs to bring them to trial. I have one hundred Irishmen, including twenty-six marines and the Irish marines were certainly to have joined the seamen and if I may be allowed to give an opinion from the purport of the letter left on the quarter deck and the vague reports of the well affected people the intention of the mutineers was to have murdered the officers and well disposed men and afterwards to have carried the ship to the enemy. I have made the ship's company acquainted with the contents of the enclosed letter, who all deny ever having heard of an intended mutiny. I wish to God some of the Irish could be taken from us.

N.B. It was folded up as a letter and addressed: 'Sir E. Gower. To be forwarded to him.'

[*Enclosure*]

[1]Ten days later, in a letter to Pole, Gardner went further and blamed Hamilton for a convoy getting into Brest.

373a.   *Anonymous letter*

Captain. There is a mutiny forming on board the ship. Lose no time in finding it out. Tyne[1] is a principal hand and many others, some of the marines are concerned: it is a most bloody plot.

374.   *Captain Jones,[2] Defiance, to Captain Bedford, Royal Sovereign*

10 August 1798

I could wish the Admiral would not send the Defiance on any detached service. We have many Irish men on board this ship and suspicious circumstances have happened that makes it necessary we should keep a good look out. The good men of the ship are afraid it was the intention of the Irish to take her from us the night that we were from the fleet from what they overheard but we cannot bring it to proof. The Irishmen came aft to me the day before yesterday and said that such a report was made by one of the men. I told them that I did not believe that such was their intention, at the same time let them know that there were many very bad men among them who were accustomed to drink improper toasts, that I had not proof sufficient of it at present but they might depend on it if I had I would bring them to punishment and then pointed out one of them who I said was a most infamous villain. I have too many Irish and foreigners. It would be a good thing before the ship is next paid, which will be due the latter end of this month, to draft many of them. We are at present quiet and as the good men are on the look out I hope we shall continue so.

375.   *Admiralty to Bridport*

14 August 1798

My Lords Commissioners of the Admiralty being desirous of ascertaining with as much accuracy as possible what may be the total number of Irish seamen and marines on board the different ships composing the fleet under your Lordship's command, as also the number in each ship respectively who may be suspected to be evil disposed, I am commanded by their Lordships to signify their direction to you to

---

[1]Tynan.
[2]Theophilus Jones (d. 1835). Lieutenant 1778; Captain 1782; Rear-admiral 1804; Vice-admiral 1809; Admiral 1819.

furnish me with such return for their information as soon as conveniently may be, causing however the utmost degree of circumspection and secrecy to be observed in respect to the measures you may take in in enabling you to prepare the said return.[1]

376. *Bridport to Admiralty*

Royal George, at sea, 21 August 1798

I have received your letter of the 13th instant transmitting a copy of one from Sir Charles Hamilton of the 4th, also one from Vice Admiral Sir Alan Gardner of the 9th on the subject of the Melpomene quitting her station off Abrewrack [Aber-wrac'h[2]] and acquainting me that their Lordships concur in opinion with Sir Alan Gardner in respect to the impropriety of Sir Charles Hamilton quitting his station without permission of his commanding officer and desiring that I will communicate the same to him accordingly.

Sir Charles Hamilton's conduct was not correct in quitting his station without the permission of the flag officer commanding the squadron off Brest but I did not state this to their Lordships as I concluded Sir Charles's reasons, viz. to land the prisoners and wounded as well as being in want of water might in some degree have removed any impression to his disadvantage, since which I have received your letter of the 11th instant communicating their Lordships' approbation of his conduct, the officers and men who were employed in cutting out L'Aventurier, which has been sent to him. As the Melpomene is in Cawsand Bay I shall transmit a copy of your letter of the 13th signifying their Lordships' disapprobation of Sir Charles Hamilton's quitting his station together with a copy of Sir Alan Gardner's letter of the 9th instant by the first opportunity.

377. *Bedford to Gardner*

Royal Sovereign, at sea, 21 August 1798

In compliance with the directions received from Admiral Lord Bridport intimating to me the desire of the Lords Commissioners of the Admi-

---

[1]The returns showed that there were 1517 Irish seamen and 460 Irish marines, of whom 328 and 83 respectively were classified as evil disposed. A certain amount of subjectivity is apparent. The *Saturn* had 140 Irishmen, none of then suspect, but the *Royal George* distrusted 57 out of 92 and the *Foudroyant* 50 out of 164. See also the return for the *Royal Sovereign* given below, document 377.

[2]See document 366.

ralty to ascertain the number of Irish seamen and marines serving under my command.

I beg leave to inform you that there are one hundred and seven Irish seamen (besides eight Irish seamen supernumeraries belonging to the Magnanime) and twenty-nine Irish marines belonging to His Majesty's ship Royal Sovereign.

From my own observations and the best information I can collect I have not the least reason to suspect any of them to be evil disposed.

378.   *De Courcy*[1] *to Bridport*

Magnanime, at sea, 25 August 1798

The principal occurrences of His Majesty's ship under my command having been detailed to your Lordship in my letter of the 21st instant, it remains for me to represent that they were followed by no event worthy of recital till the 24th, when at 2 in the afternoon while at the distance of about 15 leagues N.W. of Cape Finisterre two ships of very warlike appearance were observed in the S.W., which, steering to the S.E. under a crowd of sail, seemed as if intent upon intercepting our course.

The sea being smooth the Magnanime's crew high in courage and every circumstance such as to justify a spirit of enterprise, nothing remained but to try their force. As the ships rapidly approached each other it soon became apparent that the advanced ship and which seemed by much the larger was of French construction and no doubt was entertained of the more distant ship's being her consort. But in a little time, when the courses of the different ships were just discernible above the horizon a signal denoting an enemy which was displayed by the rear ship gave a new turn to appearances and it now became obvious that the headmost ship only had a claim upon our exertions.

And here, my Lord, I must beg to mark my admiration of the gallant spirit of Captain Pierrepont (that officer being, as was subsequently proved, in the command of the rear ship, the Naiad) who admitting no apprehension of having fresh enemies to contend with rather chose to encounter any hazard than to relinquish a pursuit which already had done him so much honour.

Measures being adopted in consequence of the signal alluded to, each of His Majesty's ships by 5 p.m. approached the flying enemy so very nearly as to be within the range of shot, the Naiad, which was the

---

[1]Hon. Michael de Courcy (d. 1824). Captain 1783; Rear-admiral 1805; Vice-admiral 1810; Admiral 1821.

nearer ship, being from the nature of the pursuit directly astern, while the Magnanime, which had the opportunity of chasing in an angular direction, approached on the broadside.

In this position the enemy, all whose efforts were addressed against the Naiad, commenced a retrograde fire, aiming in truth with such precision as to disable one of her guns, to lodge some shot between wind and water and to carry away some of her standing and running rigging; but, I am happy to add, without hurting any of that meritorious ship's company.

After the firing had been continued about an hour the enemy, deeming further resistance to be without hope, discharged his broadside, hauled down the tricoloured flag, and was, in the same moment, boarded by the Magnanime's and Naiad's boats. During the firing above spoken of His Majesty's ships, more solicitous of closing with their enemy than of fighting a distant battle, scarce did him any injury. To this statement it will scarce seem necessary to add my persuasion that the issue of a battle would have been highly honourable to the Naiad had the Magnanine been altogether out of the question.

La Decade (such is the name of the captured frigate)[1] commanded by Le Citoyen Villeneau, was manned with 336 men and armed with 44 guns, ten of which, nevertheless, appear to have been landed at Cayenne, whereunto this frigate, although no more than 4 months from France, had just conveyed into exile two members of the French Convention with 300 priests.

Captain Pierrepoint, who is superior to my power of praise, makes the strongest acknowledgment of the ardour by which his officers and men were animated during an anxious chase of 32 hours, and whilst in constant expectation of battle.

379. *Bridport to Spencer*

Royal George, at sea, 27 August 1798

I am sorry to inform your Lordship that the Surgeon of the Royal George has complained by letter to Captain Domett of the bad quality of the portable broth and tea which have been supplied him from Mr. Turner the contractor at Portsmouth. I have directed samples of each to be sent to the Sick and Wounded Board for examination and I have transmitted copies of the letters from Doctor Peckwood the Surgeon and Captain Domett at the same time. I have seen the tea, which appears to me not fit to be used.

---

[1]Taken into British service as the *Decade*.

It seems to me that an inspector should be appointed to examine the necessary chests before Mr. Turner issues them to the ships and I suppose the Inspector should be a medical man. I know no one so proper as the Physician of the Fleet and I think he may be usefully employed on shore for this service, which I imagine would prevent of abuse and of course check complaints from the surgeons in behalf of the sick under their care.

I submit this plan privately to your Lordship and when digested something similar might be adopted for the general benefit of the Navy. If your Lordship should approve of the Physician of the Fleet for the service he may also be usefully employed in superintending the sick at the hospital as well as attending all surveys upon invalids.

[*Endorsed as answered on 1 September*]

380. *Admiralty to Bridport*

27 August 1798

My Lords Commissioners of the Admiralty, having received information of the arrivals on the 22nd instant of the three French frigates named in the margin [*La Concorde, Le Medee, Franchise*] in Killala Bay on the north west coast of Ireland, from which a body of troops with arms had been disembarked, I am commanded by their Lordships to acquaint you therewith, and to signify their direction to you to keep with you, for the purpose of very closely watching the port of Brest, and preventing any farther reinforcements being sent to Ireland, as many frigates as can possibly be spared from other services.

381. *Admiralty to Bridport*

29 August 1798

I am commanded by my Lords Commissioners of the Admiralty to signify their direction to your Lordship to direct the attention of the frigates under your orders for the present principally to the watching the motions of the enemy's ships at Brest and the blocking up the port of Rochefort for the purpose of intercepting the enemy's frigates which have been at Killala Bay in case they should attempt to return to either of those ports and to prevent others with reinforcements from getting out.

382.   *Bridport to Admiralty*

Royal George, at sea, 30 August 1798

The Plymouth lugger joined me this afternoon, when I received your letters of the 27th instant acquainting me that the three French frigates therein named had arrived in Killala Bay on the N.W. coast of Ireland on the 22nd instant, from which a body of troops with arms had been disembarked. And directing me to keep as many frigates with this squadron as can possibly be spared from other services for the purpose of very closely watching the port of Brest and preventing any further reinforcements being sent to Ireland. And in answer thereto I acquaint you that I shall keep as many of the frigates under my orders employed upon the above service as may be in my power.

383.   *Spencer to Bridport*

Admiralty, 1 September 1798

I am sorry to hear that there have been any complaints about the necessaries for the sick on board the Royal George but I have no doubt that on the experimentation being made the Sick and Hurt Board will take the proper measure for rectifying the cause of them.

I should have supposed that an employment such as your Lordship points out would be incompatible with the duties of the Physician to the Fleet afloat. It might otherwise be well to have such inspection adopted: the subject shall however be considered.

384.   *Admiralty to Bridport*

3 September 1798

Having communicated to my Lords Commissioners of the Admiralty your letters to me of the 21st, 25th and 27th of last month, together with the reports inclosed therein of the state of the enemy's force at Brest, as made to you by the officers you had ordered to reconnoitre, I am commanded by their Lordships to acquaint you that they have had very great satisfaction in observing the attention your Lordship has paid to the blocking up of the port abovementioned, which has been done with such judgement as to have effectually prevented the sailing of any part of the squadron destined, as supposed, to carry troops to Ireland.

Although their Lordships judge it to be still of great consequence that every exertion should be used to keep the enemy's squadron in port, they nevertheless think fit in order to save H.M. ships from being disabled by the approaching equinoctial gales, to leave it to your Lordship's discretion to come into port with the ships of the line composing your squadron whenever the weather may be such as to render it necessary. In which case it is their direction that you send the several ships, in such proportions as you may judge proper, to Cawsand Bay and Torbay to have their stores and provisions completed as expeditiously as possible, holding them afterwards in momentary readiness to put to sea when the wind shall have become favourable for the enemy's leaving Brest, when your Lordship is to lose no time in returning to your station.

If on your arrival off Brest your Lordship should find that any of the enemy's ships have sailed from thence during your absence, it is their Lordships' further directions that you immediately detach to the coast of Ireland a force proportionate to that of the enemy which shall appear to have put to sea.

385. *Intelligence Report*

[September 1798]

Intelligence brought by M. de la Boissiere from France, which he left the 20th September 1798.

The Hoche with 6 frigates sailed from Brest (Road) on the morning of the 15th instant and was out of sight at night.

The squadron is commanded by the officer who landed the troops in Killala Bay. Two 74s, of which the Montblanc was one, were ready to sail but had no troops an board.

386. *Sickness Return*

[September 1798]

Admitted into Haslar Hospital, 1797.	6,573
Admitted into Plymouth Hospital, 1797.	6,041
Total	12,614

Admitted into Haslar Hospital the first nine months of 1798.	3,862
Admitted into Plymouth Hospital the first nine months of 1798.	4,833
Total	8,695

The whole admissions computed for the year according to the proportion above stated will amount to 10,882. Difference, 1,734.

387. *Durham to Bridport*

Anson, at sea, 16 October 1798

I have the honour to inform your Lordship that I sailed from Cawsand Bay on the 16th of September last in order to put your Lordship's orders into execution.

On the morning of the 20th following, off Belle Isle, I fell in with the enemy's squadron, consisting of one sail of the line and eight frigates, His Majesty's ship Ethalion in company with them. Captain Countess[1] ordered me to keep sight of the enemy in company with him until I should be able to determine their destination, acquainting the Government of England and Ireland by every means possible.

I have great pleasure in informing your Lordship that from the indefatigable perseverance of Captain Countess (notwithstanding the foggy and unfavourable weather) I was enabled to put his orders fully in execution. Having kept sight of them nearly three weeks and until their arrival off the coast of Ireland, between 7 and 8 in the morning of the 11th of October made the N.W. part in company with the Ethalion and at 10 joined the squadron under the command of Sir John Warren Bt. At 1/2 past 12 discovered the enemy, Sir John Warren having made the Anson's signal to keep sight of the enemy during the night. I was under the necessity of carrying a great press of sail in order to gain a proper situation to put his orders in force. During the night I had the misfortune to lose the mizen mast, the fall of which carried away the main topsail yard, which rendered it impossible for me to continue the chase.

Your Lordship will be better able to judge than I can possibly express what my feelings and those of the officers and ship's company must have been at that critical moment after the many anxious hours we had passed in keeping sight of so superior an enemy and to be disabled at the moment we were flattering ourselves of being sufficiently repaid for all our fatigue and anxiety. Notwithstanding our disabled state we had the good fortune by a change of wind and the position of the enemy to be enabled next morning to cut off four of their fast sailing frigates who were making their escape from Sir John Warren's squadron and having brought them to action for two hours and a half, three of them keeping a close connected line. The wind freshening and from the

[1]George Countess (d. 1811). Lieutenant 1774; Captain 1790; Rear-admiral 1809.

disabled state of the Anson, not having almost a sail left to the yard, our masts, yards and bowsprit shot through in several places, they escaped but I have reason to believe not without having received considerable damage.

I have every reason to be satisfied with the conduct of the officers and ship's company, who behaved with the greatest gallantry.

388.   *Durham to Bridport*

Anson, in Plymouth Sound, 27 October 1798

From the disabled state of His Majesty's ship under my command in the action of the 12th inst. and the wind remaining to the S.W. I was unavoidably separated from the squadron under the command of Sir John Warren, Bart. and drove considerably to the N.W. of Ireland.

I have great satisfaction in informing your Lordship that on the 18th at day light in the morning I discovered a large ship to leeward, fortunately for me, with the loss of her fore and main topmasts (the Anson being by no means in a situation to chase, her mizen mast gone, main yard and main crosstrees, the bowsprit and fore yard shot through in several places). I immediately bore up and got alongside of her. After an action of one hour and a quarter, most gallantly disputed, which does the highest honour to Citizen Joseph Andrieu Segune, her commander, she struck. Proved to be La Loire, one of the largest and finest frigates belonging to the Republic, presented by the city of Nantes, quite new and never before at sea, pierced for 50 guns, mounting 46 (eighteen pounders) having on board 664 men (troops included) among whom are a number of artillery, Etat Major for three regiments. La Loire had 48 men killed and 75 wounded, was one of the four frigates which the Anson engaged the 12th and was making her escape from the coast.[1]

389.   *Admiralty to Bridport*

31 October 1798

I have received and communicated to my Lords Commissioners of the Admiralty your letter of the 29th instant enclosing for their Lordships' information the copy of the letter you had received from the Honour-

---

[1]In this action the Anson had 2 killed and 13 wounded. On the 12th she had 8 wounded.

able Captain Herbert[1] of the Amelia, the only one you had received from the different squadrons under your orders since the 22nd ultimo and expressing your surprise that Sir John Warren had not written to you as well as to Vice Admiral Kingsmill on the captures made by the ships with him on the 12th instant and I am commanded by their Lordships to acquaint you that Sir John Warren having after his arrival on the coast of Ireland acted under the orders of Vice Admiral Kingsmill, he has of course judged it unnecessary to make any report excepting to his commanding officer.

390.   *Admiralty to Gardner*[2]

5 November 1798

I have received and communicated to my Lords Commissioners of the Admiralty your letters of the 2nd and 3rd instant, the former acquainting me for their information that in consequence of the very heavy gales of wind which have prevailed for some days past you had been under the necessity of proceeding into Torbay with His Majesty's ships named in the margin; the latter enclosing a report which had been made to you on the state of the defects of the knee of the head of the Ajax[3] which had rendered it necessary for you to send that ship to Portsmouth; and I am commanded by their Lordships to acquaint you that they approve of your having returned to Torbay with the ships abovementioned and that from your account of the state of the weather they would have approved of your having proceeded thither sooner than you have done.

391.   *Admiralty to Gardner*

7 November 1798

I am commanded by my Lords Commissioners of the Admiralty to acquaint you that directions have been given to the Victualling Board to send an immediate supply of provisions to Torbay for the use of such ships under your orders as may be deficient.

---

[1]Charles Herbert (d. 1808). Lieutenant 1793; Captain 1795.

[2]Addressed to Gardner in Torbay.

[3]A 74 launched in March 1798 at a cost of £57,000, she required her defects made good in December 1798 and a 'middling repair' in April 1802. Many of her knees had been 'grain cut' and broken. The two repairs cost an additional £44,000. The ship had been merchant built. St Vincent, First Lord of the Admiralty from 1801, instigated a prosecution of the builder. See Morriss, *Royal Dockyards*, 28–9.

392.   *Admiralty to Bridport*[1]

22 December 1798

I am commanded by my Lords Commissioners of the Admiralty to enclose to your Lordship for your information a copy of my letter to Vice Admiral Sir Alan Gardner of this day's date signifying to him their Lordships' direction to return with the squadron under his command to Torbay in case the wind should appear to be settled to the westward and I am to signify their Lordships' directions to you to hold a sufficient number of frigates in readiness to be sent out for the purpose of watching the port of Brest on the return of the said squadron into port.

393.   *Bridport to Spencer*

Cricket Lodge, 23 December 1798

I think the frigates under my orders have been very active and rather successful, having captured several privateers and two pretty valuable loaded ships from the East and West Indies. By letter from Captain Stopford which I have just received I find he has chased two others that escaped in the night but I believe one of them is taken by the Boadicea called the Invincible Buonaparte and is arrived at Spithead . . .

I cannot help expressing the concern I feel upon the loss of the Colossus in St. Mary's, Scilly, but it is fortunate that only one man has suffered by that event.[2]

Your Lordship is in possession of my professional sentiments upon the anchorage and in them I fully stated the dangers that might arise for His Majesty's Fleet upon the plan suggested to your Lordship by some experienced seaman, to which I could not concur.

394.   *Bridport to Admiralty*

Cricket Lodge, 24 December 1798

I have received your letter of the 22nd instant acquainting me that you are commanded by the Lords Commissioners of the Admiralty to en-

---

[1]Addressed to Bridport at Cricket Lodge.

[2]He referred to Sir William Hamilton (1730–1803), minister plenipotentiary at Naples, 1764–1800, who had embarked the cream of his collection of classical vases on board the *Colossus*. See I. Jenkins and K. Sloan, *Vases and Volcanoes. Sir William Hamilton and His Collection* (British Museum, 1996), 58–9.

close for my information a copy of your letter to Vice Admiral Sir Alan Gardner of that day's date, which I have also received, signifying to him their Lordships' directions to return with the squadron under his command to Torbay in case the wind should appear to be settled to the westward and to signify their Lordships' direction to me to hold a sufficient number of frigates in readiness to be sent out for the purpose of watching the port of Brest on the return of the said squadron into port.

And in return thereto I acquaint you that I shall give notice to Vice Admiral Sir Alan Gardner accordingly and transmit directions to the senior officer under my orders at Plymouth to hasten the refitting the frigates at that port and keep them in readiness for immediate service.

I hope their Lordships will take into consideration the putting two frigates under my orders to replace the Jason and Pique, lost on the coast of France, and I beg to suggest whether it may not be necessary to have a line of battle ship or two to cruise off Brest to command and protect the frigates on that station.

[*Endorsed that their Lordships had no frigates to spare and did not judge it necessary to keep line of battle ships off Brest*]

395.   *Spencer to Bridport*

Admiralty, 27 December 1798

I was much concerned at the loss of the Colossus, which appears by Captain Murray to be attributed to the parting of her cable and the ship, being deficient in the complement of her anchors, had not the usual resources for bringing her up after that accident had happened. I will not say how far that might or might not have happened in any other anchorage and still less can I presume to enter into any discussion with your Lordship on a point of this nature but as you have dwelt once or twice on the term experienced seaman which I happened once to make use of when writing to you on this subject I will only just observe that the person from whom I had the observation in question on the road of St. Mary's in Scilly was Sir Edward Pellew, than whom I do not believe there are many more experienced or able seamen in His Majesty's service.

396. *Gardner to Admiralty*

Royal Sovereign, at sea, 31 December 1798

Whenever the wind shall appear to be settled to the westward (from which quarter it has not blown for some time) I certainly shall endeavour agreeably to my former order to shelter the squadron in Torbay, which place, however, I consider at this season of the year (when S.E. winds are very prevalent) to be a very unsafe anchorage.

With respect to their Lordships' directions to leave a sufficient number of frigates off Brest to watch the motions of the enemy there you will please to acquaint them that the Indefatigable is the only frigate at present employed to watch the enemy's motions, which ship is not altogether in a fit state at present for that service but being the only one I have to reconnoitre the enemy I have desired her commander to keep the sea as long as he possibly can with safety and so soon as the Nymphe joins me it is my intention to order Captain Fraser[1] upon this service under the orders of Sir Edward Pellew.

The squadron under my command are all in want of sails, cordage and other stores and their provisions are growing short and whenever they may arrive in Torbay or any other place they will require a thorough caulking and refitting.

397. *Bridport to Spencer*

Cricket Lodge, 31 December 1798

With respect to the loss of the Colossus I shall utter not another word upon that unfortunate event. But nothing surprises me more than what your Lordship has stated respecting Sir Edward Pellew's opinion upon the safety of anchoring His Majesty's Fleet in St. Mary's road. And I must beg your Lordship will ask Captain Legge,[2] whenever you shall see him, Sir Edward's declaration upon that subject. I have as high an opinion of the abilities of Sir Edward Pellew as your Lordship can have and I consider him as able a seaman as any captain in His Majesty's service but I am inclined to believe his local attachments bias his mind rather too much for correct judgment.

---

[1]Percy Fraser (d. 1827). Lieutenant 1789; Captain 1795; Navy Board Commissioner 1813–23; Superannuated Rear-admiral 1823.
[2]Sir Arthur Kaye Legge (d. 1835). Lieutenant 1789; Captain 1793; Rear-admiral 1810; Vice-admiral 1814; Admiral 1830.

I saw Captain Draper[1] three days ago who came home a passenger in the Colossus and he told me that St. Mary's, Scilly, was not a safe anchorage for line of battle ships as there was not drift for them in case of parting with a cable, which occasioned the loss of that ship as she struck at low water and if the new cable had parted the day before he believed not one man could have been saved.

398. *Bridport to Admiralty*

Cricket Lodge, 31 December 1798

Lord Bridport presents his compliments to Mr. Nepean and acquaints him that he shall be at Bath the latter end of this week to which place he will be pleased to direct his letters in case he shall have occasion to write to him on service. Many returns to you upon the present season are sincerely offered.

399. *Return of Emoluments*

Pay and emoluments of the Right Honourable Lord Bridport for one year from the 1st of January to 31st December 1798.

Salary as Treasurer of Greenwich Hospital one year from the 1st January to 31st December.	£200. 0.0
Stores and table money for Ditto.	£78.12.2
Pay as Vice Admiral of England one year from 1st January to 31st December.	£434. 1.0
Flag pay, table money and compensation pay as Commander in Chief of the Channel Fleet, 1 year from 1st January to 31st December.	£1,866. 6.0
	£2,578.19.2

400. *Bridport to Admiralty*

Cricket Lodge, 5 January 1799

In my last letter to you of the 31st ultimo I acquainted you for their Lordships' information that I had directed Sir Charles Hamilton to proceed and join Vice Admiral Sir Alan Gardner off Brest as soon as

---

[1]John Draper (d. 1813). Lieutenant 1780; Captain 1795.

the Melpomene should be ready for sea; and I now acquaint you that I have directed Captain White of His Majesty's sloop Sylph to proceed to sea and join the ships cruising off Corunna and St. Andero and follow the orders of the senior officer on that station, which I hope their Lordships will approve, as from information I have received from Sir Harry Neale, Captain of His Majesty's ship St. Fiorenzo, the enemy's cruisers and their prizes keep close to the north shore of Spain on their return into port. I therefore hope their Lordships will think the Sylph cannot be better employed.

401. *Bridport to Admiralty*

Cricket Lodge, 7 January 1799

Lord Bridport presents his compliments to Mr. Marsden[1] and acquaints him that not having been able to get a house at Bath before Wednesday next, he has been obliged to remain in the country until that day but on Thursday the 11th he will certainly be there.

402. *Young[2] to Spencer*

Admiralty, 15 January 1799

I am very sorry to see some appearance this evening of the wind coming to the south-east. I think it impossible that the French should have a squadron of any consequence ready to put to sea for some little time at least but if the wind becomes fair for their sailing we must, I suppose, send our squadron off Brest, where they will be buffeted about to little good purpose. I was in hopes after the long easterly wind we have had that we should have a westerly wind for some weeks that our ships might have longer days and a chance of moderate weather when they sailed.

. . . The Arethusa has had a very narrow escape, having run on shore in a thick fog under the light house of Cape Barfleur, fortunately not near a battery. The French got some guns down but as they began to fire the ship floated. A great hole is made in the bottom.

---

[1]William Marsden (1754–1836). Second Secretary to the Board of Admiralty, March 1795–January 1804; first Secretary 1804–7.

[2]Sir William Young (1751–1821). Lieutenant 1770; Captain 1778; Rear-admiral 1795; Vice-admiral 1799; Admiral 1805. Admiralty Commissioner November 1795 to February 1801; Commander-in-Chief Plymouth 1804–7, and North Sea 1811–14.

403. *Bridport to Admiralty*

Bath, 22 January 1799

I have received your letter of yesterday's date together with the intelligence which their Lordships had received from the Prince de Bouillon relative to the enemy's convoys expected to sail from Rochefort. And in obedience to their Lordships' commands I shall send orders to Captain Countess by the first post to proceed immediately with the Ethalion and Anson and take the earliest opportunity of reconnoitring Basque Road and the port of Rochefort and to cruise between Belleisle and Rochefort for the space of one month for the purpose of intercepting the enemy's convoys abovementioned and upon falling in with them to use their best endeavours to take and destroy them and then to cruise very diligently from the latitude of Belleisle to the estuary of the Garonne and to remain on the above service until they shall be relieved or receive further orders.

I wish much to have two frigates got ready to proceed off Corunna and St. Andero as the Sylph is cruising on that station alone, the Fisgard[1] being returned to Plymouth for the reasons stated by Captain Martin[2] in his letter to me, a copy of which I transmitted to you yesterday.

[Endorsed that he is not to despatch two frigates without receiving instructions]

404. *Bridport to Admiralty*

Bath, 24 January 1799

I have received your letter of yesterday's date in answer to mine to you expressing a desire to have two frigates got ready to cruise between Corunna and St. Andero, and that you had their Lordships' commands to acquaint me that it was probable the frigates would be wanted for other services and that I was not to send any ship upon that service until I receive further directions from their Lordships, to which strict attention shall be paid.

As from the intelligence which you have transmitted to me several convoys are expected to sail from Rochefort and Bordeaux for the

[1] *Fishguard.*
[2] Sir Thomas Byam Martin (d. 1854). Lieutenant 1790; Captain 1793; Rear-admiral 1811; Vice-admiral 1819; Admiral 1830. Comptroller of the Navy, 1816–31.

supply of the enemy's ships at Brest I take the liberty to suggest the propriety of sending two frigates to cruise between the Penmarcks and L'Orient, as all convoys from the ports in the Bay must make the Penmarcks and they often take shelter, if interrupted, at L'Orient.

By Captain Home's[1] last return to me, a copy of which I transmitted to you for their Lordships' information, it appears that the San Fiorenzo and Naiad will be the next frigates ready for sea and several others, I apprehend, will soon follow. I shall therefore wait their Lordships' directions to detach those frigates upon the Penmarcks station, which I consider an important one for the purpose above mentioned and they will be ready at hand for any other services if required.

The frigates are named in the margin now in port and not under orders:

[At Plymouth: *St. Fiorenzo, Naiad, Mermaid, Amelia, Magnanime, Cambrian, Clyde, Fisgard, Indefatigable.*

At Spithead: *Boadicea.*

In Portsmouth Harbour: *Phaeton, Stag.*]

[*Endorsed 25th January to approve of his doing as he has proposed*]

405.   *Warren to Spencer*

Stonehouse, 30 January 1799

I cannot avoid trespassing upon that kindness you have expressed to me to state to your Lordship that being kept in the Channel fleet under circumstances peculiarly unpleasant I must consider as an unhandsome and very hard fate.

I am well aware that Lord Bridport's favourite argument against detaching me from the fleet is there being five or six senior officers to me in it but these gentlemen (however superior their merits may be considered) have never yet been called into detached service, consequently they cannot feel that mortification that I must ever do at remaining off Brest after having for three years successively borne a broad pendant.

[*Endorsed as received on the 2nd February*]

---

[1]Roddam Home (d. 1801). Lieutenant 1772; Captain 1779; Rear-admiral 1799.

406. *Spencer to Warren*

Admiralty, 2 February 1799

The situation in which you are at present placed was the unavoidable consequence of the nature of the naval war at the time and the circumstance of your being removed to a line of battle ship, which removal took place in consequence of a request of your own.

407. *Bridport to Admiralty*

Bath, 6 February 1799

I am sorry to find that all the frigates have waited a considerable time for rigging and sails from the dock yard at Plymouth; and I believe the Naiad has been in Hamoaze upwards of two months.

8

THE BRUIX CRUISE[1]
12 FEBRUARY–15 AUGUST 1799

In February 1799 the French still had 14 ships of the line and six frigates in good condition lying in Brest water, with another 20 vessels in the naval arsenal [408]. British frigates in the Iroise attempted to keep the harbour under observation and to block the movement of vessels along the coast to and from Brest [409, 411, 416], though some convoys close inshore got through [414]. Early in March intelligence was received of mobilisation, and of an embargo on the sailing of privateers with the transfer of their crews to Brest [410, 412]. The destination of the fleet was said to be either Ireland or Portugal [424]. By the end of March, intelligence from the continent suggested the strength of the intended fleet was 30 ships of the line, and its destination to be the Mediterranean [415].

After his winter break, Bridport was ordered urgently on 19 March to hoist his flag [417]. During this break the Admiralty had closely controlled the disposition of the frigates under the command of Bridport who acted more evidently than hitherto simply as a channel of communication [418]. After his arrival at Spithead he attended to arrangements for maintaining the sea-going capability of his force [419] and sailed from Spithead on 13 April with eight of the line [422]. Meanwhile, off Ushant Lord Hugh Seymour, who was destined for command of the Leeward Islands station [426], handed over a part of his squadron of ships of the line to Sir George Berkeley [420]. The latter took over from him at a difficult time. By mid-April several of his ships with their crews needed to return to port to refit and recover from their winter cruise. The *Mars* had been five months at sea and her leaks were affecting the health of her men. Moreover, from 16 April the French were pushing out into Bertheaume Bay and Berkeley was driven by strong easterly winds off his station [421]. It was five days before he was able to get back off Ushant where Bridport had by then arrived [427].

---

[1]For papers relating to the cruise of Admiral Bruix published earlier by the Navy Records Society, see the *Private Papers of George, Second Earl Spencer*, ed. J. S. Corbett and H. W. Richmond (4 vols, NRS, 1913 etc.), III, 41–103.

The desperate state of some frigates placed them at risk from the French as well from the weather [423]. The weather took its toll on the battle ships too [427]. Fortunately, however, Seymour's ships were in relatively good condition [425] and the number of potential reliefs at Plymouth permitted Bridport to order in the worst of his frigates [428]. An adequate number of reliefs were necessary as, under Admiralty control [429], Pointe de Penmarch had become a regular frigate station [430] and the possible southerly course of the French fleet demanded all exits from the Iroise be watched [432]. These frigates also stopped French traders and privateers, recapturing many British vessels [438]. Reliefs and reinforcing ships of the line arrived too. Bridport was ordered to keep with him only that number French preparations seemed to demand and to send in the others to replenish and be paid in turn [431].

On 25 April 1799 these arrangements were interrupted by the movements of the French fleet. Intelligence later reported operations within Brest harbour [445]. By the 26th at least 18 ships of the line had emerged into Camaret Bay or were under weigh [433] and that night they sailed. Reinforced from L'Orient shortly before, they comprised 25 ships of the line and eight frigates and corvettes under Vice Admiral Eustache Bruix[1] [441]. Fog helped to obscure their departure. Next morning their tail end rounding the Saintes was sighted by the *Nymphe*.[2] Bridport prepared his force for battle and gave chase. But on the *Nymphe* annulling her earlier sighting signal, the chase was cancelled [435]. Captain Fraser of *La Nymphe* later explained that he had lost sight of the French fleet in fog and, unable to transmit this by signal, had decided to annul his earlier signal. The French fleet was out of sight when the fog cleared and he assumed they had put about and returned to their anchorage [436]. Relayed by cutter, the interpretation attached to his conflicting signals re-echoed in England [439]. But Fraser had been mistaken. The French had not put back. Brest harbour was empty. Bruix had sailed and been lost.[3] Bridport could do nothing more than

---

[1]Eustache Bruix (1759–1805). Vice-admiral in 1799. Had left the French navy at the Revolution but rejoined and served under Villaret-Joyeuse. He was Minister of Marine when he took the Brest fleet to the Mediterranean in April 1799 and returned safely with it in August. He commanded the French flotilla of boats intended for the invasion of Britain but resigned due to ill health.

[2]W. James, *The Naval History of Great Britain from the declaration of war by France in 1793 to the accession of George IV* (6 vols, London, 1859), II, 287.

[3]Captain Percy Fraser (d. 1827). Lieutenant 1789; Captain 1795. Thereafter Fraser's mistake seems to have affected his career. He received no more promotions and became a commissioner of the navy in 1813. He was placed on the list of superannuated rear admirals in 1823.

send warnings to the Admiralty and to St Vincent, and as planned take a defensive station off Cape Clear [440].

There, Bridport was steadily reinforced [443, 444]. Among the vessels that joined was the hired armed lugger *Black Joke* which on the 27 April had captured the French National armed schooner *Rebecca* having on board a naval frigate captain with dispatches for Ireland. His instructions directed him to inform rebel leaders about the French fleet, the troops it carried and their armamament [437]. The master of the *Rebecca* revealed, however, that her capture and the failure to destroy the despatches had been deliberate. Not only did he reveal that she had been sent out as a *ruse de guerre* – to persuade the British government that Bruix was intended for Ireland when he was not – but that Bruix was supplied for a long cruise and had embarked artillery officers without guns [448]. Bridport sent the despatches and associated intelligence to London through the hands of the Lord Lieutenant of Ireland. The Admiralty was justly sceptical of the credibility of the despatches. One point of suspicion was their early dating but late interception – after the French fleet had sailed. How could something so important have been so delayed [452]? The answer lay in the poor sailing qualities of a first vessel in which the despatches had been embarked [450]. Bruix had to supply a second vessel which, for the sake of conformity with the deception, was also named *Rebecca* [451].

Meanwhile in London, the possibility of the French taking a southerly course had already been acted upon. St Vincent was reinforced, and a reserve squadron placed at readiness to sail where most needed [442]. Bridport, charged with guarding against either a landing on the west coast of Ireland or an enemy excursion into the Channel, was reinforced to 20 of the line with the availability of another three [446, 447, 449]. By 10 May the Admiralty was aware that the French had gone south. Bridport was thus directed to shelter and replenish in Bantry Bay, whence would be directed eight victuallers [454]. By then the Admiralty also had information of the sailing on 28 April of a Spanish squadron of five from Ferrol [453]. A storeship was thus sent to supply Bridport and he was directed to detach a squadron under Gardner to St Vincent [455], while he with the remainder of his force found the Spanish squadron, possibly in Rochefort or back in Ferrol, and prevented it from joining the French fleet [456, 457].

By the end of May the French newspapers confirmed that the Spanish squadron was in Aix Roads, off Rochefort [458]. Detaching 16 of the line under Gardner, Bridport with ten was off Ile de Rhe by 4 June [460]. He was sceptical of being able to inflict damage on the Spanish squadron, though it might be prompted to move higher up the Charante

River towards Rochefort by attack from bomb vessels [461]. Hoping to get the squadron to rid itself of guns and stores, the Admiralty seized upon Bridport's suggestion and made available three bomb vessels [465]. Leaving Berkeley with six of the line [463], Bridport returned to Plymouth where he was directed to take command of the bomb vessels [464]. At this point, preferring rest and recuperation to command of a mission of subordinate importance, Bridport was promptly superseded by Pole [466–9]. But his pessimism about the possible achievement of the bomb vessels was vindicated. From Aix Roads early in July, Pole could only report total failure. The shells from the bomb vessels fell no closer than a quarter of a mile from the Spanish squadron, while the mortars from French batteries on the islands of Aix and Oléron threatened serious damage to his own ships. Pole accordingly withdrew, sending Berkeley back to England while he kept station off the port [470].

Berkeley had for long been dissatisfied with his situation in the Channel fleet. From off Brest, he had wished to take leave for private reasons [434]. Off Rochefort, he was dissatisfied and in low spirits [463]. From that station he wrote to the Sick and Hurt Board expressing his frustration with the victualling of the Channel fleet. In May 1795 the Sick and Wounded Board had recommended the principle of employing lemon juice as a preventive of scurvy by general issue to all seamen [53]. The Admiralty had adopted that principle.[1] But the shortage of lemon juice at that time had limited the practice of that policy to squadrons on foreign stations. Surgeons in general had been instructed to look out for seamen with incipient symptons of scurvy and to treat them with lemon juice. The men in the Channel fleet had also been served as well as possible with fresh meat and vegetables. Nevertheless, as Berkeley pointed out, ships on blockade duty in that fleet were often far longer at sea than ships on foreign voyages. With lemon juice being used on the Channel station only as a cure once scurvy appeared, the disease still broke out about nine weeks after the termination of adequate supplies of fresh vegetables. Berkeley's letter had effect. The Admiralty demanded a return of the incidence of scurvy in Berkeley's

[1] The failure for four years to include ships on home stations (including the Channel fleet) in the policy of issuing lemon juice generally to crews as a preventive is overlooked by C. Lloyd, 'The introduction of lemon juice as a cure for scurvy', *Bulletin of the History of Medicine* XXXV (1961), 123–32; by Lloyd in his 'Victualling of the fleet in the eighteenth and nineteenth centuries', in *Starving Sailors. The Influence of Nutrition upon Naval and Maritime History* (National Maritime Museum, 1981), 9–15; and by K. J. Carpenter, *The History of Scurvy and Vitamin C* (Cambridge, 1986), 95. However, Lloyd and Coulter in *Medicine and the Navy 1200–1900* (4 vols, Edinburgh, 1957–63), III, 325, note that 1795 'did not see the final conquest of scurvy'.

ships, which revealed, for example, over a hundred cases in the *Renown* [492].[1] Prompted by Berkeley, the Sick and Wounded Board recommended the provision of sourkraut to ships on home stations. More important, realising that supplies of lemon juice in stock now permitted the issue in greater quantities. More widely, the Sick and Wounded Board recommended its supply to all ships on stations in home waters, though in half the proportions supplied for foreign stations [471].

At the end of July, on receiving information of the fleet under Bruix returning north, Pole on his own initiative withdrew his ships of the line from Aix Roads into the Channel [472–4]. Bruix's fleet had managed to inject great alarm and activity into the British naval establishment, but had done little actual harm in the Mediterranean.[2] He had, however, united to his force the Spanish squadrons both from Carthagena [462] and Cadiz [475], with which he now sailed north. After leaving Cadiz on 21 July, when his destination was still unsure, the defence of the English and Irish coastlines from invasion again became vital [476]. Bridport was ordered to rehoist his flag and to prepare the fleet in Torbay to resist attack [477, 478]. It was a test of both flag officers and strategic readiness. Gardner, whose health had begun to suffer, refused to leave the fleet even for a prestigious shore appointment [480, 481, 483, 486, 491, 494]. Meanwhile Bridport reinforced the watch on Brest [479], which on 8 August Bruix re-entered with a fleet of 59 sail including 40 ships of the line: 25 French and 15 Spanish [482]. Together with the vessels already there, intended as the nucleus of a second French fleet [462], his return established in Brest an enemy force of at least 45 ships of the line. In September the Spanish squadron in Aix Roads attempted to join the combined fleet but, on finding Brest then too well guarded, instead re-entered Ferrol.[3]

408. *Gore to Admiralty*

Triton, at sea, 12 February 1799

On the 5th I fell in with a Danish brig which sailed from Brest that morning. I learned from the master that the enemy had 14 sail of the

---

[1]Lloyd and Coulter in *Medicine and the Navy*, III, 325–6, attribute the extension of the general issue of lemon juice to all ships, on home as well as foreign stations, to Gilbert Blane. The influence of Berkeley's letter is not noticed.

[2]See A. N. Ryan, 'In search of Bruix, 1799', in *Français et Anglais en Méditerranée de la Révolution française a l'indépendance de la Grèce (1789–1830)* (Service Historique de la Marine, Paris, 1992), 81–90.

[3]James, II, 303.

line (3 of them three deckers) and 6 frigates lying in Brest water, apparently in good condition but very short of men – that in the arsenal they had 20 sail of ships of all descriptions, all of which were undergoing repairs and a great number of artificers were employed about them and that the general subject of conversation was an intended invasion of Ireland in large force.

409. *Admiralty to Thompson*[1]

26 February 1799

I am commanded by my Lords Commissioners of the Admiralty to signify their direction to you to send the Cambrian or Fisgard to join the frigates cruising off Brest and to send the other to join the Ethalion off of Rochefort, it appearing that the Anson, which was intended for that service, has arrived in a disabled state at Spithead.

It is their Lordships' further direction that you inform the officers commanding the frigates cruising off of Brest that there is reason to believe the enemy intend to send some of their ships or transports close along shore to the southward and direct them to look out for and endeavour to intercept them if possible.

410. *Intelligence report from Sir James Craufurd*

Hamburg, 26 February 1799

Certain accounts have been received from France that the Directory have sent orders to Brest for the equipment of 24 ships of war. The number of ships of the line is not specified.

411. *Legge to Admiralty*

Cambrian, 3 March 1799

Yesterday I observed in Brest Road 15 sail of the line and 7 or 8 frigates and corvettes, 4 of the line of battle ships were apparently ready for sea. In general they appeared to be lying with topmasts struck and the topsail yards fore and aft in the top. Two of them were three deckers, one of which carried a flag at the fore.

---

[1] Addressed to Thompson in Torbay.

412.   *Intelligence report*

3 March 1799

The most positive orders were given that no more privateers were to sail or be fitted out from any port after the 4th instant but that the crews of all those now in port and all others as they arrived were to be immediately sent to the fleet at Brest, which is yet in want of a great many seamen, and it was expected that all privateers now at sea, hearing of such orders, would go into Spanish ports to refit.

413.   *Intelligence report from Mr Boys*[1]

8 March 1799

A fleet of ships of the line is certainly getting ready at Brest, reported to consist of 20 sail of the line and to be destined for Portugal, but generally believed for Ireland. They have been sending stores by land from Dunkirk and other places to Brest for the purpose of fitting out the above force.

414.   *Cunningham to Admiralty*

Clyde, 13 March 1799

On the 11th instant we saw a squadron of the enemy's ships consisting of five frigates and four corvettes and passed very near one of them. Inshore of them we saw a large convoy working into Brest. On the morning of the 12th eight of the enemy's ships were under weigh and one at anchor close to the Toulinquet Passage.

415.   *Intelligence report from George Leuchar*

Frankfort [Frankfurt], 17 March 1799

I left Paris six days ago and embrace the first opportunity of communicating to your Excellency some news which may be of the greatest importance to the safety of the British Government.

I know from a friend of mine who left Brest about three weeks ago that there is a great expedition preparing at that port.

---

[1]From Mr Boys who left France on 2 March.

A Mr. Forfait, Commissaire de Marine, the same man who fitted out Bonaparte's expedition at Toulon is pushing with the greatest vigour.

Three weeks ago there were already 17 sail of the line, 6 frigates and 6 corvettes in the road. 2 three deckers were lying alongside of the wharfs and had taken their guns in and many were in the inner harbour which could not be well observed, with their topmasts and rigging up. They are besides expecting a new three decker from Rochefort (which has already been launched there) at Brest. The fleet will consist, after all the ships are got ready, of 30 sail of the line, among which are be [sic] 4 three deckers, 6 or 7 of eighty guns and all the rest seventy fours.

One of the great reasons why they could not send out their whole fleet last year was owing to an absolute want of cables but they have since grown a considerable quantity in Brittany which they drag daily into Brest by cart loads. They are still badly off for sailors but they have got a great many cannoniers trained for to fight the guns and they began when I left Paris to take away all the sailors from the privateers. They have for some time refused them all lettres de marques. They intend to board the English fleet if they should meet with it, for they are very much flushed with success since the taking of the Ambuscade frigate by the Bayonaise corvette [in December 1798]. The English fleet therefore must try to keep them to leeward as the French will be superior in men. I daresay this fleet is intended for Ireland but a great many well informed men think it destined for the Mediterranean. It would be well therefore to give Lord St. Vincent notice of it.

I hope to God the English fleet will meet them and then their last efforts will be defeated but I repeat that they will be perhaps the strongest fleet the French ever sent to sea this war. I shall be myself in a month's time [in] London and shall be extremely happy to give your Lordship all further information in my power.

His Excellency the Russian Minister at Frankfort will have the goodness to forward this letter in the most expeditious manner.

416. *Legge to Seymour*

Cambrian, at sea, 17 March 1799

On the afternoon of the 14th I stood in, in His Majesty's ship under my command to reconnoitre the enemy in the port of Brest: the ships appear nearly in the same state as when I last reported. Out of eighteen sail of the line four only appeared in a state of forwardness, one of them, which I could distinguish to be the Berwick, appeared ready for sea with all her sails bent, the rest are in a dismantled state without any sails bent. There are now a flag and two broad pendants flying in the harbour, a large three decked ship appears to be fitting in the port.

On the morning of the 14th the Triton, having chased to the southward by signal, captured a French brig called the Victoire from Bordeaux, bound to Brest laden with wine, cordage and pitch; at the same time we fell in with the St. Fiorenzo and Naiad, the latter in chase of a sloop, which she captured.

417.   *Spencer to Bridport*

Admiralty, 19 March 1799

As our accounts from Brest have of late given us reason to suppose that great exertions are making there for an expedition probably destined to Ireland and as it seems most likely that the latter end of this month or the beginning of the next will be the time at which they will be disposed to put to sea, it will be advisable for your Lordship to hoist your flag again in order to be ready to move at a short warning if it should be necessary; on this view of the subject an order has been given for that purpose which you will receive from the Board officially and I write these few lines to say what the grounds are on which this measure is taken and to point out how desirable it will be for your Lordship to be at Spithead again as soon as possible.

418.   *Bridport to Admiralty*

Cricket Lodge, 20 March 1799

I have received your letter of the 18th instant acquainting me that their Lordships approve of my sending the Phaeton and Stag to cruise off Rochefort and also of my sending the Indefatigable to relieve the Mermaid but it was their Lordships' directions that I should keep the Amelia in constant readiness for service until they shall have received some further information relative to the enemy's preparations for putting to sea from Brest; she will therefore remain at the port of Plymouth accordingly.

You will please to acquaint their Lordships that I have sent orders to the respective captains of the Phaeton and Stag and Indefatigable agreeably to their approbation and the Anson will remain at Spithead as directed in your letter of yesterday's date which I have just received; and agreeably thereto I shall repair to Spithead to hoist my flag on board the Royal George, and I intend being there before the end of this month unless their Lordships shall judge the King's service shall allow me to be absent a week longer from my duty.

[*Endorsed 22 March that their Lordships are desirous he should repair to Spithead to resume the duties of his command as soon as he conveniently can.*[1]]

419.   *Bridport to captains of cruisers*

Royal George, Spithead, 29 March 1799

In the event of your making captures and having many prisoners on board which may make it necessary for your returning to Cawsand Bay to land them you are immediately to apply to Sir Richard King, the Port Admiral, by letter for permission to send them on shore; and in case they cannot be received at Plymouth you are to proceed immediately to Spithead for that purpose and lose no time in removing them out of your ship. Having so done you are to return to Cawsand Bay if necessary to recruit your water and provisions and then return to your former station.

420.   *Seymour to Admiralty*

Sans Pareil, at sea, [14?] April 1799

I beg you will acquaint the Lords Commissioners of the Admiralty that I had the honour to receive their Lordships' order of the 10th by the Constitution cutter which joined me on the 13th instant, in compliance with which I have placed the ships named in the margin [*Mars, Dragon, Caesar, Impetueux, Ajax, Magnificent, Cambrian, Childers* brig, *Lady Duncan* lugger, *Lurcher* cutter] under the command of the Honourable Rear Admiral Berkeley and have given him the order of which the enclosed is a copy, together with copies of all the papers in my possession containing any intelligence respecting the enemy.

. . . I had placed the Lurcher cutter under Admiral Berkeley's orders but another cutter having joined the squadron before they separated I judged it expedient that she should accompany me into port.

[*Enclosure*]

[1]He arrived there on 28 March.

420a.   *Seymour to Berkeley*

13 April 1799

You are hereby required and directed to take under your orders the ships named in the margin and with them diligently to cruise off the port of Brest, keeping as close to the said port as circumstances will permit and using your best endeavours to prevent any small squadron from putting to sea from thence or to take and destroy them should they attempt to do so.

421.   *Berkeley to Admiralty*

Mars, at sea, 16 April 1799

Lat. 48.57N. Long. 6.06W. Ushant S. by E. distance 15 leagues.
Wind S.W.

As the Joseph cutter received considerable damage in the late gales I send her to Plymouth to repair it and take that opportunity of informing their Lordships of the situation of this squadron.

Vice Admiral Lord Hugh Seymour left me the 14th instant the morning with the ships named in the margin [*Mars, Dragon, Caesar, Impetueux, Ajax, Magnificent*[1]] to follow their Lordships' orders, which I received the 13th and he will probably have pointed out the state in which the Cambrian's masts, etc. are at present, a state which renders her very unfit for the service she is employed upon, especially as she is the only frigate now left to reconnoitre Brest water and from the last intelligence conveyed by Captain Gore of the Triton their Lordships will see that the enemy have anchored a superior force in Bertheaume road to frustrate any such intention. I shall, however, when the weather permits reinforce Captain Legge with a line of battle ship but I trust that the representations already made by Lord Hugh will induce them to order out some other frigates immediately to take the service upon them.

It has blown so very hard from the eastward that from the time I parted with Lord Hugh I have been able to make very little progress towards my station but as the wind has backed to the northward and westward I shall resume it today. Having therefore no fresh intelligence to communicate I must very reluctantly represent to their Lordships the

[1]This list seems to be an error. Seymour later writes to the Admiralty and to Bridport of his arrival in Cawsand Bay with *Sans Pareil, Formidable, Saturn, Atlas, Canada* and *Triumph.*

present condition of the Mars, whose crew as well as the ship itself may suffer very much by a longer continuance at sea. It is now near five months since her orders came to be held in instant readiness for sea and in that state of expectation she has waited in Cawsand Bay during the period abovementioned and of course did not shift any of the running rigging or employ the artificers from the dockyard to remedy her defects. The consequence is that she has not a single part of her running rope but what is as rotten as touch paper, nor is any part of the standing rigging much better except the lower shrouds. Her sails were blown to rags the first gale of wind we experienced and those which we bent in lieu have been split in the last and obliged to be repaired before we could make sail. The decks and sides are so leaky that the men are constantly wet and the effect of their bedding being in that state has begun to show itself by symptoms of fever and other complaints arising from damps and cold and the leaks in the after part of the ship have damaged some of the bread and other stores. I think it therefore my duty to add the above particulars to those which have caused her already to be reported in real want of refitting and docking.

P.S. The wind is now come to the S.W, and I am standing in for Ushant.

422. *Bridport to Admiralty*

Royal George, at sea, 16 April 1799

Ushant S.E. by E. 6 or 7 miles.

I acquaint you for the information of the Lords Commissioners of the Admiralty that I sailed from St. Helens on the morning of the 13th instant and yesterday afternoon arrived on my station, and at 5 p.m. Ushant bore E.S.E. 2 or 3 miles. This morning the Lady Duncan lugger and His Majesty's sloop Childers joined me, when I was informed that Vice Admiral Lord Hugh Seymour had left Rear Admiral Berkeley on the 14th but I have not fallen in with either squadron, neither have I had an opportunity of sending any ships to reconnoitre the enemy's force at Brest but I conclude that Lord Hugh Seymour will have communicated to their Lordships the observations made of that port to the time of his leaving the command with Rear Admiral Berkeley.

The first eight ships named in the margin [*Royal George, Prince, St. George, Neptune, Glory, Achilles, Pompee, Anson*] are now with me and the last seven [*Mars, Atlas, Dragon, Caesar, Magnificent, Impetueux, Ajax*] I suppose are with Rear Admiral Berkeley.

423. *Neale to Bridport*

St Fiorenzo, at sea, 16 April 1799

I have the honour to inform your Lordship that on the 9th instant, after reconnoitring two French frigates at anchor in the port of L'Orient, I stood towards Belle Isle. On our approach I saw some ships at anchor in the Great Road but as the weather was hazy and the ships under the land I could not sufficiently ascertain their strength until we had run the full length of the island, when I clearly distinguished them to be three French frigates and a large sailing gun vessel with their topsail yards ready hoisted to come out to us. At this instant a heavy and sudden squall from the N.W. carried away the Amelia's main topmast and her fore and mizen topgallant masts, the fall of the former tearing a great part of the mainsail from the yard.

The enemy, who were apparently waiting our near approach, got under weigh immediately and made sail towards us in line ahead.

Circumstanced as we now were, I felt we had but one duty to perform and that we could do nothing more than testify our readiness to meet them. I therefore made the signal to prepare for battle and when they had advanced a little to leeward of us I shortened sail so as for the Amelia to keep under command with her fore and mizen topsails only and made the signal to bear up, preserving the weather gage and fighting in close order. The enemy tacked to meet us and we instantly commenced an action, receiving the fire from one of the batteries on the island at the same time. The enemy were so little disposed to close quarters we were under the necessity of bearing down upon them three times until they were close upon the islands of Houat and Hedic [Hoedic]. After engaging them one hour and fifty-five minutes they hove ship and stood from us. I am extremely sorry we had it not in our power to do anything more with the enemy (who had a port close on each side of them) than compel them to relinquish an action which from their superiority and the crippled state of the Amelia previous to the action had inspired them with the hope of success. Soon after the action ceased they bore up for the Loire, two of them apparently much shattered and the gun vessel returned to Belle Isle.

424. *Intelligence report from W. Grenville*

Berlin, 18 April 1799

I am apprized by Count Kaugnitz that he is informed here by un-doubted authority from Paris that the expedition preparing at the port of

Brest was originally destined for Ireland but in case that expedition should appear to be too hazardous it is intended to be applied to an attack upon Portugal.

425. *Seymour to Bridport*

Sans Pareil, Cawsand Bay, 18 April 1799

I have the honour to inform your Lordship that I arrived at this anchorage on the 16th instant with the ships named in the margin [*Sans Pareil, Formidable, Saturn, Atlas, Canada, Triumph*] and that they are completing their provisions and stores with all the expedition the weather will admit of. Their defects, which I am happy to say do not appear to me to be very considerable, have been reported to the dockyard and will be made good without delay on the part of the officers afloat.

426. *Seymour to Bridport*

Sans Pareil, Cawsand Bay, 18 April 1799

My public letter will inform your Lordship of my having reached this anchorage on Tuesday last with the squadron under my orders, when I was rather surprised at learning that you was at sea as the Admiralty orders which directed me to leave a small squadron with Admiral Berkeley had led me to believe that the principal part of the Channel fleet was detained at Spithead. The weather since my arrival has been so very bad as to have prevented my seeing those officers from whom I might obtain exact information respecting the state of your ships at this port but I will accompany this letter by the best account that I can receive of them previous to closing it. The San Fiorenzo and Amelia yesterday anchored in Plymouth Sound having been forced there by damages which they received in action with three French frigates off Belleisle. The weather prevented Sir Harry Neale from communicating to me the circumstances of the action which he appears to have ended with success but he sent a copy of his official letter to your Lordship to the Admiralty and the original will now reach you by Captain Crawford,[1] the Childers being ready for sea and intended to sail this afternoon. I have stopped the Lady Jane cutter until Saturday morning, when she will convey to your Lordship any letters which may then have reached

---

[1]James Coutts Crawford (d. 1828). Lieutenant 1783; Commander February 1799; Captain 1802.

this place and I will endeavour to send some vessel to the fleet every three days, directing the masters to call at Falmouth in case of their being able to do so without the loss of much time as I am uncertain whether your correspondence with Government passes entirely through this place and I know how much you must wish it to be regularly kept up at this time. The papers, as well as the world in general, having given me the command at the Leeward Islands, I am led to regret that I had not the pleasure of seeing you before I quitted the station off Brest, that in the case of that report being realized, which I expect it will, I might have received any commands which your Lordship may have to execute in that part of the world and to have expressed on taking my leave of you the very great satisfaction which I have always had in being employed under your command. I beg you will now accept my best thanks for the attention which I have received from you during that period and with them the assurance of my ever remaining your Lordship's very faithful friend and servant.

427.   *Bridport to Admiralty*

Royal George, at sea, 21 April 1799

In my letter of the 16th instant I acquainted you for their Lordships' information with my arrival on my station and on the 17th at 9 a.m. I was joined by Rear Admiral Berkeley with the ships named in the margin [*Mars, Caesar, Dragon, Impetueux, Magnificent, Ajax*], in the afternoon of that day by His Majesty's ship Naiad from Plymouth and on the 19th instant by His Majesty's ships Cambrian and Terrible, but the weather has been so extremely tempestuous that I have not yet been able to have any communication with the Rear Admiral.

I am also to acquaint you that the ships of the squadron do not appear to have received any material damage except the Neptune, that ship having carried away her fore and both topsail yards on the 17th instant in a heavy squall of wind.

I am also to inform you that I have received your letter of the 13th instant by the Naiad directing me to employ the Nymphe on the service of watching the enemy's fleet in the port of Brest, which station I have allotted for her. I have expected her to join me for some days past.

428. *Bridport to Admiralty*

Royal George, at sea, 22 April 1799

Herewith you will receive a copy of a letter from the Honourable Captain Legge of His Majesty's ship Cambrian stating the defects of that ship. Under these circumstances and there being so many ships belonging to the squadron at Plymouth, I have judged it for His Majesty's service to order Captain Legge to proceed to Spithead (where there is a sheer hulk) for the speedier purpose of refitting his ship and then to rejoin me without loss of time.

429. *Bridport to Admiralty*

Royal George, at sea, 22 April 1799

I acquaint you that His Majesty's ship Superb from Spithead and the Fowey and Lady Jane cutters from Plymouth joined the squadron in the evening of the 21st inst. and the following morning I received your three letters of the 12th and two of the 13th instant together with a copy of the report made by Captain Gore of the enemy's force at Brest the 6th.

. . . P.S. I shall immediately give orders to the Anson and Naiad with the Fowey cutter to take the St. Fiorenzo and Amelia's station off the Penmarcks.

430. *Bridport to Durham*

Royal George, at sea, 22 April 1799

You are hereby required and directed to proceed with His Majesty's ship under your command[1] and the ship and vessel named in the margin [*Naiad, Fowey*] and cruise off the Penmarcks and between that land and Port L'Orient for the purpose of intercepting any convoys that may pass or repass from Rochefort and Bordeaux to Brest or from thence to the same ports, taking care not to go to the southward of Belleisle except in chase but strictly to keep on the above station, communicating to me from time to time such information as you may be able to obtain from any vessel you may meet with and in case you should fall in with the enemy at sea you are to order the Naiad or Fowey to join me with all

[1]The *Anson* (44).

possible dispatch and to endeavour by every means in your power to keep sight of them until you shall ascertain as well as circumstances will permit to what coast they appear destined, when you are to lose no time in acquainting me therewith on my station off Brest and not finding the squadron there you are to proceed to the nearest port, acquainting the Secretary of the Admiralty with your arrival and transmitting such information as you may have to communicate for their Lordships' information.

You are to continue on the above station and service until you shall receive further orders or are called in by signal and to take such other ships and vessels under your command as may be sent to you during your continuance on the above station.

431. *Admiralty to Bridport*

26 April 1799

I am commanded by my Lords Commissioners of the Admiralty to acquaint you that the Russel was to leave Cork on the 22nd to join your Lordship on your rendezvous; that the Ramillies (which is ready for sea) has been ordered to join you from Cawsand Bay, that the Robust will sail from Plymouth, and the Renown and Venerable from Spithead for the same purpose; and to signify their direction to you to keep with you as many ships as the preparations of the enemy may require, sending the rest to complete their stores and provisions, with orders to rejoin you as expeditiously as possible, and on their rejoining you are to send in others with similar orders so that by relieving the ships as frequently as circumstances will admit the fleet may be kept as complete as possible in their stores and provisions.

Your Lordship is likewise to order the captains going into port, whose ships will be in course of pay to have their books ready to send to the Navy Board the moment they arrive, that their ships may not be delayed on that account, and when you send the Mars to Plymouth your Lordships will order her to be docked.

432. *Admiralty to Bridport*

26 April 1799

I am further to acquaint your Lordship that the Aimable will be ordered to join you immediately and that their Lordships will send you as many frigates as other necessary services will admit, which you will employ in watching the enemy's ships in Brest, particularly directing their commanders to be careful that it does not escape unperceived to the southward for though the absolute necessity of protecting the coast of Ireland must make that the first object of your attention if the enemy should be able to put to sea without being seen by your cruisers, yet there is very great reason to believe that the expedition fitting out at Brest is intended against Portugal, the success of which undertaking it is most essentially necessary to prevent.

433.   *Bridport to Admiralty*

Royal George, at sea near Ushant, 26 April 1799

Herewith you will receive a copy of the report made to me of the enemy's forces at Brest the 24th instant by Captain Sir James Saumarez[1] of His Majesty's ship Caesar, together with the observations of the Master of that ship. The wind being to the eastward I ordered the Caesar, Dragon, Superb and Terrible to reconnoitre the enemy fleet the following morning and stood close to the Black Rocks with the rest of the squadron and herewith you will also receive a copy of the report made to me by Captain Campbell, which with the above from Sir James Saumarez are transmitted for their Lordships' information.

They will perceive by the above reports that it is necessary this squadron should be reinforced by some of the ships under my command either from Plymouth or Portsmouth and they may probably judge it expedient to order Admiral Sir Alan Gardner to join me without loss of time. I also acquaint you for their Lordships' information that from the reports made to me and my own observations I am of opinion the enemy fleet will put to sea and should they do it unobserved I shall lose no time in proceeding with the whole of my present force off of Cape Clear or other parts of the coast of Ireland as intelligence may direct me. But if only part of the Brest fleet should quit their anchorage, in that case I shall leave such a force as circumstances may make necessary under one of the Rear Admirals off of Brest and proceed myself with the rest of the squadron in quest of the enemy.

[*Enclosures*]

---

[1]James Saumarez, Baron de Saumarez (1757–1836). Lieutenant 1778; Captain 1782; Rear-admiral 1801; Vice-admiral 1807; Admiral 1814. Defeated the French at Algeciras in 1801. Commander-in-Chief in the Baltic 1808–12. Created a peer in 1831.

433a.   *Report of Captain Sir James Saumarez of His Majesty's ship*
Caesar of the state of the French fleet at Brest the 24th April 1799

7 sail of the line at anchor in Camaret Bay.
5 sail of the line under sail and coming to, outside of Brest road.
7 sail of the line in the road besides frigates.
The whole apparently getting under sail.
Total 19.

433b.   *Observations made by the Master of the Caesar on the*
enemy's force at Brest the 24th April 1799

At 5 St. Matthew Point N.E. by compass.
Point du Raz south.
Ships in Brest road E. by N. to N.
8 sail of the line in Camaret Bay.
4 sail of the line under weigh.
6 sail of the line in the inner road, two of which are 3 deckers, and
some frigates.
Total 18.

433c.   *Report of the enemy's ships at Brest reconnoitred by Captain*
George Campbell of His Majesty's ship Dragon the 25th April 1799

At an anchor in the outer road 19 sail, two of which are three decked
ships, 12 are two decked ships and 5 are frigates or sloops.
   Two sail under weigh from the inner road, one of which is a two
decked ship.
   Seven sail under weigh, three of which are two decked, one a frigate
and three are sloops.
   Six sail in the outer road, size not known.
   Of the ships at an anchor in the outer road, one of the three decked
ships has a flag at the mizen, the other a broad pendant and one of the
two decked ships a broad pendant.

434.   *Bridport to Spencer*

Royal George, at sea very near Ushant, 26 April 1799

Your Lordship has been informed that Rear Admiral Berkeley wishes
for private considerations to be allowed to return into port when the

Mars is ordered to be docked and refitted. I have also been told that the Rear Admiral is intended for another service. Should this be the case and another rear admiral should be sent to me to replace him in this squadron under my command I request to know if Rear Admiral Sir Richard Bickerton stands upon your Lordship's list for employment. If that should be so I beg to inform your Lordship that I have a good opinion of the abilities and zeal of Sir Richard Bickerton and that I shall be much pleased to see his flag flying under my orders if your Lordship has not allotted another service for him.

It also appears probable that a vice admiral might be appointed to compose the flag staff under me to replace Lord Hugh Seymour, who, I understand, is going, if not already gone, to a foreign command.

I have never presumed to ask your Lordship for the appointment of a particular flag officer since I had the honour to command the Channel fleet,[1] neither do I solicit this mark of attention now but only state to your Lordship such flag officers as would be perfectly acceptable to me and if a vice admiral shall be appointed to serve with me in the Channel fleet I should be glad to see Vice Admiral Linzee's[2] flag as third in command, having been informed that he was offered to hoist his flag in the North Sea squadron which manifests that your Lordship had received a favourable opinion of his services.

This letter was written before I received intelligence that the Brest fleet had put to sea and I send it without alteration.

[*Endorsed as received on 10 May and answered the same day*]

435.   *Lord Bridport's Journal*[3]

Friday 26th. Winds N. Ushant E.1/2 S. Distance 4 Leagues.

P.M. Fresh breezes and cloudy weather, made the signal and tacked, at six parted company His Majesty's Ship Nymphe. Ditto weather. Made the signal and tacked. 6.30 made the look out ships (Superb and Dragon) signals to keep their stations. 8.0 Ushant E. by N. 3 Leagues. A.M. moderate and cloudy with rain 4.30 wore ship – at 6.0 made the Cambrian's signal to examine strange sail N.W. At 9.0 the Mars made

---

[1]But see his correspondence of 19–20 December 1796 about the appointment of Rear-admiral Pole, documents 156, 157.

[2]Robert Linzee (d. 1804). Lieutenant 1761; Captain 1770; Rear-admiral 1794; Vice-admiral 1795; Admiral 1801. A brother-in-law of Samuel, Lord Hood.

[3]This extract runs from noon on 25 April to noon on 27 April.

the signal for land. East. 9.30 Made the signal and wore. Ushant Light House E. by S. 1/2 South 5 or 6 Miles. Joined company His Majesty's Ship Russel.

Saturday 27th. Winds N. by W., N. by E., E.N.E. Outer Rocks of the Saints S. by E. 1/2 E., distance 7 miles.

P.M. Fresh breezes and hazy weather. 12.50 made the Childers signal to examine a strange sail, E. by N. At 1.8 the Dragon repeated the Nymphe's signal for the enemy in sight and on the starboard tack. At 1.15 made the Superb and Dragon's signals to denote the number of the line etc. At 1.20 the Superb made the signal of inability to comply with the preceding signal. At 1.26 made the general signal to alter course together to S.W. At 1.30 bore up. At 1.44 made the Dragon and Superb's signals to reconnoitre the enemy. Not answered by the latter. At 2.10 made the general signal to alter course together to S.E. At 12.15 [sic] made the general signal to prepare for battle. Foggy weather. 2.5 the Impetueux made the signal ships seen are of the line. At 2.56 made the general signal for the fleet to chace and made sail. At 3 the Impetueux made the signals ships seen are of the line and 11 in number. At 3.19 the Superb repeated the Nymphe's signal of annul. At 3.22 made the general signal to leave off chace and shortened sail. 3.23 made the Nymphe's signal to pass within hale. Hauled to the wind on the starboard tack. At 3.29 the Prince made the signal for having occasion to lye by. Hove to. At 4.18 the Prince made the signal for being ready to make sail, etc. Filled at 4.30. Made the general signal to tack, missed stays, and wore. At 4.55 made the Nymphe's signal for a lieutenant. Made and shortened sail as necessary. Parted company His Majesty's Ship Nymphe. At 8 Ushant N.N.E. ½ E. dist. 5 leagues. Light airs and cloudy weather. A.M. Ditto weather. At 4.30 sprung up a light breeze. At 5.10 the Nymphe made the signal for ships seen are at anchor, with the annulling flag. At 7.20 bore up the entrance of Brest East, Black Rocks N.E. by E. distant 7 Miles. Light airs and hazy weather. 9.15 sounded 48 fathoms. Made sail. Parted company His Majesty's Sloop Childers with dispatches for Earl St. Vincent and the Dolly cutter for Plymouth.

436. *Fraser to Pole*

La Nymphe, 26 April 1799

I suppose from the Admiral's signal to speak the Nymphe you are at a loss to understand what all the signals that have been made today meant and as it is possible the officer who will answer it may not feel quite competent to the explanation I send him armed with these few lines. According to the Admiral's wishes I stood into Brest Bay last night after dark and, bringing Ushant light to the westward of me, I brought to with the ebb with my head to the westward. It came on so thick at 11 that I lost sight of both St. Matthews and Ushant Light. At 5 I wore and stood in to the Black Rocks but it was so thick I could not see anything. At half past 8, it appearing to promise better weather, I again stood in, and at 9, when I had just gained the length of the Black Rocks, I discovered through the haze (to appearance) the body of the French fleet under weigh, that is to say, I counted eleven sail, in two divisions or lines, standing out with a large frigate far advanced ahead of them. The rest of the fleet were partly at an anchor and some appeared to have their sails loose. I tacked in the wake ahead of the lee division and the frigate gained upon me a good deal and set her topgallant sails for a moment. About ½ past I discovered the two ships, the Superb and Dragon, and as it was extremely hazy I thought the fewer flags likely to be the best understood. I made the signal for the enemy on the starboard tack and afterwards their bearing. I kept sight of the enemy till half past 12 when the fog was so thick I lost them. At 1 (or before) I wore but could not again see them. I suppose they put about and stood in again to their anchorage as the headmost frigate wore at ½ past twelve. When the fog cleared up the Dragon made my signal, that the preceding one was not distinct, which I made early in the forenoon. I then repeated it and of course stood in to make the anchorage if possible before dark to observe the motions of the enemy but upon the Dragon's repeating my signal the Admiral made the signal for a general chase, as if the enemy was that moment in sight, and observing several of the ships of the line making a great deal of sail and fearing the consequences I made the signal of annul and which signal, I conclude, has made the Admiral suppose that I had not seen anything but there is no signal in the book that I could make to indicate that I had lost sight of the enemy and I did not think proper to make the signal for the enemy being again at anchor until I was certain they were so, though it appeared to me that they had returned again as I ran down and must have crossed within sight of them had they run to the southward.

437.   *Lieutenant James Nicolson*[1] *to Bridport*

H.M. Lugger Black Joke, at sea, 28 April 1799

I have the honour to inform your Lordship that yesterday at 8 p.m., Ushant bearing E.N.E. distant six leagues, I fell in with and captured La Rebecca (a French National armed schooner mounting eight swivel guns with small arms) from Brest bound for Ireland, having on board a National officer charged with despatches which I have the satisfaction to inform your Lordship have fallen into my hands and which I have the honour to send herewith.

[*Enclosure*][2]

437a.   *Secret instructions for Citizen Le Breton, commanding the Aviso Rebecca, signed E. Bruix*

16th Germinal,[3] 7th year of the Republic

The Citizen Le Breton commanding the Aviso, the Rebecca, will weigh from the Road of Brest as soon as the wind will permit.

He will take the greatest precautions to avoid the sight of the English ships cruising on the coast and when he learns by the signal the position of the enemy he will pass by the Passage du Raz, through the Four or L'Iroise.

When he hath run about 30 leagues W.N.W. he will direct his course in such a manner as to make the N.W. of Ireland from 12 to fifteen leagues from the west coast in order to avoid the stations which the enemy keep from Cape Clear to the Isles of Durseys. He will then run to the north to gain the latitude of the Isle of Mullet which he will approach, taking care to keep at a distance if he should perceive any ships of war of the enemy, if not he will approach within sight of the houses on the coast with the English flag at his masthead, taking care to brail up the lee part of his topsail every quarter of an hour.

Then without doubt the fishing boats will present themselves on board and if not he will run along the coast repeating the signal at each principal point and manoeuvring as above directed.

---

[1]James Nicholson (fl. 1791–1805). Lieutenant 1795; [Commander ?1805].
[2]The three separate documents emanating from the *Rebecca* that are printed here (see also 450 and 451) are in Bridport's private papers. It is not clear who translated them.
[3]The 16th Germinal was 5 April.

If he should find amongst the fishermen who accost him one who gives him the first word <u>Convenu</u> he will conduct him to the place where the correspondent should be and he will ask from him the second word in order to assure himself that this is the true individual in whom he ought to place confidence. As soon as he hath obtained this certainty he will give the dispatches with which he is charged. He will explain by word of mouth to this correspondent the details of the fleet and its situation in troops and ammunition. He will receive equally from him token of the disposition of the minds of the people in the different counties and cities, and particularly of Dublin. He will inform himself whether the two letters of marque sent in Ventose from the port of Brest and that from Dunkirk have delivered their packets and what steps have been taken after the instructions given.

The return of Citizen Le Breton being very urgent, he will not stay in Ireland longer than absolutely necessary for this communication. He will take the answer of the correspondent as well as the signal agreed on and he will give and receive their watch words, <u>Mots d'Ordre</u>.

If the correspondent thinks it necessary to send to Brest one of his own people for the continuance of the common disposition, the Citizen Le Breton will receive him on board.

It is useless to recommend to him, <u>Citizen Le Breton</u>, to testify to the Irish to whom he will address himself the fraternal regard which the republicans and all the country owe to them reciprocally.

The Citizen Le Breton will return as fast as possible to Brest and if he finds the enemy near the coast of this port he will enter at L'Orient and repair immediately to Brest to deliver his despatches to the commander of the fleet.

During his passage he shall avoid with the greatest care every sail seen and if unfortunately he should be joined by a ship of war he is expressly recommended to throw into the sea these instructions, the despatches annexed and the signal of reconnaissance and those of convention [sic]:

The Minister depends on the zeal, activity and prudence of Citizen Le Breton and he is persuaded that he will execute his mission to the satisfaction of the Government at Brest.

438.   *List of captures*

A list of captures and recaptures brought to Plymouth between the 1st March and 30th April 1799.

No.	Name		C Captured R Recaptured	When	By what ship
1.	L'Heureux Hazard	Priv.	C	5th March	Naiad
2.	Indefatigable	Priv.	C	6th March	Ethalion
3.	Aurora		R	8th March	Fisgard
4.	Le St. Joseph		C	9th March	Clyde
5.	Le Debut		C	21st March	Sylph
6.	Fanny		R	22nd March	Atalante
7.	Golondrina		C	23rd March	Mermaid & Sylph
8.	Le Resolue	Priv.	C	31st March	Spitfire
9.	L'Argus	Priv.	C	3rd April	La Pomone
10.	Bellona		C	6th April	Phaeton
11.	Nymph		R	11th April	Phaeton
12.	L'Entrependut		C	13th April	St. Fiorenzo
13.	Le Decidé		C	13th April	St. Fiorenzo

439.   *Commissioner Fanshawe to Spencer*

Plymouth Yard, 30 April 1799

Although it is probable that your Lordship's being at Bath is generally known and that intelligence of material events will be immediately conveyed to you thither by persons whose situations enable them to give you more circumstantial information I will beg leave to send you with my daily official return intelligence which I have today learnt of the Dolly cutter having last night arrived at this port from Admiral Lord Bridport to announce the sailing of the Brest fleet and of his Lordship's being in pursuit of it on Friday evening – another cutter, the Fowey, is since arrived and it is reported to me that she brings intelligence of the French fleet having returned into port.

440.   *Admiralty to Bridport*

1 May 1799

I received this morning by express from Plymouth and immediately communicated to my Lords Commssioners of the Admiralty your Lordship's two letters of the 26th and 27th of last month, the former (in duplicate) containing the report which had been made to you of the state of the enemy's fleet at Brest, the latter inclosing the copy of a letter from Captain Fraser of the Nymphe giving an account of its having put to sea and acquainting us for their Lordships' information that upon satisfying yourself of the authenticity of that intelligence you were proceeding with the squadron under your command off Cape Clear in quest of the enemy.

It is much to be lamented that Captain Fraser had not been able to keep sight of the enemy's squadron and to have given your Lordship more satisfactory information by which you might have been enabled to fall in with it before it had reached any considerable distance from Brest, or to have followed it to the point of its actual destination. Under the present state of uncertainty however, their Lordships cannot but approve of the decision you have pursued of proceeding in the first instance off Cape Clear, where your Lordship will continue until you shall have gained some further account of the enemy and where you will be joined by the Polyphemus from Cork.

By letters received from Portsmouth, it appears that the Venerable had sailed from thence on the 26th and the Renown on the following day to join your Lordship on your rendezvous of Brest, and by letters received from Vice Admiral Kingsmill it is probable that the Russel would sail from Cork for the same purpose on the 22nd, in which case it is hoped that she will have joined you before you had left your rendezvous.

Although there is reason to believe that Vice Admiral Sir Thomas Pasley, on receiving the intelligence from your Lordship by the cutter, will have hastened to sea the Ramillies and Robust (which ships have been some days under orders to join you) yet to insure their immediate departure from Plymouth, their Lordships have sent orders by express for that purpose: they will in the first instance [repair] off Cape Clear, as will the three frigates named in the margin [*Beaulieu, Aimable, Mermaid*] which have been ordered to sail from Spithead, so that in the event of your finding it proper to quit your station off Cape Clear, your Lordship will in such case leave some one of your cruizers with such orders as you may deem necessary for the commanders of these ships.

It may also be proper to mention to your Lordship that Sir Thomas Pasley has been directed to send two cutters or luggers off Brest with orders to any one of your ships on that station to follow you off Cape Clear, and that Admiral Sir Alan Gardner has been ordered to proceed with the Royal Sovereign and Repulse to Cawsand Bay, to hold the said ships and any others that he may find there in readiness to put to sea the moment any intelligence shall be received that can enable their Lordships to dispose of those ships to any purpose of advantage.

441.   *Intelligence report from Captain Lane*[1]

3 May 1799

A person whom I despatched to Morlaix was privately informed by an American gentleman who had just returned from Brest that the French fleet sailed from that place on the 25th ultimo consisting of 25 sail of the line and 8 frigates, part of which joined a few days before from L'Orient and Rochefort and that its destination was generally understood to be for Cadiz, as no troops were on board but a great many supernumerary naval officers who, it was supposed, were intended to act on board the Spanish men of war.

442.   *Pitt to Windham*[2]

Downing Street, 4 May 1799

In consequence of the intelligence yesterday confirming the probability that the French may be gone southward, five ships of the line have been ordered to proceed immediately from Cawsand Bay to join Lord St. Vincent. Six or seven will be in readiness at a minute's warning either for the same destination or any other which fresh intelligence may point out.

With the force at our disposal it seems to be thought better not to send any provisional instructions to Lord Bridport, especially as I find the opinion at the Admiralty is that he is not likely to receive <u>certain</u> accounts from the southward so soon as we are; and the bare knowledge of their having at first steered that way would not be sufficient to justify his leaving Ireland and the Channel open. Every precaution has been taken to put Lord St. Vincent and all our squadrons in the Mediterranean on their guard and to apprize them of the reinforcements sent and of that in readiness.

---

[1]Charles Henry Lane (d. 1807). Lieutenant 1777; Captain 1790.
[2]William Windham (1750–1810). Politician; Secretary for War, 1794–1801.

443. *Admiralty to Bridport*

4 May 1799

I have received and communicated to my Lords Commissioners of the Admiralty your Lordship's letter of the 28th of last month by the Fisgard inclosing the duplicate letter therein referred to, and acquainting me for their Lordships' information of your intention upon reaching Cape Clear with the squadron under your command to continue upon that station until you should receive their Lordships' further directions, having left the Lady Jane cutter upon your late rendezvous off Ushant for the purpose of apprizing such ships as may be sent to join you there to repair forthwith off the abovementioned Cape; and I am commanded by their Lordships to acquaint you that they approve therof.

444. *Fanshawe to Spencer*

Plymouth Yard, 5 May 1799

With the official return transmitted this day to your Lordship I beg leave also to communicate the purport of a letter which I received late last evening from Falmouth, where an American vessel had arrived on the 3rd instant whose master reports having met Lord Bridport's fleet and been boarded from the Caesar the preceding Wednesday [1 May] at noon in latitude 49-2, longitude 9-30.

Since the arrival this morning of Admiral Gardner I have seen another large ship, said to be the Captain, coming from the eastward.

445. *Intelligence report from D'Auvergne*

Substance of communication received from Brest the 6th May 1799.

Brest 16th April. A convoy of thirty sail under the protection of the cabane, the Richmond, came into the road from Nantes, L'Orient and the other ports on the western coast, principally loaded with provisions which were, as well as the men that navigated it, immediately distributed among the ships in the road that were prepared for sea with redoubled activity.

17th April. The ship La Convention of 74 guns was got out of dock and ordered to be fitted with every expedition.

18th to 23rd. Strict search was made everywhere for all seamen and every able man met in the streets, whether seafaring or not, for the service of the Republic was taken up and embarked by force and only one boat from each ship allowed to come for orders and every person else closely kept on board.

22nd. The ship Convention was complete all but with cables and ready to go in the road.

25th. The ship Convention hauled into the road during the last night.

This morning 15 ships of the line by signal sailed from the road and anchored without accident at Bertheaume.

This morning at 8 o'clock the Minister Bruix, preceded by the music of the garrison, was conducted in grand cortege, all the garrison being under arms, from his house to the boat waiting at the slip. He was followed by all the general officers and as soon as the boat passed the boom the forts saluted with 23 guns, as did the ship, the Ocean. When he arrived on board the signal was immediately made and the whole fleet put to sail and joined the other divisions already at Bertheaume.

Citizen Bruix's baggage being embarked in the Creole frigate, it is conjectured he will leave the Ocean when at sea and go on board the frigate, which is esteemed the fastest sailer in the fleet.

April 27th. This morning at 6 o'clock the ship Convention is preparing to join the fleet.

At 9 a.m. the whole fleet is under sail and proceeding to sea from Bertheaume. It is composed as follows:

26 sail of the line of battle as by list transmitted the 15th. The ship Convention replacing the Wattigny that struck on a rock when going to Bertheaume. 8 large frigates and 5 corvettes.

The ships are all full of men prepared for the service but in very small proportion seamen.

150 soldiers, and no more, are embarked on board each line of battle ship. They consist of the Belgic conscription of 3,500 men, recruits who scarce have ever seen arms. The surplus are Cannoniers de la Marine.

The last convoy arrived completed the provisions of the fleet to five months of the most necessary articles and they have water for the same time at short rations.

There remains at Brest the 4 ships reported to be in the harbour by the return of the 15th and the Wattigny who has joined them with the Precieuse frigate at the boom. The crews of the above have all been taken away in the fleet.

446. *Admiralty to Bridport*

7 May 1799

I have the honour of enclosing to your Lordship an extract from one of the Paris papers received this day by which it appears that the enemy's fleet which lately sailed from Brest consisted of 25 ships of the line besides frigates and sloops. In consequence of this and other intelligence to the same effect which leaves their Lordships in no doubt as to the extent of the enemy's force they have thought proper to order Sir Alan Gardner in the Royal Sovereign, now in Cawsand Bay, to proceed with that ship and the Atlas without a moment's loss of time and endeavour to fall in with your Lordship off of Cape Clear or wherever else he may learn you may be, upon the junction of which ships, and those which have sailed from the different ports to join you, the force then with your Lordship will consist of no less than 23 ships of the line and in the event of your meeting the enemy, though superior in numbers, their Lordships have the fullest confidence that you will give a very satisfactory account of them.

Their Lordships have directed me to suggest to you the propriety of your keeping some of your frigates cruising to the westward to discover the enemy's fleet if it should be destined for Ireland and that you should keep to the westward in order to get unperceived to the northern coast of that kingdom and to signify their direction to you to take the Polyphemus and whatever frigates you may happen to find off Cape Clear under your command but not to detach any of them from the Irish station, excepting on urgent service and when those already under your immediate orders shall not be with you.

I have their further commands to signify their direction to your Lordship in the event of the enemy's fleet being accompanied by any considerable number of transports you should in such case employ all your frigates in endeavouring to destroy them.

447. *Bridport to Admiralty*

Royal George, off Mizen Head, 8 May 1799

I have this morning received your letter of the lst instant together with a duplicate of the same date acknowledging the receipt of mine of the 26th and 27th ult. and communicating their Lordships' approbation of my proceeding off of Cape Clear with directions for my remaining in that station until I shall receive further accounts of the enemy. Also informing me that Sir Thomas Pasley[1] had been directed to send two cutters or luggers off of Brest with orders to any of the ships in that station to follow me to Cape Clear. And that Admiral Sir Alan Gardner with the Royal Sovereign and Repulse had been ordered to proceed to Cawsand Bay and to hold the said ships or any others which he may find there in readiness to put to sea the moment any intelligence shall be received that can enable their Lordships to dispose of those ships to any proper advantage.

I acquaint you for their Lordships' information that on my arrival off Cape Clear this morning I was joined by the ships and cutters named in the margin [*Venerable, Renown, Ramillies, Robust, Beaulieu, Aimable, Megaera, Lurcher, Nimrod, Dolly*] in addition to those belonging to Admiral Kingsmill's squadron as mentioned in my other letter of this day's date. And I have already acquainted you that the Russel joined me on the morning of the 27th ultimo.

As my present force is twenty ships of the line and the Polyphemus is out of repair I shall order Captain Lumsdaine[2] to return to Cork as Admiral Kingsmill seems to wish to have that ship with him. I have ordered Captain Brace[3] of the Kangaroo to proceed to the town of Bantry for the purpose of taking charge of any despatches or letters that may be there for me as well as to obtain intelligence and I shall take my station for the present off Achill Head, stretching my ships between the Blaskets and Lough Swilly for the purpose of intercepting the enemy's fleet should it appear on this coast and I shall order two of Admiral Kingsmill's frigates to remain off Cape Clear, agreeably to their Lordships' directions.

448.   *Pasley to Unknown*

Plymouth, 8 May 1799

Last night a small chasse marée, prize to the Black Joke lugger, arrived. By her I had a letter from the officer commanding her which I sent to Lord Spencer at Bath, but as the post was with difficulty saved I had no time to take a copy.

---

[1]Pasley, who lost a leg at the battle of the Glorious First of June 1794, had just become Commander-in-Chief at Plymouth.

[2]George Lumsdaine (d. 1812). Lieutenant 1776; Captain 1787; Rear-admiral 1807; Vice-admiral 1811.

[3]Sir Edward Brace (d. 1843). Lieutenant 1792; Commander 1797; Captain 1800; Rear-admiral 1830; Vice-admiral 1838.

In it he said that he had taken her, Ushant bearing E.S.E. six leagues: that he boarded her by surprise in the night by which he had had the good fortune to seize the despatches which they were in the act of throwing overboard slung with a weight and that he was going in quest of Lord Bridport to deliver them to his Lordship. This morning I have had the French master on shore, examined and cross-examined him by which it appears clear to me that this vessel was sent out with an officer and despatches on purpose to be taken, to mislead, by giving in a false destination. He says they sailed two days before, the men being dissatisfied were told by their officers that they were safer than on board the fleet as they would have no fighting; that it was probable they would be taken but should not remain above a month in England; that when they saw the lugger they stood towards her, when boarded they made no resistance nor an attempt to throw the despatches overboard though slung with a lead and line, though it might have been easily done by the officer if he had so pleased. She sailed on the 25th and was taken on the 27th.

The man further says that the fleet had no transports with them nor any army on board but a number of artillery officers and men, 6 months provisions and spare rigging, cordage and sails of every kind.

449. *Admiralty to Bridport*

9 May 1799

I received this morning and immediately communicated to my Lords Commissioners of the Admiralty your Lordship's letter to me of the 30th of last month, inclosing the copy of a letter you had received from Lieutenant Nicholson of the Black Joke lugger, giving an account of the capture of a French schooner called the Rebecca with a French officer on board, and of his having had the good fortune to intercept the dispatches entrusted to the care of that officer, as also the instructions which had been given to him for his guidance, and acquainting me for their Lordships' information that you had judged it proper to transmit the dispatches and instructions in original to His Excellency the Lord Lieutenant.

The same messenger that brought your Lordship's dispatch to me was also charged with a letter from His Grace the Duke of Portland, with the papers so intercepted, which have since been communicated by His Grace to their Lordships, and I have their commands to signify to you their full approbation of your proceedings on this occasion, by which the government of Ireland has been fully apprized of all the information of which your Lordship was in possession.

Although no doubt can be entertained of the instructions to Monsieur Lebreton being authentic papers, yet at the same time there are circumstances attending them, amongst which are their receipt date (so far back as the 5 of last month) and the little caution which appears to have been observed by the officer with whom they were entrusted, that lead their Lordships to think their contents should be treated with a certain degree of caution, but in your Lordship's situation circumstances must very shortly arise that must tend to remove every degree of doubt, and you will of course be guided by them; under any circumstances however, it will be proper that your Lordship should station a frigate or two off the Mullet to bring intelligence if the enemy should appear on the N.W. coast of Ireland, or apprize you of any thing else which may appear to be worthy of your notice.

By intelligence which has been received today it appears probable that the object of the enemy is a descent upon Ireland, and that the squadron from Brest is likely to be reinforced by the Spanish squadron from Ferrol, consisting of six ships of the line, and about 4000 troops, which are to join at a certain rendezvous. I transmit a précis of that intelligence to which I have referred, and in order that your Lordship may be put into a condition to meet the combined force, their Lordships have judged it proper (as your Lordship will see by the inclosed orders) to direct Captain Thornbrough in the Formidable with the three other ships named in the margin [*Triumph, Canada, Agincourt*] to join you immediately from Plymouth on your rendezvous off Cape Clear.

It will be highly important that your Lordship should transmit as frequently as possible to Admiral Kingsmill and to me information of the different positions you may be likely to take that their Lordships may be enabled with as much certainty as possible to communicate with your Lordship all the various circumstances which must arise, connected with the important services with which you are now intrusted, and that unless you should receive certain information of the enemy's intention so as to be able to follow their fleet to its point of destination, you should keep your squadron in such a situation as to be able to come up Channel in case the enemy should direct their operations that way.

I enclose a copy of orders which have been given to Sir Thomas Williams,[1] for proceeding with the three ships therein mentioned, between Cape Clear and Ushant for your Lordship's information.

---

[1]Sir Thomas Williams (d. 1841). Lieutenant 1779; Captain 1790; Rear-admiral 1809; Vice-admiral 1814; Admiral 1830.

450. *Le Breton to Bruix*

Ushant, 27th Germinal, Year 7[1]

I have the honour to transmit the substance of the Rebecca's journal by which you will find that I have been as yet disappointed in my views by the wind and other unexpected accidents.

I took the command of the vessel the 17th at 8 o'clock in the morning and got under way from the road of Brest a quarter of an hour afterwards. I stood into the Iroise passage, when many leaks were discovered and as no signal was made for the enemy I returned and anchored in Camaret Bay in order to stop them. The next day I found five leaks on the larboard and one on the starboard side and I have since been told that on her last voyage many was caulked in Conquet. I was detained in Camaret until the 23rd, when I sailed, but abreast of the Black Rocks I was becalmed and the flood tide drifted me back to Conquet, where I anchored. The following day, 24th, I weighed from thence and stood to the northward of Ushant, where I saw an English frigate. I stood across her in hopes of inducing her to chase me. She was three miles to windward of me and I was a league and half from the shore but she set her studding sails and ran towards her fleet, which was reefing their topsails and standing to the N.W. As I ought not, agreeable to your orders, allow myself to be taken but with such precautions as should give the appearance of truth to the commission with which you had honoured me I could not without exposing it follow the enemy and also risking the loss of the vessel and her crew had I passed the night in the offing, the Rebecca not being able to carry sail after the ships reefed their topsails or stand the sea in her present condition she certainly would have been lost.

This vessel came from Ireland and has been at Brest. The truck of her mainsail hauled down in the hold by the step of the mast in order to make it stand they gave her mast 5 feet longer (here he mentions a great many things of considerable weight upon the deck which he would have hove overboard had he been sure of not wanting them again and adds that the alterations that were made had rendered the vessel unfit to keep the sea[2]). Under those circumstances I found myself obliged to anchor at Ushant in order to hold myself in readiness to seize the first favourable opportunity to carry your wishes into execution. It is with pain I have seen the weather oblige the enemy to keep at a distance and

---

[1] 16 April 1799.
[2] Interjection by translator.

deprive me yet of proving my zeal to the country and my obedience to your orders.

After so much delay I thought it my duty to acquaint you of all these accidents and to wait your orders for my further proceedings. I lament that I did not give you this information the moment I was able but the hopes of seizing a fortunate moment to execute my orders was the cause of my committing this fault and I pray you will judge me according to my intentions.

I beg also to observe that the Rebecca is not at present in a state to proceed on her supposed destination. Part of her provisions is consumed, she has but three days water and we want utensils. She cannot carry sail and consequently makes but little way. With the most prudent precautions her situation altogether will destroy the intention of what I am charged with and weaken your expectations on the result of it.

I wait your orders at Ushant.

451. *Bruix to Le Breton*

Brest, 29th Germinal, Year 7[1]

The Minister of the Marine and Colonies to Citizen Le Breton.

I have just received, Citizen, the letter which you wrote to me on the 27th of this month by which you inform me of your being in the harbour of Ushant after having made useless efforts during several days to arrive at your destination.

I wish you had informed me earlier of this event that I might have taken measures to refit you. However, I have equipped a small vessel in which there is embarked forty days provisions. She is a vessel of good quality as to sailing, etc. You will move yourself and crew into her and will not lose a moment in getting under sail. It is not necessary for me to tell you that it is more and more urgent that you fulfil your mission; having lost so much time the least delay will render it altogether useless. The new vessel which you are to embark in will be named also the Rebecca.

[1] 18 April 1799.

452.   *Marsden to Spencer*

Admiralty Office, 9 May 1799, 4 o'clock

The information received this morning which I take for granted your Lordship will have read before you open this letter affords much room for speculation. The circumstances are extraordinary.

A despatch dated the 5th April announcing the intention of the French fleet's proceeding to sea but not until the return should be made to that despatch is intercepted on the 27th a few leagues from Ushant the day after the sailing of the fleet. What could have occasioned such a delay? The Board in general seems inclined to think of a ruse de guerre and that it was intended to be intercepted in order to mislead us.

[*Endorsed as received on the same day*]

453.   *Admiralty to Bridport*

Admiralty Office, 10 May 1799

Since I had the honor of conveying to your Lordship yesterday the message communicated to me by telegraph, I have received a letter from Sir Peter Parker which tends to confirm the accuracy of the message, and from the Danish ships having sailed from Bilbao, as you will perceive by Captain Butt's[1] letter to Sir Peter (accompanying this), no doubt remains of he having fallen in with the French fleet in the situation, or nearly so, which he has stated.

I also inclose to your Lordship the copy of a letter from Captain Curzon[2] of the Indefatigable giving an account of the sailing of the squadron from Ferrol which, from its proceedings and a variety of circumstances, is evidently designed to reinforce the fleet from Brest; and from the intelligence received today from Captain D'Auvergne, Prince de Bouillon, from Jersey, (a copy of which is likewise transmitted) there is the strongest reason to believe consists of not less than 25 or 26 sail of the line besides frigates and sloops.

The extract of a private letter from Sir Thomas Pasley to Vice Admiral Young, which I also inclose for your Lordship's information, tends to confirm the suspicion entertained of the authenticity of the intelligence to be collected from the instructions and letters, taken on

---

[1]Henry Samuel Butt (d. 1838). Lieutenant 1792; Commander 1797.
[2]Henry Curzon (d. 1846). Lieutenant 1783; Captain 1790; Rear-admiral 1810; Vice-admiral 1814; Admiral 1830.

board the Rebecca, of the enemy's designs, are not without sufficient ground.

[*Endorsement*]

Sent to Lord Castlereagh to be forwarded to Cork. Duplicate by Rear Admiral Collingwood.[1]

454.   *Admiralty to Bridport*

13 May 1799

The Cambrian having anchored yesterday afternoon at Spithead, your Lordship's several despatches dated the 8th instant which you had committed to the charge of Captain Legge reached me this morning and have since been communicated to my Lords Commissioners of the Admiralty.

Their Lordships have commanded me to acquaint you that they have great satisfaction in finding by these letters that your Lordship has been joined by the ships therein mentioned which had been ordered to reinforce the squadron under your orders; and they hope very shortly to learn from you that the ships named in the margin [*Royal Sovereign, Atlas, Formidable, Canada, Triumph, Agincourt*] will have also joined you, excepting the latter, which they have directed Sir Thomas Pasley to detain at Plymouth if she should not have sailed from thence before my letter to him of this day's date should reach [sic].

Your Lordship will have been informed by Sir Alan Gardner, who Captain Legge informs me he had fallen in with off the Dodman, of the disaster the Atlas had met with. It appears, however, by a letter from Captain Thornbrough of the 11th instant that the damages she sustained had been nearly repaired and that he expected she would be in a fit condition to sail from Plymouth with the Formidable, Canada and Triumph by yesterday.

By my letter to your Lordship of the 9th instant you will have perceived it to be their Lordships' intention that you should have continued with your squadron off Cape Clear so as to have been enabled the more readily to come into the Channel if circumstances had rendered it necessary for you to do so rather than to have proceeded to the N.W. coast of Ireland; and I have it now in command from them to

[1]Cuthbert Collingwood, First Baron Collingwood (1750–1810). Lieutenant 1775; Captain 1780; Rear-admiral 1799; Vice-admiral 1804.

signify their direction to you, in the event of your not receiving any well grounded intelligence of the enemy's being upon or approaching the coast of Ireland to lose no time in proceeding with your squadron to Bantry Bay, where you are to cause its provisions and stores to be completed as speedily as possible, leaving such of your frigates on the coast as you may think requisite for the purpose of bringing intelligence of any proceedings which may be worthy your Lordship's notice.

I have written to Admiral Kingsmill by this conveyance to take every practicable means for forwarding to Bantry Bay such supplies of stores and provisions as can be collected at Cork in order that your squadron may be put into the best state that circumstances will admit to enable your Lordship to carry into execution such further service as may be judged necessary, upon which subject your Lordship may expect very soon to receive instructions.

In the completion of the several ships it will be desirable for reasons which I shall have the honour of communicating to your Lordship that such of them as are not mentioned in the margin [*Royal George, Atlas, Achilles, Mars, Agincourt, Polyphemus*] should have a preference to the six ships therein named; though at the same time your Lordship will of course not omit to make use of any means that can be exerted for their speedy conclusion also.

455.   *Admiralty to Bridport*[1]

16 May 1799

I am commanded by my Lords Commissioners of the Admiralty to acquaint your Lordship that they have ordered H.M. ship the Chichester loaded with naval stores to proceed without a moment's delay to Bantry Bay, and to signify their directions to your Lordship to cause the said stores to be distributed on board the ships to be put under Sir Alan Gardner, but if the squadron should have proceeded to its destination before the arrival of the Chichester your Lordship will bring that ship with you to England, or leave orders for her to follow you if she should not reach that place before your leaving it.

As the success of the expedition under Sir Alan Gardner must in a great measure depend on the celerity with which he is despatched, it is their Lordships' commands that you do hasten that officer by every possible means in execution of his orders, and if by unloading the Chichester after her arrival its departure should be thereby likely to be

[1]Addressed to Bridport in Bantry Bay.

delayed, your Lordship is, rather than suffer such delay to take place, to order that ship to accompany the squadron to its place of destination.

456. *Admiralty to Bridport*

21 May 1799

Your Lordship is hereby required and directed, after detaching Sir Alan Gardner with the 16 ships of the line as directed by our orders to you of this day's date, to proceed with the remainder of the ships of the line which may be with you and six frigates off of Rochefort, and if you shall find a squadron of the enemy's ship in that port, you are to use your best endeavours to take or destroy it, but if from the position of the enemy you should find such a measure to be impracticable, your Lordship is to cruize off of that port and prevent its putting to sea. If the number of the enemy's ships be such as shall require the whole of your force, you are to continue with it on that service, but if not, you are in such case to leave a sufficient force under the order of Rear Admiral Berkeley and return with the ships which are most in want of supplies or repairs to Cawsand Bay. If your Lordship should not find any squadron of the enemy at Rochefort, you are then to proceed off of Ferrol, and finding a squadron there, you are to remain with the whole of the force, or to leave a part, as the number of the enemy's ships may require. If you should find a French squadron at Rochefort, but no Spanish ships, you are to leave a sufficient number of ships to watch them and proceed off of Ferrol, and finding a Spanish squadron to be in that port, you are to cruise and prevent it from putting to sea, but finding no squadron there, your Lordship is to lose no time in proceeding to Cawsand Bay. In the event of your Lordship not finding any squadron either at Rochefort or Ferrol, you are in that case to return with all the ships of the line to Cawsand Bay, excepting the four which by our orders to your Lordship of the 14th instant, were to have sailed with Sir Alan Gardner, which four ships your Lordship is to send to join Lord St. Vincent off of Cadiz or at Gibraltar, or whereever else his Lordship may be; but if you shall obtain certain information of the enemy's fleet having been disabled or separated, or of any part of it having returned to the French ports, your Lordship is to endeavour to intercept such ships which shall appear to be still at sea, or proceed off of the ports to which they may have returned, as from the nature of the information you may receive shall appear to you to be most expedient. Your Lordship is to continue off the ports where you shall find it necessary to cruize, so long as the provisions of your squadron will admit, sending frequent accounts to our secretary for our information, of your movements and of your intended proceedings, that their Lordships may know where to find your Lordship, and to furnish you with any intelligence or instructions which may be necessary for your guidance. Your Lordship is to send to Cawsand Bay as soon as possible any frigates belonging to your squadron which you may happen to have with you, excepting those you are to detach with Sir Alan Gardner, and those which you are to take with you as above directed, in order that their stores and provisions may be completed and that they may be put into a proper condition for further service.

457. *Bridport to Admiralty*

Royal George, Bantry Bay, 27 May 1799

I received last night their Lordships' two orders to me of the 21st instant, also your two letters of that date but the one of the 20th to which I am referred has not yet reached me. And I acquaint you that I shall give the necessary orders and instructions to Admiral Sir Alan Gardner agreeably to their Lordships' directions. I understand the Hindostan[1] and some brigs laden with stores and provisions sailed from Cork the 24th instant. The moment they arrive in this bay all possible dispatch shall be used in completing the several ships as well as circumstances will permit, as most of them already are nearly so, with water, when the detachment shall be made under the orders of Sir Alan Gardner. In one of their Lordships' orders I an directed to proceed off Rochefort with the remainder of the ships of the line and six frigates and if I should find no squadron of the enemy there to proceed off Ferrol and on finding no squadron in that port to send the four ships which were to have sailed with Sir Alan Gardner to join Lord St. Vincent off of Cadiz or at Gibraltar or wherever his Lordship may be and directing me to continue off of the ports where I may find it necessary to cruise so long as the provisions of the squadron will admit, sending to you frequent accounts of my intended proceedings and I acquaint you that I shall repair as expeditiously as possible, after the stores and provisions have arrived and are distributed with the force that will remain with me, consisting of the ships and vessels named in the margin [*Royal George, Mars, Atlas, Ajax, Achilles, Agincourt, Venerable, Ramillies, Robust, Renown, Anson, Naiad, Phaeton, Stag, Clyde,*

---

[1]A 54-gun ship purchased from the East India Company in 1795 and used as a storeship.

Sylph sloop, *Megaera* fireship, *Black Joke, Lurcher, Nimrod, Dolly, Lady Jane*] agreeably to their Lordships' directions. I have already informed you that I had directed Captain Stopford to procure such supplies for the Phaeton, Stag and Clyde as Lough Swilly would afford, those ships having been near ten weeks at sea, and when they arrive here, which I daily expect, I shall order such further supplies as circumstances will permit.

458. *Bridport to Admiralty*

Royal George, Bantry Bay, 28 May 1799

I this morning received your letter of the 20th instant informing me that intelligence had been received through the channel of the French papers that the Spanish squadron which lately sailed from Ferrol has arrived at the Isle of Aix and that five other ships supposed to be ships of war were seen by the packet on her passage from Lisbon on the 12th instant, Scilly North 23 East, distant 112 leagues, standing to the eastward, which ships their Lordships conceive may be part of the Brest fleet and enclosing extracts of the intelligence therein mentioned and I acquaint you that the direction for detaining Admiral Sir Alan Gardner and the squadron I have been ordered to put under his command has been superseded by their Lordships' order of the 21st instant, which I acknowledged the receipt of yesterday by His Majesty's ship Sirius.

The Hindostan with eight sail of victuallers anchored here from Cork last night and this morning. I have given directions for a proper distribution of the stores and provisions but there will not be near sufficient to complete Sir Alan Gardner's squadron to four months and I shall not wait for more being sent round from Cork as I hope to leave this anchorage by the latter end of the week or sooner if possible.

459. *Bridport to Captain Edwards*[1]

Royal George, at sea, 31 May 1799

It was yesterday reported to me that Mrs. Edwards and your family were on board the St. George. I acquaint you that I heard it with astonishment and concern. And I am to inform you that it is impossible they can be allowed to continue in your ship and I am under the

---

[1]Sampson Edwards (d. 1840). Lieutenant 1774; Captain 1781; Rear-admiral 1801; Vice-admiral 1806; Admiral 1814. At this time he was captain of the *St George*.

necessity of directing you to remove the whole into the Kangaroo and Captain Brace will be desired to land them at Cork with such other women as you may have permitted to be carried to sea.

You will see by my orders to you, which you will this day receive, that I have put you under the orders of Admiral Sir Alan Gardner for your future guidance, who will proceed on distant service when the fleet separates.

460. *Durham to Bridport*

Anson, off the Isle of Rhé, 4 June 1799

I beg leave to acquaint your Lordship that in obedience to your Lordship's order I this evening reconnoitred Basque Roads and perceived lying at anchor near the Isle d'Aix five sail of the line, one of which apparently a three decked ship, having a Spanish flag at the fore topgallant masthead without a bowsprit: (her foreyard rigged for getting it in) also three frigates and one frigate lying in Rochelle roads, all the ships have their lower yards and topgallant masts struck.

461. *Bridport to Admiralty*

Royal George, off Isle d'Aix, 5 June 1799

In my letter of the 1st instant I acquainted you for their Lordships' information with the squadron having left Bantry Bay and with my having made the detachment under the command of Admiral Sir Alan Gardner when I left the coast of Ireland.

I made Belleisle the 3rd instant, the next morning Isle Dieu and in the afternoon I sent the Anson and Black Joke lugger to look into Rochefort, supported by the Venerable, and enclosed is a copy of Captain Durham's report by which their Lordships will see that the Spanish squadron is at the anchorage of Ile d'Aix, notwithstanding the report made to him, which is also enclosed, though it is not improbable but the Spanish squadron may have put to sea on the 24th ultimo and been driven back by contrary winds.

The anchorages of Basque Road and Ile d'Aix are so well known, upon record at the Admiralty, that it is unnecessary for me to make any observations upon them. I shall therefore only state that the destroying of that squadron appears to be impracticable and the keeping it from putting to sea very uncertain unless a squadron shall be ordered out to anchor in Basque Road under the command of some officer of experience and, if bombs were sent with that officer, the squadron at anchor under the protection of Ile d'Aix might be disturbed and obliged to move up the Charente for shelter and security.

462. *Admiralty to Bridport*

8 June 1799

I have it in command from my Lords Commissioners of the Admiralty to transmit to your Lordship herewith for your information transcripts of intelligence which has been received from the Prince de Bouillon, respecting the enemy's fleet in the Mediterranean, together with an account of the farther preparations of the enemy at Brest to equip another fleet . . .

[*Enclosures*]

462a. *Substance of communications received at Jersey the 3rd June 1799*

St Brieux, 2 June 1799

Letters have just been received from officers in Citizen de Bruix fleet dated at Toulon the 21st May that give the following particulars of their voyage thither.

Very advantageous winds and weather favoured the progress of the fleet to the southward till the 4 May when it obtained sight of the English fleet under Admiral St. Vincent about 12 or 14 leagues west of the Straits mouth; dispositions were immediately made to attack it with prospects of advantage, when a storm arose which separated the fleets, and Admiral Bruix entered the Mediterranean and got safe before Carthagena on the 7th May. An Aviso was sent in which brought out 6 ships with whom the fleet proceeded to Toulon. One of the ships had been dismasted and gave some trouble, and an opportunity to the English to come up and attack the fleet, which however, after some skirmishing got safe into port where it remained the 21st May with nine Spanish ships, having found three there on its arrival. One or two efforts had been made to put to sea with the avowed purpose to withdraw from the coast of Italy the division of General McDonald (for whom orders were found there pursuant to a decree of the Directory to evacuate the Italian Meridional Republic) and to take it to Malta or the Levant; but the project appears now suspended by the appearance in the offing of, it is said forty sail, great and small, of the combined fleets under the English Admiral St. Vincent in the act of blockading the port.

Brest, 31st May
The artificers that have been collected by the forced levies since the departure of the fleet are again actively employed in the rope houses and sail loft. The shipwrights work on the Indivisible and two razees. Stores continue to arrive by land carriage, and it is expected that in the course of a month there will again be collected in the road a force of 13 ships of the line, including the 6 Spanish and one French from Rochefort that are daily expected round, with one from L'Orient laying there ready for sea, with the Indivisible and two razees fitting in the harbour. There are now in the road 3 line of battleships, one frigate and two corvettes.
   D'Auvergne – Prince de Bouillon
   Jersey June 3d 1799

P.S. The levies of the last military conscriptions are all retained at St. Brieux and openly protected.

   462b.   *Further intelligence despatched by D'Auvergne*

4 June 1799

I add here the state of Brest road and harbour on the 31st ultimo that reached me yesterday.
   'In the road three line of battle ships, one frigate and two corvettes.'
   'In the harbour, two line of battle ships fitting after a thorough repair and razey.[1] The Patriote and Eole.' The Indivisible a three decker intended to mount 30 carronades upon her quarter deck, gangways and forecastle, which will make her a 130 gun ship of immense dimensions; artificers are finishing to plank her upper works, and she is expected to be in the water and fitted in the course of a month. The Patriote and Eole are still in the Great Dock, and a large frigate almost ready for launching on the slip of the Montagne, that, with three or four rotten hulks constitutes the contents of the harbour. The ships in the road are the Dugoucies 74, Berwick 74, and Mutius 74. The Entreprenant is at the boom, she is also a 74. The two last did belong to the fleet when it sailed, one of them returned from Bertheaume the day before it dropped

---

[1]Razee. A ship was razeed by cutting off upperworks or entire decks. The term comes from the French.

there, having run foul of the Mont Blanc, and the other returned since, which on examining and comparing my lists I judge to be the Mutius as she sailed with the fleet, and has got in a lower mast since her return. The Chef de division Vienne commands them at present and has delivered a Tableau (an order) of anchorage for thirteen ships which he expects to have assembled in the course of a month, order having been given for that purpose. They will be composed as follows:

The three at present in the road. The Eole and Patriote from the harbour. Six Spanish ships from Rochefort. One new French 74 from ditto coming round with the preceding. The ship that put into Lorient which is also ordered round when the Rochefort division passes.

The Precieuse is the frigate in the road.

My confidential messenger Monsieur L., scrupulously examined, is positive that all the letters agree at St. Brieux that a combined fleet was before the port of Toulon and blocked them in it on the 21st of May the date of the letter.

463. *Bridport to Spencer*

Royal George, Cawsand Bay, 14 June 1799

The Board will know by my public letter to Mr. Nepean what ships I have left under the command of Rear Admiral Berkeley off of Rochefort. I wish I had left him in better spirits and with less feeling of dissatisfaction.

[*Endorsed as received on the 16th and answered on the 21st*]

464. *Bridport to Admiralty*

Royal George, Cawsand Bay, 20 June 1799

I have received their Lordships' order of 18th instant for taking the Explosion, Sulphur and Volcano bomb vessels under my command. Also their Lordships' secret order of the above date directing me so soon as the two first mentioned bomb vessels shall arrive at Plymouth to proceed with them to sea as expeditiously as possible on the service therein stated and to send Rear Admiral Berkeley in the Mars to Cawsand Bay with directions to remain there for further orders. I have also received and shall deliver their Lordships' order of the 18th instant to Captain Crawford of His Majesty's sloop Childers. And I acquaint you that the Royal George will be in course of payment the 1st of July and her books will be sent to London so as to be returned to the Pay Office at this port by that time.

465.   *Spencer to Bridport*

Admiralty, 21 June 1799

I have to acknowledge the receipt of your letter of the 14th June on your arrival in Cawsand Bay and I agree with your Lordship in wishing that Rear Admiral Berkeley had been left off Rochefort in better spirits and with less dissatisfaction. As it appears not at all improbable that a successful attempt may be made on the Spanish squadron in the anchorage off the Isle of Aix either by destroying them or by driving them up the River Charente (into which I understand they cannot go without getting rid of their guns and part of their stores) we have thought it best for the King's service to direct your Lordship to undertake that operation and have in pursuance of this intention conveyed in your public letter placed what bomb vessels we had at hand under your direction for that purpose. I cannot help feeling rather sanguine on this subject, more especially as I am informed that in the opinion of some French officers in this country of considerable experience ships of as large a draft of water as the Spanish Admiral's ship must be cannot anchor so near the shore as to be properly protected by the batteries. If this should be the case I am persuaded your Lordship will make the best use of the advantage which would thereby be given you and as I feel confident in your experience and judgment on these subjects it appears to me that the conduct of any enterprise of this nature could not be trusted to better hands. It is quite unnecessary for me to point out how important its success could prove in the present state of the war.

466.   *Bridport to Admiralty*

Royal George, Cawsand Bay, 22 June 1799

By their Lordships' order of the 18th instant I am directed to proceed to sea with His Majesty's ship Royal George and three bomb vessels when they shall be assembled at this port and I am to send Rear Admiral Berkeley in the Mars to Cawsand Bay on my arrival off Rochefort.

As the flag officers and ships detached with Admiral Sir Alan Gardner are no longer under my orders I take for granted their Lordships do not intend that I should proceed to sea to relieve Rear Admiral Berkeley without other flag officers and ships to accompany me upon my intended service, which appears to have arisen upon the subject of the Spanish squadron at anchor at Isle d'Aix and upon which I stated the taking or destroying them to be impracticable but I suggested that it was possible they might be disturbed by bomb vessels, but I fully consider that to be the extent of such operations as undoubtedly the ships will remove higher up and not allow shells or shot to injure them. I take this to be the purport of the bomb vessels attending me off Rochefort as no limitation of time for my cruising is stated in their Lordships' order.

The caulkers will not finish caulking the Royal George before tomorrow or Monday. As soon as she is refitted and paid, which I understand by Captain Domett she will be on the 1st of July if her books are returned from London I will lose no time in proceeding to sea with only three bomb vessels and their tenders and make all possible despatch off of Rochefort where Rear Admiral Berkeley will join me with six ships of the line, when the Rear Admiral shall be sent to Cawsand Bay in the Mars and I apprehend other ships will soon require to be sent also into port.

I trust I have not misunderstood my orders of the 1st instant brought to me by Sir Harry Neale by returning into port when it was their Lordships' intentions that I should have remained at sea as the hastening me out in the manner I am ordered seems to imply. If there was no absolute necessity for my commanding six ships of the line and repairing off Rochefort I should certainly request some relaxation from my public duty which I feel my health requires.

467. *Bridport to Admiralty*

Royal George, Cawsand Bay, 24 June 1799

I have received your letter of the 22nd instant acquainting me that the Royal George's pay books will be ordered to be returned whenever I shall next arrive in a King's port where her crew can be paid. And I inform you that I shall proceed to sea either tomorrow or Wednesday with the three bomb vessels and their tenders, agreeably to their Lordships' orders and I shall take the Dolly and Lurcher cutters with me.

I shall order the ships and vessels named in the margin [*Phaeton, Stag, Melpomene, Naiad, Anson, Clyde, Childers*] to proceed and join me on my station whenever they are ready for sea, also the Melpomene as soon as the court martial has been held on her carpenter, unless their several captains should receive directions to the contrary from their Lordships.

The Lady Duncan lugger arrived in Plymouth Sound this morning from Rear Admiral Berkeley. I shall give directions to Lieutenant Nicolson, her commander, to remain here seven days after my sailing and the master of the Nimrod cutter three days for the purpose of taking charge of any letter or dispatches that may arrive here for me.

The bottoms of the bomb tenders which came from Plymouth being very foul and Captain Wainwright[1] and Captain Butt having requested that their masters might be permitted to lay them on shore for the purpose of cleaning them I complied with their request and they will be afloat tomorrow morning – at present the wind blows fresh at south-west.

468. *Admiralty to Bridport*

24 June 1799

I have received and communicated to my Lords Commissioners of the Admiralty your Lordship's letter to me of the 22nd instant and I have their Lordships' commands to acquaint you in answer thereto that under their orders to you of the 18th instant for proceeding to sea with the Royal George and the three bomb vessels therein mentioned and for sending Rear Admiral Berkeley into port it was certainly their Lordships' intention that you should sail from Cawsand Bay without other flag officers and ships to accompany you, the force of the enemy not requiring more ships and the state of the Mars, from your Lordship's representation, making it necessary that she should be sent into port to refit and that their hastening you to sea was not in consequence of your having mistaken the nature of the orders you had received by Sir Harry Neale but because their Lordships meant to entrust to you the execution of the only service which the present situation of the enemy's force will admit of being attempted by the ships under your Lordship's orders and because the best hope of success in such an attempt resting on its being made before the enemy, suspecting it, should move their ships too far up the river to be within reach of the shells it is necessary the ships should proceed in execution of that service without the smallest delay, but as it appears that your Lordship's health requires relaxation from your public duty their Lordships have been pleased to grant you permission to go on

---

[1] John Wainwright (d. 1810). Lieutenant 1760; Captain 1782; superannuated 1804.

shore for the reestablishment of it, having ordered Rear Admiral Pole to hoist his flag on board the Royal George and proceed immediately off of Rochefort to endeavour to destroy the Spanish squadron and to take or destroy such other of the enemy's ships and vessels as he may happen to meet with.

469. *Bridport to Admiralty*

Royal George, Cawsand Bay, 26 June 1799

I acquaint you for their Lordships' information that the tenders of the Explosion and Sulphur bomb vessels were afloat yesterday afternoon and I had made the necessary arrangements for proceeding to sea early this morning but there was little wind at S.S.W. I shall lose no time in causing my flag to be hauled down and go on shore agreeable to their Lordships' permission when Rear Admiral Pole will give directions for hoisting his flag in the Royal George and proceed to sea according to the order he has received for that purpose.

470. *Pole to Bridport*

Royal George, at anchor in the Portuis [Pertuis] d'Antioch,
3 July 1799

We anchored with the squadron yesterday morning in Basque Road at 11 a.m. and, having previously given directions to Captain Keats to place the bomb vessels, they commenced their fire about one p.m. and continued until ½ past three when, although the enemy shells and shot reached them, yet not one of ours fell within a quarter of mile of the Spanish ships. At ½ past three it fell calm and I was obliged to send our boats to tow the bombs out, the enemy having sent forth fifteen mortar and gun boats which were rapidly advancing from many points. All the change that took place in the enemy's position was previous to the fire of the bombs. The frigate which lay the furthest out removed to within the ships of the line and the Spanish Admiral moved about a cable and half or two cables. As the bombs could not be placed nearer without being destroyed by the enemy's fire and as they were of no use where they were I determined to desist from any further use of them, not feeling myself authorized to stand in with the ships to engage them and indeed I see no object which could be obtained by so doing, as Captain Keats' pilot and himself say they have no doubt but the Admiral might move within if he thought proper without taking out a single gun or shot. Therefore I apprehend it would be madness to attempt going with the squadron under the fire of the batteries merely to make their ships move in. It hath been calm the greater part of the last 24 hours and Admiral Berkeley is still in sight from the mast head.

471. *Sick and Wounded Board to Admiralty*

Office for Sick and Wounded Seamen, 19 July 1799

We request you will be pleased to inform the Right Honourable the Lords Commissioners of the Admiralty that we have received a letter dated the 1st instant from the Honourable Rear Admiral Berkeley, of which a copy is enclosed, stating that the crews of the ships under his command have suffered by the scurvy from not being allowed a sufficient supply of refreshments, particularly sour krout and lemon juice.

We have taken the same into our consideration and we beg you will remark to their Lordships that when the supply of lemon juice and sugar was originally proposed by us, it was recommended to be general in all His Majesty's ships while at sea, and after the small beer was expended, and that beside what was in the surgeons' charge a sufficient quantity should be put in the pursers' charge for the men in health. But, from the scarcity and high price of lemons, this supply was limited to ships fitted for foreign service, and the surgeons were also directed by the 13th article of their new instructions when the stock of lemon juice was not sufficiently ample for the whole complement of men to examine the ship's company, by the captain's permission, and to select such cases as had obscure symptoms of scurvy in order that they might be served lemon juice and sugar, without being put on the sick list.

We beg leave further to state to you for their Lordships' information that in consequence of the demands from the Victualling Office being much less than was expected, the stock of lemon juice now on hand is such as to afford a supply to the ships serving on the coasts of Great Britain and Ireland, over and above what is furnished for the use of the sick, and we are humbly of opinion that it would be for the advantage of His Majesty's service if their Lordships would please to give directions to the Commissioners of the Victualling to supply all the ships on the said service with half the proportion supplied for foreign service, and that the surgeons be directed to comply with the above cited article of their instructions by selecting such men as may require lemon juice or sugar from the pursers' stores in the proportion of one ounce of the former and two ounces of the latter to each man daily after the expenditure of small beer.

We are further of opinion that such a supply, together with the usual supply of sour krout, which we beg also to recommend, will save great part of the expense now incurred in the several ports of England for vegetables furnished for scorbutic men.

[Endorsement]

20 July. Direct them to let me know the number of scorbutic cases in that fleet.

[Enclosure]

471a.   *Berkeley to Sick and Wounded Board*

Copy   Mars, at sea, 1 July 1799

Having been employed chiefly in the Channel fleet this war I cannot help taking notice of a circumstance relating to the health as well as the comfort of the crews of His Majesty's ships on that service which falling more immediately under the cognisance of the department you fill I dare say would be altered upon your representation to the Admiralty.

The ships fitted for foreign service are allowed various refreshments and antiscorbutics which are denied to those upon the home stations, a circumstance which from observation has most forcibly struck me as an error, for the ships ordered abroad are rarely or ever six weeks on that passage to any part of the world without touching at some ports, where refreshments of fresh meat, vegetables and fruits can be procured for the men, whereas the Channel ships are seldom out less than six, but very often their cruises are extended to nine, twelve and sometimes fourteen weeks without a possibility of getting either fresh provisions or vegetables for the crews.

The ships upon foreign stations are allowed sour krout, which the home ships are not, and lime juice in greater proportions which perhaps is needless as there is scarcely a foreign station where it may not be procured in a fresher state or in the fruit itself. In this climate therefore and after the cruise has been of a certain duration (say one month) if fresh beef and vegetables are not sent out, surely it would be right to give them sour krout, and if spirits <u>must</u> be served to qualify their deleterious nature with lime juice and sugar or molasses which certainly would be means of keeping off the scurvy, for I never knew an instance of a ships being out nine weeks that the scurvy did not begin to shew itself, although kept under and certainly very much lessened by the lime juice which is medicinally allowed to all ships. But this lime juice is never made use of until a a scorbutic patient discovers himself which is rarely or ever until the disease has gained a considerable head, where as if it was mixed with his drink from the time the beer was expended and that he was allowed sour krout with his beef or to eat as a salad it might keep him free from the scurvy, or at least operate upon him so as to keep the disorder from bursting forth in the violent manner which we always see instances of at the period I have mentioned.

I have taken the liberty therefore of writing this public letter that you may make use of it, if it should be thought necessary, as a representation from an officer the ships of whose squadron are at present examples of the necessity of some allowance.

472. *Pole to Admiralty*

Royal George, at sea, Barges d'Olonne east 13 miles, 29 July 1799

From the information which I have received from Sir Thomas Pasley of the enemy's fleet coming to the northward I have judged it expedient to endeavour to bring the ships under my command into the Channel, as I apprehend it must be their Lordships' wish to collect the force. I have therefore not waited for orders to that purpose in presuming to do this. I know I take on myself much responsibility but I have weighed in my mind the probable consequence of not moving from hence and have decided to make sail for the Channel and wait off the Lizard for their Lordships' orders. If I have erred in judgment I must throw myself on their Lordships' clemency for protection.

473. *Pole to Admiralty*

Royal George, at sea, 29 July 1799

I have the honour to acknowledge the receipt of their Lordships' order of the 20th instant by the Fanny lugger. Only two hours previous to the receipt of that order I had addressed a letter to you for the information of my Lords Commissioners of the Admiralty to say that in consequence of intelligence received from Sir Thomas Pasley I was proceeding to the Channel. I now make the best of my way to Torbay instead of the Lizard.

474.   *Pole to Admiralty*

Royal George, Torbay, 2 August 1799

I have the honour to acquaint you for the information of my Lords Commissioners of the Admiralty that I am this moment anchored in Torbay with the ships of the squadron under my orders, as noted in the margin [*Royal George, Sans Pareil, Venerable, Renown, Robust, St. Fiorenzo, Megaera* fire ship, *Lurcher* cutter], the Boadicea, Mondovi and Uranie being on the look-out, the two first within the Portuis d'Antioche and the latter between Belle Isle and Sable d'Olonne. I sent the Black Joke lugger to Captain Keats and the Dolly cutter to Captain Towry[1] to order them hither and I expect their arrival every moment.

My letter to you by the Railleur sloop and Joseph cutter will have made their Lordships acquainted with my proceedings since I received from Vice Admiral Sir Thomas Pasley intelligence of the enemy . . . I found at anchor here His Majesty's ships Atlas and Saturn.

475.   *Grenville[2] to Bridport*

Plymouth, 3 August 1799

I was just going to write to you yesterday to acquaint [you] with the confirmation of the account of the combined fleets having got into Cadiz which was brought by the Louisa brig but Captain Durham informed me that he had just despatched a letter to you with the above news etc. of their fleet. When in a condition to avail themselves of this piece of good fortune and that they should have a sufficient land force on board they may do infinite mischief by an attack upon Ireland. I find that we are assembling all the ships we can collect to form a fleet in Torbay, which appears to me to be the wisest thing we can do in the present situation of affairs. If the five Spanish ships should join from Rochefort and two or three from Brest, Lord Keith will not be in sufficient force to hazard a battle as he cannot leave the Mediterranean without a certain number of ships to protect the coast of Italy and to favour our operations in that part of the world. In short I think that the French have the game in their hands in the present moment if they are in a condition to profit of their good fortune.

---

[1]George Henry Towry (d. 1809). Lieutenant 1790; Captain 1794.
[2]William Wyndham Grenville, Baron Grenville (1759–1834) was Secretary of State for Foreign Affairs 1791–1801.

476.   *George III to Spencer*

Windsor, 42 minutes past 6 p.m., 5 August 1799

The hearing that the combined fleets of the enemy have sailed from Cadiz the 21st of the last month and that there is no account of Lord Keith later than the 25th of that month is certainly unpleasant but I have that complete trust in the protection of divine providence that I do not doubt we shall speedily hear of our fleet having passed the straits of Gibraltar and giving such an account of the enemy as will set every person's mind at ease. The collecting as strong a force as possible in the Channel seems to be highly proper.

I am sorry to find that Earl Howe died this morning. His public services and private virtues make him a serious loss.

[*Endorsed as received on the 6th*]

477.   *Admiralty to Bridport*

5 August 1799

... I am commanded by my Lords Commissioners of the Admiralty to signify their direction to your Lordship to repair immediately to Torbay, and hoisting your flag on board the Royal George, take under your command such ships and vessels as are now collected at that anchorage and may hereafter have orders to join you.

478.   *Admiralty to Pole*

5 August 1799

My lords Commissioners of the Admiralty having received intelligence by the Triton frigate, arrived at Plymouth, that the combined fleets of the enemy left Cadiz on the 21st ultimo and were seen on the following day standing to the northward, I have it in command from their Lordships to signify their direction to you to arrange the ships in Torbay in the best manner you may be able for resisting any attack which may be made upon them by the enemy's fleet.

479.   *Bridport to Admiralty*

Royal George, Torbay, 11 August 1799

I have ordered the Mondovi brig to proceed off Brest, directing her commander, Captain Selby,[1] to put himself under the command of Captain Cunningham of His Majesty's ship Clyde and follow his orders for his further proceedings and as I have judged it for His Majesty's service that their Lordships, as well as myself, should be informed as early as possible of the motions of the enemy at Brest as well as that of the combined fleets of the enemy and for these purposes I have directed Captain Cunningham to send the Mondovi back to Torbay with such intelligence as he may have collected, keeping the Fowey cutter with him to answer any future communication.

480.   *Spencer to Gardner*

Admiralty, 12 August 1799

From the uncertain state of your health of late which I have not observed without much concern it has occurred to me that it might perhaps not be disagreeable to you to be placed in a situation which required rather less active exertion and was liable to less constant anxiety than that in which you have hitherto been serving and I am therefore induced to avail myself of the opportunity which is offered by the arrangements produced by Lord Howe's death and to propose to you the appointment of Commander-in-Chief at Portsmouth in the room of Sir Peter Parker who succeeds to that of Admiral of the Fleet. The situation I propose to you is the highest and most reputable of its kind and though there are several other admirals more senior who would I believe very willingly take it I have judged it due to your services and present situation in the fleet to make you the offer and shall have great satisfaction if it will be agreeable to you to accept it.

481.   *Gardner to Spencer*

Bath, 13 August 1799

I had the honour of receiving your Lordship's letter this evening acquainting me that from the arrangements which are about to take place

---

[1]William Selby (d. 1811). Lieutenant 1793; Commander 1 October 1798; Captain 25 December 1800.

on account of the death of Lord Howe you have been induced to propose to me the appointment of Commander-in-Chief at Portsmouth in the room of Sir Peter Parker ... I cannot, my Lord, sufficiently express the obligations I am under to your Lordship for this mark of your attention and consideration and for the favourable opinion you are pleased to entertain of my services but as I hope my health is sufficiently re-established to enable me to return to my duty in my present situation in the Channel fleet, I cannot consistent with my feelings withdraw myself at this time from active service. I must therefore beg leave to decline the offer which your Lordship has done me the honour to make and I hope so doing I shall not forfeit your good opinion.

482. *Pellew to Keith*

Impetueux, 13 August 1799

Report of the state of the enemy's fleet at Brest.

In the outer road are from 45 to 50 large ships of war, chiefly of the line.

There appeared 1 Spanish admiral, 1 vice admiral, 2 rear admirals but I could see only 10 private ships under the same colours.

There were 1 French admiral, 2 vice admirals, 1 rear admiral and 1 commodore and 25 ships under the French colours. Four three deckers appeared stripped to the lower masts.

Most of the others had lower yards and topmasts struck, with their sails loose as if for unbending.

Three or four of the northernmost French ships (the commodore one of them) had topgallant yards across and sails loose as if ready for sea.

In addition to the above information I have to state to your Lordship the report of a French pilot on board a Prussian dogger examined by me as he came out of Brest this afternoon and for which I waited.

Upon interrogatory he says the fleet arrived on Wednesday afternoon the 7th instant consisting of 25 French sail of the line and 8 frigates.

The Spanish fleet of 15 sail of the line, 6 frigates and 4 corvettes.

There was at anchor in the outer road before, 5 sail of 74s ready for sea and L'Indivisible of 80 guns, a new ship in port, nearly ready, so that in all in the outer road are 44 sail of the line.

Many of the ships had sprung topmasts and one Spanish three decker only had been obliged to go into the port.

He also says there are no more troops at Brest than form the usual garrison and that all the troops in the neighbourhood were gone into La Vendée to quell insurrections before the fleet arrived.

Says there is no want of masts and yards in the Arsenal but a great scarcity of rope and sail cloth.

Provisions of every sort are abundant, both fresh and salt.

And lastly he says that Bruix was received at Brest with great applause and called a great admiral for having brought the fleet back in safety.

No expedition was at all talked of and to himself and many others the return of the fleet was quite unexpected and he believes also by people in office as the signal posts on their approach had announced them as the English fleet.

483.   *Spencer to Gardner*

Admiralty, 15 August 1799

The sentiments conveyed to me in your letter of the thirteenth instant are such as it is impossible not to enter into and to consider as doing you great credit. I shall, of course, say nothing more upon the subject at the present moment but when the immediate pressure of the moment is removed, which I take it for granted it will be very shortly, I should then think that there might no longer exist those objections to my proposal which you have so properly felt and that the reasons which I stated to have been my inducement for making it will weigh with you to accept it.

9

THE COMBINED FLEET IN BREST
18 AUGUST 1799–24 APRIL 1800

With an enemy fleet totalling over 40 ships of the line in Brest in August 1799, the British naval establishment responded with noteworthy calm. To be sure, the frigate guard was reinforced and Bridport was refused further leave [485, 486]. But for the spectacle of a large fleet gathered together Spencer took time out of London to visit Bridport in Torbay, from where George III invited him to Weymouth [487, 488]. However, off Brest the shortage of frigates permitted the French to send out a frigate squadron to meet convoys of naval stores and provisions [495] and, though he himself was awaiting a storeship and victuallers, Bridport was once again urged to sea by the Board [489, 490]. Following the northward redistribution of the Franco-Spanish fleet, Lord Keith had reinforced Bridport from the Mediterranean command and he was blamed for thinning the frigates off Brest, so permitting French squadrons to emerge [493]. Yet from the Iroise, Keats pointed out the difficulties of seeing French convoys approaching, and of intercepting them once they were through the Passage du Raz and provided with an escort [495].

To civilians at the Admiralty these observations were academic. Never having experienced the combined effects of geography and weather off the port of Brest, their limited understanding of the difficulties of mounting a complete blockade compromised Admiralty control. It was a handicap notable both in Spencer and Nepean, the Secretary to the Board. To compensate for this lack of first-hand knowledge, the navy had painters provide views of the coastline against which the British navy was expected to act. Just as Nicholas Pocock was employed to paint views of the royal dockyards for the Navy Board,[1] so John Serres, marine painter to George III and draughtsman to the Admiralty was sent to work off Brest [496]. His despatch corresponded with an evaluation, drawn up by Spencer following conversations with officers, of the landing places around Brest from which an amphibious attack might be made on the port.[2] Spencer favoured a main landing in

---

[1] D. Cordingly, *Nicholas Pocock 1740–1821* (London, 1986), 66–9.
[2] *Private Papers of George, Second Earl Spencer*, ed. J. S. Corbett and H. W. Richmond (4 vols, NRS, 1913 etc.), III, 105–30.

Douarnenez Bay, with a supplementary landing on the Conquet peninsula. However, the idea of such an attack was eventually abandoned.

Off Ushant early in September, Bridport commanded a fleet of 32 ships of the line. His immediate concern was to block access into Brest to further reinforcements and incoming convoys, and to check the coastal trade and privateers. He thus specifically stationed frigates as they joined him [502], checked their performance on station, and authorised their refitting [504]. Relative strengths in frigates permitted the French to station an advance squadron in Bertheaume Bay, which in September was able to deter Keats's squadron from approaching too close. Observations of the French fleet thus only coincided with the retirement of the advance squadron on account of bad weather [500]. In October the French occupied Camaret Bay from where they were harassed by British frigates [505].

In spite of this immediate task, Bridport still agitated to put more frigates on the north coast of Spain. However, the Admiralty still declined to consider that station a priority, [498, 499]. Almost in retaliation, Bridport reacted to his frigate shortage by ordering his captains to take under their command all frigates belonging to other squadrons not under Admiralty orders. He was reprimanded for doing so [501]. But he was positively jubilant in reporting captures on the north coast of Spain [506] and took delight in the commandeering of one of St Vincent's frigates that had strayed from the Mediterranean station, justifying the act by reference to precedents, though they were not considered appropriate ones at the Admiralty [507]. Indeed the Admiralty now reacted quickly and sharply to evidence of frigates straying from their designated stations. Bridport had to answer for unexplained alterations in deployments [508]. He was also reproved for weakening his battle fleet strength by deploying even single ships of the line on unauthorised stations [509].

Supervision of the blockade by the Admiralty was based on intelligence received from France, not only of the state of readiness of the Brest fleet, but of the movements of its admirals [511]. Internal political changes, notably the establishment of Napoleon as First Consul of France and the progress of the Chouan revolt in Brittany, informed the Admiralty's direction of the blockade [514]. The latter was particularly important in denying the French government control of land communications around Brest and in determining the dependence of the French fleet on supplies by sea. The French had virtually free movement in the Iroise, permitting frigate squadrons to sail and convoys to be escorted into Brest [515]. It was a freedom the Admiralty now desired to restrict, a responsibility that in early December 1799 fell to Gardner, as

Bridport was permitted leave. However, Gardner's efforts were frustrated by the winter gales which drove the fleet off station and back into Torbay at the end of the year [516, 518].

The enlargement and concentration of the Channel fleet raised problems of reprovisioning and refitting, especially at times when it returned to the English coast together. The combined numbers of the fleet in Torbay and Cawsand Bay placed a great strain on the victualling department at Plymouth. In addition the supply of ships in Torbay could be hampered by the easterly winds, which prevented victuallers getting round Berry Head [512]. To reduce the pressure on Plymouth's facilities, specific squadrons of ships of the line were diverted to Spithead to refit and reprovision [513]. Even so, prodigious quantities of provisions were shipped to Torbay, the amounts restricted in part by the limited number of victuallers available [517].

In January 1800 the report of a French squadron of 15 ships of the line having put to sea prompted the hasty return of Gardner off Brest. His instructions, demanding the despatch of a squadron in pursuit, if necessary into the Mediterranean, anticipated a series of similar orders that attempted to cover every conceivable eventuality that might result from the presence at Brest of the combined fleet [519]. This growing body of instructions formed a legacy inherited hereafter by all the fleet and squadron commanders blockading Brest during the remainder of the wars against Napoleonic France.

Not that Bridport seemed to share in the Admiralty's preoccupation with the enemy fleet in Brest. He persisted in attempting to deploy frigates on the north coast of Spain and off the Garonne, efforts the Admiralty continued to resist, not even permitting him to order ships to sea without Admiralty permission [520–22, 524]. Yet, once the whole of the combined fleet seemed to be established in Brest, if only temporarily, frigates were posted, partly as Bridport desired, off the Garonne and off Cape Finisterre. However, the principal purpose of the latter was not to take privateers but to track and provide information of a squadron that might escape from Brest [523, 525]. Furthermore, the Admiralty continued to keep control of the frigates ordered to cruise off Ferrol, a service on which Bridport was reduced simply to offering advice [544].

Bridport was encouraged to focus purely on closing the port of Brest. The strength and capabilities of the combined fleet depended on the naval stores available to it. But in February 1800 the British navy proved itself still incapable of stopping large ships from carrying stores and provisions into Brest [526]. Gardner was accordingly required to improve his guard over the entrances and exits, employing his 'most active, audacious and intelligent' captains for the purpose [527]. The sheer number of enemy ships of the line ready for sea posed a logistical challenge. With the possibility of the greater part sailing at a moment's notice, the absence of even part of the British force in port refitting markedly reduced Gardner's capability of meeting the enemy on equal terms [528]. In consequence in March Bridport was ordered out with reinforcements and directed to keep 28 battleships always with him. He was also to receive more smaller vessels to be devoted solely to watching Brest harbour and attacking convoys.

Bridport's instructions permitted the detachment of a pursuing squadron 'to any part of the world' so long as that pursuit was based on credible information of the enemy. Should Bridport himself with his main force be given the opportunity of destroying any part of the combined fleet, his main target was to be the French contingent [530]. Yet, when reinforcement permitted Gardner to return with a squadron into Torbay, Bridport felt as unequal to the combined fleet as Gardner had done, and no more capable of stopping ships getting in and out of Brest [532]. All that the Admiralty could do was to ensure Bridport kept with him all the frigates in their opinion available for the blockade of Brest, to keep him constantly reinforced, and to ensure provisions were always available in Torbay for ships returning to revictual [534, 535].

The supply of the quantity of stores and provisions required by the blockading fleet posed some problems. There was a shortage of cordage for ships refitting at Plymouth [549]. Also in the spring of 1800 the poor harvest of 1799 was felt in a national grain shortage. The southwest, which drew provisions from as far north as Gloucestershire, was to suffer particularly bad food shortages. In April the Victualling Board was obliged to insure against deficiencies by ordering provisions from Portsmouth and Dover [545]. Payments to crews for savings of bread, otherwise smuggled for sale on shore, were introduced [547]. In addition the Victualling Board had its Plymouth agent report precisely what had been done to supply the fleet in Torbay. His report exonerated the efforts of the Victualling department; it indicated that delays in the deliveries of victuallers in Torbay mainly resulted from adverse weather [550].

Fortunately in April 1800 reprovisioning for a long pursuit did not appear imminently necessary. Intelligence suggested that an expedition to Ireland was intended, to be escorted by at least 30 ships of the line. The Admiralty promptly increased Bridport's main force to 30 [538, 540, 541]. However, severe weather acted to drive the fleet into Torbay [546] where, though urged to sea [543], Bridport took the opportunity to strike his flag for the final time [548]. Now 73 years old, he had for some while been feeling frail [532] and had received permission to come on shore if the state of his health required him to do so [542]. Indeed, rather to his discomfiture, the Admiralty had felt the necessity to prepare his flag captain, Sir Charles Morice Pole, to succeed him in the event of his death [531, 536]. St Vincent, back from the Mediterranean, stood in the wings [537] and was to replace Bridport as Commander-in-Chief in the Channel later that month [551, 552]. Along with the death of Lord Howe in August 1799 [476], the event marked the transfer of command at sea in the Channel to a new generation of naval officers.

484. *Bridport to Admiralty*

Royal George, in Torbay, 18 August 1799

I have received your letter of the 16th instant acquainting me that His Majesty's ship Amelia was ordered to proceed immediately from Plymouth and join me in this bay and directing me to employ as many of the frigates as possible to watch the motions of the enemy at Brest; and to cause the caulkers of the fleet to be employed in caulking such ships as may require it. And in answer thereto I acquaint you that the Naiad and Amelia, together with the Lady Jane and Fowey cutters, anchored here yesterday afternoon.

I stated to you in my letter of the 16th instant that I had ordered Captain Keats with the ships and cutter named in the margin [*Boadicea, Uranie, Lurcher* cutter] to proceed on the station off Brest and on falling in with the Clyde, Diamond and Mondovi sloop to take them also under his orders and in my letter of yesterday's date I acquainted you that Vice Admiral Lord Keith had sent the ships named in the margin [*Prince George, Princess Royal, Hector, Defence*] to Spithead, which I suggested to him though he had, previous to his arrival here, made the Princess Royal's signal to put into Plymouth but it not being obeyed and the ship very leaky he directed her to repair to the above anchorage.

485. *Admiralty to Keith*[1]

19 August 1799

The Earl Spencer having communicated to my Lords Commissioners of the Admiralty your Lordship's letter of 16th instant desiring a few

---

[1] Addressed to Keith in Torbay.

days leave of absence from your duty on your private affairs, I have received their Lordships' commands to acquaint you that with every disposition to attend to your accommodation they feel it impossible in the present moment to comply with your Lordship's request.

486.   *Gardner to Spencer*

Royal Sovereign, Torbay, 20 August 1799

I have had the honour of receiving your Lordship's letter of the 15th instant and in answer beg leave to repeat the obligations I feel myself under for the offer you have been pleased to make me of the chief command at Portsmouth but feeling exactly as I did when I had the honour of answering your Lordship's first letter on that subject and however desirable the appointment may be in time of peace it is a situation I am by no means desirous of holding during the continuance of war so long as my health admits of my being more actively employed.

487.   *Spencer to Bridport*

Admiralty, 23 August 1799

As I can never have a better opportunity of seeing a large fleet collected together than the present one and as the service at the moment will allow of my quitting Town for a few days without inconvenience I propose myself the pleasure of paying your Lordship a visit in Torbay, where I mean to be (if not prevented by any unforeseen occurrence) on Monday morning next. My first object will of course be to pay my respects to your Lordship on board the Royal George and I shall be obliged to you to let a boat be ready to take me on board at Brixham Quay, where I hope to be by about nine o'clock or ten at latest on Monday morning. I shall only have my son and his tutor with me, whom I shall beg your permission to introduce to you and if the weather should prove favourable I look forward with great pleasure to passing a day or two in the midst of the very fine fleet now under your Lordship's command.

488.   *George III to Spencer*

Weymouth, 23 August 1799

Though not apprized of the particular motive of Earl Spencer's sudden departure for Torbay, I cannot but look on it as highly proper. I shall be glad of seeing him here on his return. If the weather should prove favourable I strongly recommend his coming from Torbay by sea as the passage will probably be very short.

489.   *Keats to Bridport*

Boadicea, at sea off Brest, 24 August 1799

It was not until the 22nd that I was able to get upon my station off Brest with the Uranie and Lurcher cutter and this day was the first that an opportunity offered of standing in with any prospect of reconnoitring the enemy; as we approached for that purpose five of the enemy's ships, frigates, and a sixth of, I believe, also the same rate, stood out, as we thought, to keep us off. The day passed in our standing in or off as circumstances would allow. Towards the evening the enemy's ships stood up with seeming intent to anchor in Camaret Bay but when sufficiently high bore up and stood (the six ships accompanied by a brig and lugger) towards the Raz, through which passage they all passed soon after sunset. Not having been joined by either the Diamond, Clyde, Mondovi or Fowey, doubtful if at liberty to consider these frigates as a squadron according to the spirit of my orders at sea and of sufficient importance to follow with both ships and thus leave the station entirely destitute of cruisers at a time when so very large a force of the enemy lay in Brest, I determined (especially as it appeared to me the service of watching them might probably be as well performed by one as two ships) to detach the Uranie on that service, which sails well, to send the Lurcher to your Lordship and remain with the Boadicea on this station. In so doing I trust I have acted, if not to the letter, to the spirit of my orders and to the satisfaction of your Lordship.

The Uranie parted at 8 p.m. but as there is no moon till late and she must pass without the Saintes and the course the enemy will steer cannot be ascertained there must be some doubt of her being in sight of them in the morning.

I have not spoke with any vessel from Brest nor do I believe from the winds and weather we have had that any one since we sailed from Torbay has been able to get out of that port before this day; we could not get sufficiently near to make any observation of the numbers, force or situation of the enemy's ships in the road. The commanding ship of the six wore a distinguishing pendant, they were all French and nothing was discovered that appeared to indicate having troops on board.

490.   *Bridport to Admiralty*

Royal George, Torbay, 26 August 1799

I acquaint you for their Lordships' information that I have received their secret order of the 23rd instant directing me to put to sea with such of His Majesty's ships under my command as may be in Torbay and proceed on the service therein stated and in return I acquaint you that most of the ships are in want of stores and provisions as neither the Empress Mary from the Nore or the Hindostan and Lascelles from Portsmouth have yet arrived here, nor any stores from Plymouth. Their Lordships will therefore be pleased to give such directions to hasten them as they shall judge necessary.

[*Endorsements*]

28th August: acquaint his Lordship that the Hindostan has sailed from Spithead to join him in Torbay for some days past and that the Victualling Board have been desired to hasten supplies of provisions to the ships which may be in want as speedily as possible.

Victualling Board to report what has prevented the supplies from reaching Torbay.

Acquaint him that it is so necessary he should proceed off of Brest before the convoys now at Spithead can go to sea that he should not wait either for the Hindostan or for further supplies of provisions but to send in his ships from time to time to be supplied as they can be spared or as their wants may render it necessary.

491.   *Young to Spencer*

Admiralty, 28 August 1799

I had very little hopes of your succeeding in persuading the Admirals to do what you wished. It is not a pleasant thing to allow oneself to be unfit for one's situation and indeed I feared that some of them might not be quite pleased at its being hinted to them that they were so.

492. *Sick and Wounded Board to Admiralty*

Office for Sick and Wounded Seamen, 30 August 1799

We have received your letter of the 20th ultimo signifying the directions of the Right Honourable the Lords Commissioners of the Admiralty that we should let you know for their Lordships' information the number of scorbutic cases in that part of the Channel fleet under the command of the Honourable Rear Admiral Berkeley.

In obedience thereto we enclose a list of the ships with the number of scorbutic cases which occurred on board each, either during their cruize, or which were on board at their arrival in port and we beg to observe that the surgeon of the Renown has stated that beside the 112 which he has returned, the scurvy became very general through the ship towards the end of the the cruize.

[*Enclosure*]

492a. *List of the ships under the command of the Honourable Rear Admiral Berkeley, with the number of scorbutic cases on board each ship*

Venerable	19
Renown	112
Robust	3
Ramillies	1
Ajax	5
Mars	12
	152

[*Endorsement*]

31 August: Let me see the paper which occasioned the application.

493. *Bridport to Admiralty*

Royal George, Torbay, 31 August 1799

As soon as the Hindostan has delivered to the fleet the stores she has on board to supply it or the vessel from Plymouth is cleared, it is my intention to carry the fleet under my command to sea, agreeably to their Lordships' directions, the moment I can quit this bay to arrive on my station without hazard and that I shall not wait for any further supplies. I have sent the frigates named in the margin [*Boadicea, Amelia, Diamond, Uranie, Triton, Unicorn, Sylph* sloop, *Fowey* cutter, *Lady Duncan* lugger] on that station as I consider it of the utmost importance to prevent as much as possible any supplies being carried into the port of Brest and I am sorry to find that Lord Keith judged it necessary to remove the Clyde and Diamond from the orders those ships were under when his Lordship came off Brest, which were placed there upon an original order from their Lordships and afterwards repeated by subsequent orders from me, these frigates being strictly put under my command. If they had not been removed there was an apparent probability that Captain Keats, under whose orders they were put, would have had strength sufficient to attack the six frigates that lately put to sea from that port. On that ground I shall leave the measure, trusting that I shall have no blame laid to my charge upon their escape.

When Lord Keith came to the northward of Cape Finisterre he fell in with the Stag and judged it for His Majesty's service to order her from her station to England, then cruising under my orders with the Fisgard, and when he had with him the Caroline, Beaulieu, Ethalion and Nymphe. When his Lordship came off of Brest three of the four were with him. It surely could not be necessary to fix on the Clyde to go off Rochefort and the Diamond to Cork.

494. *George III to Spencer*

Weymouth, 6 September 1799

I am sorry to find by Earl Spencer's note that Sir Alan Gardner still persists in not accepting of the command at Portsmouth which would have been an appointment highly pleasing to the officers of the Navy and with his disinclination to command a fleet might at some occasion have taken him out of an unpleasant predicament.

495. *Keats to Bridport*

Boadicea, off Brest, 6 September 1799

The object of the enemy's squadron mentioned in my letter of the 3rd by the Sylph, it seems pretty clear, is merely at present to favour and protect the arrival of their supplies – and I am sorry they have succeeded so well in it. On the 3rd, as it forced us to retire without the

Iroise, a convoy of nearly 30 sail entered through the Passage du Four. In the night a more numerous one got through the Passage du Raz, 14 of which, laden with naval stores, provisions, wine, etc. were taken and destroyed. Learning from the prisoners that three of the enemy's frigates had been that day in Hodierne [Audierne] Bay and seven sail of men of war supposed by them to be the Spanish squadron from Rochefort at nearly the same time off the Penmarks [Pointe de Penmarch], I passed the Raz with the Uranie in the night in the expectation of falling in with them in the morning; but the alarm had probably been given, for nothing was to be seen in the morning. Three ships were afterwards discovered, a frigate and 2 corvettes, which we chased into the rocky bay within the Glenans [Isles de Glénan] – returning I was called by signal to Rear Admiral Sir J. Warren who detained the Amelia and charged me with the accompanying letter. This morning I re-entered the Iroise through the Raz, reconnoitred the enemy and having afterwards been rejoined by the Diamond and learned from Captain Griffith[1] that your Lordship had expressed satisfaction in the supposition that Sir John Warren had taken me and the other frigates in pursuit of the Spanish squadron, I determined, as I felt convinced the enemy's fleet were not in sufficient readiness to put to sea, to leave one ship, the Unicorn, to look out in the Iroise and to proceed with the Diamond and Uranie to the southward of the Saintes in expectation of joining your Lordship and being useful in the pursuit of the Spaniards or serviceable in Hodierne Bay or off the Penmarks during the continuance of the westerly wind in intercepting any further supplies. For I feel persuaded with the present winds that in that situation the ships may be more advantageously employed for the public service than they can be in the Iroise, where their convoys can never be seen before they are through the Raz and in a situation to be protected by the squadron seemingly destined for that purpose.

P.S. 7th September. I take the liberty to add in a postscript that having this morning fallen in with Sir J. Warren, who does not at present detain me, I purpose proceeding off the Penmarks or into Hodierne Bay as circumstances may make necessary to intercept supplies and to vary my station from thence to the Iroise as circumstances according to my judgment shall render necessary to complete the object of your Lordship's commands.

[1]Sir Edward Griffith Colpoys. See biography in Chapter 2.

496.   *Nepean[1] to Bridport*

Admiralty, 9 September 1799

I have engaged Mr Serres,[2] the marine painter whose father I dare say your Lordship very well remembers, to go out in one of the ships from Plymouth for the purpose of taking views of Brest and the environs and to continue at sea during your present cruise. It is somewhat extraordinary that, excepting a sketch taken by the schoolmaster of the Sans Pareil there is not one view of that port or of any part of the coast in its vicinity to be found in this or any other of the public offices, though every possible search has been made, and is not now for your Lordship to know that views of that description give landsmen a better idea than the best constructed charts.[3] I flatter myself that your Lordship will receive Mr. Serres kindly and that you will give him every opportunity of performing the service required of him by putting him on board the frigates and other ships you may order to reconnoitre and the more extended his views are along the coast the better. I am to give him a large sum for this service.

497.   *Bridport to Admiralty*

Royal George, at sea, 5 a.m., 10 September 1799

I foresee that it will be for His Majesty's service to take my station with the fleet off the Saints and to watch narrowly the Passage du Raz, as the enemy may push through it to answer its immediate purposes. I write my sentiments for their Lordships' information as they occur to me.

498.   *Bridport to Admiralty*

Royal George, at sea, 10 September 1799

The number of ships of the line now with me is thirty-two and I wish to send two of them to cruise off the Penmarks to intercept the two ships

---

[1]First Secretary to the Board of Admiralty.

[2]John Thomas Serres (1759–1825), marine painter to George III. As marine draughtsman to the Admiralty from 1793 he received £100 a month. His father, Dominic Serres (1722–93) was born at Auch, Gascony, and served as a seaman and master of a trading vessel before being captured and brought to England, c. 1758. He became a member of the Royal Academy in 1768 and marine painter to George III.

[3]The practice of conveying geographical impressions to naval board members by means of paintings was already well established. From 1785 Joseph Farrington and Nicholas Pocock were commissioned to paint aerial views of the royal dockyards to be hung on the walls of the Navy Board boardroom. See Cordingly, *Nicholas Pocock*, 66–9.

that are intended to sail from Lorient for Brest, both new and both reported to be ready for sea. I wish also to send a frigate with a small vessel to cruise to the northward of the [Chenal du] Four but I have but one with the fleet, which is the Beaulieu and a repeater. The Magnanime, the other repeater, besides the Megara, parted company the day I came upon my station and has not yet rejoined me. The Sylph sloop was detached by Captain Keats to look after the fleet on the 3rd instant and I have not yet seen her. I am much surprised that the Magnanime and Sylph have not repaired to their rendezvous.

I have also expected out the Nymphe, Indefatigable and Stag as some of the frigates have been out their full time, particularly the Fisgard, which ship is cruising on the north part of the coast of Spain, and the Naiad I ordered to join her. It appears necessary that two frigates should always be upon that station, if not three or even four, as all the privateers out of Bordeaux pass and repass with their prizes along that coast and many captures have been carried into Port Passage.

499.   *Admiralty Secretary to Bridport*

Admiralty Office, 13 September 1799

I have received and communicated to my Lords Commissioners of the Admiralty your Lordship's letter of the 10th instant with its several enclosures; and I am commanded by their Lordships to acquaint you in answer thereto that by letters from Plymouth it appears Rear Admiral Collingwood has sailed from thence to rejoin your Lordship with the Triumph and Stag, and that Rear Admiral Berkeley in the Mars expected to be able to follow him with the ships named in the margin [*Terrible, Bellona, Indefatigable, Nymphe*] on the 11th instant.

In addition to the ships abovementioned, their Lordships have ordered the Cambrian to join you from the Downes and the Fisgard from Plymouth, to which port she has lately returned: with these reinforcements their Lordships trust you will be enabled to provide for the most necessary of the different services pointed out in your abovemention'd letter.

With repect however to the detaching of frigates to the north coast of Spain, as proposed by your Lordship, I have it in command to acquaint you that however proper it may be to have a squadron of frigates on that station, they are so impressed with the great importance of intercepting the enemy's coasting convoys bound to Brest with supplies, and of watching the proceedings of the enemy's fleet at that port, that until frigates can with more convenience be spared, they think it adviseable that the lesser consideration of intercepting the enemy's cruizers on the north coast of Spain should for the present give way.

500.   *Keats to Bridport*

Boadicea, off Brest, 15 September 1799

The accompanying letter from Rear Admiral Sir J. Warren was brought to me on the 10th, with which I then despatched the Lurcher to your Lordship but the latter having missed the fleet and rejoined me yesterday, I embrace the opportunity to inform your Lordship that the advanced squadron of the enemy has quitted its anchorage at Bertheaume and I have no doubt re-entered Brest on account of the late gale, since we had yesterday a good view of their fleet and by several different reports make it to consist of 60 ships of the line and frigates – 43, if not more, we take to be of the line. Two only of that class were made out to be incomplete in their equipment. Nearly all had their yards and topmasts struck or lower yards and topgallant masts lowered which some were then employed swaying up. We believe their sails to be bent and observed the Spanish ships had been lately freshly painted.

The Diamond and Amelia are in Hodierne [Audierne] Bay to watch the Passage du Raz and interrupt its navigation. The Uranie is with me. The Unicorn separated Friday evening. I am yet ignorant of the cause. The Triton was taken by Sir John Warren the 10th. The Sylph and Fowey I understand to be employed by your Lordship.

The few laden vessels going to Brest have been chased into Hodierne or the Penmarks and several light ones from it compelled to return or seek protection elsewhere.

501.   *Admiralty Secretary to Bridport*

Admiralty office, 5 October 1799

I have received and communicated to my Lords Commissioners of the Admiralty your letter of the 23d ultimo, acquainting me for their Lordships' information with the orders you had given to the commanders of your cruizers to take under their command all frigates belonging to other squadrons not under Admiralty orders, which they might fall in with upon your station; and inclosing the copy of a letter your Lordship had received from Captain Pierrepont of the Naiad who, in consequence of those orders, had taken the Alcmene under his command and brought her with him into port: and in return thereto, I have it in command to acquaint you that their Lordships do not approve of Captain Pierrepont's having taken the Alcmene under his orders (as you will have perceived by my letter to you of yesterday's date) and to signify their direction to your Lordship, except in situations where the urgency of the public service shall require it, not to take under your command any ship or vessel not put under your orders by them; and that when you give orders in future to the captains of ships of your squadron to take others under their command, you instruct them to take such only as shall be under your own immediate orders, it being their Lordships' intention that you should not interfere with the ships under the orders of any other officer.

Their Lordships approve of your never having sent ships to cruize to the southward of Cape Finisterre; and it is their direction that you continue to keep your cruizers to the northward of that cape, it being their intention that ships should be kept within the limits of the command of the admiral under whose orders they are placed, and have in consequence directed the captain of the Alcmene to account for his being found on this side of the cape abovementioned.

The strength of the enemy's fleet in Brest being such as to make it probable that all the ships of the line composing your Lordship's squadron will be required to watch it, especially if it should be found necessary that the squadron should cruize for that purpose during the winter, their Lordships do not for these reasons approve of your sending any ship of the line to cruize off Ferrol, as you have proposed.

502. *Bridport to Admiralty*

Royal George, Torbay, 6 October 1799

I acquaint you for their Lordships' information that the Fisgard joined me on the evening of the 4th instant and the following day I detached her to proceed off of Brest with orders to Captain Martin to take the Fowey cutter under his command and, on joining the Boadicea, to follow the orders of Captain Keats. The Childers came into the bay yesterday and I immediately gave Captain Crawford an order to proceed and cruise off Abreverack [Aber-Wrac'h] and when the Sirius shall be ready for sea it is my intention to send Captain King[1] on that station to prevent convoys getting through the Passage du Four and to take the Childers under his command.

[1]Sir Richard King (d. 1834). Lieutenant 1791; Captain 1794; Rear-admiral 1812; Vice-admiral 1821.

503.   *Bridport to Admiralty*

Royal George, Torbay, 9 October 1799

Enclosed is a letter from Captain White of His Majesty's ship Windsor Castle [not reproduced] which I transmit for their Lordships' information and I conclude they will cause that ship to be completed with men. I also beg to call their Lordships' attention to the ships of this fleet in general, which by the last weekly return they will perceive are fifteen hundred and twenty nine seamen short of the full complement.

504.   *Bridport to Captain Pierrepont*[1]

Royal George, off the Berry Head, 24 October 1799

In answer to your letter of the 23rd instant I acquaint you that it does not appear to me to be necessary for the Naiad to go into the harbour to refit. If it is, you must apply to the Admiralty for that purpose as I have never ordered a ship into Hamoaze but upon urgent occasions.

I am very glad to know that your two valuable prizes are safe in the harbour and that you are preparing to land the whole of the bullion, as it appears right and necessary that you should do so. I am also glad to know that the recaptured tobacco ship is arrived in the Sound.

I have received your journal, which you sent by the post and being above privilege was charged five shillings and five pence. This you will attend to in future as that expense would have been avoided if you had sent it by any of the ships ordered to join me from Plymouth.

505.   *Cunningham to Bridport*

Clyde, 27 October 1799

I was favoured with your Lordship's letter by the Fowey cutter but beg leave to inform you that it has become doubtful to me what were the motives of the enemy's motions on the 25th instant, for I now think they meant nothing more than to occupy Camaret Bay during the fine weather.

Yesterday, upon the approach of the fleet, two of them which were anchored at the mouth of the Goulet returned into the harbour (one of

[1]Of the *Naiad*.

the line) and left out only three of the line, one frigate and two corvettes. The division under Rear Admiral Berkeley working up put them into some confusion and I observed them to be sending people from Brest in boats to man the batteries at Camaret. The French admiral appeared not to know whether to weigh or to remain at anchor and was constantly making signals until the other two ships bore up to him.

By this time the Clyde and Fisgard were about gun shot from them and I thought it more proper to bear down upon the weathermost line of battle ship than to expose the two frigates to the fire of at least two of the enemy's ships of the line, which were close together, although the Rear Admiral had previously made the signals 13 and 48 but at the time we bore up our signal of recall was made and soon after that of the division.

The enemy continued under sail till the evening and then anchored in Camaret Bay, where they remain. Some small vessels are coming out of Brest and are, I apprehend, going to the southward.

506. *Bridport to Spencer*

Royal George, Torbay, 3 November 1799

I feel myself extremely obliged to your Lordship for the honour of your congratulations in the success of the frigates upon the north coast of Spain by which a valuable cargo has been brought into England and carried off from an enemy.

I rejoice equally with your Lordship that our friends in the Triton will have a share in the captures and it appears to me, as well as to your Lordship, that the bringing the Santa Brigida off in the face of a superior Spanish squadron does all the officers much credit . . .

P.S. I have just heard some very extraordinary reports on the subject of Lord St. Vincent's claims. I am persuaded neither your Lordship nor the Board of Admiralty will offer a partial judgment upon the occasion.

[Endorsed as received on the 5th]

507. *Young to Spencer*

Admiralty 5 November 1799

Your Lordship will have seen by the letter of yesterday that Lord Bridport is in Torbay, which is a most fortunate circumstance as we have had some very hard gales for the last three days. You will see a long letter on the subject of the Alcmene written in better temper than any I ever saw and you will probably have a letter from him on the same subject. The precedents he quotes are by no means similar to his case but as his letter does not appear to require an answer we have not told him so.[1]

508. *Bridport to Admiralty*

Royal George, Torbay, 6 November 1799

I received last night by express from Plymouth your letter of the 2nd instant signifying their Lordships' directions that I should call upon the captains of the Sirius and Childers sloop to report why they were not upon their station off Abbervrack [Aber-Wrac'h]. And in return I acquaint you that in consequence of their Lordships having directed me by your letter of the 9th ultimo to send the Boadicea to Spithead and the Amelia having been ordered by Captain Keats to proceed to Plymouth, where she arrived an the 15th, in consequence of her mainmast being sprung, which left only the Clyde and Fisgard on the service of watching the enemy's motions at Brest, I judged it necessary to send the Sirius, on her joining me the 18th, to reinforce Captain Cunningham. On my arrival off Brest the 25th ultimo I found the Childers had chased a small convoy through the Passage du Four and, on falling in with the Clyde, Captain Cunningham detained her in order to follow some chasse marées through the Bec du Raz; when I ordered Captain Crawford to repair to his station, where he now is, unless driven off by the late tempestuous weather.

509. *Bridport to Admiralty*

Royal George, Torbay, 8 November 1799

I have received your letter of the 6th instant signifying their Lordships' direction for me not to send the Dragon again off the Penmarks nor any ship of the line in her stead. Also to order the captains of the respective ships in this bay to complete their provisions to at least four months with all possible expedition. And in return I acquaint you that demands for that purpose shall be sent to the agent victualler at Plymouth with-

---

[1]Bridport had found one of St Vincent's frigates, the *Alcmene*, in the area of his command and had taken her over. The precedents he irrelevantly quoted were those of Kingsmill in October 1798 and Keith in August 1799.

out a moment's delay, and I beg to be informed if it is their Lordships' pleasure that the fleet should remain at this anchorage until the ships are completed with provisions to four months, which may take some time as the fleet has already been here a week and prevented from receiving any beer by the severity of the weather.

[*Endorsed that he should proceed to his station off Brest if the wind should come to the eastward*]

510. *Bridport to Admiralty*

Royal George, Torbay, 9 November 1799

Captain Countess having represented to me that His Majesty's ship Robust, under his command, is much infested with rats, he has shown me one of his cartridges very much eaten by them and enclosed is a statement signed by the Gunner of that ship which is transmitted for their Lordships' information. As the above ship was in course of payment the 1st of September last, it is my intention to send her to Cawsand Bay to refit the first opportunity.

[*Enclosure*]

510a. *Henry Davis, Gunner, to Countess*

Robust, 9 November 1799

Cartridges destroyed by rats, etc.	32 prs.	640
....	18 ..	737
....	9 ..	453
Carronade	18 ..	136
....	32 ..	103
	Total	2069

Henry Davis. Gunner

511. *Young to Spencer*

Admiralty, 15 November 1799

I am very sorry for the necessity of our fleet going out but with an easterly wind we must not wish them in Torbay. We have, however, directed Lord Bridport to take with him only thirty ships, for by the papers received today the Spanish admiral appears to have been very lately at Paris, which will prevent the whole of their fleet sailing, and the messages by telegraph, if true, will show them to be in such a state as to prevent their sending out expeditions till the new order of things[1] is a little settled, so that had our ships been in a safer anchorage I should have wished them to remain there.

512.   *Bridport to Admiralty*

Royal George, Torbay, 15 November 1799

The wind having come to the eastward I caused the signal to be made for the fleet to unmoor and if it continues in that quarter I shall proceed to sea either this evening or tomorrow morning but it is with regret I state to you that the ships are much shorter of provisions now, except beef and pork, than on their arrival in this bay and I apprehend the port of Plymouth cannot be depended upon through the winter season for supplying a fleet with provisions at this anchorage and in Cawsand Bay amounting to more than forty ships of the line exclusive of frigates and smaller vessels. In making these suggestions I mean no complaint against any department, the disappointment having been occasioned by the inclemency of the weather and what has taken place now may happen again as I have been here a fortnight and the only supplies have been fresh beef and about one hundred and thirty tuns of beer.

513.   *Bridport to Admiralty*

Royal George, at sea, 19 November 1799

I have received your letter of the 15th instant signifying their Lordships' directions that I should only keep with me thirty ships of the line, sending such ships to Spithead to be refitted as I may think proper above that number. And in the event of my putting to sea, to return to Torbay when the wind shall shift to the westward, without waiting till it blows hard. In return I acquaint you that I have ordered Rear Admiral Sir Charles Cotton[2] in the Prince together with the ships named in the

---

[1]Napoleon had seized power six days before.
[2]Sir Charles Cotton (d. 1812). Lieutenant 1777; Captain 1779; Rear-admiral 1797; Vice-admiral 1802; Admiral 1808.

margin [*Superb*, *Pompee*, *Agamemnon*] to proceed to that anchorage to be refitted and paid. I have also ordered the Rear Admiral to direct and superintend the speedy re-equipment of the several ships at Spithead under my command.

514. *Intelligence report*

Intelligence obtained from French fishermen by the Dolly cutter, 19 November 1799.

That the reason of the ships being dressed is that Buonaparte has dissolved the Directory and placed himself at the head of the government and that the people were well pleased with the measure.

That Quimper has been stormed by the Chouans and all prisoners of every description liberated.[1]

515. *Intelligence report*

Substance of the last communications from Brest received at Jersey, 24 November 1799.

Jersey, 26 November 1799

October 7th. The Bravoure frigate sailed from L'Orient with the following corvettes: L'Eole, La Belagie, La Cerf, La Bichu.

18th. The Terrible went out of the harbour and joined the fleet in the road. The frigate La Vengeance sailed for L'Orient.

The corvette La Chevrette and an armed lugger went out of the harbour in the road.

21st. Forty tons of gunpowder and two hundred stand of arms escorted by a company of infantry sixty strong came in from the country, the stores were deposited at the Arsenal.

25th. The following line of battle ships and frigates under the command of Citizen Le Targée went out of the road and anchored at Bertheaume. Viz. – The line of battle ships La Convention, Le Patriote, Le Jean Bart, Le Tourville. Frigates. La Bravoure, La Precieuse and another, the name not reported.

The Tactique corvette that had sailed yesterday returned with the Chevrette this morning; the cutter L'Aiguille went out to Bertheaume.

---

[1]Although the Chouans gained some successes during October the revolt was put down by General Hedouville by mid-December.

The movements of this division are intended to protect the arrival of a convoy expected with provisions. If the coast is clear it has orders to go and meet it as far as L'Orient.

Nov. 4th. The above division that cruised in the Iroise returned to Bertheaume.

5th. A convoy of twenty sail arrived from Nantes loaded with grain and flour for the fleet.

10th. The division at Bertheaume has received men to convey to L'Orient to fit the ships that are there.

It is expected to sail the first favourable moment.

The fleet having been subsisted on its sea provisions for some time are now reduced to a three months' proportion, exclusive of bread, which the convoy arrived the 5th will complete to four months.

The Chouans continue to intercept and interrupt all unprotected communications with the country up to the very suburbs, the field and out works of which have lately been repaired and on which working parties of the garrison are still employed.

516.   *Bridport to Admiralty*

Royal George, at sea, 5 December 1799

I have received your letter of the 2nd instant acquainting me that directions have been given for provisions to be sent from Plymouth to Torbay so soon as any part of the fleet under my command arrives there or on its way thither. And, agreeably to their Lordships' instructions, I shall direct Admiral Sir Alan Gardner during his continuance off of Brest to use his utmost endeavours to prevent supplies being carried into that port or the enemy's ships of the line from going out to protect their convoys from His Majesty's frigates and, when he returns into port, to leave as many frigates as possible to watch the motions of the enemy fleet and to intercept their convoys.

517.   *Victualling Board to Admiralty Secretary*

Victualling Office, 27 December 1799

Inclosed we beg leave to send you, for the information of the Right Honourable the Lords Commissioners of the Admiralty, an account of provisions shipped by our agent at Plymouth on board sundry vessels between the 28th ultimo and 24th instant, as well as for the supply of the squadron of His Majesty's ships in Torbay under the command of

Rear Admiral Whitshed,[1] as for the use of the Channel fleet on its return to that place; shewing also the period for which the provisions proposed for each service are respectively calculated to serve 10,000 men: – and as the detention of the vessels containing the provisions designed for the Channel fleet is attended with considerable expense to the Crown, we submit to their Lordships how far it may be adviseable to ship any further supplies of provisions for Torbay for the service of the said fleet until we hear of its return to that place.

[*Endorsement*]

28 December: Not to ship any further supplies until its return.

[*Enclosure*]

517a. *An account of the provisions shipped from His Majesty's victualling stores at Plymouth on board sundry vessels for Torbay, between the 28th November and 24th December 1799*[2]

	For the squadron now in Torbay under the command of Rear Admiral Whitshed.	Which will serve 10,000 men.	For the Channel Fleet on its return to Torbay.	Which will serve 10,000 men.
Biscuit	2,761 cwt.	30 days	4,400 cwt.	49 days
Beer	215 tuns	5	644 tuns	16
Wine	23,251 galls	18	13,511 galls	10
Spirits	3,655 galls	5	10,031 galls	16
Beef	5,966 eight lb pieces	19	7,548 pieces	15
Pork	11,437 four lb pieces	16	10,445 pieces	14
Flour	45,651 lbs ⎫	included in the beef.	25,167 lbs ⎫	included in the beef.
Suet	7,665 lbs ⎭		– ⎭	
Raisins	600 lbs		5,429 lbs	
Pease	976 bushels	21	957 bushels	21

[1]Sir James Hawkins Whitshed (d. 1849). Lieutenant 1778; Captain 1780; Rear-admiral 1799; Vice-admiral 1804; Admiral 1810.

[2]In the original this table is presented horizontally.

Oatmeal	281 bushels	4	799 bushels	11
Molasses	22,800 lbs	7	95,133 lbs	30
Butter	13,646 lbs	4	23,922 lbs	6
Cheese	28,673	19	22,680 lbs	13
Sugar	4,038 lbs	} included	–	} included
Rice	8,077 lbs	in butter & cheese.	2,628 lbs	in butter & cheese.
Vinegar	1,243 lbs	13	767 lbs	8
Tobacco	2,000 lbs	–	969 lbs	–

518. *Gardner to Admiralty*

Royal Sovereign, at sea, Lat. 49.02 N., long. 6.49 W.,
28 December 1799

I herewith enclose duplicates of my letter to you dated the 12th instant, forwarded to Falmouth by the Telemachus cutter, since which time we have had continual gales of wind from the E.N.E. to the E.S.E. with very little variation and the fleet have therefore been unable to maintain their station off Brest and have been driven upwards of sixty leagues to the westward of Ushant, frequently obliged to lay to under a close reefed maintopsail only. I have the satisfaction to add that the squadron have not hitherto suffered any material injuries in their masts, yards or sails.

519. *Admiralty to Gardner*

12 January 1800

Having ordered Rear Admiral Sir Charles Cotton in His Majesty's ship Prince with the others named in the margin [*Superb*, *Saturn*, *Cumberland*, *Glory*, *Hector*, *Agamemnon*] to proceed immediately to Torbay, you are hereby required and directed upon his appearance to put to sea with the squadron under your orders, and taking the Rear Admiral and the ships abovementioned with you, proceed as expeditiously as possible off Brest, from which port a squadron (as appears by the intelligence herewith transmitted to you) is reported to have sailed, consisting of 15 ships of the line.

If, on your arrival off Brest, you should find that the whole of the enemy's fleet still remains there, you are to cruize off that port to watch it until the wind shall settle to the westward and then to return to Torbay; but in case of obtaining information that a part of the enemy's ships have put to sea, you are to detach Sir Charles Cotton with such a number of ships of the line (best fitted for foreign service) as may be equal to that of the enemy, or with twelve sail of the line if the force of the enemy cannot be ascertained, together with two or three frigates and two cutters and luggers.

You are to direct Sir Charles Cotton to proceed with all possible dispatch off Ferrol, sending a frigate ahead to reconnoitre that port, and in case it should appear that the French squadron has put in there, to cruize off that port to prevent its' sailing; but not finding it there, to make the best of his way to the southward, detaching a frigate to Lisbon to obtain information and directing Rear Admiral Duckworth to join him, if he should be there.

In case Sir Charles Cotton should not obtain intelligence of the enemy's having taken some other direction, he is to cruize off Cadiz, and finding the French squadron there, to cruize off that port, using his best endeavours to prevent its' sailing; and you are to instruct him, whilst he shall be on the coast of Portugal to detach some vessel to Tangier Bay for the purpose of ascertaining whether the enemy's squadron has proceeded up the Straits keeping near the coast of Barbary; and, if he shall find that it has passed the Straits, to follow it, sending into Gibraltar for information respecting it.

Should he not obtain any intelligence from thence which may enable him to determine what may be the enemy's destination, he is to proceed off Mahon, and not meeting with Lord Keith there, nor receiving intelligence of the course the enemy has steered, to repair off Malta, sending a frigate to Cagliari to obtain information, and some vessel for the like purpose to Leghorn or to such other place as he may learn the Commander in Chief [Mediterranean] to be, apprizing him of his arrival and intended proceedings.

If the Rear Admiral should arrive off Malta without receiving accounts of the enemy, he is to remain there until he shall receive orders from the Commander in Chief. In case he should not find the French squadron in Cadiz, nor obtain information of it having passed the Straits, he is to proceed to Lisbon and wait there for orders.

If however he finds the enemy's squadron in Cadiz, or follows it into the Mediterranean, he is in that case to put himself under the orders of Vice Admiral Lord Keith, or the Commander in Chief for the time being.

As soon as you shall have ascertained the state of the enemy's force at Brest, you are immediately to send an account thereof to our Secretary for our information; and in case of you detaching Sir Charles Cotton as abovementioned, to instruct him to transmit in like manner the intelligence he shall have obtained respecting it.

If previously to your leaving Torbay you should receive certain information of the enemy's fleet having sailed from Brest, you are upon being joined by Sir Charles Cotton immediately to make the detachment without waiting until you shall have looked into that port.

520.   *Bridport to Admiralty*

London, 20 January 1800

I acquaint you for their Lordships' information that agreeably to their permission communicated by your letter of the 17th instant I have sent instructions to Sir Alan Gardner in the event of his finding the enemy's fleet still in Brest to detach the Clyde and any other frigate he can conveniently spare to cruise from Belle Isle to the Garonne. And as their Lordships have permitted me to send some frigates to the southward I beg to know if I may be allowed to order any ships to cruise between Cape Penas and Port Passage, that place being a rendezvous of a number of the enemy's privateers and as one of the best stations to intercept captures they may make. The Danae and some other frigates at Plymouth will soon be ready for sea.

[*Endorsed that their Lordships cannot allow him to detach the frigates to that station at present*]

521.   *Bridport to Admiralty*

London, 24 January 1800

I have received your letter of the 22nd instant acquainting me that their Lordships have found it necessary to employ the Danae[1] on a temporary service with the Loire and that I was not to send any orders to her captain for the present. Their Lordships may be assured that every attention shall be paid to their directions communicated by your letters of the 13th and 21st instant and I shall not order any ship to sea until I receive their permission for that purpose. At the same time I beg to state to their Lordships that it has always been my wish to have two or three frigates cruising off the Garonne and I regret that there was not one with the Amethyst, in which case there is no doubt but the two

---

[1]On 25 March Captain Edward Griffith wrote to Bridport informing him that the *Danae* had been captured by her crew and carried into Brest. PRO, ADM. 1/115, 25 March 1800. For Collingwood's observation regarding the *Danae* Mutiny see the Note by R. Saxby in *The Mariner's Mirror*, 74 (1988), 328.

French frigates seen by Captain Cooke the 6th instant would have been captured.

522. *Admiralty to Bridport*

24 January 1800

I have received and communicated to my Lords Commissioners of the Admiralty your letter to me of this day's date upon the subject of some frigates to be employed in cruising off the Garonne and I have their Lordships' command to acquaint you that they cannot allot any frigate at present to that particular service.

523. *Admiralty to Bridport*

31 January 1800

His Majesty's ships Amethyst and Nymphe, at Plymouth, being ready for sea, I have it in command from my Lords Commissioners of the Admiralty to acquaint your Lordship therewith in order to your giving their commanders such instructions as you may judge necessary for their proceeding to cruise with the said ships off the Garonne.

524. *Bridport to Admiralty*

London, 1 February 1800

I have received your letter of the 31st ultimo acquainting me that the Amethyst and Nymphe are ready for sea and directing me to send such instructions as I may judge necessary for their commanders to proceed and cruise with the said ships off the Garonne, which shall be complied with.

By letters lately received from Lord Ranelagh[1] and Captain Gore I am informed their respective ships will soon be ready for sea. It has always been my intention to send the Triton off of Brest to relieve the Sirius and when she is refitted and ready for service to have ordered the Doris and that ship to cruise to the southward of the Garonne if their Lordships shall approve of this arrangement.

[1]The Honourable Charles, Viscount Jones (d. 1800). Lieutenant 1782; Captain 1793. Created an English peer 1797.

[Endorsed that at present it is not their Lordships' intention to allow him to send ships south of the Garonne]

525.   *Admiralty to Bridport*[1]

9 February 1800

Your Lordship is hereby required and directed to order three of the frigates under your command now at Plymouth to proceed with all possible dispatch off Ferrol, and cruize off that place and Cape Finisterre, keeping a very vigilant look out for the purpose of discovering a squadron of the enemy's ships which are expected shortly to sail from Brest, and upon discovering the enemy's squadron, one of the said frigates is to remain off Ferrol in order to give information thereof to a squadron of His Majesty's ships which may be expected to follow the enemy, whilst the other two (which are to be the fastest sailing ships), are to follow the enemy and use their best endeavours to ascertain their course, keeping the enemy's squadron in sight until it shall have entered the Straits of Gibraltar, in case it should be proceeding thither.

Having so done, one of the last-mentioned frigates is to cruize off the Straits for the purpose of giving information to the British squadron which may be in quest of the enemy (taking, however, particular care not to be carried by the current into the Straits) and the other is to proceed to Minorca and Malta with intelligence, unless any other of His Majesty's frigates belonging to the squadron employed in the Mediterranean should proceed on the last-mentioned service, in which case the frigate sent by your Lordship is to keep company with the enemy's squadron, and having ascertained its course, her captain is to endeavour to fall in with His Majesty's squadron which may probably pass near to Carthagena. But if the enemy's squadron instead of steering a course for the Straits should steer to the westward, the two frigates sent by your Lordship are to follow it until it shall have got so far as to make it highly improbable that it should be destined for the Mediterranean, at which time one of them is to proceed with all possible expedition to Tangier, and land an officer with such information as her captain shall have obtained, with directions to the said officer to proceed with such information immediately to Gibraltar in order to its being sent after any squadron of His Majesty's ships which may have gone up the Mediterranean, a duplicate and triplicate

[1]Addressed to Bridport 'in Town'.

of which information he is to send to the British Consul at Tangier, to be forwarded by safe & speedy conveyances to Gibraltar. The captain of the frigate is then to proceed off the Tagus, and send the like information to His Majesty's Minister and the commanding officer of His Majesty's ships at Lisbon, and having so done make the best of his way to the nearest port in England and transmit to our Secretary with all possible dispatch an acccount of his arrival and proceedings. If, however, he should fall in with any other of His Majesty's frigates before he goes to Tangier or Lisbon, he is in that case to send her with the information to those places, and is to come himself to England as above directed. The other frigate which follows the enemy's squadron is to keep sight of it until her captain shall have been able to determine its destination, and then proceed with all possible expedition to inform the commander of His Majesty's ships of its approach, making the best of his way to Martinique and Jamaica if the enemy should be bound to the West Indies.

If whilst cruizing off Ferrol, the captains of the said frigates should obtain information that the enemy's squadron has passed to the southward though not seen by them, one of the frigates is to remain off the last-mentioned port as above directed; another of them is to proceed with all possible dispatch to the Straits of Gibraltar in order to ascertain whether the enemy's squadron has passed that way; and the third is to proceed to Madeira, and not hearing of it there, to go on to Teneriffe, and not being able to obtain information of it at that place, to proceed as expeditiously as possible to Martinique and Jamaica with information of the enemy's squadron having sailed, and of its destination being uncertain; but if her captain should fall in with or obtain certain information of the course it has steered, he is, in that event, to proceed as before directed.

As the determining the destination of any squadron which may sail from Brest must be of the greatest consequence, the commanders of the said frigates are not to suffer themselves to be led away from their stations in chace, and they are to be particularly attentive whenever the wind shall be such as may admit of the enemy's sailing from Brest.

Your Lordship will direct the captains of the frigates which you may appoint for this service to continue upon it so long as their provisions or water will allow, and then make the best of their way to Plymouth for further orders.

526.   *Curzon to Gardner*

Indefatigable, at sea, Stevenet S.E. by S. 4 miles, 15 February 1800

From the unusual number of large vessels which are constantly attempting and generally with success to pass into Brest by channels of the Four and Toulinquet[1] I have reason to believe it has received a large supply of stores and provisions. Today I gave chase and was in great hopes of cutting off two large ships passing from the Raz to the Toulinquet but the wind southering brought us to leeward and they went away large into Brest. One of them appears to be a ship of the line under reduced masts and the poop taken off, the other a large merchant ship. A large transport at anchor between the Parquet [La Parquette] and St. Mathieu was obliged to cut and run into [Le] Conquet. Near forty sail of large vessels came down the Four last Monday evening and another convoy (if I may judge by the number of signals made in that channel) passed through in the night of Wednesday.

527.   *Admiralty to Gardner*[2]

20 February 1800

I have it in command from my Lords Commissioners of the Admiralty to send you herewith copies of intelligence received from Lisbon in order that you may inform the officers whom you may detach after any squadron of the enemy's ships of the possibility of its being destined as therein mentioned. From the variety of information which has been received respecting the squadron said to be ready to sail from Brest and the variety of destinations to which it is supposed to be intended their Lordships are confident that you will see, without their more particularly pointing out to you, the absolute necessity there is for its being so closely watched as to make it impossible for it to put to sea without your being so immediately informed of it as to enable you to bring it to action before it can leave the coast; to do which it will be necessary that you keep some of the frigates and smaller vessels under your orders constantly watching the Passage du Raz and the Goulet that every movement of the enemy may be observed as soon as made; and the commanders of the frigates and other vessels so employed should be directed to consider the watching of the enemy as the sole object of their attentions and not to suffer themselves on any account to be led

---

[1]There is a Pointe du Toulinquet close to Camaret Bay.
[2]Addressed to Gardner off Brest.

away from that object by chasing or by any other circumstance whatever. But as far as may be consistent with that service they are to
prevent supplies being carried into Brest by taking or destroying the
convoys bound thither and for the more perfect performance of this
service their Lordships do not doubt but that you will see the propriety
of employing upon it the most active, audacious and intelligent captains
under your orders.

528.   Gardner to Admiralty

Royal Sovereign, at sea, Ushant S.E. about 6 leagues,
25 February 1800

By His Majesty's ship Stag, which joined me this evening, I received
your letter of the 18th instant acquainting me that Rear Admiral Whitshed
has been directed to proceed with the ships named in the margin [*Royal
George, Temeraire, London, Pompee, Ramillies, Hector, Montagu, Venerable*] to Torbay in order that if anything in the movements of the
enemy's fleet should indicate an intention to send the whole or the
greatest part of it to sea I may send orders to those ships to join me . . .
Their Lordships, however, trust that I will not call them out unless I
shall see sufficient grounds to justify me for so doing. In answer thereto
I beg leave to state that their Lordships are in possession of all the
intelligence respecting the enemy's fleet which has come to my knowledge, by which it appears that there are forty-one or forty-two sail of
the line in Brest, with the flags of nine admirals, and Captain Curzon in
his last report is of opinion that about thirty sail of the line appear to be
perfectly ready for sea, which (with respect to numbers) corresponds
with the intelligence you received from Captain D'Auvergne, Prince of
Bouillon, which you transmitted to me in your letter of the 15th instant,
fourteen of which are said to be completed to five months and twelve
others to three mouths, besides fifteen sail of Spanish ships of the line
and several frigates which I am to suppose are also ready. Their Lordships therefore must be the best judges whether the force they have put
under my command is or is not sufficient for the service expected from
it. Previous to my sailing from Torbay their Lordships directed me by
your letter of the 20th January not to proceed to sea with more than
twenty sail of the line, since which I have had their Lordships' authority to send for the ships I left in Torbay and also those in Cawsand Bay
if from the apparent size of the enemy's force in Brest I should think it
necessary to do so, which I had no difficulty whatever in determining
upon, and if from any subsequent intelligence which their Lordships

have received through me or from any other quarter they should at this critical conjuncture deem it advisable to reinforce me I trust they will send their orders to Rear Admiral Whitshed accordingly, as it is most probable that the only information I may receive of the enemy's movements will be that of their getting under weigh, when it will be too late for me to send orders for the ships in Torbay to join me, neither (in all probability) will it be in my power to send the Rear Admiral a rendezvous where to join me or to direct him to what quarter he is to proceed in quest of me.

You further acquaint me that it is their Lordships' intention to employ under my orders as many frigates and smaller vessels as other services will admit. The sooner they are ordered the better as I shall have only three frigates left with the fleet when the Diamond leaves me (who must go into port for a new bowsprit) and these are very insufficient for the several services for which they are wanted at present and in the event of the enemy's putting to sea I shall feel the want of frigates and other smaller vessels exceedingly, indeed without an addition it will be impossible for me to fulfil the different orders and instructions that I have received from their Lordships.

529.   *Admiralty to Bridport*[1]

4 March 1800

Having communicated to my Lords Commissioners of the Admiralty your Lordship's letter to me of this date acquainting me for their Lordships' information that in pursuance of their directions to you to proceed without a moment's loss of time to Torbay you intended leaving Town either this evening or tomorrow morning, expecting to arrive there on Saturday or Sunday week, I am commanded by their Lordships to acquaint you that as there is an intention of ordering your Lordship to sail from the anchorage abovementioned as soon as possible with the ships which may be assembled there, their Lordships are desirous you should repair thither as soon as you can and which they hope you will be enabled to do long before the time you have mentioned.

---

[1] Addressed to Bridport 'in Town'.

530. *Admiralty to Bridport*[1]

17 March 1800

Your Lordship is hereby required and directed to put to sea immediately with all the ships in Torbay, and proceed as expeditiously as possible off Brest, and having joined Admiral Sir Alan Gardner who is now on that staion your Lordship is to keep with you twenty-eight sail of the line and all the frigates which you may find on that station and to send Sir Alan Gardner with all the ships of the line more than the number above-mentioned into port, with directions to him to repair with six ships in addition to the Royal Sovereign to Cawsand Bay, selecting for that purpose such ships as may be in the course of pay or that may stand most in need of repair or a supply of stores, and sending the others to Torbay, there to remain until they receive further orders, directing the captains of the whole of the said ships to complete their stores and provisions and get their ships ready for sea with all possible dispatch.

In case any of the ships named in the margin [*Impetueux, Robust, Canada, Russell, Defence*] should not join your Lordship in Torbay, you are to leave directions for them to follow you off Brest, sending similar orders to the four first mentioned of those ships which are now at Plymouth.

From the variety of intelligence which has been received relative to the destination of the enemy's fleet at Brest (copies of which you will receive herewith), it is extremely difficult to determine for what object it may be really intended; it will therefore be of the utmost consequence that your Lordship should use every possible precaution and exertion to prevent its putting to sea without your having such early information of its movements as may enable you to bring it to action before it leaves the coast, to enable you to do which as many frigates and smaller vessels as can be spared from other services will be sent to your Lordship, all of which you are to employ on that duty alone, arranging them in such manner as you shall judge best for watching the enemy, with instructions to their captains to consider that service as the object to which their attention is at all times to be directed and never to suffer themselves to be led away by chacing or by any other circumstance whatever; but, they are to use their utmost endeavour to prevent supplies of every description being carried into Brest so far as it can be done without drawing off their attention from the principal object upon which they are employed.

If, notwithstanding your Lordship's endeavours to prevent it, a squadron of the enemy's ships should put to sea, and escape without your

[1]Addressed to Bridport in Torbay.

being able to bring it to action, you are immediately to proceed to the coast of Ireland with the whole force under your command or with such part of it as shall be at least equal in number and force (as far as from the information you may receive you shall be able to determine) to the enemy's squadron, leaving in the latter case one of the Flag officers with the remainder to watch the enemy's ships left in Brest.

But if your Lordship should obtain information on which you may with certainty depend that there are no troops embarked in the enemy's ships, or if any, not more than four or five thousand, you are to detach a squadron equal in number and force to that of any squadron which may escape from Brest, selecting for that purpose (as far as other circumstances will admit) the faster sailing ships and putting them under the command of one or more flag officers, as from their number you may think fit, under the instructions hereinafter mentioned.

If the enemy's squadron which may put to sea should be composed entirely of French ships, your Lordship is in that case to direct the officer commanding the detachment which you may send in pursuit of it to proceed immediately off Ferrol in order to obtain information from the frigates stationed there for the purpose of looking out for it, but not obtaining from the captains of the frigates, nor by any other means information of the enemy, he is in that event to send a frigate along the coast to Lisbon for the purpose of obtaining such information with directions to any of His Majesty's ships which may be in the Tagus to join him when he appears off that river, instructing the captain of the frigate to look into Vigo in his way, if he can do so without losing time.

In case the said commanding officer should not receive intelligence of the enemy's squadron at Lisbon, he is to proceed with the ships under his command off Cadiz, sending a frigate before him to Tangier Bay with orders to her captain to ascertain, if possible, whether the enemy's squadron has proceeded up the Straits; and not obtaining any information thereof, he is to repair with the said ships to Lisbon and wait there for further orders, leaving some frigates cruizing off the Straits to carry him information if the enemy should arrive there after he had gone away, transmitting to our Secretary with all possible dispatch an account of his arrival and proceedings and completing with all possible dispatch the water and provisions of the ships. But if he should learn that the enemy's squadron has gone through the Straits, he is to follow it, sending into Gibraltar for any intelligence he may be able to obtain of it there, but not obtaining any such intelligence, he is to proceed off Mahon, looking into Carthagena if it can be done without loss of time.

On his arrival off Mahon, if he should not find Vice Admiral Lord Keith at that place, nor obtain information which may enable him to follow the enemy, he is immediately to proceed off Malta, sending information of his arrival and intended proceedings to the said Vice Admiral either at Leghorn or wherever he shall have reason to believe he may be; and in case the said commanding officer shall arrive off Malta without having obtained intelligence of the enemy, he is to remain there until he obtains it, or until he receives orders from the Commander in Chief of His Majesty's ships in the Mediterranean for his further proceedings. But if on his arrival off Malta, he should receive certain information of the French squadron having raised the blockade of that island and that the said squadron had proceeded to some other place, he is in that case to follow it according to the best intelligence he may be able to obtain, and upon coming up with it to use his best endeavours to take or destroy it.

If, after having passed the Straits he should discover that he has been misinformed and should obtain certain information that the enemy had not gone into the Mediterranean, he is to go immediately to Lisbon and wait there 'til he receives orders from us, or information which may enable him to follow the enemy.

If he should find the enemy's squadron on any port or place in which he cannot attack it, he is to cruize off that port or place for the purpose of preventing its putting again to sea, taking care to send immediately information of his situation to our Secretary, and if within the Mediterranean to Vice Admiral Lord Keith whose orders he is to follow in the event either of his finding the enemy's squadron at Cadiz or following it through the Straits.

Your Lordship will direct the officer commanding the squadron you detach to follow that of the enemy to any part of the world to which it may go as long as he shall be able to obtain information on which he may with certainty depend of the route it has taken; and if it should go to the West Indies he is in that case to repair with all possible expedition to Martinique, and not hearing of them there to make the best of his way to Jamaica, and follow the orders of Admiral Sir Hyde Parker[1]. But, as it is of the utmost consequence that the British squadron should not go to the West Indies, nor to any other very distant part unless the enemy's squadron should go there, he is to be extremely cautious how he gives credit to any information he receives, and to proceed in consequence of such only as will not admit of his doubting of its truth; and whenever he shall determine to go to the West Indies or to any other

---

[1] Sir Hyde Parker (1739–1807). Lieutenant 1758; Captain 1763; Rear-admiral 1793; Vice-admiral 1794; Admiral 1799.

very distant part he is immediately to send a frigate to England with an account thereof to our Secretary for our information.

In case the squadron which may sail from Brest should be composed of Spanish and French ships, and the commanding officer of the squadron which your Lordship may detach in pursuit of it should find that the Spanish ships had put into port and that the French ships had proceeded on, he is to leave such a number of ships as he can spare to watch the port in which the Spanish ships may be, and proceed himself in pursuit of the French ships with a force equal to theirs, considering in all his operations the taking or destroying the French squadron as the principal object of his attentions.

If he should fortunately take or destroy the enemy's squadron before it gets to the Mediterranean, he is to return with the ships which may be with him to England. But if the capture or destruction of it should happen within the Straits, he is to repair either to Gibraltar or Mahon as circumstances may require.

As it is probable the enemy may intend to employ their force on different objects, the commanding officer abovementioned is, in case he should learn that they have divided their squadron, to divide his also in the same manner following one part himself with one division, and detaching the other division after the other part of the enemy's force. But if he should obtain information of one part only, he is to follow that and send the other division to Lisbon to wait for orders.

If the force of the enemy should be such as to render it necessary for your Lordship to follow it with all the ships under your command, you are to follow it accordingly, taking care to send to our Secretary for our information the earliest intelligence of your having so done, and to transmit to him also during your continuance at sea frequent accounts of your proceedings, and every intelligence you may be able to obtain proper for our knowledge.

In case upon your Lordship's falling in with the enemy's fleet, you should find it composed of French and Spanish ships, and should have no prospect of bringing the whole to action, you are, in that event, to use your best endeavours to take or destroy the French ships in preference to those belonging to Spain.

If on your arriving off Brest you should find the enemy had put to sea, and that Admiral Sir Alan Gardner was gone in pursuit of them, you are, if the information you obtain will enable you so to do, to follow them, unless there should be a considerable force of the enemy remaining in Brest, in which case you are to remain off that port and prevent the enemy from putting to sea; but if there should be no such force remaining in Brest and you should not obtain information of the course the squadron has taken, you are to go off the Lizard and wait for orders, transmitting to our Secretary an account of your arrival and proceedings.

By a messenger at ½ past 12 at night.

531.   *Admiralty to Bridport*

12 March 1800

I have it in command from my Lords Commissioners of the Admiralty to transmit to your Lordship the enclosed order to be delivered to Rear Admiral Pole empowering him to hoist his flag on board the Royal George in case of your Lordship's death while he may be employed as your first Captain; an event which they sincerely trust is not likely to happen, though they have judged the measure of precaution to be necessary.

532.   *Bridport to Spencer*

Royal George, at sea, 20 March 1800[1]

I beg to call your Lordship's attention to the active appearance of the force at Brest on the 14th instant when Captain Gore looked into that port and when he clearly saw forty-three ships of the line with nine flags hoisted and one broad pendant with eight frigates and many smaller ships also. The number allotted to meet this force consists of twenty-eight ships of the line and three admirals. I shall therefore have, if the whole force puts to sea and I should see it, fifteen ships more than my line and six more admirals and one broad pendant. Under these circumstances I must request that more ships may be immediately sent to me and all the admirals belonging to the fleet which I have now the honour to command.

. . . let me also add that I hope to see Sir Alan Gardner with the fleet as soon as possible and I am to request that he may bring me permission to return into port and retire from the service in case I should find myself unable to continue longer to keep my employment from the want of health and bodily infirmities which I feel fast coming upon me.

. . . Your Lordship and the Board will see that a convoy is got into Brest, by Captain Keats's letter to me, from the eastward and that another was approaching through the Raz. I am sorry that convoys cannot be cut off but I am aware of the difficulty of doing it and I fear

[1]This letter is dated fully in Bridport's papers but in Spencer's only bears the month and the year. Hence Spencer's reply of the 25th.

also that ships will get out of Brest notwithstanding every attention is paid to keep them in by the most watchful care.

[Endorsed as received on the 25th]

533. *Admiralty to Admiral Milbanke*[1]

21 March 1800

The Right Honourable Mr. Windham, His Majesty's Secretary at War, having requested that a cutter may be appointed for the conveyance of three gentlemen to Tres-port, who it is much wished should sail on Sunday morning next, I have it in command from their Lordships to signify their direction to you to appoint a proper vessel for the performance of the said service, with directions to the commander to receive the said gentlemen on board and having landed them at Tres-port to make the best of his way back to Portsmouth for further orders, victualling them during their continuance on board in the same manner as his ship's company.

534. *Bridport to Admiralty*

Royal George, at sea, 24 March 1800

I request to be informed if it is their Lordships' intention that all the frigates which may join me shall be employed for the express purpose of watching Brest, as it appears to me necessary that the several ports to the southward from which the enemy receive their supplies should also be attended to. The Amethyst and Nymphe, stationed off the Garonne, have been near seven weeks at sea and the Doris and Alcmene employed with the Uranie off Ferrol have been cruising about that time and I apprehend all but the Nymphe and the latter ship will soon return to Plymouth Sound to complete their water and provisions. I therefore request to know if it is their Lordships' pleasure that I should send ships from time to time to relieve ships upon those stations, taking care not to keep less than four frigates in succession, with smaller vessels, watching the port of Brest.

[Endorsement]

[1]Mark Milbanke (d. 1805). Lieutenant 1744; Captain 1748; Rear-admiral 1779; Vice-admiral 1780; Admiral 1793. From 14 September 1799 until 1803 Commander-in-Chief Portsmouth.

He is to keep all his frigates with the fleet unless he receives directions to the contrary.

535.   *Admiralty to Bridport*[1]

25 March 1800

I have received and communicated to my Lords Commissioners of the Admiralty your letter of the 18th instant requesting their Lordships' instructions respecting the eventual return of the squadron under your command to Torbay and I have it in command from their Lordships to acquaint you that in case during your continuance off Brest the wind should come to the westward and there should be an appearance of blowing weather your Lordship is, rather than run the risk of your ships being disabled by continuing at sea, to return with the ships of the line to Torbay, taking care to leave your frigates so stationed off Brest as to be able to watch the motions of the enemy to give you the earliest intelligence of their proceedings.

Whenever the wind shall again change to the northward or eastward so as to enable the enemy to put to sea your Lordship is to return with all possible despatch to your station and continue to carry into execution the orders you may be under.

I have their Lordships' further commands to inform you that they have ordered a further number of ships of the line to join your Lordship immediately and have also directed the Victualling Board to have supplies of provisions in readiness for the use of the squadron in case of your finding it necessary to return to Torbay.

536.   *Spencer to Bridport*

Admiralty, 25 March 1800

I have this morning received your letter dated at sea without the day of the month and conveyed to me by Sir A. Gardner on his return to Cawsand Bay.

. . . On the subject of the order which was sent to the Rear Admiral, which your Lordship seems by your public letter to think unprecedented I have only to say that in the situation in which the flag officer in the fleet would have stood (if unfortunately any such fatal event as is therein provided for had happened) the awkwardness of his situation would have

---

[1] Addressed to Bridport off Brest.

been such as seemed to require some similar precaution; and though it may perhaps never have occurred before, a case something similar to it occurred within my knowledge in the land service at the time of the invasion of Ireland by General Humbert, when a commission actually passed the great seal authorizing Lords Justices to take upon them the government of that kingdom in the event of the Lord Lieutenant's death, which was deemed a possible event, though not a probable one, when Lord Cornwallis marched at the head of the army to meet the enemy.[1]

Your Lordship will perceive by the letter you will have from Mr. Nepean that we shall comply with as little delay as possible with your request for an addition to your force and it will become very necessary when so large a portion of our disposable force is at sea at once to endeavour if possible to prevent their being disabled by bad weather by bearing up for Torbay whenever the wind shall come to blow from the westward; we have had so long a course of easterly winds that it is to be apprehended when the wind changes (especially at this season of the year) that there will be blowing weather and I am not without suspicion that the enemy's object is rather by making demonstrations to induce us to expose our fleet to an equinoctial gale than that they have any serious intention to come out in force.

537. *Spencer to St Vincent*

Admiralty, 27 March 1800

I was truly concerned at the receipt of your note of the 24th by which I learnt that you were so much indisposed as to prevent your giving me the pleasure of your company on this day sennight. I hope you are getting well fast as it is not improbable that I may have to call on you soon for your services.

538. *Intelligence report from D'Auvergne*

28 March 1800

19th February. Orders received for the ships destined for the expedition to be kept in momentary readiness. It is reported they are to separate into two divisions. They have on board a complete train of artillery with 30,000 stand of arms.

2nd March. The whole fleet received orders to prepare to cover the departure of the expedition to a safe offing (it consists of 41 or 42 sail –

---

[1]This was in the autumn of 1798.

but it is very certain that not more than 17 French and 15 Spanish ships of the line are fitted to keep the sea any time and only 14 of the former are yet, 28 March, under orders for it; although the Ocean is manifestly destined to bear the commanding admiral).

21st March. General Brune arrived at Brest. He had been preceded by General Humbert and 7,000 troops, who are embarked on the ships in addition to their garrisons, viz. 14 of the line, 7 frigates and 4 avisos which make demonstrations of being ready for sea, as do the Spaniards. It is reported that General Kleber has agreed to a suspension of hostilities with Sir S. Smith and that in consequence a part of the expedition will be suspended.[1]

26th March. It is generally believed that Ireland is the object of the expedition and that they will be able to disembark 14,000 men.

539.   *Sick and Wounded Board to Admiralty*

Office for Sick and Wounded Seamen, 2 April 1800

We have received your letter of the 31st ultimo, enclosing an extract of one which you had received from Admiral Sir Alan Gardner, respecting a contagious fever which had broken out among the company of His Majesty's ship Pompee arrived at Plymouth, that we may take such measures as the occasion appears to require, enquiring at the same time whether the cause of this alarming malady can be traced, and if so, to report the same to you for their Lordships' information.

We request you will be pleased to acquaint their Lordships that having received from Mr James Wilkes, the surgeon of the Pompee, a letter dated the 28th of last month, of which a copy is enclosed on the subject of the fever on board that ship. We on the 31st directed Doctor Farr one of the Physicians of the Royal Hospital at Plymouth to report to us his opinion of the fever with which the men received from the Pompee are afflicted, and in regard to the man whom Mr Wilkes mentions to have been received from the Royal William, we have called on the surgeon of that ship to account for his having been sent from thence in such a state.

So soon as we receive the information which we have required on these points, we will transmit the same to you, in order to its being laid before their Lordships.

[*Enclosure*]

[1]Kleber had ratified the Convention of El Arish on 28 January.

539a.   *James Wilkes to Sick and Wounded Board*

His Majesty's ship Pompee, Cawsand Bay, 28 March 1800

I beg leave to inform you a fever made its appearance on board His Majesty's ship Pompee on the 2nd March, which attacked two men who were in the habit of frequent intoxication. It came on with vomiting of bile, very great pain at the scorbiculis cordis, foul tongue, quick pulse and great pain in the head, back, and loins. I immediately gave emetics, and applied blisters to the part. In a few hours they were taken with delerium; one died the following day, the other was sent to sick quarters at Dartmouth. On the 6th we received a man sent from the Royal William in a wretched state, his legs anasarcous, with bloated countenance, intolerable stench of breath, and eruptions all over his body, sore throat, and excessive debility. He immediately took to his bed, complained much of his throat, he was blistered under the throat, and was supported by wine bark, and sago, and in a few days died in a most putrid state. On the 9th we had several taken ill with typhus fever which has daily increased to the present time, we have had seventy patients with the fever since we sailed, and am very sorry to add we have had the misfortune to lose seven, as it continued contagious adding from six to ten to the list every day, and our efforts to stop the progress of infection ineffectual. I represented our situation to Captain Stirling, and we are now arrived in Cawsand Bay. This dreadful disorder has given me much uneasiness. We have been extremely healthy, not having lost a man this last 21 months or occasion to send many to the hospital. I impute the infection gaining ground to our being four months in harbour, the men receiving twelve months pay, and the very great excesses which seamen will commit, which has rendered them liable to infection.

P.S. We have sent thirty six to the hospital this morning, there are twenty convalescents on board, and four taken ill last night with symptoms of fever.

540.   *Admiralty to Bridport*[1]

4 April 1800

I have it in command from my Lords Commissioners of the Admiralty to signify their directions to your Lordship to keep with you only thirty

---

[1]Addressed to Bridport off Brest.

ships of the line, and to send such ships as may be with you more than that number to Plymouth, with orders to their captains to cause their stores and provisions to be completed with all possible dispatch. It is their Lordships further direction that as other ships of the line shall hereafter join your Lordship you send an equal number into port for the purpose abovementioned.[1]

[*Answered by Bridport on 7 April that their Lordships' directions would be complied with.*[2]]

541. *Keats to Bridport*

Boadicea, off Ushant, 6 April 1800[3]

Remarks on the situation of the Boadicea, Naiad, Triton and Stag at the close of the day on the 24th ultimo, which were the only ships at that time under Captain Keats' orders.

At noon and till half past 3 the Boadicea and Naiad were anchored, the outer Black Rock bearing N. by W. by compass, St. Mathieu N.E. by E.

The Triton and Stag, on the wind becoming southerly in the preceding night, had been ordered by me off the Passage du Raz to prevent the arrival of supplies. They were both well in the entrance of Douarnenez Bay at the above time.

At ½ past the Boadicea and Naiad weighed and worked farther to windward, as well for the purpose of observing if the enemy in Brest made any movement as to leave them at the close of day uncertain as to our situation in the night.

. . . The Triton and Stag were actually four miles to the eastward of Cape Raz and close in shore in the act of examining the wreck of the Repulse,[4] which had been discovered by them that afternoon.

The Boadicea and Naiad were at this time under easy sail expending the time and making observations until dark when they bore up and anchored very near the same situation they had quitted at ½ past 3.

---

[1]Copy in COR/11 endorsed by St Vincent.
[2]ADM. 1/115, 7 April 1800.
[3]This is part of a report on an unidentified sighting. It is given here as a rare picture of a quiet afternoon on the blockade.
[4]Lost the previous month.

542.   *Spencer to Bridport*[1]

Admiralty, 8 April 1800

Understanding from Admiral Gardner that my last letter to your Lordship [that dated 25th March] in answer to that which I had the honour of receiving from you of the[2]   had not reached you and learning that by being sent to sea in search of the fleet it may have missed you, entirely I enclose a duplicate of it and shall only at present add to what is therein contained that, in consequence of the representation your Lordship has made on the subject of your health, I have thought it advisable to send you the conditional permission to come on shore which you will receive from Mr. Nepean by the present conveyance, and in case Sir Alan Gardner's not having found you before the wind is fair for the fleet to put to sea again according to the orders you will receive at the same time should render it necessary for your Lordship to proceed again yourself, that officer will be directed to follow you that his presence may enable you to avail yourself of the leave of absence then granted should the state of your health make it necessary.

P.S. Since writing the above I perceived that the conditional leave of absence to which I alluded is drawn up in the form of an order, which I had supposed would have been a letter, which I only mention that your Lordship may understand to what I alluded.

543.   *Admiralty to Bridport*[3]

8 April 1800

Secret

Admiral Sir Alan Gardner having acquainted us that His Majesty's ships named in the margin [*St George, Bellona, Dragon*] had anchored in Cawsand Bay, and that he had been informed your Lordship had proceeded with the rest of your squadron to Torbay, your Lordship is hereby required & directed (without waiting for the completing of the stores and provisions of the ships) to put to sea with all the ships you may have with you the moment the wind shall change so as to admit of the enemy's fleet sailing from Brest, or so soon you shall receive

---

[1] Addressed to Bridport in Torbay.
[2] There is here a blank. The original letter, to which Bridport referred, was itself without date. See Althorp G215.
[3] Addressed to Bridport in Torbay.

information by signal or otherwise that the enemy are making any movement which indicates an intention to sail; using every possible exertion to arrive off Brest in time to prevent the enemy's fleet from putting to sea, or to bring it to action if it should attempt to do so.

If on your Lordship's arrival off Brest, or before you arrive there, you should obtain certain information that only a part of the enemy fleet had sailed without your being able to determine their destination, you are either to proceed yourself with a squadron equal in number to that of the enemy to the coast of Ireland, or send such squadron thither under the orders of some other flag officer, as from circumstances you shall judge most proper; and you are either to repair yourself, or direct some other flag officer to repair, with the remainder of your squadron off the Lizard in order to meet the enemy in case they should attempt to enter the Channel.[1]

544. *Bridport to Admiralty*

Royal George, Torbay, 8 April 1800

I acquaint you for their Lordships' information that His Majesty's ship Amelia from Plymouth joined me yesterday afternoon, when I received your letter of the 3rd instant acquainting me that after the repeated directions I had received not to detach any of my frigates their Lordships cannot approve of my sending any from off of Brest to reinforce the squadron off Ferrol as they intend to send out such ships as may be necessary to relieve others which may require coming into port. Also that their Lordships have ordered Sir Alan Gardner to send the Cambrian off of Brest if she should not have proceeded off of Ferrol. And in return I acquaint you that, as Lord Viscount Ranelagh had been obliged to send the Alcmene into port and the Uranie had separated from him without being seen or heard of by his Lordship for three weeks, there appeared to be a need for sending one or two frigates to join him in the execution of the service in which their Lordships had judged three frigates to be necessary in February last and certainly not less so on the 1st instant when I detached the Fisgard on that service, the enemy having a squadron actually at sea on the date of his Lordship's despatch. I should have judged it expedient from the urgency of the case to have sent two frigates to him if they could have been spared from the fleet.

---

[1]Copy endorsed by St Vincent.

I did not receive their Lordships' order for taking the Cambrian under my command till last night but I have seen nothing of her. Had I known their intention of sending that ship or any other to join Lord Ranelagh I should not have detached the Fisgard as above stated. The Clyde was ordered to cruise off the Penmarcks with the Agamemnon but as she returned into port with that ship and their Lordships have ordered Captain Cunningham to join me I apprehend there is no frigate on that station as I understand the Nereide is arrived at Plymouth. I consider it of great importance to have ships cruising between the Penmarcks and the Saintes for the purpose of watching the Bec du Raz and I shall send the Thames upon that service should it meet with their Lordships' approbation to cruise with the Clyde that is now at Plymouth.

545.   *Victualling Board to Admiralty*

Victualling Office, 9 April 1800

We have received your letter of this date inclosing an extract of one the Right Honourable the Lords Commissioners of the Admiralty have received from Admiral Lord Bridport dated the 7th instant representing the want of beer and coals for the supply of the ships of the fleet under his Lordship's command which had arrived in Torbay; and signifying their lordships' directions to us to take measures for sending the necessary supplies of those articles to that anchorage without loss of time.

In reply to which we beg leave to acquaint to for the information of their Lordships that we yesterday sent orders to our agent at Plymouth for his forwarding without delay ample supplies of provisions and beer for the use of the fleet under the command of Admiral Lord Bridport in Torbay; and also wrote to our agent at Portsmouth and Dover requiring them likewise to send thither with all possible despatch such quantities of the latter article as the stores under their care might conveniently allow; and we have this day issued directions to provide and forward without loss of time such supplies of coals as it may be in their power to procure for the use of the several ships composing the said fleet.

546.   *Bickerton to Bridport*

Portsmouth, 9 April 1800

I am honoured with your Lordship's letter and have the satisfaction of informing you that the fleet has escaped the severe weather we have experienced for the last two days, having arrived in Torbay on Sunday. I have seen a letter from Captain Domett expressing the highest satisfaction at the conduct of the crew of the Royal George, which I mention as reports of an opposite tendency have got about. I never gave the smallest credit to such reports but as they were evidently propagated with a bad intention it is to be lamented that the author cannot be discovered and punished.

547. *Bridport to Admiralty*

Royal George, Torbay, 10th April 1800

I have received your letter of the 8th instant informing me that their Lordships for the reasons stated have determined to make a very considerable addition to the allowance paid to the ships' companies for their savings of bread to be continued as long as the scarcity of corn shall last, which will be paid if circumstances will admit of it once every month, for which their Lordships will give orders immediately. And in return I acquaint you that the Royal George's company would have been paid this afternoon for their savings of bread to the 31 ultimo had I not received the above letter. I have therefore suspended the payment and I shall give secret directions to the captains of the several ships in this bay to prevent any sums from being paid on this head until their Lordships' pleasure is made known upon it. I am informed that the ships' company of the Royal George appear perfectly satisfied with the price already ordered for provisions saved and I have not heard of a single murmur upon this, or any other subject, in any of His Majesty's Ships under my command and I suggest to their Lordships, if their intentions have not been divulged, either let the price remain as at present established or to make such an addition to it, on a general principle, as they shall judge necessary; as I am of opinion the varying the price to be paid for the savings that may be made in consequence of any scarcity which may arise both at present and in future might induce the ships' companies of the fleet to be at all times dissatisfied, unless they receive from Government the same sums they could get for their savings on shore, were they permitted to dispose of them.

[Endorsement by Admiralty Secretary]

12 April: Acquaint him that their Lordships were not induced to adopt this measure from a knowledge of any dissatisfaction prevailing in the ships under his Lordship's command on account of the present allow-

ance but because it was understood that the men took up the whole of their bread and found means to have it conveyed on shore at a time when it is of the utmost consequence to H.M. service, at a time when so alarming a scarcity exists in the Kingdom, that every method should be devised for retaining on board His Majesty's ships as much as possible of their stock of provisions and particularly of bread.

548. *Bridport to Admiralty*

Royal George, Torbay, 10 April 1800

I have received their Lordships' order of the 8th instant authorizing me to send the fleet I command to sea under the orders of Admiral Sir Alan Gardner in case he should join me in this bay and come on shore myself if the state of my health should render it necessary for me to do so.

I have not yet moved out of the Royal George but if the weather moderates I intend going on shore this day and I apprehend their Lordships will order Admiral Sir Alan Gardner to bring the Royal Sovereign to Torbay with such ships now at Plymouth as are refitted and paid. When he arrives I shall avail myself of their Lordships' order and come on shore if I feel myself unable to do my duty in the responsible command committed to my charge.

549. *Admiralty to Navy Board*

11 April 1800

I am commanded by my Lords Commissioners of the Admiralty to transmit to you an extract of a letter which I have received from Admiral Sir Alan Gardner with a copy of the letter therein referred to from the Honourable Captain Curzon of His Majesty's Ship Indefatigable representing that the equipment of the ships at Plymouth is very much retarded from the want of cordage, for your information.

550. *Victualling Board to Admiralty*

Victualling Office, 16 April 1800

We received your letter of the 12th instant inclosing an extract of one the Right Honourable Lords Commissioners of the Admiralty had received from Admiral Lord Bridport, and signifying their Lordships' direction to us to report to you for their information what measures have been taken in consequence of Mr Nepean's letter to us of the 25th of last month, ordering two months' provisions for eight thousand men to be sent to Torbay, in order that the ships of the Channel fleet might be completed on their arrival at that anchorage without delay.

In return to which we beg leave to acquaint you, for the information of their Lordships, that immediately upon the receipt of your letter, our Secretary wrote to our agent at Plymouth requiring him to state to us very fully the steps that have been taken ... and having this day received our agent's report upon the occasion, we beg leave to transmit you a copy thereof, and of the papers which accompanied it, from which we trust it will appear to their Lordships' satisfaction that every possible exertion has been used in forwarding supplies to Torbay for the beforementioned fleet.

[*Enclosures*]

550a.   *Thomas Miller to the Commissioners for Victualling His Majesty's Navy*

Plymouth Victualling Office, 14 April 1800

... I beg leave to acquaint you that immediately upon receipt of your said directions, the utmost exertions were used by myself and your other officers here to procure hired craft, and load them accordingly; that such craft as could possibly be obtained were thereupon forthwith engaged and the greatest diligence used in loading them, as will appear by the inclosed list of such vessels and their ladings. The adverse winds and bad weather which have some time past prevailed have prevented the arrival of those vessels in Torbay as early as could be wished, but by letters I have received from my clerk, Mr Elizeus Jessep junior, superintending the delivery of provisions there, I am informed of the arrival of the following craft with their cargoes, great part of which I presume, if the weather would permit, have been e're now delivered, and, the very moment the weather moderates, all the remainder of those vessels, as well as such others as we can possibly procure, to load will depart from hence to complete fully the whole demands that have been received for the supply of the said fleet. It has given me extreme concern that the weather should have so long protracted the hired craft from leaving this port for Torbay and especially in the instance of the beer vessels which for the most part are open craft and cannot proceed to sea with safety while the weather is at all boisterous.

Inclosed I beg leave to send you a letter from Mr John Slight, your Storekeeeeper, accounting for the seeming delay in forwarding the before-mentioned supplies.

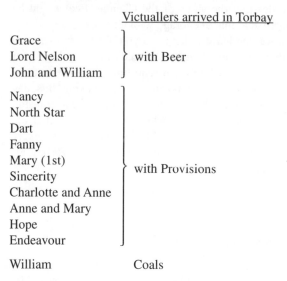

Victuallers arrived in Torbay

Grace
Lord Nelson   } with Beer
John and William

Nancy
North Star
Dart
Fanny
Mary (1st)   } with Provisions
Sincerity
Charlotte and Anne
Anne and Mary
Hope
Endeavour

William   Coals

550b.   *John Slight, Storekeeper, Plymouth to the Victualling Agent, Plymouth*

[No date]

In consequence of your directions that I would explain to you the reasons why the demands from the fleet in Torbay have not been completed, I beg to observe that utmost and every possible exertion has been used to comply with them, but the late boisterous weather with almost constant rain for the last three or four days have so much retarded the business ... I herewith send you an account of the provisions put on board vessels for the fleet.[1]

An account of provisions put on board vessels and consigned to the fleet under the command of Admiral Lord Bridport at Torbay.

Bread	bags	4,517
Wine	gallons	12,314
Spirits	gallons	4,845
Beef	8lb ps	12,616

[1]John Slight also sent a detailed account of the provisions shipped on each victualler, which will be found in ADM. D/42, 16 April 1800.

Pork	4lb ps	22,604
Flour	pounds	76,820
Suet	pounds	4,520
Raisins	pounds	7,972
Pease	bus	1,807
	galls	7
Oatmeal	bus	1,039
	galls	4
Butter	pounds	42,268
Cheese	pounds	43,640
Vinegar	galls	2,592

551. *St Vincent to Spencer*

Grosvenor Place, 21 April 1800

I return you many thanks for the communication of last evening, will wait upon you tomorrow and with your Lordship's permission read over the instructions which are preparing.

I sent my secretary to Portsmouth some days ago to make what preparations he could without discovering the object of them and I will set about what is necessary for my own departure, which I did not feel myself at liberty to do before.

552. *Bridport to Admiralty*

Royal George, Torbay, 24 April 1800

I have received their Lordships' order of the 22nd instant directing me to strike my flag and come on shore, leaving with Admiral Sir Alan Gardner attested copies of all orders and directions relative to my late command which may either in part or in whole remain un-executed with directions to him to carry the same into execution, which has been complied with.

10

ST VINCENT TAKES COMMAND
25 APRIL–28 JUNE 1800

Appointed to replace Bridport on 22 April, St Vincent embarked upon his command of the Channel fleet with energy. Although only eight years younger than his predecessor, in attitude and vigour he represented a younger generation of senior officers. Bridport's friends naturally claimed that Ushant would soon sap St Vincent's drive [577]. But having already condemned his predecessor's management of the Channel fleet [342], he arrived in his new post with the belief that he would do better; and indeed the period of his command was to be characterised by an effort to maintain a closer blockade of the port of Brest than had ever before been attempted during the French Revolutionary War. With a persisting fear of mutiny in the fleet, the blockade raised questions about the best management of the seamen. St Vincent's response was to expect a new discipline of the officer corps. He also demanded higher standards in the support services provided by the Sick and Wounded, Victualling and Navy Boards. To effect these changes, the new Commander-in-Chief revealed extraordinary determination and sense of purpose.

His first task was to win the loyalty and support of his immediate subordinates. Revealing a grace not often associated with him, St Vincent was by turns complimentary, encouraging and supportive to the senior officers serving under him. Gardner, whom he might have deprived of the chance of higher command, was treated with delicate diplomacy [556]; of Keats and Gore, alternately commanding the frigates in the Iroise, he was unashamedly laudatory [563]; to Berkeley, commanding the ships of the line off the Black Rocks, he gave unstinted approval and discretion to use his independent judgement as the movements of the enemy dictated [564]. In discussing their responsibilities, British tactical arrangements, and the intelligence available to squadron commanders, he was forthright, clear and logical. With Spencer, he was the same [561]. Communication was direct, specific and economical. It had the effect, so far as these letters suggest, of inspiring confidence, understanding and harmony of operation.

As under Bridport, St Vincent's command stretched as far south as Ferrol. Down to the smallest cutters, it included over 90 vessels [600].

Pellew commanded a large number covering troopships in Quiberon Bay [588]. Frigates continued to be stationed at points of interception between the French ports [589, 591]. Most ships of the line remained with St Vincent, off Ushant. Initially, as before, these were restricted to 30 while others replenished and refitted [558], but in June 1800 they were reduced to the number he judged necessary to match the threat from Brest [605]. More than Bridport had ever expressed, he demonstrated his seamanship to evaluate what was going on around the Goulet [563, 564] and to position and direct his ships [596]. His pride was his professionalism. No longer was energy devoted to scoring points over the Board of Admiralty. In the opening months of his new command, St Vincent devoted himself entirely to directing and maintaining the efficiency of his fleet.

Although the more southerly French ports had to be considered intermittently [570], St Vincent's concentration was otherwise fully on Brest. He devoted himself to closing that port completely. The organisation of his fleet into in-shore frigates, an outlying squadron of ships of the line, backed by the main fleet off Ushant, all working in mutual support [620], was to come close to achieving this objective. Closure of the port demanded the prevention of naval supplies getting in as much as the destruction of the Franco-Spanish fleet if it came out. Initially, in May 1800, convoys were still getting into Brest [557]. Then up to six French ships of the line stationed themselves at the mouth of the Goulet to cover in-coming vessels [559]. At other times smaller vessels took their place [595]. These manoeuvres, the threat of a large Franco-Spanish force putting to sea, the expectation that the Spaniards at least would take the first opportunity to get out [593], and the movements of vessels within the Bay of Brest, made the estimation of enemy intentions particularly difficult [560, 562, 565]. Keats tried the dangerous expedient of sending a fast rowing boat into the Goulet [566]; otherwise he interrogated fishermen [567, 601, 612]. The information he and Gore gathered generated intelligence sufficiently accurate [604] to enable St Vincent to question that provided provided by the spies of Captain D'Auvergne, Prince de Bouillon [618, 620]. It also enhanced the British capability to wage unceasing war on convoys and on the vessels coming out to assist them [603, 606, 611]. By June 1800 the tactic had begun to succeed to the extent that convoys were deterred from attempting the final dash into the Goulet [608].

On the rocky uncharted coast, the work of the in-shore frigates was hazardous in the extreme [568]. Too easily St Vincent was deprived of effective ships [568, 569]. Perhaps the most dangerous work was performed by the guard St Vincent attempted to establish in the Goulet at night. It demanded the finest sailing cutters then available [594]. Nevertheless these operations placed the French under British control. Information gained of sickness among the Spaniards and desertion by the French reinforced British confidence. It encouraged the Admiralty to reduce the size of the fleet St Vincent was directed to keep off Ushant, albeit after a demonstration of its potential force [578, 582, 584]. So close did the French feel the pressure of the blockade that in June 1800 they anticipated a British attack overland on Brest. Encampments were established on the high land overlooking Camaret Bay [608]. Reports varied as to whether they contained armed peasants, soldiers or marines from the French ships [612], but St Vincent felt entitled to describe the whole coast as 'petrified' [610].

The rigour of the blockade was maintained by St Vincent for one ulterior motive: to prevent the minds of seamen from dwelling on the views of the disaffected. In March 1800 the *Danae* had been carried into Brest by her mutinous crew and there were still repeated reports and rumours of plots [599]. St Vincent was particularly conscious of a threat posed by the Irish [614]. Nevertheless he realised that the majority of men were well-disposed, an opinion reinforced by Pellew, who could point out that his ship had twice already been purged of undesirable men [628]. St Vincent was sufficiently worried to feel himself responsible for defeating discontent, which he believed Bridport had neglected [597]. The task was the more difficult because letters of complaint received at the Admiralty were anonymous and targeted particular captains. Yet the Admiralty was clearly cautious of communicating these declared threats to the captains concerned [628].

The discipline of the officers also concerned him.[1] He knew that many of them, as well as the seamen, were tired of the war and its demand for ceaseless duty. But he knew too that it was upon the self-discipline of the officers that the blockade depended [597]. He felt his own task to be the more difficult because of his predecessor's neglect of discipline in the officer corps [607]. He was particularly incensed by the report that a toast against his 'Mediterranean discipline' had been drunk in the Channel fleet at the very table where Bridport had presided [622]. Correction of the report was, if anything, the more damning of Bridport, though it clearly removed suspicion from other officers still serving in the fleet [627]. To reinforce them St Vincent wished to bring on younger men whom he regarded as meritorious [614]. But

---

[1]For St Vincent's opinions of sea officers in 1799–1800, see the *Private Papers of George, Second Earl Spencer* ed. J. S. Corbett and H. W. Richmond (4 vols, NRS, 1913 etc.), IV, 2–24.

Spencer was gently sensitive to the wear and tear that service in the Channel fleet had imposed on experienced officers and clearly unwilling for them to suffer on account of the mental toll it had taken [627].

The support derived from on shore was fundamental to St Vincent's attempt to maintain a close blockade. That support was not promoted by a pre-existing prejudice against the servants of bureaucracy. There was, for example, a decided dislike of the care provided for seamen in naval hospitals. With a persistent shortage of seamen [503, 607], the hospitals were considered a route by which men were lost by desertion, undue invaliding or infection. In the *Pompee* in March 1800, for example, there had been a contagious fever [539] which her surgeon blamed on the bedding in the naval hospital. From a knowledge of other outbreaks, the Sick and Wounded Board could deny this, attributing sickness to conditions on board individual ships and in receiving ships [555]. The state of men delivered from a receiving ship [554] tended to support the board's opinion. So also did an infestation of rats, discrete to a particular ship [510]. The sea officers' prejudice against the hospital at Plymouth was reinforced, however, by none other than Trotter, the Physician of the Fleet [571], and immediately echoed by St Vincent [572]. He promptly gave his agreement to a survey under Trotter's authority of men proposed for sick quarters on shore and for reports of clothes that came back unclean from hospital [574, 575]. However, Trotter had maintained a running conflict with the management of Plymouth Hospital. Indeed this circumstance prompted Spencer to warn St Vincent against the 'colouring and exaggeration' which it was likely to produce [581].

Yet, regardless of these animosities, practical provision had to be made for invalids. The Sick and Wounded Board pressed ahead to obtain, convert and man a building at Goodrington for men necessarily landed from ships in Torbay. This was to be ready in September 1800 [609, 615, 626]. St Vincent, on the other hand, aimed to prevent men becoming sick in the first place. He pressed for the Channel fleet to obtain the same provision for the prevention of scurvy as fleets on foreign stations. Having already seen on the Mediterranean station the preventive effects of lemon juice,[1] he realised more fully than his predecessor can have done the need for its general issue in the Channel fleet and requested orders to that effect be issued by the Admiralty [598]. By June 1800 the stock of juice for general issue maintained by

---

[1]Through the recommendations of Dr. John Harness, lemon juice had been used to combat scurvy in the Mediterranean fleet since 1793. See J. J. Keevil, C. Lloyd and J. L. S. Coulter, *Medicine and the Navy 1200–1900* (4 vols, Edinburgh, 1957–63), III, 322.

the Victualling Board, as well as the new supply being obtained by the Sick and Wounded Board, was sufficient for both boards to comply with St Vincent's request. The Board of Admiralty consequently acceded to the demand [619, 621]. Subsequently St Vincent also demanded more fresh fruit and vegetables, and for the issue of wine and beer instead of spirits [629].

As well as the nature and amount of provisions issued, the Victualling Board was also obliged to improve the promptitude of its supplies. The time ships took to reprovision deprived the fleet off Ushant of effective ships. St Vincent believed some ships of the line failed to take on board as much water as they could stow in order to reduce the length of their cruise [572]. The belief was without evident foundation. The captains themselves attributed their shortages and delays to failures in the supply of beer and water to their ships from Plymouth [585]. In consequence in May 1800 a Victualling Board commissioner was despatched from London to Plymouth to remove the causes of the delays [587]. He was able to clear the victualling department of culpability and to reveal they had been caused primarily by ships refusing to receive water when it was delivered and by failing to make their demands sufficiently explicit [592]. He was also able to show that masters of vessels carrying water and beer to the Sound and Cawsand Bay overloaded their vessels, thereby making them unseaworthy in blowing weather. He consequently drafted regulations to prevent overloading in future. For the supply of victuals and water to ships in Torbay, he recommended a depot of provisions and water on shore, a proposal approved at the Admiralty [602, 625]. Meanwhile, still dissatisfied, for his own information St Vincent devised a questionnaire for the agent victualler at Plymouth and for ships' pursers to complete, recording the precise time when demands and deliveries of provisions were made [617, 623, 624].

At the same time the operations performed at the dockyards, under the auspices of the Navy Board, were hastened. In spite of its great size, the Channel fleet now relied for small scale work almost wholly on the services provided at Plymouth dockyard. This meant that there were invariably more ships in the Sound, Cawsand Bay and Hamoaze than the yard officers could attend to soon after their arrival. The replacement of worn rigging demanded a survey and condemnation by the surveying masters employed under the Master Attendant. Delays before ships' rigging was surveyed led the Admiralty to direct that the number of surveying masters at Plymouth be increased [586]. St Vincent also requested that the dockyard officers take no notice of 'frivolous' faults included in lists of defects drawn up by ships' carpenters. The yard officers were directed to confine themselves to repairs which were absolutely necessary, and leave minor or inessential faults to the carpenters and their mates [613]. By these means St Vincent aimed to keep more of his ships at sea.

553.   *Admiralty to Navy Board*

25 April 1800

I am commanded by my Lords Commissioners of the Admiralty to signify their directions to you to hasten the payment of His Majesty's Ships Montagu and Dragon by every means in your power.

554.   *Sick and Wounded Board to Admiralty*

Office for Sick and Wounded Seamen, 30 April 1800

Mr Felix, surgeon of His Majesty's ship Mars, having by his letter to us of the 7th instant represented the very improper state of three men, part of a draught sent from the Royal William to the Namur and received from that ship on board the Mars, we beg to enclose an extract of Mr Felix's said letter, and request you will be pleased to lay the same before the Right Honourable the Lords Commissioners of the Admiralty, for their Lordships information.

[*Endorsement*]

1 May. Send to Admiral Milbank directing him to make particular inquiry into the circumstances of the sending these men in so improper a state from the Royal William.

[*Enclosure*]

554a.   *Felix to Sick and Wounded Board*

27 April 1800

In my last return, I boasted of my prospect of having the Mars very healthy this cruise. I am not at present so confident, the three patients marked Continued Fevers were part of a draught sent from the Royal William to us; it was not till late in the next day (they being put on board in the middle of the night) that we discovered them laying about the deck covered with dirt and vermin and half naked. It is strange that with all the regulations that have been adopted, receiving ships should still continue to pour infection through the fleet. From the opinion that Admiral Berkeley has, that sick quarters are the certain loss of men, he would not suffer them to be sent on shore. We have therefore adopted the best means that presented to prevent any ill consequences. The rest that came with them (one hundred) have been sent to the fleet. Those men have been very ill but appear better today.

555.   *Sick and Wounded Board to the Admiralty*

30 April 1800

We beg leave to enclose for the information of the Right Honourable the Lords Commissioners of the Admiralty, a copy of a letter dated the 26th instant which we have received this day from Mr Wilkes, surgeon of His Majestys' ship Pompee, from which it appears most probable to us that the late sickness in that ship has originated from the state of the bedding, as mentioned in the said letter, and we beg further that you will be pleased to signify to their Lordships that, having made minute inquiry into the cause of the sickness which has of late arisen in some other of His Majesty's ships, we are of opinion that it may in them all have originated from causes existing on board of these ships, or in receiving ships and tenders, and not from men returned from the hospital as had in some cases been alleged.

[*Enclosure*]

555a.   *James Wilkes to Sick and Wounded Board*

His Majesty's Ship Pompee, Cawsand Bay, 26 April 1800

I have taken every pains in my power to purify His Majesty's ship Pompee by fumigating and having windsails of large dimensions down the hatchways. We still have one or two men taken ill every twenty-four hours but the disease is more mild and appears on the decline. From the filthy state of the bedding of the men at the hospital reported to me by Dr Farr I have requested they may be destroyed and have recommended cleanliness and the necessity of bedding and slops of every description being issued to the men in the want of those articles.

556. *St Vincent to Gardner*

Ville de Paris, 3 May 1800

In answer to your letter of this date I have the honour to repeat to you that no man thinks higher of your pretensions than I do and that I am the last person to supplant you in them; how it has come to pass that a universal opinion has obtained of your determination not to take a command in chief I know not but I have conversed with no man either before I joined this squadron or since that was not impressed with it.

557. *Keats to St Vincent*

Boadicea, off St Matthews [Pointe de St Mathieu], 3 May 1800

The wind and weather having been peculiarly favourable both yesterday and this day for the enemy to put to sea with some prospect under cover of thick weather of avoiding our fleet, I have thought under such circumstances you would be desirous of hearing from me and of being informed that certainly no ship of the line and we believe no frigate either has got out. I was in Camaret Bay this morning, when we made out 44, if not 45, ships of the line in the road, one excepted, all complete in their rigging and we believe having sails bent. Three had their topsails hanging by their head earings, the robins cast off, either having or being in preparation to block the yards.

This morning a convoy of 30 sail escorted by two brigs and 2 small armed vessels entered the Four from the eastward. It was directed by signal from the shore to anchor under the protection of the batteries at Conquet, where it now lays. The difficulty of the navigation there, added to the ignorance of all but one pilot[1] renders an attack on it by the squadron hazardous, perhaps, with any wind but impracticable from this side with the present, which is at north. I can therefore only hope to delay its getting to Brest while the wind shall allow me to maintain this state.

The enemy, perhaps in order to deprive us of that satisfaction, are putting some ships in motion in Brest. One is already under sail, a

---

[1]The first British charts of the Bay of Brest to be printed and made generally available to blockading ships were those made by Captain John Knight in 1800, published by William Faden in 1802. For the origin of these charts see documents 680, 707. Before publication of these charts the British fleet had available to it only the *Neptune François*, the standard French atlas published by Jaillot in 1693. See S. Fisher, 'Captain Thomas Hurd's survey of the Bay of Brest during the blockade in the Napoleonic Wars', *The Mariner's Mirror*, 79 (1993), 293–304.

second from her situation we conclude to be preparing to weigh. The Sylph brig with the Joseph and Fowey cutters, growing short of water and some other species of provisions I ordered home yesterday to be completed to three weeks from the Beaulieu.

P.S. The ship which was under sail has anchored, being compelled so to do, I believe, from the tide.

558.   *Admiralty to St Vincent*

3 May 1800

I have it in command from my Lords Commissioners of the Admiralty to signify their directions to your Lordship to keep with you thirty ships of the line and to send such ships of the line as may be with you more than that number to Cawsand Bay with orders to their captains to complete their water and provisions with all possible dispatch.

559.   *Berkeley to St Vincent*

Mars, off St Matthews lighthouse, 9 p.m., 4 May 1800

I received yours by the Nimrod, which cutter I dispatched back as soon as possible with Captain Keats' report; your letter has relieved me from much anxiety as no signal was made for my squadron to proceed as far as I did. The enemy's advanced squadron consisted of three line of battle ships under a rear admiral and three frigates, whose object was, I apprehend, to drive away our frigates and protect a small convoy which came through the Four passage from the eastward which has anchored under the Conquet in Lochrist Bay. Upon our appearance three more line of battle ships weighed from Brest and joined them and at sunset a fourth had her topgallant yards up and seemed to be weighing but they all returned up the Goulet upon our starting towards them. From some ideas, however, which the advanced ships entertained that their ships had troops on board and might have a view of putting to sea through the Toulinquet Passage I thought it right to drive them to a decision and at sunset, after chasing them back, I brought to as near as I could with safety to the squadron and after sunset perceived the enemy returning along the south shore towards Camaret Bay, where I dare say they will anchor. The flood tide, however, making strong I had thought it right to stand out under an easy sail to stem it but near enough to be apprized of their motions by Captain Keats, of whose uncommon vigilance and attention I have so frequently borne testimony. I do not myself imagine they have any other view than protecting the convoy as they were the self same squadron in number and ships which I once before drove in. If the wind remains to the north or eastward I shall keep as near the Black Rocks [Les Pierres Noires][1] as I can but should it come to the westward at all I shall stand out as the number and size of the squadron will not permit me to risk anything in so narrow a passage. Two of the enemy's frigates ran foul of each other, by which one of their bowsprits was carried away. The utmost number I could count of the enemy in Brest was thirty-four sail of ships, besides the six sail which were out as an advanced squadron. One of the Spaniards' main topmast was down but in other respects they seemed ready but no topgallant yards across.

560. *St Vincent to Keats*

Ville de Paris, 5 May 1800

I am much obliged by your very satisfactory account of the 3rd instant and I have no doubt you have designed the object the detachment of enemy's ships which came out had in view; nevertheless it is highly probable his whole force is preparing to put to sea and every effort on our parts must be made to prevent him. To this effect Rear Admiral Berkeley will continue off the Black Rocks and I will endeavour to be close in with Ushant at daylight every morning.

The small convoy anchored under the batteries of Conquet is certainly not an object of enterprise with so many more important before us.

561. *St Vincent to Spencer*

Ville de Paris, off the bay of Brest, 5 May 1800

I have placed Rear Admiral Berkeley with the Mars, Superb, Impetueux, Captain and Centaur off the Black Rocks and shall use every means to be close under Ushant with the squadron every morning at daylight while the easterly wind continues. I am of opinion that the enemy was not ready for sea on Saturday or he would have attempted to come out, as the weather was unusually favourable to him for the season, so thick and rainy we could not see any distance. Your Lordship will observe a great difference in the number of his ships of the line between the

[1]West of Pointe de St Mathieu.

reports of Rear Admiral Berkeley and Captain Keats. Little reliance seems to be placed on the intelligence conveyed by the persons who act under the orders of the Prince of Bouillon; yet it must be very defective indeed if the number of ships at Brest in readiness for sea is not ascertained daily as I understand a number of persons are employed in it.

P.S. I have this moment received an account from Captain Keats which reconciles the reports before made by Rear Admiral Berkeley and him. I send a copy of it in the public despatch, not believing it possible any ships of the line could have come out of Brest and put to sea on the 3rd instant after the close of day.

562.   *Keats to St Vincent*

Boadicea, off Bertheaume, 5 May 1800

It becomes my unpleasant duty to inform your Lordship that the number of the enemy's fleet in Brest water is decreased without my being able satisfactory [sic] to account for it. By every observation and we have been as high up as possible, there is no more than 37 ships of the line at present in that road. I include those which returned this morning and 14 frigates or ship corvettes. On the 3rd I have no doubt of the usual number having been there on that night, which was rainy with little wind and at times thick, my attention particularly directed to the convoy in Conquet. The Toulinquet was, from the state of the weather, thought to be impassable by the pilots. No vessels, I can answer, passed between St. Matthew and the Parquette. The ships do not usually anchor so far to the southward as not to be visible from the situation we can occupy; still, any number may be removed out of sight there. To whatever cause is to be ascribed the deficiency I entreat your Lordship not to spare me if I shall appear to have been negligent or inattentive to the important duty entrusted to me or if I shall have failed to exercise my judgment to the best of my ability. The state of the atmosphere has not been favourable this day to the view of the enemy but in numbers I do not think it possible we can be much out even though it is very difficult to count ships in clusters. We did not observe the usual number of Spanish ensigns but several ships had not any colours hoisted. I will use my endeavours to get hold of some fishermen this evening if the weather proves moderate.

563.   *St Vincent to Keats*

Ville de Paris, 5 May 1800

I am extremely concerned that you should be under the smallest apprehension of my not giving the fullest credit to the abilities you have displayed in the arduous service imposed on you: it is hardly within possibility that any ships of the line could have come out of Brest after the close of day on Saturday. I very much doubt whether such an event ever happened when French ships of war were better handled than they appeared to be yesterday and today. We had very little wind in the offing and you must have had less in the bay.

Our latest intelligence from the persons employed by the Prince of Bouillon, brought by the Diamond on Friday, states seventeen sail of the line French and fifteen Spanish in readiness and ten French neither fitted, victualled or manned inside the abovementioned. What degree of credit is to be given to this I am not a competent judge and I only mention it that you may form your conclusions. Be the event what it may no blame can possibly attach to you.

The Toulinquet Passage I conceive to be hazardous to large ships in the most favourable weather by day and the most desperate enterprise in little wind at night and not to be attempted without every precaution of vessels placed with lights and it is not probable they could have got clear without being seen by Sir Edward Pellew and by Sir Richard Strachan[1] who were in a situation on Sunday morning to have perceived anything passing without the Saints and the frigates stationed in Hodierne Bay must have fallen in with them on that side so that upon the whole I am inclined to believe that some change of position in the harbour has occasioned the different appearance you have remarked today. Sure I am the Spaniards, sickly and helpless as by all accounts they are, have not ventured to escape in the night.

564.   *St Vincent to Berkeley*

Ville de Paris, 5 May 1800

Nothing could be more correct than your whole conduct of yesterday and last night: the bearings of the enemy not having been pointed out by compass signal I judge it expedient to direct ships from the squadron to chase, relying on your judgment to act according to circumstances,

---

[1]Sir Richard John Strachan (d. 1828). Lieutenant 1779; Captain 1783; Rear-admiral 1805; Vice-admiral 1810; Admiral 1821.

which the officer commanding the Corps de Reserve is left the free exercise of. I very much approve your plan of operations, wishing you to keep without the Black Rocks in the night, taking care to be in with them early in the morning.

So long as the wind continues in this quarter every exertion will be made to have the squadron well in with Ushant at day break in the mornings. Fortunately the flood tide does not make early, which I think will prevent the enemy breaking loose before we approach the Black Rocks. You certainly have more ships with you than can be managed without hazard within the bay. Therefore reduce your detachment to the size your experience directs, keeping the ships with you whose commanders are best practised in the Bay of Brest, which I understand to be Captain Sutton,[1] Captain Sir Edward Pellew, Sir Richard Strachan and Captain Markham.[2]

565.   *St Vincent to Berkeley*

Ville de Paris, Monday evening, 5 May 1800

Captain Keats is under an impression that some ships of the line slipped out of Brest on Saturday night which I hardly think possible. He made out 44 ships of the line (Spaniards inclusive) on Saturday and counted 37 only this morning, with 10 sail of frigates and corvettes.

566.   *Keats to St Vincent*

Boadicea, 6 May 1800

I take the liberty to mention to your Lordship that considering I might obtain intelligence by a small four oared fast rowing boat I ordered a Master's Mate (Mr. Burke) last night to the mouth of the Goulet for that purpose – not meeting with success he was induced to remain until the day broke when a boat with 6 swivels, one piece of cannon and manned with 15 or 16 men lay between him and the Joseph cutter. As it was necessary to fight his way out, which he did with great gallantry, in which two out of his four men were wounded, though not materially, I beg I may be allowed to mention his name to your Lordship.

---

[1]Sir John Sutton (d. 1825). Lieutenant 1778; Captain 1782; Rear-admiral 1804; Vice-admiral 1809; Admiral 1819.
[2]John Markham (d. 1827). Lieutenant unknown; Captain 1783; Rear-admiral 1804; Vice-admiral 1809; Admiral 1819. Served as an Admiralty commissioner on St Vincent's board 1801–4, and with the whigs 1806–7. MP for Portsmouth 1801–18, 1820–26.

567. *Keats to St Vincent*

Boadicea, off St Matthews, 6 May 1800

I last evening sent three different ways to procure intelligence, one succeeded; Captain Dashwood[1] of the Sylph has brought to me two fishing boats, one of Douarnenez, one of Dinant [Dinan]. The men have been separately and very particularly examined, their different relations agree and confirm the opinion your Lordship has formed of the cause of the alteration we had observed in the road: nine ships of the line and two frigates (whose names I enclose) are taken into the port to have their bottoms looked at. They all agree in stating the Spaniards to be sickly and in perpetual brawls with the French seamen. That their seamen are not paid, discontented and desert on all occasions. That no troops are or have been embarked that they have heard of, nor are there any extra at Brest. Reports, they add, state that their fleet is to put to sea but amongst them they are of opinion that seven ships of the line and three frigates, which they term the Bertheaume squadron, are only seriously intended to put to sea and if it were proper to give full credit to their accounts their ships are generally in no condition to put to sea, neither being complete in men, provisions or stores. In confirmation that some of their ships are in the state they mention and that your Lordship represents the ten sail to be in, I had, in my first report of the 3rd and which I afterwards erased, taken notice that about that number appeared too high out of the water for ships ready for sea. In my report of the 22nd of March to Lord Bridport I took notice that the enemy were observed at work strengthening their fortifications on both sides the Goulet. These people assure us that they have been repaired and more guns mounted in them but that no new works have been thrown up.

568. *Keats to St Vincent*

Boadicea, off the Black Rocks, 7 May 1800

I am exceedingly concerned that it becomes my duty to inform your Lordship that the Alcmene had the misfortune to get on shore at 1/2 past 3 this morning. Having lost her rudder, thrown some of her guns and stores overboard and otherwise received considerable damage, I have ordered Captain Digby (the Sylph accompanying him) to your

[1]Sir Charles Dashwood (d. 1847). Lieutenant 1794; Commander 1799; Captain 1801; Rear-admiral 1830; Vice-admiral 1841.

Lordship or Rear Admiral Berkeley for further directions. The wind shifting yesterday in the afternoon to the S.W. with unfavourable appearances of weather, it became necessary to withdraw the squadron from the situation off St. Matthieu. It afterwards changing, I anchored off the Black Rocks. A fog, dispersed by a fresh wind from the land this morning, afforded an opportunity to the convoy off Conquet to weigh with a prospect to get round St. Matthieu. In pursuit of them to defeat this object we discovered an armed brig and 5 gunboats proceeding from Conquet, evidently with an intention of attacking the Alcmene, then high and dry. I therefore gave up the doubtful object of pursuing the chase to send the remainder of our boats to the Alcmene. Captain Dashwood, with some risks and great judgment, succeeded in placing the Sylph in a protecting situation; the enemy vessels, after a feeble attack, retreated. The Alcmene at high water was got off but the convoy safe to Brest.

569.   St Vincent to Admiralty

Ville de Paris, off Ushant, 8 May 1800

I desire you will represent to the Lords Commissioners of the Admiralty that the necessity I am under of sending in the Diamond (in want of water and provisions) with His Majesty's ship Alcmene leaves me very bare of frigates and therefore I have to request their Lordships will be pleased to order those under my command that are in port to join me as soon as possible.

570.   Spencer to St Vincent

Admiralty, 8 May 1800

This letter will be delivered to you by Colonel Maitland, with whom you had some communication on the subject of his plan[1] before you set off from London. As I am much disposed to think that you will be able best to judge upon the fact of the properest means for seconding him in his enterprise I have caused the official orders to be couched in as general terms as possible. Colonel Maitland seems inclined to think that Sir Edward Pellew would be the best calculated of any of the captains of the line of battle ships to cooperate with him in this service, from the local experience as well as his other good qualifications as an

---

[1]For taking Belle Isle.

officer. I wish, however, to leave that to your Lordship's better judgment and discretion as well as what ships you may think it right to send to cover the operation. If it be true (as we are informed) that there is a French 74, the Argonaut, ready at Lorient it seems absolutely requisite that one ship of the line at least should accompany even the first division of the force and as it is desirable not to diminish your force off Brest at present below the number prescribed of thirty, whatever you send with Colonel Maitland must be considered as exclusive of that specified number. It will probably be necessary to send also one or two frigates.

571.   Trotter[1] to St Vincent

Plymouth Dock, 10 May 1800

The sick man, labouring under real affliction, has of course been neglected, while the imposter has passed unpunished. For the defection of men, in proportion to the number sent to hospitals, exceeds all decency. I have made many attempts to expose and eradicate these practices, but having no authority or instructions the evil has now arrived at that magnitude that it is swallowing up all order. Captains Buller[2] and Stirling etc. will be able to give your Lordship some information on this subject.

I humbly think that much good might be done by immediate directions to the Governor of this hospital to permit no patient belonging to the fleet to be put on the list for survey unless he is under medicine, or manifestly disabled. Men that may be afterwards found objects for being discharged might be surveyed at stated periods, as the squadrons arrive in port, without being sent on shore. This would, at least, check the present mode of invaliding our people.

It was formerly the practice that every object should be reported to me, or inspected, before sent to an hospital, whether officers or seamen, unless in cases of accident, and your Lordship knows the value of such a form as this.

Your Lordship's directions for the officers of the fleet to report, when the clothes of the people are returned from hospitals uncleaned, I believe, might be a check on that department, hitherto most shamefully

---

[1] After an accident in 1795, Trotter, though Physician of the Fleet, resided mainly on shore. This proximity to the naval hospital at Plymouth possibly contributed to the hostility that developed between them.
[2] Sir Edward Buller (d. 1842). Lieutenant 1782; Captain 1790; Rear-admiral 1808; Vice-admiral 1812.

conducted. The Pompee and Russell's infections were imported from Haslar and Plymouth.

Much valuable matter relating to the preservation of health having been obtained by the surgeons' reports to me at stated periods, I have to request your Lordship will be pleased to order me to be furnished with a general history of health for the last six months, and by monthly returns afterwards, to be transmitted through the flag ship as convenient. This method has tended to keep alive just habits of study, and correct forms of medical duty; while it enables us to record for the benefit of our successors a mass of evidence on every essential point of service that would be otherwise lost.

572. *St Vincent to Spencer*

Ville de Paris, 13 May 1800

I am very much hurt by the manner in which the ships of the line come to me so very deficient in water. Their consumption both in port and at sea is much greater than it ought to be and I am circulating my opinion upon this subject, not judging it expedient to issue an order until I have tried the effect of the aforementioned hint. It is evident that the stowage is reduced very much below the capacity of many ships for the express purpose of short cruises and to avoid being sent on foreign service. The Edgar is reported to be capable of stowing one hundred and seventy-eight tons only. She is certainly of the smaller class,[1] yet I am persuaded ought to carry two hundred tons at least with four months provisions.

After I had closed my public letter enclosing the statement Captain de Courcy and the surgeon of the Canada make of the sickness in that ship, Mr. Baird, surgeon of the Ville de Paris, investigated it thoroughly and assured me there was no ground for the representation that the disorder was infectious and with care and attention the whole on the sick list might very soon be recovered. I thereupon gave a positive direction to Captain de Courcy not to send any of them to the hospital at Plymouth, which I have reason to believe is not conducted as it ought to be, very few sick sent there being returned to their ships, and great abuses are suspected in the invaliding.

[*Endorsed as received on the 18th and answered on the 20th*]

---

[1] At 1644 tons she was up to the size for 74s when launched in 1779, but they had got bigger since then.

573. *St Vincent to Admiralty*

Ville de Paris, off Ushant, 13 May 1800

I am to acknowledge the receipt of your letter of the 8th instant signifying their Lordships' direction to me to order Daniel Ward to be discharged from the Prince and to call upon Captain Sutton to account for his having impressed a man enrolled as a Sea Fencible. I herewith transmit you Captain Sutton's reply to my enquiries respecting this man and as it appears that he was not within his district when he was impressed I deem it necessary to wait their Lordships' further directions before I order him to be discharged.

[*Enclosure*]

573a. *Sutton to St Vincent*

Prince, at sea, 12 May 1800

In reply to your Lordship's directions I beg to inform you that Daniel Ward, a seaman serving on His Majesty's ship under my command, was not impressed by me or any officer belonging to the Prince; that he was drafted into this ship from the Royal William on the 27th of April last and on examining the man he says that he was impressed by the Regulating Officer at Ryde and from thence sent to the guardship at Spithead.

[*Endorsement*]

19 May: to acquaint his Lordship that the man had a leave from the commanding officer of the district to be absent and must in consequence be discharged.

574. *St Vincent to Trotter*

Ville de Paris, off Ushant, 14 May 1800

I cannot possibly enter into that part of the subject of your letter of the 10th instant relative to transactions which took place before my appointment to the command of this squadron but you may rest assured of my support in the discharge of the important office you fill, more particularly the counteracting the alarming account you give of invaliding men who are not real objects in Plymouth Hospital.

Directions are given that no sick in future shall be sent thither from the ships of the squadron in Cawsand Bay without your authority and a report to be made to me whenever clothes or necessaries are sent unclean with recovered men – an order will also be issued to the surgeons of the squadron to report to you monthly the state of their sick from the date of my taking the command – all retrospect I decline for obvious reasons.

I conclude you have represented to the Secretary of the Admiralty the observations you have made on the conduct of Plymouth Hospital, over which I have no jurisdiction; lest you should not have so done I have sent an extract of that part of your letter which relates to it.

575.   *St Vincent to Admiralty*

Ville de Paris, off Ushant, 14 May 1800

I enclose for the consideration of the Lords Commissioners of the Admiralty an extract of a letter which I have received from Doctor Trotter, Physician to the Fleet; and, in the mean time, presuming their Lordships will approve thereof, I have given directions that no sick shall be sent in future from the ships of the squadron under my command to Plymouth Hospital without his authority; and I have also directed the captains to report to me whenever clothes shall be sent from the hospital uncleaned; and the surgeons to send a monthly report of their respective sick to the Doctor, from the date of my taking the command.

[*Enclosure*: extract of a letter from Doctor Trotter, Physician of the Fleet, to Admiral the Earl of St Vincent KB, dated Plymouth Dock 10th May 1800.] *See document 571*

576.   *Keats to St Vincent*

Boadicea, off St Mathieu, 14 May 1800

Intelligence collected from prisoners taken last night, which left Brest yesterday. NB The men reside at Brest.

That seventeen sail of the line, all French, and of two decks, with two Spanish and two French frigates have lately been removed from Brest water into port, where they remain rigged.

That the Ocean is to be taken in this tide, and it is believed others are to follow them.

That five or six hospitals are filled with sick, particularly the Spaniards, and that great numbers die.

That it is reported Admiral Villaret Joyeuse is to command the fleet, but that Admiral Bruix's flag is still flying in the Ocean.

That some weeks ago troops embarked for an expedition, were relanded, and have marched from Brest.

That some time ago, the sick Spaniards were taken from the hospitals on shore to their ships, but have been since relanded.

That the French ships are generally very short of men. The seamen not being paid, are discontented and desert on every occasion.

That no ship of the line or frigate has put to sea from Brest.

The reason which public report assigns for ships being removed from the road into the port is sickness, their shortness of men, and some ships to have their bottoms looked at. There is no talk of their sailing.

577.   *Domett to Bridport*

Royal George, Torbay, 18 May 1800

I am just come from the Ville de Paris but did not see the commander-in-chief as he was in bed and I believe very ill, though they say a little fatigued only in consequence of the very bad weather we have had. He will find Ushant a very different climate to that of Cadiz I imagine, both with respect to his own health and the management of the fleet, and I do not think that he will be able to stand it long.

578.   *Admiralty to St Vincent*

19 May 1800

I am commanded by my Lords Commissioners of the Admiralty to signify their direction to your Lordship that instead of keeping with you thirty sail of the line, as before directed, your Lordship should retain only such a number as from the apparent state of the enemy's fleet in Brest, you shall think sufficient to prevent it from putting to sea in addition to the number necessary for performing the services mentioned in my letter to your Lordship of the 8th instant, sending such of the ships above that number as are in course of pay or in want of repairs to Cawsand Bay and the rest to Torbay to complete their stores and provisions. Their Lordships are further pleased to direct that when your Lordship sails from Torbay you should send a small vessel with the information to Admiral Kingsmill at Cork.

579.   *Admiralty to Commander Malbon*[1]

19 May 1800

You are hereby required and directed to receive on board the sloop [*Cynthia*] you command the French gentleman named in the margin [Monsieur Magon] and putting to sea the moment wind and weather will permit proceed down Channel and when you get off the Lizard you are to open the enclosed sealed pacquet and carry into execution the orders you will find therein contained for your further proceedings.

Secret. You are hereby required and directed to land the French gentleman whom you have been directed to receive on board the sloop you command on such part of the coast of France, in the Morbihan, as he may point out and having so done return with as little delay as possible to Spithead for further orders.

580.   *Admiralty to Malbon*

19 May 1800

I have it in command from my Lords Commissioners of the Admiralty to signify their direction to you in addition to their orders of this day's date to receive on board the sloop you command the sum of £20,000 and to dispose of it in such a manner as Monsieur Magon shall desire, taking care to acquaint me therewith for their Lordships' information.

581.   *Spencer to St Vincent*

Admiralty, 20 May 1800

With respect to the charges brought by Dr. Trotter against the administration of the hospital, it is fit that your Lordship should be informed of the sort of differences which have long subsisted between the Doctor and the Faculty belonging to those establishments and his statements must be taken with a suitable allowance for some degree of high colouring and exaggeration which these differences are very apt to produce.

---

[1]Micajah Malbon (d. 1813). Lieutenant 1783; Commander 1795; Captain 11 August 1800.

582.   *St Vincent to Admiralty*

Ville de Paris, in Torbay, 21 May 1800

After acknowledging the receipt of your letter of the 19th instant signifying the directions of the Lords Commissioners of the Admiralty that instead of keeping with me thirty sail of the line I should retain such a number as from the apparent state of the enemy's fleet in Brest I should think sufficient to prevent it from putting to sea, in addition to the number necessary for performing the services mentioned in your letter of the 8th instant, I beg leave to submit to their Lordships whether it would not be good policy to make demonstration of thirty-four sail of the line, if I can collect that number, before the wind enables me to get under weigh and afterwards detach to Cawsand Bay or to this anchorage in conformity to their Lordships' orders according to the intelligence which I may receive: such was the plan I had in contemplation before the receipt of your letter and I am the more confirmed in it because of the reports spread in this quarter of the squadron having suffered the most serious disasters, which will doubtless reach France and may cause all the ships at Brest to be put into a state of equipment.

583.   *Captain Marsh[1] to St Vincent*

Temeraire, in Torbay, 23 May 1800

I beg leave to represent to your Lordship that Henry Lishnow, a Prussian styling himself a natural son of the King of Prussia, is serving as a landsman on board His Majesty's ship under my command. He has already represented his case to Baron de Jacobi, the Prussian Minister, and notwithstanding the Baron believes him to be an impostor, yet as the man is a foreigner that cannot speak English, has never done any duty and is so far from being useful that he is a nuisance in the ship, I have therefore to request your Lordship will be pleased to represent him to the Lords Commissioners of the Admiralty as an object not worth keeping in the service.

---

[1]Edward Marsh (d. 1812). Lieutenant 1780; Captain 1797.

584. *Admiralty to St Vincent*

23 May 1800

I have received and communicated to my Lords Commissioners of the Admiralty your Lordship's letter of the 21st instant submitting for the reasons thereinmentioned whether it might not be for the good of the public service to make demonstration of 34 sail of the line in case you could collect that number before the wind enables you to get under weigh and afterwards detach to Cawsand Bay or Torbay in conformity to their Lordships' directions (signified to you in my letter of the 19th instant) according to the intelligence which your Lordship may receive; and I have it in command from their Lordships to acquaint you that they are pleased to permit you to do as you have proposed.

585. *Admiralty to Victualling Board*

23 May 1800

The supplying so large a fleet as may probably frequently be in Torbay and Cawsand Bay requiring particular exertions, and complaints having been made to my Lords Commissioners of the Admiralty by several of the captains of His Majesty's Ships at Plymouth that supplies of beer and water have not been sent to their respective ships as expeditiously as they might have been, I am commanded by their Lordships to signify their directions to you to send one of the members of your Board to Plymouth for the purpose of enquiring into the causes of any delay which may have taken place in the supplying of provisions to His Majesty's Ships at that port, and of taking such measures as may be judged necessary for their being supplied with the least possible delay in future.

586. *Admiralty to Navy Board*

23 May 1800

The refitting of His Majesty's ships at Plymouth being frequently delayed by their number being so great that the surveying masters cannot attend to survey their rigging when required, I am commanded by my Lords Commissioners of the Admiralty to signify their direction to you to send two additional surveying masters to the said port and to keep them there till further order.

587.   *Victualling Board to Admiralty*

Victualling Office, 24 May 1800

We have received your letter of the 23rd instant representing . . . it is their Lordships' direction that one of the members of this Board do proceed to Plymouth for the purpose of enquiring into the cause of any delays which may have taken place in the supplying of provisions to His Majesty's ships at that port; and of taking such measures as may be judged necessary for their being supplied with the least possible delay in future.

In return to which we beg leave to acquaint you for the information of their Lordships, that the Honourable John Rodney,[1] one of the members of this board, will immediately proceed to Plymouth for the purpose of strictly investigating the causes of the complaints which have been preferred to their Lordships, as set forth in your letter, and of duly attending to their Lordships' direction.

588.   *Young to Spencer*

Admiralty, 29 May 1800

Your Lordship will receive a letter from Sir Edward Pellew to Lord St. Vincent by which you will perceive that he requires forty-eight frigates, sloops and cutters, besides flat boats, to blockade the little island of Belle Isle. This is indeed a magnificent mode of doing business.[2]

589.   *St Vincent to Cunningham*

Ville de Paris, 1 June 1800

I have received your letter of the 29th instant enclosing intelligence of the squadron of the enemy's force at Lorient, in consequence of which I have ordered Captain Stopford of His Majesty's ship Excellent to cruise between the Glenans and the Isle de Groix for the purpose of intercepting any ships that may endeavour to get to Brest.

In the event of your observing any detachment of the enemy attempting to get through the Passage du Raz, I desire you will immediately

---

[1]John Rodney (1765–1847). Lieutenant 1780; Captain 1780. Lost a leg in an accident 1795 and superseded. Chief secretary to the government of Ceylon 1803–32.

[2]Pellew's list of the 'small force' he required is printed in *Spencer Papers*, III, 337. It comprised 6 frigates, 8 sloops or brigs, 28 cutters or luggers, 6 gunboats, and 6 flat boats in addition to ships' launches.

despatch a frigate with information thereof to Sir Edward Pellew (who is employed with a squadron in Quiberon Bay) directing her captain to communicate with Captain Stopford in his way if it can be done without loss of time.

590.   *St Vincent to Marsh*

Ville de Paris, 2 June 1800

Having transmitted to the Lords Commissioners of the Admiralty your letter respecting Henry Lishnow, the Prussian serving on board His Majesty's ship under your command, it is their Lordships' direction that you make him as useful as possible.

591.   *St Vincent to Admiralty*

Ville de Paris, off Ushant, 3 June 1800

As it appears by the report of Captain Fayerman[1] the whole force of the enemy is in preparation to come out, I have repeated the orders given by Rear Admiral Berkeley to the captains of the Windsor Castle, Bellona and Gibraltar to join me immediately. The Pompee and Russell are, I fear, not yet in a state to put to sea.

Having judged it expedient to place the Excellent between the Glenans and Isle Groix to watch the French Argonaut and frigates ready for sea in Port L'Orient as per enclosed intelligence from Captain Cunningham and to detach the Ramillies with the Diadam and Inconstant, which joined this morning, I am reduced to thirty ships of the line, from which a further reduction must be made as other troop ships join.

P.S. The Windsor Castle and Bellona are this instant signalled.

592.   *Victualling Board to Admiralty*

Victualling Office, 3 June 1800

We received your letter of the 19th and 21st ultimo, the former transmitting an extract of a letter which you had received from Admiral the Earl of St. Vincent, dated off Ushant the 12th of May, representing the shortness of water on board His Majesty's ships Atlas and Edgar, and

---

[1]Francis Fayerman (d. 1822). Lieutenant 1777; Captain 1793; Rear-admiral 1810; Vice-admiral 1815.

the latter enclosing a copy of one his Lordship has received from Captain Graves of His Majesty's ship Cumberland complaining of delay in the supplying of the stores therein mentioned to the ships under his orders at Plymouth and signifying the directions of the Lords Commissioners of the Admiralty to us to call upon the officers of the Victualling department at the before mentioned port to account for the delay which has taken place in the supplies to those ships.

In return to which we have to request you will be pleased to represent to their Lordships that the Honourable John Rodney, one of the members of the board, having, at our desire, in the course of his present visitation of the Victualling Department at Plymouth, entered into a strict investigation of the grounds of the several complaints which have been laid before their Lordships, and having, in consequence, reported to us in detail the whole of the circumstances attached thereto, we beg leave to transmit herewith a copy thereof for their Lordships' information, from which we trust it will appear to them, as it does to us, that not any neglect or delay of the nature complained of is justly imputable to this department.

[*Enclosure*]

592a.   *Rodney to Victualling Board*

Pope's Head Inn, Plymouth, 31 May 1800

Upon my arrival at this place on the 28th instant, I received your letter of the 26th transmitting two letters which you had received from Mr Nepean (with their enclosures) upon the subject of complaints which had been made to the Right Honourable the Lords Commissioners of the Admiralty by two letters from Admiral the Earl of St Vincent, the one with respect to the shortages of the water on board His Majesty's ships Atlas and Edgar at the time of their joining his Lordship off Ushant after their departure from Plymouth on the 11th instant, and the other from a representation made to his Lordship by Captain Graves of the Cumberland, that at the period when his letter was written (being on the 13th instant) 'only 30 butts of beer and 16 of water had been received, notwithstanding he has been in Cawsand Bay a time more than sufficient to have completed all the ships that had been put under his orders', and desiring me to make such enquiries as may lead to a full investigation of the matter and to report to you the result.

In compliance with your instructions, I have strictly investigated the measures which were pursued by the officers of His Majesty's Victualling Department at this port in furnishing His Majesty's ships Atlas,

Edgar and Cumberland with supplies of the several articles previously referred to, and I have in consequence to report to you so far as the subject relates to His Majesty's ship

<u>Atlas</u>

that on the 24th ultimo a demand was made upon this office for a supply of 30 butts of water, prior to which all former applications for that article appear to have been duly executed.

Whereupon 40 butts were on the same day shipped for and immediately forwarded to her, but when the craft came alongside the Atlas the water was refused to be received because as was alleged 'the ship was painting', and it was therefore delivered to the Montagu.

In the evening of the next day (the 25th) 30 butts – correspondent with the demand – were shipped for the Atlas with which the vessel sailed the next morning, the craft also taking a supply for the Raileur sloop, proceeding first, as more convenient, to the Raileur, she delivered the quantity consigned to her, when the people of the ship putting a number of empty casks on board the craft which they were desirous of returning, and which filled her up, she was necessitated for the purpose of getting rid of the empty casks to carry back to the office the water which had been designed for the Atlas. But on the following day (the 27th) she again sailed with the 30 butts in question and delivered them.

On the 29th in the evening, 30 punchions of water were shipped for the Atlas, for which not any <u>regular or written demand</u> was made, but which, it is believed, was sent from a representation of the master of some one of the office craft, that he had been hailed by the ship and was desired to mention that a supply was wanted for her. The quantity was delivered on the 30th.

The next demand was dated on the 4th (though not received until the 5th) instant for 30 butts. On the 5th 36 butts were in consequence shipped for her but although the master of the craft, it is said, used every means to proceed to the ship the weather was at that time so stormy and tempestuous that she could not get to the Atlas until the 7th when, upon making towards her, he was ordered <u>not</u> to come alongside, the reason assigned for which has been 'that the ship's company were then being paid their wages'. The water was thereafter delivered to the Russel.

Notwithstanding the 36 butts above mentioned were refused to be received, a demand was made on the 7th for 25 butts, and accordingly 26 butts were shipped for her on the 8th and delivered on the 9th, from which period, until the 11th instant, when she sailed from Cawsand Bay, no further demands were received from or supplies of water sent to her.

From the above statement it evidently appears that the Atlas was supplied with 1 butt and 30 punchions of water beyond the quantity regularly demanded, and that in two instances the supplies forwarded to her were refused to be received.

The circumstances, therefore, of her being, as is stated in the letter from Admiral the Earl of St. Vincent, '70 tuns shorter than she ought to have been' at the time of her joining the fleet after her departure from Plymouth, cannot, I presume be said to attach to this department.

———————

With regard to His Majesty's ship the
Edgar
the whole of the demands of water for the supply of this ship having been executed previously to the 15th ultimo, an application was received on that day for 150 tons equal to 300 butts of water.

	Butts [*supplied*]
In part compliance therewith there were delivered on the 17th	54
.............idem..............18th	56
.............idem..............21st	44

	Butts [*demanded*]
Another demand was made on 1st for	70

	Butts [*supplied*]	Butts [*demanded*]
Shipped and delivered in execution of these demands on the 27th	54	
Shipped on the 29th and delivered on the 30th	20	
A still further demand was made on the 9th inst for		20
Making the aggregate	228	390

In addition to the 228 butts forwarded and delivered to the Edgar, as above specified, 14 butts were shipped for her on the 9th instant, but though the Master is said to have used his utmost efforts to get into Cawsand Bay where the Edgar was at anchor, he was unable from bad weather to do so until the 11th when she got under sail before he could run the craft alongside her.

It will appear by the aforegoing representation, that the Edgar proceeded to sea deficient in the quantity of water demanded for her by 162 butts supposing that the two subsequent demands of 70 and 20 making together 90 butts were intended as an addition to the 300 first applied for, though I am of opinion (notwithstanding there are no traces in office to prove it) that they formed a part of the original demand, and were merely sent to state when they were wished to be forwarded, in which case the supply would be equal to the demand within 72 butts.

As however, at the time her demands were under execution there were a very considerable number of other ships in port for which supplies of water were required in a pressing and particular manner, and as nothing of an urgent nature was brought forward to induce more immediate attention to the Edgar, I have reason to think that she was furnished with as much despatch as the immensity of service carrying on at the time would reasonably admit; and if there had been the slightest hint given to the officers of this department that a greater exertion in her completion was necessary, the requisite supplies of water would doubtless have been delivered.

The complaint of the Edgar being short of water may thus, I apprehend, be attributed more to the demands not being sufficiently explicit as to the despatch necessary to have been used, than to any want of attention on the part of this office.

In answer to the complaint preferred by Captain Graves of the
Cumberland
I have to inform you that I find she arrived with other ships under his orders on the evening of the 9th instant; and that in order to expedite the service the agent immediately on their appearing in sight, without waiting for regular demands, sent a warrent to Southdown to forward a supply of beer and water forthwith for the use of the squadron.

Six vessels were accordingly laden on the 9th and 10th with 100 tuns of beer and 56 tuns of water for this purpose; but from the tempestuous state of the weather, two only of the vessels with 32 tuns of beer and 16 tuns of water could get out to Cawsand Bay where the squadron had anchored, which they delivered on the 11th and of which the Cumberland received 15 tuns of beer and 8 tuns of water; the four other vessels being compelled to deliver to Hamoze.

Upon the 11th instant, the first demand was made from the Cumberland for 70 tuns of water, soon after which Captain Wickey[1] waited upon the agent and signified to him that it was the direction of the Port Admiral[2] that all vessels laden for Captain Graves's squadron should be consigned expressly to the Cumberland for orders. Eight vessels were thereupon laden on the 13th, 14th and 15th instant (which it is said was as expeditious as the general press of service for every description of vessels would then allow) with

[1]John Wickey (d. 1833). Lieutenant 1778; Captain 1781; Rear-admiral 1801; Vice-admiral 1805; Admiral 1813.
[2]Sir Thomas Pasley.

Beer   64 tuns

Water   154 tuns

and consigned to the Cumberland agreeably to the orders given: the whole of which was delivered to the different ships on the 14th and 15th instant; the Cumberland however only taking 40 butts of water out of a vessel that contained 60, declining to receive the remaining 20, which were afterwards returned into store on the 15th instant.

On the 18th, another demand was made for the Cumberland of 14 tuns of beer and 14 tuns of water; and on the same day 13 tuns of the former and 12 of the latter were shipped, which were delivered on board her on the 19th. A further quantity of 5 tuns of beer was also furnished to her by the ship's boat on the 21st instant and on the 24th she sailed from Cawsand Bay; making the aggregate quantity of beer and water demanded for and supplied to her as follows viz.

	Beer	Water
	Tuns	Tuns
Demanded	14	84
Supplied	33	40
	19	44
	over	short

Upon which it may be proper to remark that though the supply of water to the Cumberland appears to fall short of the demand by 44 tuns, yet 20 butts were returned from her on the 15th instant, having been refused to be received as previously stated, and it was at the option of Captain Graves to have furnished the ship with such a quantity as he might have judged proper from the supplies consigned to him for the use of the squadron under his orders.

I have been led to state the whole of the proceedings relating to the Cumberland while she remained in port that the board might be better enabled to determine how far there has been cause for complaint, and I beg leave to submit the same to your consideration.

To prevent any future complaints, I am taking such measures as appear to me to be proper, which I shall fully make known to you on my return to Town.

593.   *St Vincent to Gore*

Ville de Paris, 6 June 1800

I am much obliged by the information of the enemy's movements contained in your letter of this morning – respecting which I always

suspect imposture and notwithstanding appearances I am strongly inclined to think that the Spaniards will embrace the first opportunity of
getting out.

594.   *St. Vincent to Admiralty*

Ville de Paris, off Ushant, 6 June 1800

Rear Admiral Berkeley, who commands the advanced squadron stationed to support the frigates employed to watch the movements of the
combined fleets in Brest harbour, having represented the Joseph and
Fowey armed cutters, particularly the latter, as totally unfit for the
service they are necessarily employed on, viz. watching the Goulet
during the night, and that they are in constant danger of capture from
two corvettes anchored in Camaret Bay, I desire you will state to the
Lords Commissioners of the Admiralty the great benefits that would be
derived from cutters similar to those engaged in the service of the
revenue. The Lieutenant [Darby[1]] of the Fowey describes her as old and
water soaken [sic] and is of opinion that the owners wish her to be
captured that they may receive the value she was originally estimated
at.

595.   *Berkeley to St Vincent*

Mars, off the Black Rocks, 7 June 1800

The enemy have made no movement with their fleet in Brest but have
detached a frigate to anchor close in with the fort at Camaret and a
corvette and cutter to cruise in Bertheaume road. The cutter was driven
in again by our cutters this morning.

This manoeuvre is in consequence of the capture of a coasting sloop
by the Joseph cutter yesterday close to the enemy's batteries, from
under whose fire he very gallantly brought her off.

596.   *St Vincent to Warren*

9 June 1800

With the wind to the eastward of north or even one point to the westward
of it I wish you to show your squadron to the northward of the Saints so

---

[1]John Derby (d. 1831). Lieutenant 1796.

as to be observed from Douarnenez. Rear Admiral Berkeley will be off the Black Rocks whenever the wind blows so as to enable the enemy to get out of Brest and the squadron as near him as possible . . .

It sometimes happens that frigates from the East Indies push for the Raz to avoid our cruisers to the southwards. Therefore while the wind continues to the westward you may allow your frigates to chase out of sight when there is a moral certainty of coming up with the chase ascertained to be an enemy but during an easterly wind it is absolutely necessary to keep them within call.

597. *St Vincent to Pasley*[1]

Ville de Paris, off Ushant, 10 June 1800

I am very much obliged by your communication of the relation made by Captain Hurlock's[2] servant. The Pompee is very badly composed and I am not surprised at the propagation of any doctrine from that quarter and I have learned from Captain Wolseley[3] that his people are for the most part Irish of the very worst description. It is also certain that before I was appointed to command this squadron anonymous letters in greater numbers than since the mutiny had been received at the Admiralty complaining of ill-treatment from officers. Nevertheless from all the information I have obtained the major part of the crews of the squadron seem well disposed, the good men feel the comforts and advantages they enjoy and do not permit the miscreants to insult and oppress them as they formerly did . . .

The licentious conversation of the wardroom officers and in some instances at the tables of officers of high rank in the navy has occasioned infinite mischief, for it soon diffuses through the ship . . . Everybody appears tired of the war and the abominable drunkenness of the men both in port and at sea works up the passions and produces evils that were formerly unknown . . .

From the little knowledge I have of the conduct of my immediate predecessor it appears he took no kind of responsibility upon himself in cases of the greatest exigency, which renders my situation the more critical . . .

My maxim is to keep the squadron in constant movement . . . The most certain means of discovering anything improper carrying on in

[1]Commander-in-Chief Plymouth.
[2]Hurlock was not a naval officer.
[3]William Wolseley (d. 1842). Lieutenant 1778; Captain 1782; Rear-admiral 1804; Vice-admiral 1809; Admiral 1819.

His Majesty's fleet would be for the letters to be secretly opened at the Post Office, which must proceed from high authority and be done in a way that cannot be discovered.

598.   *St Vincent to Admiralty*

Ville de Paris, off Ushant, 10 June 1800

The scurvy having made its appearance on board some of the ships of the squadron, I beg leave to submit to the consideration of the Lords Commissioners of the Admiralty the propriety of granting an order that lemon juice may be issued for the general use of the crews as a preventive, being by the present regulations respecting what is provided by the Sick and Hurt Board confined to the sick only and the Victualling Board not furnishing any for ships employed in the Channel service.

599.   *Admiralty to St Vincent*

Secret

Admiralty Office, 10 June 1800

I have the command of my Lord Commissioners of the Admiralty to transmit to Your Lordship the enclosed copy of letter which has this day been received from Vice Admiral Graeme[1] with copies of the letters therein referred to in order that your Lordship may be on your guard against the proceedings therein alluded to, and take such measures as you may judge prudent to counteract them if you should have grounds for believing that any designs of a criminal nature are now forming on board of the fleet under your Lordship's command.

[*Enclosures*]

599a.   *Graeme to Admiralty*

Copy

Sheerness, 9 June 1800

I have received a letter from Captain Briscoe[2] of H.M.S. Iris enclosing one Lieutenant Robinson of the marines received from [sic] Sergeant of

---

[1]Alexander Graeme (d. 1818). Lieutenant 1760; Captain 1778; Rear-admiral 1795; Vice-admiral 1799; Admiral 1804.
[2]Not in Syrett and DiNardo. Thus presumably of the Royal Marines.

the said ship, which you will be pleased to lay before their Lordships and acquaint them that I have seen Lieutenant Robinson who informs me that the Sergeant had his information from the Drummer who had been drinking on shore with some men belonging to the Veteran, and upon the Sergeant asking him when sober if he recollected what he had said, he said he did, but could not recollect the men's names.

599b.   *Briscoe to Graeme*

Iris, Little Nore, 9 June 1800

I have this moment received the enclosed letter from Lieutenant Robinson of the marines of H.M.S. which I have the honor to command; I have therefore sent it to you, by him, to give you every information on it.

599c.   *Lieutenant Robinson, R.M., to Briscoe*

[n.d.]

The duty and allegiance I owe my sovereign obligates me to inform you of the following particulars. I have learned that there is some business of a very serious nature carrying on in the Channel fleet which may be attended with dangerous consequences if not detected before two months. Their designs are communicated to the fleet at Yarmouth, and there are papers relative to the same business concealed on board the Veteran. I have heard no more and remain with the utmost respect.

P.S. Though I consider this information as consistent with the strictest honour, yet I request my name may be kept secret.

599d.   *Extract of a letter from Plymouth dated 7 June 1800*

A marine is just returned from the hospital who says that he was one night called into one of the nurses' cabins by two men belonging to the Pompee, one belonging to the Ethalion and one to the Terrible, with some others drinking. They desired him to take a glass. When he sat down they told him that whenever the fleet arrived in port again that there would be a general and more terrible mutiny than ever yet had happened on board the large ships, that it was all arranged and settled, but with much more secrecy than the last. On asking their cause of complaint, they said they had none against Government, but the tyranny of their captains whom they were resolved to sacrifice to a man.

600.   *St Vincent to Admiralty*

Ville de Paris, off Ushant, 10 June 1800

I herewith transmit for the information of the Lords Commissioners of the Admiralty the present disposition of His Majesty's squadrons under my command.

[*Enclosures*]

600a.   *Disposition of a squadron of His Majesty's ships and vessels under the command of Admiral the Earl of St Vincent K.B., 10 June 1800*

Ships	Commander	How disposed of
Ville de Paris	Admiral the Earl of St Vincent	
	Captain George Grey	
Royal Sovereign	Admiral Sir A. Gardner Bt	
	Captain William Bedford	
Prince	Rear Admiral Sir C. Cotton	
	Captain Samuel Sutton[1]	
Barfleur	Rear Admiral C. Collingwood	
	Captain G. H. Stephens[2]	
Temeraire	Rear Admiral J. H. Whitshed	
	Captain Edward Marsh	
Cumberland	.. Thomas Graves	
St George	.. Sampson Edwards	
Venerable	.. Sir W. G. Fairfax[3]	
Saturn	.. Thomas Totty[4]	
Caesar	.. Sir J. Saumarez	Cruising off
Windsor Castle	.. Albemarle Bertie	Ushant with
Neptune	.. James Vashon	Admiral the
Glory	.. Thomas Wells[5]	the Earl of
London	.. J. C. Purvis[6]	St Vincent.
Atlas	.. Theophilus Jones	

[1]Samuel Sutton (d. 1832). Lieutenant 1783; Captain 1797; Rear-admiral 1821.

[2]George Hopewell Stephens (d. 1819). Lieutenant 1778; Captain 1794; Rear-admiral 1813.

[3]Sir William George Fairfax (d. 1813). Lieutenant 1757; Captain 1782; Rear-admiral 1801; Vice-admiral 1806.

[4]Thomas Totty (d. 1802). Lieutenant 1775; Captain 1782; Rear-admiral 1801.

[5]Thomas Wells (d. 1811). Lieutenant 1780; Captain 1782; Rear-admiral 1804; Vice-admiral 1808.

[6]John Child Purvis (fl. 1778–1819). Lieutenant 1778; Captain 1782; Rear-admiral 1804; Vice-admiral 1809; Admiral 1819.

Terrible	..	William Wolseley
Magnificent	..	Edward Bowater[1]
Triumph	..	Eliab Harvey[2]
Marlborough	..	Thomas Sotheby[3]
Gibraltar	..	Wm. H. Kelly[4]
Edgar	..	Edward Buller
Defiance	..	T. R. Shivers[5]
Elephant	..	Thomas Foley[6]
Resolution	..	A. Hyde Gardner[7]
Namur	..	Wm. Luke[8]
Bellona	..	Sir T. B. Thompson[9]
Robust	..	George Countess
Uranie	..	G. H. Towry
Megara	..	P. T. Bover[10]
Dolly		Watson
Fowey		Lieutenant Derby

Mars	Rear Admiral the Hon.	Advanced
	G. Berkeley	squadron
	Captain John Monkton[11]	to support the
Superb	.. John Sutton	frigates in the
Centaur	.. John Markham	Bay of Brest . . .

[1]Edward Bowater (d. 1829). Lieutenant 1776; Captain 1783; Rear-admiral 1804; Vice-admiral 1810; Admiral 1819.

[2]Sir Eliab Harvey (d. 1830). Lieutenant 1779; Captain 1783; Rear-admiral 1805; Vice-admiral 1810; Admiral 1819.

[3]Thomas Sotheby (d. 1831). Lieutenant unknown; Captain 1783; Rear-admiral 1805; Vice-admiral 1810; Admiral 1821.

[4]William Hancock Kelly (d. 1811). Lieutenant 1776; Captain 1783; Rear-admiral 1805; Vice-admiral 1810.

[5]Thomas Revell Shivers (fl. 1777–1825). Lieutenant 1777; Captain 1790; Rear-admiral 1808; Vice-admiral 1812; Admiral 1825.

[6]Sir Thomas Foley (d. 1833). Lieutenant 1778; Captain 1790; Rear-admiral 1808; Vice-admiral 1812; Admiral 1825.

[7]Lord Alan Hyde Gardner (d. 1815). Lieutenant unknown; Captain 1790; Rear-admiral 1808; Vice-admiral 1813.

[8]William Luke (d. 1818). Lieutenant 1777; Captain 1790; Rear-admiral 1809; Vice-admiral 1814.

[9]Sir Thomas Boulden Thompson (d. 1828). Lieutenant 1782; Captain 1790; Rear-admiral 1809; Vice-admiral 1814.

[10]Peter Turner Bover (d. 1802). Lieutenant 1794; Commander 1798; Captain August 1800.

[11]John Monkton (d. 1826). Lieutenant 1777; Captain 1795; Superannuated Rear-admiral 1814.

Renown	Rear Admiral Sir J. B. Warren	
	Captain Thomas Eyles[1]	
Excellent	.. Hon. R. Stopford	Cruising off the
Defence	.. Lord H. Paulett	Passage du Raz
Fisgard	.. T. B. Martin	
Unicorn	.. Philip Wilkinson[2]	
Triton	Captain John Gore	
Nymphe	.. Percy Fraser	Cruising in the
Lurcher	Lieutenant Forbes[3]	Bay of Brest . . .
Joseph	.. Lapenotiere[4]	
Naiad	Captain William Pierrepont	Cruising off
Childers	J. Coutts Crawford	Abreverack to
Lady Duncan	Lieutenant Coet[5]	watch the
		Passage du Four
Impetueux	Captain Sir E. Pellew	
Ajax	.. Hon. A. F. Cochrane[6]	
Canada	.. Hon. M. De Courcy	
Ramilles	.. R. Grindall	
Stag	.. Robert Winthrop[7]	
Magicienne	.. J. Ogilvy[8]	
Brilliant	.. Hon. J. Paget[9]	
Thames	.. William Lukin[10]	
Amethyst	.. John Cook	
Amelia	.. William Spranger[11]	

[1]Thomas Eyles (d. 1835). Lieutenant 1790; Captain 1796; Rear-admiral 1819; Vice-admiral 1830.

[2]Philip Wilkinson (d. 1846). Lieutenant 1790; Captain 1794; Rear-admiral 1813; Vice-admiral 1821; Admiral 1837.

[3]Syrett and DiNardo lists six lieutenants with this surname in the navy at this time.

[4]John Richards Lapenotiere (d. 1834). Lieutenant 1794; Captain 1811.

[5]William Coet (d. 1837). Lieutenant 1793; Retired Commander 1828.

[6]Hon. Sir Alexander F. I. Cochrane (d. 1832). Lieutenant 1778; Captain 1782; Rear-admiral 1804; Vice-admiral 1809; Admiral 1819.

[7]Robert Winthrop (d. 1832). Lieutenant 1790; Captain 1796; Rear-admiral 1819; Vice-admiral 1830.

[8]Although given as *J.* Ogilvy, the only captain of this surname at this time was Sir William Ogilvy (d. 1823). Lieutenant 1780; Captain 1797; Superannuated Rear-admiral 1821.

[9]Again, although given as *J.* Paget, the only officer of this surname at this time was the Honourable Sir Charles Paget (d. 1839). Lieutenant 1796; Captain 1797; Rear-admiral 1823; Vice-admiral 1837.

[10]Listed in Syrett and DiNardo as William Windham (d. 1833). Lieutenant 1793; Captain 1795; Rear-admiral 1814; Vice-admiral 1830.

[11]John William Spranger (fl. 1790–1819). Lieutenant 1790; Captain 1795; Rear-admiral 1814.

Requin brig	Lieutenant Fowell[1]	
Telemachus cutter	.. Spencer[2]	
Nimrod cutter	.. William Marsh[3]	
Viper cutter	.. Forster[4]	Under the orders
Europa troop ship	Captain J. Stephenson[5]	of Sir Edward
Cyclops	.. J. Fyffe[6]	Pellew
Thisbe	.. J. Merrison[7]	
Winchelsea ..	.. J. Hatley[8]	
Blonde	.. J. Burne[9]	
Diadem	.. Sir T. Levingston[10]	
Inconstant	.. J. Ayscough[11]	
Rose revenue cutter	William Yeates[12]	
Diligence	William Dobbins	
Speedwell	J. Hopkins	
Swan	William Ferris	
Dolphin	R. Johns	
Greyhound	R. Wilkinson	
Falcon	J. Wharton	
Repulse	G. E. Munnings	
Swallow	T. Amos	
Indefatigable	Captain Honourable H. Curzon	
Cambrian	.. Honourable A. K. Legge	Cruising off
Sirius	.. Richard King	Ferrol . . .
Earl of St Vincent	Lieutenant Boys[13]	

[1]There were two lieutenants of this surname at the time: Samuel Fowell (d. 1823), Lieutenant 1794, Commander 1808; and William Fowell (d. 1837), Lieutenant 1795, Retired Commander 1830.

[2]This was either Christopher Spencer, Lieutenant 1795; or George Allen Spencer, Lieutenant 1794.

[3]William Marsh (d. 1818). Lieutenant 1778.

[4]Mathew Forster (d. 1824). Lieutenant 1790; Captain 1806.

[5]Although given as J., this was probably Thomas Stephenson (d. 1809). Lieutenant 1778; Captain 1798.

[6]John Fyffe (d. 1835). Lieutenant 1782; Commander 1798; Captain 1807.

[7]Probably John Morrison (d. 1806). Lieutenant 1790; Commander 1797; Captain 1806.

[8]John Hatley (d. 1832). Lieutenant 1782; Commander 1797; Captain 1802.

[9]Probably John Burn (d. 1813). Lieutenant 1790; Commander 1799.

[10]Sir Thomas Livingstone (d. 1853). Lieutenant 1790; Commander 1796; Captain 1800; Rear-admiral 1830; Vice-admiral 1838; Admiral 1848.

[11]John Ayscough (d. 1863). Lieutenant 1793; Commander 1797; Captain 1806; Rear-admiral 1841; Vice-admiral 1849; Admiral 1855.

[12]The masters of revenue cutters were not naval officers.

[13]There were four lieutenants named Boys at this time: Charles Worsley (d. 1809), Edward (d. 1827), Henry (d. 1816), and Thomas (d. 1840).

In Portsmouth Harbour

Juste	Captain Sir H. Trollope
Formidable	.. E. Thornborough

At Spithead

Achille	Captain George Murray
Warrior	Charles Tyler[1]

In Torbay

Royal George	Captain William Domett

In Cawsand Bay

Pompee	Captain Charles Stirling	
Russel	.. Herbert Sawyer[2]	Ordered to join
Captain	.. Sir R. Strachan	the squadron.

In Hamoaze

Montagu	Captain John Knight[3]	
Agamemnon	.. R. D. Fancourt[4]	
Boadicea	.. R. G. Keats	} Ordered to join
Alcmene	.. Henry Digby	the squadron as soon as completed.

In Plymouth Sound

Doris	Captain Rt. Hon. Ld Ranelagh	Ordered to join
Diamond	.. Edward Griffith	the squadron
Sylph	.. Charles Dashwood	immediately
Beaulieu	.. F. Fayerman	Gone in to complete water
Clyde	.. C. Cunningham	and provisions
Suwanow	Lieutenant J. Nicholson	and ordered to rejoin the squadron the instant that shall be effected.

---

[1]Sir Charles Tyler (d. 1835). Lieutenant 1779; Captain 1790; Rear-admiral 1808; Vice-admiral 1813; Admiral 1825.

[2]Sir Herbert Sawyer (d. 1833). Lieutenant 1780; Captain 1789; Rear-admiral 1807; Vice-admiral 1811; Admiral 1825.

[3]Sir John Knight (d. 1831). Lieutenant 1830; Captain 1781; Rear-admiral 1801; Vice-admiral 1805; Admiral 1813.

[4]Robert Devereaux Fancourt (d. 1826). Lieutenant 1777; Captain 1789; Rear-admiral 1808; Vice-admiral 1812; Admiral 1825.

600b.   *Distribution of the force under the command of Sir Edward Pellew Bart*

Ramilles	Amethyst Amelia Rose cutter Swan cutter	N.E. of Belle Isle to cover from L'Orient.
Thames	Cynthia Telemachus cutter Nimrod cutter	Passage of Lomaria in Quiberon
Stag	Diligence cutter	Off Houat
Canada Brilliant	Falcon cutter Requin brig Repulse cutter	Palais Road Croisic, Villamic and Pou passage
Diadem	Thisbe Swallow cutter	Quiberon Bay, Crac, Carnac and Palice
Magicienne	Speedwell cutter	South end of Belle Isle
Europa	Viper cutter	Morbihan
Impetueux	Dolphin cutter Greyhound cutter	Centre Quiberon Bay
Troop Ships		Off Houat, two regiments, 36th and 92d encamped on the island.

601.   *St Vincent to Berkeley*

Ville de Paris, off Ushant, 11 June 1800

Although I place little faith in the accounts given by fishermen, yet, if an opportunity offers, it may not be amiss to interrogate them as to the state of the French and Spanish fleets distinctly with respect to men and time for which they are victualled.

It is evident that the seven French ships with all sails bent intend to put out the very first favourable opportunity but which I have no doubt your vigilance will prevent.

602.   *Victualling Board to Admiralty*

Victualling Office, 11 June 1800

We received your letter of the 23rd past, representing that the supplying of so large a fleet as may probably frequently be in Torbay and Cawsand Bay requiring particular exertions, and complaints having been made to the Right Honourable the Lords Commissioners of the Admiralty by several of the captains of His Majesty's ships at Plymouth, that supplies of beer and water have not been sent to their respective ships so expeditiously as they might have been; it was their Lordships' direction that we should send one of the members of this Board to Plymouth for the purpose of enquiring into the cause of any delay which may have taken place in the supplying of provisions to His Majesty's ships at that port; and of taking such measures as may be judged necessary for their being supplied with the least possible delay in future.

In return to which we beg leave to acquaint you for the information of their Lordships, that the Honourable John Rodney, one of the members of this board, immediately after the receipt of their Lordships' directions, proceeded to Plymouth and Torbay (agreeably to our letter to you of the 24th past) for the purpose of attending to the objects pointed out by your letter; and having, on the 6th instant, presented to us a report of his proceedings, we, herewith, transmit a copy thereof, requesting you will be pleased to lay the same before their Lordships.

Conceiving that the several measures which he has therein suggested will be productive of considerable advantage to this department, and essentially tend to accelerate the future victualling of His Majesty's ships, we have given directions that the whole be forthwith carried into execution except in two instances viz.

> 'The taking up of vessels to be stationed in Brixham pier, with a depôt of provisions equal to a proportion for 15,000 men (or about 23 sail of the line) for one month, for the more immediate supply of the fleet whenever it may return to Torbay, in aid of the usual shipments from Plymouth; and the forming of a pier contiguous to that part of the victualling premises at Plymouth particularised in the report, with a bason within to shelter the vessels loading from the wharfs agreeably nearly to a former design, but with the addition of gates to inclose the water and keep the vessels in the bason at all times afloat; and the erecting theron of further storehouses for the use of this office.'

neither of which we deemed ourselves authorised to carry into effect without the directions of their Lordships.

Respecting the former, we beg to recommend to their Lordships that it be adopted without loss of time, in like manner as was, upon a suggestion of this board, directed by their Lordships' order of the 3rd of April 1794 for the greater expedition in the victualling of the fleet then under the command of Admiral Earl Howe, (which was discontinued by their order of the 2nd of December following) and in the event of their Lordships approving thereof we have to desire you will move them for orders to us accordingly.

And should it appear to their Lordships, as it does to us, that the execution of the works contained in the latter proposition will also materially conduce to the benefit of the victualling service at the port of Plymouth, we submit whether it may not be expedient for them to refer the matter to the Inspector General of Naval Works for his consideration and report thereon.

[Enclosures]

602a.   *John Rodney to Victualling Board*

Victualling Office, Somerset Place, 6 June 1800

You having been pleased verbally on the 24th past to signify to me your desire that I would proceed to Plymouth in consequence of complaints which had been made ... by several of the captains of His Majesty's ships ... 'that supplies of beer and water have not been sent to their respective ships as expeditiously as they might have been', and that I would enquire into the cause of any delay which may have taken place in the supplying of provisions to His Majesty's ships at Plymouth, taking such measures as I might judge necessary for their being supplied with the least possible delay in future ...

It is to the not receiving of the supplies of beer and water from South-down for the use of ships in Plymouth Sound and Cawsand Bay so expeditiously as they have been requested that the complaints have been more immediately confined; but great allowances should be made for the distance at which South-down is situated from Plymouth (from where the warrants for the issue of those articles are necessarily sent) and the obstacles which afterwards but too often occur from tempestous and stormy weather to the prevention of the vessels getting out with that despatch which might otherwise be used.

Admitting however the force of these impediments, I am free to confess there has not been that exertion practiced to overcome them, but more especially in the transportation of the supplies, that there ought to have been; for I find it has been frequently the custom when the weather has become what might be termed rough or blowing, though not stormy, for the masters of vessels which have been laden expressly for the ships in the Sound or Cawsand Bay to take upon themselves, without any authority from the office, and to the counteraction of the service upon which they have been ordered, to deliver their cargoes in Hamoaze, although the demands for the ships lying there can at all times be easily complied with.

The reason why the masters of these vessels have been desirous of delivering their cargoes in Hamoaze, in preference to the Sound and Cawsand Bay, has been that as they were anxious to make the most advantage by their freight they have laden their vessels, which are open, to such an extent by placing the casks one upon the other to an extreme height as to preclude their being able to face the sea usually to be met with in the Sound and Bay, except in the most favorable seasons, and therefore to avoid trouble and risque they have discharged in Hamoaze.

From hence it has happened that they have been detained a considerable time after the discharge of their cargoes at this place waiting for the return of the tide to enable them to proceed back to South-down to reload; and, in the event of the weather becoming favourable in the interim, a material delay has arisen as well from their detention on account of the tide, as from the loss of time occupied in reloading them for the former service, supposing as must often occur that not any vessel in the mean time returns.

Instead therefore of their having gone into Hamoaze had they waited a reasonable period for an alteration of weather they would have been in readiness to have proceeded to the Sound or Cawsand Bay the instant it would have admitted; and thus in most cases have delivered in a far less space of time than had been taken up in going into Hamoaze waiting the return of the tide to carry them back to South-down, and reloading afterwards for the service first intended.

To remedy this in future, I have issued strict orders that not any master of a vessel shall presume to deliver his cargo to any other ship than that to which he is expressly consigned by the bill of lading, unless under very peculiar circumstances or he has the sanction of the agent. And the better to enable the vessels hereafter to proceed to the Sound or Cawsand Bay in most weather, I have thought it proper to desire the contractor to cause six of them to be fitted with gratings and tarpaulins and although by this alteration a less quantity of beer and water may be delivered at a time, yet a certain supply for the ships at these places may thereby be calculated upon generally.

In further aid of this service, I recommend, in case of a continuation of such weather as may prevent the vessels that may have been laden from proceeding to Plymouth Sound or Cawsand Bay, in order to meet the consumption which must arise on board ships during their detention, to keep up a proper activity in this department at Southdown, and more especially to expedite the completion of the supplies required for His Majesty's ships as soon as opportunity occurs, that the agent be directed to engage (if the contractor cannot furnish them), and load with all possible despatch, such an additional number of vessels as may be competent to answer the full demands in the office at least, in order that they may go off the moment the weather may admit.

By the adoption of these measures, and a due exertion on the part of the officers belonging to this department which they assured me should be rigidly adhered to, I trust the complaints of this description will in future be completely obviated.

Much [in-]convenience having arisen to this department by its being often inserted in the demands which have been made from His Majesty's ships on their arrival in port for a full proportion of provisions etc. to complete them 'that they were wanted <u>immediately</u>' though the ships has not probably been in a fit state to receive them when they have come alongside, thereby occasioning the supplies to be either brought back to the office or sent to other ships at much trouble, I have desired the agent to endeavour to learn from the officer who may bring the demand, or by any other expeditious means, the actual or probable time or times when it may suit the ship to receive the supplies, and to govern himself accordingly.

For the more effectually ascertaining, in cases of any future complaints, to whom the neglect may be properly attributed, I have likewise desired the agent to insert in each demand in a more particular manner than has heretofore been done, the precise time it may be actually received at his office. I have also desired that the officers at Southdown do furnish the Agent with an account daily of the progress they make in the execution of his warrants for supplies of beer and water to His Majesty's ships to the end that he may henceforth ascertain more correctly than he has been able to do from the daily progress ar present rendered whether they have been duly attended to, and that he may take the necessary steps if he discovers any negligence therein.

Observing likewise that the agent does not make any entry of his warrants to the storekeeper or to the officers at South-down for supplies for His Majesty's ships, but merely obtains the demands upon which they are grounded as the official record, which are liable to be mislaid, I have desired that he will enter the same in future in a book to be kept for that purpose.

Thus having laid before you all that has occurred to me upon the subject of complaints of the nature before referred to, and pointed out the measures which appear to me the best adapted to prevent them happening in future, I have to conclude my report upon the subject of my mission to Plymouth with a few remarks respecting the pier which has been built in Sultan Pool, for the protection and improvement of the harbour, as stated in a letter from the agent victualler dated the 22d past, delivered to me previously to my leaving London . . .

Attending to the former part of Mr Marsden's beforementioned letter pointing out the necessity of particular exertions being used in supplying the fleet while in

Torbay

I took an opportunity of visiting that place as stated in my letter to you of the 27th past, and have maturely considered the measures most likely to conduce to this important end.

For accelerating the victualling of the fleet whenever it may return to this anchorage, I am decidedly of opinion that a depot of provisions, consisting of a regular assortment of the different species equal to a supply for 15,000 men, or about 23 sail of the line, for one month (omitting beer, butter, cheese and molasses, by reason of their liability to spoil and waste) should be kept on board vessels of an easy draught of water, to lie in Brixham pier, of from 150 and not exceeding 200 tons burthen; to be there in readiness to go off and deliver to the fleet as soon as it comes into Torbay, by which means a seasonable supply will be consistently afforded previously to the arrival of the usual shipments from Plymouth; and the victualling of the fleet will immediately commence from the time of its arrival and progressively go forward until its completion.

As soon as the stationed victuallers have delivered their cargoes, they should proceed to Plymouth, and having been laden with further supplies should return therewith to the fleet, continuing to do so, from time to time in concert with the other vessels, until it proceeds to sea, when they should be laden and form a depot again in Brixham pier. In the event of the execution of this plan, which I strongly recommend to the Board, it would be adviseable to keep the wine and spirits in a vessel or vessels distinct from the other species.

Understanding from Mr. Bartlett, who superintends the watering of the fleet in Torbay, that much confusion arises on its return, from the number of boats that repair to the wharf for supplies of water, I am of opinion that these inconveniences would be entirely done away, and the fleet most essentially expedited in the completion of that article if 100 tuns of empty casks in butts, with a necessary quantity of spare hoops, bungs, bung cloths etc., etc., were to be sent from Plymouth and deposited under his care, in order that as soon as the fleet is seen to be coming in, he may cause them to be immediately filled, and hiring vessels for the purpose run them alongside the ships as soon as they drop their anchors. And as there is a loft belonging to Mr. Bartlett adjoining the watering wharf well suited to contain the casks etc., I recommend that it be forthwith engaged and appropriated to this purpose.

The expenses that will arise from the adoption of these measures I am persuaded will be more than counterbalanced by the facility and despatch with which the fleet will be hereafter supplied, and submitting the whole to your consideration, I have the honor to be with great regard . . .

[*Endorsements*]

13 June
Approve of what has been done by Commissioner Rodney and direct that the measures he has suggested be adopted; acquaint them at the same time that the Inspector General will be directed on his intended visitation to examine and prepare a plan and estimate of the intended pier etc.

Send extract to General Bentham with directions accordingly.

Orders accordingly

603.   *Gore to St Vincent*

Triton, off Point St Mathieu, 11 June 1800

At first light this morning I observed a fleet of 32 brigs, sloops and chasse-marées, under convoy of a large brig, a cutter and lugger come through the Four and anchor between Points Coquet and Ninotiere and have been all day planning an attack upon them by the boats of the Triton and La Nymphe covered by Sylph and the cutters.

At three p.m. I saw a cutter come out of Brest and push along shore and from her appearance judged her to be sent as a reinforcement to the convoy, and consequently sent the cutters to cut her off. No words I can divine can convey an adequate idea to your Lordship of the gallantry displayed on this occasion by the lieutenants and crews of the Joseph and Lurcher hired cutters; they followed her within the rocks under a tremendous fire of round and grape and, although I made their signal to leave off pursuit, their zeal had withdrawn their attention so much that they did not see it. The Lurcher, from a superiority of sailing, followed her up a creek where Lieutenant Forbes boarded her, but being fast aground, could not get her off and had the boatswain and two men wounded, the latter I fear mortally, in the attempt. The Lurcher has received several shot through the hull and rigging; but I trust we can find means in the squadron to repair all damages, as also those of Joseph, though I am apprehensive it will defer my attack until tomorrow night. Your Lordship may rest assured they shall not get into Brest if my exertions can prevent them.

I beg further to inform your Lordship that another Spanish two decked ship got under weigh in Brest and is gone to the southward of Point Espagnolle; from the manner she got under sail I judge her to be very badly handled.

I have given my fullest approbation to the lieutenants and crews of the cutters and that I shall endeavour to express my sense of their service to your Lordship.

604.   *St Vincent to Admiralty*

11 June 1800

Since my last, the enclosed detailed accounts of the combined fleet in Brest have been received from Rear Admiral Berkeley . . .

[*Enclosures*]

604a.   *Berkeley to St Vincent*

Mars, off the Black Rocks, 3/4 past 7 o'clock p.m., 10 June 1800

Lieutenant Derby returned at six o'clock this afternoon with the enclosed answer from the commandant at Brest by which I hope the two corvettes may yet be safe as undoubtedly some traces of them would have been seen upon the coast, if they could not have weathered it, and the only misfortune to apprehend is their having foundered. Lieutenant Derby was not able to procure any information; it seems however that the idea at Brest is that our fleet consist of forty sail of the line and ten frigates. I have sent the Fowey with this letter that your Lordship may see the lieutenant if you wish it, and Captain Gore will keep the Lurcher instead of her. The frigates made sail close in this evening covered by the Centaur; the enemy's batteries fired at them from each side, as they made the best use of the opportunity the weather gave of pushing their reconnoitring very far up the Goulet, and enclosed you have Captain Gore's account; but I beg to add that Captain Gore describes his situation to be such as not to have been able to see the southern part of the bay, where the Spanish ships who weighed the other day are gone to the anchorage of Greve D'Anglois.

P.S. I beg to add in justice to Lieutenant Derby that I think he has conducted himself with a very becoming zeal and alacrity. I also enclose Captain Markham's report although I think he has mistaken a broad pendant for a Spanish Admiral's flag.

604b. *Commandant of Brest to Berkeley*

Le Commandant des Armee, à Monsieur Le Contre-Amiral de L'escadre bleue . . .

Il serait aussi consolant pour le bien l'humanité qu'agréable au commandant de l'azuir de la marine a Brest de pouvoir vous donner quelque renseignement sur le sort de deux corvettes <u>Le Railleur</u> et <u>La Trompeuse</u>, qui manquent depuis le dernier coup de vent, et occasionment en angleterre des inquiétude fondée mais cela lui est impossible.

C'est avec une peine vivement sentie qu'il annonce à Monsieur Le Contre-amiral de l'escadre bleue qu'il n'en a aucune connaissance, il eut rendre avec plaisir service à la societé en tranquilisant quelque familière d'angleterre.

[*Translation*]

The Commander of the armed forces to his Lordship the Rear-Admiral of the Blue squadron.

It would be as comforting to mankind as it would be agreeable to the commander of the navy in Brest to give you some information on the fate of the two corvettes <u>La Railleur</u> and <u>La Trompeuse</u>, both of whom are missing since the last wind and who are rightly giving cause for concern in England but it is not possible.

It is with deeply felt pain that he has to announce to his Lordship the Rear-Admiral of the Blue squadron that he has no knowledge of their whereabouts, though he would have gladly rendered service to society by reassuring a few families in England.

604c.　*Gore to St Vincent*

Triton, off the Goulet de Brest, 10 June 1800

I have the honour to inform your Lordship that I this afternoon availed myself of a steady breeze to reconnoitre the enemy's combined fleet in Brest and find them as per enclosed report which I took on the spot. What are become of the rest of the Spanish fleet I am sorry it is not in my power to inform your Lordship, but presume to suppose they may have followed the ships I saw go to the southward of Point Espagnolle.

If your Lordship wishes it, I will take care to detach boats by night and gain what information is to be obtained from fishermen.

604d.　*Gore's account of the combined fleet in Brest*

Triton, off the Goulet, ½ past 5, 10 June 1800

French ships of the line at anchor in the Rade de Brest　30
of which　　three are of 3 decks
　　　　　　twenty-seven are of 2 decks
　　　　　　and nine are frigates

Spanish ships of the line in the Rade de Brest　8
of which　　four are of 3 decks
　　　　　　four of 2 decks
　　　　　　and one frigate

French flags flying
　　two Vice Admirals
　　three Rear Admirals
Spanish flags flying
　　one Vice Admiral
　　two Rear Admirals
　　one commodore

In the harbour of Camaret
　　two ship and one brig corvettes
　　two gun brigs

N.B. The Spanish ship which had her topmasts down on the 5th instant has now got them up – but her top gallant masts are down and top sail yards.

One Spanish three deck ship and one two decker and the frigate have all their sails unbent. All the French ships appear ready for sea, have all sails bent and top gallant yards across.

604e.   *Markham's account of the combined fleet in Brest*

10 June 1800

French line
French line sails unbent
French line
French line
French line
French Rear Admiral, French frigate
French line
French line
Spanish line Rear Admiral sails unbent
French line, French frigate
Spanish line sails unbent
Spanish frigate
French line, Spanish line
French Rear Admiral
French line 1, French line 2, French line 3.
French line 1, French line 2
French Rear Admiral   } within these ships are several
French Vice Admiral   } small ships of war
Spanish line with topmasts struck
French line, French frigate
French line
Spanish admiral
Spanish line
Spanish line
French line
French line
French Rear Admiral
Spanish Vice Admiral
French line
Spanish line
Spanish line
French line sails unbent
French line
French line
Spanish Rear Admiral sails unbent
French line, French line
French Rear Admiral sails unbent

Spanish force
One Admiral, one Vice Admiral, two Rear Admirals.
Total of Spanish force: ten sail of the line, one frigate.

French force
One Vice Admiral, five Rear Admirals.
Total of French force: twenty-nine sail of the line, four frigates, two corvettes and other small vessels of war not distinct.

Camaret Bay
Two ship corvettes, one brig ditto, two merchant brigs.

N.B. The French Admiral struck his flag between 12 and 3.

605. *Admiralty to St Vincent*

12 June 1800

It being of the utmost consequence to His Majesty's service that the squadron under your Lordship's command should continue off Brest as long as possible, your Lordship is hereby required and directed not to detach more ships to cooperate with the expedition[1] under the direction of Brigadier General Maitland than may be absolutely necessary; to keep with you as many ships as you shall judge sufficient to watch the enemy's squadron at Brest and to send all above that number to Cawsand Bay with directions to their respective captains to complete their provisions and water and to rejoin your Lordship with all possible despatch.

On being rejoined by the last mentioned ships your Lordship is to send such other ships of your squadron to Cawsand Bay as may stand most in need of a supply of provisions and water with directions to their commanders to act in like manner, that the necessity of the whole of the squadron under your Lordship's command returning into port at the same time may be prevented or, if it cannot be avoided, be put off as long as possible.

---

[1]The expedition was destined for Quiberon Bay to cooperate with insurgent French royalists in the Morbihan and to take Belle Isle. The garrison on the island was found to be too strong to achieve that objective and the troops were eventually landed on the island of Houat, from where they were later shipped to the Mediterranean.

606. *Forbes to St Vincent*

Lurcher cutter, off Ushant, 12 June 1800

In obedience to your Lordship's directions I am to acquaint you that at three p.m. on the eleventh of June, a cutter being seen steering along shore from Brest to St. Mathews, I chased in company with the Joseph by signal from Triton, which, on the enemy's discovering, she hauled close in with the land under cover of the batteries. At four p.m. I commenced firing within half a mile of the shore, tacking occasionally, the batteries keeping up a heavy fire of shells, round and grape shot, which the enemy perceiving had not the desired effect of keeping His Majesty's cutter off they ran on shore close under the guns of Conquet. I immediately boarded her with five men in the boat, the Frenchmen leaving their cutter by their boats and jumping from the end of their bowsprit on shore among the rocks. I instantly cut both her cables and hoisted her sails to endeavour to force her off the ground but found it impossible. I then attempted to burn her by setting fire to some loose powder, there being no fire on board her, which had not the desired effect. Having no other means of destroying her and having two men mortally wounded and a heavy fire of musketry increasing from all quarters on us, I was under the necessity of leaving her. Lieutenant Pelletier[1] of the Joseph gave every assistance and from a well directed fire was highly serviceable in keeping numbers off with small arms which would otherwise have much annoyed us.

I beg leave to mention to your Lordship that the Master's Mate, Boatswain and company behaved in a very spirited and gallant manner during the whole of the affair, which was nearly two hours from the time of our first firing. During the action I had two men mortally wounded, the Boatswain shot through the thigh and myself slightly in the leg. Our damage in the hull and rigging is considerable, having six shot between wind and water, fourteen in other parts of the hull, the sternpost shot through and through. The sails and rigging much cut with the bowsprit and main boom wounded.

607. *St Vincent to Spencer*

Ville de Paris, off Ushant, 13 June 1800

Captain Gore watches the motions of the enemy with a zeal and ability not to be surpassed and conducts these enterprises so ably that I perse-

[1]Lapenotiere.

vere in my intention to send the Boadicea off Ferrol and the Clyde along the coasts of France, Spain and part of Portugal to enable Mr. Serres to complete his views.[1] The conduct my predecessor observed to the captains of these frigates had very nearly broke them down. I never saw either until the other day, yet I am bound by every principle not to allow men who have performed such eminent services to be deprived of a fair proportion of the few good chances within my sphere.

The Royal George is ninety short of complement with many convalescents in a very feeble state but the zeal of Captain Domett prompted him to join in this weak state.

[Endorsed as received on the 10th]

608.   *Berkeley to St Vincent*

Mars, off the Black Rocks, 14 June 1800

I received yours by the Megara and have the honour to acquaint you since the last report, the enemy yesterday evening sent seven more line of battle ships to the southward in Brest harbour, viz. five French with a vice and two Spanish under a rear admiral. The number of tents on the Heights of Camaret was considerably increased. I am in great hopes from Captain Gore's report of this morning that the cutter has got some fishermen but I confess I have no great faith in any intelligence we can obtain from them. The convoy which was in Conquet road is separated, the large vessels went back yesterday to the eastward and the small ones are hauled into the dry harbour of Conquet.

609.   *Sick and Wounded Board to Admiralty*

Office for Sick and Wounded Seamen, 14 June 1800

Having in our letter to you of the 11th instant on the subject of the accommodation for the sick sent on shore from the ships in Torbay, acquainted you . . .

We beg to acquaint you that a house which appears to us from the description we have received of it well adapted for the purpose can be obtained. It is situated close to a fine sandy bay called Goodrington sands, lying about one mile to the south of Paignton and four to the north of Brixham and at a distance of half a mile from any other

[1]See document 496.

building. The premises are 100 feet in front with a plot of ground sufficient for an airing ground; they consist of five rooms on the ground floor and five rooms on the second floor and we are of opinion, when properly fitted, they might be capable of receiving such a number of patients as might be a great accommodation to the fleet in Torbay and may probably do away with the necessity of sick quarters at Dartmouth.

The proprietor is willing to let the greater part of these premises for twenty-five pounds per annum for one year certain from the 4th instant, and as long as the war may continue he will whitewash, paint and put the whole in good repair, and will make any additions or alterations hereafter that may be wanted to the amount of three hundred pounds, allowing him five per cent for his money, and when the term of the occupation of the smaller part, consisting of two rooms on a floor expires, he agrees to let that at five pounds per annum which is the rent now paid.

Should the Right Honourable the Lords Commissioners of the Admiralty be pleased to approve of this building being appropriated to the purpose proposed, we beg to recommend that a member of this Board may be directed to proceed thither, to give the necessary directions on the spot for the same being properly fitted.

We beg to be favoured with their Lordships' determination as soon as conveniently may be, the proprietor having been desired to keep the premises unlet until he hears from us.

[*Endorsement*]

16 June: acknowledge and approve of their doing as they have proposed.

610.   *St Vincent to Pellew*

Ville de Paris, 15 June 1800

More Spaniards and some French ships of the line are gone into La Rade Anglaise out of our view and a number of large ship tents are erected on the heights of Quelorne and one on St. Mathieu. Whether sickness or defensive has occasioned this I am ignorant but it is evident the whole coast is petrified, for a large convoy did not think itself safe in Conquet road and is gone back to the eastward and acted wisely for Captain Gore of the Triton would otherwise have carried some of them last night.

611.   *St Vincent to Pierrepont*

Ville de Paris, off Ushant, 15 June 1800

The convoy which came round Point St. Mathieu the 13th has been at anchor at Conquet, from whence they proceeded in consequence of some demonstration being made by Captain Gore for attacking them. The vessels are loaded with provisions for the combined fleet which no doubt they will endeavour to convey by land to Brest. Therefore if you could make a coup with your boats as has been done successfully by Sir J.B. Warren at St. Croix it would at this period be attended with the happiest effect.

612.   *Gore to St Vincent*

Triton, off the Black Rocks, 15 June 1800

I have the honor to inform your Lordship that I directed Captain Dashwood of His Majesty's brig Sylph to proceed yesterday evening after dark into the bay Dinan (to which place I have observed fishing boats go every morning) and intercept some fishing boats that I might if possible obtain some information respecting the late extraordinary movements of the enemy's fleet.

He captured three boats in which are 13 men who all agree that it was intended for the whole naval armament in Brest to have put to sea on the 28th ultimo when they came out; but that the French division had scarcely cleared the harbour when a courier arrived from Paris with countermanding orders. The force they report in Brest to be, in commission 53 sail of the line and 12 frigates, out of which 8 sail of the line are refitting in the harbour and 45 are in the Road; that it almost daily happens that one ship goes into the Road and another takes her place in the harbour; that they are far from sickly, and are better manned than they have been since Lord Howe's victory; and that desertion is nearly at an end in consequence of all the arrears being paid; and before the Minister Bruix left Brest, he promised they should be paid regularly every six months.

They say that the ships have moved to the southern part of the Rade de Brest in consequence of information that your Lordship meditated an attack upon the heights of Camaret, and that the troops are encamped there to defend them against such attack; but they disagree respecting what those troops are, some say they are four regiments of armed peasants, others that they are the marines of the combined fleets.

The tents as I have before informed your Lordship are formed of spars and sails of ships.

They declare there is no idea of the fleet sailing and that no person knew their destination when they were going to sea.

I am sorry to inform your Lordship that the Joseph's boat inadvertently landed at Bertheaume last night and brought off the flags from the signal post and the two men stationed there; the man who had charge of the post says he would have given them had they required it as they will be changed immediately which I shall take care to notice. This man is by far the most intelligent amongst them, and says that a descent from our fleet is daily expected in the neighbourhood of Brest; that they are under a considerable degree of alarm as there are only two regiments of militia in the town of Brest, and that the marines of the French and Spanish have been landed on the heights of Camaret for the purpose of defending them.

The French Admiral Bruix and Spanish Massaredo are both at Paris, and not expected down; he does not know who commands in their absence.

The ship which got on shore on the Fillettes, when the squadron came out under Contre Admiral Gentheame[1] to protect the convoy, was with difficulty got off, and the injury she received is irreparable.

The ships which have moored to the southward are lashed together in tires of three and four ships and have unbent all their sails.

Such, my Lord, is the best information I have been able to collect through this uncertain channel; as they differ in many respects and all plead the most abject ignorance (as being poor fishermen it is not their business to know or enquire about anything of the kind) I trust that should any part of it hereafter be found incorrect that no discredit will attach to me, for my anxiety to do everything in my power has prompted me to try this means of corroborating my observations.

613.   *St Vincent to Fanshawe*[2]

Ville de Paris, off Ushant, 16 June 1800

Observing that very frivolous matters such as repairing ladders, gratings, etc. which ought constantly to be kept in order by the carpenters' crews are mentioned in the defects delivered to me by the captains of several

---

[1]Honore-Joseph-Antoine Ganteaume (b. 1755). Officier auxiliaire 1778–83; Souslieutenant 1786; Lieutenant 1793; Captain 1794; Commodore 1795; Rear-admiral 1798.
[2]Commissioner, Plymouth dockyard.

of the ships under my command which have been sent into port for the purpose of completing their water and provisions only and which I conclude have been inserted by the carpenters for the sole purpose of detaining those ships in port, I must request you will be pleased to give strict injunctions to the officers of the dockyard not to pay attention in future to any such like defects nor to take in hand any work on board the ships appertaining to this squadron but what shall appear to be of serious moment and absolutely necessary to be put to rights.

614. *St Vincent to Spencer*

Ville de Paris, before Brest, 16 June 1800

Nothing would produce a better effect at this moment than the promotion of Captain Bover and continuing him in active employ for his incomparable behaviour in the hour of severe trial[1] and his being the son of a gallant officer and worthy man with whom I was acquainted half a century ago . . .

Botts, the Corresponding Society man who was executed on board the Princess Royal, conveyed to me by the clergyman who attended him in his last moments that the only atonement he could make for the heinous crime he had committed was to warn me against the machinations of the Irish in the fleet, whose oaths of allegiance and professions of loyalty were never to be relied on, and entreating me to keep a constant vigilant eye over them – the Scotch, when bad, are worse than the Irish.

615. *Admiralty to Sick and Wounded Board*

16 June 1800

Having laid before my Lords Commissioners of the Admiralty your letter to me of the 14th instant, relative to a house which can be obtained for the accommodation of the sick who may be sent on shore from the fleet in Torbay, I am commanded by their Lordships to acquaint you that they approve of your doing as you have proposed.

---

[1]While serving as a lieutenant on board the *London* at Spithead in May 1797, Peter Bover had shot a mutineer dead.

616. *St Vincent to Legge*

Ville de Paris, off Ushant, 18 June 1800

I am impelled by public duty to express the dissatisfaction I feel at the length of time the frigates under my command pass in port, the experience of half a century having brought me to know that a week, even passing a tide in dock, is ample. I therefore hope you will cause your officers to exert every nerve in filling up the water and provisions of His Majesty's ship under your command, for there never was a period which required greater exertions; relying as I do upon your zeal and activity I cannot entertain a doubt of seeing the Cambrian here in ten days after her arrival at Plymouth.

617. *St Vincent to Pasley*[1]

Ville de Paris, off Ushant, 18 June 1800

The unaccountable delay in port of His Majesty's ships and vessels under my command, particularly the frigates, when sent in to complete their water and provisions only, has impelled me to write a letter to the agent victualler at Plymouth, of which I enclose a copy and have to request you will be pleased to give every aid in your power towards expediting the victualling of such ships as shall be sent in for that purpose and you will discourage by all possible means the meddling and rigging etc except in cases of positive necessity.

[*Enclosure*]

617a. *St Vincent to Thomas Miller, Agent Victualler, Plymouth*

Copy

Ville de Paris, off Ushant, 18 June 1800

The exigencies of the service requiring that the utmost possible exertion should be used in completing the water and provisions of such of His Majesty's ships and vessels under my command as shall from time to time be sent into port for that purpose, particularly frigates and sloops, I desire you will be pleased to send me by the earliest conveyance after

[1]Sir Thomas Pasley, Port admiral Plymouth.

each ship etc. shall be completed a report agreeable to the form on the other side hereof, and I request you will communicate this letter and form of report to the pursers the instant of their arrival, as they shall be held responsible if the smallest delay is occasioned by their not giving in timely demands to complete their respective ships with beer, water and provisions to the time for which they are ordered to be victualled.

[*On the reverse side*]

His Majesty's Ship.................
Time she arrived in port
Time the demands for beer and water were received
Beer: quantity demanded
     : when sent on board
Water: quantity demanded
     : when sent on board
Provisions: when demanded
          : when sent on board
Remarks, etc. Here to be mentioned if any delay has been occasioned by bad weather or other circumstances or if any request has been made that the beer, water or provisions may not be sent off as soon as possible, and particularly if, when sent off, it shall have been returned or not taken on board immediately.

618.   *St Vincent to Berkeley*

Ville de Paris, off Ushant, 19 June 1800

I enclose intelligence [*not reproduced*] forwarded to the Admiralty by the Prince of Bouillon which militates so strongly against our observations that I wish you to communicate it to Captain Gore with the annexed extract of Captain Cunningham's log. I have not ventured to assert a contradiction of Captain D'Auvergne's correspondent but I think it must be erroneous.

619.   *Victualling Board to Admiralty*

Victualling Office, 19 June 1800

We have received your letter of the 16th instant[1] inclosing one which the Right Honourable the Lords Commissioners of the Admiralty had

[1]See ADM. G/792, 16 June 1800.

received from Admiral the Earl of St. Vincent proposing that lemon juice may be supplied for the general use of the crews of His Majesty's ships and vessels under his orders, and signifying their Lordships' direction to us to report to them how far the state of the present stock of lemon juice will admit of a general supply of the article.

In return to which, we beg to acquaint you for the information of their Lordships that the lemon juice at present remaining in His Majesty's several victualling stores in London, Portsmouth and Plymouth is sufficient to serve 20,000 men for 231 days, and that by a letter we have received from the Commissioners for Sick and Wounded Seamen, who provide and furnish this board with the said article, dated this day (to whom we thought it proper to make application on the subject), they have reported to us that from the state of their present stock of lemon juice they shall be able in future to furnish us with the usual supplies for His Majesty's ships and vessels on particular stations abroad, as well as to supply it for the use of the sick in general, and also to furnish us with a general supply for the use of the crews of His Majesty's ships and vessels under the orders of Admiral the Earl of St. Vincent.

620.   *Berkeley to St Vincent*[1]

Mars, off the Black Rocks, 20 June 1800

I beg leave to enclose a letter from Captain Gore relative to the supposed sailing of the seven ships from Brest contained in Captain D'Auvergne's intelligence, which I hope is perfectly clear and satisfactory but I have experienced the fallacy of intelligence from that quarter before and therefore am not surprised at it now.

This morning in consequence of the signals from Ushant denoting the English fleet to bear N.N.W. and the advanced squadron W.S.W., both steering to the westward, it gave confidence to four large frigates to weigh from Brest and, having joined the two corvettes in Camaret, they chased our frigates as far as the Black Rocks but upon the signal being made for my squadron standing in and the Triton shortening sail to offer battle and support the Nymphe, whom they were coming up with very fast, they returned and three of them are anchored in Camaret this evening; Captain Gore had some idea that they meant to put to sea but I rather ascribe their motions to the above reasons, as our frigates and cutters destroy their supplies to the new work on Camaret Point, which is carried on with unceasing labour and the stores and materials

[1]Enclosed in St Vincent to Admiralty, 30 June 1800.

conveyed in the Spanish launches, many of which Lieutenant Seymour[1] of the Nile cutter saw this morning at daylight sailing down with their colours hoisted and landed their cargoes in Camaret.

621.   *Admiralty to St Vincent*

21 June 1800

I have received and communicated to my Lords Commissioners of the Admiralty your Lordship's letter to me of 10th instant submitting for their Lordships' consideration the propriety of granting an order that lemon juice may be issued for the general use of the crews of His Majesty's ships and vessels under your command; and I am commanded by their Lordships to acquaint you that orders are given to the Victualling Board for that purpose.

622.   *St Vincent to Spencer*

Ville de Paris, off Ushant, 21 June 1800

Your Lordship probably knows that the following toast was given by a Captain when sitting at a numerous table on board the Royal George, 'May the Mediterranean discipline never be introduced into the Channel Fleet' and neither my illustrious predecessor nor any person present as far as I have heard expressed the smallest disapprobation, although I do know that some were shocked at it, after which I appeal to you whether the authority of the Admiralty should not appear on all proper occasions in support of your Lordships . . .

[*Endorsed as received on the 21st*]

623.   *Admiralty to St Vincent*

23 June 1800

I have communicated to my Lords Commissioners of the Admiralty your Lordship's letter of the 18th instant, inclosing for their Lordships' information a copy of one you had judged it necessary to send to the agent victualler at Plymouth, together with a form of a report which

---

[1]Probably Richard Seymour (d. 1806), Lieutenant 1794; but there was a William Seymour who became a lieutenant in 1795 whose career thereafter is untraced.

you are of opinion would expedite the supply of stores to His Majesty's ships and vessels under your command; and I am commanded by their Lordships to acquaint you that they have sent a copy of the abovementioned form to the Victualling Board with directions to them to order their agent at Plymouth to comply with the same.

624. *Victualling Board to Admiralty*

Victualling Office, 24 June 1800

We have received your letter dated yesterday inclosing a copy of one which Admiral the Earl of St Vincent had been impelled to write to the agent victualler at Plymouth for the unaccountable delays in port of His Majesty's ships and vessels under his Lordship's command, when sent in to complete their water and provsions, and signifying the direction of the Right Honourable the Lords Commissioners of the Admiralty to us to order our agent to comply with the directions therein contained.

In return to which we beg leave to acquaint you for the information of their Lordships that having yesterday received a letter from Admiral the Earl of St Vincent to a similar effect, we immediately gave directions to our agent at Plymouth to take particular care that his Lordship's requisition be strictly attended to.

625. *Admiralty to Victualling Board*

24 June 1800

Having laid before my Lord Commissioners of the Admiralty your letter to me of the 11th instant, enclosing a report of the Honourable John Rodney, one of the members of your Board who had been sent to Plymouth in pursuance of their Lordships' directions to you of the 23rd ultimo; I have their Lordships' commands to acquaint you that they approve of the measures which have been taken by Commissioner Rodney on the several occasions therein stated, and that they have been pleased to give directions to the Inspector General of Naval Works on his intended visitation to Plymouth to prepare a plan and estimate of the proposed pier.

626.   *James Johnston[1] to Admiralty*

Paignton, 26 June 1800

The house rented here for an hospital is now ready for receiving about twenty sick, and the new building I have contracted for will be ready the first of September and will contain about one hundred men.

The builder is bound to lay out £400 for which he is to receive only five per cent.

As the first step to receiving sick men is the appointment of a surgeon, I beg leave to recommend Mr Mathew Ball, late surgeon of the Terrible to be surgeon of the hospital. He is a most respectable man and in all respects adequate to the situation, and I have put him in complete possession of my ideas in arranging the various appendages requisite to an hospital and none other could be adequate to see them carried into effect, from the circumstance of his having daily attended me with the contractor and workmen.

[*Endorsements*]

8 June. To be appointed.

Sir, as this appears to be a new appointment, what salary is Mr Ball to have?

1 July. Sick and Wounded Board to be directed to propose a salary.

627.   *Spencer to St Vincent*

Admiralty, 27 June 1800

I agree entirely with your Lordship . . . relative to the expediency, if possible, of having men of firm and vigorous minds at the head of line of battle ships in times like these but from the very nature of things it is impossible to have so large a fleet of that description as is now under your orders commanded only by those who are equally of that description. Some allowance must be made for the impossibility of knowing accurately how far an officer's nerves have kept up to the mark who has been battered and worn in the service and to supersede a man who has many years of good service to cite as his claim merely because he is a little the worse for wear would be a harsher measure than could well be

[1]Commissioner for Sick and Wounded Seamen.

justified, though we should undoubtedly desire to place in the command of ships to be actively employed only such as are fully equal to it.

As your Lordship has been informed of the anecdote of the toast on board the Royal George I think it fair to let you know how (as I was confidentially informed on enquiry) the real issue was. The sentiment was expressed by the Admiral on their breaking up but it was not given by anyone as a toast. The subject of discussion had been on the topic and on going out of the cabin, I am told that Lord B said, 'God forbid that the discipline of the Mediterranean fleet should be established in the Channel'.

628.   *Pellew to St Vincent*

Impetueux, at Palais Road, 27 June 1800

The only report that I feel myself justified to make with respect to the infamous and diabolical plan said to be in agitation among the seamen of His Majesty's fleet is that I have no reason from the behaviour of the ship's company under my command at present to suspect them of being implicated in so wicked a design; and I believe, if the secret is known in the ship to some whose behaviour and activity on former occasions make them suspicious characters, yet there are many perfectly ignorant of it.

I wish, however, to be clearly understood as having no confidence or reliance on the fidelity of any description of seamen whatever on such an occasion but understanding anonymous letters have been received at the Admiralty complaining of the conduct of particular captains, of whom I may be one, I trust their Lordships will consider it proper (commanding secrecy) to refer such letters to the officers therein named, that they may be on their guard in their own defence from murder and assassination; the delegates and principals on the first mutiny had deserted before I commanded this ship and by your Lordship's protection the remainder were completely rooted out off Minorca.[1]

---

[1]The *Impetueux* was one of the ships sent to the Mediterranean from the Channel at the time of Bruix's cruise. Lord Keith, writing to his sister, recorded on 13 July that five of her crew had been hanged. See *The Keith Papers*, ed. W. G. Perrin and C. Lloyd (3 vols, NRS, 1926, 1950 and 1955), II, 40.

629.   *Sick and Wounded Board to Admiralty*

Office for Sick and Wounded Seamen, 28 June 1800

We beg leave to enclose for the information of the Right Honourable the Lords Commissioners of the Admiralty a copy of a letter dated the 24th instant which we have this day received from Earl St Vincent, representing the state of health of the fleet under his Lordship's command and suggesting certain means for checking and preventing the prevalence of these diseases incident to it, from the nature of the service in which it is now engaged.

We are of opinion with his Lordship that a great share of the ill health now prevailing in His Majesty's ships is imputable to the use of ardent spirits and are of opinion that a supply of malt liquor or wine in lieu of spirits would be highly conducive to the health of the men.

We beg leave also humbly to recommend that the supply of roots, fruits, and other vegetables suggested by Lord St Vincent be carried into effect, being of opinion that these, together with the lemon juice already directed, are the only means of maintaining the state of health which may enable the fleet to keep the sea for a great length of time.

[*Endorsement*]

30 June. Directions for their supplying vegetables as proposed by the commander in chief.

[*Enclosures*]

629a.   *St Vincent to Sick and Wounded Board*

Copy   Ville de Paris, off Ushant, 24 June 1800

The dissolute and profligate life the seamen of that squadron have led when in port, and the increase of the allowance of ardent spirit at sea has so contaminated their juices, that the ship fever, in my opinion improperly termed typhus, and scurvy are appearing in many of them and unless you send out onions, turnips and carrots in very large quantities and keep the surgeons well supplied with necessaries, I foresee that the important measure of keeping the combined fleets in check by an adequate force constantly cruising before Brest will not be achieved. I have represented to the Lords Commissioners of the Admiralty the benefit likely to be derived from an allowance of prepared lemon juice being served to the whole people of the squadron, which will do something, but I have much reliance on fresh vegetables, and ripe fruits of every kind I have always found very salutary.

Mr Baird was occupied in visiting the sick of the squadron the whole time we were in Torbay, and went to Dartmouth to inspect the sick quarters, if worthy to be called by that name, for the men were quartered on the lowest inhabitants and in some instances two in a bed, and when able to crawl about, exposed to the allurement of gin shops and other concomitant vices.

I wish to have a copy of the report Doctor Harness made of the state of Plymouth hospital and all other information touching the medical departments the sick of this squadron are likely to be sent to, without which I cannot form a just judgement of what is fit for me to do respecting them.

629b. *Sick and Wounded Board to St Vincent*

Office for Sick and Wounded Seamen, 28 June 1800

We have received your Lordship's letter of the 24th instant . . . We are of opinion with your Lordship that a great share of the bad health now prevailing in the fleet is imputable to the use of ardent spirits and we have therefore recommended to the Lords Commissioners of the Admiralty to cause malt liquor and wine to be supplied to the fleet off Brest as far as may be practicable.

The supply of refreshments enumerated by your Lordship for the men in health falls under the victualling department but in transmitting your representation to the Lords Commissioners of the Admiralty we have at the same time recommended that it may be carried into effect.

We beg also to inform your Lordship that there is a new set of instructions for navy surgeons about to be issued, in the 15th article of which we have laid down the regulation which we conceive to be most beneficial with regard to the diet for the sick.

In further answer to your Lordship's suggestions, we have to acquaint you that there is a supply of surgeons' necessaries for three months at Plymouth and Torbay, and we shall take care to keep up a stock adequate to all future demands.

With regard to the service at Dartmouth, we are so sensible of the defective state of it, that a member of this board had been at that place for the purpose of putting the accommodation of the sick on a better footing and we have come to a resolution of abolishing the sick quarters and have actually hired a house and directed additional buildings to be erected at Goodrington sands contiguous to the anchorage at Torbay which is so frequently the resort of the Channel fleet.

We are sorry we cannot immediately comply with your Lordship's wish respecting Dr Harness's report upon Plymouth hospital as it makes part of our correspondence with the Right Honourable the Lords Commissioners of the Admiralty without whose concurrence we should not be competent to communicate any part of it, and have therefore referred this also to their Lordships.

[Endorsements]

[At the Admiralty]
14 April. Send in the report of Dr Harness, if the report has been read, and send in the Victualling Board's letter on this subject if one has been received.

Inclosed is Dr Harness's report. I cannot trace any letter from the Victualling Board on the subject.

[By St Vincent]
In reply to my letter of the 24th.

11

THE MEDITERRANEAN DISCIPLINE
29 JUNE–21 OCTOBER 1800

Bridport's alleged dislike of the 'Mediterranean discipline' aggravated St Vincent [699]. Undoubtedly it fuelled his contempt for the state of the Channel fleet when he joined it. He later claimed that on his appointment the internal management of ships compared unfavourably with those of Russia and Spain, while their cleanliness was inferior to those of Turkey and the North African Barbary states [663]. Yet little more than two months after his appointment, St Vincent rejoiced in the impact of his regime. Early in July 1800 he claimed the fleet already worked together better and that individual ships were more efficiently managed [634]. By August, he asserted discipline was above mediocrity and would arrive at perfection within three more months [665]. Conspicuously proud, he despatched, for the information of the Admiralty, copies of the orders he had seen fit to issue. They related to matters as various as the airing of beds, the employment of convalescent men, the speed of replenishing in port and the rigging of masts and sails [638].

The more he was confirmed in the salutary effects of discipline and subordination, the more did he stress their importance [649, 682]. On the rotten apple principle, he targeted individuals: a recent chaplain of the *St George* alleged to have sold spirits to seamen [630, 633, 636]; the surgeon of the *Pompee* for indolence and incompetence [637, 646, 657]. In each case, he aimed to terminate their careers. To avoid such cases in future, he expected senior officers to support him in discouraging their juniors from becoming discontented [709], and he intervened directly himself to prevent drunkenness in officers [708]. Not surprisingly, the indulgences and conspiracies of seamen remained a concern [632, 640], sometimes a source of despair [697]. After the Spithead and Nore mutinies, he felt unable to place his confidence in them [711]. Instead he aimed to mitigate their excesses by insulating them from the shore [641], of which even officers could expect only fleeting experience [684], especially as ships were consistently expected to be self-sufficient in performing minor repairs [701].

St Vincent's pleasure in tightening discipline coincided with renewed outbreaks of scurvy [640]. The heightened tenor of his own language suggests that he himself, at least temporarily, was not immune from the effects of inadequate nutrition. He was himself to a large extent master of his own diet but had committed himself to remaining afloat for the rest of the war and was likely to have suffered from some vitamin deficiencies [659, 660].[1] The scurvy generated renewed activity on the part of the Victualling Board in despatching victuallers to the fleet [642]. This board was also authorised to establish a depot of provisions in Torbay [635]. At the same time the Sick and Wounded Board increased its purchases of fruit and vegetables for despatch off Brest whenever opportunities offered [655]. Meanwhile the initiatives of individual officers for the supply of cattle from islands off the Brittany coast were not discouraged [648]. St Vincent trusted these measures, with lemon juice issued generally as a preventive, would contain the scurvy and equally well treat it at sea as in port. Thus, while Trotter, Physician to the fleet, was commended for his part in securing vegetables for ships arriving at Plymouth, he was also immediately reprimanded for affecting their detention in port [641, 643].

Trotter, still operating largely from on shore on account of the injury received in 1795, was insufficiently in communication with St Vincent to achieve satisfactory understanding with him. Relations between them completely failed. Excluded even from receiving relevant copies of correspondence between the Commander-in-Chief and the shore boards, Trotter does not appear even to have been made aware of the introduction of lemon juice as a general preventive to scurvy. He himself maintained that its daily use would weaken the constitutions of seamen, and persisted in advocating the use of lemon juice only as a cure once scurvy appeared, combined with the issue of fresh vegetables, especially once ships returned to port, but if necessary shipped off to them. These supplies were still continued; indeed, were to be supplied from Portsmouth as well as Plymouth [686]. Yet ignored, and at odds with the new use of lemon juice as a preventive, Trotter was hurt by St Vincent's reprimand. Refusing to reply, he consciously withdrew his cooperation with the Commander-in-Chief.[2]

Within a fortnight he had been replaced as Physician of the Fleet by the surgeon Dr Andrew Baird, whom St Vincent had found in the *Ville*

---

[1]Mental symptoms accompanied outbreaks of scurvy. Contemporaries described them as madness or idiocy. See J. Watt, 'Some consequences of nutritional disorders in eighteenth century British circumnavigations', in *Starving Sailors. The Influence of Nutrition upon Naval and Maritime History*, ed. J. Watt, E. J. Freeman and W. F. Bynum (National Maritime Museum, 1981), 59.

[2]*The Health of Seamen. Selections from the Works of Dr. James Lind, Sir Gilbert Blane and Dr. Thomas Trotter*, ed. C. Lloyd (NRS, 1965), 244–6.

de Paris on joining the Channel fleet. Baird's merit lay in supporting St Vincent's adoption of lemon juice as a general preventative and his enthusiasm for its efficacy.[1] He also recommended himself by proposing a reduction in the amount of sugar to be issued to seamen for consumption with their lemon juice; in undertaking to improve the enlargement of sick berths, the space available in the cock pit, the cleanliness and ventilation of store rooms, and conversion of the space under the forecastle, where pigs were kept, to a dispensary [667, 669].[2] This last alteration was subsequently extended throughout the Channel fleet, and indeed became general throughout the navy. Later Baird claimed that these new arrangements resulted in the despatch to hospital of only 16 men in September 1800 when the fleet returned to Torbay after a cruise of four months. Sir Gilbert Blane, Commissioner for Sick and Wounded Seamen at the time, maintained they made a major impact on the morale of the sick.[3]

Initially Baird was not well received by all commanders of vessels in the fleet [679, 681]. But, possibly encouraged by the change in chief Physician, Baird's appointment coincided with proposals from surgeons within the fleet to vaccinate with cowpox seamen who had never had smallpox. One of their arguments was that the navy would act as a medium by which the population on shore would be convinced of the value of the vaccine [670]. Edward Jenner had done his first experiment in 1796, published his work in 1798, further observations in 1799, and a *Complete Statement of Facts and Observations* in 1800. The Admiralty did not oppose trials in the fleet [683], the first of which were reported in September 1800. Vaccination was subsequently made available to anyone in the fleet that desired it [700, 704].

Though determined to preserve seamen in health at sea, St Vincent refused to accept any extravagance in their use of vital supplies. He personally surveyed returns of water remaining on board ships in the fleet, and questioned the rates of consumption they provided [673]. Without regard to rank, civil or military, the same officers were held to account, with the same compunction, for the stations their ships were

---

[1]Lloyd and Coulter attribute the recommendation for the general issue of lemon juice as a preventive to Baird. J. J. Keevil, C. Lloyd and J. L. S. Coulter, *Medicine and the Navy 1200–1900* (4 vols, Edinburgh, 1957–63) III, 167. But this is by no means clear. St Vincent too would have realised its effect from his Mediterranean days. See Chapter 10, document 598.

[2]For further details of sick berth arrangements, see *The Health of Seamen*, 263. B. Lavery, *The Arming and Fitting of English Ships of War 1600–1815* (London, 1987), 204–6, carries a contemporary illustration of the sick bay on board the *San Domingo* in 1811.

[3]*The Health of Seamen*, 186, 204.

seen to keep around the Iroise [672, 717, 718]. His most senior subordinates, Berkeley and Warren, commanding the squadron of ships of the line off the Black Rocks and Passage du Raz, were formally dictated their duties [631, 645]. This firmness in his mind reflected the state of the war on the continent. French military successes on shore strengthened his resolve to keep Brest closed [644].

It was a policy not without benefits. Close experience of the Brittany coastline permitted unknown passages to be closed [647, 680]. Publicly, St Vincent was not for marginal improvements in hydrographical knowledge for its own sake. His commanders had copies of charts made at the time of Colbert for *Neptune François*, the official French collection of charts, and St Vincent opposed resources being used to improve on them [652] even though he was glad of fresh soundings when they were available [693]. It was a view reflecting the permanence achieved by blockade stations, some of which were now equipped with anchors and buoys: that for example of the advance squadron off the Black Rocks [653]. An uninhabited island among the rocks known as the Saintes was even explored with a view to occupation [707]. However, at the same time, in contrast to this apparent immobility, to facilitate communication from particular stations to supporting forces, rapid reinforcement and understanding of tactics, St Vincent expected every ship to be equipped and capable of making and repeating signals [661].

St Vincent brooked no concessions, even in the face of the worst weather. Although the main fleet might be forced into Torbay, the advanced squadron off the Black Rocks was expected to remain off Ushant, ready to return into the Iroise the moment winds permitted [666]. Inevitably, the strain of the close blockade took its toll. Berkeley was invalided from command of the support squadron and Warren was forced against his will to take his place [664]. On the basis of meritorious service, Warren was anxious for release to the north coast of Spain [656], and defied St Vincent's wrath in demanding release from the support squadron after six weeks [668]. He was replaced by Captain John Knight, who consequently obtained and received sanction for every movement of his squadron [675, 677, 687], before himself being replaced by Sir James Saumarez [703, 719]. Yet St Vincent himself in September 1800 could not avoid being driven off station by a northwesterly gale [706]. He, like his predecessors, took refuge in Torbay, prompting a recommendation, like others before it, for the use by the fleet of Douarnenez Bay [705].

Since June Sir Edward Pellew with seven 74s and smaller vessels had occupied Quiberon Bay with troopships carrying 5000 troops and

200 artillery. The force had been intended to support the Chouans in their resistance to the French government. After a landing was made at Quiberon, Belle Isle was intended as the next operation. On account of potential resistance, Houat was occupied instead. However, in August the force was earmarked for an attack on Ferrol [671] and sailed, under Warren's escort, on the 21st of that month [693]. The removal of the squadron from Quiberon Bay opened the way to further French coastal convoys with supplies for Brest. A good harvest already gave incentive for such movements [676, 695, 718, 720], which were co-ordinated with French frigates patrolling between Camaret and Bertheaume Bays [678]. Better supplies seem to have reactivated the French fleet [680, 710, 719]. Napoleon himself was expected at Brest, as were large numbers of troops and pressed seamen under guard [685, 688]. The Admiralty authorised St Vincent to recall ships of the line and promised reinforcement [690, 698]. At the same time, St Vincent attempted to block off supplies getting into Brittany further south and being conveyed to Brest overland [702].

Ministers placed complete faith in the blockade maintained by St Vincent [654]. Yet he was allocated ships no less strictly than Bridport had been, and was permitted no flexibility in their deployment [658]. While his quota of ships of the line was tightly prescribed, with frigates he had greater latitude. This permitted him to maintain the patrols in the Bay of Biscay and off Cape Finisterre [639, 651], which took large privateers on several occasions [662, 691]. However, these detachments again left the main fleet short of frigates and prevented the release of any surplus even for the most pressing escort duties [692]. To even the odds, especially in frigates, St Vincent was glad to support even the most optimistic suggestion for destroying French ships. A proposal for a fireship attack on the frigates in Camaret and Bertheaume Bays received every encouragement but was eventually abandoned [689, 693, 694, 703].

St Vincent's commitment and command might have reassured ministers. But his uncompromising language did not preclude differences of opinion with the Admiralty. Consistently outspoken, his private correspondence with Spencer did not exclude animadversions on the professional capabilities of officers, particularly those of high standing, holding senior posts in his fleet, and even current Admiralty commissioners [714, 715, 716]. Spencer was not one to allow injustice to go unanswered, thereby provoking adamantine declarations of ineptitude [715, 722]. At the Admiralty St Vincent aimed at his 'pseudo friend', Vice-admiral Young, who not only prohibited St Vincent from intercepting Spanish ships carrying bullion but subsequently brought Sir

John Warren to account for deliberately extending his detachment in order to remain longer on the coast of Portugal than was deemed absolutely necessary at the Admiralty [656, 713, 721].

These cross-currents apart, the main thrust of St Vincent's energy was directed to raising the standard of discipline in the Channel fleet and it had decided effects. During the summer of 1800, the fleet off Brest became increasingly self-sufficient. As well as provisions, water and stores came out to the fleet in its own ships [724]. Scurvy was kept at bay. Virtually insulated from shore, the desertion of seamen became more difficult. The blockade remained close and virtually unbroken. British security was preserved; indeed the security of islands off the French coast was preserved from the 'depredations' of privateers [696]. Meanwhile the shore establishments were able to improve their facilities. The hospital at Paignton was completed [650]. The enlargement of the basin and number of docks at Portsmouth approached completion. The dock and victualling yards established a routine of refitting and supply, their standards scrupulously monitored. Imperfections in ships' equipment were unequivocally condemned. Second only to the competence of officers was the criticism levelled at the attitudes of dockyard artificers [712]. The breadth of St Vincent's concerns anticipated his appointment in February 1801 to First Lord of the Admiralty after Spencer. However, the immediate future was to demonstrate that, though this attention to detail raised the rigour of the blockade, it still did not deter the French from planning expeditions from Brest [723] and indeed escaping when they had an intention to do so.

630.   *St Vincent to Captain Edwards*[1]

Ville de Paris, off Ushant, 29 June 1800

Having seriously reflected upon what you related touching the late chaplain of the St. George, I think it a duty incumbent upon me, holding the high and important situation I do, to represent his conduct to the Archbishop of Canterbury. I therefore desire you will send me a detailed report of the conversation which was overheard by the cook of the St. George, the steps he took in consequence, with all the measures which were afterwards pursued to bring the proof home to the chaplain, with his name, place of nativity, present residence and the college he was educated at, signed by you, that his Grace may be enabled to judge whether such a character is worthy to be continued a member of the Church.

[1]Of the *St George*.

631.   *St Vincent to Berkeley*

Ville de Paris, off Ushant, 30 June 1800

To avoid a possibility of mistake in my intention touching the duties to be performed by the squadron of reserve during the continuance of an easterly wind I judge the following explanation necessary. The object of your anchoring off the Black Rocks or cruising near them as occasions may require is to support the squadron of frigates under the orders of Captain Gore, not to control the exercise of his judgment, unless the enemy should come out in such force as to require it. Otherwise the responsibility of an arduous duty respecting the movements in Brest harbour could not in fairness rest with him where it is now lodged and his reports should uninterruptedly come to me, he making others to you. The moment I have the means you shall have a cutter to communicate between us.

632.   *St Vincent to Berkeley*

Ville de Paris, 2 July 1800

I have received further proofs of a conspiracy among the seamen, a swearing in at Haslar Hospital has been discovered . . . Much drunkenness and some insolence with a slack manner of doing the duty of this ship has appeared evident to me since we left Torbay. Some filthy habits have also been contracted by the evil communication which has happened on shore.

633.   *St Vincent to Edwards*

Ville de Paris, off Ushant, 2 July 1800

I am very much dissatisfied with the report you have made touching the execrable conduct of your late chaplain. I expect a detail of the expressions the cook of the St. George heard which induced him to enter the berth with every other minute circumstance relative to this abominable transaction. I trust you did not so far forget your duty as to suffer the investigation to be made by any person but yourself – you are now amenable under a peremptory order to comply strictly with the letter. The place of this person's nativity is of such notoriety I am surprised at the reply you have made on that head but neither it nor the college he was educated at are unknown to, Sir, your most obedient, . . .

P.S. I demand also to know whether the chaplain was confronted with the witnesses against him, whose names I require, and what justification if any he set of; in short every syllable which passed on this momentous occasion.

634.   *St Vincent to Fanshawe*

Ville de Paris, without Ushant, 3 July 1800

I have the satisfaction to acquaint you that the Mediterranean discipline so much deprecated is introducing into this squadron by slow degrees and no open resistance made to it. The improvement in our movements and general economy is hardly to be credited considering the short time we have been at it and the repugnance felt by some to change old and bad habits.

635.   *Admiralty to Victualling Board*

3 July 1800

Admiralty Order. To take up a number of vessels to be stationed in Brixham Pier with a depot of provisions equal to a proportion for 15,000 men (or about 23 sail of the line) for one month.

636.   *St Vincent to the Archbishop of Canterbury*

Ville de Paris, before Brest, 3 July 1800

There is no offence of so dangerous a tendency as the selling spirituous liquors to the people, whose daily allowance keeps them in an inflamed state. Mr. Bingham, late chaplain of the St. George, having been detected in the practice of it during the command of my predecessor and let off without a trial by court martial and having been guilty of petty larceny (as I am credibly informed) when chaplain of the Duke, under the command of Captain (now Rear Admiral) Holloway, I feel it to be my indispensable duty to lay the enclosed copies of correspondence and reports before your Grace that this unworthy member of the Church may not meet with encouragement.

637.   *St Vincent to Dr Gilbert Blane*[1]

Ville de Paris, off Ushant, 5 July 1800

Your Board have a great deal to answer for by appointing Mr. Wilkes surgeon of the Pompee, as to his excessive indolence, etc., may be justly imputed the loss of a great number of men by death and invaliding in that sink of corruption, Plymouth Hospital.

638.   *St Vincent to Admiralty*

Ville de Paris, off Ushant, 8 July 1800

I enclose for the information of the Lords Commissioners of the Admiralty copies of several orders which I have found it necessary to issue to the respective captains and commanders of His Majesty's ships and vessels under my command, . . .

[*Enclosures*]

638a.   *St Vincent to respective captains*

Ville de Paris, 2 July 1800

Experience having proved that most of the infectious diseases in His Majesty's ships originate in pent-up foul air and that none is so noxious as that which proceeds from the human body, the following regulation is to be observed in future on board every ship under my command; the times when the bedding is aired and the number of hours it is exposed each day to be entered in the Log Book.

The bedding of the respective ships' companies of the fleet is to be shook, and aired if possible, once a week during the summer months and as frequently in winter as the weather will permit; and a report is to be made on the back of the state and condition of the times the bedding was aired and how long it remained exposed to the air each day since the last account.

---

[1]Sir Gilbert Blane F.R.S. (1749–1834). A commissioner for Sick and Wounded Seamen 1795–1802. Physician to the Fleet under Rodney, 1779–83, he printed privately *A Short Account of the Most Effectual Means of Preserving the Health of Seamen*, and published in 1785 *Observations on the Diseases of Seamen*. The latter is printed in *The Health of Seamen*, ed. C. Lloyd (NRS, 1965) along with his paper *On the comparative health of the British Navy, from the year 1799 to the year 1814, with proposals for its further improvement*.

638b.

Ville de Paris, off Ushant, 5 July 1800

It is my direction that the captains and commanders of His Majesty's ships and vessels under my command do cause the beer, water and provisions, which may be necessary to complete them to the time for which they are ordered to be victualled, to be demanded the instant they shall be moored in Cawsand Bay or Plymouth Sound; and it is my positive order that no rigging shall be lifted or meddled with which is not restored before sun set, unless a lower mast is to be shifted.

638c.

Ville de Paris, off Ushant, 6 July 1800

In addition to my order of yesterday, the necessary demands for sails, cordage, top masts, yards, and spars are to be made the instant the ship, arriving in Plymouth Sound or Cawsand Bay, is moored, that I may know where to attach the blame if she is not at sea in a reasonable time; which never ought to exceed a week, unless a mast is to be shifted – and in that event not more than ten days.

638d.

Ville de Paris, off Ushant, 6 July 1800

It is my direction that the ships of the fleet always keep their convalescent men employed picking oakum, in order to have a sufficient quantity ready for caulking the ships.

638e.

Ville de Paris, off Ushant, 6 July 1800

The Commander in Chief is very much surprised to find that, when the ships under his command go into port for the express purpose of filling up with water, there is the smallest space in the hold left unoccupied; and he requires in future that every possible means be used to stow, even to a barrel, and no pretence of 'room to stow away chests' or other accommodation, at the whim of the master or mates of the hold, will be admitted.

638f.

Ville de Paris, off Ushant, 8 July 1800

The Admiral, having observed a main topsail split in tacking yesterday for want of a crowfoot, and that several topsail yards have been crippled since he took the command of the squadron entirely owing to the lifts not being bowsed taut, particularly when the reefs were in, and that some lower yards have been in danger, if not actually sprung, from the same cause, directs that the crowfeet be full reeved immediately and strict attention paid to keeping the lifts of the lower and topsail yards taut in all His Majesty's ships under his command.

639.   *St Vincent to Keats*

Ville de Paris, off Ushant, 8 July 1800

Being extremely solicitous to mark my approbation of your meritorious services and those of Captain Cunningham of the Clyde, I hereby authorize you to water at Oporto in the Boadicea and to direct Captain Cunningham should he fall in with you to do the same and to cruise as long as your and his provisions last and you are at liberty to send any or all the three frigates under your orders, one by one, to Oporto for the same purpose and to keep them with you as long as their provisions last, giving their captains the most precise orders to return to the northward of Cape Finisterre the moment the object of anchoring off the Bay of Oporto is accomplished, for I wish that the utmost degree of delicacy may be observed in avoiding a trespass on the limits of Vice Admiral Lord Keith's command.

640.   *St Vincent to Admiralty*

Ville de Paris, off Ushant, 8 July 1800

I desire you will represent to the Lords Commissioners of the Admiralty that the scurvy is making its appearance in a more progressive way than it has yet done and I am very apprehensive that should we have any bad weather the disorder will increase in an alarming degree; and I am sorry to observe that sending ships into port is not likely to give a check to it from the profligate and abandoned life the crews of the Channel fleet have been and still are in the habit of leading when in port, their only gratification being in getting beastly drunk with ardent spirits in the lowest brothels, from whence they return to their ships with their blood in a state to receive every disorder arising out of such practices. The westerly winds being, to all appearances, set in for the summer, the lemon juice and sugar to be supplied from the Victualling Office should be sent in a ship of war or we shall not receive them in time to stop the progress of this rapid disease and whatever refreshments are intended should come from Ireland, for it will be difficult for anything that does not swim upon copper to get out of the Channel, a proof of which is that the Iphigenia and Thetis have not yet joined.

641.   *St Vincent to Trotter*

Ville de Paris, off Ushant, 9 July 1800

I am to acknowledge the receipt of your letter of the 3rd instant and highly commend your exertions towards procuring vegetables for the use of His Majesty's ships under my command that arrive at Plymouth. At the same time I must desire you will discourage by all possible means the propensity to remain in port on account of sickness as I am persuaded the ships' companies will be far more healthy at sea, particularly now that lemon juice and sugar is directed to be supplied for the general use.

642.   *Victualling Board to Admiralty*

Victualling Office, 11 July 1800

The following is an extract of a letter we have just received from our Agent Victualler at Plymouth dated the 9th instant viz.

'I beg to inform you the Zenety brig, John Bishop master, and the Sophia Magdalena galliot, John Johnson master, being laden with provisions to be sent to Admiral the Earl of St. Vincent, and the Adventure brig, Thomas Longford master, now taking in a cargo of provisions for the said service, will be completed by tomorow evening if the weather continues favourable. I have this day requested Vice Admiral Sir Thomas Pasley will be pleased to appoint a convoy to proceed with the aforesaid victuallers off Brest, according to your orders.'

643.   *St Vincent to Trotter*

Ville de Paris, off Ushant, 13 July 1800

I very much disapprove your officious interference to prevent His Majesty's ships under my command from putting to sea the moment their beer, water and provisions are completed, which is ordered to be done with the utmost possible dispatch, and I desire you will discontinue this practice.

644.   *St Vincent to Warren*

Ville de Paris, off Ushant, 14 July 1800

I highly approve the enterprise which you directed against the enemy's convoy near the island of Noirmoutier[1] ... but, as my force is very much reduced and the state of the country becoming extremely critical from the reverses which the Emperor's armies have experienced in Italy and on the Danube which there can be no doubt have compelled him to make peace, I must request you will keep with His Majesty's ships under your orders in sight of the Passage du Raz with a westerly wind and when the wind shall be to the eastward that you cruise between the Saints and this squadron, within sight of signals.

645.   *St Vincent to Warren*

Ville de Paris, near Ushant, 14 July 1800

You must be stationary off the Penmarks with the wind westerly and when it blows on any point of the compass that the combined fleets can sail out of the Goulet you must be in sight of me with the Renown and Elephant or my force will not be in any degree adequate to that of the enemy.

Rear Admiral Berkeley is laid up by a very severe fit of the gout which seems likely to send him in. When that happens you will be ordered to take the command of four or five ships of the line stationed to support the frigates in the Bay of Brest and to anchor within the Black Rocks when the wind blows out of the Goulet.

[1] Now joined to the mainland, south of St Nazaire.

646.   *St Vincent to Blane*

Ville de Paris, 14 July 1800

Mr. Wilkes[1] killed Sir Richard Onslow's[2] son as much as if he had shot him on board the Barfleur.

647.   *St Vincent to Berkeley*

Ville de Paris, 15 July 1800

Captain Knight has deserved well of his country for ascertaining the passage between Ushant and Banec [Ile de Bannec[3]] which the French have taken a great deal of pains to keep us in ignorance of, as they politically and wisely did for more than a century of the easy navigation of the Gulf of the River St. Lawrence, which in my conscience I believe Sir Charles Saunders would have turned his back upon even after Admiral Durell got up to the Traverse if I had not been his first lieutenant and virtually his captain . . .

   When the Ville de Paris goes in to be new coppered, her false keel restored and an addition made to her post to throw the rudder out I shall hoist my flag on board the Formidable, Captain Thornbrough having been very obliging on the subject, as, I dare say, Captain Domett would, but there are, as you may imagine, many reasons why I wish to give the Royal George a good berth.[4]

648.   *St Vincent to Warren*

Ville de Paris, close to the Black Rocks, 16 July 1800

Nothing can be properer than your endeavouring to obtain supplies of cattle from Isle Dieu [Ile D'Yeu[5]], always keeping in mind that, with an easterly wind, your presence in the vicinity of Brest is indispensable.

[1]Surgeon of the *Pompee*.
[2]Sir Richard Onslow (d. 1818). Lieutenant 1758; Captain 1762; Rear-admiral 1793; Vice-admiral 1794; Admiral 1799.
[3]South-east of Ushant.
[4]But see letters from 24 July 1800, document 656.
[5]Between St Nazaire and les Sables-d'Olonne.

649.   *St Vincent to Pellew*

Ville de Paris, near the Black Rocks, 16 July 1800

I honour and respect all your feelings about the captains of the Naiad and Alcmene, yet I cannot possibly relax an iota upon their subject, for although discipline and subordination seem to be given up by all my brethren it never shall be said that the smallest dereliction from these essentials has been made by, ... [St Vincent].

650.   *Admiralty to Sick and Wounded Board*

16 July 1800

Having laid before my Lords Commissioners of the Admiralty your letter to me of the 14th instant, inclosing a copy of the report which had been made to you by Doctor Johnstone of his visitation to Paignton, to give directions for fitting an hospital at that place for the reception of sick men from His Majesty's ships and vessels in Torbay, I have their Lordships' commands to acquaint you that they approve of the arrangements made by the doctor for the care of the sick at Paignton.

I have also their Lordships' commands to desire you will let me know when the hospital shall be established, that application may be made for a guard.

651.   *St Vincent to Keats*

Ville de Paris, off Ushant, 17 July 1800

This despatch will be delivered to you by Captain Towry of His Majesty's ship Uranie, who is directed to put himself under your command and she shall be followed by the Fisgard, Beaulieu and Cambrian as soon as I have the means of replacing them where they are at present employed, which I think will enable you to spread from latitude 46.00 to Cape Finisterre so as to intercept the frigates and numerous privateers of the enemy which are now at sea.

652.   *St Vincent to Berkeley*

Ville de Paris, 19 July 1800

I cannot agree with you upon the value of Ushant, which, if in our possession, would not furnish any of the objects your sanguine mind exhibits. Besides that, the enemy would dispossess you of it with disgrace in forty-eight hours.

Captain Knight will love the Montague if he is permitted to make use of her in surveying, which I very much disapprove; a cutter and his own boats in the day are <u>tante</u> to all his views . . . all he has done and will do is not worth, to the public, a coil of twice laid rope . . . do you think the French during the reign of Louis Quatorze under the auspices of le grand Colbert did not make a better survey of Brest than Captain John Knight will do and have not you got it in the Neptune?[1]

653.   *Berkeley to St Vincent*

Mars, off the Black Rocks, 20 July 1800

We were in the midst of our supplies to the Triton when the Cumberland made the signal, not very distinctly, with the Spanish flag at the main and, seeing a ship standing out of Brest, I made the interrogatory with the same signal but afterwards, perceiving it to be the advanced frigates only under weigh, I made the proper signal to you, which I believe was understood although, our Spanish ensign being torn, I was obliged to make it with a jack.

I rather imagine this alert was in consequence of the enemy seeing our launches busily employed and wishing to make a push at the Nymphe and as their whole force came very boldly down before the wind I was obliged to make the Montague's and Saturn's signals to slip and support the advanced ships. Their launches, however, being left at their buoys with hawsers, they will easily resume their situations without losing their anchors. The Cumberland made the signal for the enemy returning to Brest but this I apprehend he is mistaken in, as I think, after manoeuvring in the Goulet, they will again anchor in Bertheaume and Camaret. The Triton had fortunately just got everything in except a few coals and wood which I have sent up in my launch to her, as Captain Gore's usual alacrity prompted him to weigh instantly. It is possible that this may be a relief of some of the enemy's advanced ships and the whole squadron may have got under weigh and manoeuvred to exercise or to conceal the change of ships.

---

[1] The *Neptune François*, the official French collection of charts.

654.   *Dundas to a correspondent*

Wimbledon, 22 July 1800

Attacking Belle Isle is not worth the expense. How then can the disposable forces best be employed against France – and against Spain? The French fleet in Brest must be left to Earl St Vincent. It has been suggested that we could capture Ferrol, where there is a Spanish fleet. Lord St Vincent says that with all the force at present under Abercrombie[1] he could take Carthagena, Cadiz and the Canaries. This would certainly make the enemy give up hope of prevailing against us.[2]

We have, however, since we had a disposable force used it for the benefit of others. We should employ it for our own benefit. It was by annihilating the enemy's colonial and commercial resources at the start of the war that we have been able to maintain our pre-eminence since. By reverting to this policy we can bring the French to make peace. Whatever the harshness of the terms we must exclude them from the West Indies.

655.   *Sick and Wounded Board to Admiralty*

23 July 1800

The Right Honourable the Lords Commissioners of the Admiralty having been pleased by their order of the 7th instant to direct that we should cause a supply of roots, fruits and other vegetables to be purchased and sent out by every opportunity which may offer, to the fleet under the command of Admiral the Earl of St Vincent, we caused inquiry to be made at the different ports in order to ascertain what quantity of the vegetables named in the margin [onions, leeks, turnips, carrots and cabbages] could be supplied and at what rates.

The enclosed paper will shew the result of such inquiry but the prices at which these vegetables have been offered at Plymouth, Paignton, and Falmouth exceeding in general so much what has been asked at Portsmouth, as well as the prices paid by the Victualling Board for certain

[1]General Sir Ralph Abercromby (1734–1801). Fought in Flanders and the West Indies earlier in the French Revolutionary War. Commanded the troops in the Mediterranean in 1800; defeated the French at Alexandria, where he died of his wounds.

[2]This letter appears to have been written the day after Dundas saw Colonel Maitland. *Historical Manuscripts Commission 14th Report, Appendix part V: the Manuscripts of J. B. Fortescue, Esq., preserved at Dropmore*, vols ii–vi (London, 1894 etc.) VI, 273. St Vincent had written to Spencer on 9 July advising against an attack on Ferrol, 'the least vulnerable of any part of the coast of Spain', and suggesting only that Cadiz and Cartagena might be within Abercrombie's capability if he had as many troops as common report gave him.

kinds of vegetables at Plymouth (which is also shown in the said paper), we have judged it most adviseable to request you will be pleased to lay the matter before their Lordships and we beg to be favored with their further direction for our guidance in the business and particularly as to the ports from which the supplies should be forwarded and by what vessels.

[*Endorsements*]

24 July. Let me see the orders given to them. Direct them to send them from Plymouth by every ship that sails from thence to join Lord St Vincent.

[*Enclosure*]

655a. *Prices at which sundry sorts of vegetables have been offered to the Commissioners for Sick and Wounded Seamen with the quantity of each sort tendered*

	Onions	Leeks	Turnips	Carrots	Cabbages
Portsmouth	14 Cwt/wk at 18s/8d per Cwt	–	–	2 Cwt/wk at 18s/8d per Cwt	14 Ton/wk at 4s/– per Cwt
Plymouth*	3 Tons at 31s/6d per Cwt	–	1 Ton at 21s/– per Cwt	–	77 Tons at 10s/6d per Cwt
Paignton	Quantity not mentioned 28s/6d per Cwt	–	–	–	Quantity not mentioned 10s/6d per Cwt
Falmouth	2,000 Bundles per week at 1d per bundle for 2 weeks, and as the season advances a larger supply.	–	3,000 Weight per week at 9s/4d per Cwt.	–	3,000 Weight per week at 9s/4d per Cwt.

* The Plymouth report not stating clearly whether the quantity offered is what can be supplied weekly, or during three months, the Sick and Wounded Board have required more particular information on the subject.

Prices paid by the Victualling Board for vegetables at Plymouth.

Cabbage ....   4s/– per Cwt
Onions .... 13s/– per Cwt
Turnips .... 10s/– per Cwt.

656. *St Vincent to Warren*

Royal George, near the Black Rocks, 24 July 1800

Your confidence in me is not thrown away and I will do everything in my power to aggrandize you in my present situation and in any future I may be advanced to.

   . . . The Admiralty having prohibited my sending the Superb and Bellona to intercept the two Spanish seventy-fours with eleven millions of dollars on board, which I impute to my pseudo friend Vice Admiral Young, I fear there is no chance of your making a coup on the north coast of Spain.

657. *St Vincent to Blane*

Royal George, 24 July 1800

If Mr. Wilkes is not removed I will bring a direct charge against your Board, for the said Wilkes is a butcher of men and I impute the death of all who have been lost to the King's service in the Pompee to him.

658. *St Vincent to Warren*

Royal George, very near the Black Rocks, 27 July 1800

I am absolutely and positively forbid to detach any ship of the line and the Renown and Elephant are considered as composing a part of my actual force before Brest and I am sorry to tell you that Admiral Berkeley either is or pretends to be so ill he must go into port. I have told him he may but must not keep the Mars there. Should he close with these conditions you must come immediately and take the command of the advanced squadron, which is to continue at anchor so long as I command the Western Squadron during an easterly wind, winter or summer.

659. *St Vincent to Monsieur Fenwick*[1]

Royal George, before Brest, 27 July 1800

Would it be possible to obtain forty or fifty dozen of the best claret that is produced in the vintage near Bordeaux. You will oblige me very much if this can be managed and I do not think the First Consul would object to it.

660. *St Vincent to Sir Charles Saxton*[2]

Royal George, before Brest, 27 July 1800

I am sure she [the *Ville de Paris*] will come out of dock everything I wish and as I am not to put my foot out of her during the war, unless my health makes it indispensably necessary (of which my rivals, competitors or what you please to call them, seem to have now no hopes) . . .

661. *St Vincent to Hamond*[3]

Royal George, before Brest, 27 July 1800

I certainly wish that every ship in the Western Squadron may be supplied with the pendants in the sheet I sent to the Board, for all repeat occasionally, which contributes to the rapidity of our movements, which are improving daily malgré the pious ejaculation of my predecessor.

662. *Towry to Keats*

Uranie, at sea, 28 July 1800

Cruising according to your instructions in His Majesty's ship under my command, I beg leave to acquaint you of my having captured this day La Revanche, a French schooner privateer mounting fourteen six-pounders, with eighty men, belonging to Bayonne; had been out from thence about four months but last from Vigo (nineteen days) to which port she had carried three prizes, an English brig called the Marcus, a Portuguese ship and a Spanish brig, prize to the Minerve.

[1] 'Négociant a Bordeaux'.
[2] Commissioner, Portsmouth dockyard.
[3] Comptroller of the Navy Board.

663.   *St Vincent to Berkeley*

Royal George, 28 July 1800

I could not have conceived it possible that this squadron should have been in so many instances worse arranged and economized than the ships of Spain or Russia; I do assure you the armed vessels of the Porte, Tunis, Tripoli and Algiers are so clean in every part that the officers of many of the ships of this fleet ought to blush at the comparison. I heartily hope you are better and remain very sincerely yours . . .

664.   *St Vincent to Berkeley*

Royal George, 29 July 1800

I am extremely concerned to learn by your letter of yesterday that your indisposition increases and I have in consequence come to a resolution to order you to proceed to Cawsand Bay in the Mars the moment the Agamemnon joins and has received from the Mars water to fill her quite up, provisions, wine and necessaries to complete her to four months, which Captain Moncton[1] will have in readiness to furnish. You will be directed to leave the unexecuted orders with Captain Knight, who is to command at the advanced post until the arrival of Sir John Warren, and you will inform him that Captain Stopford commands in Hodierne Bay and that his squadron is composed of the Excellent, Elephant and Defence (the last named stationed off Isle Groix to block L'Orient) the Lord Nelson cutter and Suwarrow schooner.

Samuel Hood[2] joined yesterday in the Courageux, built upon a plan of your friend Admiral Gambier's.[3] She is eight feet broader than the Defence at the fore part of the quarter deck and six inches narrower at the waterline, carries her lower deck ports eleven inches lower than the

---

[1]Monkton. For career see Chapter 10.

[2]Sir Samuel Hood (1762–1814). Lieutenant 1780; Captain 1788; Rear-admiral 1807; Vice-admiral 1811. Younger brother of Captain Alexander Hood, who had been killed in April 1798. He served mainly in the Mediterranean but also in the West Indies and lost an arm off Rochefort in 1805. He died while Commander-in-Chief East Indies.

[3]James, Lord Gambier (1756–1833). Lieutenant 1777; Captain 1778; Rear-admiral 1795; Vice-admiral 1799; Admiral 1805. A nephew of Margaret Middleton (née Gambier), wife of Sir Charles Middleton, Lord Barham. Admiralty commissioner 1795–1801, 1804–6, 1807–8. Commander-in-Chief and Governor of Newfoundland 1802–4; commanded the Copenhagen expedition in 1807 and raised to the English peerage November 1807; then commanded the Channel Fleet. He had religious views 'bordering upon the Methodist principles'. The *Courageux* was built by the Surveyor Sir John Henslow and launched in March 1800.

designer's calculations and yet will not stand upright in moderate weather but when in our language she comes to her bearings she will not go lower. In short the ship does not answer at all, being of Gulf of Finland build above the line of flotation and an indian proa below.

665.   *St Vincent to General O'Hara*[1]

Royal George, between Ushant and the Black Rocks, 1 August 1800

I am sure it will give you pleasure to know that this fleet which, when I came to it was at the lowest ebb of wretched and miserable discipline, is now above mediocrity and will, in three months if we are not driven into Torbay by tempestuous weather, be to perfection. We keep the combined fleets completely in check by anchoring a small squadron of ships of the line in the Iroise, near the Parquet Rock, and by a squadron of frigates and cutters plying night and day when the weather will permit in the opening of the Goulet between Camaret and Bertheaune, two ships of the line with a cutter and lugger are placed off the Raz de Frontenac and are generally at an anchor in Hodierne Bay during an easterly wind, one of the line off Isle Groix to block L'Orient and Sir Edward Pellew's squadron in Quiberon Bay with three regiments encamped on Houat – what they are intended for I know not as our expedition seems likely to end in vapour.

666.   *St Vincent to Captain Sutton*[2]

Royal George, off Ushant, 3 August 1800

With a westerly wind the ships under your orders are not to join the squadron but keep as close to the Black Rocks as circumstances will admit and in the event of my being compelled by tempestuous weather to take shelter in Torbay you are on no account to go into port but keep as close to Ushant as possible to be in readiness to support the advanced squadron which will resume its present position in the Iroise with the first spurt of easterly wind.

---

[1]Charles O'Hara (1740?–1802). Lieutenant-general 1793; General 1798. Fought in Germany, India, North America; captured at Yorktown, 1781, and at Toulon, 1793. Governor of Gibraltar 1795–1802.

[2]Of the *Superb*. This same letter went to Captain Knight of the *Montagu*. Copies of the latter exist in COR/7 and 11.

667.   *St Vincent to respective captains*

Royal George, off Ushant, 3 August 1800

It having been found by experience that one ounce of sugar is sufficient to mix with the same quantity of lemon juice and a pint of water to make good sherbert, it is my direction that it be mixed in that proportion accordingly, which is to be considered as each man's daily allowance in future; and the respective pursers are to be held responsible for the sugar which will be saved.

668.   *St Vincent to Pellew*

Royal George, before Brest, 3 August 1800

Sir J. Warren says he cannot endure to be chained to the Black Rocks longer than six weeks. I have therefore urged a promotion that I may have the benefit of Captain Thornbrough and Sir J. Saumarez's services at that important post in the character of flag officers.

669.   *Sick and Wounded Board to Admiralty*

Office for Sick and Wounded Seamen, 7 August 1800

Admiral the Earl of St Vincent, Commander in chief of the Channel fleet, having by his letter of the 1st instant acquainted us that he had directed Mr Andrew Baird,[1] late surgeon of the Ville de Paris, but now of the Royal George, to correspond with us and to state such observations as might occur to him in discharging the function of Physician and Inspector of the Squadron, we enclose a copy of his Lordship's said letter, which we request you will be pleased to lay before the Right Honourable the Lords Commissioners of the Admiralty for their Lordships' information.

   We also enclose a copy of Mr Baird's letter to us of the 2nd instant, acquainting us of the good effects which have attended the use of the lemon juice and sugar. In regard to that part of the letter wherein a reduction of the quantity of sugar is proposed, we beg you will acquaint their Lordships that we are of opinion from the experiments we have

---

[1]Dr Andrew Baird (fl. 1757–1843). Commissioner for Sick and Wounded Seamen 1803–4; Inspector-General of Naval Hospitals in 1804. Baird's relationship with St Vincent continued even after the latter's retirement and he attended him in his last illness in 1823.

made since receipt of the beforementioned letter that the proportion of one ounce of sugar is sufficient for one ounce of lemon juice, and we beg leave to suggest to their Lordships that directions should be given accordingly to the Victualling Board for their guidance in supplying these articles to His Majesty's ships and vessels.

[*Endorsement*]

8 August. Orders accordingly.

[*Enclosures*]

669a.   *St Vincent to Sick and Wounded Board*

Royal George, off Ushant, 1 August 1800

The benefits derived from the intelligence and active zeal of Mr Baird in discharging the functions of Physician and Inspector of the sick of the squadron during our anchorage on Torbay and since we sailed from thence are of such magnitude that it would be the height of injustice to delay the communication of them to your board, and I have directed him to correspond with you, and to state such observations as occur to him.

669b.   *Baird to Sick and Wounded Board*

Royal George, off Ushant, 2 August 1800

In obedience to Lord St. Vincent's commands, under whose orders I have continued to visit the sick of the fleet since my last report to you, I now beg to acquaint you that the use of the citric acid and sugar has been attended with the happiest effects. When its use first became general among the people of the Ville de Paris I had upwards of twenty under cure of scurvy and fresh ones daily appearing, but before that ship quitted the fleet I had not a single case ill enough to make trial of Corwell's Concrete on. On my coming into the Royal George I found a few cases, but at present every symptom has disappeared. In seven ships of the line that have been longest at sea, which I visited within the last three days, I have not found a single case (where scurvy was the sole disease) that was incapable of duty. So I can now say it is near subdued in all those ships where this wholesome beverage has been used for a few weeks, and where the counteracting effects of excess and intemperance have not been felt.

We have just received a supply of vegetables which cannot fail to do much good, and are highly relished by the people.

In addition to visiting the sick of the fleet the Commander in Chief has directed me to see that the necessary means is pursued for the preservation of health as well as the removal of disease and with this view he requires that I shall see the sick berths enlarged where it is necessary and rendered comfortable; that I shall also recommend the removal of all bulk heads forming berths in the cock pit and substitute hanging screens; the removal of the lattice work bulk heads separating the wings from the cable tiers; and also required that I shall inspect the different store rooms below and see that they are kept perfectly clean and well ventilated; and that the sick may no longer be annoyed by the nauseous stench of hogsties, his Lordship has given out in public orders that they shall be removed from under the forecastle, which additional space is given to the surgeon as a dispensatory where he is to dress and see his patients instead of the cock pit, except during time of action; so that I trust those regulations will be attended with the most salutary effects both as to the comfort and accommodation of the sick, and the prevention of disease, it being Lord St Vincent's opinion, as it is strictly mine, that disease is much oftener generated on board than imported and the duty I am daily employed on convinces me more and more of the fact.

As economy of the good things allowed becomes necessary, permit me to observe that experience has proved to me that the quantity of sugar allowed is too much by one half: previous to the order given by Lord St Vincent, that the acid and the sugar should be made into sherbert, the people both in the Royal George and the Neptune complained of their punch being too sweet until the quantity of sugar on the former ship was reduced to half the full allowance; in the Ville de Paris at my request it was always issued as sherbert in the reduced quantity of one ounce of sugar to the ounce of lemon juice, and a pint of water; it was then sufficiently palatable and the effect was as I have already stated. In the Royal George we now observe the same proportion. Thus it appears that every advantage is desired by serving of sherbert agreeable to the plan I have adopted as above, and were it to become general on the calculation of six hundred men to every line of battle ship and sugar purchased at six pence per pound there would be a saving to the government of upwards of eleven thousand pounds sterling a year in a fleet of thirty-two sail of the line independent of frigates etc.

Thirty boxes of lemon juice have lately been received here from Plymouth hospital which I have signed for and shall deliver them to such surgeons of the fleet as may want them, taking care to receive the receipts which I shall forward to you.

670. *Sick and Wounded Board to Admiralty*

Office for Sick and Wounded Seamen, 7 August 1800

We enclose a copy of a letter from Mr Veitch surgeon of His Majesty's ship Magnificent requesting our opinion in the expediency of inoculating with the cow pox such of the men on board that ship as have never had the small pox, and who are willing to submit to the operation, which we beg you will lay before the Right Honourable the Lords Commissioners of the Admiralty.

As Mr Veitch's proposal is new in the service, we deem it our duty to submit this point to their Lordships' determination, and to add that we have of late heard so many respectable testimonies in its favour that we are of opinion it may be adviseable to make trial of it on board of the Magnificent for the reasons assigned in the inclosed letter.

[*Endorsement*]

8 August. To remain for the present. To try it on board the Triumph at Portsmouth on any men desirous of being so inoculated.

[*Enclosure*]

670a. *James Veitch to Sick and Wounded Board*

Copy

Magnificent, off Ushant, 26 July 1800

The vaccine inoculation has since my return from the West Indies attracted very general notice and seemingly most deservedly as it apparently offers the most eminent and permanent advantages to society. Enquiring at the small pox hospital, which I visited early after my arrival in England, and reading has convinced me of its utility and I feel animated by a desire provided the board approve of it, of extending its advantages to the Magnificent by inoculating in a gradual and limited way all those men who have not suffered from small pox as a security against its irruption at any future period. The cow pox from every idea I have been able to collect relative to its nature appears not to be communicable from the person inoculated to another unless through the medium of inoculation; it likewise seems not to be strictly a pusticular disease, of course not loathsome either in point of smell or otherwise; and the person who has been subjected to its action is not only secured against its influence but is insulated as to the powers of the variolous contagion and, to crown all, the fever and excessive excitement consequent to its absorption scarcely merit the appellation of disease, circumstances recommending it in the fullest degree for naval practice, as the necessarily crowded situation of men on board of ship would render the introduction of a contagious disease, however mild, into a healthy man of war with the view of superceding the attack of one more virulent, active and deadly, subject to be considered an unpleasing and dangerous clew for the medical man to wind from. Independent of securing our naval exertion from any depression by small pox during the time of war, there is a period approaching when ambition will be taught its limits and we may cease contending for our security and independence; it is then that this practice may shine forth with peculiar lustre and advantage, and prove one great means of restoring rapidly the depopulation necessarily flowing from war. Men who have fought the battles of their country are drawn from all, and a great many from the remotest, parts of three kingdoms where the prejudices of education, religion amd ignorance operate injurious to society from the bulk being in some degree guided by such principles. It therefore becomes a national and material point to gain an accession of opinion in favor of this mild mode of inoculating, which ought not to be allowed to pass unobserved by these men provided it were introduced into the navy, and the reduction of prejudice eventually arising from examples of its utility would adhere to the mind and at the conclusion of the war would prove the means of disseminating its advantages widely amongst the descendants of those who have served and who are likely to become themselves in their turn the bulwark of their country and our commercial interests. Gratitude and the knowledge of the number who have fallen during the pending contest demand the extension of a fostering hand to this order of men.

The discovery of the circulation of the blood which for a time injured the fame and reputation of the immortal Harvey is a wonderful example of the narrowness and perversions of ignorance and the opposition which the introduction of the inoculation for the small pox met in London and throughout England is fresh in the memory of thousands. Hence the necessity for annihilating prejudice in bringing about a revolution of so much importance and pointing out by every possible means the track proper to be followed. I am in possession of the vaccine virus but I conceive it my duty to avoid any application for its being carried into effect until I receive the opinion of the Board who may perceive dangers I am not aware of.

671.   *St Vincent to Stopford*

Royal George, off Ushant, 8 August 1800

The scene is materially changed within the few days last passed respecting Sir Edward Pellew and the force both of ships and troops in Quiberon Bay, which are ordered to proceed on service to attack Ferrol so soon as Lieutenant General Pulteney[1] and a large force from Netley and Swinley camps join. You will therefore only have to attend to the coast from L'Orient to the Raz, [which has] become of much greater importance than before by the extreme scarcity of provisions in the district of Brest, so that you may expect attempts to be made to pass convoys through the Glenans and Penmarks the moment Sir Edward Pellew shall have retired from Quiberon. They are now endeavouring to get provisions round in small vessels from lower Normandy and I fear they will succeed, malgré the efforts of our cruisers from the nature of the coast, environed as it is with rocks and intricate passages which, with the uncertainty of the tides, renders the navigation very dangerous to any but the people who reside on the spot. The blockade of L'Orient is discontinued by order of the Admiralty.[2]

672.   *St Vincent to Lord Ranelagh*[3]

Royal George, off Ushant, 8 August 1800

It is with a considerable degree of surprise that I have been to the eastward of Ushant without observing the Doris in the station positively prescribed to her, the more so because Captain Domett explained to your Lordship succinctly that it was expected of you to place His Majesty's ship under your command in a situation to command the Passage du Four and the enclosed intelligence will show you that a neglect of the duty your Lordship is specially appointed to perform may be attended with the most serious consequences to the State.

---

[1]Sir James Murray-Pulteney (1751?–1811). Lieutenant-colonel 1780; Major-general 1793; Lieutenant-general 1799; General 1808. Served in America and the West Indies; temporarily occupied the heights of Ferrol in 1800. Assumed the name of Pulteney on his marriage with Henrietta Laura Pulteney, Baroness Bath, 1794.

[2]This announcement appears to refer to the technical and legal concept of blockade as a complete ban on all traffic.

[3]Honourable Charles, Viscount Jones.

673.   *St Vincent to Knight*

Royal George, off Ushant, 9 August 1800

I have some suspicion from a rough calculation of the daily consumption of water in His Majesty's ship under your command that six butts instead of four are used and should you have women on board without the authority of the Lords Commissioners of the Admiralty and the Commander-in-Chief and this apparent waste of water has been occasioned by them you will in course send them to England by the first conveyance.

674.   *St Vincent to Knight*

Royal George, off Ushant, 9 August 1800

I have not the smallest objection to your anchoring with the advanced squadron under your orders in Douarnenez Bay with a westerly wind, taking care to be at your post off the Black Rocks when the wind shall come to the northward or eastward.

675.   *St Vincent to Knight*

Royal George, off Ushant, 9 August 1800

I enclose for your guidance in the event of the enemy putting to sea, when I may be forced from the rendezvous by tempestuous weather, a secret instruction which is on no account to be opened but under the circumstances abovementioned, and you will observe that the ships said to be in Quiberon Bay, in the copy of the order for commanding the advanced squadron which you have received from Rear Admiral Sir J. B. Warren, are no longer to be taken into consideration.

[*Endorsement*]

Secret Instruction from the second paragraph to the last, in the most secret order number 3 dated 7 March 1800.

676.   *St Vincent to Knight*

Royal George, off Ushant, 10 August 1800

I enclose for your information the copy of intelligence received from Mr. Secretary Nepean, by which it appears that a convoy of the enemy from lower Normandy will shortly endeavour to get into Brest. The movements of the frigates with the additional one from Brest demonstrate the approach of the convoy abovementioned.

677.   *St Vincent to Knight*

Royal George, off Ushant, 13 August 1800

I am to acknowledge the receipt of your letter of yesterday and in reply have to observe that you have my permission to move your berth as you shall judge most proper for accomplishing the service on which you are ordered but you must not go to Douarnenez Bay with the wind to eastward.

When I am joined by additional cutters, of which I am in hourly expectation, one shall be placed under your orders.

678.   *Knight to St Vincent*

Montagu, at anchor off the Black Rocks, 16 August 1800

Having no doubt that your Lordship heard the cannonade of this afternoon I cannot be silent on the occasion although nothing of consequence has occurred.

Being induced by the commanding breeze to take a near view of La Goulette [Goulet de Brest], as also the anchorage of the enemy's advanced ships, I weighed and stood in with His Majesty's ships you had placed under my orders; as the Montague (being considerably advanced) drew abreast of the four frigates in Bertheaume road they weighed and stood under easy sail towards Camaret. That gave hope of closing with them, which was effected as this ship got within range of the surrounding mortar and gun batteries, who made it necessary to tack and return a pretty harm [sic] fire from the enemy's ships, who had then reached Camaret Bay.

679.   *St Vincent to Sawyer*

Royal George, off Ushant, 16 August 1800

Your letter, this moment received, has not contributed in the smallest degree to alter the opinion I had formed of your having determined to avail yourself of this influenza to get the Russel again into port. The most serious charge I make against you is the savage rudeness offered to Mr. Baird on the quarter deck of the Russel yesterday, wholly unbecoming the

character of her commander and particularly reprehensible in the despond-
ing state your improper conduct has placed the crew of His Majesty's ship
under your command. If you continue to court enquiry in the style of the
letter I am replying to, it will come sooner than you are aware.

680.   *Domett to Bridport*

Off Brest, 16 August 1800

The enemy is said to be again very much alive at Brest. Ships are
coming out of the harbour and the number in the road apparently ready
for sea increasing. We make out about thirty sail of the line. The wind
and weather have been remarkably favourable for blocking up the port,
enabled the advanced squadron to continue constantly at anchor near
the Black Rocks and the frigates to keep close in with St. Mathieu's
Point, which has prevented even a chasse marée from getting in and
occasioned the markets at Brest to be very ill supplied. The advanced
squadron is now commanded by Captain Knight, who has been able,
from the very extraordinary long run of fine weather to survey almost
all the small islands and rocks within Ushant and confirmed what we
supposed, that there was a tolerable passage between Ushant and the
Isle of Molene [Ile Molène]. Stopford is off the Bec du Raz with three
sail of the line and a cutter or two and Sir John Warren is the colleague
of Sir James Pulteney for carrying on the operations of the army.

681.   *St Vincent to Sawyer*

Royal George, off Ushant, 18 August 1800

Having conveyed to you such reproof as I judged fit for the occasion,
though short of what you merited, I shall give myself no further trouble
on that score and I positively forbid your presuming to write at me in
the manner you have lately done or to make a signal for having intelligence to communicate when you have none.

682.   *St Vincent to Blane*

Royal George, before Brest, 19 August 1800

You see I have still obstacles to surmount which do not discourage me in
the smallest degree and I have not the smallest doubt of trampling all
opposition to the weal of His Majesty's service underfoot, all the officers

of the squadron whose good opinion is worth a rush affording me every support in their power and testifying upon all occasions the incalculable benefits this squadron has derived from my taking the command of it.

683.   *Admiralty to Sick and Wounded Board*

19 August 1800

Having laid before my Lords Commissioners of the Admiralty your letter to me of the 7th instant inclosing a copy of a letter from Mr Veitch surgeon of the Magnificent respecting the expediency of inoculating with the cow pox such of the men on board that ship as have not had the small pox and are willing to submit to the operation, I have their Lordship's command to signify their direction to you to cause a trial of that inoculation to be made on board the Triumph at Portsmouth on any men who may be desirous of being inoculated.

684.   *St Vincent to the Admiralty*

Royal George, off Ushant, 20 August 1800

I desire you will communicate the enclosed report to the Lords Commissioners of the Admiralty and acquaint their Lordships that I learn, from the best source of information, it has been no uncommon thing for two or more lieutenants of one, or more, ships to be left behind when the squadron has sailed from Torbay before I was appointed to command it; and I entreat of their Lordships to put a stop to this shameful dereliction of duty by wholesome correction.

[*Enclosure*]

684a.   *Totty to St Vincent*

Saturn, at sea, 20 August 1800

In obedience to your Lordship's order directing me to state the reason why Lieutenant Wingate[1] of His Majesty's ship Saturn, under my command, was left behind at Plymouth, I have the honour to inform your Lordship that I am unable to assign the particular cause which may have detained him on shore. He, the said Lieutenant Wingate, had my

---

[1]George Thomas Wingate (fl. 1793–1814). Lieutenant 1798; Commander 1814.

permission to go on shore on Saturday last and the Saturn sailed from Cawsand Bay early the following morning.

685.   *Intelligence report: D'Auvergne to William Huskisson*[1]

Jersey, 21 August 1800

I have the honor to acquaint you for the information of Mr Secretary Dundas that advice has reached me that the different Republican Generals and Prefects in the Western Departments have received the most pressing orders for a prompt and general levy of all the seafaring men of their districts, to convey them guarded to Brest where an armament is directed to be prepared with every diligence by the time of the arrival of Bonaparte there, expected to be about the close of the present republican month, the disposable troops in the four departments amounting to about fifteen thousand men are marched for Brest, twenty two thousand men are announced, from the interior as soon as they can be collected.

An abundant harvest that is gathering all over the country will afford them an ample stock of provisions, every information from different parts of the province announces very active preparations in the maritime ports by the arrival of the first consul; I trust His Excellency will be persuaded that I shall have their movements watched with all the activity and intelligence in my power.

686.   *Sick and Wounded Board to Admiralty*

Office for Sick and Wounded Seamen, 22 August 1800

It appearing that the quantity of vegetables which can be procured at Plymouth, for the service of the Channel fleet, is not so large as could be wished, and that the price is extremely high, we request you will be pleased to submit for the consideration of the Right Honourable the Lords Commissioners of the Admiralty whether it may not be advisable also to send occasional supplies from Portsmouth where vegetables can be purchased at much less expense and in much larger quantities.

[*Endorsement*]

Acknowledge receipt. To send them also from Portsmouth whenever a favourable opportunity offers.

[1]Copy also in ADM. 1/6034.

687.   *St Vincent to Knight*

Royal George, off Ushant, 25 August 1800

I think it necessary to observe that in case of the squadron being driven from the anchorage from the advanced post with the wind from the N.W. and not being able, or not judging it advisable, to anchor in Douarnenez Bay, it may not be possible to preserve a position so as to make Ushant frequently, in which event a station near the Penmarks appears the most judicious step that can be taken.

688.   *Stopford to St Vincent*

Excellent, Hodierne Bay, 26 August 1800

The Lord Nelson cutter joined me on the 24th instant; Lieutenant Percy[1] informs me that on the 22nd instant he spoke a neutral vessel coming from Concarneau from whom he received the intelligence that all the fishermen from that part of the coast have been ordered to Brest and that the seamen who have been absent upon leave were ordered to return to their duty.

689.   *King to St Vincent*

Sirius, off St Mathieu, 27 August 1800

The eight frigates and corvette which were in Camaret Roads are now moored close into Camaret, shut in with Point du Convent, moored close to each other; and it strikes me, from their present position, that a fire ship might be thrown in with effect; therefore, if your Lordship could spare Captain Rickets[2] for a few days, I will carry him up to make him conversant of their situation.

690.   *Admiralty to St Vincent*

Admiralty office, 29 August 1800

Mr Secretary Dundas having transmitted to my Lords Commissioners of the Admiralty a letter which he had received from Captain D'Auvergne by which it appears that the greatest exertions are making to enable the

---

[1]Probably Robert Percy (fl. 1783–1800). Lieutenant 1783.
[2]William Henry Ricketts (d. 1840). Lieutenant 1782; Captain 1790.

enemy's fleet to proceed to sea, I enclose to your Lordship a copy of Captain D'Auvergne's letter and I have their Lordships' commands to signify their direction to you to call in any ships of the line which you may have detached to the southward, excepting those under the command of Sir John Warren, and to keep the ships under your orders so situated that you may be enabled to collect the whole together whenever the enemy's fleet shall shew a disposition to put to sea.

I have their Lordships' further commands to acquaint you that they have directed every possible exertion to be made for completing the repairs of the ships named in the margin [*Ville de Paris*, *Prince of Wales*, *Triumph*], that they have ordered men to be sent to Plymouth to complete the complement of the Princess Royal, and that the said ships will be ordered to join your Lordship as possible.

691. *Samuel Hood to Warren*

Courageux, Vigo Bay, 30 August 1800

Perceiving yesterday afternoon the French privateer in the harbour had removed for security near the narrows of Redondella, close to the batteries, where I thought there was a probability of her being attacked with success, I ordered two boats from each ship named in the margin [*Amethyst, Stag, Amelia, Brilliant, Cynthia*] with those of the Renown, Impetueux and London you sent me and from the Courageux, commanded by lieutenants volunteering their services, to be ready at 9 o'clock and placed them under the direction of Lieutenant Burke[1] of the Renown, whose gallant conduct has so often merited your commendation; about 40 minutes past twelve they attacked her with the greatest bravery, meeting with desperate resistance, her commander having laid the hatches over to prevent her people giving way; and cheered as the boats advanced but notwithstanding this determined opposition she was carried in 15 minutes.

I am sorry to add Lieutenant Burke has received a severe wound but I hope not dangerous; our loss has been as per enclosed list [4 killed, 20 wounded], the greater part occasioned by this desperate conduct of her commander, who was mortally wounded; too much praise cannot be given to those deserving officers and men who so gallantly supported Lieutenant Burke and towed her out with much courage through the fire of the enemy's batteries. I need not, sir, comment on the ability and courage of the commanding lieutenant, his former services having gained

[1]Henry Burke (d. 1804). Lieutenant 1796; Commander 4 October 1800.

your esteem; and I have no doubt the sufferings of his wound will be alleviated by that well known attention shown to officers who have so gallantly distinguished themselves, for which I beg leave to offer my strongest recommendation.

The privateer is a very fine ship named La Guêpe of Bordeaux, with a flush deck, 300 tons, pierced for 22 guns, carrying 18 nine-pounders and 161 men, commanded by Citoyen Dupan, stored and provisioned in the completest manner for four months; she had 25 killed and 40 wounded.

692.   *St Vincent to Lieutenant General Sir James Pulteney*

Royal George, off Ushant, 30 August 1800

I am extremely concerned I cannot comply with your request by adding frigates to the escort ordered by the Lords Commissioners of the Admiralty to the troops under your command. The fact is that I have not half the number of frigates necessary for the various services under my directions. There never ought to be less than ten constantly attached to this fleet and I have not one.

693.   *St Vincent to Knight*

Royal George, off Ushant, 30 August 1800

Before I received your letter of yesterday I had despatched the Megara fireship to you, which if you can burn to the destruction of one frigate I shall feel that a brilliant service is performed under your auspices. You will find Mr. Ricketts a man of great precision and cool bravery.

I return you many thanks for your observations on the bay of Brest and I take the liberty to send you a copy of a chart lent me by Sir James Saumarez which was taken out of a French ship of war in the year 1747 by his intrepid uncle, Captain Philip Saumarez[1] of immortal memory, and you will oblige me very much by filling it up with soundings, views of headlands etc.

MOST SECRET AND CONFIDENTIAL. I have the pleasure to acquaint you that the armament sailed from Quiberon Bay on the 21st destined against Ferrol with every prospect of complete success. Sir

---

[1]Philip Saumarez (d. 1747). Lieutenant 1737; Captain 1743. An uncle of Sir James, Lord de Saumarez (1757–1836), he was a survivor of Anson's circumnavigation and was killed in Hawke's battle off Cape Finisterre, 14 October 1747.

James Pulteney has twelve thousand effective soldiers and Sir John Warren nine thousand seamen and marines with every supply we could furnish him with.

694.   *Knight to St Vincent*

Montagu, Black Rocks, evening of 1 September 1800

Having this morning again anchored the advanced ships off the Black Rocks, I availed myself of the flood tide, accompanied by Sir Richard Strachan and Lieutenant Ricketts (both admirably calculated to execute, as to judge of the projected enterprize). We embarked with Captain King in the Sirius and took a near and favourable view of the situation of the enemy's frigates in Camaret, who remain as they were, compact in the Bay, and are of opinion, however practicable the attempt might be, to insure success, notwithstanding the apparent preparation by gun and guard boasts of the enemy, who make their apppearance on all occasions, that it might be a night assault, to which the moon, your Lordship will admit, is at present an obstacle, who can equally judge of the watchful vigilance of the enemy, as of the anxious zeal of the officers your Lordship has selected to make the attempt.

695.   *Intelligence report: D'Auvergne to Dundas*

Jersey, 2 September 1800

I have the honor to transmit to your Excellency the continuation of the movements at Brest up to the 19th ultimo inclusive: the very abundant harvest that is gathering has a little eased the distress of the place with respect to bread; the most industrious activity is put by the administration on the coast to convey other species of provisions to that town where all minds are absorbed by the expectation of receiving the consul Bonaparte; the admirable vigilance with which Audierne and L'Iroise are guarded leaves them for access but the River Morlaise [Morlaix]: the general rendezvous now of the supplies that Normandy and the northern coasts of Britanny can furnish, and this access will continue I trust to be successfully intercepted by our cruisers off Isle de Bas [Ile de Batz].

696.   *St Vincent to D'Auvergne*

Royal George, off Ushant, 3 September 1800

The Mayor of Isle Dieu having represented to me that privateers belonging to Guernsey and Jersey have frequently committed violent depredations on the property of the defenceless inhabitants of that island, calling themselves at the same time tenders belonging to His Majesty's fleet under my command, I am to request you will be pleased to signify to the masters of privateers that I shall not fail to inflict every mark of displeasure in my power on the vessels that may hereafter be guilty of such disgraceful transactions. I have the honour to be with great esteem and regard, your Highness's most obedient, humble servant.

697.   *St Vincent to the Navy Board*

Royal George, off Ushant, 7 September 1800

. . . the much to be lamented change in the character of seamen which I find far worse in this squadron than I did in the Mediterranean. Here they are a drunken, slovenly, lazy and filthy race and although the discipline and subordination is somewhat improved I despair of seeing it perfectly restored during the present war.

698.   *St Vincent to Admiralty*

Royal George, off Ushant, 7 September 1800

By His Majesty's ship Caesar I have this day received your letter of the 29th ultimo enclosing the copy of intelligence from Captain D'Auvergne which Mr. Secretary Dundas had transmitted to the Lords Commissioners of the Admiralty and in obedience to their Lordships' direction to call in any ship of the line which may have been detached to the southward, excepting those under the command of Sir John Warren, the Dolly cutter was despatched with the necessary orders for that purpose to the captains of His Majesty's ships Excellent, Elephant, Defence and Canada which had been stationed off the Passage du Raz, Isle Groix and in Quiberon Bay.

699.   *St Vincent to John Lloyd*[1]

Royal George, near Ushant, 13 September 1800

You perhaps don't know that my illustrious predecessor uttered the following ejaculation at the table I am now writing upon before most of the admirals and captains of his squadron, 'God forbid the Mediterranean discipline should ever be introduced into the Channel Fleet'.

700.   *Sick and Wounded Board to Admiralty*

Office for Sick and Wounded Seamen, 13 September 1800

Mr James Moffat, surgeon of His Majesty's ship Endymion, having in his letter of the 10th instant transmitted to us a list of twelve inoculations with vaccine matter performed on board that ship, we enclose a copy of Mr Moffat's said letter, and of the list which accompanied it, and beg to submit for the consideration of the Right Honourable the Lords Commissioners of the Amiralty whether, from this additional testimony in favor of the practice, it may not be adviseable to introduce it generally through the fleet.

[*Endorsement*]

15 September. Directions to inoculate any persons who wish to be so inoculated. Acquaint Lord St. Vincent.

[*Enclosures*]

700a.   *James Moffat to Sick and Wounded Board*

Endymion, Spithead, 10 September 1800

I have enclosed a report of sick now on board His Majesty's ship Endymion together with one of twelve inoculations with vaccine matter as a substitute for the small pox, which from the mildness of the symptoms as well as the incapability of its being communicated by contagion cannot fail of recommending its general use in the navy.

---

[1]John Lloyd of Pound, Devon. Clerk of the Cheque, Plymouth dockyard, 1762–1801, and for many years a friend of St Vincent. *Letters of the Earl of St. Vincent 1801–4*, ed. D. Bonner Smith (NRS, 2 vols, 1921, 1926), II, 207n.

[*Second enclosure*: report of cases inoculated on board His Majesty's ship Endymion on her passage to and from Gibraltar, dated Spithead, 9 September 1800.]

701.   *St Vincent to Commissioner Fanshawe*

Ville de Paris, off Ushant, 14 September 1800

I send no ship in that has occasion for a shipwright or joiner or house carpenter to be sent on board her, and I highly disapprove any boat being sent on shore for repair, and request you will refuse to receive any boat in future.

702.   *St Vincent to Captains Bowater and Sotheby*[1]

14 September 1800

You are hereby required and directed to proceed without a moment's loss of time in His Majesty's ships under your command and cruize between Glenan Islands and Point Quiberon for the express purpose of intercepting the supplies intended for the combined fleets which are collected at Noirmoutier and other places with a view of being pushed into Quimper River to be conveyed from thence by land to Brest, and which are daily stealing along shore for that purpose. It being of the utmost consequence that those supplies should, if possible, be cut off, you are not to be diverted from this important service by chasing, or any other circumstance whatever, and if the line of battle ship and frigates which are ready for sea at L'Orient should ever come out, you are to use your utmost endeavours to draw them towards the Saintes Islands where you may expect to find Captain Knight in His Majesty's ship Montagu and the frigate and vessels named in the margin [*Naiad, Suwarrow, Lord Nelson*] to whom you are at all times not only to look for support in case of being overpowered by the enemy, but also communicate any intelligence you may obtain which you shall judge necessary either for him to be informed of, or to be forwarded to me.

You are to continue on this service until you receive further order, and on no pretence whatever to put into port, but in the event of experiencing heavy gales of wind from the westward that will not admit of your preserving the aforementioned station, you are to seek shelter in Quiberon Bay where the ship you command may, with the

---

[1]Of the *Magnificent* and *Marlborough* respectively.

detachment under the orders of Captain Knight who has received similar instructions, be usefully exerted in intercepting any vessels of the enemy that shall attempt to pass that way.

703.   *St Vincent to Saumarez*[1]

Ville de Paris, off Ushant, 19 September 1800

I herewith transmit you copies of letters which I have received from Captains King and Knight and as the moon is now favourable for the enterprise therein suggested have dispatched the Megara fireship to you for that purpose and desire you will join the Sirius, accompanied by Captains Stopford and Hill,[2] and carefully examine the position of the enemy's frigates in Camaret and Berthoaume Days and if it shall appear feasible to burn them or even one of them I desire you will direct the same to be carried into execution by the said fireship assisted with the launches, barges and such other boats of both the advanced squadrons (of which you will apprize Captain Sutton) as you shall think proper the instant that circumstances shall render the attempt expedient, the whole enterprise to be conducted and carried into execution by the Honourable Captain Stopford of His Majesty's ship Excellent.

704.   *St Vincent to Admiralty*

Ville de Paris, off Ushant, 23 September 1800

I have to acknowledge the receipt of your letter of the 15th instant acquainting me that in consequence of reports which had been made to the Lords Commissioners of the Admiralty by the Commissioners for taking care of Sick and Wounded Seamen of the favourable effects of the vaccine inoculation, their Lordships had directed those Commissioners to cause any seaman who may be desirous of it to be so inoculated.

705.   *Knight to St Vincent*

Montagu, Douarnenez Bay, 24 September 1800

My position south of the Raz in the late gale induced me to take refuge in Douarnenez Bay and I am the more satisfied in having done so as the

[1]Copy also in COR/11.
[2]Henry Hill (d. 1849). Lieutenant 1793; Commander 1795; Captain 1801; Rear-admiral 1830; Vice-admiral 1841.

ground I took up, being in the S.E. part of the bay, became exposed to the gale, which blew right in at W.N.W. and N.W. by W., the angle between the two outer points was 28° being between N. 50° W. the Bec de la Chevre and N. 78° W. the Bec du Raz, on clean fine sand 10 fathom depth at low water and two miles from the shore. I changed situation in the bay to the N.W. part thereof, when the Bec bore W.½ N., 2½ miles out of range of shot and the entrance two points open.

When the wind drew to the N.W. I repassed the Raz, from whence, being this morning near the Penmarks, on the change of wind to the S.W. I returned hither and found the advanced squadron quiet at anchor, sheltering from the gale.

If I presume to venture an opinion I trust you will at least pardon me, that the fleet under your Lordship's command might equally ride here safe and undisturbed, there being no hidden corners where Brulots may be expected in the quarter the wind blows from that would detain it here.

By such a situation your Lordship can best judge of the saving to the Crown, as ground tackle is far less liable to wear than in Cawsand or Tor Bays.

706.   *St Vincent to Admiralty*

Ville de Paris, in Torbay, 25 September 1800

I desire you will acquaint the Lords Commissioners of the Admiralty that I contended against the elements with a view to preserve the important position assigned me as long as I possibly could without crippling the ships under my command or being driven to the eastward of Torbay, either of which events might have had the worst effect at this critical period.

The Barfleur, Neptune, Mars, Juste and Russel were directed by signal to proceed to Cawsand Bay, the three first named being in course of pay, the Juste having a number of the Repulse's men on board unpaid[1] and the Russel in want of stores. Every effort shall be made to get the squadron in this bay, named on the other side hereof [*Ville de Paris, Royal Sovereign, Windsor Castle, Prince George, St George, Princess Royal, Formidable, Glory, Atlas, Namur, Achille, Spencer, Saturn, Venerable, Ramillies, Defiance, Bellona*] to sea the first favourable moment.

The Caesar, Pompee, Captain, Marlborough, Defence, Sirius, Alcmene, Megara fireship, Admiral Mitchell and Joseph cutter are left

---

[1]The *Repulse* had been lost off Brest in March. See document 541.

to watch the port of Brest. The Superb, Centaur and Warrior to support them.

The Montagu, Naiad, Lord Nelson cutter and Suwarrow schooner are stationed between the Saintes and Penmarks and the Magnificent from the Glenans to Quiberon Point; it is, however, probable that the three ships have taken shelter from the violent north-west gales in Quiberon Bay. The Lady Duncan lugger is off Abreverack.

I enclose a journal of my proceedings since I left Torbay and am, . . .

6 p.m. The wind being come far to the northward with an appearance of lasting, I shall hold the squadron in readiness to put to sea the moment the rigging is set up and masts secured and I have sent orders to the ships in Cawsand Bay to hold themselves in readiness to join me.

707.   St Vincent to Knight

Ville de Paris, Torbay, 26 September 1800

I did not receive your letter of the 19th by the Lord Nelson cutter until last night, the bad weather having occasioned Lieutenant Percy to take shelter in Torbay before we were compelled to do it. The weather has been very unfavourable for your exploring the danger of the Saintes and I am very agreeably surprised to learn that you have ascertained so much.[1] I will thank you to observe critically the surface of the inhabited island, what variety there is on it as to hillocks, the depth of soil, whether there are many large loose stones or rocks which could be used in masonry with every other remark which occurs to you, but in performing this I request you will let as little appear to your own people and to the French fishermen, who are an acute race, as possible.

708.   St Vincent to Admiralty

Ville de Paris, off Torbay, 26 September 1800

I desire you will represent to the Lords Commissioners of the Admiralty that the excessive drunkenness in several of the wardrooms of ships of this squadron, occasioned by the pursers being compelled through menace to supply spirits to the officers ad libitum, has been the cause of the scandalous scenes which have produced so many courts

---

[1]Captain Stopford had suggested the possibility of seizing and fortifying the Saintes.

martial; to correct this and many other abuses growing out of it I have issued the enclosed order, which I hope their Lordships will confirm throughout the Navy.

[*Enclosure*]

708a.   *General Order*

The Commander-in-Chief, highly disapproving a practice which has too long prevailed in His Majesty's naval service of the pursers issuing a greater quantity of spirits and wine to individuals than the stated allowance, does most positively direct that this breach of good order and regulation be discontinued; and the respective pursers of the squadron under his command are hereby forbid at their peril to serve out more than the authorized allowance to any person or on any pretence and to pay no debts whatsoever of provisions in kind.

709.   *St Vincent to Trollope*

Ville de Paris, Torbay, 1 October 1800

The mass of heterogeneous and improper matter contained in your letter of 12th ultimo occasioned my overlooking the dangerous tendency of the postscript. I advise you in future to beware of encouraging your officers in thinking themselves aggrieved by any specific order the Commander-in-Chief thinks fit to give or presume to question the propriety of them yourself, perhaps not the first instance of attempts to incite resistance to the orders of the admiral who presides over this fleet.

710.   *King to St Vincent*

Sirius, off Brest, 6 October 1800

I beg leave to inform your Lordship I had yesterday afternoon the satisfaction of reconnoitring Brest, the wind moderating and coming round to south; the ships appear to lay very thick and apparently ready for sea, all fully rigged but none had topgallant yards across. I could plainly distinguish 28 or 29 sail but I do not imagine they were all of the line, as just as I raised their hulls the weather came on hazy. I could not perceive any ships in Camaret, therefore suppose those frigates compose part of the above number; there were nine ships with Spanish colours and only seven ships with flags flying.

711.   *St Vincent to National Endeavour*[1]

Ville de Paris, in Torbay, 6 October 1800

I am honoured with your letter of the 3rd instant and do not disapprove an application being made to the officers and seamen of the fleet from the office but, after the execrable conduct of the seamen in the mutiny without a just pretext of grievance, I never will be the instrument of making any proposal to them until they show a proper sense of past misconduct.

712.   *St Vincent to Admiralty*

Ville de Paris, in Torbay, 6 October 1800

I desire you will represent to the Lords Commissioners of the Admiralty that before many of the squadron had hove up their lee anchors, the wind backed to the S.S.E. and the sea rose, insomuch several of them veered and could not purchase their lee anchors, when perceiving others to have hove in to a cable on the weather anchor, the signal was made to veer cable, in doing which the splice of the Royal Sovereign's cable upset in going round the bitts. The Master of the Formidable pretends that her cable parted a foot without the splice, but I have no doubt the splice upset. The Mars parted the cable of her lee anchor a fathom or two from it in heaving up, and the cable, a patent one, appears to be quite rotten; I do not, however, apply this to any defect in the invention but to the careless manner in which our ropemakers manufacture the cables, an allegation which holds good against the whole of our cordage, and unless there is an entire change of system in that branch, as well as in every other in His Majesty's Dock yards, and wholesome laws enforced to govern the artificers by, the navy will be put to continued hazard, and the country ruined by incapacity, waste, idleness, corruption and every other vice.

The Neptune has also parted a cable but her report is not yet received.

The Neptune's report, this instant received, is also enclosed.

---

[1]Addressed to the 'National Endeavour' at Paddington. It is unclear precisely what its proposed application was.

[Endorsement]

8 October. Send reports to Navy Board respecting the cables.

713.   *Young to Spencer*

Admiralty, 8 October 1800

The easterly wind was so short as not to admit of our fleet getting out of Torbay nor the French, I should hope, out of Brest. As for Warren, I fancy he will stay out till he will feel that nothing but some very successful stroke will justify him; and he will continue doing wrong in hopes of catching an excuse.

I don't know Captain Browne[1] but I have heard him well spoken of. Lord St. Vincent's commendation does not always imply merit in its object but if Captain Browne be a favourite we should hear no more complaints of the Robust.

714.   *St Vincent to Spencer*

Ville de Paris, in Torbay, 8 October 1800

There is one berth near the old Fish House in Cawsand Bay where the ground is so rubbly no ship can take it without destroying her cables but chain moorings may be laid down with safety. If Penn, the pilot, does not know this, I do. This suggestion is made on account of the Juste being ordered to Spithead, she having lost fourscore men by desertion when she docked at Portsmouth, the disease of all ill-governed ships and she is the worst on record except the Fortitude when commanded by the present Vice Admiral Young, the Robust of this day and the Russell when Sir H. Trollope commanded her.

715.   *Spencer to St Vincent*

Clermont Lodge, 12 October 1800

I will speak to the Navy Board on the subject of the berth in Cawsand Bay where you think a mooring chain might be usefully laid down; but the cause of the Juste being ordered to Spithead was on account of her

---

[1]William Brown (d. 1814). Lieutenant 1788; Captain 1793; Rear-admiral 1811.

masts being reported defective and I should hope that from Spithead she will not lose her men by desertion.

If your Lordship has been correctly informed respecting the prevalence of desertion on board the Fortitude when commanded by Admiral Young I should infer from thence that the practice does not wholly originate in the want of proper attention to discipline in the commander of a ship, for from what I have observed of that officer since I have had the pleasure of knowing and acting with him I am confident that he can never have been negligent of his duty and whatever other failings he may be supposed to have, he is the last man I should suspect of relaxation of discipline.

716.   *St Vincent to Spencer*

Ville de Paris, near Ushant, 13 October 1800

My cough increases and I am full of apprehension that I shall be compelled to retire from this command unless you give me the winter's sun in the region of Torbay. If Sir Hyde Parker comes it will be best to fix him at once in the Royal George. I can with confidence assure your Lordship that Captain Domett had rather command any ship in the fleet than her, – entre nous, he has no authority in her, the people are masters and the government, such as it is, goes on by coax and managements. There is not an officer in her except the Captain and Lieutenant Rosenhagen.[1] In course she never can be better without a total change. The Royal Sovereign is gone to the Devil also owing to the mistaken lenity and kindness of Sir H. Harvey.

[*Endorsed as received on the 17th*]

717.   *St Vincent to Lieutenant Coet*

Ville de Paris, off Ushant, 13 October 1800

To my astonishment I found this morning that the Lady Duncan lugger was not on her station and a convoy of the enemy passing through the Four. I therefore desire you will immediately join me to account for this neglect of your duty.

---

[1]Philip Lewis Rosenhagen (d. 1813). Lieutenant 1795; Captain 1806.

718.   *St Vincent to Admiralty*

Ville de Paris, off Ushant, 13 October 1800

I desire you will acquaint the Lords Commissioners of the Admiralty that at daylight this morning twelve sail of sloops and hoys under convoy of an armed brig were seen standing along shore to the S.W. The Excellent and Saturn were instantly sent in chase but before they could get up with them the whole got into the Four Passage. The Lady Duncan lugger was not on her station and it is evident Lieutenant Coet has not been attentive to his duty. I have therefore sent orders to him, at Plymouth, to join me immediately to account for his conduct.

719.   *Saumarez to St Vincent*

Caesar, off the Black Rocks, 13 October 1800 at 5 p.m.

I have recalled the Joseph cutter to acquaint your Lordship that the convoy I stated to be coming through the Four this morning have taken shelter in Locris[1] River on this side of Conquet. The frigate with an armed brig and lugger are anchored under protection of their batteries and I fear will get into Brest notwithstanding our endeavours to prevent them.

I stood in towards the Goulet this afternoon and find all the ships with yards and topmasts up but several without having their sails bent. Enclosed is a report I have received from Captain King which perfectly agrees with my observation. His signals this morning denoting their coming out of port were in consequence of having their topsail yards hoisted and having the appearance of coming out to protect their convoy but which was prevented by the signals from Ushant announcing your Lordship's fleet being in sight with all sails set.

720.   *St Vincent to Knight*

Ville de Paris, off Ushant, 14 October 1800

Having delivered to Captain Pierrepont of His Majesty's ship Naiad such orders and instructions as you shall deem necessary for performing the important duties of watching the Passage du Raz (copies of which you are to forward to me) and placed under his command either

---

[1] A village in this locality is named Lochrist.

the Lord Nelson cutter or Suwarrow schooner, you are hereby required and directed to proceed without a moment's loss of time, accompanied either by the schooner or cutter, and cruize between the mouth of the Loire and Belle Isle as well for the purpose of intercepting the supplies which are collected on the coast (as per enclosed intelligence) to be conveyed to Brest and which are daily stealing along shore, as for aiding His Majesty's ship Marlborough, placed under your orders to watch the port of L'Orient.

721.   *Warren to Admiralty*

Renown, Cawsand Bay, 16 October 1800

I have received your letter of the 14th instant in which their Lordships require that I would let you know for their information why I did not immediately rejoin the Earl of St Vincent after sailing from Vigo.

I must therefore represent that the situation of the convoy from having suffered in their masts and yards whilst in Vigo Bay by driving in the hard gales of wind on board each other, it was necessary they should be repaired by the ships of war and all of them not being finished until the squadron and convoy were beyond Oporto rendered it impossible for me to quit them until they were in a state to pursue their voyage.

The wind upon the coast of Portugal and Spain is generally three parts of the year to the northward as well as the current, which obliges every ship that is homeward bound to stand to the westward to obtain a wind or to fetch the Cape: which I endeavoured to do by every means in my power; it therefore gives concern to understand that their Lordships entertain a doubt of the least time having been lost in following my orders from the Commander in Chief, who has expressed his entire approbation of my conduct upon that service.

[Endorsement]

18th October. Inform Sir John Warren that although it might be necessary to accompany the convoy as far as Oporto to complete the repairs of the transports, yet when their Lordships observe in his journal that after leaving the convoy he had run three degrees to the southward, that for several days, though already far to the westward, he had run to the westward with an easterly wind instead of making the best of his way to the northward; and when by the journals of three packets which sailed from Lisbon, one on the day he left Vigo Bay, one on the 17th

September and one on the 4th October, it appears that all those packets arrived in Falmouth before he arrived in Cawsand Bay their Lordships cannot but be of opinion that if he had taken proper measures to do so he might have joined Lord St. Vincent with the squadron under his command sooner than he did.

722.   *St Vincent to Spencer*

Ville de Paris, near Ushant, 18 October 1800

I mean to say what will not be contradicted by any officer of intelligence who served in the Mediterranean and particularly by Rear Admiral Holloway, that the relaxation of discipline on board the Fortitude was proverbial, appeared upon <u>every</u> occasion and beggared all description.

[*Endorsed as received on the 22nd*]

723.   *Ralph Abercromby to Keith*

21 October 1800

From the information I have received which may be considered as authentic, the combined fleet at Brest have received orders to proceed to the Mediterranean and that preparations are now making at Barcelona for their reception as they could not stop at Cadiz on account of the epidemic disorder which now rages there; Sicily is said to be their destination.

724.   *St Vincent to Admiralty*

Ville de Paris, off Ushant, 21 October 1800

I cannot too much applaud the conduct of Captain Hood of His Majesty's Ship the Courageux who, by stowing a great quantity of water on his gun deck, has brought out the stores stated in the enclosed schedule; nor Commissioner Fanshawe's unremitted exertions in causing them to be put on board at a very short notice.

[*Enclosure*]

724a.   *List of stores brought out to the fleet*
by His Majesty's Ship Courageux

For the Ville de Paris
12 large brushes
300 yards of old canvas
2 coils of 5   inch hawser
2   ..   4½ ..
5   ..   4   ..
4   ..   3½ ..
5   ..   3   ..
5   ..   2½ ..
5   ..   2   ..
6   ,,   1½   ..
6   ..   1   ..
6   ..   ¾   ..
20 log lines
70 lb twine
2 grindstones
100 sail needles
100 thimbles
6 lb beeswax
200 lb tallow
Forty thrums
10 nine inch blocks
12 ten inch   ..
12 ten inch   ..   single
12 nine inch   ..   ..
12 eight inch   ..   ..
2 twenty-one inch   ..   ..
20 buckets
12 serving mallets
2 four inch cables
2 three inch   ..
30 spars
One cutter
One bower cable
One hawser 5½ inch
Two of 5 inch

Elephant
Two bower cables

Royal Sovereign
Two bower cables

Bellona
Two bower cables
Main topsail yard

St George
One bower cable
One ensign

12

THE ESCAPE OF GANTEAUME
21 OCTOBER 1800–9 FEBRUARY 1801

In mid-October 1800, on account of a persistent cough, St Vincent was given permission by the Admiralty to reside on shore at Tor Abbey and to delegate command of the fleet off Brest to his second-in-command [725, 731]. Accordingly, Sir Henry Harvey was instructed to take over the command off Brest [734, 744, 760], where temporarily Sir Hyde Parker presided. Spencer at the Admiralty was content with the arrangement. The fleet had received an infusion of the 'Mediterranean discipline' which Spencer applauded, at least in response to claims of its new efficiency on the part of St Vincent [737]. Meanwhile, against the drift of political patronage, the Commander-in-Chief took pains to ensure captains of whom he approved were appointed to ships demanding new management [730, 768, 778]. He expressed himself confident that the manoeuvres in which he had drilled the fleet off Ushant would be maintained [744], and made a point of sending to the Admiralty copies of his orders relating to the formation, watch-keeping and the seamanship required of ships [808].

St Vincent's release from command off Ushant came at a time when the greater part of the Franco-Spanish fleet in Brest harbour seemed to be preparing to sail on a variety of expeditions [726–8, 736]. According to intelligence, six of the line were intended to relieve Malta or provide support to the French army in Egypt [733]; the main fleet was to destroy the expedition under Sir Ralph Abercromby intended for Egypt and to invade Sicily [735]; another detachment was to sail for the Indian Ocean [738, 739]. An attempt to sail made in mid-October was halted by the appearance of British ships of the line [742]. Gales, causing collisions in harbour, forced some back to Brest dockyard for repair. Nevertheless throughout November the smaller detachments remained ready to sail, keeping the British fleet in high alert [746, 748].

However, late in November intelligence suggested that, though one of the French expeditions was still likely, the greater part of the French fleet would be laid up for the winter. The Admiralty accordingly prepared to reduce the force off Brest to 20 ships of the line, with six in Torbay and six in Cawsand Bay [752]. The reduction would save the fleet from some wear and tear, especially in its rigging, now all the more necessary because of events in the north. The peace settlement between France and Russia laid the foundation for the 'Armed Neutrality of the North' aimed at ending the British blockade of members' trade with France. It threatened to impose restrictions on the supply to Britain of naval stores from the Baltic and also to extend British operations to the northern seas [749, 788]. More immediately it demanded the detention of Russian, Danish and Swedish ships [780, 800].

St Vincent, who now divided his life between Tor Abbey and *Ville de Paris* in Torbay, accepted the reduction in the force off Brest without demur [754]. He remained supremely confident that the commanders of the in-shore squadron, Saumarez, Pellew and Thornbrough, would keep any French expedition in port [750, 753, 786] but nonetheless took the precaution of providing his deputy off Brest with detailed instructions for the pursuit of any French squadron should it escape [756, 757]. St Vincent was kept informed of the situation in Brest on a daily basis [758] and from warning signs anticipated an imminent attempt to escape [759, 765, 767]. Intelligence from Captain D'Auvergne, Prince de Bouillon, confirmed this view [762], and in mid-December St Vincent reinforced the in-shore squadron to nine ships of the line [764, 776].

St Vincent's residence in Torbay now placed him in closer communication with the Admiralty. He remained on good terms with Spencer even if suspicious of the attitude of the rest of the Board towards himself [761, 795]. However, on issues that mattered the Board reinforced St Vincent's orders, ensuring, for example, that captains of ships at Plymouth slept on board and that refitting excluded the removal of lower masts unless sanctioned by the Admiralty itself [740, 741].

From Torbay St Vincent was also able to police the contacts of the ships with the shore. He still considered that seamen were at risk of being incited to discontent from contact with malcontents on land [784]. He thus placed great importance on captains remaining on board when in port [743], attributing desertion to the absence of captains and negligence on the part of junior officers [751, 770, 797, 810, 811]. He likewise blamed the ability of a French convoy to get along the north coast of Brittany into Brest on the tardiness of ships getting to sea after sheltering in English ports after a gale [763]. He thus regarded his own presence in Torbay as indispensable, now driving rather than leading his ships to sea, but still effectively maintaining its discipline [781]. There he could also enhance the supply of fresh vegetables to the fleet at sea [747, 755] and ensure the defence of the anchorage when the fleet returned to the bay for shelter [783].

Though in St Vincent's opinion 'uncommonly favourable', the winter weather took its toll on sails and rigging [765, 771]. Late in December Harvey was driven into Torbay [769]. Alternating easterly and westerly winds then prevented him from getting back off Ushant for over a week [772, 773]. On 8 January 1801 the French took the opportunity to send to sea a squadron of seven ships of the line and two frigates under Rear-admiral Ganteaume. He escaped through the Passage du Raz but, encountering British ships, he put back to Camaret bay, then returned into Brest [775–9]. Nevertheless the French fleet remained ready to sail, and in mid-January another spell of gales drove Harvey into Torbay and Pellew out of the Iroise [782, 785, 787]. Harvey was able to leave Torbay on 23 January, but that very night Ganteaume sailed from Brest. Next morning he may have been sighted by the few ships remaining off Ushant, but the weather remained so bad that identification was virtually impossible [790]. In the event Ganteaume with seven large ships was next seen off Cape Finisterre.[1]

The gales prevented the advance squadron reassembling in the Iroise until 25 January. The Franco-Spanish force in Brest was observed to be smaller than before, but poor visibility prevented confirmation of Ganteaume's departure [791, 794]. Belatedly, the Admiralty ordered Harvey to be reinforced [789]. Both the Admiralty and St Vincent impatiently awaited a precise count of the fleet in Brest. The clean escape, unaccosted by any ships, defied belief [799, 800]. Not until 3 February, was the escape confirmed and only then by intelligence from D'Auvergne [796, 801]. The Admiralty promptly ordered pursuit by six of the line, to command of which Sir Robert Calder was appointed. However, by then two weeks had passed since Ganteaume's departure and even more time was lost from the pursuit having to be mounted from Torbay [803, 806]. Needless to say, Ganteaume had made good his escape. He entered the Mediterranean on 9 February. His ships carried 5000 troops intended for Egypt. North of Cape de Gata, however, he took the frigate *Success*, from whom he was informed of the likelihood by that time of British landings in Egypt. Rather than continue towards that destination, he turned north and entered Toulon on 19 February.[2]

Meanwhile the fleet off Ushant had been warned of an intention for a second squadron to leave Brest [796]. The Admiralty had ordered the destruction of French fishing boats and capture of fishermen in order to

[1]W. James, *The Naval History of Great Britain from the declaration of war by France in 1793 to the accession of George IV* (6 vols, London, 1859), III, 69. Ganteaume's squadron actually consisted of three 80-gun ships, three 74s and two frigates.
[2]James, III, 73.

deprive the warships of crews [793]. The blockade was also succeeding in deterring the inward convoy of supplies, but French shipping was accumulating to the south of Brest and intelligence suggested the French would send out ships to escort a convoy into the port [805]. Supply vessels were cut out wherever possible [732]. But for these purposes, as well as for the capture of privateers [804], St Vincent needed frigates and cutters, and of these he now felt a severe want [803], so much so indeed that he was cautious of encouraging any new diversion of resources [809].

Despite St Vincent's criticisms, the officers and men of the fleet revealed remarkable endurance. Under the new regime of a daily dose of lemon juice, the scurvy had been kept at bay. For those invalided on shore, facilities were now available in Torbay. Although the proposal of St Vincent for a hospital at Brixham was rejected by the Sick and Wounded Board [745], the hospital at Paignton approved by the Sick and Wounded Board was ready to receive staff by January 1801 [792]. Morale was a more widespread problem. The return of *Ville de Paris* into Torbay triggered a period of 'slackness' on board St Vincent's own flagship [774]. Measures to reduce drunkenness generated a mutinous spirit aboard the *Naiad* [807]. St Vincent tended to blame the officers of the fleet. Indeed by February 1801 he used the same terms to describe their conduct afloat as he applied to disorder on shore, particularly at Plymouth [812]. British society seemed to be in a state which St Vincent believed could only be altered by a change of government [810]. It was a radical solution in which, so far as the navy was concerned, he can hardly have expected to perform the central role.

725.   *Admiralty to St Vincent*

21 October 1800

The Earl Spencer having communicated to my Lords Commissioners of the Admiralty a letter he had received from your Lordship representing that from the state of your health it was necessary you should come on shore and with a view to its re-establishment desiring so to do and to reside in the vicinity of Torbay, I have their Lordships' commands to acquaint you that they are pleased to indulge your Lordship with the leave you have solicited on your arrival in Torbay and that in the event of its being found expedient that the squadron should return to its station off Brest before you shall find yourself sufficiently recovered your Lordship will in such case deliver to the officer next in seniority to you such orders and instructions as may be necessary for his direction and guidance in the execution of the service committed to your care during your absence.

726.   *John Cook[1] to St Vincent*

Amethyst, off the Black Rocks, 23 October 1800

A report of the enemy's fleet in Brest Water October 22nd 1800.

I think there are about thirty-three or thirty-four sail of the line but they lay so near each other that it is impossible to count them distinctly. They all had their top gallant masts up, nine ships have flags hoisted, and the same number of ships have their sails bent. In Camaret Bay there is a frigate with her lower yards down

727.   *De Courcy to St Vincent*

23 October 1800

Report of His Majesty's Ship Canada

Stretched across the Goulet by signal from the Caesar, when abreast of Camaret Bay, reconnoitred the enemy's force; saw in the fair opening 26 sail of the line, of which nine were three deckers; observed also the mast heads of 5 other sail over the larboard point of the harbour which, from the great space between the masts, were supposed to be ships of the line. Eight admirals flags were flying; in addition to this force viewed 8 frigates and corvettes, and many sail, with yards and topmasts struck, farther off, and of uncertain size.

Returning from Camaret, took possession of a fishing boat manned by Spanish seamen belonging to the Prince of Asturias.

728.   *Saumarez to St Vincent*

23 October 1800

Intelligence from three Spanish prisoners taken by His Majesty's Ship Canada, belonging to the Principe de Asturias.

The Spanish squadron consisting of fifteen sail of the line, three frigates and two brigs are ready for sea; they have about forty days

[1]John Cooke.

provisions on board most species except wine or spirits, of which the crews are only served half allowance. They have only received two months wages since they have been in the port of Brest.

The French have also thirty sail of the line said to be ready for sea and provisioned in the same manner. The Vengeur of three decks and two other line of battle ships in a state of equipment are nearly ready. The whole are reported to be in great want of stores having received no supplies for several months, except by small craft and that very rarely.

The Spanish admiral Don Mazzareo is at Paris and no expectation of the fleet putting to sea.

729.   *Thomas Foley to St Vincent*

Elephant, at sea, 26 October 1800

I have enquired into the case of John Dean Swift, who says he was born in the year 1750 in West Chester county, fifteen miles from New York, was brought up to be a coasting pilot and was so employed in the last war. He is married, his wife lived at New York but he has not heard from her since he has been in our service. He left America in 1794, having piloted a ship out of the Capes of Virginia in such very bad weather as not to allow of his pilot boat taking him out of her. The ship belonged to Boston, was called the Nancy and arrived in the River Thames, where he was pressed, having no protection from the circumstances of his being carried off. He was sent to the Sandwich, Edgar, Goliath and Elephant. He has no document to prove his citizenship. He had made a voyage to England in September 1793 in the ship Hazard of Boston and was pressed in London but was able by the help of his Master, Mr. Ephraim Delano, so to prove his being an American that he was liberated from the Enterprise receiving vessel at the Tower.

[Endorsement]

He is to be discharged if Captain Foley has reason to believe what is stated to be fact.

730.   *St Vincent to Spencer*

Ville de Paris, in Torbay, 28 October 1800

Captain Browne will soon set the Robust to rights and Captain Domett will be well pleased with the Belleisle. I shall have much to say to your

Lordship upon the subject of the Royal George when we meet. If Captain Domett had not been overruled by those old women Admirals Bridport and Pole he would have set her to rights. His nerves are so shook he is not up to it now.

[*Endorsed as received on the 30th*]

731.   *St Vincent to Blane*

Ville de Paris, in Torbay, 28 October 1800

I have kept close in the after cabin, which is as warm as possible without fire, but I am confident another cruise would finish me. Happily Lord Spencer has communicated the real state of my health to the Board and I am indulged with the permission I asked to reside on shore in the vicinity of Torbay and I intend to remove to Tor Abbey (which commands the anchorage and is a well sheltered delightful situation in all respects) as soon as I can arrange matters for the next in command.

732.   *Stopford to St Vincent*

Excellent, off Abreverack [Aber-wrac'h], 28 October 1800

I have the honour to acquaint your Lordship that I sent the boats of His Majesty's ship under my command last night under the direction of Lieutenant Bain[1] to cut out three large brigs which I had observed in a creek to the eastward of Abreverack.

The service was very dexterously and completely executed and they are all brought out through a very intricate navigation.

One of the brigs mounts three carriage guns and her crew, being in some measure prepared for the attack, made some resistance, which was, however, soon overcome by boarding but (I am sorry to add) with the loss of one seaman (a quartermaster) who was mortally wounded.

One of the vessels is loaded with biscuits for Brest, another with wood for the same place and the third is in ballast.

---

[1]Henderson Bain (d. 1862). Lieutenant 1800; Captain 1813; Retired Rear-admiral 1846; Retired Vice-admiral 1855; Retired Admiral 1861.

733.   *St Vincent to Harvey*

Torbay, 28 October 1800

I herewith transmit you the copy of intelligence which I received last night from Mr. Secretary Nepean respecting which it is necessary to apprize you that the six sail of the line therein mentioned are part of a much larger force which has been held in constant readiness to slip out from Brest for some months past having on board a great quantity of ordnance, fused ammunition and every other apparatus of war destined as was believed for the relief of Malta and support of their army in Egypt. There is no forming any conjecture of what may be the enterprise at present in contemplation from any intelligence I am in possession of but as there can be no doubt but the whole force in Brest will come out to cover this squadron into the sea, everything will depend on our rapid movement upon the first blush of a north-east wind.

734.   *St Vincent to Harvey*

28 October 1800

The Right Honourable Lords Commissioners of the Admiralty having been pleased to grant me permission to reside on shore for the reestablishment of my health, you are hereby required and directed to take under your command the flag officers and captains of His Majesty's ships, named on the otherside hereof, they being respectively instructed to obey your orders, and the instant the wind shall come to the northward or eastward, so as to admit of the combined fleets sailing from the port of Brest, to make the best of your way with the ships abovementioned to the rendezvous off Ushant for the purpose of watching the said fleets and giving them battle in the event of their coming out, governing yourself in the execution of this service by the orders and instructions from the Lords Commissioners of the Admiralty mentioned in the accompanying schedule No 1 to 20, and by such orders as you may hereafter receive from their Lordships, or me, for the purpose: . . .

You are to forward to me at this anchorage from time to time, as opportunity shall offer, or as you may deem necessary, every information you shall obtain respecting the enemy's force, position or movements, together with particular occurrences of the ships under your immediate orders, and also of those detached, which may be communicated to you.

735.   *Keith to St Vincent*

29 October 1800

Most secret.

I am informed from undoubted authority that the combined fleets are to sail if possible for the express purpose of destroying the armament under the direction of Sir Ralph Abercromby and me, and for the invasion of Sicily. This was the object of General Berthiers mission to Madrid. Bread is said to be ordered for them at Carthagena, Toulon etc., it being recommended that on account of the sickness at Cadiz the fleet should not enter that port, my last accounts are that 400 die daily at Seville, 10 at Rota, 180 on the island of Leon, and 60 at St. Mary's

736.   *St Vincent to Admiralty*

Bellona, in Torbay, 30 October 1800

I desire you will acquaint the Lords Commissioners of the Admiralty that a boat with three Spaniards on board belonging to the Principe de Asturias, bearing the flag of Don Gravina, having been driven into the Bay of Brest, was picked up by the Canada, one of the advanced squadron, when I directed Sir James Saumarez to send them to Brest with a flag of truce and complimentary letter to the Spanish admiral and I herewith transmit for their Lordships' information copies of Sir James's letter and note on the occasion.

[*Enclosure*]

736a.   *Saumarez to Spanish Admiral*

Caesar, Bay of Brest, 25 October 1800

His Britannic Majesty's squadron under my command stationed in the Bay of Brest having detained three seamen belonging to one of His Catholic Majesty's ships named the Principe de Asturias, bearing as I understand the flag of your Excellency, I am happy in conforming with the orders of my Commander-in-Chief, the Earl of St. Vincent, to have it in my power to release the said three prisoners, together with the boat in which they were captured, for which purpose I send a flag of truce with a British officer to the French advanced post.

I profit of the opportunity afforded me of assuring your Excellency of the high respect with which I have the honour to be your Excellency's most obedient and very humble servant . . .

737. *Spencer to St Vincent*

Admiralty, 5 November 1800

I was rather surprised that the fleet did not bear up with the last S.W. gale. There is no use in keeping out too long while it blows so in that quarter, especially when they can put to sea in so short a time as you mention in your letter to the Board, which gives a most satisfactory proof that the discipline of the Mediterranean may very wholesomely be applied to the Channel fleet.

738.   *W. Wickham to Lord Grenville*

Crems, Munster, 13 November 1800

I have received certain information from Paris that an expedition is now preparing at Brest, and nearly ready to sail, for the Islands of France and Bourbon. It is to be comprised of several ships of war and frigates, and is to be commanded by Admiral Joyeuse, and a Mr Mogan is to sail with it, who is appointed Governor of those colonies, and Commissary General for the affairs of India.

Both are furnished with their commissions and I am given to understand that they are detained only on account of the want of money necessary for the carrying such an enterprise into effect at this moment, and the difficulty and danger of clearing the Bay of Biscay in the present station of the British fleets.

I have not been able to learn the extent of the force to be sent out, but I am inclined to think that it is meant to be considerable.

I have forwarded a copy of this despatch to the Marquis of Wellesley, through the channel of Lords Minto and Elgin.

739.   *Intelligence report from Captain D'Auvergne, Prince de Bouillon*

14 November 1800

The voyage of the Villant to India has been long preparing 'a la sourdins'. The military means that are prepared to accompany him do not amount to much; they may perhaps cover some political project of greater importance which the quantity of presents in the oriental taste he has embarked may be destined to forward. His voyage thither appears however decided and to be at the eve of proceeding. The usual active success of our cruisers will, I hope, yet defeat its intentions.

740.   *Admiralty to Sir Thomas Pasley*[1]

14 November 1800

I am commanded by my Lords Commissioners of the Admiralty to signify their direction to you to give orders to the respective captains and commanders of His Majesty's ships and vessels in Plymouth Sound and in Cawsand Bay to sleep constantly on board their respective ships.

741.   *Admiralty to Pasley*

14 November 1800

Having laid before my Lords Commissioners of the Admiralty your letter to me of the 12th instant desiring instructions in respect to the ordering the Edgar into Hamoaze, I have their Lordships' commands to refer you to my letter of the 10th instant upon this subject and to acquaint you that you are at liberty to order any ship directed to be refitted up into Hamoaze when ever it shall appear by the representations of the Commissioner that her defects cannot be made good in Cawsand Bay or the Sound, excepting when the occasion may be for the purpose only of shifting their lower masts, in which case they are not to be brought into Hamoaze without orders from their Lordships.

742.   *Intelligence report from D'Auvergne*

Jersey, 15 November 1800

13 October–13 November 1800

Brest October 13th. Yesterday morning the division for sea (Admiral La Touche's) got under sail and was proceeding for sea when the signal posts repeated the appearance of thirteen large English ships off Ushant and the division returned to its anchorage.

[1]Port Admiral, Plymouth.

Admiral La Touche had the preceding day reconnoitred the Iroise in a light tender, and having seen nothing was induced to make the movement he demonstrated yesterday. He has embarked sixty supernumerary *assistants* chosen amongst the most robust and best seamen of that class all armed with pistols and poniards and prepared to lead boarders; the first division consists of six French line of battle ships and the second is designed of seven; they have completed their sea provisions from the other ships, and the small portions that could be found in the different magazines.

743. *St Vincent to Isaac Coffin*[1]

Tor Abbey, 15 November 1800

Seven eighths of the captains who compose this fleet (subtracting from the number all who served <u>long</u> under me in the Mediterranean) are practising every subterfuge to get into harbour for the winter . . . I am at my wits' end to compose orders to meet every shift, evasion and neglect of duty.

744. *St Vincent to Hyde Parker*

Tor Abbey, 17 November 1800

Sir Henry Harvey proceeded off Brest this morning and you will find him very near Ushant.

The principle on which the squadron acts with the wind easterly is to wear the sternmost and leewardmost first, which we are pretty expert in the practice of, once during the night so as to be within a couple of leagues of Ushant at daylight in the morning. This is the more necessary when the flood makes early and if it flows strong you will find much shelter between Ushant and the Black Rocks during the day and when at a greater distance the communication is well kept up by the inner advanced squadron at anchor between the Black Rocks and the Parquette and the outer under sail between them and Ushant.

---

[1]Sir Isaac Coffin (d. 1839). Lieutenant 1779; Captain 1782; Rear-admiral 1804; Vice-admiral 1808; Admiral 1814. Dockyard commissioner, Sheerness, 1801–5.

745.   *Sick and Wounded Board to Admiralty*

Office for Sick and Wounded Seamen, 21 November 1800

Admiral Earl St Vincent having in his letter of the 10th instant acquainted us that General Bentham[1] had informed him that he is planning magazines for provisions intended to be constructed at Brixham, and his Lordship having suggested to us the propriety of furnishing the General with our ideas upon the subject of a naval hospital which it is his Lordships opinion ought to come into the general plan, and that space for two or three hundred patients would be sufficient as Portsmouth and Plymouth hospitals may be at all times resorted to, we enclose a paper containing some observations and suggestions on the subject which have been communicated to us by Doctor Johnston, one of the members of this Board, and we request you will be pleased to lay the same before the Right Honourable the Lords Commissioners of the Admiralty for their Lordships consideration.

[*Endorsement*]

22 November. Send copy to General Bentham.

[*Enclosure*]

745a.   *James Johnston to Sick and Wounded Board*

Observations relative to the naval hospital at Paignton with suggestions on the hospital proposed to be built at Brixham.

The hospital at Paignton is situated on a rocky amd dry foundation within thirty yards of high water mark, there is no stagnating water, high trees or building in its vicinity, the nearest house is three quarters of a mile distant, and at all times there is free ventilation, and it is considered by the neighbourhood as possessing a salubrious air.

In the premises there is a well with a pump, and nearly adjoining a large stream of fine running water. There is a gravel walk seven feet in breadth from the entrance along the front of the dwelling house hospital, continued along the sea wall to the boundary wall and about half an acre of grass plat in the centre, for an airing ground.

---

[1] Sir Samuel Bentham (1757–1831). Brother of Jeremy Bentham. Apprenticed as a shipwright in the Royal dockyards; travelled in Russia and Siberia 1780–82; entered Russian service and promoted to Brigadier-general. Returned to England in 1791 and became Inspector General of Naval Works in 1796.

The new building when completed, with the dwelling house, will contain about 125 cradles, which it is presumed will be sufficient to contain the number of sick that may be proper objects for an hospital, as the Channel fleet are seldom in Torbay, but when driven in by stress of bad weather from southerly and westerly gales, and the commander in chief has most judiciously directed that no sick shall be sent on shore that can be cured on board.

Should unfortunately any contagious disorder prevail in particular ships, the sick may be sent to Haslar or Plymouth, according to the circumstances of the wind, as suggested by Earl St Vincent. There is another regulation which, if adopted, would tend to prevent the unnecessary accumulation of patients. It frequently happens that men who are deemed unfit for further service are sent from His Majesty's ships to hospitals for the purpose of being invalided. These men occupy the room which ought to be allotted to such as are really sick, it would therefore be a great relief to this hospital were such invalids sent to Haslar or Plymouth.

The only inconveniences that appear to me to attend this hospital are that when the wind is at south east, the sea is so great on the beach no boats can land, but in that case the fleet generally puts to sea. When the wind is in any other quarter it is smooth water on the beach.

At low water and until it is half flood boats are prevented from coming to the beach by a flat which runs out about thirty yards; this inconvenience is remedied by a light cart drawn by men or a horse which will receive the sick from the boats whilst they are afloat. From half flood to high water boats can conveniently land.

The present expence to Government is thirty five pounds per annum for the dwelling house lately inhabited by Bishop the proprietor and now filled with 13 cradles. The adjoining tenement at five pounds per annum contains on the ground floor a kitchen sufficient for the whole hospital, a room for the use of the surgeon, and for holding surveys, two rooms above for the dispensary, and lodgings for medical assistants.

On the new building £400 is to be expended by the proprietor for which he is to receive 5 per cent per annum so long as government may think proper to retain it.

There is a wall for defense to be built with some additions to the garret story of the large building and a small erection at the entrance gate, for which the proprietor is to receive 10 per cent per annum. In both cases Government may quit the premises on giving six months notice, but the proprietor has not that advantage and after all the buildings are finished and made complete, the proprietor will sell the whole for £1600.

With respect to the suggestion of erecting an hospital at Brixham for two or three hundred patients, the observations I shall submit on the point must be taken from general report, as when on two visitations to Paignton I never heard it was in contemplation to erect an hospital at Brixham, therefore did not visit it. From what I learn it would be great objection to that situation that the stench from the fish is at all time offensive, but in very hot weather almost insupportable. I am also informed that the navy slaughter house is a great nuisance and that its smell extends to a considerable distance. An hospital situated within the sphere of these offensive and deleterious effluvias must be greatly annoyed by them.

The vicinity of an hospital to the town of Brixham and the Victualling Office store houses where there must be when the fleet is in the bay a great concourse of seamen, bumboat women, strumpets and dealers in spiritous liquors must render it difficult to preserve regularity and discipline.

Finally, I must beg leave to observe that to erect an hospital capable of containing two or three hundred patients with a surrounding wall of defence with houses for the officers, medical assistants and clerks, storehouses for every description of stores, ovens, bathing and fumigating rooms, and many other appendages necessary for a permanent establishment would require long time in the erection and be attended with a most serious expense.

746. *Saumarez to Harvey*

Caesar, off the Black Rocks, 21 November 1800

I beg to acquaint you that yesterday I stood in toward the Goulet with this ship, the Triumph and Amethyst. The weather being very clear had a good view of the enemy's fleet who all appeared with their yards and topmasts struck and except very few ships had their sails unbent.

Having sent the Nimrod cutter with a boat from the Caesar to one of the small islands with the view of obtaining intelligence, they picked up a small boat on her way to Ushant with two French pilots on board, one belonging to the Jean Jacques, the other to the Spanish ship Neptuna. They had quitted Brest the same morning and gave me the following information.

Seven sail of the line and three frigates are ready to put to sea on a secret expedition, having eight months stores and provisions on board, commanded by the French admiral Manouard, whose flag is on board the L'Indivisible. They are reported as perfectly ready and only waiting for a favourable opportunity to put to sea. They have from five to seven hundred troops on board each of the line of battle ships and all been paid their wages previous to their sailing. A French vice admiral came to Brest three weeks since who is senior to La Touche Treville and has his flag on board the Ocean. It was by many supposed that Admiral La Touche Treville was to have commanded on the above expedition. They describe most of the line of battle ships, as well French as Spanish, to be laid up for the winter.

747. *St Vincent to Sick and Wounded Board*

Ville de Paris, in Torbay, 25 November 1800

I have reason to believe that forty bags of carrots, far the best root for taking to sea, may be purchased in the neighbourhood for the supply of His Majesty's squadron under my command if you will send the necessary directions to your correspondent here for that purpose or I will order them to be purchased if you prefer that mode of procuring them.

748. *Intelligence report from D'Auvergne*

25 November 1800

Intelligence down to 21st November 1800; received 22nd December.

Brest, 5th November 1800
The arrival of Admiral Ganteaume from Paris has given fresh activity to the first division prepared for sea, always consisting of the six line of battle ships and three frigates detailed in a preceding report, their sea provisions continue to be completed to six months.

The Legion des Tranes, consisting of between two and three thousand men, have been embarked under the orders of General Saliuguet, who returned from Paris with Ganteaume. This last ones most special mission here appears to be to give effect to the new organisation of the lower classes of the officers of the marine. A number, consisting of from three to four hundred mulatoes and blacks, have likewise arrived with several inhabitants of St Domingo, destined to accompany the expedition. It appears as if this opportunity was to be embraced to free the 'Pavi' of Paris of the men of colour, that the distress of the colonies have for some time past brought there. They are provisionally disposed of at the temporary quarters in the re-trenched camp at Recouvrance.

The ship the Jean Bart, prepared to bear Villaret[1] to the Isle of France, is in the road ready for sea, and is to sail with the expedition to an offing; the expedition [of] which there are now no doubts, is des-tined for the Antilles, is always composed of the following ships, with six months provisions kept complete, all except <u>wine or spirits</u> of which there is not fifteen days, the vigilance of the English cruizers, letting none pass even to the ports at a reasonable distance for land carriage, by which some however is expected,

L'Indivisible
L'Constitution
L'Dix Août
L'Marengo
L'Zélé
L'Cisalpin

And three 40 gun frigates, the Jean Bart and one frigate for Villaret expedition.

15th. The division is complete for sea, all but the <u>want</u> of <u>wine</u> or <u>spirits</u>, the troops are strictly kept on board, 500 in each ship of the Legion and Artillery, the Legion was completed at Rennes with the most exceptionable subjects among the troops marched towards the frontiers.

16th. The ship <u>Cisalpin</u> and <u>Wattigny</u>, having in the late gales driven on board each other as the <u>Wattigny</u> returned from Rescauvel, have been obliged to come into the harbour to repair the damages they sustained. This last ship and another likewise of the line of battle are intended (if sea provisions sufficient can be got for them) to join the division for the secret expedition in the place of the two frigates that have likewise been damaged by boarding each other in the storm.

The Terrible (French) and Neptune Spanish, line of battle ships, boarded each other also in the storm.

24th. The above two ships, besides the Indomptable one of the frig-ates, and another Spanish ship that suffered in the gales of the 19th have been obliged to come into the harbour to repair their damages. The ship La Revolution, although not damaged, is got into harbour.

25th. The division for the secret expedition and Villarat's ships and frigates continue ready for the sea, all but the <u>want</u> of <u>wine</u> or <u>spirits</u>

---

[1]Louis-Thomas, Comte Villaret de Joyeuse (1748). Officier auxiliaire 1778–83; Lieu-tenant 1784; Captain 1792; Rear-admiral 1793; Vice-admiral 1794. Governor of Martinique during the Napoleonic War for the loss of which in 1809 he was demoted by court martial.

that are expected by land from L'Orient. The Blacks and people of colour at Recouvrance are to embark in the two ships destined to replace the frigates that have been damaged in the storm, they do not appear to embark with a good grace, as they are closely guarded [in] the retrenched camps.

[*Endorsement*]

Information from Prince Bouillon down to November 25th 1800. Received December 22.

749.   *Spencer to St Vincent*

Admiralty, 28 November 1800

The hostile measure taken by the Emperor of Russia (which will, I fear, deprive us of a considerable quantity of hemp) will make it necessary to economize our stores as much as possible and a circular order to that effect has accordingly been issued. Your Lordship will also receive an instruction founded on our late intelligence from Brest which I hope will enable us to get our ships in as perfect a state as possible in point of repairs against the opening of the weather after the winter, when it is not improbable that we may have a more extended naval war on our hands than we have ever yet had. On this subject I propose by and by to write more fully.

750.   *St Vincent to Keith*

Tor Abbey, 29 November 1800

Sir James Saumarez with a well chosen squadron anchors in Iroise with every wind that favours ships coming out of the port. He will be relieved by Sir Edward Pellew in eight or ten days, for, entre nous, I never will employ an admiral on any critical service when in my judgment there are captains more capable of performing it and by this means (which subjects me to some hatred and malice) I hope to keep you upon velvet.[1]

---

[1] On 1 November St Vincent had told Warren that the service could not be carried on as it ought to be without Pellew's promotion.

751.   *St Vincent to Hamond*[1]

Tor Abbey, 29 November 1800

. . . the warrant officers are nefarious rascals and many of the lieutenants, with some captains, deal largely in embezzlement . . .

752.   *Admiralty to St Vincent*

29 November 1800

Whereas by the intelligence transmitted by your Lordship to our Secretary in your letter of the 25th instant there appears reason to believe that the enemy has an intention of laying up the most considerable part of their fleet at Brest for the winter and to take the advantage of the first favourable opportunity that may offer of sending a squadron from thence on a secret expedition, the destination of which cannot be ascertained; and whereas we have judged it expedient in consequence that until you receive further orders your Lordship should keep only twenty sail of the line off Brest for the purpose of watching the motions of the enemy whenever the weather will admit of your so doing; that six sail of the line should be kept in Cawsand Bay and the like number in Torbay; and that you should send to Spithead such weak ships as require repairs; your Lordship is hereby required and directed to make such disposition of the force under your command accordingly, taking all possible care that the ships in port be kept in readiness to put to sea and join the fleet to the westward in case the appearance of preparation in the enemy's fleet should render their so doing necessary.

753.   *St Vincent to Keith*

Tor Abbey, 30 November 1800

I am exceedingly obliged by your favour of the 29th ultimo acquainting me that you had received information from undoubted authority that the combined fleets are to sail, if possible, from Brest for the express purpose of destroying the armament under your Lordship's and Sir Ralph Abercromby's direction and your Lordship may rest assured that my utmost exertion shall not be wanting to defeat the enemy's view.

[1]Comptroller of the Navy.

754.   *St Vincent to Admiralty*

Ville de Paris, in Torbay, 1 December 1800

At five o'clock this morning I received by a messenger two orders from the Lords Commissioners of the Admiralty dated the 29th ultimo, ¾ past 10 p.m., directing me to keep only twenty sail of the line off Brest for the purpose of watching the enemy's motions; and in obedience thereto I have ordered the squadron to be disposed of as on the other side hereof. When the Impetueux is ready she will relieve the Caesar, which ship will be sent to Spithead and the Excellent will be relieved off Abreverack and sent to Cawsand Bay by the Boadicea and I mean to attach the Sylph sloop to that station in addition to the Lady Duncan lugger.

I have not considered the Captain and Canada as coming within the scope of their Lordships' order and they are left off L'Orient and the Loire for the purpose of blocking the former and cutting off the enemy's supplies from the latter.

I beg leave to submit to their Lordships the expediency of the captains and officers of the ships sent to Spithead sleeping on board to prevent desertion and other more serious evils.

1.   Left cruising off Brest under the orders of Admiral Sir Hyde Parker. Royal George, Royal Sovereign, Windsor Castle, Prince George, Prince of Wales, Princess Royal, Neptune, Atlas, Cumberland, Juste, Venerable, Bellona.
2.   In the bay of Brest. Caesar, Triumph, Terrible, Achille, Defiance – to be relieved by the Pompee.
3.   Off the Black Rocks. Magnificent, Ganges, Warrior.
4.   Ordered to Spithead. St. George, Mars, Ramillies, Defence, Saturn.
5.   Ordered to Cawsand Bay. Barfleur, Russell, Montague, London, Courageux.
6.   Ordered to Torbay. Temeraire, Formidable, Prince, Spencer.

755.   *St Vincent to Agent and Steward, Royal Hospital, Plymouth*

Ville de Paris, in Torbay, 1 December 1800

The squadron stationed at the Black Rocks requires every consideration and I recommend your sending once a month as opportunities present, close cabbage, turnips and leeks thither. As Sir Edward Pellew will soon relieve Sir James Saumarez in this critical command I wish you to confer with him upon the supply of vegetables beforehand.

756.   *St Vincent to Hyde Parker*

Ville de Paris, in Torbay, 1 December 1800

Whereas it appears to the Commissioners of the Admiralty from intelligence received by them that there is reason to believe that the enemy has an intention of laying up the most considerable part of their fleet at Brest for the winter, and to take the advantage of the first favourable opportunity that may offer of sending a squadron from thence on a secret expedition, the destination of which cannot be ascertained; and whereas their Lordships have judged it expedient in consequence that until further order twenty sail of the line only should be kept off Brest, for the purpose of watching the motions of the enemy whenever the weather will admit of so doing, and that six sail of the line should be kept in Cawsand Bay, and the like number at this anchorage [Torbay] in readiness to put to sea and join the squadron to the westward, in case the appearance of preparation in the enemy's fleet should render their so doing necessary, you are hereby required and directed to deliver to Rear Admirals Whitshed and Collingwood, and to Captain Edwards [the] accompanying orders, and to hasten them (and the ships put under their command respectively) in proceeding accordingly.

In proceeding in the execution of your former orders, you are to direct the captains of all the frigates which shall discover any squadron of the enemy's ships putting to sea to send you information thereof by some cutter or lugger, and to follow it themselves, and to quit it in succession for the purpose of proceeding to your rendezvous off Brest, or not finding you there, to the nearest port in England with information of the course it may steer; leaving, however, one fast sailing ship to accompany the enemy until the commander of such ship shall be able to ascertain the place of their destination, when he is to use his best endeavours to get ahead of the enemy's squadron, and carry infomation of its approach to the Commander-in-Chief of His Majesty's ships in that quarter.

On receiving information of the enemy having sailed, you are to detach a squadron equal in number and force to that of the enemy which may have escaped, with directions to the commander of the squadron which you may so detach to follow it wheresoever it may go. But if he should not be able to obtain such information as may enable him to follow it, he is to proceed immediately off Ferrol, and to act agreeably to any information he may receive from the captains of the frigates employed off that place. But if the said commander should not receive any information which can determine the place to which the enemy may be destined, he is, in that event, to proceed as expeditiously as possible off Cadiz, and in case the enemy's ships should be gone up the Straits he is to follow in pursuit of them, and, upon coming up with them, to use his best endeavours to take or destroy them.

In case, however, the said commander should not obtain, on his arrival in the Straits, any certain information of the enemy's course, he is to repair off Cartagena, Barcelona and Toulon, and upon finding the enemy ships at either of those places, he is to block up the port at which they may be; but not finding the enemy's ships at either of those places, he is to repair off the Isle of Elba, and not hearing of them there, to go on to Palermo, and not obtaining information of them there, to repair off Malta, and thence proceed in quest of Vice Admiral Lord Keith according to the best intelligence he may be able to obtain of his Lordship and, upon joining him, to put himself under his command, and follow his orders for his further proceedings . . .

In case the enemy's ships should not have proceeded up the Straits, the commanding officer of the squadron . . . is, upon being well informed of that circumstance, to proceed off the island of Madeira, and act as the information he may be able to obtain at that place shall require . . . [1]

757.   St Vincent to Hyde Parker

1 December 1800

In addition to my order to you of this day's date, you are hereby required and directed, in case you should obtain information of a squadron having sailed from Brest, . . . to detach a squadron of equal force in pursuit of it, with directions to . . . act as directed by my order abovementioned except that in the event of their not having gone through the Straits of Gibraltar, instead of proceeding as therein directed to Madeira he is to return with all possible expedition to join the squadron off Brest, or not finding it there, to proceed to this anchorage. And on receiving such information, you are also to detach a squadron, fewer in number by three sail of the line than the squadron of the enemy which had escaped; or, if their number cannot be ascertained, to send four sail of the line with some fast sailing cutter or lugger with directions to the commanding officer, to proceed with all possible expedition to Jamaica where he is to put himself under the orders of Vice Admiral Lord Hugh Seymour; taking care at proper

[1]The remainder 'Cancelled by his subsequent order'.

time to send the cutter or lugger ahead to give the Vice Admiral information of his approach.

If information should be received by you of the enemy's squadron having been seen in a situation which may leave no doubt of it being bound to the West Indies, orders are immediately to be sent to recall the squadron detached towards the Mediterranean; but if information should be received of the enemy having gone into the Mediterranean, orders are to be sent to recall the ships sent to Jamaica.

758.   St Vincent to Hyde Parker

Ville de Paris, in Torbay, 2 December 1800

I have to acknowledge the receipt of your letter of yesterday informing me that the enemy's ships continue in the same state as mentioned in your last report and show no indication of putting to sea.

P.S. Does not the extinguishing the lights on Ushant and Point St. Mathieu indicate an intention of the squadron putting to sea which our intelligence leads us to believe is in a state of preparation for that purpose.

759.   St Vincent to Spencer

Tor Abbey, 3 December 1800

The lights on Ushant and Point St. Mathieu are discontinued, which renders cruising in the Bay of Brest extremely hazardous and indicates that the enemy intends to push the squadron (which has been so long watching an opportunity to elude our vigilance) out the first favourable moment.

[*Endorsed as received on the 5th*]

760.   St Vincent to Hyde Parker

6 December 1800

The Lords Commissioners of the Admiralty having been pleased to comply with your request to be indulged with leave of absence, you are hereby required and directed, on availing yourself thereof, to deliver to Vice Admiral Sir Henry Harvey an authenticated copy of the order under which you have cruized off Ushant together with the annexed orders and instructions as mentioned in the schedule No 1 to 73, which you received from him, and all other orders and papers which you may have been furnished with since that period, relative to the most important service of watching the combined fleets in the port of Brest.

761.   *St Vincent to O'Hara*

Tor Abbey, 8 December 1800

I have worked miracles in this fleet without the smallest aid from the powers above, whence I receive nothing but little mean jealousy. I mean in the Board, for Lord Spencer is everything I would wish him to be.

762.   *Intelligence from D'Auvergne*

11 December 1800

Continuation of the substance of reports from Brest to the 11th December inclusive.

Nothing particular has occurred since the last report to the 24th Ultimo.

Brest
December 3d 1800. The crews of the ships of the division for sea have been paid <u>three months pay</u> and strict orders given to keep them on board their respective ships.
A young brother[1] of the Consul Bonaparte arrived, and was made 'Aspirant provision' and embarked on board the Indivisible, the commanding ship of the division.
   The new organisation of the corps of officers has produced the reform or dismission of 800 individuals, which has weighed more particularly on the subaltern classes, '<u>Capitaines de Frigates, Lieutenants</u> et Enseignes'; there are but eight persons put off the list of the chiefs of divisions, or captain 'de vaissau'.
   A further detachment of 800 men of the marine troops are ordered to hold themselves in readiness to march, which will reduce to a very small party those left.

December 11th. The expedition for sea is on the <u>Qui vive</u> for an opportunity to get out, ever since the crews have been paid three months; young Jerome Bonaparte proceeds in it in the Indivisible where the

---

[1]Jerome Bonaparte.

'Conseiller d'Etat' Lescallier has likewise embarked with the quality of 'Vice Consul'; his functions are not publicly defined but is said to be provided with very great powers; the scarcity of provisions has prevented the line of battle ships replacing the frigates as intimated in a former report; the latter's slight damages have been repaired and the collection of <u>swarthy</u> individuals collected at Recouvrance have been embarked in them, the troops only being distributed on the line of battle ships, which occasions conjectures with respect to the possibility of their having distinct destinations; the greatest art is put in the Bureaux to deceive observation and disguise the real object in view.

Orders have just been given for the march tomorrow morning of 300 men of the marine troops across the country for the Army of Italy, two hundred more are likewise under marching orders for Nantes.

Gratulating salutes took place in the road yesterday evening, on the recent successes of the Army of Bavaria.

Twenty eight sail of the English fleet are just now signalled to be in the offing of L'iroise.

[*Endorsements*]

Continuation of the substance of reports from Brest to the 11th December 1800 inclusive.

Received from Earl of St Vincent 10th January 1801.

763.   *St Vincent to Pasley*

Ville de Paris, in Torbay, 15 December 1800

... respecting the escape of a French convoy through the Passage du Four, to which I beg leave to observe that the vessels employed on the Isle of Bas station which put into the ports of England for shelter during gales of wind from the westward do not in my opinion get under weigh soon enough after the breaking of the gale to rejoin their station in time to prevent the enemy's convoys from passing along shore, as they always push to sea the instant the gale breaks.

764.   *St Vincent to Pellew*

Ville de Paris, in Torbay, 17 December 1800

There being every reason to suppose that the squadron which has been so long in preparation at Brest will endeavour to put to sea the very first favourable opportunity that may offer, under the command of Joyeuse, I have judged it expedient to reinforce your detachment with H.M. ship Terrible and which, including the ships with Captain Bowater, will make your detachment nine sail of the line and either the Nymphe or Uranie shall be immediately added to it.

765.   *St Vincent to Harvey*

Ville de Paris, in Torbay, 17 December 1800

The consumption of sails in the short space of time the squadron has been out and that under the circumstances of weather uncommonly favourable for the season is quite alarming. I therefore request you will issue a general order to enjoin the utmost care in reefing and setting sails and that the topsails are clewed up whenever there is occasion to take the third or fourth reef in.

I shall send you the Temeraire, Formidable and Prince in a few days if the wind continues to the eastward to relieve the Prince George, Neptune and another three decker that you may judge fittest to be sent in.

... When the wind shifts to the westward and you judge proper to return with the squadron to this anchorage I advise your leaving three frigates with Sir Edward Pellew.

... It is evident that the enemy has in contemplation to put the squadron under the command of Joyeuse to sea the first favourable opportunity, which makes it extremely necessary to keep the squadron of observation well supplied with stores.

766.   *St Vincent to Fanshawe*[1]

Ville de Paris, in Torbay, 18 December 1800

The Lords Commissioners of the Admiralty having directed me to order that the flags and standards as directed in His Majesty's Order in Council for settling the ensigns, armorials, flags and banners on the Union of the Two Kingdoms of Great Britain and Ireland to be worn and spread on board His Majesty's ships and vessels under my command on the 1st January next, I have to request that you will be pleased to cause the necessary flags and standards to be provided to this anchorage accordingly.

[1]Commissioner, Plymouth dockyard.

767. *Harvey to St Vincent*

Royal Sovereign, off Ushant, 20 December 1800

I have the honour to enclose the reports transmitted to me yesterday by Sir Edward Pellew on the state and situation of the enemy's fleet at Brest as observed by the Beaulieu and Fisgard.

Many of the enemy's ships appear in a state of forwardness for sea, whatever may be their real intentions. I shall endeavour at all times to keep His Majesty's ships under my orders in the best situation that the wind and weather will permit to fall in with them in case they should put to sea.

768. *Spencer to St Vincent*

Admiralty, 27 December 1800

Captain Brown shall have a good frigate as soon as I can fix on a proper arrangement for the Robust. He asked me for the Doris but I was under an engagement to Windham to move his nephew into an 18 pounder frigate and I wished to take the opportunity of giving the Thames to a young relation of mine, Captain John Halliday,[1] whom I venture to recommend strongly to your Lordship's protection and countenance which, unless too long an interval of London life and manners should unfortunately have spoilt him, I have every reason from his former conduct to hope he may deserve.

769. *St Vincent to Admiralty*

Ville de Paris, in Torbay, 28 December 1800

I have to acknowledge the receipt of your letter of the 25th instant enclosing the copy of a letter from Captain D'Auvergne, Prince of Bouillon, accompanying intelligence of the enemy's motions at Brest.

The wind having come to S.E. this morning, Sir Henry Harvey made the signal to weigh and immediately proceeded to sea with the ships under his orders. The empty victuallers have also sailed for Plymouth and the full ones that remained for Dartmouth to be in readiness to come hither the instant they may be required.

---

[1]John Richard Halliday, later Tollemache (d. 1837). Lieutenant 1795; Captain 1796; Rear-admiral 1819; Vice-admiral 1830.

770.   *St Vincent to Admiralty*

Ville de Paris, in Torbay, 28 December 1800

I desire you will submit the enclosed letter[1] from Captain Hotham[2] of His Majesty's ship Immortalité to the Lords Commissioners of the Admiralty and inform their Lordships that I attribute the loss of men by desertion in a great measure to the high premium given by crimps at Plymouth for manning the outward bound trade assembled at Falmouth and, in some degree, to granting leave of absence to the captains, for it is a well known fact throughout the fleet that when the captain is not on the spot the lieutenants are seldom or ever at their duty and the petty officers are for the most part children.

771.   *Lieutenant Thomas Shirley[3] to St Vincent*

His Majesty's hired cutter Admiral Mitchell, 30 December 1800

I have the honour to state to your Lordship my having received Sir Edward Pellew's permission on Monday last to put into this port in order to complete with provisions and to replace the standing rigging which is nearly gone.

I humbly beg leave to submit to your Lordship's consideration the shameful manner in which the owners have repeatedly fitted His Majesty's hired cutter – scarcely five weeks had elapsed before the Master reported to me a deficiency of provisions and the rigging, which has not been over the masthead twelve months should want replacing. I assure your Lordship that every possible exertion in my power is making to rejoin Sir Edward Pellew.

772.   *Harvey to St Vincent*

Royal Sovereign, Torbay, 2 January 1801

Having used every endeavour possible to gain the appointed rendezvous off Ushant since I sailed from Torbay the morning of the 30th ultimo, I found it impracticable from the prevailing strong S.W. and

---

[1]Captain Hotham's letter attributed the time his ship had taken getting ready for sea to a want of seamen.
[2]Sir Henry Hotham (d. 1833). Lieutenant 1794; Captain 1795; Rear-admiral 1814; Vice-admiral 1825.
[3]Thomas Shirley (fl. 1790–1800). Lieutenant 1790.

westerly winds; and being this morning at ½ past 10 2 leagues S.W. from the Eddystone with a strong W.S.W. wind, I thought proper to bear up with His Majesty's ships under my orders for this anchorage. The Windsor Castle, Montagu and Megara did not get out of the bay the morning I sailed but the latter has since joined. The Unicorn parted company the night of the 30th in thick weather.

I beg leave to observe to your Lordship that the winds and weather have been for some days past in the most unsettled state I ever met with; the easterly winds that sprung up were of short duration and soon succeeded by strong gales from the westward.

773.   St Vincent to Admiralty

Ville de Paris, in Torbay, 5 January 1801

I desire you will acquaint the Lords Commissioners of the Admiralty that during the whole of last night it blew a heavy gale of wind at S.W. by W. and as, from its extreme violence, it is probable some of the ships of the advanced squadron may have suffered in their masts and yards (of the Pompee I have great apprehensions in particular) I have thought proper to order Sir Henry Harvey to take with him the Neptune, Atlas and Courageux (in addition to the ships under his orders) in the event of the wind coming to the eastward before intelligence is received from Sir Edward Pellew.

It having been communicated to me that letters have been received from Rear Admiral Sir Erasmus Gower intimating that the Princess Royal is to be ordered to Portsmouth I desire you will represent to their Lordships that she can very ill be spared from the fleet at this juncture and that I hope the Rear Admiral will be allowed to take his passage hither in the Mars or some other ship that may be coming from Spithead to rejoin the squadron.

Several of the captains at this anchorage, lately promoted to the flag, have communicated to me your letter giving them notice thereof but as I have not received any official communication whatever on this subject, should the wind come to the eastward before their successors join, I shall feel myself under considerable embarrassment how to act, but am rather inclined to think I ought in that case to put acting commanders in their ships.

774. *St Vincent to Admiralty*

Ville de Paris, in Torbay, 5 January 1801

I enclose Sir Thomas Troubridge's[1] report of the muster and state of the Ville de Paris. The observation he makes upon the slackness of the people is very just. I remarked it on my return to her off Brest and I impute the change from what she was when I removed from her in Mahon Harbour to evil communication with the ships' companies of this undisciplined fleet which Captain Bathurst,[2] though a zealous man, could not prevent and to other causes springing from an opinion that my health was in so bad a state I never should appear more. I have, however, the satisfaction to acquaint you for the information of the Lords Commissioners of the Admiralty that no other symptom of insubordination has appeared and the ship's company will, I have no doubt, recover their wonted alacrity.

775. *Harvey to St Vincent*

Royal Sovereign, off Ushant, 10 January 1801

Having last night received the enclosed reports from Sir Edward Pellew of the movements and appearance of the enemy's fleet I lose no time in sending them for your Lordship's information, as also Sir Edward Pellew's letter and have ordered Captain Ricketts to proceed immediately to Torbay with this despatch.

The ships that are anchored in Camaret Bay will no doubt attempt to put to sea the first favourable opportunity and as the fleet in Brest Road appears to be in readiness for sailing it may possibly be their intention to cover the sailing of the Camaret squadron. I shall endeavour to keep the best possible situation for meeting them should they put to sea and I hope by the activity and vigilance of the advanced squadron they will not escape unobserved.

---

[1]Sir Thomas Troubridge (d. 1807). Lieutenant 1781; Captain 1783; Rear-admiral 1804. St Vincent had selected Troubridge to be his Captain of the Fleet and wished to see him included in the promotion of January 1801 (see document 773). In the event he became an Admiralty commissioner on St Vincent's Board 1801–4. He was lost at sea in 1807 while on his way to command in the East Indies.

[2]Walter Bathurst (fl. 1790–1827). Lieutenant 1790; Captain 1799.

776.   *Pellew to Harvey*

Impetueux, off the Black Rocks, 12 January 1801

I had the honour to receive your orders by the Montagu last night and agreeable thereto return her to make you easy – having this moment sight of the same force in Camaret Bay now getting under sail which was there before. I will keep the Courageux until evening to send you a report of their proceedings as possibly they may go into port, the weather not looking pleasant.

I am joined by Triumph and Venerable, which completes my number to nine as directed. We had much difficulty yesterday in getting into the bay and worked hard all night. Be assured, sir, of my utmost vigilance and attention and that you shall hear every minute change of appearances and I trust we shall be able to frustrate the designs of our enemies whenever they dare move out of port.

I shall have the honour to send you by the Courageux a report of the state and condition of His Majesty's ships under my orders.

777.   *Harvey to St Vincent*

Royal Sovereign, off Ushant, 13 January 1801

Since my letter to your Lordship of the 10th instant by the Megara I have received the enclosed letter from Sir Edward Pellew by which your Lordship will perceive that there is much reason to believe the French ships that were in Camaret Bay are returned into Brest Road, more especially as the wind is now at S.S.W. with an appearance of its coming more westerly.

778.   *Harvey to St Vincent*

Royal Sovereign, off Ushant, 14 January 1801

The Courageux has just joined me from the advanced squadron and I have retained her in lieu of the Prince George, which makes the whole number of ships of the line under my orders twenty-one, including the advanced squadron . . . I have received a letter by the Courageux from Sir Edward Pellew acquainting me that the enemy's squadron remained yesterday noon in Camaret Bay and the wind then appeared to be coming round to the S.W.

779.   *Pellew to Harvey*

Impetueux, off the Black Rocks, 15 January 1801

I send the Telemachus to you with the last report, by which you will see the enemy's squadron have returned into port. The atmosphere was very clear and Captain Fayerman must have had a very correct view and by the number of flags flying and the forward state of the ships would lead one to conjecture the whole may be coming out should favourable opportunity present itself.

780.   *St Vincent to Harvey*

Ville de Paris, in Torbay, 17 January 1801

His Majesty's fireship Megara arrived here last night and by her I received your letter of the 16th instant enclosing Sir Edward Pellew's reports of the state of the combined fleet in Brest. The Megara is dispatched to Captain Keats off Abreverack and the inner advanced squadron with a copy of the enclosed general order for detaining all Russians, Danes and Swedes, after which Captain Ricketts is ordered to join, but in the event of the enemy's ships returning to Camaret I desire he may be sent back to Sir Edward Pellew with directions to attempt the destruction of the enemy if it shall appear to be practicable.

781.   *St Vincent to George Rose*[1]

Tor Abbey, 19 January 1801

I am all packed up for a start to Town, where I hope I shall not be kept long, for I do assure you my presence is absolutely necessary to prevent malingering and a return to the abominable habits I found this fleet in.

---

[1]George Rose (1744–1818). Served in the navy until 1762; Exchequer clerk, then secretary to Board of Taxes, 1777. Secretary to the Treasury 1782–83, 1784–1801. Subsequently a vice-president of the Board of Trade, Paymaster-general and Treasurer of the Navy.

782. *St Vincent to Harvey*

Ville de Paris, in Torbay, 20 January 1801

I have to acknowledge the receipt of your letter of this date informing me of your having thought proper to bear up for this anchorage with the squadron under your orders, the wind being to the westward with every appearance of a continued gale, in order to prevent any of the ships being crippled when the enemy's fleet could not put to sea.

783. *St Vincent to respective captains*

Ville de Paris, in Torbay, 21 January 1801

A guard boat properly armed under the direction of a lieutenant from each of the ships at this anchorage is to assemble at the outer ship in the bay every evening at sunset and remain there until daybreak in readiness to counteract any design the enemy may have on the ships at their anchorage.

But to prevent the assembling of the guard boats alongside of one ship being made a point of general communication, an order will be issued tomorrow morning directing them to remain alongside their respective ships and to be held in constant readiness to proceed to the outer ship as a rendezvous the instant a signal shall be made for that purpose.

784. *St Vincent to Admiralty*

Ville de Paris, in Torbay, 22 January 1801

From the wicked and malignant stories which are daily in circulation at Brixham and from thence conveyed on board the ships, and letters written from people at Portsmouth to seamen in this squadron, there must be a number of dangerous incendiaries at all the ports. Captain Otway[1] told Sir Thomas Troubridge yesterday that some of the Royal George's people had received letters from the Belleisle saying they had refused to weigh the anchor until Lieutenant Rosenhagen and a mate were discharged. Directions were given to find out the names of the persons who wrote these letters without creating the least suspicion of the object in view.

---

[1]Sir Robert Waller Otway (d. 1846), Lieutenant 1793; Captain 1795; Rear-admiral 1814; Vice-admiral 1830; Admiral 1841.

785. *St Vincent to Admiralty*

Ville de Paris, in Torbay, 23 January 1801

I desire you will acquaint the Lords Commissioners of the Admiralty that, the wind being to the northward, the squadron under the orders of Vice Admiral Sir Henry Harvey lay unmoored the whole of yesterday, during which the wind backed to the westward and blew strong but it having come to north at daylight this morning Sir Henry got under weigh and all the ships were round the Berry Head before eight o'clock.

786. *St Vincent to Saumarez*

Tor Abbey, 25 January 1801

Nothing can be more propitious to your Bath excursion than the present moment, for Rear Admiral Thornbrough is just gone to relieve Sir Edward Pellew and you will not be wanted to relieve him in less than five weeks, at the expiration of which it will be proper that the Mars should come in, for in winter time no ship should be kept longer from port than six weeks if the service will admit.

787. *Harvey to St Vincent*

Royal Sovereign, off Ushant, 25 January 1801

Captain Fayerman of His Majesty's ship Beaulieu has just joined me with his foremast so badly sprung as to render his going into port necessary. I have had no communication with Sir Edward Pellew but I understand from Captain Fayerman as well as from Captain Wolseley of the Terrible, whom I spoke with this day that the advanced squadron have been much dispersed in consequence of the heavy gales that have prevailed for some days past.

I arrived off Ushant yesterday morning early with His Majesty's ships under my orders and was close in with the Isle last evening but have received no intelligence of the enemy's fleet in Brest.

788. *St Vincent to Admiralty*

Ville de Paris, in Torbay, 26 January 1801

I have to acknowledge the receipt of your letter of the 24th instant enclosing an extract of one from Lieutenant General Fraser to Mr.

Dundas containing intelligence from Portugal and also the copy of a letter from the Navy Board stating that in consequence of the shortage of the supply of hemp it will be advisable that His Majesty's ships should be furnished with only seven cables instead of eight, which measure has met with the approbation of the Lords Commissioners of the Admiralty.

In addition to the many excellent traits in the character of Captain Brown of His Majesty's ship Robust which I have often represented to their Lordships and in proof of the good effect produced by his conduct I beg leave to submit to their Lordships' consideration a letter from the petty officers of that ship requesting to be reduced to the established ration of provisions and to subscribe three months pay for the support of the war.

[Endorsed that their Lordships decline to accept the offer]

789. *St Vincent to Harvey*

Ville de Paris, in Torbay, 26 January 1801, ½ past 5 p.m.

As from the exertions which the French appear to have made lately for the purpose of manning their fleet at Brest it is probable they may have more ships ready for sea than they appeared to have when last reconnoitred, the Lords Commissioners of the Admiralty have been pleased to order that you shall be reinforced with all the ships that may be ready for that purpose. I have therefore directed Rear Admiral Collingwood to proceed and join you with such ships as are ready in Cawsand Bay and those that do not accompany him shall be dispatched to you as soon as possible.

790. *Fayerman to St Vincent*

Beaulieu, Plymouth Sound, 27 January 1801

The gale of wind which began on Thursday evening from the N.W. veering round to the N.E. dispersed the squadron (of nine sail of the line and a frigate) under the orders of Sir Edward Pellew, and also separated the Beaulieu and the two frigates, the Fisgard and Uranie, who were in company.

On Thursday the 22nd instant at 5 p.m., Ushant then bearing from S ½ E to S b W ½ W 7 or 8 miles we were with our heads to the northward, the wind at N.W. and the squadron on our lee bow, about 4 miles; it blowed extremely hard in the night. After wearing occasionally and carrying as much sail as the wind would permit, in the morning at daylight we found ourselves within two or three miles of the Portsall Rocks, off of Abreverack [Aber-Wrac'h], blowing then very hard and extremely strong in squalls with hail and sleet and the sea running very high. At that time we observed five or six sail of the squadron on our weather quarter; after pressing under reefed courses and storm staysails two points and sometimes three points free, we cleared Ushant at 1 p.m. bringing it to bear S.E. by S. 4 or 5 miles; it continued to blow very hard the remainder of that day (Friday), all that night and great part of the following day; as it moderated we made all the sail we could to gain Ushant and at 1 p.m. on Sunday, the weather hazy with the wind at S.W., we had a sight of it bearing N.E. 4 or 5 leagues and also saw the fleet in the N.W., 5 or 6 miles distant; three or four ships in sight in different directions, which I supposed to be some of Sir Edward Pellew's squadron; upon waiting on Sir Henry Harvey I found that the Terrible had joined him that day but could give no account of the other ships.

791. *Thornbrough to St Vincent*

Montagu, Ushant E.N.E, 4 miles, wind W.N.W., 27 January 1801

I arrived off the Black Rocks the morning of the 24th and found Sir Edward Pellew and frigates all absent, having been obliged to get to the westward during the late N.W. gales, and the sudden shift of wind to the N.E. kept them off. I stood in as far as the Vandree and counted 14 large ships in Brest harbour but nothing was in Berthcaume or Camaret Bays.

Sir Edward Pellew reached in from the S.W. about noon and by 8 o'clock at night got off the Black Rocks. The next morning, the 26th, I took upon me the command of the squadron and Sir Edward Pellew proceeded to cruise agreeable to your Lordship's orders.

The Nymphe went to reconnoitre but from the thickness of the weather could not see through the Goulet. Therefore cannot say whether any ships escaped during the absence of the squadron. I anchored the squadron the night of the 25th but the wind shifted suddenly to S.W. We weighed and got out safe.

792.   *Sick and Wounded Board to Admiralty*

27 January 1801

We request you will be pleased to acquaint the Right Honourable the Lords Commissioners of the Admiralty that the naval hospital at Paignton is nearly completed and that it appears to us that the service cannot be properly conducted without the assistance of an agent, we therefore beg to recommend to their Lordships that an agent should be appointed accordingly at a salary of one hundred pounds per annum, with an allowance of thirty pounds per annum for house rent being the same as is allowed to the agent of the Royal Hospital at Deal.

793.   *St Vincent to Admiralty*

Ville de Paris, in Torbay, 28 January 1801

I am to acknowledge the receipt of an order from the Lords Commissioners of the Admiralty dated the 24th instant to direct the captains and commanders of His Majesty's ships and vessels under my orders to use their best endeavours to seize or destroy any fishing boats or other vessels belonging to France which they may fall in with and to detain their crews as prisoners of war.

794.   *Harvey to St Vincent*

Royal Sovereign, at sea, 28 January 1801

In my letter to your Lordship of the 25th instant by the Beaulieu, Captain Fayerman, I mentioned that the advanced squadron were a good deal dispersed in consequence of the late heavy gales but I am now happy to inform you that they are again assembled without having received any material damage and yesterday evening I saw them well in within Ushant. The wind is now at N.W., which obliges me to keep an offing to the northward.

Sir Edward Pellew joined me on the evening of the 26th, having been relieved by Admiral Thornbrough and proceeded on the execution of your Lordship's orders. I herewith forward you his journal together with his letters and I have every reason to hope with him that the enemy's ships may not have effected their escape in consequence of the late N.E. gales, which were of short duration and being so immediately succeeded by one equally strong from the N.W.

795. *St Vincent to Lieutenant General Simcoe*[1]

Tor Abbey, 30 January 1801

Lord Spencer has not yet condescended to consult me, although he must know that I made a maritime tour of the Baltic in the year 1775 and was not idle. It is with extreme concern I learn from others that his Lordship has insuperable objections to a co-operation and I fear some of his advisers, the Neptunes at the Board (who are all incompetent to judge of a subject of this magnitude), have taught him to rely on a sea bombardment, which we all know to be an impotent operation.

796. *D'Auvergne to St Vincent*

Jersey, 31 January 1801

As a 'suite' to my letter to your Lordship of the 16th that I was obliged to send by a detour to find the Joseph cutter at Guernsey, having then none of the vessels under my orders here; your Lordship will have learnt the attempt Admiral Ganteaume's division made to get out of the Iroise on the 8th instant but forced back by the appearance of what their fears magnified to be the whole of the fleet under your Lordship's orders; I have now the honour to address you accounts that have reached me today of the <u>final departure</u> of the division under Ganteaume. My correspondent is perfectly silent with respect to Villaret although I still suspect he has secretly embarked on it with the intentions alluded to in my last letter of the 16th; the assistant surgeons gone <u>by land</u> from Brest to Toulon for Egypt would indicate that the Mediterranean is certainly not the channel by which the succours in that division are intended to be conveyed to Egypt if such as it may be adjudged by their description is their real destination; the nature of the provisions they are furnished with must eventually oblige them to a 'relache' somewhere if their destination is very distant; your Lordship will observe with satisfaction that the successful vigilance of our cruisers is one of the causes for the second division being ordered to another French port before it executes any hostile mission against us . . .

---

[1]General John Graves Simcoe (1752–1806). Commanded Queen's Rangers during the American War of Independence; first governor of Upper Canada, 1792–94; governor of San Domingo, 1794–97. In 1801 he was General Officer Commanding, Western Command, and was active in the south-west of England where poor harvests and the demands of the fleet had prompted food rioting. *Letters of the Earl of St Vincent 1801–4*, ed. D. Bonner Smith (NRS, 2 vols, 1921, 1926), I, 130; II, 167–8.

796a.   *Intelligence report*

A substance of communications from Brest received at Jersey the 31st
January 1801.

Brest, 23rd January. At 10 a.m. an express arrived from Paris for Admiral Ganteaume with orders to put to sea; the division as follows,
accordingly, having prepared, sailed at 1/2 past 4 p.m., the wind blowing a strong breeze from the northward, it got completely clear of the
Goulet and Bertheaume before dusk and at daylight in the morning,
24th, was out of sight of any of the signal posts; it is composed of the
ships that were last selected by Admiral Ganteaume, viz.

	Guns	Captains
The Formidable	80	Citoyen Alary
Indivisible	80	Gourdon
Indomptable	80	Montmuran
La Constitution	74	Faure
Le Dix-Août	74	Bergeret
Le Defraix	74	Christipature
Frigates		
La Créole	40	Gourges
La Bravoure	40	Dordelieu

24th. Various reports with respect to its destination are spread about but
most likely the real one is secret. St. Domingo is that which is most
spoken of although the best informed appear to believe it is more directly
intended for the support of the oriental interests of the Republic.

This evening arrived a covered diligence from Government with
money; it was drawn by eighteen horses and escorted by a squadron of
fifty horsemen; it is reported to have brought three millions and a half
of livres in specie.

Orders have been given for the departure hence by land of forty-five
assistant surgeons for Toulon, to be conveyed thence to Egypt; the
whole of their arrears due have been paid them to assist in facilitating
their journeys.

25th. Orders have been given this morning for the following ships to
prepare to sail within eight days; they are to proceed for Rochefort,
provisions running very short now and most of theirs having been given
to the division gone to sea. They are also intended to favour the entrance of a convoy impatiently expected from Bordeaux with some to
relieve the distress of the place, which is excessive.

Division under orders for Rochefort.

	Guns
L'Océan	120
Le Gaulois	74
Le Redoutable	74
Le Patriote	74
Le Cisalpin	74
Le Wattigny	74

Frigates	
La Fidéle	40

and another, name not certain

797. *St Vincent to Lady Dalyell*

Tor Abbey, 2 February 1801

When I took the command of this fleet the majority of the lieutenants serving in it were in a continual state of intoxication which occasioned almost a total dereliction of discipline and the most dangerously licentious conversation and to avoid the punishment due to such atrocious offences mental derangement was frequently set up in excuse.

798. *St Vincent to Bover*

Tor Abbey, 2 February 1801

I have named you twice to the Admiralty and once to an admiral whose captain was likely to go ashore and I write by this post in the strongest terms to Sir C. Cotton as you desire.

799. *St Vincent to Harvey*

Ville de Paris, in Torbay, 2 February 1801

I impatiently expect further reports of the state of the combined fleet in Brest which may tend to clear up the present doubt whether any of the enemy's ships effected their escape during the absence of the advanced ships.

800.   *St Vincent to Admiralty*

Ville de Paris, in Torbay, 2 February 1801

I have to acknowledge the receipt of your letter of the 31st ultimo signifying the direction of the Lords Commissioners of the Admiralty to inform them what orders have been given to the Impetueux and acquainting me that their Lordships rest with full confidence that I have taken care to give directions that every practicable means may be adopted for ascertaining whether any of the enemy's ships escaped from Brest during the absence of the squadron appointed to watch that port; in reply to which I desire you will acquaint their Lordships that the leading feature of the instructions to the officer commanding the advanced squadron (as reported in my journal) is to seize every possible opportunity of ascertaining the force, position and movements of the enemy's fleet and to send me from time to time the result of his observations and on the 30th and 31st ultimo I transmitted to you the communications I had received from Vice Admiral Sir Henry Harvey, Sir Edward Pellew and Rear Admiral Thornbrough; in addition to which I beg leave to observe that the Amelia and Suwarrow schooner are stationed off the Passage du Raz and that the Canada, Magicienne and Thames have arrived from the southward without seeing or hearing anything of an enemy's squadron.

Sir Edward Pellew was ordered, on being relieved by Rear Admiral Thornbrough, to cruise between Ushant and Scilly to intercept Russian, Danish and Swedish vessels for the space of ten days and at the expiration of that time to proceed to Cawsand Bay to replenish.

801.   *St Vincent to Keith*

Ville de Paris, in Torbay, 3 February 1801

By the enclosed intelligence this instant received from the Prince of Bouillon I am informed that a squadron of the enemy, owing to a sudden shift of wind, was enabled to effect their escape from Brest on the 23rd ultimo when the advanced squadron of the fleet under my command was forced by a heavy gale of wind from before that port. I have therefore judged it necessary immediately to apprize your Lordship thereof. I have directed Captain Ogilvy to communicate the purport of his mission to the senior officers of those ships off Cadiz and Gibraltar, Minorca and Malta.

802.   *St Vincent to Vice Admiral Sir Charles Cotton*

Ville de Paris, in Torbay, 4 February 1801

I am to acknowledge the receipt of your letter of yesterday by express informing me of the arrival of H.M. ship Concorde at Plymouth after having fallen in with the French squadron[1] which lately escaped from Brest.

803.   *St Vincent to Admiralty*

Ville de Paris, in Torbay, 5 February 1801

I have to acknowledge the receipt of an order from the Lords Commissioners of the Admiralty dated 3rd instant by a messenger who arrived at midnight, to send orders to Vice Admiral Sir Henry Harvey to detach a flag officer and six sail of the line, exclusive of the flag ship, in pursuit of the enemy's squadron which according to the intelligence transmitted by the Prince of Bouillon appeared to have escaped from Brest; in reply to which I desire you will acquaint their Lordships that my orderly dragoon was instantly despatched to stop the Thames and Magicienne and, by the messenger, the necessary directions were sent to be conveyed by those ships to Sir Henry Harvey, omitting that part of their Lordships' instructions to recall the squadron which may be detached in the event of Sir Henry receiving information that the enemy's had not sailed, as I conceive there can no longer remain a doubt thereof, from the circumstances which have been communicated to their Lordships from the captains of His Majesty's ships Immortalité and Concorde, copies of which were forwarded to Sir Henry and he was also informed that he was at liberty to select any ships from the advanced squadron or otherwise, excepting those named in the margin [*London*, *Achille*, *Venerable*, *Terrible*] to make the detachment, agreeable to the spirit of their Lordships' order.

The Spencer has sailed with duplicates and the Juste and Pompee have been ordered to proceed immediately to join the squadron from Cawsand Bay.

I desire you will lay before their Lordships the enclosed extract of a letter which I have received from the Honourable Captain Stopford of His Majesty's ship Excellent and represent to their Lordships that (according to my judgment) I make the best possible use of the frigates

[1]Then off Cape Finisterre. See James, III, 69–70.

under my orders but am in the most serious want of an addition of both frigates and cutters to cut off the supplies which are daily stealing to a rendezvous for the fleet in Brest or the detachment thereof which the Prince of Bouillon states to be equipping for the express purpose of meeting those succours and of which I shall apprize Captain Stopford by the Suwarrow schooner.

[*Enclosure*]

803a.   *Extract of a letter from Stopford, dated 1st February 1801*

The convoy in the Morbihan continues to accumulate as vessels come along shore from the southward.

804.   *Herbert to St Vincent*

Amelia, at sea, 5 February 1801

I have the honour to inform your Lordship that two hours ago I captured the French brig privateer La Juste of St. Maloes [St Malo] but last from L'Orient, armed with fourteen guns and seventy-eight men, commanded by Jean Pierre Charlet, had been out thirty days and captured nothing: the night being very dark and the weather being very thick we did not see her till she was close to us and she did not discover us till she was on board of us, by which she carried away her foremast and bowsprit.

805.   *St Vincent to Stopford*[1]

Ville de Paris, in Torbay, 6 February 1801

I have to acknowledge the receipt of your letter detailing the proceedings of the ships and vessels under your orders and informing me that the convoy in the Morbihan continues to accumulate as vessels come along shore from the southward. In reply to which I transmit you the copy of intelligence received from the Prince of Bouillon and as there can be little doubt but the enemy will endeavour to send out a strong detachment from Brest to escort the victuallers they stand so much in need of, I desire you will direct the captains and commanders of all the

---

[1]A similar letter was sent to Rear-admiral Thornbrough.

ships and vessels under your orders to keep a very sharp look out to prevent a surprise.

806.   *St Vincent to Admiralty*

Ville de Paris, in Torbay, 6 February 1801

Since closing my letters Sir Henry Harvey has arrived with the squadron, not having been joined by either the Thames or Spencer. I have therefore ordered Rear Admiral Sir Robert Calder[1] instantly to put to sea and proceed in pursuit of the enemy with the ships named in the margin [*Prince of Wales, Juste, Pompee, Russell, Cumberland, Montagu, Courageous, Thames, Magicienne*] and have directed him in the event of not falling in with the Juste, Pompee and Spencer to take three ships from the advanced squadron or as many as will make his detachment six sail of the line, besides the Prince of Wales, and also to take two frigates from the Bay of Brest if he is not joined by the Thames and Magicienne.

807.   *St Vincent to Admiralty*

Ville de Paris, in Torbay, 7 February 1801

A spirit of revolt having made its appearance on board the Naiad the latter end of January, originating in the necessary measures pursued to correct the perpetual drunkenness of the men at sea and total dereliction of discipline which I am sorry to say pervaded every ship of the old leaven in this fleet, Captain Ricketts judged it expedient to repair to this anchorage sooner than he intended and not being able to bring sufficient proof to convict any of the persons suspected, I have felt it my duty to remove all those he has pointed out as the most dangerous into the Ville de Paris and Spencer and to give marines in exchange from the former and blue jackets from the latter.

Captain Ricketts and his officers have met this intention with a manliness I cannot too much praise and I enclose letters from him reciting the meritorious conduct of the acting Lieutenant and Sergeant of Marines, both of whom are deserving the protection of the Lords Commissioners of the Admiralty.

---

[1]Sir Robert Calder (d. 1818). Lieutenant 1762; Captain 1780; Rear-admiral 1799; Vice-admiral 1804; Admiral 1810.

808.   *St Vincent to Admiralty*

Ville de Paris, in Torbay, 8 February 1801

I enclose copies of general orders which I have found it necessary to issue since I have had the command of the Western Squadron, by which the Lords Commissioners of the Admiralty will perceive I have not been inattentive to the risks which ships run of getting on board each other during an evolution at sea.

[*Enclosures*]

808a.   *General memorandum*

Ville de Paris, 10 May 1800

Respective captains out of port

The Commander-in-Chief has very great pleasure in expressing the satisfaction he derives from the zeal and activity shewn in the squadron he has the honour to command; and has simply to recommend keeping the columns in compact order when wind and weather will permit, which can only be done by increasing sail in small proportions the moment the ship is perceived to drop. And when the signal is made to tack or wear, more particularly in succession, by every ship clapping on as much canvas as the distance from her file leader will permit, and not to back, except to avoid an evident risk, and by not standing beyond the wake of her leader before she begins her movement. The officers commanding the middle watch are strictly enjoined to preserve close order at day-break, to facilitate an immediate attack on falling in with the enemy, more especially on his coming out of port.

808b.   *General memorandum*

Royal George, off Ushant, 12 September 1800

Respective captains

The Commander-in-Chief highly disapproves the obstinate perseverance of the Juste in backing her main and mizen topsails when the signal is made to tack or wear in succession, and this has frequently happened when her topgallant sails and stay sails have been set; and it has given the Admiral great concern to see this slovenly practice imitated by a ship ably commanded, which has recently joined the fleet. It ought to be the especial care of the captains, lieutenants and masters of His Majesty's ships to study the rate of going of the ship they serve in, with that of their file leader, and govern themselves accordingly.

808c. *General memorandum*

Ville de Paris, off Ushant, 21 October 1800

Respective captains

The very unofficer like and unseaman-like manner the Mars was conducted this morning by pushing through between the Ville de Paris and Barfleur, those ships at the time being in very close order, thereby obliging the Barfleur to lay all aback to avoid running on board the Mars, obliges the Commander-in-Chief, publicly, to reprimand Captain Monkton and the officer of the watch, and strictly to forbid the like conduct in the future.

808d. *General memorandum*

Ville de Paris, Torbay, 23 October 1800

Respective captains

The Commander-in-Chief cannot suppose it possible that any captain of a ship under his command is off the quarter deck or poop when a movement of the fleet is made, night or day, nor that he is in bed at break of day every morning: he requires that two lieutenants in a watch shall at all times be on deck in ships of the line, no excuse for a breach of which will be admitted.

809. *St Vincent to Stopford*

Ville de Paris, in Torbay, 8 February 1801

By the Nile cutter I have received your letter of the 5th instant with its several enclosures and desire you will encourage by all possible means the dispositions and plans suggested by General Georges,[1] until the Lords Commissioners of the Admiralty shall signify their pleasure thereon, but at the same time not to lose sight for an instant that the intercepting of the enemy's supplies and destruction of their convoys is the important and principal object which will increasingly demand

[1] A Chouan leader.

your utmost vigilance and also that it is possible if General Georges has made his peace with Bonaparte that this may be a manoeuvre to draw off your attention from the essential duties above mentioned.

810.   *St Vincent to Sir Francis Baring*[1]

Tor Abbey, 8 February 1801

The officers in general, with very few exceptions, are so licentious, malingering and abominable that their conduct must bring about another mutiny. In fine I see no means of saving the country from a sudden and violent concussion but the retreat of Mr. Pitt and company, to be succeeded by Lord Lansdown,[2] who will make the best possible peace and care not what becomes of him after.

811.   *Admiralty to St Vincent*

9 February 1801

I have received and communicated to my Lords Commissioners of the Admiralty your letter to me of the 7th instant acquainting me for their Lordships' information among other occurrences that His Majesty's ship the Glory had arrived in Torbay having missed the anchorage of Cawsand Bay in proceeding out of Hamoaze and that several of the officers had been left behind at the time of her sailing from Plymouth, and I have their Lordships' commands to acquaint you in answer thereto that they cannot help feeling the greatest astonishment that the captain of the Glory should have suffered those officers to be on shore at the time when every one ought to have been at his duty and that they take it for granted your Lordship has called upon Captain Draper for an explanation.

812.   *St Vincent to Admiralty*

Ville de Paris, in Torbay, 10 February 1801

It is really shocking to receive such daily reports of the licentiousness which prevails at Plymouth Dock and its neighbourhood, and as I

---

[1]Sir Francis Baring (1740–1810). Merchant-financier, founder of the house of Baring Brothers; published financial treatises including *Observations on the establishment of the Bank of England* (1797).

[2]Sir William Petty, first marquis of Lansdowne and second earl of Shelburne (1737–1805). Statesman.

conclude the enclosed is founded on fact I trust the Lords Commissioners of the Admiralty will use their utmost endeavours to prevent the serious and alarming consequences therein represented.

[*Enclosure*]

812a.   *Thomas Trotter to Sir Thomas Troubridge*

Plymouth Dock, 9 February 1801

A fever very similar to what appeared in the Glory and also owing to the same cause now prevails in the Edgar. The hulk is so ill calculated for comfort that all the exertions of officers can do little, and relief can only be exerted when the crew are removed into their own ship, which will be in a few days.

The quorum of magistrates here have licensed 200 public houses in Dock, every avenue being filled in the skirts of the town, wherever a sailor was accustomed to frequent. They have now turned their direction to the village of Cawsand. There the same system is practiced; even the spot at the Fish house, where we usually landed our sick for the benefit of air and recreation, attended by a surgeon's mate and midshipman to prevent strolling to gin shops, is now occupied by a new Inn to catch them come out of the boat!!!

It will excite your wonder when I inform you that a clergyman and a captain of the navy are two out of three Justices of the Peace that grant licences to these graves of our seamen, and that in time will equally intomb both the health and discipline of our ships.

[*Endorsements*]

12 February
Acknowledge receipt and acquaint his Lordship that my Lords have sent a copy to the Duke of Portland that his Grace may take such steps as he may judge proper for preventing the evils arising from the granting such licences.

Send to Mr King[1] for that purpose.

---

[1]Undersecretary, Home Office.

13

CORNWALLIS SUCCEEDS
26 FEBRUARY–25 OCTOBER 1801

St Vincent was appointed First Lord of the Admiralty in the administration of Henry Addington on 19 February 1801. Admiral Sir William Cornwallis was appointed Commander-in-Chief of the Channel fleet the following day, and hoisted his flag in Torbay five days later [813]. Cornwallis was not to make dramatic changes in the organisation of the blockade. Nevertheless the discipline of the fleet relaxed from the pitch to which St Vincent had screwed it, both in terms of the rigour with which he pursued malefactors and in the precision with which he demanded ships keep station in and around the port of Brest. Whereas St Vincent was prepared to pursue a chaplain so far as the Archbishop of Canterbury, Cornwallis was content to permit another behaving improperly simply to leave his situation [818]. Likewise, the main fleet under Cornwallis was permitted to adhere to Ushant less closely, though 'near enough for the purpose for which we are here'. However, as before, two or more frigates remained within the Iroise while the support squadron of ships of the line, varying in strength according to the apparent readiness of the French, served to provide reinforcement as well as to communicate with Cornwallis who remained with the main fleet off Ushant [827, 832, 834]. Other frigates continued to patrol as far south as Cape Finisterre taking privateers, both Spanish and French, one of the latter indeed carrying the Governor of Guadaloupe [817, 825].

Though the discipline was different, the blockade thus continued largely on the lines established by St Vincent. The commanders of the support squadron, Thornbrough and Saumarez, took six-weekly turns on station [814]. In March neither intelligence nor inspection of the fleet in Brest suggested an imminent excursion in force [821]. Yet some ships were being prepared for sea, in L'Orient and Rochefort [826] as well as Brest, and information was received of the French intention to concentrate their forces at Rochefort [822]. These more southerly ports were less heavily blockaded than Brest and in March one French ship of the line and one frigate escaped from L'Orient, only the latter returning to its previous anchorage [815]. Consequently, in April Pellew took a squadron down the coast to Aix Roads to blockade Rochefort. There, under a flag of truce, the French admiral in command claimed they intended an assault on the British fleet that summer [826].

By mid-April, indeed, French preparations for sea were more forward and on a larger scale than anticipated. In consequence the blockade was reinforced. The Admiralty had already decided to concentrate off Ushant line of battleships temporarily on other stations, and Cornwallis saw fit to strengthen his advance squadron [827]. Reports in April of Ganteaume free in the Mediterranean[1] [822, 826a], in May of a Spanish squadron loose from Ferrol [830], among other movements, kept him continually on his guard. Attempts by the French to place ships at the mouth of the Goulet were promptly answered. In July the corvette Chevrette was cut out of Camaret Bay with large loss on both sides.[2] Subsequently, two French line of battle ships worked their way through the Goulet, but they immediately returned on the approach of British ships in force [834].

The movements of the French at least enabled Cornwallis to take a good look at the state of their ships' sails and rigging. Their state of dilapidation confirmed the effectiveness of the British blockade in preventing naval stores getting into Brest. The French ports south of L'Orient were still full of small coasting vessels waiting to get up to Brest and convoys of these were regularly harassed. Numerous coasters were taken or destroyed [836], yet the small size of the French vessels permitted them to make progress through coastal shallows out of reach of British warships of greater draught and renewed demands for small brigs, cutters and luggers [819]. To get at these coasters, the British did arm and man small vessels themselves, but these operations were not without danger: in May one British manned chasse marée was taken by two boats from the shore [831]. The French also sought to avoid the blockade by using a newly completed canal to get their supplies into Brest [833].

The flow of intelligence from inside Brest via Captain D'Auvergne remained valuable [821, 822], especially as sightings of the Franco-Spanish fleet from the mouth of the Goulet seemed only to produce conflicting accounts. In April the number of ships of the line that could be seen varied between 17 and 24 [828]. However, Cornwallis was also

---

[1]Urged to sea by Napoleon, Ganteaume sailed from Toulon for Alexandria on 19 March but, having suffered gale damage, put back to Toulon. Ordered to sea again, he sailed for Egypt once more on 27 April and approached Alexandria on 7 June. On apparent evidence that the port was well guarded, he sailed west along the coast of North Africa intending to disembark his troops. However off Bengazi he was forced to continue his westward course by the appearance of British ships in search of him. On 24 June off Cape Derna he took the British 74 *Swiftsure* and re-entered Toulon on 22 July. W. James, *The Naval History of Great Britain from the declaration of war by France in 1793 to the accession of George IV* (6 vols, London, 1859), III, 74–7.

[2]James, III, 139–41.

able to obtain first hand knowledge of the state of the Franco-Spanish fleet from close surveillance by a pilot in the British fleet who spent four days and nights in the harbour [834].

By August 1801 some ships in the British fleet had been at sea more than five months. However, the health of the seamen remained good [835]. This reflected the new lemon juice regime now in place and the occasional supply of fresh vegetables. In May, for example, victuallers intended for Torbay were sent out to the fleet off Ushant [830]. Thomas Trotter, who had resumed his duties as Physician of the Fleet with the departure of St Vincent, still campaigned for better quality victuals for the sick [816a], and weaknesses in the care of invalids were gradually being removed. Thus the vulnerability of the sick landed by open boat for the hospital at Plymouth led to permission for provision of a decked vessel for that purpose, as at Portsmouth [816b]. In spite of such attention to the health of seamen, contagion still occasionally entered ships with men transferred from a receiving ship. Then men had to be sent on shore [816] where increased hospital accommodation was now available. For in March the hospital at Paignton was ready for the reception of seamen, only awaiting the adoption of recommendations for greater security aimed at preventing invalids from deserting [823].

These provisions, combined with the belief that seamen were better preserved from the excesses in which they indulged on shore [835], reduced losses of men and eased the manning problem. Men were still pressed as necessary from merchant ships at sea, and individuals were occasionally discharged as they revealed just cause [573, 583, 590, 729]. But otherwise stability of numbers sanctioned the practice, for example, of allowing the seamen of Guernsey and Jersey immunity from the press [829], possibly because of their privateering value[1]. This stability strengthened the position of the Admiralty in relation to the seamen, and was reinforced by St Vincent's reputation as a manager of men. It was a strength that conferred support upon its sea officers, for example, in declining to make any concession to the custom for seamen to be paid before they went to sea [820].

The Admiralty's bargaining position with regard to its seamen was complemented by the good condition of ships in the fleet. Severe squalls in April had brought about a collision between two ships in which both lost masts and one its bowsprit [824]. Otherwise, ships of the line had been refitted regularly, three at a time [835]. In consequence the fleet

---

[1]Between 1793 and 1801 nearly 10 per cent of all letters of marque were issued to the masters of 164 privateers from the Channel Islands, which took 68 per cent of all prizes condemned uncontested to British privateers. A. G. Jamieson (ed.), *A People of the Sea. The Maritime History of the Channel Islands* (London, 1986), 173–80.

remained a fully effective force when the blockade was terminated following signature of the preliminaries of peace on 1 October 1801 [837] and exchange of ratifications on 12 October. The cessation of hostilities was communicated to ships in the fleet eight days later [839], when they were withdrawn from their stations on the French coast, some to be turned to new purposes, the remainder to be kept in a state of readiness for immediate service [840]. The Board of Admiralty had already ordered the Victualling Board to cease supplying fresh provisions to the ships off Ushant [838]. Six months later, on 27 March 1802, the war was formally terminated by the signature of a treaty of peace at Amiens.

813.   *Cornwallis to Admiralty*

Ville de Paris, Torbay, 26 February 1801

I am to acquaint you for the information of the Lords Commissioners of the Admiralty that I arrived here and hoisted my flag yesterday evening; and found at anchor His Majesty's ships and hired cutters named in the margin [*San Josef*, *Immortalité*, *Megara* fire ship, *Dolly* cutter, *Suwarrow* schooner].

814.   *Thornbrough to Admiralty*

Mars, Cawsand Bay, 9 March 1801

I desire you will be pleased to acquaint their Lordships that I have this day anchored in Cawsand Bay in His Majesty's ship Mars, having been relieved from the command of the advanced squadron by Sir James Saumarez the evening of the sixth.

I received orders from the Honourable William Cornwallis to proceed to this anchorage to victual and refit without loss of time and join him either off Brest or in Torbay according to the information I might receive.

From the strong westerly winds it had not been possible to reconnoitre Brest since the 19th of last month and I am certain nothing has sailed from thence since the 23rd of January, two days prior to my taking that command.

The light house on Ushant has been lighted every night since the 1st of this month.

The 20 landsmen lately sent to this ship brought a very bad fever with them, one of them and one marine have died of it and I have ordered 10 to be sent to the hospital. When they are removed and fresh provisions for the remainder [sic] I hope we shall put a stop to it.

815.   *Captain William Brown to Stopford*

Robust, Quiberon Bay, 9 March 1801

I beg to acquaint you that being between the Island of Groa [Groix] and the Birvideaux under our topsails treble reefed, it blowing fresh with very squally weather and particularly dark, I saw on the 7th of this month at 9 p.m. two sail approaching us on our weather beam, which ships could not be more than three cables length from us. Their steering large with the wind from E.N.E. indicated their being the line of battle ship and frigate from Port Louis. I immediately wore, intending to keep the Robust as near as possible the same course till the ship was perfectly ready for action. But the time the ship took in gathering way, though every exertion was made and the strange ships certainly going very fast, we lost sight of them, it being reported to me by the Master and the signal midshipman who I had placed on the poop to watch their motions, the last they had seen of them they certainly hauled to the northward and westward. I immediately set all sail and kept rather more to the northward than they were supposed to steer in order to get them between the Robust and the land (taking care not to show any light) but she not seeing them in that position, I shaped my course for the Penmarks to do my utmost to cut them off. The position I took was immediately in their track and to deceive them the more I stood on until dark, making them suppose it was my intention to watch the passage between Groa [Groix] and the main; the not having any idea these ships were bound abroad was also an inducement to shape my course to the northward and westward under the impression they might be loaded with stores and provisions for the Brest fleet, which I thought of the greatest possible consequence to counteract. The not seeing anything off the Penmarks at daylight on the 8th and the having looked into Port Louis and finding the line of battle ship gone from that port and the frigate returned identified them to have been the ships I saw on the evening of the 7th. I therefore thought it my duty to report to you the above circumstance.

816.   *Thornbrough to Admiralty*

His Majesty's Ship Mars, Cawsand Bay, 11 March 1801

Inclosed are two letters I have this day received from Doctor Trotter, which I desire you will be pleased to lay before their Lordships for their consideration.

One of the sick men landing from the Mars died on his passage yesterday from Cawsand Bay.

[*Enclosures*]

816a.   *Trotter*[1] *to Thornbrough*

Plymouth Dock, 10 March 1801

I have just visited the Mars and directed eleven men to be sent on shore, reduced to the last degree of debility from a fever of the contagious kind. It appears that this disease was brought on board by a party of men sent from the Cambridge that had passed through different ships before they came to the Mars. It spread in the Achille to sixty or seventy men, of whom five died; in the Mars three or four deaths have happened and more than fifty have been recovered on board. The recoveries in both ships have been in a great measure owing to the kind attention of the officers in supplying them with delicacies from their tables. Such are still the imperfect arrangements of the medical department that a surgeon has it in his power to demand gratuitous medicines to an unlimited amount while the benefits to be derived from their exhibition are either lessened or entirely frustrated by a want of fresh animal food, the stronger malt liquors and a better wine to nourish and support the emaciated and languid patient. The diseases of debility which have appeared in the fleet for the last ten months, joined to the length of the cruises, strongly urge the necessity of improving the comforts of diet at sea beyond what has been observed in former times.

816b.   *Trotter to Thornbrough*

Plymouth Dock, 11 March 1801

Having on many occasions observed the inconvenience and hardship which the sick experience on being sent in open boats to the hospital from Cawsand Bay, I have to request you will be pleased to move their Lordships to allow a small decked vessel for that purpose similar to what has been long in use at Portsmouth.

---

[1]Though St Vincent had replaced Trotter as Physician of the Fleet, he appears to have resumed duties as such under Cornwallis, though still based on shore.

[Endorsement]

13 March.
Send copy to Sir Thomas Pasley with directions to him to call on the captain of the Cambridge to account for having sent men in the state in which those are represented to be from the flag ship, by which act of inattention it appears their infection has spread in a considerable degree, and direct him to give such orders as may in future guard as much as possible against evils of the same nature.

Direct him to let me know whether any vessel now at Plymouth is in his opinion well adapted for this service, and if so, without waiting for the directions from their Lordships to employ her upon it.

Acquaint Admiral Thornbrough accordingly.

817.   *Captain Cooke to Captain Ricketts*

Amethyst, at sea, 17 March 1801

I have to acquaint you that in executing your instructions of the 15th instant that on the evening of the 16th I fell in with and captured the Nostra Signora del Carmen, a Spanish schooner privateer mounting six guns and having on board 65 men, sailed from Vigo the preceding evening bound on a cruise. As she did not appear to me to be calculated for His Majesty's service I destroyed her.

818.   *Cornwallis to Admiralty*

Ville de Paris, Torbay, 27 March 1801

The Earl of Northesk,[1] captain of His Majesty's ship Prince, having represented to me that the Reverend John Griffin, chaplain of that ship, had not conducted himself with that propriety in the ship which from a person in his station was to have been wished and expected; that he had been put out of the wardroom mess and was himself desirous of being discharged. As the ship is liable to go to sea in a moment upon a change of wind and conceiving that it might be their Lordships' inclination that under such circumstances he should not continue on board I have ventured to allow the Earl of Northesk to let him go on shore, which I hope will meet with their Lordships' approbation. Mr. Griffin hath

---

[1] William Carnegie, Earl of Northesk (d. 1831). Lieutenant 1777; Captain 1782; Rear-admiral 1804; Vice-admiral 1808; Admiral 1814. Inherited title in English peerage 1792.

written a letter of thanks to his Lordship for not having exhibited him in a more public manner and perhaps their Lordships may be pleased to direct him to be discharged.

819. *Pellew to Cornwallis*

29 March 1801

On the evening of the 24th instant and next day fell in with 12 sail of light vessels from L'Orient bound to Bordeaux for provisions and wine, two brigs were taken, six brigs burnt and four drove on shore on Noirmoutier. On our arrival off Sable d'Oleron a convoy of sixty sail, all laden, were in the outer road ready to depart, all of which we drove again into the inner harbour.

There is not a little port from Bordeaux to L'Orient which are not full of loaded vessels for Brest and without an addition of small brigs, cutters or luggers no efforts of the large ships, I fear, can perfectly prevent them getting along shore, although they are very considerably retarded.

820. *Gambier[1] to Nepean[2]*

[Neptune], Portsmouth, 31 March 1801

It is a very unpleasant circumstance the Neptune's pay books not being received at the Navy Office. I am extremely anxious to get to sea on Thursday and I do not like that the Neptune's company should assert their right of their wages being paid them before they go to sea. I wish therefore that the Board would authorize me to assure them that they shall be paid at Plymouth in a short time. I will have it reported today among the ship's company that the pay books are at Plymouth and on Thursday before we sail I shall direct Captain Brace to do as I have stated in my public letter to you.

[Endorsement]

---

[1]Though an Admiralty commissioner since 1795, Gambier served in the Channel fleet at this time.
[2]First Secretary to the Board of Admiralty.

To make known to the Neptune's company the reason of the delay in the payment of their wages and to assure them that their Lordships will order their wages to be paid to them at Plymouth as soon as the nature of the service the ship is employed on will permit her going to that port.

821. *D'Auvergne to Cornwallis*

Jersey, 31 March 1801

I am this instant honoured with your letters by the Childers and am sorry to inform you that my confidential man has not returned, as I expected, from Brest. I conclude the light nights have alone detained him. The only certain accounts I have received since I had the honour to address you is the change in the command of the Spanish fleet in that port; Admiral Gravina having superseded Mazzaredo. This change may have occasioned the movements among the Spaniards observed. It has likewise been latterly circulated there that the Spaniards were to proceed to the Tagus if they got out. I have had no information of any troops in numbers sufficient for an embarkation being in that vicinity and my last account repeated the distress for sea provisions. The instant my confidential messenger arrives with anything certain I shall have the honour to transmit it to you or the squadron off Ushant by one of the cruisers under my orders.

822. *D'Auvergne to Cornwallis*

Jersey, 31 March 1801, p.m.

I have this moment information from Brest of the 21st instant that Dordelain's division, described in my communication to you, are the only ships prepared to put to sea. Every other susceptible of service are preparing to follow their destination positively for Rochefort; the distress for provisions excessive; no troops at this moment, the manoeuvres of the Spaniards under Gravina are mere exercises as they do not intend to leave Brest.

Dordelain's division is well manned but he has but one month's provisions on board . . . Ganteaume is certainly blocked in Toulon.

823.   *Captain Samuel Sutton*[1] *to Cornwallis*

March 1801

For the better security of the hospital at Paignton, the guard, now a corporal with six privates, might be increased, the present being insufficient.

The window sashes of the upper ward, which have no security to prevent the patients making their escape, might be secured by an iron bar and wirework in the same manner as the window sashes of the lower ward are.

The wall in front of the hospital, now six feet high, might be raised or the ground lowered in order to prevent the men making their escape that way and the wooden paling to be armed with nails or tenterhooks, which is not at present done.

The surgeon, Mr. Ball, residing at the village of Paignton instead of being at the hospital is probably the cause of the irregularity I found among the patients at the hospital.

The provisions of every kind I found to be perfectly good and proper and no complaint whatever from the men at the hospital upon any ground.

824.   *Cornwallis to Admiralty*

Ville de Paris, off Ushant, 12 April 1801

I request that you will be pleased to acquaint the Lords Commissioners of the Admiralty that the wind has blown fresh for several days past, shifting frequently in squalls from N.W. by N. to N. by E. About one o'clock on Friday morning the lieutenant of the watch informed me the ships had many of them been taken aback and that the Ville de Paris was boxed off. I was under considerable uneasiness lest some accident should have befallen some of the ships and when I went upon deck they told me guns had been heard in the night. As the day dawned a ship was seen upon the lee quarter without a bowsprit or foremast and one astern with her mainmast gone. As soon as it was light enough I made a signal to L'Achille to go to the assistance of the ship upon the lee quarter and the Canada, which was nearby, also went, perhaps in consequence of a signal from that ship. I sent the Belleisle to assist the other ship, which proved the Centaur. Both ships were at a considerable distance. I therefore sent the Fisgard to the ships to leeward to enquire particulars and

[1]First captain to Cornwallis.

in the evening she returned and brought me a letter (the copy of which I enclose) from Rear Admiral Thornbrough.

Captain Cunningham informed me that he saw the enemy very distinctly on the 9th in the same state as before and adds that the new three decker and two others had not yet bent their sails.

[*Enclosure*]

824a.   *Thornbrough to Cornwallis*

Mars, 11 April 1801

About ¾ past 12 the Mars was taken aback and came about on the starboard tack. Everything was done to avoid the Centaur and lights shown. She ran across us and carried away our bowsprit and head and, before I could get the ship before the wind, our foremast fell and soon after our main topmast. I was not on deck until our bowsprit was gone. Captain Lloyd was on deck.

825.   *Cooke to Cornwallis*

Amethyst, at sea, 12 April 1801

I have the honour to acquaint you that on the 9th instant in latitude 44° 35′ N., longitude 10° 00′ W. I captured the French national ship corvette Le General Brune (formerly a merchant ship) from Guadeloupe bound to Bordeaux, commanded by Citizen Martin, lieutenant de vaisseaux, mounting 14 guns (six pounders) and having on board 100 men, including General Pelard, late Governor of Guadeloupe, and suite.

826.   *Pellew to Cornwallis*

Impetueux, at sea, 15 April 1801

The ships under my orders weighed this morning after the Fisgard sailed and when daylight closed and my motions could no longer be observed I stood up for Brest.

I have the honour to enclose the report of Lieutenant Pilford,[1] the officer I sent with a flag of truce to the rear admiral laying in Isle D'Aix

---

[1]John Pilford (d. 1834). Lieutenant 1795; Captain 1805.

Road. I learn in addition to this report that the Experiment[1] is the third ship observed by him to be rigged at Rochefort with the L'Aigle and Duguay-Trouin.

The garrison on Isle D'Aix have been increased to 3,000 men and there are mounted on it one hundred and twenty-two pieces of artillery. At low water the enemy's ships have only two feet under them.

The Foudroyant has everything on board except provisions and the admiral said 350 men had arrived from Bordeaux for her that day, that all the privateers were called in and that he believed they intended to try an action with us this summer under the idea we could not bring above 25 ships off Brest after providing for the North Sea fleet.

I herewith cover a copy of my letter to the rear admiral with his answer. My motive for sending the flag to him was to discover if they had any troops embarked or appeared to be on the move. [From] all I can learn I think they will wait for the other ships from Rochefort. I suspect the troops assembled on the island are for the purpose of embarking whenever the squadron may be ready and not for the defence of the port, although the admiral said they were so numerous that the whole coast was lined with them since their return from the Rhine and that he expected more would be sent on the island. The admiral confirmed the information procured by the Indefatigable of a new 74 being launched at L'Orient after he sailed from it.

[*Enclosure*]

826a.   *Lieutenant Pilford to Pellew*

Impetueux, 6 April 1801

The French squadron lying in Isle D'Aix Road are moored in a line directly across from the inner point of Isle D'Aix to the southernmost point of the large bank and are placed in the following manner.

The Ambuscade within a cable's length of the island, then the Guerrier, Union, Argonaut, Foudroyant and bomb vessel within a half cable's length of each other, in a line from N.E. to S.W.

The Argonaut (in which ship Admiral Bedout had his flag hoisted) appeared to be well manned but by no means in good order. She was very dirty and the sailors badly clothed, the quarter deck was at all times full of men of every description and there seemed but little order

---

[1]Probably the 50-gun ship launched at Deptford in 1774 and captured by the French off the east coast of North America in September 1778.

and discipline kept up amongst them. The Argonaut was very badly finished and appeared to be of a small scantling for so large a ship and her main deck parts particularly small. The Union, Guerrier and Ambuscade were full of men but on board the Foudroyant I never observed more than one hundred men on deck at a time and I am inclined to think she has not more than two hundred men on board her. I observed in Rochefort three ships with their top gallant masts struck but haze was so great I could not determine whether they were frigates or ships of the line. The admiral informed me that two thousand men were landed on Isle D'Aix on the first day we stood in to reconnoitre them and that more troops were expected there every hour, that about a week ago 20,000 troops had passed within a few leagues of Rochelle on their route to join the Spanish troops on the frontier of Portugal. The French squadron under Admiral Ganteaume had also escaped from Toulon but no accounts had been received of them since.

827. *Cornwallis to Admiralty*

Ville de Paris, off Ushant, 16 April 1801

Your letter signifying their Lordships' commands dated the 31st of March not to recall Sir Edward Pellew did not reach me until the 14th instant owing to its having arrived in Torbay after I had sailed from that place. I had of course ordered him to join me in obedience to their Lordships' orders to call in all the line of battle ships; but afterwards, upon being joined by several ships, I thought Sir Edward Pellew, being in the bay, likely to be of so much use that upon receiving a letter of intelligence from him by the Stork sloop I sent her back immediately and in a letter to Sir Edward left it to act from circumstances as it appeared to him best for the good of the service and to be particularly watchful lest any squadron of the enemy should come at the back of him; but he had sailed and, having missed the sloop, joined me yesterday. He immediately returned with instructions to keep the ships and vessels stationed in the best manner to prevent supplies reaching Brest and to endeavour to take or destroy the enemy's ships if an opportunity afford.

It is probable a larger force may sail from Brest than has been mentioned, for by the reports of the officers who look in more ships appear to be brought forward. They have produced a force at L'Orient and Rochefort beyond what Sir Edward Pellew declared he had any conception of and he has spared no pains, I believe, to obtain information. He informed me that he had sent a boat on board the French admiral when he was in Basque Road to endeavour to learn what their intentions were; I have enclosed copies of Sir Edward Pellew's reports to me upon that head.

I beg leave to inform their Lordships that before Sir James Saumarez was withdrawn from the station before Brest he had applied to me for a reinforcement in consequence of the increased force of the enemy ready to sail. I therefore submit to their Lordships whether it would be prudent to leave half of the ships or, in fact, all the ships of two decks separated from the rest of the squadron and without any certainty of their joining me should the enemy come out in force. I am perfectly ready, however, to execute their Lordships' commands if they should think such a measure advisable. If the French squadron intended for Rochefort has not sailed within these few days that intention is, at least for the present, given up as from the violence of the wind I have been driven ten or twelve leagues to the westward. They were all at anchor on the twelfth.

The report of the Prince of Bouillon sent me by the Childers was not very material. He said as soon as he received any further intelligence he would send one of the vessels under his orders to me. I have not, however, heard from him since. I rather suspect his intelligence was of old date, before the enemy's plan was changed.

Sir Edward Pellew seems to be of opinion from all the information he has received and the observations he could make that they have an intention to make some great effort this summer. Portugal may perhaps only be held out to deceive us as it was upon a former occasion when they actually went to Ireland.

I have at present three frigates under Captain Cunningham inshore – a frigate at some distance from them – and three line of battle ships spread, during the easterly wind, between the last mentioned and the squadron to act under the direction of Rear Admiral Sir James Saumarez, who has instructions to use the utmost of his endeavours to point out their route should the enemy sail; and having communicated by signal or otherwise with me, if he should get sight of them, to endeavour to amuse the enemy until more force can get up.

I have this moment received a report from Captain Cunningham, who looked into Brest yesterday evening, by which it appears no squadron had attempted to sail during these easterly winds. I enclose Captain Cunningham's report, who appears to me to have been very diligent in his look out during the late gales.

828. *Cornwallis to Admiralty*

Ville de Paris, off Ushant, 20 April 1801

As the accounts of the force in Brest have not entirely agreed when taken by the different ships Captain Sutton went up on the 18th in a frigate to make remarks and I have enclosed his report for their Lordships' information; the reports have varied from so low as seventeen up to twenty-four of the line. I am inclined to believe that an exact estimate cannot be made from ships looking in if the enemy is at any pains to deceive. One ship had her topsail yards manned, either bending or furling her sails and the new three decker had topgallant yards across but no sails bent though there was some appearance in the tops of sails ready for bending. Sir James Saumarez counted twenty of the line, Captain Rowley twenty-one, the captain of the Caesar twenty-two, Captain Douglas[1] of the Nymphe made a signal for twenty-four of the line some days ago. Captain Cunningham, who has been constantly and diligently upon the watch and should know from having seen so frequently their positions, is positive that not a line of battle ship has sailed since the last week in February. The Océan, which was one of the ships said to be in Camaret Bay some time since with the squadron supposed to be going to sea has not now her sails bent.

829. *Captain George Tobin[2] to Cornwallis*

Dasher, off Abreverack, 20 April 1801

I have the honour to acknowledge the receipt of your letter from off Ushant of the 13th instant and in reply beg leave to acquaint you for the information of the Lords Commissioners of the Admiralty that it is true my having impressed fifteen men from the Alarm lugger of Guernsey.

I beg leave to state to you that I judged it for the good of His Majesty's service to impress as many men as possible, knowing the Oiseau, with which ship I was cruising, to be short of her complement as well as the sloop under my command.

I have to add that the Alarm was returning from her cruise at the time and within a short day's sail of her port, also that I made myself well

---

[1]This was either John Erskine Douglas (d. 1847), Lieutenant 1778; Captain 1795; Rear-admiral 1814; Vice-admiral 1825; Admiral 1838; or Stair Douglas (d. 1826), Lieutenant 1780; Captain 1797; Rear-admiral 1821.

[2]George Tobin (d. 1837). Lieutenant 1790; Commander 1798; Captain 1802; Rear-admiral 1837.

acquainted that none of the impressed men were in any way protected or natives of either of the islands Guernsey or Jersey, a description of persons I shall certainly ever avoid impressing.

I cannot conclude without observing that I am continually in the way of boarding some of the very many privateers belonging to Guernsey and Jersey – that a very great proportion of their crews are not inhabitants of the islands – there remains no doubt but that great numbers of them are deserters from the Navy, which at the same time this number is in some measure prevented from increasing from a dread many entertain of being discovered or impressed again into the service.

830.   *Cornwallis to Admiralty*

Ville de Paris, off Ushant, 14 May 1801

I request that you will be pleased to acquaint the Lords Commissioners of the Admiralty I have received information within these two days from Spanish prisoners taken in different vessels and all agreeing in the same story, that on the 20th of April a Spanish squadron sailed from Ferrol consisting of three three-decked ships, two of two decks and a lugger but were ignorant as to their destination; it appears strange, if true, that this squadron should have sailed so long since and that no information should have been received of them from any quarter.

Some victuallers intended for the fleet upon its return to Torbay have been sent to us here. I have sent some of them down under the charge of the Dasher sloop to Sir Edward Pellew and, having cleared the remainder, they are escorted to Plymouth by the Unicorn, which ship is in want of stores and some repairs.

831.   *Commander William Parker[1] to Cornwallis*

Stork, at sea, 14 May 1801

I beg to inform you that on the 26th of April 1801 in the afternoon we chased several chasse marées that were standing over from Croizic towards Ponerf but were only enabled to capture two, one light, the other loaded with bread and flour who had been run on shore after dark near the batteries at Ponerf but was brought off by the boats without resistance.

---

[1]Sir William Parker (d. 1866). Lieutenant 1799; Commander 1799; Captain 1801; Rear-admiral 1830; Vice-admiral 1841; Admiral 1851.

Conceiving we might decoy some of the enemy's vessels into our hands before they were aware of the deception I armed the light chasse marée and sent fourteen seamen, four marines and the surgeon's mate, under the command of Mr. Wilson, the Master, to look out in shore.

In the morning at daybreak she took another small chasse marée with bread and flour but unfortunately strayed out of our sight, the weather becoming excessively hazy and inclinable to calm and we were detained all morning off the Point St. Jacks to obstruct the passage of a convoy of chasse marées.

I am concerned to say the enemy discovered their situation from the Morbihan and two rowing boats with small cannon, full of men, were sent out after them – nor did we perceive any of the vessels until the commencing of firing and we had the mortification to see them taken possession of and towed into the Morbihan before we could get near enough to be of any assistance. I sent a flag of truce in the following day to obtain an exchange of prisoners but without being able to receive any of them. This loss becomes greater as the party consisted of some of the very best men belonging to the Stork.

832.   *Gambier to Spencer*

Neptune, at sea, Ushant light house 7 or 8 leagues, 6 June 1801

Your Lordship knows pretty accurately the spot upon which we usually cruise here – we are generally from five to ten leagues distant from Ushant – never so near as you may remember the fleet was accustomed to be when under the command of Lord St. Vincent, though always near enough for the purpose for which we are here, as the two frigates stationed within Ushant keep a good watch upon the enemy and two or three decked ships between them and the fleet keep the communications to the commander-in-chief, who no doubt knows how matters go on as far as can be known by sight in Brest. I understand the last report states the French ships to be eight of the line and the Spanish nine, all apparently perfectly ready for sea, and though the French government gives out that they are to put to sea we are not so sanguine in our expectations as to think they will meet us under the disadvantages of a combined force of two nations.

833. *Cornwallis to Admiralty*

Ville de Paris, off Ushant, 21 July 1801

I request you will be pleased to state to the Lords Commissioners of the Admiralty in return to that part of the intelligence sent to me by their direction 'that convoys have passed uninterruptedly and landed at Benardet [Bénodet]', Captains Rowley and Gage,[1] who are just come from their stations upon that part of the coast declare to me that it is not true and that no convoys have passed them. Perhaps it would be impossible to answer for a single chasse marée sometimes getting close along within the rocks but they both separately have told me that the enemy have lately made a canal which enables them to get their provisions with greater ease to Brest now than formerly.

I have, however, given the most positive directions to all the ships stationed along shore to keep the most diligent lookout and that the commanders will be answerable for any omission in that very material part of their duty.

834. *Cornwallis to Admiralty*

Ville de Paris, off Ushant, 27 July 1801

The morning of the 22nd two line of battle ships with a large frigate stood out of Brest. A signal was made to me that they had anchored in one of the bays. I therefore stood early in the morning to the entrance of the harbour to see whether anything could be done with them but they weighed as soon as the tide would serve and worked into the harbour. It, however, gave me an opportunity of seeing the state of those ships. They appeared to be very ill equipped, the topsails of one of them seemed out of proportion to the yards, the ropes were constantly giving way and the jib of the other was split across, which remained in the same state.

From these observations, if they should play any more tricks of that kind, it seemed to me that there is a chance of catching them before they get back. I have therefore directed Rear Admiral Thornbrough, who has three line of battle ships, besides the frigates, to take every opportunity of doing so without exposing the ships to the batteries unless there is a prospect of success and I have stationed Vice Admiral

---

[1] Sir William Hall Gage (d. 1864). Lieutenant 1796; Captain 1797; Rear-admiral 1821; Vice-admiral 1837; Admiral 1846.

Sir Andrew Mitchell[1] with five line of battle ships further out than the Rear Admiral to keep up a communication with me and still to be in a situation to support the ships more advanced should the enemy reinforce any they may send out in consequence of the first being attacked.

We had at the same time a very good view of the ships in Brest Road, which did not differ from what we have before seen. If, therefore, the intelligence received is correct there must be several ships hid from our sight and that there are more than we can see was confirmed by James Hamon, the pilot of the Immortalité, who some time since was four nights and days in the harbour and came off again in a French boat that he seized. He is a most daring man and is very deserving of encouragement.

835. *Gambier to Spencer*

Neptune, off Ushant, 25 August 1801

We detach three ships at a time to Cawsand Bay to replenish but there are not enough to bring the turns to the different ships so soon as they should go into port. Several of them have been more than twenty-one weeks at sea. The men are, I believe, all in good health. We have not a man sick in this ship, which would not be the case if we were in port as they would have opportunities of getting at liquor and other indulgences and debaucheries that they are out of the way of at sea. While the weather continues fine we are best at sea but it is dull work.

836. *Commander James Coutts Crawford to Cornwallis*

Childers, off Ushant, 14 September 1801

Having been detached by Sir Edward Pellew to cruise in the Portuis Breton, I discovered in the morning of the 11th instant a small convoy of the enemy's vessels making for Les Sables d'Olonne. I immediately chased them but could not arrive up with them before they got under the batteries of that place; however, I captured one brig, drove another onshore on the rocks and made them abandon six chasses marées. I could do no more. The heavy fire from the batteries, together with a gun brig and three armed luggers, and the shore lined with troops

[1]Sir Andrew Mitchell (1757–1806). Lieutenant 1777; Captain 1778; Rear-admiral 1795; Vice-admiral 1799; Admiral 1805. He commanded the naval support force at the Helder in 1799 and was knighted in 1800; Commander-in-Chief North America from 1802.

prevented me from taking possession and bringing them off. The brig I have brought off is laden with cannon, shot, nails, etc. The Childers has received two 42 pounders besides other shot in her hull, the masts and yards not damaged and I am happy to say only one man wounded.

837.   *Cornwallis to Admiralty*

Belleisle, off Ushant, 8 October 1801

You will be pleased to inform their Lordships that I yesterday received a message by a flag of truce from the French admiral commanding in chief at Brest communicating to me an account of the preliminaries of peace having been signed at London on the 1st instant and transmitting to me the enclosed telegraphic despatch to which I returned an answer agreeable to the enclosed copy.

[*Enclosures*]

837a.   *Commander-in-Chief at Brest to Cornwallis*

Dépêche Télégraphique. A 10 de la République Française, une et indivisible, la Paix a été signée à Londres le 9 Vendemiaire.

[*Translation*]

Telegram. At 10 of the French Republic, one and indivisible, the peace has been signed in London on the 9th Vendemiaire.

837b.   *Cornwallis to Commander-in-Chief at Brest*

Belleisle, off Ushant, 7 October 1801

Sir, I have received the honour of your very obliging message by a flag of truce communicating to me the account of the preliminaries of peace having been signed in London on the first of this month, on which happy event I beg leave to offer you my most sincere congratulations.

838.   *Admiralty to Victualling Board*

17 October 1801

Abstract of order

To discontinue the sending out bullocks for the supply of the Channel fleet.

839.   *Cornwallis to Admiralty*

Belleisle, at sea, 20 October 1801

I have received their Lordships' order of the 11th instant directing me immediately to abstain from all acts of hostility against the possessions and citizens of the French Republic and its allies; and if I should fall in with any French squadron or detached ships, or any squadron or detached ships of its allies, to notify by a flag of truce to the commander of such squadron or detached ships the exchange of the preliminary articles of peace and not make use of the force under my command unless (notwithstanding the aforesaid notification) such commander or commanders should prepare to attack me.

Also directing me to give the like orders to the captains and commanders of all His Majesty's ships and vessels under my command, with directions to them to communicate the same to the captains and commanders of all other British ships and vessels, etc., which they may fall in with.

To all which I shall pay immediate attention.

840.   *Cornwallis to Admiralty*

Belleisle, at sea, 25 October 1801

I received the 20th instant by the Halifax express boat their Lordships' orders of the 11th of this month – one marked secret – and the others most secret. The first, expressing the time limited for taking prizes (which has been communicated to the ships) and directing me to withdraw the ships under my command from their stations upon the French coast but to keep the squadron in a state of preparation for immediate service and for dividing them to the stations therein appointed, which has been done as far as it is possible at present and the ships with me would admit by detaching Vice Admiral Sir Andrew Mitchell with nine sail of the line, the rest to join as soon as they can, and the same will be duly attended to with regard to stationing of the other ships.

APPENDICES

APPENDICES

APPENDIX 1

LIST OF BRITISH SHIPS AND VESSELS MENTIONED IN THE TEXT[1]

	Guns	Built	
Achille	74	1798	
Admiral Mitchell	12		Hired cutter, 1800–1801.
Adventure	44	1784	
Agamemnon	64	1781	
Agincourt	64	1796	Built for the East India Company.
Aimable	32		French, captured 19 April 1782.
Ajax	74	1798	
Alarm	32	1758	
Alcmene	32	1794	
Alexander	74	1778	Captured by the French 1794; recaptured 23 June 1795.
Alfred	74	1778	
Amazon	36	1795	
Ambuscade	32	1773	
Amelia	38		French, captured 13 June 1796.
America	64	1777	
Amethyst	36	1799	
Amphitrite	28	1778	
Anson	64	1781	Reduced to a 44 in 1794.
Aquilon	32	1786	
Ardent	64	1796	Formerly an East India Company ship.
Arethusa	38	1781	
Argo	44	1781	
Argonaut	64		French, captured 1782.
Artois	38	1794	
Astrea	32	1781	
Atalante	16		French, captured 10 January 1797.
Atlas	98	1782	
Audacious	74	1785	
Aurora	28	1777	
Babet	20		French, captured 3 April 1794.
Barfleur	98	1768	
Beaulieu	40	1791	
Bedford	74	1775	
Belleisle	74		French, captured 23 June 1795.

[1]Data derived from the first volume of J.J. Colledge, *Ships of the Royal Navy* (2 vols, London, 1987); and from D. Lyon, *The Sailing Navy List* (London, 1993).

Bellerophon	74	1786	
Belliqueux	64	1780	
Bellona	74	1760	
Black Joke			Hired cutter, 1793–1800.
Blonde	32	1787	
Boadicea	38	1797	
Bridgewater	24	1744	
Brilliant	28	1779	
Brunswick	74	1790	
Caesar	80	1793	
Cambrian	40	1797	
Cambridge	80	1755	
Canada	74	1765	
Captain	74	1787	
Caroline	36	1795	
Centaur	74	1797	
Centurion	50	1774	
Charon	44	1783	Hospital ship, 1794–1800.
Chichester	44	1785	Storeship, 1799.
Childers	14	1778	
Cleopatra	32	1779	
Clyde	38	1796	
Colossus	74	1787	
Commerce de Marseille	120		French, captured 29 August 1793.
Concorde	36		French, captured 15 February 1783.
Constitution	14		Hired cutter, 1796–1801.
Courageous	32		French, captured 18 June 1799.
Courageux	74	1800	
Crescent	36	1784	
Culloden	74	1783	
Cumberland	74	1774	
Cyclops	28	1779	Troopship, March 1800.
Cygnet	12		Hired cutter, 1796–99.
Cynthia	18	1796	
Danae	20		French, captured 7 August 1798.
Dasher	18	1797	
Defence	74	1763	
Defiance	74	1783	
Diadem	64	1782	Troopship, May 1798.
Diamond	38	1794	
Diana	38	1794	
Diligence			Hired cutter, 1800.
Dolly	8		Hired cutter, 1796–1801.
Dolphin	12		Hired cutter, 1793–1801.
Doris	36	1795	
Dover	14		Hired cutter, 1794–1801.
Dragon	74	1798	
Druid	32	1783	
Duke	90	1777	
Duke of York	6		Hired cutter, 1796–1800.

Earl St Vincent	16		Hired cutter, 1799–1801.
Edgar	74	1779	
Elephant	74	1786	
Empress Mary	16		Storeship, purchased 1799.
Endymion	50	1797	
Enterprise	28	1774	
Ethalion	38	1797	
Europa	50	1783	Troopship, 1798.
Eurydice	24	1781	
Excellent	74	1787	
Explosion	12		Bomb vessel, purchased 1797.
Falcon	14	1782	Fireship, June 1800.
Fame	74	1759	
Fanny	16		Hired lugger, 1799–1801.
Fisgard	44		French, captured 9 March 1797.
Flora	36	1780	
Formidable	90	1777	
Fortitude	74	1780	
Fowey	14		Hired cutter, 1798–1800.
Galatea	32	1794	
Ganges	74	1782	
Gibraltar	80		Spanish, captured 16 March 1780.
Glory	90	1788	
Goliath	74	1781	
Greyhound	12		Hired cutter, 1798–99.
Hebe	38		French, captured September 1782.
Hector	74	1774	
Hindostan	54		Purchased from East India Co. 1795.
Hope	3		Gun vessel, purchased 1794.
Hope	12		Hired lugger, 1795–97.
Hussar	28	1784	
Illustrious	74	1789	Wrecked March 1795.
Immortalité	42		French, captured 20 October 1798.
Impetueux	74		French, captured 1 June 1794.
Impregnable	98	1789	
Incendiary	16	1782	Fireship
Inconstant	36	1783	
Indefatigable	64	1784	Reduced to 38 in 1795.
Invincible	74	1765	
Iphigenia	32	1780	
Iris	32	1783	
Irresistible	74	1782	
Isis	50	1774	
Jason	38	1794	
Joseph	12		Hired cutter, 1796–1801.
Juste	80		French, captured 1 June 1794.
Kangaroo	16	1795	
Lady Duncan	12		Hired lugger, 1798–1801.
Lady Jane	6		Hired cutter, 1795–1800.

Lascelles			Hired vessel, 1800–1801.
Latona	38	1781	
Leda	36	1783	
Leopard	50	1790	
Leviathan	74	1790	
Lion	64	1777	
Loire	40		French, captured 18 October 1798.
London	90	1766	
Lord Nelson	12		Hired cutter, 1798–1801.
Lurcher	12		Hired cutter, 1796–1801.
Magicienne	32		French, captured 2 September 1781.
Magnanime	64	1780	Reduced to 44 in 1795.
Magnificent	74	1766	
Majestic	74	1785	
Marlborough	74	1767	
Mars	74	1794	
Medusa	50	1785	
Megaera	14	1783	Fireship
Melampus	36	1785	
Melpomene	38		French, captured 10 August 1794.
Mercury	28	1779	
Mermaid	32	1784	
Minerve	38		French, captured 24 June 1795.
Minotaur	74	1793	
Monarch	74	1783	
Mondovi	16		French, captured 13 May 1798.
Monmouth	64	1796	Laid down for East India Company.
Montagu	74	1779	
Naiad	38	1797	
Namur	90	1756	
Nassau	64	1785	
Neptune	98	1797	
Nereide	36		French, captured 20 December 1797.
Niger	33	1759	
Nimrod			Hired cutter, 1794–1802.
Northumberland	74	1798	
Nymphe	36		French, captured 10 August 1780.
Oiseau	36		French, captured 18 January 1793.
Orion	74	1787	
Pallas	32	1793	
Penelope			Hired cutter, 1795–99.
Penelope	32	1783	
Perseus	20	1776	
Phaeton	38	1782	
Phoebe	36	1795	
Phoenix	36	1783	
Pique	38		French, captured 6 January 1795.
Polyphemus	64	1782	

Pomone	44		French, captured 23 April 1794.
Pompee	80		French, captured 28 August 1793.
Porcupine	24	1777	
Powerful	74	1783	
Prestwood	6		Hired cutter, 1793–1801.
Prince	90	1788	
Prince George	90	1772	
Prince of Wales	98	1794	
Princess Royal	90	1773	
Proserpine	28	1777	
Queen	98	1769	
Queen Charlotte	100	1790	
Railleur	20		French, captured 17 November 1797
Raisonnable	64	1768	
Ramillies	74	1785	
Rattler	10		Hired cutter, 1793–96.
Raven	14	1796	
Renown	74	1798	
Repulse	64	1780	
Resolution	74	1770	
Revolutionaire	38		French, captured 21 October 1794.
Robust	74	1764	
Rose	10		Hired cutter, 1794–1800.
Royal George	100	1788	
Royal Sovereign	100	1786	
Royal William	100	1692	Rebuilt 1719 as an 84. Guardship.
Ruby	64	1776	
Russell	74	1764	
St Albans	64	1764	
St Fiorenzo	38		French, captured 19 February 1794.
St George	98	1785	
San Joseph	114		Spanish, captured 14 February 1797.
Sandwich	98	1759	Receiving ship.
Sans Pareil	80		French, captured 1 June 1794.
Saturn	74	1786	
Sceptre	64	1781	
Scourge	22		French, captured 15 January 1796.
Sheerness	44	1787	
Sirius	36	1797	
Speedwell	14		Hired cutter, 1797–1801.
Spencer	74	1800	
Spitfire			French schooner, captured 1798.
Stag	32	1794	
Standard	64	1782	
Stork	18	1796	
Success	32	1781	
Suffolk	74	1765	

Sulphur	8		Bomb vessel, purchased April 1797.
Superb	74	1798	
Surprise	24		French, captured 20 April 1796.
Suwarrow			Hired schooner.
Swallow	18	1795	
Swan	14		Hired cutter, 1799–1801.
Swiftsure	74	1787	
Sylph	18	1795	
Telemachus	14		Hired cutter, 1796–1801.
Temeraire	98	1798	
Terrible	74	1785	
Thalia	36	1782	
Thames	32	1758	
Theseus	74	1786	
Thetis	38	1782	
Thisbc	28	1783	
Thunderer	74	1783	
Tigre	80		French, captured 23 June 1795.
Trent	36	1796	
Triton	32	1796	
Triumph	74	1764	
Unicorn	32	1794	
Unité	38		French, captured 1 April 1796.
Uranie	38		French, captured 5 January 1797.
Valiant	74	1759	
Valiant	11		Hired lugger, 1794–1801.
Venerable	74	1784	
Veteran	64	1787	
Ville de Paris	110	1795	
Viper	14		Cutter, purchased January 1797.
Virginie	38		French, captured 3 April 1796.
Volcano	8		Bomb vessel, purchased March 1797.
Warrior	74	1781	
Winchelsea	32	1764	
Windsor Castle	98	1790	

APPENDIX 2

LIST OF DOCUMENTS AND SOURCES

The documents used in this volume are to be found in the Public Record Office, the National Maritime Museum and the British Library.

Public Record Office

Admiralty In-letters	ADM. 1/100–120
	ADM. 1/393
	ADM. 1/6034
Admiralty Out-letters	ADM. 2/132–3
	ADM. 2/626–7
	ADM. 2/943–9
	ADM. 2/1003
	ADM. 2/1346–9
Admiralty Minutes	ADM. 3/136
Admirals' Journals	ADM. 50/124
Sick and Wounded Board Out-letters	ADM. 98/20

National Maritime Museum

Admiralty In-letters from Victualling Board	ADM. D/39–43
Admiralty In-letters from Sick and Wounded Board	ADM. F/25–31
Victualling Board In-letters	ADM. G/791–2
Papers of the Honourable Sir William Cornwallis	COR/3–4, 7, 11.
Papers of Charles Middleton, first Baron Barham	MID/1/140, 14/24.

British Library

Log of HMS Russell	Add. Mss. 22113
Papers of John Jervis, Earl of St Vincent	Add. Mss. 31163–4, 31167
Papers of Alexander Hood, Viscount Bridport	Add. Mss. 34933, 35194–210
Papers of William Windham	Add. Mss. 37844, 37866
Papers of Henry Dundas, first Viscount Melville	Add. Mss. 40102, 41079
Papers of George Spencer, second Earl Spencer	Althorp Papers

At the time this volume was being compiled the Althorp Papers were in the class of unbound manuscripts in the British Library. Detailed specific reference therefore seemed unwise. They are, however, so well indexed that finding a specific document should present no problems. The odd letter which was out of place is specified.

At the National Maritime Museum, Cornwallis Papers which remain unused, but which will throw more light on the management of the Channel fleet by the Honourable Sir William Cornwallis in 1801–2, include COR/8, 34, 38–9, 44–6.

Numerical list of documents used in this volume

No.	Description	Date	Reference
I	THE CHANNEL FLEET		
1	Admiralty to Alexander Hood	12 June 1793	Add. Mss. 35194
2	Admiralty to Howe	3 July 1793	ADM. 2/1346
3	Admiralty to Howe	13 August 1793	ADM. 2/1346
4	Admiralty to Howe	12 October 1793	ADM. 2/1346
5	Admiralty to Howe	11 December 1793	ADM. 2/1346
6	Admiralty to Howe	17 April 1794	ADM. 2/1347
7	Howe to Admiralty	18 April 1794	ADM. 1/100
8	Howe to Admiralty	23 April 1794	ADM. 1/100
9	Admiralty to Howe	21 May 1794	ADM. 2/1347
10	Admiralty to Montagu	2 June 1794	ADM. 2/1347
11	Howe to Admiralty	2 June 1794	*The Times*, 12 June 1794

12	Admiralty to Montagu	3 June 1794	ADM. 2/1347
13	Occurrences at Plymouth	12 June 1794	*The Times*, 16 June 1794
14	Occurrences at Portsmouth	13 June 1794	*The Times*, 16 June 1794
15	Occurrences at Plymouth	14 June 1794	*The Times*, 17 June 1794
16	Occurrences at Portsmouth	15 June 1794	*The Times*, 17 June 1794
17	Admiralty to Howe	14 June 1794	ADM. 2/1347
18	Middleton to Patton	27 June 1794	MID/1/140
19	Middleton draft memorandum	June 1794	MID/10/3
20	Alexander Hood to Chatham	5 July 1794	Add. Mss. 35195
21	Middleton to Dundas	26 July 1794	Add. Mss. 41079
22	Middleton to Dundas	Undated	Add. Mss. 41079
23	Middleton to Dundas	10 December 1794	Add. Mss. 41079
24	Howe to Spencer	17 December 1794	Althorp Mss.
25	Spencer to Howe	25 December 1794	Althorp Mss.
26	Howe to Spencer	26 December 1794	Althorp Mss.
27	Admiralty to Bridport	26 December 1794	Add. Mss. 35195
28	Bridport to Admiralty	28 December 1794	Add. Mss. 35195
29	Howe to Spencer	28 December 1794	Althorp Mss.
30	George III to Spencer	6 January 1795	Althorp Mss.
31	George III to Spencer	8 January 1795	Althorp Mss.
32	Spencer to Bridport	10 January 1795	Add. Mss. 35195
33	Bridport to Spencer	11 January 1795	Add. Mss. 35195
34	Howe to Admiralty	22 January 1795	ADM. 1/102
35	Lord Hood to Bridport	26 January [1795]	Add. Mss. 35199 (Misplaced)
36	Howe to Admiralty	27 January 1795	ADM. 1/102
37	Howe to Admiralty	1 February 1795	ADM. 1/102
38	Howe to Spencer	8 February 1795	Althorp Mss.
39	Spencer to Howe	11 February 1795	Althorp Mss.
40	Seymour to Spencer	11 February 1795	Althorp Mss.
41	Spencer to Gardner	23 February 1795	Althorp Mss.
42	Howe to Bridport	28 February 1795	COR/4
43	Warren to Admiralty	2 March 1795	ADM. 1/102
44	Powlett to Colpoys	14 April 1795	ADM. 1/102
45	Warren to Admiralty	24 April 1795	ADM. 1/102
46	Lord Hood to Admiralty	28 April 1795	ADM. 1/393
47	Seymour to Spencer	3 May 1795	Althorp Mss.
48	Seymour to Spencer	4 May 1795	Althorp Mss.
49	Seymour to Spencer	9 May 1795	Althorp Mss.
50	Seymour to Spencer	12 May 1795	Althorp Mss.
51	Dr Trotter to Howe	15 May 1795	ADM. 1/102
52	Admiralty to Bridport	27 May 1795	Add. Mss. 35195
53	S. & W. Board to Admiralty	27 May 1795	ADM. F/25
54	S. & W. Board to Admiralty	5 June 1795	ADM. F/26

II   THE BLOCKADE INITIATED

55	Admiralty to Howe	6 June 1795	Add. Mss. 35195
56	Howe to Bridport	7 June 1795	Add. Mss. 35195
57	Admiralty to Bridport	9 June 1795	Add. Mss. 35195
58	Spencer to Bridport	10 June 1795	Add. Mss. 35195
59	Seymour to Spencer	10 June 1795	Althorp Mss.
60	Seymour to Spencer	10 June 1795	Althorp Mss.
61	George Fox to Admiralty	16 June 1795	Add. Mss. 35195
62	Warren to Bridport	17 June 1795	Add. Mss. 35195
63	Admiralty to Bridport	19 June 1795	Add. Mss. 35195
64	Warren to Bridport	19 June 1795	Add. Mss. 35195
65	Log of HMS Russell	22–23 June 1795	Add. Mss. 22113
66	Seymour to Spencer	24 June 1795	Althorp Mss.
67	Gardner to Bridport	24 June 1795	Add. Mss. 35195
68	Spencer to Bridport	29 June 1795	Add. Mss. 35195
69	Warren to Bridport	3 July 1795	Add. Mss. 35196
70	Howe to Bridport	5 July 1795	Add. Mss. 35196
71	Palliser to Bridport	6 July 1795	Add. Mss. 35196
72	Bridport to Spencer	7 July 1795	Althorp Mss.
73	Seymour to Spencer	8 July 1795	Althorp Mss.
74	Admiralty to Bridport	9 July 1795	Add. Mss. 35196
75	Spencer to Sidney Smith	11 July 1795	Althorp Mss.
76	Sidney Smith to Spencer	13 July 1795	Althorp Mss.
77	Admiralty to Bridport	14 July 1795	Add. Mss. 35196
78	Spencer to Bridport	14 July 1795	Add. Mss. 35196
79	Gardner to Bridport	20 July 1795	Add. Mss. 35196
80	Sidney Smith to Spencer	21 July 1795	Althorp Mss.
81	Sidney Smith to Spencer	22 July 1795	Althorp Mss.
82	Howe to Spencer	24 July 1795	Althorp Mss.
83	Spencer to Howe	24 July 1795	Althorp Mss.
84	Admiralty to Warren	27 July 1795	Add. Mss. 35196
85	George III to Spencer	27 July 1795	Althorp Mss.
86	Spencer to George III	[27 July 1795]	Althorp Mss.
87	George III to Spencer	28 July 1795	Althorp Mss.
88	Seymour to Spencer	28 July 1795	Althorp Mss.
89	Admiralty to Bridport	29 July 1795	Add. Mss. 35196
90	Admiralty to Bridport	31 July 1795	Add. Mss. 35196
91	Spencer to Bridport	31 July 1795	Add. Mss. 35196
92	Buckingham to Bridport	1 August 1795	Add. Mss. 35196
93	Abstract of sick returns	8 August 1795	Add. Mss. 35196
94	Bridport to Spencer	9 August 1795	Add. Mss. 35196
95	Admiralty to Bridport	10 August 1795	Add. Mss. 35196
96	Spencer to Bridport	15 August 1795	Add. Mss. 35196
97	Spencer to George III	15 August 1795	Althorp Mss.
98	George III to Spencer	16 August 1795	Althorp Mss.
99	Seymour to Spencer	18 August 1795	Althorp Mss.
100	Bridport to Admiralty	19 August 1795	Althorp Mss.
101	Bridport to Admiralty	24 August 1795	Add. Mss. 35196
102	Bridport to Admiralty	24 August 1795	ADM. 1/103

103	Abstract of sick returns	24 August 1795	Add. Mss. 35196
104	Seymour to Spencer	24 August 1795	Althorp Mss.
105	Bridport to Admiralty	26 August 1795	ADM. 1/103
106	Seymour to Spencer	29 August 1795	Althorp Mss.
107	Gardner to Bridport	29 August 1795	Add. Mss. 35196
108	Victualling Board to Warren	29 August 1795	Add. Mss. 35196
109	Admiralty to Bridport	30 August 1795	Add. Mss. 35196
110	J. Stewart to S. & W. Board	31 August 1795	ADM. F/26
111	Admiralty to Bridport	1 September 1795	Add. Mss. 35196
112	Warren to Bridport	3 September 1795	Add. Mss. 35196
113	Warren to Bridport	4 September 1795	Add. Mss. 35196
114	Cornwallis to Bridport	6 September 1795	Add. Mss. 35196
115	Sidney Smith to Spencer	12 September 1795	Althorp Mss.
116	Bridport to Howe	15 September 1795	Add. Mss. 35196
117	Bridport to Admiralty	19 September 1795	Add. Mss. 35196
118	George III to Spencer	19 September 1795	Althorp Mss.
119	Abstract of sick returns	September 1795	Add. Mss. 35196

III   THE LOGISTICAL PROBLEMS

120	Log of HMS Russell	2–3 October 1795	Add. Mss. 22113
121	Seymour to Bridport	8 October 1795	Add. Mss. 35196
122	Spencer to Bridport	20 October 1795	Althorp Mss. (Misplaced with correspondence for 1798)
123	Bridport to Spencer	22 October 1795	Althorp Mss.
124	S. & W. Board to Admiralty	9 December 1795	ADM. F/26
125	S. & W. Board to Admiralty	1 January 1796	ADM. F/26
126	Harvey to Bridport	3 January 1796	Add. Mss. 35197
127	Seymour to Spencer	4 January 1796	Althorp Mss.
128	Harvey to Admiralty	5 January 1796	ADM. 1/105
129	Seymour to Spencer	6 January 1796	Althorp Mss.
130	Dr Blair to Admiralty	4 February 1796	ADM. F/26
131	S. & W. Board to Admiralty	16 February 1796	ADM. F/26
132	Spencer to Gardner	25 February 1796	Althorp Mss.
133	S. & W. Board to Admiralty	11 March 1796	ADM. F/26
134	Spencer to Hood	20 March 1796	Althorp Mss.
135	George III to Spencer	23 March 1796	Althorp Mss.
136	Warren to Admiralty	24 March 1796	ADM. 1/105
137	Admiralty to Vict. Board	29 March 1796	ADM. G/791
138	Gardner to Spencer	30 March 1796	Althorp Mss.
139	Colpoys to Admiralty	14 May 1796	ADM. 1/105
140	Seymour to Spencer	14 May 1796	Althorp Mss.
141	Keats to Warren	19 May 1796	ADM. 1/105
142	S. & W. Board to Admiralty	25 May 1796	ADM. F/27
143	Vict. Board to Admiralty	27 May 1796	ADM. D/40
144	Vict. Board to Admiralty	15 June 1796	ADM. D/40
145	Vict. Board to Admiralty	6 September 1796	ADM. D/40
146	Gardner to Spencer	16 September 1796	Althorp Mss.

147	Spencer to Gardner	23 September 1796	Althorp Mss.
148	Admiralty to Gardner	7 October 1796	ADM. 2/943
149	Bridport to Spencer	24 October 1796	Althorp Mss.
150	Spencer to Bridport	26 October 1796	Add. Mss. 35197
151	Vict. Board to Admiralty	8 November 1796	ADM. D/40
152	S. & W. Board to Admiralty	21 November 1796	ADM. F/27
153	Spencer to Bridport	5 December 1796	Add. Mss. 35197
154	Colpoys to Spencer	7 December 1796	Althorp Mss.
155	Colpoys to Spencer	11 December 1796	Althorp Mss.
156	Spencer to Bridport	19 December 1796	Althorp Mss.
157	Bridport to Spencer	20 December 1796	Althorp Mss.

IV   TOWARDS A SYSTEM

158	Admiralty to Bridport	20 December 1796	ADM. 2/1351
159	Bridport to Admiralty	21 December 1796	Add. Mss. 35197
160	Admiralty to Bridport	22 December 1796	ADM. 2/1351
161	Admiralty to Bridport	24 December 1796	ADM. 2/1351
162	Bridport to Admiralty	24 December 1796	Add. Mss 35197
163	Admiralty to Kingsmill	24 December 1796	ADM. 2/1351
164	Seymour to Spencer	27 December 1796	Althorp Mss.
165	Seymour to Spencer	29 December 1796	Althorp Mss.
166	Warren to Spencer	30 December 1796	Althorp Mss.
167	Seymour to Spencer	31 December 1796	Althorp Mss.
168	Admiralty to Bridport	31 December 1796	ADM. 2/1351
169	Admiralty to Bridport	31 December 1796	ADM. 2/1351
170	Admiralty to Colpoys	31 December 1796	ADM. 2/943
171	Admiralty to Bridport	1 January 1797	ADM. 2/1352
172	Spencer to Warren	2 January 1797	Althorp Mss.
173	Bridport to Spencer	3 January 1797	Althorp Mss.
174	Warren to Spencer	12 January 1797	Althorp Mss.
175	Seymour to Spencer	16 January 1797	Althorp Mss.
176	Admiralty to Bridport	28 January 1797	ADM. 2/1352
177	Admiralty to Bridport	28 January 1797	ADM. 2/1352
178	Seymour to Spencer	1 February 1797	Althorp Mss.
179	Bridport to Spencer	3 February 1797	Althorp Mss.
180	Admiralty to Miles	21 February 1797	ADM. 2/1352
181	Admiralty to Bridport	25 February 1797	ADM. 2/1352
182	Admiralty to Bridport	26 February 1797	ADM. 2/1352
183	Admiralty to Bridport	26 February 1797	ADM. 2/132
184	Bridport to Spencer	28 February 1797	Althorp Mss.
185	Spencer to Bridport	1 March 1797	Althorp Mss.
186	Bridport to Spencer	10 March 1797	Althorp Mss.
187	Spencer to Warren	10 March 1797	Althorp Mss.
188	Pellew to Spencer	10 March 1797	Althorp Mss.
189	Spencer to Pellew	14 March 1797	Althorp Mss.
190	Warren to Admiralty	14 March 1797	ADM. 1/107
191	Pellew to Spencer	18 March 1797	Althorp Mss.
192	Warren to Spencer	24 March 1797	Althorp Mss.
193	Spencer to Pellew	28 March 1797	Althorp Mss.

194	Bridport to Spencer	30 March 1797	Althorp Mss.
195	Spencer to Bridport	31 March 1797	Althorp Mss.
196	Seymour to Spencer	2 April 1797	Althorp Mss.
197	Bridport to Spencer	13 April 1797	Althorp Mss.

V THE SPITHEAD MUTINY

198	Bridport to Spencer	13 April 1797	ADM. 1/107
199	Spencer to Bridport	14 April 1797	ADM. 3/136
200	Admiralty to Bridport	15 April 1797	ADM. 3/136
201	Admiralty to Bridport	15 April 1797	ADM. 2/133
202	Bridport to Spencer	15 April 1797	Althorp Mss.
203	Bridport to Admiralty	15 April 1797	ADM. 1/107
204	Bridport to Admiralty	16 April 1797	ADM. 1/107
205	Admiralty to Bridport	16 April 1797	ADM. 3/136
206	Bridport to Admiralty	16 April 1797	ADM. 1/107
207	Bridport to Admiralty	17 April 1797	ADM. 1/107
208	Admiralty to Bridport	17 April 1797	ADM. 3/136
209	Bridport to Admiralty	17 April 1797	ADM. 1/107
210	Windham to Spencer	17 April 1797	Althorp Mss.
211	Admiralty to Bridport	18 April 1797	ADM. 2/943
212	Board of Admiralty minutes	18–21 April 1797	ADM. 3/136
213	Keats to Warren	21 April 1797	ADM. 1/107
214	Bridport to Spencer	22 April 1797	Althorp Mss.
215	Delegates to Bridport	[22 April 1797]	Add. Mss. 35197
216	Spencer to Bridport	22 April 1797	Althorp Mss.
217	Bridport to Spencer	23 April 1797	Althorp Mss.
218	Spencer to Bridport	24 April 1797	Althorp Mss.
219	Bridport to Spencer	24 April 1797	Althorp Mss.
220	Admiralty to Bridport	24 April 1797	ADM. 2/943
221	Spencer to Bridport	25 April 1797	Althorp Mss.
222	Bridport to Spencer	26 April 1797	Althorp Mss.
223	Spencer to Bridport	28 April 1797	Althorp Mss.
224	Bridport to Admiralty	1 May 1797	ADM 1/107
225	Spencer to Kingsmill	4 May 1797	Althorp Mss.
226	Spencer to Bridport	4 May 1797	Althorp Mss.
227	Bridport to Spencer	5 May 1797	Althorp Mss.
228	Spencer to Bridport	6 May 1797	Althorp Mss.
229	Bridport to Spencer	7 May 1797	Althorp Mss.
230	Bridport to Admiralty	7 May 1797	ADM. 1/107
231	Bridport to Admiralty	8 May 1797	ADM. 1/107
232	Spencer to Bridport	8 May 1797	Althorp Mss.
233	Admiralty to Bridport	9 May 1797	ADM. 2/943
234	Bridport to Admiralty	9 May 1797	ADM. 1/107
235	Bridport to Spencer	[19 May 1797?]	Althorp Mss.
236	Admiralty to Curtis	9 May 1797	ADM. 2/1352
237	Admiralty to Bridport	10 May 1797	ADM. 2/943
238	Spencer to Bridport	10 May 1797	Althorp Mss.
239	Spencer to Howe	10 May 1797	Althorp Mss.
240	Bridport to Pitt	11 May 1797	Add. Mss. 35197

241	Howe to Spencer	11 May 1797	Althorp Mss.
242	Vict. Board to Admiralty	11 May 1797	ADM. D/40
243	Bridport to Admiralty	13 May 1797	ADM. 1/107
244	Chatham to Bridport	13 May 1797	Add. Mss. 35197
245	Admiralty to Bridport	13 May 1797	ADM. 2/1352
246	Admiralty to Bridport	13 May 1797	ADM. 2/1352
247	Spencer to Bridport	14 May 1797	Althorp Mss.
248	Admiralty to Bridport	14 May 1797	ADM. 2/1352
249	Delegates to Bridport	14 May 1797	Add. Mss. 35197
250	Spencer to Bridport	14 May 1797	Althorp Mss.
251	Bridport to Spencer	15 May 1797	Althorp Mss.

VI   THE GROWTH OF CENTRAL CONTROL

252	Admiralty to Bridport	15 May 1797	ADM. 2/1352
253	Admiralty to Orde	20 May 1797	ADM. 2/1352
254	Admiralty to Bridport	27 May 1797	ADM. 2/943
255	Admiralty to Bridport	10 June 1797	ADM. 2/1352
256	Admiralty to Bridport	10 June 1797	ADM. 2/1352
257	Admiralty to Bridport	11 June 1797	ADM. 2/1352
258	Bridport to Spencer	18 June 1797	Althorp Mss.
259	Admiralty to Bridport	20 June 1797	ADM. 2/943
260	Vict. Board to Admiralty	21 June 1797	ADM. D/40
261	Alexander Hood to Bridport	26 June 1797	Add. Mss. 35197
262	Spencer to Bridport	29 June 1797	Althorp Mss.
263	Bridport to Spencer	30 June 1797	Althorp Mss.
264	Spencer to Bridport	2 July 1797	Althorp Mss.
265	S. & W. Board to Admiralty	4 July 1797	ADM. F/28
266	Bridport to Admiralty	5 July 1797	ADM. 1/108
267	Bridport to Admiralty	14 July 1797	ADM. 1/108
268	Bridport to Admiralty	15 July 1797	ADM. 1/108
269	Warren to Bridport	18 July 1797	Add. Mss. 35198
270	Keith to Spencer	20 July 1797	Althorp Mss.
271	Warren to Bridport	24 July 1797	Add. Mss. 35198
272	Gore to Warren	24 July 1797	ADM. 1/108
273	Bridport to Spencer	27 July 1797	Althorp Mss.
274	Admiralty to Bridport	29 July 1797	ADM. 2/944
275	Spencer to Keith	30 July 1797	Althorp Mss.
276	Spencer to Bridport	30 July 1797	Althorp Mss.
277	Pellew to Admiralty	30 July 1797	ADM. 1/108
278	Nagle to Warren	31 July 1797	ADM. 1/108
279	Bridport to Spencer	6 August 1797	Althorp Mss.
280	Bridport to Admiralty	8 August 1797	ADM. 1/108
281	Pellew to Bridport	8 August 1797	Add. Mss. 35198
282	Bridport to Admiralty	9 August 1797	ADM. 1/108
283	Bridport to Admiralty	13 August 1797	ADM. 1/108
284	Admiralty to Bridport	16 August 1797	ADM. 2/944
285	Bridport to Admiralty	16 August 1797	ADM. 1/108
286	Bridport to Admiralty	20 August 1797	ADM. 1/108
287	Pellew to Spencer	25 August 1797	Althorp Mss.

288	Spencer to Pellew	28 August 1797	Althorp Mss.
289	Admiralty to Bridport	30 August 1797	ADM. 2/944
290	Admiralty to Bridport	2 September 1797	ADM 2/1352
291	Duckworth to Bridport	3 September 1797	Add. Mss. 35198
292	Admiralty to Bridport	8 September 1797	ADM. 2/944
293	Nepean to Spencer	11 September 1797	Althorp Mss.
294	Admiralty to Bridport	13 September 1797	ADM. 2/944
295	Bridport to Admiralty	14 September 1797	ADM. 1/108
296	Spencer to Bridport	18 September 1797	Althorp Mss.
297	Spencer to Warren	22 September 1797	Althorp Mss.
298	Windham to Spencer	14 October 1797	Althorp Mss.
299	Admiralty to Bridport	11 November 1797	Add. Mss. 35198
300	Bridport to Spencer	14 November 1797	Althorp Mss.
301	Keith to Bridport	25 November 1797	Add. Mss. 35198
302	Admiralty to Curtis	29 November 1797	Add. Mss. 35198
303	Admiralty to Bridport	29 November 1797	ADM. 2/944
304	White to Bridport	2 December 1797	Add. Mss. 35198
305	Hall to Spencer	2 December 1797	Althorp Mss.
306	Cherry to Spencer	20 December 1797	ADM. D/40
307	Curtis to Admiralty	31 December 1797	ADM. 1/108
308	Admiralty to Bridport	2 January 1798	Add. Mss. 35198
309	Bridport to Admiralty	5 January 1798	ADM. 1/109
310	Thompson to Admiralty	13 January 1798	ADM. 1/109
311	Thompson to Admiralty	14 January 1798	ADM 1/109
312	Thompson to Admiralty	16 January 1798	ADM. 1/109
313	Thompson to Admiralty	22 January 1798	ADM. 1/109
314	White to Bridport	23 January 1798	Add. Mss. 35198
315	Thompson to Admiralty	25 January 1798	ADM. 1/109
316	Spencer to Keith	15 February 1798	Althorp Mss.
317	Spencer to Keith	19 February 1798	Althorp Mss.
318	Bridport to Spencer	4 March 1798	Add. Mss. 35199
319	Spencer to Bridport	5 March 1798	Add. Mss. 35199
320	Bridport to Spencer	6 March 1798	Add. Mss. 35199
321	Spencer to Bridport	9 March 1798	Add. Mss. 35199
322	Warren to Admiralty	14 March 1798	ADM. 1/109
323	Bridport to Spencer	21 March 1798	Althorp Mss.
324	Spencer to Bridport	23 March 1798	Althorp Mss.
325	Bridport to Spencer	31 March 1798	Althorp Mss.
326	Spencer to Bridport	1 April 1798	Althorp Mss.
327	Spencer to Bridport	7 April 1798	Althorp Mss.
328	Spencer to Bridport	9 April 1798	Althorp Mss.
329	Comptroller to Spencer	13 April 1798	Althorp Mss.
330	Admiralty to Bridport	15 April 1798	ADM. 2/1353
331	Bridport to Spencer	18 April 1798	Althorp Mss.
332	Bridport to Admiralty	22 April 1798	Add. Mss. 35199
333	Seymour to Spencer	25 April 1798	Althorp Mss.
334	Spencer to Bridport	1 May 1798	Althorp Mss.
335	Spencer to Bridport	1 May 1798	Althorp Mss.
336	Bridport to Admiralty	4 May 1798	ADM. 1/109
337	Seymour to Spencer	15 May 1798	Althorp Mss.

338	Admiralty to Bridport	15 May 1798	ADM. 2/1353
339	Bridport to Spencer	17 May 1798	Althorp Mss.
340	Admiralty to Bridport	17 May 1798	ADM. 2/945
341	Spencer to Bridport	19 May 1798	Add. Mss. 35199

VII   THE FRENCH EXPEDITIONS TO IRELAND

342	St Vincent to Spencer	28 May 1798	Althorp Mss.
343	Admiralty to Bridport	31 May 1798	ADM. 2/1353
344	Bridport to Admiralty	31 May 1798	ADM. 1/109
345	Spencer to Camden	4 June 1798	Althorp Mss.
346	Admiralty to Bridport	5 June 1798	ADM. 2/945
347	Stopford to Gardner	5 June 1798	Add. Mss. 35199
348	Bridport to Admiralty	11 June 1798	ADM. 1/109
349	Bridport to Admiralty	11 June 1798	ADM. 1/109
350	Bridport to Spencer	19 June 1798	Althorp Mss.
351	Bridport to Admiralty	28 June 1798	ADM. 1/109
352	Bridport to Admiralty	2 July 1798	Add. Mss. 35199
353	Bridport to Admiralty	5 July 1798	ADM. 1/110
354	Bridport to Admiralty	11 July 1798	ADM. 1/110
355	Bridport to Admiralty	11 July 1798	ADM. 1/110
356	Bridport to Admiralty	11 July 1798	ADM. 1/110
357	Bridport to Admiralty	11 July 1798	ADM. 1/110
358	Bridport to Admiralty	19 July 1798	ADM. 1/110
359	Neale to Lady Bridport	20 July 1798	Add. Mss. 35199
360	Spencer to Seymour	21 July 1798	Althorp Mss.
361	Bridport to Admiralty	24 July 1798	ADM. 1/110
362	Thompson to Admiralty	26 July 1798	ADM. 1/110
363	Admiralty to Pole	29 July 1798	Add. Mss. 35199
364	Intelligence report	30 July 1798	ADM. 1/6034
365	Bridport to Admiralty	31 July 1798	ADM. 1/110
366	Hamilton to Bridport	4 August 1798	Add. Mss. 35199
367	Pellew to Gardner	5 August 1798	ADM. 1/110
368	Keats to Gardner	6 August 1798	Add. Mss. 35199
369	Gardner to Admiralty	7 August 1798	ADM. 1/110
370.	Pellew to Gardner	8 August 1798	Add. Mss. 35199
371	Gardner to Admiralty	9 August 1798	ADM. 1/110
372	Bridport to Admiralty	9 August 1798	ADM. 1/110
373	Gower to Gardner	9 August 1798	ADM. 1/110
374	Jones to Bedford	10 August 1798	Althorp Mss.
375	Admiralty to Bridport	14 August 1798	ADM. 2/1353
376	Bridport to Admiralty	21 August 1798	ADM. 1/110
377	Bedford to Gardner	21 August 1798	Add. Mss. 35199
378	De Courcy to Bridport	25 August 1798	Add. Mss. 35199
379	Bridport to Spencer	27 August 1798	Althorp Mss.
380	Admiralty to Bridport	27 August 1798	ADM. 2/1353
381	Admiralty to Bridport	29 August 1798	ADM. 2/945
382	Bridport to Admiralty	30 August 1798	ADM. 1/110
383	Spencer to Bridport	1 September 1798	Althorp Mss.
384	Admiralty to Bridport	3 September 1798	ADM. 2/1353

385	Intelligence report	September 1798	ADM. 1/6034
386	Sickness return	September 1798	Althorp Mss.
387	Durham to Bridport	16 September 1798	Add. Mss. 35199
388	Durham to Bridport	27 September 1798	Add. Mss. 35199
389	Admiralty to Bridport	31 October 1798	Add. Mss. 35199
390	Admiralty to Gardner	5 November 1798	ADM. 2/945
391	Admiralty to Gardner	7 November 1798	ADM. 2/945
392	Admiralty to Bridport	22 December 1798	ADM. 2/945
393	Bridport to Spencer	23 December 1798	Althorp Mss.
394	Bridport to Admiralty	24 December 1798	ADM. 1/111
395	Spencer to Bridport	27 December 1798	Althorp Mss.
396	Gardner to Admiralty	31 December 1798	ADM. 1/111
397	Bridport to Spencer	31 December 1798	Althorp Mss.
398	Bridport to Admiralty	31 December 1798	ADM. 1/111
399	Return of emoluments	31 December 1798	Add. Mss. 35199
400	Bridport to Admiralty	5 January 1799	ADM. 1/112
401	Bridport to Admiralty	7 January 1799	ADM. 1/112
402	Young to Spencer	15 January 1799	Althorp Mss.
403	Bridport to Admiralty	22 January 1799	ADM. 1/112
404	Bridport to Admiralty	24 January 1799	ADM. 1/112
405	Warren to Spencer	30 January 1799	Althorp Mss.
406	Spencer to Warren	2 February 1799	Althorp Mss.
407	Bridport to Admiralty	6 February 1799	ADM. 1/112

VIII THE BRUIX CRUISE

408	Gore to Admiralty	12 February 1799	ADM. 1/6034
409	Admiralty to Thompson	26 February 1799	ADM. 2/946
410	Intelligence report	26 February 1799	ADM. 1/6034
411	Legge to Admiralty	3 March 1799	ADM. 1/6034
412	Intelligence report	3 March 1799	ADM. 1/6034
413	Intelligence report	8 March 1799	ADM. 1/6034
414	Cunningham to Admiralty	13 March 1799	ADM. 1/6034
415	Intelligence report	17 March 1799	Add. Mss. 35200
416	Legge to Seymour	17 March 1799	ADM. 1/112
417	Spencer to Bridport	19 March 1799	Althorp Mss.
418	Bridport to Admiralty	20 March 1799	ADM. 1/112
419	Bridport to captains	29 March 1799	ADM. 1/112
420	Seymour to Admiralty	[14?] April 1799	ADM. 1/112
421	Berkeley to Admiralty	16 April 1799	ADM. 1/112
422	Bridport to Admiralty	16 April 1799	ADM. 1/112
423	Neale to Bridport	16 April 1799	Add. Mss. 35200
424	Intelligence report	18 April 1799	ADM. 1/6034
425	Seymour to Bridport	18 April 1799	Add. Mss. 35200
426	Seymour to Bridport	18 April 1799	Add. Mss. 35200
427	Bridport to Admiralty	21 April 1799	ADM. 1/112
428	Bridport to Admiralty	22 April 1799	ADM. 1/112
429	Bridport to Admiralty	22 April 1799	ADM. 1/112
430	Bridport to Durham	22 April 1799	ADM. 1/112
431	Admiralty to Bridport	26 April 1799	ADM. 2/1354

432	Admiralty to Bridport	26 April 1799	ADM. 2/1354
433	Bridport to Admiralty	26 April 1799	Add. Mss. 34933
434	Bridport to Spencer	26 April 1799	Althorp Mss.
435	Bridport's journal	26–27 April 1799	ADM. 50/124
436	Fraser to Pole	26 April 1799	Add. Mss. 34933
437	Nicolson to Bridport	28 April 1799	ADM. 1/112
	Bruix to Le Breton	5 April 1799	Add. Mss. 35200
438	List of captures	30 April 1799	Add. Mss. 35200
439	Fanshawe to Spencer	30 April 1799	Althorp Mss.
440	Admiralty to Bridport	1 May 1799	ADM. 2/1354
441	Intelligence report	3 May 1799	ADM. 1/6034
442	Pitt to Windham	4 May 1799	Add. Mss. 37844
443	Admiralty to Bridport	4 May 1799	ADM. 2/1354
444	Fanshawe to Spencer	5 May 1799	Althorp Mss.
445	Intelligence report	6 May 1799	Add. Mss. 35200
446	Admiralty to Bridport	7 May 1799	ADM. 2/946
447	Bridport to Admiralty	8 May 1799	ADM. 1/112
448	Pasley to unknown	8 May 1799	Add. Mss. 35200
449	Admiralty to Bridport	9 May 1799	ADM. 2/1354
450	Le Breton to Bruix	16 April 1799	Add. Mss. 35201
451	Bruix to Le Breton	18 April 1799	Add. Mss. 35200
452	Marsden to Spencer	9 May 1799	Althorp Mss.
453	Admiralty to Bridport	10 May 1799	ADM. 2/1354
454	Admiralty to Bridport	13 May 1799	ADM. 2/1354
455	Admiralty to Bridport	16 May 1799	ADM. 2/1354
456	Admiralty to Bridport	21 May 1799	ADM. 2/1354
457	Bridport to Admiralty	27 May 1799	ADM. 1/112
458	Bridport to Admiralty	28 May 1799	ADM. 1/112
459	Bridport to Edwards	31 May 1799	Add. Mss. 35200
460	Durham to Bridport	4 June 1799	ADM. 1/113
461	Bridport to Admiralty	5 June 1799	ADM. 1/113
462	Admiralty to Bridport	8 June 1799	ADM. 2/1355
463	Bridport to Spencer	14 June 1799	Althorp Mss.
464	Bridport to Admiralty	20 June 1799	ADM. 1/113
465	Spencer to Bridport	21 June 1799	Althorp Mss.
466	Bridport to Admiralty	22 June 1799	Add. Mss. 35200
467	Bridport to Admiralty	24 June 1799	ADM. 1/113
468	Admiralty to Bridport	24 June 1799	Add. Mss. 35200
469	Bridport to Admiralty	26 June 1799	Add. Mss. 35200
470	Pole to Bridport	3 July 1799	Add. Mss. 35200
471	S. & W. Board to Admiralty	19 July 1799	ADM. F/30
472	Pole to Admiralty	29 July 1799	ADM. 1/113
473	Pole to Admiralty	29 July 1799	ADM. 1/113
474	Pole to Admiralty	2 August 1799	ADM. 1/113
475	Grenville to Bridport	3 August 1799	Add. Mss. 35200
476	George III to Spencer	5 August 1799	Althorp Mss.
477	Admiralty to Bridport	5 August 1799	ADM. 2/1356
478	Admiralty to Pole	5 August 1799	Add. Mss. 35200
479	Bridport to Admiralty	11 August 1799	ADM. 1/113
480	Spencer to Gardner	12 August 1799	Althorp Mss.

481	Gardner to Spencer	13 August 1799	Althorp Mss.
482	Pellew to Keith	13 August 1799	Add. Mss. 35200
483	Spencer to Gardner	15 August 1799	Althorp Mss.

IX   THE COMBINED FLEETS IN BREST

484	Bridport to Admiralty	18 August 1799	ADM. 1/113
485	Admiralty to Keith	19 August 1799	ADM. 2/946
486	Gardner to Spencer	20 August 1799	Althorp Mss.
487	Spencer to Bridport	23 August 1799	Add. Mss. 35200
488	George III to Spencer	23 August 1799	Althorp Mss.
489	Keats to Bridport	24 August 1799	ADM. 1/113
490	Bridport to Admiralty	26 August 1799	ADM. 1/113
491	Young to Spencer	28 August 1799	Althorp Mss.
492	S. & W. Board to Admiralty	30 August 1799	ADM. F/30
493	Bridport to Admiralty	31 August 1799	ADM. 1/113
494	George III to Spencer	6 September 1799	Althorp Mss.
495	Keats to Bridport	6 September 1799	Add. Mss. 35200
496	Nepean to Bridport	9 September 1799	Add. Mss. 35200
497	Bridport to Admiralty	10 September 1799	ADM. 1/113
498	Bridport to Admiralty	10 September 1799	ADM. 1/113
499	Admiralty to Bridport	13 September 1799	ADM. 2/1356
500	Keats to Bridport	15 September 1799	Add. Mss. 35200
501	Admiralty to Bridport	5 October 1799	ADM. 2/1356
502	Bridport to Admiralty	6 October 1799	ADM. 1/114
503	Bridport to Admiralty	9 October 1799	ADM. 1/114
504	Bridport to Pierrepont	24 October 1799	Add. Mss. 35200
505	Cunningham to Bridport	27 October 1799	ADM. 1/114
506	Bridport to Spencer	3 November 1799	Althorp Mss.
507	Young to Spencer	5 November 1799	Althorp Mss.
508	Bridport to Admiralty	6 November 1799	ADM. 1/114
509	Bridport to Admiralty	8 November 1799	ADM. 1/114
510	Bridport to Admiralty	9 November 1799	ADM. 1/114
511	Young to Spencer	15 November 1799	Althorp Mss.
512	Bridport to Admiralty	15 November 1799	ADM. 1/114
513	Bridport to Admiralty	19 November 1799	ADM. 1/114
514	Intelligence report	19 November 1799	ADM. 1/114
515	Intelligence report	26 November 1799	Add. Mss. 37866
516	Bridport to Admiralty	5 December 1799	ADM. 1/114
517	Vict. Board to Admiralty	27 December 1799	ADM. D/41
518	Gardner to Admiralty	28 December 1799	ADM. 1/114
519	Admiralty to Gardner	12 January 1800	ADM. 2/1357
520	Bridport to Admiralty	20 January 1800	ADM. 1/115
521	Bridport to Admiralty	24 January 1800	ADM. 1/115
522	Admiralty to Bridport	24 January 1800	Add. Mss. 35201
523	Admiralty to Bridport	31 January 1800	Add. Mss. 35201
524	Bridport to Admiralty	1 February 1800	ADM. 1/115
525	Admiralty to Bridport	9 February 1800	ADM. 2/1357
526	Curzon to Gardner	15 February 1800	ADM. 1/115
527	Admiralty to Gardner	20 February 1800	ADM. 2/1357

528	Gardner to Admiralty	25 February 1800	ADM. 1/115
529	Admiralty to Bridport	4 March 1800	ADM. 2/1357
530	Admiralty to Bridport	7 March 1800	ADM. 2/1357
531	Admiralty to Bridport	12 March 1800	Add. Mss. 35201
532	Bridport to Spencer	20 March 1800	Add. Mss. 35201
533	Admiralty to Milbanke	21 March 1800	ADM. 2/1357
534	Bridport to Admiralty	24 March 1800	ADM. 1/115
535	Admiralty to Bridport	25 March 1800	ADM. 2/1357
536	Spencer to Bridport	25 March 1800	Althorp Mss.
537	Spencer to St Vincent	27 March 1800	Althorp Mss.
538	Intelligence report	28 March 1800	ADM. 1/6034
539	S. & W. Board to Admiralty	2 April 1800	ADM. F/30
540	Admiralty to Bridport	4 April 1800	COR/11
541	Keats to Bridport	6 April 1800	ADM. 1/115
542	Spencer to Bridport	8 April 1800	Althorp Mss.
543	Admiralty to Bridport	8 April 1800	COR/11
544	Bridport to Admiralty	8 April 1800	ADM. 1/115
545	Vict. Board to Admiralty	9 April 1800	ADM. D/42
546	Bickerton to Bridport	9 April 1800	Add. Mss. 35201
547	Bridport to Admiralty	10 April 1800	ADM. 1/115
548	Bridport to Admiralty	10 April 1800	ADM. 1/115
549	Admiralty to Navy Board	11 April 1800	ADM. 2/626
550	Vict. Board to Admiralty	16 April 1800	ADM. D/42
551	St Vincent to Spencer	21 April 1800	Althorp Mss.
552	Bridport to Admiralty	24 April 1800	ADM. 1/115

X   ST VINCENT TAKES COMMAND

553	Admiralty to Navy Board	25 April 1800	ADM. 2/626
554	S. & W. Board to Admiralty	30 April 1800	ADM. F/30
555	S. & W. Board to Admiralty	30 April 1800	ADM. F/30
556	St Vincent to Gardner	3 May 1800	Add. Mss. 31167
557	Keats to St Vincent	3 May 1800	ADM. 1/116
558	Admiralty to St Vincent	3 May 1800	ADM. 2/1358
559	Berkeley to St Vincent	4 May 1800	ADM. 1/116
560	St Vincent to Keats	5 May 1800	Add. Mss. 31163
561	St Vincent to Spencer	5 May 1800	Althorp Mss.
562	Keats to St Vincent	5 May 1800	ADM. 1/116
563	St Vincent to Keats	5 May 1800	Add. Mss. 31163
564	St Vincent to Berkeley	5 May 1800	Add. Mss. 31163
565	St Vincent to Berkeley	5 May 1800	Add. Mss. 31163
566	Keats to St Vincent	6 May 1800	Althorp Mss.
567	Keats to St Vincent	6 May 1800	ADM. 1/116
568	Keats to St Vincent	7 May 1800	ADM. 1/116
569	St Vincent to Admiralty	8 May 1800	ADM. 1/116
570	Spencer to St Vincent	8 May 1800	Althorp Mss.
571	Trotter to St Vincent	10 May 1800	ADM. 1/116
572	St Vincent to Spencer	13 May 1800	Althorp Mss.
573	St Vincent to Admiralty	13 May 1800	ADM. 1/116
574	St Vincent to Trotter	14 May 1800	Add. Mss. 31163

575	St Vincent to Admiralty	14 May 1800	ADM. 1/116
576	Keats to St Vincent	14 May 1800	ADM. 1/116
577	Domett to Bridport	18 May 1800	Add. Mss. 35201
578	Admiralty to St Vincent	19 May 1800	ADM. 2/1358
579	Admiralty to Malbon	19 May 1800	ADM. 2/1358
580	Admiralty to Malbon	19 May 1800	ADM. 2/1358
581	Spencer to St Vincent	20 May 1800	Althorp Mss.
582	St Vincent to Admiralty	21 May 1800	ADM. 1/116
583	Marsh to St Vincent	23 May 1800	ADM. 1/116
584	Admiralty to St Vincent	23 May 1800	ADM. 2/1358
585	Admiralty to Vict. Board	23 May 1800	ADM. 2/626
586	Admiralty to Navy Board	23 May 1800	ADM. 2/626
587	Vict. Board to Admiralty	24 May 1800	ADM. D/42
588	Young to Spencer	29 May 1800	Althorp Mss.
589	St Vincent to Cunningham	1 June 1800	Add. Mss. 31163
590	St Vincent to Marsh	2 June 1800	Add. Mss. 31163
591	St Vincent to Admiralty	3 June 1800	ADM. 1/116
592	Vict. Board to Admiralty	3 June 1800	ADM. D/42
593	St Vincent to Gore	6 June 1800	Add. Mss. 31163
594	St Vincent to Admiralty	6 June 1800	ADM. 1/116
595	Berkeley to St Vincent	7 June 1800	ADM. 1/116
596	St Vincent to Warren	9 June 1800	Add. Mss. 31167
597	St Vincent to Pasley	10 June 1800	Add. Mss. 31167
598	St Vincent to Admiralty	10 June 1800	ADM. 1/116
599	Admiralty to St Vincent	10 June 1800	COR/11
600	St Vincent to Admiralty	10 June 1800	ADM. 1/116
601	St Vincent to Berkeley	11 June 1800	Add. Mss. 31163
602	Vict. Board to Admiralty	11 June 1800	ADM. DP/42
603	Gore to St Vincent	11 June 1800	ADM. 1/116
604	St Vincent to Admiralty	11 June 1800	ADM. 1/116
605	Admiralty to St Vincent	12 June 1800	ADM. 2/1358
606	Forbes to St Vincent	12 June 1800	Althorp Mss.
607	St Vincent to Spencer	13 June 1800	Althorp Mss.
608	Berkeley to St Vincent	14 June 1800	ADM. 1/116
609	S. & W. Board to Admiralty	14 June 1800	ADM. F/31
610	St Vincent to Pellew	15 June 1800	Add. Mss. 31167
611	St Vincent to Pierrepont	15 June 1800	Add. Mss. 31163
612	Gore to St Vincent	15 June 1800	ADM. 1/116
613	St Vincent to Fanshawe	16 June 1800	Add. Mss. 31163
614	St Vincent to Spencer	16 June 1800	Althorp Mss.
615	Admiralty to S. & W. Board	16 June 1800	ADM. 2/626
616	St Vincent to Legge	18 June 1800	Add. Mss. 31163
617	St Vincent to Pasley	18 June 1800	COR/11
618	St Vincent to Berkeley	19 June 1800	Add. Mss. 31163
619	Vict. Board to Admiralty	19 June 1800	ADM. D/42
620	Berkeley to St Vincent	20 June 1800	ADM. 1/116
621	Admiralty to St Vincent	21 June 1800	ADM. 2/948
622	St Vincent to Spencer	21 June 1800	Althorp Mss.
623	Admiralty to St Vincent	23 June 1800	ADM. 2/948
624	Vict. Board to Admiralty	24 June 1800	ADM. D/42

625	Admiralty to Vict. Board	24 June 1800	ADM. 2/626
626	Johnston to Admiralty	26 June 1800	ADM. F/31
627	Spencer to St Vincent	27 June 1800	Althorp Mss.
628	Pellew to St Vincent	27 June 1800	ADM. 1/116
629	S. & W. Board to Admiralty	28 June 1800	ADM. F/31

XI   THE MEDITERRANEAN DISCIPLINE

630	St Vincent to Edwards	29 June 1800	Add. Mss. 31163
631	St Vincent to Berkeley	30 June 1800	Add. Mss. 31163
632	St Vincent to Berkeley	2 July 1800	Add. Mss. 31167
633	St Vincent to Edwards	2 July 1800	Add. Mss. 31163
634	St Vincent to Fanshawe	3 July 1800	Add. Mss. 31167
635	Admiralty to Vict. Board	3 July 1800	ADM. G/792
636	St Vincent to Archbishop	3 July 1800	Add. Mss. 31167
637	St Vincent to Blane	5 July 1800	Add. Mss. 31167
638	St Vincent to Admiralty	8 July 1800	ADM. 1/116
639	St Vincent to Keats	8 July 1800	Add. Mss. 31163
640	St Vincent to Admiralty	8 July 1800	ADM. 1/116
641	St Vincent to Trotter	9 July 1800	Add. Mss. 31163
642	Vict. Board to Admiralty	11 July 1800	ADM. D/42
643	St Vincent to Trotter	13 July 1800	COR/11
644	St Vincent to Warren	14 July 1800	Add. Mss. 31163
645	St Vincent to Warren	14 July 1800	Add. Mss. 31167
646	St Vincent to Blane	14 July 1800	Add. Mss. 31167
647	St Vincent to Berkeley	15 July 1800	Add. Mss. 31167
648	St Vincent to Warren	16 July 1800	Add. Mss. 31167
649	St Vincent to Pellew	16 July 1800	Add. Mss. 31167
650	Admiralty to S. & W. Board	16 July 1800	ADM. 2/627
651	St Vincent to Keats	17 July 1800	Add. Mss. 31163
652	St Vincent to Berkeley	19 July 1800	Add. Mss. 31167
653	Berkeley to St Vincent	20 July 1800	ADM. 1/116
654	Dundas to correspondent	22 July 1800	Add. Mss. 40102
655	S. & W. Board to Admiralty	23 July 1800	ADM. F/31
656	St Vincent to Warren	24 July 1800	Add. Mss. 31167
657	St Vincent to Blane	24 July 1800	Add. Mss. 31167
658	St Vincent to Warren	27 July 1800	Add. Mss. 31167
659	St Vincent to Fenwick	27 July 1800	Add. Mss. 31167
660	St Vincent to Saxton	27 July 1800	Add. Mss. 31167
661	St Vincent to Hamond	27 July 1800	Add. Mss. 31167
662	Towry to Keats	28 July 1800	ADM. 1/116
663	St Vincent to Berkeley	28 July 1800	Add. Mss. 31167
664	St Vincent to Berkeley	29 July 1800	Add. Mss. 31167
665	St Vincent to O'Hara	1 August 1800	Add. Mss. 31167
666	St Vincent to Sutton	3 August 1800	Add. Mss. 31163
667	St Vincent to captains	3 August 1800	ADM. 1/117
668	St Vincent to Pellew	3 August 1800	Add. Mss. 31167
669	S. & W. Board to Admiralty	7 August 1800	ADM. F/31
670	S. & W. Board to Admiralty	7 August 1800	ADM. F/31
671	St Vincent to Stopford	8 August 1800	Add. Mss. 31167

672	St Vincent to Ranelagh	8 August 1800	Add. Mss. 31163
673	St Vincent to Knight	9 August 1800	Add. Mss. 31163
674	St Vincent to Knight	9 August 1800	Add. Mss. 31163
675	St Vincent to Knight	9 August 1800	COR/11
676	St Vincent to Knight	10 August 1800	Add. Mss. 31163
677	St Vincent to Knight	13 August 1800	COR/11
678	Knight to St Vincent	16 August 1800	ADM. 1/116
679	St Vincent to Sawyer	16 August 1800	Add. Mss. 31167
680	Domett to Bridport	16 August 1800	Add. Mss. 35201
681	St Vincent to Sawyer	18 August 1800	Add. Mss. 31163
682	St Vincent to Blane	19 August 1800	Add. Mss. 31167
683	Admiralty to S. & W. Board	19 August 1800	ADM. 2/627
684	St Vincent to Admiralty	20 August 1800	ADM. 1/116
685	Intelligence report	21 August 1800	ADM. 1/6034
686	S. & W. Board to Admiralty	22 August 1800	ADM. F/31
687	St Vincent to Knight	25 August 1800	COR/11
688	Stopford to St Vincent	26 August 1800	ADM. 1/116
689	King to St Vincent	27 August 1800	COR/11
690	Admiralty to St Vincent	29 August 1800	COR/11
691	Hood to Warren	30 August 1800	ADM. 1/117
692	St Vincent to Pulteney	30 August 1800	Add. Mss. 31163
693	St Vincent to Knight	30 August 1800	Add. Mss. 31163
694	Knight to St Vincent	1 September 1800	COR/11
695	Intelligence report	2 September 1800	COR/11
696	St Vincent to D'Auvergne	3 September 1800	Add. Mss. 31163
697	St Vincent to Navy Board	7 September 1800	Add. Mss. 31163
698	St Vincent to Admiralty	7 September 1800	ADM. 1/117
699	St Vincent to Lloyd	13 September 1800	Add. Mss. 31167
700	S. & W. Board to Admiralty	13 September 1800	ADM. F/31
701	St Vincent to Fanshawe	14 September 1800	COR/11
702	St Vincent to captains	14 September 1800	COR/11
703	St Vincent to Saumarez	19 September 1800	Add. Mss. 31163
704	St Vincent to Admiralty	23 September 1800	ADM. 1/117
705	Knight to St Vincent	24 September 1800	ADM. 1/117
706	St Vincent to Admiralty	25 September 1800	ADM. 1/117
707	St Vincent to Knight	26 September 1800	Add. Mss. 31163
708	St Vincent to Admiralty	26 September 1800	ADM 1/117
709	St Vincent to Trollope	1 October 1800	Add. Mss. 31163
710	King to St Vincent	6 October 1800	ADM 1/117
711	St Vincent to National Endeavour	6 October 1800	Add. Mss. 31167
712	St Vincent to Admiralty	6 October 1800	ADM. 1/117
713	Young to Spencer	8 October 1800	Althorp Mss.
714	St Vincent to Spencer	8 October 1800	Althorp Mss.
715	Spencer to St Vincent	12 October 1800	Althorp Mss.
716	St Vincent to Spencer	13 October 1800	Althorp Mss.
717	St Vincent to Coet	13 October 1800	Add. Mss. 31163
718	St Vincent to Admiralty	13 October 1800	ADM. 1/117
719	Saumarez to St Vincent	13 October 1800	ADM. 1/117
720	St Vincent to Knight	14 October 1800	COR/11

721	Warren to Admiralty	16 October 1800	ADM. 1/117
722	St Vincent to Spencer	18 October 1800	Althorp Mss.
723	Abercromby to Keith	21 October 1800	COR/7
724	St Vincent to Admiralty	21 October 1800	ADM. 1/117

XII   THE ESCAPE OF GANTEAUME

725	Admiralty to St Vincent	21 October 1800	ADM. 2/1359
726	Cook to St Vincent	23 October 1800	COR/11
727	De Courcy to St Vincent	23 October 1800	COR/11
728	Saumarez to St Vincent	23 October 1800	COR/11
729	Foley to St Vincent	26 October 1800	ADM. 1/117
730	St Vincent to Spencer	28 October 1800	Althorp Mss.
731	St Vincent to Blane	28 October 1800	Add. Mss. 31167
732	Stopford to St Vincent	28 October 1800	ADM. 1/117
733	St Vincent to Harvey	28 October 1800	Add. Mss. 31163
734	St Vincent to Harvey	28 October 1800	COR/7
735	Keith to St Vincent	29 October 1800	COR/7
736	St Vincent to Admiralty	30 October 1800	ADM. 1/117
737	Spencer to St Vincent	5 November 1800	Althorp Mss.
738	W. Wickham to Grenville	13 November 1800	COR/7
739	Intelligence report	14 November 1800	COR/7
740	Admiralty to Pasley	14 November 1800	ADM. 2/1003
741	Admiralty to Pasley	14 November 1800	ADM. 2/1003
742	Intelligence report	15 November 1800	COR/7
743	St Vincent to Coffin	15 November 1800	Add. Mss. 31167
744	St Vincent to Hyde Parker	17 November 1800	Add. Mss. 31167
745	S. & W. Board to Admiralty	21 November 1800	ADM. F/31
746	Saumarez to Harvey	21 November 1800	COR/7
747	St Vincent to S. & W. Board	25 November 1800	Add. Mss. 31163
748	Intelligence report	25 November 1800	COR/7
749	Spencer to St Vincent	28 November 1800	Althorp Mss.
750	St Vincent to Keith	29 November 1800	Add. Mss. 31167
751	St Vincent to Hamond	29 November 1800	Add. Mss. 31167
752	Admiralty to St Vincent	29 November 1800	ADM. 2/1359
753	St Vincent to Keith	30 November 1800	Add. Mss. 31167
754	St Vincent to Admiralty	1 December 1800	ADM. 1/117
755	St Vincent to hospital	1 December 1800	Add. Mss. 31164
756	St Vincent to Hyde Parker	1 December 1800	COR/7
757	St Vincent to Hyde Parker	1 December 1800	COR/7
758	St Vincent to Hyde Parker	2 December 1800	Add. Mss. 31164
759	St Vincent to Spencer	3 December 1800	Althorp Mss.
760	St Vincent to Hyde Parker	6 December 1800	COR/7
761	St Vincent to O'Hara	8 December 1800	Add. Mss. 31167
762	Intelligence report	11 December 1800	COR/7
763	St Vincent to Pasley	15 December 1800	Add. Mss. 31164
764	St Vincent to Pellew	17 December 1800	Add. Mss. 31164
765	St Vincent to Harvey	17 December 1800	Add. Mss. 31164
766	St Vincent to Fanshawe	18 December 1800	Add. Mss. 31164
767	Harvey to St Vincent	20 December 1800	ADM. 1/117

768	Spencer to St Vincent	27 December 1800	Althorp Mss.
769	St Vincent to Admiralty	28 December 1800	ADM. 1/117
770	St Vincent to Admiralty	28 December 1800	ADM. 1/117
771	Shirley to St Vincent	30 December 1800	ADM. 1/118
772	Harvey to St Vincent	2 January 1801	ADM. 1/118
773	St Vincent to Admiralty	5 January 1801	ADM. 1/118
774	St Vincent to Admiralty	5 January 1801	ADM. 1/118
775	Harvey to St Vincent	10 January 1801	ADM. 1/118
776	Pellew to Harvey	12 January 1801	ADM. 1/118
777	Harvey to St Vincent	13 January 1801	ADM. 1/118
778	Harvey to St Vincent	14 January 1801	ADM. 1/118
779	Pellew to Harvey	15 January 1801	ADM. 1/118
780	St Vincent to Harvey	17 January 1801	Add. Mss. 31164
781	St Vincent to Rose	19 January 1801	Add. Mss. 31167
782	St Vincent to Harvey	20 January 1801	Add. Mss. 31164
783	St Vincent to captains	21 January 1801	ADM. 1/118
784	St Vincent to Admiralty	22 January 1801	ADM. 1/118
785	St Vincent to Admiralty	23 January 1801	ADM. 1/118
786	St Vincent to Saumarez	25 January 1801	Add. Mss. 31167
787	Harvey to St Vincent	25 January 1801	ADM. 1/118
788	St Vincent to Admiralty	26 January 1801	ADM. 1/118
789	St Vincent to Harvey	26 January 1801	Add. Mss. 31164
790	Fayerman to St Vincent	27 January 1801	ADM. 1/118
791	Thornbrough to St Vincent	27 January 1801	ADM. 1/118
792	S. & W. Board to Admiralty	27 January 1801	ADM. 98/20
793	St Vincent to Admiralty	28 January 1801	ADM. 1/118
794	Harvey to St Vincent	28 January 1801	ADM. 1/118
795	St Vincent to Simcoe	30 January 1801	Add. Mss. 31167
796	D'Auvergne to St Vincent	31 January 1801	ADM. 1/118
797	St Vincent to Lady Dalyell	2 February 1801	Add. Mss. 31167
798	St Vincent to Bover	2 February 1801	Add. Mss. 31167
799	St Vincent to Harvey	2 February 1801	Add. Mss. 31164
800	St Vincent to Admiralty	2 February 1801	ADM. 1/118
801	St Vincent to Keith	3 February 1801	Add. Mss. 31164
802	St Vincent to Cotton	4 February 1801	Add. Mss. 31164
803	St Vincent to Admiralty	5 February 1801	ADM. 1/118
804	Herbert to St Vincent	5 February 1801	ADM. 1/118
805	St Vincent to Stopford	6 February 1801	Add. Mss. 31164
806	St Vincent to Admiralty	6 February 1801	ADM. 1/118
807	St Vincent to Admiralty	7 February 1801	ADM. 1/118
808	St Vincent to Admiralty	8 February 1801	ADM. 1/118
809	St Vincent to Stopford	8 February 1801	Add. Mss. 31164
810	St Vincent to Baring	8 February 1801	Add. Mss. 31167
811	Admiralty to St Vincent	9 February 1801	ADM. 2/949
812	St Vincent to Admiralty	10 February 1801	ADM. 1/118

XIII   CORNWALLIS SUCCEEDS

813	Cornwallis to Admiralty	26 February 1801	ADM. 1/118
814	Thornbrough to Admiralty	9 March 1801	ADM. 1/118

815	Brown to Stopford	9 March 1801	ADM. 1/119
816	Thornbrough to Admiralty	11 March 1801	ADM. 1/118
817	Cooke to Ricketts	17 March 1801	ADM. 1/119
818	Cornwallis to Admiralty	27 March 1801	ADM. 1/119
819	Pellew to Cornwallis	29 March 1801	ADM. 1/119
820	Gambier to Admiralty	31 March 1801	ADM. 1/119
821	D'Auvergne to Cornwallis	31 March 1801	ADM. 1/119
822	D'Auvergne to Cornwallis	31 March 1801	ADM. 1/119
823	Sutton to Cornwallis	March 1801	ADM. 1/119
824	Cornwallis to Admiralty	12 April 1801	ADM. 1/119
825	Cooke to Cornwallis	12 April 1801	ADM. 1/119
826	Pellew to Cornwallis	15 April 1801	ADM. 1/119
827	Cornwallis to Admiralty	16 April 1801	ADM. 1/119
828	Cornwallis to Admiralty	20 April 1801	ADM. 1/119
829	Tobin to Cornwallis	20 April 1801	ADM. 1/119
830	Cornwallis to Admiralty	14 May 1801	ADM. 1/119
831	Parker to Cornwallis	14 May 1801	ADM. 1/119
832	Gambier to Spencer	6 June 1801	Althorp Mss.
833	Cornwallis to Admiralty	21 July 1801	ADM. 1/119
834	Cornwallis to Admiralty	27 July 1801	ADM. 1/119
835	Gambier to Spencer	25 August 1801	Althorp Mss.
836	Crawford to Cornwallis	14 September 1801	ADM. 1/120
837	Cornwallis to Admiralty	8 October 1801	ADM. 1/120
838	Admiralty to Vict. Board	17 October 1801	ADM. G/792
839	Cornwallis to Admiralty	20 October 1801	ADM. 1/120
840	Cornwallis to Admiralty	25 October 1801	ADM. 1/120

INDEX

NAVY RECORDS SOCIETY
(FOUNDED 1893)

The Navy Records Society was established for the purpose of printing unpublished manuscripts and rare works of naval interest. Membership of the Society is open to all who are interested in naval history, and any person wishing to become a member should apply to the Hon. Secretary, Professor A. D. Lambert, Department of War Studies, King's College London, Strand, London WC2R 2LS, United Kingdom. The annual subscription is £30, which entitles the member to receive one free copy of each work issued by the Society in that year, and to buy earlier issues at reduced prices.

A list of works, available to members only, is shown below; very few copies are left of those marked with an asterisk. Volumes out of print are indicated by **OP**. Prices for works in print are available on application to Mrs Annette Gould, 5 Goodwood Close, Midhurst, West Sussex GU29 9JG, United Kingdom, to whom all enquiries concerning works in print should be sent. Those marked 'TS', 'SP' and 'A' are published for the Society by Temple Smith, Scolar Press and Ashgate, and are available to non-members from the Ashgate Publishing Group, Gower House, Croft Road, Aldershot, Hampshire GU11 3HR. Those marked 'A & U' are published by George Allen & Unwin, and are available to non-members only through bookshops.

Vol. 8. *Naval Accounts and Inventories in the Reign of Henry VII*, ed. M. Oppenheim. **OP**.

Vol. 9. *Journal of Sir George Rooke*, ed. O. Browning. **OP**.

Vol. 10. *Letters and Papers relating to the War with France 1512–1513*, ed. M. Alfred Spont. **OP**.

Vol. 11. *Papers relating to the Spanish War 1585–1587*, ed. Julian S. Corbett. TS.

Vol. 12. *Journals and Letters of Admiral of the Fleet Sir Thomas Byam Martin, 1773–1854*, Vol. II (see No. 24), ed. Admiral Sir R. Vesey Hamilton. **OP**.

Vol. 13. *Papers relating to the First Dutch War, 1652–1654*, Vol. I, ed. Dr S. R. Gardiner. **OP**.

Vol. 14. *Papers relating to the Blockade of Brest, 1803–1805*, Vol. I, ed. J. Leyland. **OP**.

Vol. 15. *History of the Russian Fleet during the Reign of Peter the Great, by a Contemporary Englishman*, ed. Admiral Sir Cyprian Bridge. **OP**.

*Vol. 16. *Logs of the Great Sea Fights, 1794–1805*, Vol. I, ed. Vice Admiral Sir T. Sturges Jackson.

Vol. 17. *Papers relating to the First Dutch War, 1652–1654*, ed. Dr S. R. Gardiner. **OP**.

*Vol. 18. *Logs of the Great Sea Fights*, Vol. II, ed. Vice Admiral Sir T. Sturges Jackson.

Vol. 19. *Journals and Letters of Admiral of the Fleet Sir Thomas Byam Martin*, Vol. II (see No. 24), ed. Admiral Sir R. Vesey Hamilton. **OP**.

Vol. 20. *The Naval Miscellany*, Vol. I, ed. Professor J. K. Laughton.

Vol. 21. *Papers relating to the Blockade of Brest, 1803–1805*, Vol. II, ed. J. Leyland. **OP**.

Vol. 22. *The Naval Tracts of Sir William Monson*, Vol. I, ed. M. Oppenheim. **OP**.

Vol. 23. *The Naval Tracts of Sir William Monson*, Vol. II, ed. M. Oppenheim. **OP**.

Vol. 24. *The Journals and Letters of Admiral of the Fleet Sir Thomas Byam Martin*, Vol. I, ed. Admiral Sir R. Vesey Hamilton. **OP**.

Vol. 25. *Nelson and the Neapolitan Jacobins*, ed. H. C. Gutteridge. **OP**.

Vol. 26. *A Descriptive Catalogue of the Naval MSS in the Pepysian Library*, Vol. I, ed. J. R. Tanner. **OP**.

Vol. 27. *A Descriptive Catalogue of the Naval MSS in the Pepysian Library*, Vol. II, ed. J. R. Tanner. **OP**.

Vol. 28. *The Correspondence of Admiral John Markham, 1801–1807*, ed. Sir Clements R. Markham. **OP**.

Vol. 29. *Fighting Instructions, 1530–1816*, ed. Julian S. Corbett. **OP**.

Vol. 30. *Papers relating to the First Dutch War, 1652–1654*, Vol. III, ed. Dr S. R. Gardiner & C. T. Atkinson. **OP**.

Vol. 31. *The Recollections of Commander James Anthony Gardner, 1775–1814*, ed. Admiral Sir R. Vesey Hamilton & Professor J. K. Laughton.

Vol. 32. *Letters and Papers of Charles, Lord Barham, 1758–1813*, ed. Professor Sir John Laughton.

Vol. 33. *Naval Songs and Ballads*, ed. Professor C. H. Firth. **OP**.

Vol. 34. *Views of the Battles of the Third Dutch War*, ed. by Julian S. Corbett. **OP**.

Vol. 35. *Signals and Instructions, 1776–1794*, ed. Julian S. Corbett **OP**.

Vol. 36. *A Descriptive Catalogue of the Naval MSS in the Pepysian Library*, Vol III, ed. J. R. Tanner. **OP**.

Vol. 37. *Papers relating to the First Dutch War, 1652 1654*, Vol. IV, ed. C. T. Atkinson. **OP**.

Vol. 38. *Letters and Papers of Charles, Lord Barham, 1758–1813*, Vol. II, ed. Professor Sir John Laughton.

Vol. 39. *Letters and Papers of Charles, Lord Barham, 1758–1813*, Vol. III, ed. Professor Sir John Laughton.

Vol. 40. *The Naval Miscellany*, Vol. II, ed. Professor Sir John Laughton.

*Vol. 41. *Papers relating to the First Dutch War, 1652–1654*, Vol. V, ed. C. T. Atkinson.

*Vol. 42. *Papers relating to the Loss of Minorca in 1756*, ed. Captain H. W. Richmond, R.N.

*Vol. 43. *The Naval Tracts of Sir William Monson*, Vol. III, ed. M. Oppenheim.

Vol. 44. *The Old Scots Navy 1689–1710*, ed. James Grant. **OP**.

Vol. 45. *The Naval Tracts of Sir William Monson*, Vol. IV, ed. M. Oppenheim.

*Vol. 46. *The Private Papers of George, 2nd Earl Spencer*, Vol. I, ed. Julian S. Corbett.

Vol. 47. *The Naval Tracts of Sir William Monson*, Vol. V, ed. M. Oppenheim.

Vol. 48. *The Private Papers of George, 2nd Earl Spencer*, Vol. II, ed. Julian S. Corbett. **OP**.

*Vol. 49. *Documents relating to Law and Custom of the Sea*, Vol. II, ed. R. G. Marsden.

*Vol. 50. *Documents relating to Law and Custom of the Sea*, Vol. II, ed. R. G. Marsden.

Vol. 51. *Autobiography of Phineas Pett*, ed. W. G. Perrin. **OP**.

Vol. 52. *The Life of Admiral Sir John Leake*, Vol. I, ed. Geoffrey Callender.

Vol. 53. *The Life of Admiral Sir John Leake*, Vol. II, ed. Geoffrey Callender.

Vol. 54. *The Life and Works of Sir Henry Mainwaring*, Vol. I, ed. G. E. Manwaring.

Vol. 55. *The Letters of Lord St Vincent, 1801–1804*, Vol. I, ed. D. B. Smith. **OP**.

Vol. 56. *The Life and Works of Sir Henry Mainwaring*, Vol. II, ed. G. E. Manwaring & W. G. Perrin. **OP**.

Vol. 57. *A Descriptive Catalogue of the Naval MSS in the Pepysian Library*, Vol. IV, ed. Dr J. R. Tanner. **OP**.

Vol. 58. *The Private Papers of George, 2nd Earl Spencer*, Vol. III, ed. Rear Admiral H. W. Richmond. **OP**.

Vol. 59. *The Private Papers of George, 2nd Earl Spencer*, Vol. IV, ed. Rear Admiral H. W. Richmond. **OP**.

Vol. 60. *Samuel Pepys's Naval Minutes*, ed. Dr J. R. Tanner.

Vol. 61. *The Letters of Lord St Vincent, 1801–1804*, Vol. II, ed. D. B. Smith. **OP**.

Vol. 62. *Letters and Papers of Admiral Viscount Keith*, Vol. I, ed. W. G. Perrin. **OP**.

Vol. 63. *The Naval Miscellany*, Vol. III, ed. W. G. Perrin. **OP**.

Vol. 64. *The Journal of the 1st Earl of Sandwich*, ed. R. C. Anderson. **OP**.

*Vol. 65. *Boteler's Dialogues*, ed. W. G. Perrin.

Vol. 66. *Papers relating to the First Dutch War, 1652–1654*, Vol. VI (with index), ed. C. T. Atkinson.

*Vol. 67. *The Byng Papers*, Vol. I, ed. W. C. B. Tunstall.

*Vol. 68. *The Byng Papers*, Vol. II, ed. W. C. B. Tunstall.

Vol. 69. *The Private Papers of John, Earl of Sandwich*, Vol. I, ed. G. R. Barnes & Lt. Cdr. J. H. Owen, R.N. **OP**. Corrigenda to *Papers relating to the First Dutch War, 1652–1654, Vols I–VI*, ed. Captain A. C. Dewar, R.N.

Vol. 70. *The Byng Papers*, Vol. III, ed. W. C. B. Tunstall.

Vol. 71. *The Private Papers of John, Earl of Sandwich*, Vol. II, ed. G. R. Barnes & Lt. Cdr. J. H. Owen, R.N. **OP**.

Vol. 72. *Piracy in the Levant, 1827–1828*, ed. Lt. Cdr. C. G. Pitcairn Jones, R.N. **OP**.

Vol. 73. *The Tangier Papers of Samuel Pepys*, ed. Edwin Chappell.

Vol. 74. *The Tomlinson Papers*, ed. J. G. Bullocke.

Vol. 75. *The Private Papers of John, Earl of Sandwich*, Vol. III, ed. G. R. Barnes & Lt. Cdr. J. H. Owen, R.N. **OP**.

Vol. 76. *The Letters of Robert Blake*, ed. the Rev. J. R. Powell. **OP**.

*Vol. 77. *Letters and Papers of Admiral the Hon. Samuel Barrington*, Vol. I, ed. D. Bonner-Smith.

Vol. 78. *The Private Papers of John, Earl of Sandwich*, Vol. IV, ed. G. R. Barnes & Lt. Cdr. J. H. Owen, R.N. **OP**.

*Vol. 79. *The Journals of Sir Thomas Allin, 1660–1678*, Vol. I (1660–1666), ed. R. C. Anderson.

Vol. 80. *The Journals of Sir Thomas Allin, 1660–1678*, Vol. II (1667–1678), ed. R. C. Anderson.

Vol. 81. *Letters and Papers of Admiral the Hon. Samuel Barrington*, Vol. II, ed. D. Bonner-Smith. **OP**.

Vol. 82. *Captain Boteler's Recollections, 1808–1830*, ed. D. Bonner-Smith. **OP**.

Vol. 83. *Russian War, 1854, Baltic and Black Sea: Official Correspondence*, ed. D. Bonner-Smith & Captain A. C. Dewar, R.N. **OP**.

Vol. 84. *Russian War, 1855. Baltic: Official Correspondence*, ed. D. Bonner-Smith. **OP**.

Vol. 85. *Russian War, 1855. Black Sea: Official Correspondence*, ed. Captain A.C. Dewar, R.N. **OP**.

Vol. 86. *Journals and Narratives of the Third Dutch War*, ed. R. C. Anderson. **OP**.

Vol. 87. *The Naval Brigades in the Indian Mutiny, 1857–1858*, ed. Cdr. W. B. Rowbotham, R.N. **OP**.

Vol. 88. *Patee Byng's Journal*, ed. J. L. Cranmer-Byng. **OP**.

*Vol. 89. *The Sergison Papers, 1688–1702*, ed. Cdr. R. D. Merriman, R.I.N.

Vol. 90. *The Keith Papers*, Vol. II, ed. Christopher Lloyd. **OP**.

Vol. 91. *Five Naval Journals, 1789–1817*, ed. Rear Admiral H. G. Thursfield. **OP**.

Vol. 92. *The Naval Miscellany*, Vol. IV, ed. Christopher Lloyd. **OP**.

Vol. 93. *Sir William Dillon's Narrative of Professional Adventures, 1790–1839*, Vol. I (1790–1802), ed. Professor Michael Lewis. **OP**.

Vol. 94. *The Walker Expedition to Quebec, 1711*, ed. Professor Gerald S. Graham. **OP**.

Vol. 95. *The Second China War, 1856–1860*, ed. D. Bonner-Smith & E. W. R. Lumby. **OP**.

Vol. 96. *The Keith Papers, 1803–1815*, Vol. III, ed. Professor Christopher Lloyd.

Vol. 97. *Sir William Dillon's Narrative of Professional Adventures, 1790–1839*, Vol. II (1802–1839), ed. Professor Michael Lewis. **OP**.

Vol. 98. *The Private Correspondence of Admiral Lord Collingwood*, ed. Professor Edward Hughes. **OP**.

Vol. 99. *The Vernon Papers, 1739–1745*, ed. B. McL. Ranft. **OP**.

Vol. 100. *Nelson's Letters to his Wife and Other Documents*, ed. Lt. Cdr. G. P. B. Naish, R.N.V.R. **OP**.

Vol. 101. *A Memoir of James Trevenen, 1760–1790*, ed. Professor Christopher Lloyd & R. C. Anderson. **OP**.

Vol. 102. *The Papers of Admiral Sir John Fisher*, Vol. I, ed. Lt. Cdr. P. K. Kemp, R.N. **OP**.

Vol. 103. *Queen Anne's Navy*, ed. Cdr. R. D. Merriman, R.I.N. **OP**.

Vol. 104. *The Navy and South America, 1807–1823*, ed. Professor Gerald S. Graham & Professor R. A. Humphreys.

Vol. 105. *Documents relating to the Civil War, 1642–1648*, ed. The Rev. J. R. Powell & E. K. Timings. **OP**.

Vol. 106. *The Papers of Admiral Sir John Fisher*, Vol. II, ed. Lt. Cdr. P. K. Kemp, R.N. **OP**.

Vol. 107. *The Health of Seamen*, ed. Professor Christopher Lloyd.

Vol. 108. *The Jellicoe Papers*, Vol. I (1893–1916), ed. A. Temple Patterson.

Vol. 109. *Documents relating to Anson's Voyage round the World, 1740–1744*, ed. Dr Glyndwr Williams. **OP**.

Vol. 110. *The Saumarez Papers: The Baltic, 1808–1812*, ed. A. N. Ryan. **OP**.

Vol. 111. *The Jellicoe Papers*, Vol. II (1916–1935), ed. Professor A. Temple Patterson.

Vol. 112. *The Rupert and Monck Letterbook, 1666*, ed. The Rev. J. R. Powell & E. K. Timings.

Vol. 113. *Documents relating to the Royal Naval Air Service*, Vol. I (1908–1918), ed. Captain S. W. Roskill, R.N.

*Vol. 114. *The Siege and Capture of Havana, 1762*, ed. Professor David Syrett.

Vol. 115. *Policy and Operations in the Mediterranean, 1912–1914*, ed. E. W. R. Lumby. **OP**.

Vol. 116. *The Jacobean Commissions of Enquiry, 1608 and 1618*, ed. Dr A. P. McGowan.

Vol. 117. *The Keyes Papers*, Vol. I (1914–1918), ed. Professor Paul Halpern.

Vol. 118. *The Royal Navy and North America: The Warren Papers, 1736–1752*, ed. Dr Julian Gwyn. **OP**.

Vol. 119. *The Manning of the Royal Navy: Selected Public Pamphlets, 1693–1873*, ed. Professor John Bromley.

Vol. 120. *Naval Administration, 1715–1750*, ed. Professor D. A. Baugh.

Vol. 121. *The Keyes Papers*, Vol. II (1919–1938), ed. Professor Paul Halpern.

Vol. 122. *The Keyes Papers*, Vol. III (1939–1945), ed. Professor Paul Halpern.

Vol. 123. *The Navy of the Lancastrian Kings: Accounts and Inventories of William Soper, Keeper of the King's Ships, 1422–1427*, ed. Dr Susan Rose.

Vol. 124. *The Pollen Papers: the Privately Circulated Printed Works of Arthur Hungerford Pollen, 1901–1916*, ed. Professor Jon T. Sumida. A. & U.

Vol. 125. *The Naval Miscellany*, Vol. V. ed. Dr N. A. M. Rodger. A & U.

Vol. 126. *The Royal Navy in the Mediterranean, 1915–1918*, ed. Professor Paul Halpern. TS.

Vol. 127. *The Expedition of Sir John Norris and Sir Francis Drake to Spain and Portugal, 1589*, ed. Professor R. B. Wernham. TS.

Vol. 128. *The Beatty Papers*, Vol. I (1902–1918), ed. Professor B. McL. Ranft. SP.

Vol. 129. *The Hawke Papers: A Selection, 1743–1771*, ed. Dr R. F. Mackay. SP.

Vol. 130. *Anglo-American Naval Relations, 1917–1919*, ed. Michael Simpson. SP.

Vol. 131. *British Naval Documents, 1204–1960*, ed. Professor John B. Hattendorf, Dr Roger Knight, Alan Pearsall, Dr Nicholas Rodger & Professor Geoffrey Till. SP.

Vol. 132. *The Beatty Papers*, Vol. II (1916–1927), ed. Professor B. McL. Ranft. SP

Vol. 133. *Samuel Pepys and the Second Dutch War*, transcribed by Professor William Matthews & Dr Charles Knighton; ed. Robert Latham. SP.

Vol. 134. *The Somerville Papers*, ed. Michael Simpson, with the assistance of John Somerville. SP.

Vol. 135. *The Royal Navy in the River Plate, 1806–1807*, ed. John D. Grainger. SP.

Vol. 136. *The Collective Naval Defence of the Empire, 1900–1940*, ed. Nicholas Tracy. A.

Vol. 137. *The Defeat of the Enemy Attack on Shipping, 1939–1945*, ed. Eric Grove. A.

Vol. 138. *Shipboard Life and Organisation, 1731–1815*, ed. Brian Lavery. A.

Vol. 139. *The Battle of the Atlantic and Signals Intelligence: U-boat Situations and Trends, 1941–1945*, ed. Professor David Syrett. A.

Vol. 140. *The Cunningham Papers*, Vol. I, *The Mediterranean Fleet, 1939–1942*, ed. Michael Simpson. A.

Occasional Publications:

Vol. 1. *The Commissioned Sea Officers of the Royal Navy, 1660–1815*, ed. Professor David Syrett & Professor R. L. DiNardo. SP.

Vol. 2. *The Anthony Roll of Henry VIII's Navy*, ed. C. S. Knighton and D. M. Loades. A.